WOMEN'S BUDDHISM
BUDDHISM'S WOMEN

WOMEN'S BUDDHISM
BUDDHISM'S WOMEN

TRADITION, REVISION, RENEWAL

Edited by Ellison Banks Findly

WISDOM PUBLICATIONS • BOSTON

Wisdom Publications
199 Elm St
Somerville MA 02144 USA

Library of Congress Cataloging-in-Publication Data
Women's Buddhism, Buddhism's women: tradition, revision, renewal / edited by Ellison Banks Findly.
p. cm.
Includes bibliographical references and index.
ISBN 0-86171-165-3 (alk. paper)
1. Buddhist women. 2. Women in Buddhism. 3. Buddhist nuns. 4. Monastic and religious orders for women, Buddhist. I. Findly, Ellison Banks.

BQ4570.W6 W66 2000
294.3'082—dc21

99-088200

ISBN 0-86171-165-3
05 04 03 02 01
5 4 3 2

Cover design by Graciela Galup
Interior designed and typeset by Gopa Design
Cover photo by Monica Lindberg Falk

Wisdom Publications' books are printed on acid-free paper and meet the guidelines for the permanence and durability of the Production Guidelines for Book Longevity of the Council on Library Resources.

Printed in Canada

Dedicated to my mother, Anne Johnson Banks,

and in memory to my father,

William Ross Banks

TABLE OF CONTENTS

LIST OF ILLUSTRATIONS

Title page: Nuns from Keydong Thuk-Che-Cho Ling Nunnery in Kathmandu making an Avalokiteśvara *maṇḍala* at Trinity College (photo by Ellison Banks Findly)

Page 15: The assembly of nuns at Karsha Nunnery in Zangskar, northwest India. They range in age from fourteen to seventy-three, and follow the Gelugpa school of Tibetan Buddhism (photo by Kim Gutschow)

Page 131: Praying together (photo provided by Venerable Thubten Chodron)

Page 227: Sujātā's Army marching in the "Foot Pilgrimage" *(Dhamma Jyotī Pad Yātrā)* at Bodhgaya (photo by Owen M. Lynch)

Page 317: Entrance to the meditation hall at the Redwood Creek Dharma Center (photo by Sarah D. Buie)

Page 391: Hi-ah Park wearing shamanic ritual costume, 1994 (photo by Rob Sims).

ACKNOWLEDGMENTS

All projects begin with seeds planted in the fertile fields of our lives, and then grow to fruition with the help of many midwives. The seeds of this project would never have been sown had it not been for my dear friend and colleague Judy Dworin, whose vision, energy, and determination supported me from beginning to end, and whose "yankee friendship"—long-knowing and long-growing—has provided rich nurture for my own internal growth over the years. Along with Blu, Missy, Chris, and, of course, the seven "Trinity nuns," this midwife has urged me when I needed urging, consoled me when I needed consoling, and celebrated when there was much to celebrate. I thank her with all my heart, knowing full well that our work together continues to hold much promise.

I thank, as well, all those who helped out in the detailed work of compiling so many things in such a timely and efficient fashion. Gene Smith of Wisdom Publications has offered tremendous support and encouragement ever since I first came to him with the idea of this book, and I thank him—as well as all those at the press—for such wise counsel and gracious advocacy. Ron Spencer read an early draft of the manuscript and, with his usual keen ear and ever-present pencil, went through the text and offered suggestions large and small. Laurie MacFarlane tackled the job of consolidating many bibliographies into one and, in quick but careful order, assembled a useful document that reflects both the depth of scholarship informing the contributions and the breadth of materials available to our readers. As always, Gay Weidlich of the Religion Department at Trinity provided genial and diligent assistance at every level and, with the monumental efforts of Pat Kennedy of the Theater and Dance Department, facilitated the 1998 "Nuns' Circle" out of which this project developed. Most importantly, I thank the contributors themselves whose conscientious hard work, willing flexibility, and helpful suggestions made the task much easier.

In all I do, the love of my children, Caroline and Ross, nourishes and sustains me. I hope, in some small way, to give back to them what they have given me—acceptance of where we have been, contentment in who we are now, and joy in how we may be. May my life and work abide in their affection, and reflect the integrity of spirit they continue to offer me.

I am sustained as well by the good company of Fred Pfeil—friend, teacher, and confederate in the Dharma. I thank him for sharing his cat, his music, and his food, and for giving me the title of this book. May its wisdom bear fruit in the years ahead.

And, finally, I thank my beloved parents, whose lives are examples of traditions made new. Although my father passed on in the middle of this project, I carry with me his unflagging support and generous good will. And to my mother I give my most heartfelt thanks, for she has always been my dearest friend. May she be counted among the courageous women of this book as they bring new shape to the many forms of our ordinary lives.

INTRODUCTION

"Let's bring the nuns to Trinity..."

The lights were on, and Adele Broitman was first to speak. Melissa Kerin had just finished a slide lecture on nuns from the Keydong Thuk-Che-Cho Ling Nunnery in Kathmandu who had learned the meditative practice of sand *maṇḍala*-making. Their teacher had been a monk from a brother monastery in south India, and their training had begun in 1993. These women were among the first Tibetan Buddhist nuns to learn such a practice, and Missy had been present in Kathmandu, while a Trinity undergraduate and later as a Watson Fellow, as a witness and facilitator to the process. Her lecture was part of a 1996 conference on "revoicing the feminine sacred," and Adele's idea moved through the hundred or so members of the audience with such assent that the conference organizers had to respond. Judy Dworin and I rose from the speakers' platform to detail the difficulties and costs that would be involved in such an undertaking, and our final words were to dismiss the possibility altogether.

Within two weeks, however, we were meeting daily to see how impossible it really would be. The two previous *maṇḍala* projects at Trinity, in 1994 and 1996, had been much smaller in scale, and the visit of a group of nuns for a whole semester meant marshalling all the resources available at the college, and enlisting the help of people from all over New England as well as from India and Nepal. However, Trinity's renewed commitment to international programs, including those in the arts, and its efforts to diversify the population of the campus and the scope of the curriculum meant, ultimately, that the project was possible.

The nuns arrived in Connecticut in January 1998. For several months, five *maṇḍala*-makers, one *thangka*-painter, and an English translator lived on campus. They mingled with students, faculty, and hundreds of visitors who came daily to watch the progress of an Avalokiteśvara *maṇḍala* and a Green Tārā *thangka*. The dark red galleries of the art center were home to daily meditations and *pūjās*, public lessons in the scrubbing of *chakpus* (brass funnels used in the rhythmic laying down of the sand), demonstrations in the precise measurements and color applications of traditional *thangka* practice, and gallery talks and films on Tibetan Buddhist art and the contemporary role of nuns in diaspora culture. The Chenrezig meditation group from Middletown, formed in the wake of the first Trinity *maṇḍala* project in 1994, lent their support. Local school children, some of whom had participated in the second Trinity *maṇḍala* project at Sanchez Elementary School in 1996, took their current lessons and built them into their own performance of an extravagant outdoor *maṇḍala* dance held later that spring in Hartford's Elizabeth Park.

Nuns from Keydong Thuk-Che-Cho Ling Nunnery in Kathmandu making an Avalokiteśvara maṇḍala *at Trinity College (photo by Ellison Banks Findly)*

All who came to see the nuns and their work gradually formed a close-knit community, aware of the historic nature of what was happening. The Keydong nuns, who had been among the first renunciant women to learn sand *maṇḍala*-making and *thangka*-painting techniques, were also the first women to bring their practice of these meditative arts to the West. In doing so, they were not challenging Buddhist doctrine on gender questions, or especially any gender bias in the availability of Buddhist perfection. Rather, they were challenging years of traditional obstacles placed in the way of women who wanted access to all of the same practices available to men, practices that would provide them with the same effective and powerful tools for their spiritual quests as were available to their male colleagues. Those of us who witnessed this process were fully aware that history was being made, and were soon to see the teaching of these techniques among peer renunciant women in India and Nepal complement similar initiatives at other nunneries such as Dolma Ling in India and Kopan (Jangchup Omeng Gakey Cho

Ling Nunnery) in Nepal. Moreover, although we onlookers knew of the historic importance of the event, the nuns themselves were primarily attuned to the fact that as renunciants, and not necessarily as women, they were now lucky enough to be able to use these techniques for their own and others' spiritual benefit.

In addition to the making of a *maṇḍala* and a *thangka*, the 1998 project at Trinity sponsored, as its closing events, a conference and a weekend performance. The performance of *Wheel* by the Judy Dworin Performance Ensemble brought together groups of Native Americans, Eastern Europeans, Tibetans, and Christian gospel singers who, together with the nuns, created a truly international work. This piece emphasized the way women from diverse traditions could explore new forms of spiritual expression in a performance art that, by its very nature, reflected the Buddhist teaching that all things are impermanent. The conference, "Women Changing Contemporary Buddhism," brought together scholars whose own work focused on the ways women from a variety of Buddhist traditions were already laying claim to forms, practices, and institutions that had hitherto been open only to men. The work of many of these scholars focused on the ways in which women, in the contemporary setting, were reshaping these very same forms, practices, and institutions not only to suit their own needs and concerns but also to respond to the particular demands of life in late-twentieth-century culture. The papers given at the conference became the core of this book.

Where Buddhist Women Have Been

Historically, there are at least four areas in which Buddhist women have found obstacles in their spiritual lives. The first area is religious practices, that is, lifestyle customs, instructional opportunities, meditational forms, and institutional structures, many of which are routinely available to lay men and monks but are infrequently or never available to lay women and nuns. In spite of the misogynistic tone of some of their rhetoric, canonical texts clearly state that women can experience enlightenment as women. However, channels through which women can progress to this experience are often severely truncated. The full and irreversible transformation of Buddhist enlightenment is reached primarily through lengthy and arduous disciplines, which, though they vary by tradition, are each designed to move the adept to a posture of non-attachment and compassionate activity within the world. With limited access to these traditional disciplinary opportunities, women practitioners have been hampered in their efforts to actualize the fullness of their spiritual lives.

Second, the disciplinary rules that govern the monastic lives of nuns have clearly delineated them as second-class citizens in relation to monks. The best examples of this, of course, are the eight disciplinary rules said to have been laid down for nuns by Gautama Buddha at the time of the admission of the first group of women into the Buddhist life of the "gone forth," a disciplinary guide still normative in the Buddhist world today. These eight rules, for example, require all nuns to pay homage to all monks regardless of how senior a nun might be or how junior a monk might be; to be instructed by monks in the teachings and conduct of the tradition but not vice versa; to refrain from criticizing or reprimanding monks though the reverse may happen; and to be ordained by the orders of both nuns and monks though the reverse does not happen. This unevenness in institutional governance places nuns' daily lives directly under the jurisdiction of monks, thus curtailing any possibility of the kind of full self-governance for nuns that has been the norm for their brother monks.

Third, although women are, by doctrine, fully capable of experiencing enlightenment, the recognition of that highest of experiences in terms of title and status has often been withheld from them at various points in Buddhism's history. The Pali term *arahant,* for example, though applied to specific women in the later and commentarial traditions, is not applied to specific women in earlier texts—even though the conversion and enlightenment narratives of a number of individual women clearly show that the women, like their corresponding male colleagues, deserve the title. This same imbalance in the application of terms reflecting spiritual achievement and status is true in later Mahāyāna traditions as well—in the use, or lack of use, of the term bodhisattva, for example, as it recognizes women of committed practice who work for the benefit of all sentient beings.

Finally, female renunciants have at many times in Buddhist history been refused the kind of material support that male renunciants have received. Both as individuals and as members of Sangha communities, nuns have received donations, but this material support has lagged well behind that given to comparable monks and their communities. In the Pali canon, nuns are known as those who receive things only with difficulty *(kicchalābha, dullabha).* The evidence of early inscriptions, in which there are many women donors but many fewer nun receivers, and the dying back of the nuns' order in India for lack of support are good illustrations that donor support has been much greater for renunciant men than for renunciant women.

Why women in Buddhist history are discriminated against in terms of the structures by which their Buddhist lives can be carried out is not necessarily in the evidence documenting their discrimination. We may surmise, however, based on what is otherwise presented in the archives of the tradition, that the reasons have to do with the prevailing social and cultural milieus in which Buddhist women practice. It is eminently probable that as tolerant, egalitarian, and non-gendered as Buddhism may be in theory, in reality, the values of the prevailing social and religious systems in which Buddhists find themselves help to shape the current working attitudes of local Buddhist communities, as well as those of the donors who contribute to them. And often these attitudes work negatively against women. Moreover, it is quite possible that, over time, the characteristics of prevailing venues of Buddhist life have not only been adopted in part or in whole by Buddhist communities, but have accrued to the tradition passed down through teaching and disciplinary lineages and today belong to the powerful Buddhist heritage bequeathed to women. And because these unfortunate social views constitute part of the cultural baggage of twentieth-century tradition, they are currently being deemed separable from more egalitarian Buddhist doctrine by women practitioners who hope to reshape the forms, but not the content of, their spiritual quests in the contemporary setting.

Where Buddhist Women Are Going

In 1985, Yvonne Yazbeck Haddad and I published a group of articles under the title *Women, Religion and Social Change.* This collection came out of a conference of the same name, and each piece in it was to address a hypothesis we proposed, using data from many of the major world religious traditions and covering a range of historical periods. The hypothesis was that, in times of great social upheaval and cultural change, women come forward and participate more actively than in quiescent times in the transitions taking place. Moreover, we hypothesized, the nature of women's participation is twofold. First, women are publically active and prominent in the actual changes themselves, moving against older, more outdated forms with a revolutionary seriousness, an organizational zeal, and a quick-sighted attention to the details of movements and trends among peoples. Second, women are equally active and prominent in public as the new order is envisioned; they are well-to-hand in thinking through the broad schemas of what new values are to be emphasized, how new structures can authentically reflect these values, and how the new vision can be made to work viably for as many people as possible. As expected, the reactions to our hypothesis were mixed, as each cultural process examined had its own tangle of causes and conditions bearing on it. We did find, however, that the hypothesis was borne out in many of the cases and that women indeed occupied prominent places as catalysts, workers, and visionaries during times of significant social change.

For this book, I have done something similar. Each contributor has been asked to use current research and writing materials to test a hypothesis. This hypothesis is that, in the contemporary setting, women are playing a significant and even decisive role in the way the forms, practices, and institutions of Buddhism are changing to meet the needs and demands of life in late-twentieth- and early-twenty-first-century culture. These needs and demands, however, may not necessarily be solely those of women themselves, but of those not ordinarily given place in traditional structures of privilege—including those who have been disenfranchised by caste or class, race, education, social upheaval such as war, and any number of life-altering circumstances. Most of the players in these pieces are women themselves but, as you will see, many of the changes that have come and are coming about involve men, in roles as inspirational guides, as mentors, and as helpful facilitators. These men include people like Ānanda, the companion of Gautama Buddha; Dr. Bhimrao Ramji Ambedkar, the Mahar Dalit who converted masses of Dalits to Buddhism in 1956; His Holiness the Fourteenth Dalai Lama; the Venerable Maha Ghosananda, a Cambodian monk who works tirelessly on behalf of victims of the genocide by Khmer Rouge soldiers in the 1970s; as well as countless partners and friends of individual women who seek to create new and more efficacious forms of Buddhist practice in the contemporary setting.

The pieces in this collection cover a wide range of material about Buddhist life. There are historical, archival pieces that document and analyze the roles that women in past times have had in reshaping monastic and lay life to provide parity in teaching and educational matters, in using their often substantial economic resources to create and support great Buddhist institutions, and in establishing ritual traditions that are especially responsive to the enrichment of women's lives. There are contemporary ethnographic pieces, which examine the role of women victims of war in highlighting the brutal oppression of armed conflict, in bringing about peaceful solutions, and in creating therapeutic responses to the war experience. They examine a range of issues, from new solutions to the ordination question for women who seek life as full Buddhist renunciants, to questions of Sangha affiliation and teacher lineage, to questions of patronage and reciprocity in relation to renunciant communities, and to questions of social and political action in which women seek to rectify access to pilgrimage sites, to leadership positions, and to involvement in the rehabilitation of prisoners. There are pieces that focus on new forms of artistic expression and the way these forms can enhance meditational means to perfection, can include a wider, more globally responsive message and form, and can provide architectural spaces more meaningful to those who use them. There are pieces that deal with questions of healing and the ways in which traditional medical practices can be revised so that both body and mind work in tandem to produce optimum health. And there are pieces that focus on lifestyle issues of race, reproductive choices, and the ethics of intimacy.

The range of this collection is broad not only in terms of subject but also in terms of geographical spread. Buddhist women all over the world are working for change, and this collection addresses their work in India, Sri Lanka, Myanmar, Thailand, Kampuchea, Nepal, Tibet, Korea, Japan, Germany, France, England,

and the United States. Moreover, there is a great range in style. Because the topic is so current, I was able to be more faithful to what is happening now by including not only pieces *about* what changes women have been and are making, but also pieces *by* the women who are actually making these changes. Hence, some of the material here will be in formal, traditional, more scholarly formats, which focus on external observations of social and cultural processes, and some will be in more personal, even confessional formats, which, through third-person interviews and first-person reflections, give voice to the individual joys and pains of tackling critical issues and of coming up with often difficult solutions. These latter, more personal works are distinguished by floret designs both in the table of contents and in the text itself.

The organization of the book is thematic. Although most of the pieces address a range of issues, they are grouped together schematically by their main issue. In addressing ordination, affiliation, and relation to the Sangha, Nancy Barnes examines the early inscriptions at Sanchi in India and notes substantial evidence of monastics who were also donors to the site. Although nuns and monks are normally prohibited from having householder property and from handling money, inscriptions throughout South Asia prove the contrary. Most significant is her finding that while donor monks are identified by their religious titles, donor nuns are identified by the names of the villages, towns, and cities they come from—a difference that can only be attributed to the customs of local Sanchi society rather than to any conclusion about gender bias in spiritual attainment. Monica Falk turns to contemporary Thai nuns *(mae chi)* and charts the labyrinth they occupy in the space between being lay women and fully ordained nuns *(bhikkhunīs)*. Overcoming the traditional stereotypes of such women as destitute and bearers of bad karma, Falk shows that in recent times these women, while retaining a traditional absence from public activities such as officiating at ceremonies and going on alms rounds, are in fact undertaking broadened and more independent roles in nunneries more analogous to the roles of Thai monks—especially in the area of self-governance. Pieces compiled by Martine Batchelor illustrate the cases of Voramai Kabilsingh, who is one of the few fully ordained nuns in Thailand and a role model for younger women aspirants, and her daughter, Chatsumarn Kabilsingh, who works and writes actively on behalf of both Thai women seeking full ordination as nuns and Thai prostitutes trying to escape the devastation of AIDS.

Continuing the focus on Thai women, H. Leedom Lefferts explores the relationship between lay women and the monks of the Sangha. He posits that lay women, in their roles involving the exchange of things (for example, food, robes, lodgings, sons) and words, bring about transformations that perpetuate the cyclical universe of Theravāda Buddhism and Thai-Lao life. However, with modernization and Westernization, which both have considerable potency in gender areas, the traditional significance of lay women for Sangha maintenance has come under pressure and may ultimately be undermined. As women increasingly move to cities and find success in other arenas, there may be serious consequences for Thai male monastic life.

Questions for Western women are taken up by Bhikṣuṇī Thubten Chodron and Rotraut Wurst. Chodron tells of being a nun in the Tibetan tradition, ordained as a novice in Dharamsala in 1977 and as a full *bhikṣuṇī* in Taiwan nine years later. She is now living in the United States, and her experiences as a public woman, whose looks and actions conform to almost nothing normative for most Americans, are both funny and edifying. The real bite, however, is in her discussion of the impoverishment of monastic possibilities in this country for women who want to renounce. True to tradition, however, it is the Buddhist view of how "to be" rightly in the world and the meditative practices of compassion, open-heartedness, and equanimity that help women renunciants like her ride the tide of Buddhism in a new land. Rotraut Wurst, on the other hand, a former coordinator for the organization of Buddhist women Sakhyadhītā in Europe, describes a much more gruesome situation for would-be women renunciants in Germany. In contrast to their American sisters, who have more sophisticatedly networked communities and at least some hope of legitimate institutional progress, European women portray their own situation as one where information about opportunities for Buddhist women, and the opportunities themselves, are very hard to find.

Opportunities for the Tibetan nuns of Zangskar are also limited. Kim Gutschow focuses on their attempts to make novice ordination, with head-shaving and full monastic robes, a normative aspect of their religious lives. Although ordination is a crucial issue for these women, an even greater one is economic survival. Because lay patronage for Zangskari nuns is very low—in terms of both alms donations and payment for participation in lay rites of passage—they have to work hard for their material maintenance, and many are forced to live at home and work in the villages. Thus, the nuns' livelihood is supported mostly by their own labors, either in domestic or in agrarian settings.

Empowerment through ritual is a mainstay for Sōtō Zen nuns. Paula Arai reaches back into the history of Japanese nuns to show how they have used a unique ritual of gratitude dedicated to Ānanda, the early monk associated with the entrance of women into Sangha life, to provide enfranchisement and identity. These Sōtō Zen nuns, in using the Ānanda ritual, have been unflagging in their resistance to male-dominated authority and today rely on the ritual to provide affirmation for their own conviction that all women can attain enlightenment as women.

Turning to the theme of teachers, teaching, and lineages, Ellison Banks Findly focuses on two issues. The first is the degree to which nuns in the early Pali tradition lack self-governance, particularly in questions of ordination and teaching. Here it becomes clear that, while nuns have to be sanctioned by the monks' order for their full ordination, this sanction is in fact pro forma, as most of the transformative work for ordination has been done previously by the nuns' Sangha. Moreover, this transformative work has been carried out by educated and highly learned women teachers who have substantial stature in their own right. The second is the tension in the nuns' order between status given by seniority and status given by merit. While both are found in the early tradition, status given by merit—judged on the basis of experience, competence, and the "ability to inspire confidence"—has been preeminent. Both of these issues (self-governance for nuns and internal status based on merit) are of importance today, and the patterns of the early Pali tradition may well provide useful models as women monastics experiment with the structures of their contemporary communities. As Martine Batchelor's piece on the Thai lay teacher Achaan Ranjuan shows, however, not every Buddhist woman who is well taught and gifted in meditation necessarily wants official institutional affiliation and may, in fact, find that lay-nun distinctions are not fully helpful in establishing life in the Dharma.

In Myanmar, women religious are distinguished by their marital status, education, and precept vows and, as Hiroko Kawanami notes, many of these nuns are learned teachers and scholars. In the contemporary Burmese tradition, the primary distinction is between nuns who enter the nunnery young and before they are sexually experienced and are, hence, "virgin nuns," and those who come into the monastic life after marriage and sometimes after widowhood. Generally, the former become well educated and are often well-known teachers, while the latter spend much of their time in meditation. Among the changes taking place at the present time are the entry of women into the monastic life due to the presence of female relatives, the increasing number of nuns who feel comfortable taking on public preaching roles, and the new view of nuns as well-educated members of society rather than as broken-hearted old widows. Changing roles for women teachers are explored as well by Trudy Goodman who, in a short piece, notes some of the ambiguities in the lives of women practicing in the American Zen tradition, and the role these women can play as meditation teachers for both men and women.

Nirmala Salgado turns to Sri Lanka and describes the tension between renunciation and "domestication," or the day-to-day accommodation with the world, which takes place among contemporary Theravāda nuns. This tension is expressed most notably in that, unlike monks, female renunciants rarely own the land they occupy. Moreover, the attitude of contemporary nuns to land ownership is bound to their definitions of kin, and therefore monastic, lineage and has ties to inheritance patterns among lay Buddhists: because inheritance and succession rights to land favor men, monks are deemed better able to handle issues of land and property. As prospects for nuns improve in Sri Lanka, however, most efforts focus on education and ordination, but Salgado argues that ownership and control over land should also move now to the center of these discussions.

In a biographical narrative, Amy Schmidt details the life and contributions of a South Asian *vipassanā* teacher, Dipa Ma Barua, who, through her many students, has had a tremendous influence on the contemporary history of the Theravāda meditational tradition in the Western world. A village-born housewife and mother, Dipa Ma followed her own needs for meditation practice and, after working with a number of teachers, became a prominent teacher herself. Her Western students include Jack Engler, Joseph Goldstein, Jack Kornfield, Sharon Salzberg, and Kate Wheeler. The personal dimension of the teaching relationship is examined as well in a piece by James Whitehill, who explores an "ethic of intimacy" as reflected in the style of his late wife, Miko. A Japanese-American Buddhist who embodied the ideals of mother and spiritual friend, Miko's friendship taught others about the paradoxical posture of compassionate dispassion—a Buddhist-inspired ideal of interpersonal relationships.

Moving into the arena of political and social change, Serinity Young focuses on the role Tibetan nuns play in leading the opposition to the Chinese presence in Tibet. It is the nuns in Lhasa, for example, rather than the monks, who are the most vociferous in bringing attention to the oppression experienced by lay and monastics alike, and it is the nuns, therefore, who are most likely to be arrested, imprisoned, and tortured. Young examines the activist role of female monastics and finds that one of the things their arrest and torture reveals is an ambiguity in Chinese social policy: in spite of their rhetoric supporting gender parity, Chinese officials cannot accept nuns as independent agents and, instead, search for male instigators behind their actions. Like Tibet, Ladakh has suffered from the intrusion of the modern world and, like Young, Helena Norberg-Hodge finds that this intrusion has had serious effects on the women there. As women have gradually lost much of their self-confidence, strength of character, and dignity and have begun to spend much of their time lethargically watching television, the Women's Alliance in Ladakh has begun to play an important role in involving women in the promotion and preservation of their culture—most effectively, at the beginning, in discussion groups about the impact of "development."

Owen Lynch and Eleanor Zelliot examine the political and literary legacy of Dr. B. R. Ambedkar among the Dalit Buddhist women of north India. Lynch focuses on a group of Agra-based women who work—under the rubric of "Sujātā's Army"—on a number of local issues that have implications not only for the welfare of women and Dalits themselves, but for the overall nature of social activism undertaken as a form of Buddhist practice as well. Highlighting, particularly, the Liberate Bodh Gaya movement, the Ban the Lottery campaign, and the Subvert Hierarchy campaign, Lynch makes it clear that women are among the leaders, if not the primary leaders, of much of the vigorous involvement in controversial social issues in north India at the present time.

Zelliot returns to the legacy of Dr. Ambedkar and looks at the female leadership emerging from his original Buddhist-based political movement in Maharashtra. Consistently oriented towards rectifying the treatment of those most socially disadvantaged, two kinds of activities have evolved. The first, an organization known as the Trilokya Bauddha Mahasangha Sahayaka Gana (TBMSG), is based in the work of several *dhammacāriṇīs* who, as well-organized and highly trained Buddhist lay women, run hostels for young girls. These hostels have, in the past decade, become models for other fledgling institutions dedicated to the humanistic education of women. The second is the individual effort made by a number of women to bring attention to and change the dismal social conditions of many of their Dalit compatriots through writing, publishing, and grass roots campaigning. These efforts have borne particularly creative fruit in poetry and song, and Buddhist Dalit women have been able to carve out of the Dalit literature movement the even more specialized phenomenon of Buddhist literature.

Short compilations by Martine Batchelor highlight some of the social service work currently being done by Korean nuns. Jamin Sunim, for example, gives Dharma talks in prisons and engages inmates in examining the personal and circumstantial backgrounds of their crimes in a Buddhist context. Myohi Sunim has organized a home for elderly women, where she provides basic living care and assistance as well as daily Buddhist instruction; she is also planning a similar home specifically designed for elderly Buddhist nuns. And Pomyong Sunim provides therapeutic services to a wide range of Korean lay people through the practice of flower arrangement and offering.

Women's social efforts have been prominent in the settings of war and oppression as well, and Tessa Bartholomeusz describes the tension around women's roles in the Tamil-Sinhala struggle in Sri Lanka. This tension is played out between those who advocate the government's devolution package, which would give semi-autonomy to the Tamils in the north, but also peace to the country, and those who insist on retaining the geographic unity of the island at whatever the cost. The search for peace becomes gendered through the work of Women for Peace, a group of Buddhist women who strive for a political rather than a military solution and who, therefore, find the government's devolution package a reasonable option. The conjunction of Women for Peace with the devolution issue is controversial not only because it is considered anti-Buddhist (for example, anti-Sinhala) but also because, as an autonomous female activity, it challenges the traditional patriarchal bias in Sri Lankan culture.

Traditional forms of social engagement for contemporary Buddhist women are reflected in the stories of two Thai nuns described in short pieces by Martine Batchelor. Mae Chi Boonliang, for example, runs a nunnery and a charitable foundation set up to educate young women in basic studies and to train them in marketable skills, such as sewing and work with flowers. And Mae Chi Sansenee runs schools for students of all ages, including students with disabilities, on land she bought at the suggestion of her monastic teacher.

Social change sometimes takes the form of slow, persistent knocking at the door. In this context, Janice Willis raises questions of race and ethnicity in Buddhist America through interviews with four African-Americans. Representing three major sectarian traditions found in America (Theravāda *vipassanā,* Tibetan, and Zen) as well as the academic study of Buddhism, Willis' informants discuss how race and ethnicity have and have not been an issue in their study and practice of Buddhism and, if an issue, whether it has been positive or negative. Interpreting her colleagues' observations alongside her own, she explores the additional issue of gender, as developed in the account of Lori Pierce.

Under the theme of art and architecture, Melissa Kerin documents the training and early practice of *maṇḍala*-making and *thangka*-painting by nuns from the Keydong nunnery in Kathmandu. Although supported by His Holiness the Dalai Lama, and facilitated by monks from their brother nunnery in south India, the steps these nuns took were unusually courageous as they expanded their meditative practices into areas previously reserved for their male colleagues. Inspired by the work of these nuns, Judy Dworin created a performance, "Wheel," which draws on the resources of international women artists to plumb the depths of *saṃsāra* and to rework patterns of the spiritual quest to respond effectively to women's needs. *Maṇḍala* structures not only proved transformative for mature women artists but, under the leadership of Dworin and her Performance Ensemble, became especially accessible to a group of Hispanic elementary students who created a large outdoor production based on Buddhist themes of suffering, impermanence, freedom, and compassion.

Ann Norton concentrates on new work done in the arts by women who use Buddhist themes. Some of these are visual artists who use recognizable Buddhist forms such as the *maṇḍala* (Suzanne Wind Greenbaum) and the *vajra* and *mudrā* (Mary Laird), for example, and others who rework their own Buddhist heritage into contemporary images. One such artist is Haruko Okano, a Japanese-Canadian who experiments with shrine settings, while another is the Laotian-American artist Ammala Douangsavanh, who expresses her tradition in cross-cultural dance and poetry. Mayumi Oda of Tokyo is well known for her banner series, many of which explore the transformation of goddess images. And Sarah Buie examines the creation of architectural and landscaped environments by three American Buddhist women who, as teachers, seek to integrate Dharmic, feminine, environmental, and traditional Buddhist values into their spaces. Joan Halifax's "Upaya" is a residential teaching center near Santa Fe whose structures emphasize interrelatedness, attentiveness, and intimacy; Tsultrim Allione's "Tara Mandala" in Colorado combines the design of Tibetan summer encampments with current, progressive thinking on proper relationships between humans and the environment; and Yvonne Rand's slowly evolving "Redwood Creek Temple" near Muir Beach emphasizes the cyclical interdependence of birth and decay.

The section on body and health begins with the story of Hi-ah Park, a Korean Buddhist who was formally trained in Korean court dance and music. She describes her own arduous mystic illnesses, which led to and included her shamanic initiation in 1981 and, eventually, to world-renown as a shamanic Buddhist healer. Her initiation experiences were intense and profound and, in many ways, mirror traditional stages along the mystic pathway experienced by earlier Christian, Sufi, and Hindu mystics. In a Martine Batchelor piece, Tokwang Sunim, a Korean nun and long-time medical student, describes her practice as a medical technician. She treats men and women without discrimination, and promotes both strict medical hygiene and the development of proper mental culture. Although the success of her medical work is substantial, she stresses that much depends on the mental state and hard work of the patient him- or herself.

In a thoughtful muse on human reproduction, Kate Lila Wheeler addresses the very personal question of how a Buddhist decides whether or not to have a baby. After looking at conflicting aspects of the question herself, and after gathering personal views from a wide range of sources, Wheeler decides against motherhood as a personal choice. It is clear from the responses of many of her informants, however, that the Buddhist tradition supports either option. Generativity and continuity, and Buddhist women's role in them, are central themes of the work of Theanvy Kuoch as well. A Cambodian refugee in Hartford, she founded Khmer Health Advocates in 1981. Her hope was, and is, to address the multiple mental health disorders afflicting Cambodians fleeing a decade of war, torture, and starvation in their homeland. Kuoch's work focuses especially on women's and family issues that are not only deeply influenced by the experiences of Khmer Rouge persecution, but reflect assimilation pressures in America as well.

A cornerstone of the body and health section is its last contribution, a piece by Vincanne Adams and Dashima Dovchin on Tibetan medicine and women. In addition to highlighting the teachings of traditional Tibetan medicine and its relationship with Buddhist religious practice, Adams and Dovchin investigate the details of gynecological disorders and one of their most ardent investigators, Tibet's first female doctor in modern times, Kandro Yangkar (1904–1972/3). Among Kandro Yangkar's accomplishments are substantial efforts to preserve the Tibetan medical system by creating a wide range of new medicines and by focusing on women's health problems. These efforts are now drawing much attention from Western doctors who hope to integrate Tibetan medicine's healing techniques into those of the West.

While this collection represents only a sampling of the work that contemporary women are engaged in as the forms, practices, and institutions of Buddhism undergo change, it shows how great the variety is among their ranks. Activist women play roles at almost every point in the spectrum of human life, working in many types of Buddhist contexts and in many geographical locations. They question how "worldly" or "otherworldly" a Buddhist practice might be, how involved in social and political issues to get, where to find and how to relate to spiritual advisers, and how to access the most beneficial teachings and practices. Contemporary Buddhist women are also fully committed to aesthetic questions of creating meaningful spaces, movements, sounds, and visual images for their practice. And they seek, as well, ways to evolve forms of lifestyle conducive to the most balanced mental and physical health, expressive of the most humane personal relationships, and supportive of the most harmonious communal ties. While this modest collection cannot reflect all of the rich responses present in the contemporary environment, it can suggest some of the things women are now doing, and perhaps inspire others in the future.

PART I

Ordination, Affiliation, and Relation to the Sangha

THE NUNS AT THE STŪPA:
Inscriptional Evidence for the Lives and Activities of Early Buddhist Nuns in India

Nancy J. Barnes

The Nuns' Order in Buddhist Texts

A *bhikkhunī* IS A FEMALE RELIGIOUS MENDICANT who has renounced ordinary worldly life to follow the Buddha's path to enlightenment and liberation from unhappiness. She has no livelihood other than her religious life, and she receives donations of food, clothing, and shelter from the lay faithful to sustain her. The word *bhikkhunī* is usually rendered in English as nun, but the analogy between Buddhist and Christian nuns is only approximate. Like her male counterpart, the *bhikkhu*, the *bhikkhunī* undergoes a period of religious training as a novice, after which she is ordained as a full-fledged member of the nuns' order in a formal ceremony known as *upasampadā.*[1]

A woman who wishes to join the nuns' order goes to an ordained *bhikkhunī* and has her hair shaved off, as a symbol of her renunciation of ordinary lay life. She requests two senior *bhikkhunīs* to act as her instructors during her two-year training period, and these two *bhikkhunīs* present her to the whole local chapter of nuns when she is ready for ordination. The spokeswoman for the chapter asks the novice a prescribed series of questions about her health, her legal status as a free woman, and her fitness to join the order. After she has answered satisfactorily, she is presented with the nun's basic possessions: the five-part monastic robes (saffron-colored in much of the Buddhist world) in which she vows to dress henceforth, and an alms bowl with which she may beg her daily food from the laity. Then her ordination as the newest member of the chapter is announced, and she formally accepts the list of all the rules contained in the Vinaya (book of monastic discipline) that are to regulate her conduct as a *bhikkhunī.* After she has been ordained by her fellow *bhikkhunīs,* she must present herself before a quorum of the local chapter of *bhikkhus* for ordination by their community. Only then is she recognized as a *bhikkhunī* who has received double ordination from both the *bhikkhunī* and *bhikkhu* Sanghas, or religious communities. The *upasampadā* of a *bhikkhu* is nearly the same as a *bhikkhunī's* except that he receives ordination only from the monks' Sangha, not from the nuns.

According to Buddhist scriptures, the orders of *bhikkhunīs* and *bhikkhus* were founded by Gotama the Buddha soon after he had attained enlightenment. Men and women who felt a powerful desire to devote their lives to the quest for liberation from worldly suffering were drawn to him, and he accepted them as his followers, organizing them into a religious community, the Sangha. *Bhikkhunīs* and *bhikkhus* learned moral discipline, meditated, preached the Dhamma[2] to lay disciples, and presided over various life cycle rituals for the laity.[3] Buddhist sūtras (Pali suttas; discourses) and the Vinaya[4] recount stories of many *bhikkhunīs* who are said to have lived at the time of the Buddha: women who had experienced *nibbāna* (liberation) through insight into the true nature of existence and the causes of human suffering; women who were learned and became skilled and eloquent teachers; women who acted as guides and counselors to other nuns.

An old story of how the *bhikkhunī* order began is recounted in Buddhist texts.[5] A few years after the Buddha had established the order of *bhikkhus*, Mahāpajāpatī, Gotama's aunt and stepmother, came to him and asked him to receive her and her companions as female mendicants. Three times he refused her request, and she left in tears. But she did not give up her quest. She and her friends shaved their own heads, as the *bhikkhus* did, put on saffron robes, and followed the Buddha and his monks in their wanderings. Exhausted after her long journey, and fully aware that the Buddha had rejected her, Mahāpajāpatī stood weeping outside the place where the monks had gathered. The young monk Ānanda, who was related to both Mahāpajāpatī and Gotama, found her there and asked why she was so troubled. When she told him, he took it upon himself to speak on her behalf to the Buddha, but he, too, was refused. Ānanda was as determined as Mahāpajāpatī, however, and he asked the Buddha whether women were as capable of attaining enlightenment as men. When the Buddha affirmed that there was no difference in women's and men's potential for highest realization, Ānanda asked again whether Mahāpajāpatī, the woman who had raised Gotama after his own mother had died, could be received into the Buddhist Sangha along with her women companions, and the Buddha agreed. But the Buddha imposed on the women eight special rules, which would have the effect of keeping the nuns permanently subordinated to the monks, and barred from attaining positions of authority in the Sangha.

This is what the texts say. But modern scholars now ask, do these texts actually present an accurate history of events during the lifetime of the Buddha? In fact, very few Buddhist texts now extant can be definitely dated, in their present form, to earlier than the fourth or fifth centuries C.E.—that means as much as a thousand years after the time of the Buddha.[6] Certainly there were oral traditions about the teachings of the Buddha and the early years of his Sangha, and some of these accounts were committed to writing in the first century B.C.E.—a few hundred years after the death of the Buddha. However, these written texts were probably revised before they reached the state in which we now have them, so that what they now present is a carefully constructed interpretation of what Buddhism was originally like. The story of the founding of the nuns' order is one example of this process of revision and refinement. It was created by monks at some unknown time for a particular purpose: to settle the matter of the relative status of monks and nuns in the Sangha.

If Buddhist sūtras, the Vinaya, and even traditional histories do not paint an accurate picture of nuns and monks at the time of the Buddha or in the centuries immediately following his death, is there some more reliable source for information about real Buddhists in ancient times? Fortunately, there is.

Inscriptions from Early Buddhist Monuments

A number of ancient Buddhist sites have been discovered and excavated by archeologists since the mid-nineteenth century. Some of them are monastic cave complexes, which were hewn out of the sides of cliffs; some are free-standing monuments surrounded by residences for monastics. Some sites are quite modest; others are large and impressive. Among the latter are Bodhgaya, the place where the Buddha attained enlightenment; Sarnath, where he first taught the Dhamma; and the magnificent reliquary stūpas (Pali *thūpa*)[7] of Amaravati, Bharhut, and Sanchi. Portions of the structures at these sites were donated to the Buddha or the Sangha, and the donated stones were inscribed with the records of the donations. The body of inscriptions that have so far been discovered from several sites is large, and dates from the third century B.C.E. to as late as the fourteenth century C.E. The earliest of these, dating from the third century B.C.E. to the second century C.E., include a very large number of records of gifts made by *bhikkhunīs* and *bhikkhus*. Although the inscriptions are very brief, usually giving only the donor's name, religious title, perhaps a place of residence, or the name of the donor's religious teacher, a surprising amount of information can be derived from them about the Buddhist Sangha and the condition of Buddhism in the years not long after the Buddha's death. One of the best-preserved of these ancient sites is Sanchi, which also produced the richest body of inscriptions found at any single site—more than eight hundred inscriptions altogether. Some 129 record gifts of monks, and 125 are gifts that name nuns as donors. These gifts by monastics represent nearly a third of the total donations.[8]

The Monuments of Sanchi

The Sanchi site was probably founded in the third century B.C.E., for there is a pillar in the main precinct with an inscription of the Mauryan emperor, Aśoka. The oldest foundations of the principal monument, Stūpa I, and the nearby building known as Temple XL, are at the same level as Aśoka's pillar, and thus were begun at the time the pillar was erected.[9] There are three very well preserved and restored stūpas on the Sanchi Hill: Stūpa I, the largest, which is dedicated to the Buddha and once contained some of his relics; Stūpa III, which housed the relics of the Buddha's two chief disciples, Mahāmogallāna and Sāriputta, who pre-deceased him; and Stūpa II, located part way down the hill outside the main precinct, which contained relics of several revered local monks.[10] There are also remains of a number of other structures in the main precinct on the hilltop—small stūpas, temples, and monasteries. Most of the inscriptions were on paving stones and parts of the railings surrounding the three main stūpas, but some were found on stones and images from the other buildings. Aside from Aśoka's third-century B.C.E. inscription on the pillar, the inscriptions date from the second century B.C.E. to the ninth century C.E., with all but a handful dating from the second and first centuries B.C.E.[11]

The Sanchi Hill is in north central India, in the modern-day state of Madhya Pradesh. It rises from the plains about four miles from the town of Vidisha, which was an important trading center and capital of the local territory in the last few centuries B.C.E. Major east-west and north-south trade routes that linked both coasts and many important cities and ports crossed near Vidisha. Traveling merchants passing through Vidisha could stop at Sanchi to see the Buddha's stūpa, or to visit some of the other Buddhist cult centers in the vicinity. Inscriptions from Sanchi indicate that prosperous lay people from many nearby towns donated stones when the great stūpa of Sanchi was enlarged and adorned in the second century B.C.E. Presumably the place was quite familiar to them.

Although Gotama the Buddha never visited this region of northern India during his lifetime, some of his relics were brought there, probably in the third century B.C.E., and deposited in the new stūpa built to protect them. Wherever his relics were, there was the living presence of the Buddha, and people went there to be in his presence, to see his presence in the stūpa that enclosed his relics.[12] By the last quarter of the second century B.C.E., the Sanchi Hill with its Buddha relics had become important enough as a cult center to inspire the local monastic community to enlarge the main stūpa, face it with stone slabs, and surround it with a massive stone railing. Between the railing and the base or drum of the stūpa, a paved *pradakṣiṇā,* or walking path, was laid down on which the visitor could circumambulate the sacred mound. A stairway was also built to an upper *pradakṣiṇā* path with its own railing atop the drum about a third of the way to the crest of the stūpa. From that crest a mast arose surmounted by stone discs (*chattras* or ceremonial umbrellas) and enclosed by still another railing. It was the stones that made up these railings, and that paved the ground level *pradakṣiṇā* path, that were donated by nuns, monks and lay people and inscribed with their names. A little later, in the first century B.C.E., four monumental gateways *(toraṇa)* covered with sculpted panels and three-dimensional figures were added. On the gateways, too, donations were recorded.[13]

Nuns at Sanchi

The Sanchi inscriptions record gifts made and paid for by *bhikkhunīs, bhikkhus,* and lay people. All of these donors clearly had sufficient wealth to make such gifts. Although it had long been assumed by scholars of Buddhism that those who entered the Sangha gave up their personal property and all claim to their family's wealth, these inscriptions (and many from other monuments) demonstrate that this was not so. That individual monastics did own property is confirmed by several passages in the books of regulations for monks and nuns, the Vinaya.[14] Nuns and monks did themselves receive gifts of food and other articles from lay people, but some of them were not wholly dependent on the generosity of the laity. In the last few centuries B.C.E., lay people made gifts to Buddha stūpas and other holy places as acts of devotion, and to earn religious merit for themselves or for others. They also gave to nuns and monks to earn merit. In return, monastics performed religious services for their lay donors, such as preaching to them and participating in their life cycle rituals. When Sanchi's Buddha stūpa was expanded and Stūpas II and III were erected, nuns and monks presented themselves in great numbers as donors, shoulder to shoulder with prosperous lay men and women.[15]

The number of donations by nuns and monks is about equal: 125 from nuns, 129 from monks at all Sanchi's edifices. Nuns were just as likely as monks to have the means to make religious gifts, and just as likely to step forward and actively support the construction of an important monument. Monastic women were a significant element in the development of major cult centers like Sanchi. Their gifts also contributed to the creation of a new Buddhist architectural landscape in India, a landscape dotted with large and imposing stūpas like those at Sanchi, and those that once existed at Bharhut, Amaravati, and elsewhere.

At Sanchi, nuns' gifts were presented mostly to Stūpa I, the Buddha's stūpa, and to Stūpa II, which held the relics of ten local monks. These two monuments were also most favored by monks and lay donors. How much the stones cost is not recorded. Most of the inscriptions are on paving stones that were walked on, or on sections of the stūpa railing that visitors would pass while circling the monument but would hardly notice. The gifts were not made for glory. They were made to the Buddha, and the inscribed stones remained in his presence long after the donors had died.

Nuns came from other places to make their gifts to the Buddha at Sanchi.[16] Their inscriptions do not call them residents of Kākanāva, the ancient name for the religious center on Sanchi Hill. None of the monk donors is called a resident, either, although a relic casket from Stūpa II was the gift of religious pupils of a Kākanāva monk. Seventy-three of the nuns' inscriptions identify the donor by the place she came from: for example, the gift of *bhikkhunī* Yakhī from Vadivahana, the gift of *bhikkhunī* Isidatā of Kurara.[17] All the nuns whose homes are named came from just twelve cities or towns, the exact locations of most of which have not been determined, though probably none were very distant from Sanchi Hill. There are eight inscriptions of nuns from the city of Vedisa (Vidisha), which was very close by. There are also eight from Ujeni (Ujjain), another important city further to the west. But by far the largest groups of nuns came from Kurara and Nadinagara, whose locations are not known. A total of seventy-eight cities and towns are mentioned in all the inscriptions from Sanchi. Lay donors hailed from a much larger array of places than nuns did. Although the numbers of nun and monk donors at Sanchi were nearly equal, the thirty-four monks' inscriptions that mention where they resided name twenty-two places. It seems likely that there were communities of nuns in the towns named in their inscriptions, and those at Kurara and Nadinagara may have been particularly large, for at that moment in history when all these donations were made a significant number of nuns from those places chose to make gifts.

Monks' residences are harder to pin down, for the great majority of monks' inscriptions do not mention names of cities or towns at all, and those that do tally up to one or two monks each from quite a number of places. The fact that a larger number of places is mentioned in monks' records, even though so few individuals came from them, at least suggests that there were more monks' communities in the areas around Sanchi than there were nuns' communities. Monks may also have been more mobile than nuns, traveling at will, alone or in pairs. Nuns seem to have been more likely to travel to a place like Sanchi in groups. Four gifts were made to Stūpa I by groups or pairs of nuns, and one gift to Temple XL.[18] It is also important to note that nuns most often identified themselves by their places of residence, and monks did not. Lay people, too, frequently identified themselves by the names of the towns or cities where they lived.

Names of cities, towns, or villages are mentioned in the nuns' and monks' inscriptions, but not the names of monasteries. It is not clear, then, that Buddhist monastics lived in settled and self-conscious monastic communities in the second and first centuries B.C.E. On Sanchi Hill itself, none of the monasteries that have been excavated date from this early period. In these laconic inscriptions, at least, there seems to be little evidence for the existence of the kind of highly organized communities living in well-built monasteries that are described in the Vinayas.

Nuns' inscriptions at Sanchi refer to the donors as *bhikkhunīs,* who are more often than not further identified by their place of residence. One woman, however, who donated three separate railing stones to Stūpa I and one rail pillar to Stūpa II[19] is referred to as *sutatika,* one who is versed in the sūtras. Six inscriptions record gifts from women who were pupils of five different women religious teachers; two students of one of these teachers made separate gifts. There is some evidence from the inscriptions, therefore, that a woman could be recognized as learned (versed in the sūtras), and that some women were venerated by their female pupils.[20]

Monk donors, however, are often identified by religious titles other than *bhikkhu,* which indicate the monk's learning or seniority. Two monks are called by the respectful title *bhadata,* reverend.[21] One is called *thera,* elder.[22] Two are called *bhāṇaka,* reciters or preachers; another is *dhammakathika,* preacher of Dhamma.[23] One is *sutatika,* versed in the sūtras; another is *pacanekayika,* versed in the five bodies of scripture.[24] One is called *sapurisa,* true or worthy man.[25] Seventeen inscriptions record the gifts from men who identify themselves as pupils, *antevāsin,* of twelve different teachers, and the teachers are all called *aya* (*ārya*), noble or worthy.[26] *Aya* is the most commonly used religious title in the inscriptions, next to *bhikkhu.* It is used in eleven other inscriptions besides those just mentioned.[27] In some cases, a monk is identified by more than one title: *Aya Passanaka bhichu, Thera aya Naga bhichu* of Ujeni.[28] Among donor monks, then, a variety of religious titles is used, and an individual is more likely to be identified by his title than by his place of residence. This is strikingly different from the way nuns are identified.

Inside Stūpa II, a stone box containing four smaller steatite caskets was found. In the caskets were some of the ashes of ten revered local monks.[29] All the boxes were inscribed. The inscription says that the stone box contains the relics of the *vinayakas,* masters of Vinaya. The caskets name each of the deceased. One is called *ācariya,* teacher. A second is a pupil of another monk. One casket refers to *kākanāva pabhāsa,* the Light of Kākanāva (the ancient name for Sanchi). All ten monks are called *sapurisa,* true or worthy men.[30] Some of the relics of these same monks were also found in stūpas a few miles from Sanchi Hill, at Sonari and Andher, which indicates that they were held in especially high esteem in the whole area around Sanchi.[31] In the inscriptions they are called by what must have been particularly reverent titles. *Sapurisa* is not very commonly found in inscriptions from other sites, although it does occur in Buddhist scriptures. It may have been a title used among local monastics, just as *kākanāva pabhāsa* obviously was. In any case it must have been a very respectful title since it was used for these ten men whose remains were interred in large stūpas built specifically for them.[32]

Several questions suggest themselves after this analysis of how nuns and monks are identified in the Sanchi inscriptions. First of all, why were monks so frequently identified by their religious titles, while nuns were identified by the names of the cities, towns, or villages they came from? Only one woman is identified by a religious title, *sutatika.* The religious titles used indicate the seniority of a monk, or the respect with which he was regarded, or his learning. Does this mean that monks were more likely to be respected or to become learned in the sūtras and the Vinaya, which in the second and first centuries B.C.E. were probably only handed down by oral instruction from teacher to pupil? If so, did monks have more opportunities to study with a teacher, or were they more eager for learning than nuns were? Was there something about the monastic communities that offered men more support for study than women? The donative inscriptions name at least twelve learned monk teachers and their male students. They also name five learned nuns who had female pupils. Neither number is large, and the difference between them is not great, but nonetheless there were more monks than nuns in the Sanchi inscriptions who were teachers with a following of pupils. Is this fact some small indication that more monks had studied and gained sufficient mastery of Dhamma to become teachers? In that case, if a nun wanted to learn the scriptures, but could find no learned nun to teach her, could she ask to be taught by a learned monk?[33] What we do know is that there were at least five women teachers in the communities around Sanchi, and that some of their pupils valued their relationship with them so much that they identified themselves first and foremost as their disciples.

However, not even these women teachers are called by religious titles that testified to their learning. All the monk teachers were. Perhaps the monk teachers were simply more senior in the Sangha than any nuns in the inscriptions were, although a monk or nun who taught pupils had to be qualified, and that normally required years of study. Perhaps the *bhikkhunī* Sangha near Sanchi was a younger entity than the *bhikkhu* Sangha. Monk donors were drawn from a larger number of local religious communities than nuns were, according to the inscriptions. The nuns' Sangha may have been more recently introduced into the region. Without more archaeological data from other Buddhist sites in the wider area around Sanchi it is impossible to say. But the problem of why even nun teachers were not called by respectful religious titles is troubling.

But there may be other reasons for this. Who decided how the inscriptions were to read? The donors obviously supplied the basic information, but the second and first century B.C.E. inscriptions seem to follow a single pattern, which suggests that the overseer of the Sanchi building projects had something to say about how they read. The overseer certainly controlled the overall design of the railings and walking paths: the stones are all cut to regular shapes, and all are carefully finished and carefully fitted together. The overseer would also have been responsible for having the inscriptions carved into the donated blocks.[34] The overseer, *navakammika*, of a Buddhist construction project was usually a monk, and often a high-ranking monk.[35] He was appointed to this position by the local Sangha, and represented the monks' interests while he had the project carried out.

By the time the Sanchi stūpas were constructed, local traditions prescribing the designation of senior or accomplished monks had been established. It is possible that there was no local tradition of designating and differentiating nuns by such titles, no matter what their religious accomplishments; perhaps it was simply the convention to call all women monastics by one term: *bhikkhunī*. If this speculation is correct, it would suggest that the difference in the way the Sanchi monastics and laity perceived and addressed monks and nuns had more to do with custom and even with pressure from the local society than with an imbalance in ability or attainment between male and female monastics: *bhikkhunīs* are women of place, *bhikkhus* are men of accomplishment. This may also have been the way nuns and monks perceived themselves.[36]

It is worth considering, also, whether very many donors, monastic or lay, could read the inscriptions on their own donated stones. Obviously some monastics could read and write, for it was probably literate monks who were given the job of writing the inscriptions on the stones (that were then carved into the surface by other hands). But it may not have been important at all whether donors, monastic or lay, could read the inscriptions on their stones. Once the stones were set in place, it is quite possible that no one ever bothered to look at them, much less read them. It was not only that they would have been hard to read, being too high up on railing or gateway to be made out, or under one's feet as one circumambulated the stūpa, but that the inscriptions were never meant for living human eyes.

The stūpa is not just a symbol of the Buddha, nor does it merely belong to him. The stūpa is the Buddha himself. When a person made a gift to the stūpa and had her name cut into the stone, her name was permanently fixed in the living presence of the Buddha. It was the Buddha who "read" it. And the donors had every reason to have themselves identified as exactly as possible, so that their names would not be confused with anyone else's. In ancient Indian thought, a person's name was inseparable from her essential character, and her name inscribed on a stone made her present there herself. The living nun remained permanently in the presence of the living Buddha. The overseer who received the donors' money and had their names inscribed on their stones made this enduring relationship possible.[37]

Sanchi Stūpas II and III contained relics of deceased monks, not of the Buddha. Stūpa III is dedicated to the Buddha's two greatest disciples, Sāriputta and Mahāmogallāna, who figure prominently in many sūtras. According to Chinese pilgrims who visited India in the fifth and seventh centuries C.E., many stūpas were erected over their relics, which had been dispersed to Buddhist centers all over the country.[38] Relic boxes from another of their stūpas were found at Satdhara, only a few miles from Sanchi. At Sanchi, Stūpa III was built close to the Buddha's Stūpa I, within the main monastic precinct at the top of the hill. According to the Vinaya, this was the proper place for the highest ranking monks, who had experienced *nibbāna*.[39] Sāriputta and Mahāmogallāna were the Buddha's contemporaries and close companions. They had died long before any cult center was founded on Sanchi Hill. Their memory obviously survived among Buddhists all over India, but the two great disciples had no specific connection with Kākanāva-Sanchi. Their stūpa did not attract the enthusiasm that donors felt toward the Buddha's stūpa, or toward Stūpa II, which covered the relics of ten local monks. Stūpa III received only sixteen donations. Seven of these were from nuns or monks, the rest from lay people. Both monastics and laity reserved most of their gifts for the other two stūpas.

By contrast with the paucity of inscribed donations found at Stūpa III, about one hundred recorded donations are extant on the railings and pavements of Stūpa II, and more than half of these are from monks and nuns. The monks whose relics were found in Stūpa II were clearly greatly revered, enough so that a special stūpa was built for them at Sanchi, and at two nearby sites, Sonari and Andher, and their stūpas were well endowed with donations. However, their attainments were not of the highest, evidently, because Stūpa II is placed outside the main precinct, down the hill from Stūpa I and Stūpa III, which accords with instructions given in the Vinaya as to where to locate stūpas of monks of various ranks.[40] Their status was not equal to Sāriputta's or Mahāmogallāna's; they were what the Vinaya calls "ordinary monks."

Sanchi Stūpa I was still surrounded by many small stūpas when the site was discovered in the nineteenth century, but they were cleared away by excavators during the operations between 1881 and 1883. Other Buddhist sites are still crowded with small stūpas, which cluster close to the sacred monument, as at Bodhgaya, or are set at some distance from the principal structure, as at Bhaja, Kanheri and many other cave monastery complexes.[41] These small stūpas are mortuary stūpas that held the ashes of the local monastic dead. With their relics buried near the Buddha's stūpa or holy place, these people, too, remained permanently in the presence of the living Buddha. Not many of the surviving small stūpas bear inscriptions identifying the deceased. The few that do name monks.

Since most small stūpas are anonymous burials, we cannot know whether any of them contained the remains of nuns. The larger relic stūpas that are known, like Sanchi Stūpa II, were all raised for monks. Since nuns had the resources to make gifts to monks' stūpas and to the great monuments of the Buddha, they presumably would have had the wealth to build stūpas for their dead sisters. I wonder what happened to the remains of nuns.

Figure 1 *(see p. 30)*

Figure 2

Figure 3

Texts say that when *bhikkhunī* Mahāpajāpatī—the woman who had been the Buddha's stepmother and was the first *bhikkhunī,* according to the scriptures—died, a great funeral was held for her. The four most venerable monks carried her bier, and the Buddha himself walked beside it with his hand on it. In the Buddhist tradition, she is one of the most venerable nuns who ever lived. But no texts mention that a stūpa was erected for her relics after her body was cremated. After the death of the venerable Sāriputta, not just one but eventually many stūpas were built to contain his relics.[42]

A story is told in the Theravāda Vinaya about a stūpa that some nuns built for the remains of a sister they deeply venerated. A senior monk was annoyed when he found them lamenting at the new stūpa, and he demolished it before their eyes. The horrified nuns then plotted to kill the monk, but another monk warned him, and he escaped their vengeance. The nuns then went to the monk who had warned the stūpa destroyer, and reviled and insulted him for interceding. When the case was brought to the Buddha, he had nothing to say about the first monk's destruction of the stūpa, nor about the nuns' assassination plot. Instead he made a new regulation, a Vinaya rule, that no nun was allowed to verbally abuse or revile any monk.[43]

Although this story need not be accepted as history, it represents a monastic attitude that prevailed in the centuries when many of the later monastic cemeteries and mortuary stūpas were constructed. According to the Vinaya, the destruction of a stūpa was an exceedingly serious offense; it was the same as killing a living person—that is, the person whose remains the stūpa contained. The person in question was, moreover, an ordained *bhikkhunī.* Yet a senior *bhikkhu,* who knew the rules, was not chastised by anyone for committing this act of ritual murder—nor, of course, were the nuns penalized for attempting to exact blood vengeance against an ordained monk. The issue of interest to the monks who compiled this Vinaya tale was the monks' right to authority in the Sangha. Nuns were not to be permitted to establish ritual centers of their own—for that is what their stūpa was—independent from the monks. And judging from the account of Mahāpajāpatī's funeral, the monks were unlikely to establish a stūpa for a deceased nun themselves. These accounts do not inform us about attitudes or practices prevailing in the second or first centuries B.C.E. But they do suggest that the monks who composed these stories, whenever they were composed, wanted to control the actions of nuns and curtail their inclinations toward independence.

The Sanchi inscriptions make it very clear that nuns did act independently in real life: they made gifts to the stūpas of their own accord, and did not wait for monks to give them orders. Perhaps they were not addressed with the full vocabulary of religious nomenclature that the monks were honored with, but they were financially independent and played a major role in creating the cult center on Sanchi Hill. We may never know whether they also erected anonymous stūpas somewhere for their own special dead.

Conclusions

The Sanchi material used here comes from one site only, a cult center in north-central India that had local fame but may not have been well known beyond its limited geographical area. It is true that it is better preserved than any other ancient Buddhist structural site, and is, moreover, the richest single repository of early inscriptions yet discovered in India. We can be sure that the information in the Sanchi inscriptions opens a window on Buddhism in a particular region in the second and first centuries B.C.E., and even somewhat after that because of a few later inscriptions. Comparison with inscriptions from other sites that date from about the same time shows that the Sangha near Sanchi had much in common with the Sangha elsewhere, but the present lack of significant bodies of inscriptions from a significant number of other sites[44] suggests caution is in order before too many generalizations are made.

I can say that in the records from Sanchi, women played roles as important as men's. Not only were *bhikkhunīs* as active as donors as *bhikkhus* were, but lay women were often the leaders in making religious gifts, either with male and female relatives, or independently. Among those pious lay people known as *upāsakas* or *upāsikās*, there were about three times as many women *(upāsikās)* as men *(upāsakas)* who left records of gifts at the stūpas. The donors were indispensable in making Sanchi what it is.

Nuns seem not to have held ranks in the Sangha that were equal to men's, but that does not appear to have held them back. From the inscriptions we know them only as donors. We don't know any of the details of these women's daily lives. We don't know whether they lived together in communities, or how they interacted with each other or with the lay people in their towns. The only hint we find of communal action comes from the records of joint gifts made by two or more *bhikkhunīs*.[45] We also know that at least one nun made a joint gift in company with some monks and lay people, but the record tells us nothing about the relationship between these individuals.[46] We can conclude that mothers of nuns were sufficiently proud of their daughters' vocation to call themselves the mother of the nun so-and-so in the records of their own donations.[47] (There were also mothers of monks who identified themselves similarly.) My impression after closely examining the Sanchi inscriptions is that there was a vibrant population of nuns and lay women who enlivened the religious life of the Sanchi region. The last two centuries before the common era were a good time to be a *bhikkhunī* there.

At this time nuns were influential and active. Inscriptions from other places dating from the first two centuries of the common era prove that nuns continued to be influential in shaping Buddhist practices and Buddhist art. As Gregory Schopen has thoroughly demonstrated, it was nuns and monks who commissioned the first images of the Buddha ever made, and paid to have them carried to important cities to become the center of a new cult of the Buddha in human form.[48] In fact, nuns were so prominent that monks kept promulgating rules to keep them in check, as we find in the stories from the Vinaya discussed above. Monks would have had no need to make special rules to limit nuns' actions and rights if nuns hadn't already shown monks how independent they could be.

Nuns were active supporters of the Kākanāva cult center on Sanchi Hill in the second and first centuries B.C.E., but after that their inscriptions cease. Elsewhere in India, also, nuns' inscriptions became rarer, and from the fourth or fifth centuries on they disappear from the annals of donors to Buddhist monuments. Nuns did not cease to exist, for there are records of nuns' communities in later centuries, but they apparently ceased to be active and influential in the larger Buddhist world. It seems likely that the nuns lost their impact because the monks asserted their own primacy in the Sangha, and created regulations that would keep the women permanently in their place. The Vinaya texts, where these rules were preserved, were largely codified in their present form in about the fourth or fifth centuries C.E. And if Schopen's conclusions are correct, by that time the Mahāyāna movement in Buddhism was in the ascendancy, and where Mahāyāna inscriptions are found, there seem to be no nuns.[49]

But at Sanchi, in the second and first centuries B.C.E., nuns were thriving. It was then that the *bhikkhunī* Sangha seems to have reached its peak, at Sanchi and probably in many other places in India. Sanchi itself remains, an inspiring testimony to the accomplishments of women of the past, who worked with men to create one of the magnificent monuments of the ancient world.

Photo Captions

1. Sanchi, Stūpa I. View from the south, showing the South Gateway *(toraṇa)* and the double stairway to the upper walking path. The broken base of the column erected by Emperor Aśoka Maurya in the third century B.C.E. can be seen beside the gateway to the viewer's right. The core of the Buddha stūpa also dates from the third century B.C.E. It was expanded in the second century B.C.E., and the monumental gateways were added in the first century B.C.E. The railings, gateways, and stones paving the walking paths around the stūpa are inscribed with the names of donors. Photo by Nancy Barnes.

2. Sanchi, Stūpa II. Built in the second century B.C.E., it contained relics of ten revered local monks. The boxes containing the relics, the massive stone railing surrounding the stūpa, and the stones paving the walking path were the gifts of donors and were inscribed with their names. Photo by Nancy Barnes.

3. Sanchi, view of the main terrace just south of Stūpa I. The foundations of several small stūpas of various sizes dating from between the sixth and eighth centuries C.E. can be seen. The lovely small Temple XVII, with its pillared portico, is in the middle distance (ca. fifth century C.E.), and several tall columns of Temple XVIII rise behind it (ca. seventh century C.E., with foundations dating from the second century B.C.E.). Photo by Nancy Barnes.

Notes

1. This summary of the *bhikṣuṇī upasaṃpadā* is taken from the Mahāsāṅghika Vinaya. See Akira Hirakawa, *Monastic Discipline for the Buddhist Nuns, An English Translation of the Chinese Text of the Mahāsāṅghika-Bhikṣuṇī Vinaya* (Patna: K. P. Jayaswal Research Institute, 1982), 50–68.
2. Dhamma (Skt. Dharma) means the teachings of the Buddha, which were preached by him and by his disciples.
3. Gregory Schopen's study of Vinaya texts and inscriptions from ancient monuments has transformed our understanding of Indian monastic Buddhism. I have referred extensively to several of his publications when writing this essay. He has recently presented a great deal of evidence to demonstrate that monks and nuns were very much involved in life cycle rituals in the homes and for the families of lay devotees of the Buddha. These rites included marriages and funerals. See for example Schopen, "The Ritual Obligations and Donor Roles of Monks in the Pali Vinaya," in *Bones, Stones,*

and Buddhist Monks, Collected Papers on the Archaeology, Epigraphy, and Texts of Monastic Buddhism in India (Honolulu: University of Hawai'i Press, 1997), 72–85.

4. An enormous number of sūtras belonging to several Buddhist sects survive in several languages (Pali, Sanskrit, Chinese, Tibetan, and others). Some Pali texts that are exclusively about nuns are the *Bhikkhunī* chapter of the Theravāda Saṃyutta Nikāya (Book of the Kindred Sayings), and the *Therīgāthā (Songs of the Venerable Sisters).* Six Vinayas of six ancient Buddhist sects survive: Theravāda, Mahīśāsaka, Dharmaguptaka, Mahāsāṅghika, Sarvāstivāda, and Mūlasarvāstivāda. They contain lists of the rules monks and nuns must observe, explanations of why the rules were instituted, and a great many stories about the lives of Buddhist monastics and the lay people they lived among.
5. The story is found in all the Vinayas cited in note 4, and in some sūtras as well. The most accessible account is in the translation of the Theravāda Vinaya by I. B. Horner, *The Book of the Discipline (Vinaya-Piṭaka)*, vol. V *(Cullavagga)* (London: Luzac and Co., 1963), 352–58. For a fuller examination of the founding of the *bhikkhunī* Sangha and an exposition of the eight special rules for nuns, see I. B. Horner, *Women Under Primitive Buddhism* (Delhi: Motilal Banarsidass, 1990; originally published 1930), 95–161.
6. For a summary of scholars' criticisms of the traditional dating of scriptures belonging to all the Buddhist sects, see Gregory Schopen, "Two Problems in the History of Indian Buddhism, The Layman/Monk Distinction and the Doctrines of the Transference of Merit," *Bones,* 24–25. See also K. R. Norman, "The Value of the Pali Tradition," *'Jagajjyoti' Buddha Jayanti Annual* (Calcutta: 1984), 1–9, and Schopen, "The *Stūpa* Cult and the Extant Pali Vinaya," *Bones,* 91–92 and note 23, and "On Avoiding Ghosts and Social Censure, Monastic Funerals in the *Mūlasarvāstivāda-Vinaya,*" *Bones,* 205. On the historical value of the Vinayas, see Schopen, "Ritual Rights and Bones of Contention: More on Monastic Funerals and Relics in the *Mūlasarvāstivāda-Vinaya,*" *Journal of Indian Philosophy* 22 (1994): 60–61. The traditional date of the Buddha's death, long accepted by most scholars, is about 480 B.C.E. This date has recently been challenged and is being reevaluated.
7. A stūpa (Pali *thūpa*) is a hemispherical structure that contains relics of the Buddha or of his disciples. The core of an ancient stūpa was earth or rubble, which was then faced with brick or stone. The grandest stūpas were surrounded by a stone fence, which was often ornamented with carvings. Most of the stūpas built for the Buddha's followers were small, and were placed near a larger Buddha stūpa or temple. I use the Sanskrit term stūpa here because it will be the most familiar to the reader. For consistency, I use the Sanskrit for other architectural terms as well, such as *toraṇa, pradakṣiṇā,* and *chattra,* as well as *sūtra* for Buddhist sermon.
8. The most thorough study of Sanchi is by its excavator and restorer, John Marshall, in collaboration with Alfred Foucher and N. G. Majumdar, *The Monuments of Sanchi,* 3 vols. (Delhi: Swati Publications, 1983; originally published in Calcutta, 1940). It contains all the inscriptions with Majumdar's translations. Some other important publications are Alexander Cunningham, *The Bhilsa Topes; or, Buddhist Monuments of Central India* (New Delhi: Munshiram Manoharlal, 1997; originally published in London, 1854); Debala Mitra, *Sanchi* (New Delhi: Archaeological Survey of India,

1957; sixth edition 1992); and *Unseen Presence: The Buddha and Sanchi*, ed. Vidya Dehejia (Mumbai: Marg Publications, 1996). On the Sanchi inscriptions, see also Vidya Dehejia, "The Collective and Popular Basis of Early Buddhist Patronage: Sacred Monuments, 100 B.C.–A.D. 250," in *The Powers of Art: Patronage in Indian Culture*, ed. B. S. Miller (Delhi: 1992), 35–45.

9. Mitra, *Sanchi*, 16, 57–58; Mitra, "Discovery and Restoration of the Monuments," *Unseen Presence*, 16; Marshall, *Monuments of Sanchi*, 23ff, 64ff.
10. Schopen, "An Old Inscription from Amarāvatī and the Cult of the Local Monastic Dead in Indian Buddhist Monasteries," *Bones*, 178 and note 61.
11. Controversy over the precise dates of the Sanchi monuments, their art, and their inscriptions continues. I have followed the dates given by Vidya Dehejia: ca. 120–ca. 80 B.C.E. for Stūpas I and II, except for the four *toraṇas* of Stūpa I, which Dehejia dates to ca. 80–ca. 25 B.C.E. She dates Stūpa III to ca. 30 B.C.E. See Dehejia, *Early Buddhist Rock Temples: A Chronology* (London: Thames and Hudson, and Ithaca, N.Y.: Cornell University Press, 1972), 35–48, 186–88, and Table 11 (208–9). Dates suggested in the 1930s by Marshall and Majumdar, *Monuments of Sanchi*, are slightly earlier. A. H. Dani, *Indian Palaeography* (Oxford: Clarendon Press, 1963), 64–5, dates the inscriptions on the three stūpas 100 B.C.E.–50 B.C.E. Basing her conclusions on a study of the style and content of the sculptures on the railing of Stūpa II, Mireille Benisti has argued for a date of 200–150 B.C.E. for that stūpa: "Observations concernant le *stupa* no. 2 de Sanci," *Bulletin d'ẽtudes Indienne* 4 (1986): 165–70.
12. To be in the living presence of the Buddha, to see him in the stūpa that contains his relics, is *darśana*, seeing the divinity. This is the same profound impulse that motivates Hindus to visit the temples, the dwelling places of their gods. As Schopen has pointed out, the term *darśana* is explicitly used in Buddhist texts to explain what the faithful do when they visit a Buddhist holy place. Although the Buddha himself was gone from the world, the ashes collected after his cremation were preserved, and these relics were believed to be informed or pervaded with the characteristics of the living Buddha. A second-century B.C.E. inscription from northwest India speaks of another relic of the Buddha that "is endowed with life." For all of this, see Schopen, "Burial *Ad Sanctos* and the Physical Presence of the Buddha in Early Indian Buddhism," in *Bones*, 116–17, 125–28, and notes 9 and 10.
13. Although the four gateways are enormous and adorned with many beautiful sculpted panels and figures, only eleven donative inscriptions are found on them. Most of these record gifts by lay people. One is from a monk, and two are from the pupil of a monk. No inscription on the gateways belongs to a nun.
14. Schopen, "What's in a Name: The Religious Function of Donative Inscriptions," *Unseen Presence*, 60–61. See also some of Schopen's earlier publications: "On Monks, Nuns, and 'Vulgar' Practices: The Introduction of the Image Cult into Indian Buddhism," *Bones*, 238–57; "Archaeology and Protestant Presuppositions in the Study of Indian Buddhism," *Bones*, 3–4; "The Ritual Obligations and Donor Roles of Monks in the Pali Vinaya," *Bones*, 77.
15. Some of the arguments in Nancy Falk's well-known essay, "The Case of the Van-

ishing Nuns: The Fruits of Ambivalence in Ancient Indian Buddhism," in *Unspoken Worlds, Women's Religious Lives in Non-Western Cultures*, ed. Nancy Falk and Rita Gross (San Francisco: Harper & Row, 1980), 207–24, need to be reevaluated in light of more recent research. Falk argues that the *bhikkhunī* Sangha declined and vanished from India because of lack of support from the laity, which effectively starved them out of existence. In the early period of Buddhism that Sanchi represents, however, nuns were neither poor nor disadvantaged, nor did they require the economic support of lay people to survive. But it is true, as Falk says, that after the first few centuries B.C.E. nuns' inscriptions seem to disappear, implying a significant change in their situation, and the reasons for this certainly need to be further examined.

16. B. C. Law published a short paper sixty years ago in which he made use of ancient inscriptions to analyze the situation of nuns. In it, he briefly mentions some of the points I have discussed in this essay: "Bhikshunis in Indian Inscriptions," *Epigraphia Indica* 25 (1939): 31–34.
17. Majumdar's list of Sanchi inscriptions numbers 198 and 227, both from Stūpa I: Marshall et al, *Monuments of Sanchi.* Some of the eight hundred-plus inscriptions from Sanchi are fragmentary or damaged, and names of nuns' places of residence have been lost from some inscriptions, just as their personal names have been lost from others.
18. Majumdar's list numbers 22, 341, and 370, and 372 record group gifts to Stūpa I. Number 780 is a group gift to Temple XL.
19. Majumdar's list numbers 304, 305, 540, and 680. The donor is not designated as a *bhikkhunī,* only as one who knows the sūtras. In this essay I use the Prakrit spellings for words as they are actually found in the inscriptions—for example, *sutatika.*
20. Majumdar's list numbers 85, 118, 637, 645, 673, and 806. Three of these inscriptions are from Stūpa I, and three from Stūpa II. Only one of the donors and none of the teachers in these inscriptions are said to be *bhikkhunīs.* It is possible that the other donors were pious lay pupils, *upāsikās,* but that is not stated in the inscriptions either. I assume that the teachers were *bhikkhunīs,* but that of course is not certain.
21. Majumdar 102 and 206.
22. Majumdar 303.
23. Majumdar 399, 529, and 691.
24. Majumdar 242 and 631.
25. Majumdar, 288.
26. Majumdar, ii, 52, 214, 229, 242, 265, 267, 269, 270, 399, 402, 572, 632, 633, 634, 671, and 803. Majumdar also reads 348 and 349 as inscriptions by pupils, *antevāsins,* but this reading seems less certain. In these inscriptions many but not all of the pupils are specifically called *bhikkhus* as well as *antevāsins.* Thus there is some question whether the ones not designated *bhikkhus* were monks or pious lay men, *upāsakas*—the same question that arises with respect to the female *antevāsinīs* discussed above.
27. Majumdar 144, 190, 209, 294, 303, 338, 352, 377, 431, 675, 693, and 695. Although there are no nuns in the Sanchi inscriptions who are called *aya,* Law remarks that the woman who donated major portions of the surviving railing from Bodhgaya is

referred to in several inscriptions as *aya* Kurangi: B. C. Law, "Bhikshunis in Indian Inscriptions," 33. The use of this term for a woman may be rare, then, but it is not unknown.

28. Majumdar 144 and 303.
29. When Cunningham discovered and read the inscriptions on these relic containers, he assumed the names were those of monk missionaries of the third century B.C.E. who were sent by Emperor Aśoka to convert neighboring countries and who are mentioned in histories of early Buddhism composed in Sri Lanka. Many other scholars have accepted this view. Schopen's conclusions, that the Sanchi monks were local individuals, are more convincing; see "An Old Inscription from Amarāvatī," *Bones*, 199, note 61. See also Maurizio Taddei, "The First Beginnings: Sculptures on *Stūpa* 2," *Unseen Presence*, 77; and G. Yamazaki, "The Spread of Buddhism in the Mauryan Age—with Special Reference to the Mahinda Legend," *Acta Asiatica* 43 (1982): 1–16.
30. Majumdar 2–12.
31. On the remains and the inscriptions found at four Buddhist sites on hills near Sanchi—Satdhara, Sonari, Bhojpur, and Andher—the publication by Cunningham, who excavated them in the nineteenth century, is still the major source of information: Alexander Cunningham, *The Bhilsa Topes*, 309–50.
32. It is interesting to find that one of the donors to Stūpa I is also called *sapurisa* (Majumdar 288). He, too, must have been very highly esteemed. It should also be observed that two very famous disciples of the Buddha, Mahāmogallāna and Sāriputta, some of whose ashes were interred in Stūpa III at Sanchi and in a stūpa at the nearby site of Satdhara, are given no titles at all. Apparently their sanctity was so well known that no titles were necessary. Locally used titles like *sapurisa* would probably not have sufficed.
33. There is one inscription, 704, that Majumdar reads as the record of a gift by a female pupil of a monk called *aya* Padana. The inscription does not say whether the pupil was a nun or a pious lay woman, and does not actually call her a pupil, either. I tentatively accept Majumdar's reading, despite problems I find with it. Law, "Bhikshunis in Indian Inscriptions," 33, mentions two nuns in the Amaravati inscriptions who are pupils of monk teachers.
34. Dehejia, "The Collective and Popular Basis of Early Buddhist Patronage," *Powers of Art*, 37–38; Schopen, "An Old Inscription from Amarāvatī," *Bones*, 176. On overseers of Buddhist construction projects, see Marlene Njammasch, "Der *navakammika* und seine Stellung in der Hierarchie der buddhistischen Kloster," *Schriften zur Geschichte und Kultur des alten Orients* 1 (1974): 279–93.
35. Njammasch, "Der *navakammika*," 280–81. Nothing is known about the *navakammika*, the overseer in charge of new constructions, at Sanchi. But inscriptions of *navakammika* themselves from other early projects survive. Isipalita was *navakammika* of the Bharhut stūpa, which was roughly contemporary with the Sanchi stūpas, and his own inscription says he was not only the project overseer but also a learned senior monk: the reverend *(bhadanta)*, the worthy *(aya)*, and the reciter of Dharma *(bhāṇaka)* Isipalita. Schopen, "An Old Inscription from Amarāvatī," *Bones*, 190–91;

and "On the Buddha and his Bones: The Conception of a Relic in the Inscriptions of Nāgārjunikoṇḍa," *Bones*, 158–59.

36. There are a few inscriptions from other monuments or sites that include religious titles for ordained women. The most famous are those on the earliest known inscribed images of the Buddha, which were donated by *bhikkhu* Bala and *bhikkhunī* Buddhamitrā, each of whom is *trepiṭaka*, "one who knows the three collections of scriptures" (first or second century B.C.E.). Schopen, "Monks, Nuns and 'Vulgar' Practices," *Bones*, 239–57, discusses the implications of these inscriptions at length. But despite Schopen's protestations, such religious titles given to women monastics are not common in early inscriptions. At the Bharhut stūpa, which was roughly contemporary with Sanchi, sixteen donative inscriptions of nuns have been found, and all of the women are called simply *bhikkhunīs*. Nine of them are further identified by place of residence. In the twenty-three surviving monks' inscriptions, however, each and every one of them is *bhadanta*, *aya*, *sutatika*, *bhāṇaka*, or *pacanekayika*. See H. Lüders, *Bharhut Inscriptions*, revised by E. Waldschmidt and M. A. Mehendale (Ootacamund: Government Epigraphist for India, 1963): A11, 12, 24, 29, 37, 42–44, 52, 74–80 (nuns); A8, 38–40, 51, 54, 56–59, 61–73 (monks). The pattern we find at Sanchi, therefore, may be more than just a local custom.

37. Schopen, "What's in a Name," *Unseen Presence*, 63–66, 71–72; Schopen quotes Louis Renou and Jan Gonda from Gonda, *Notes on Names and the Name of God in Ancient India* (Amsterdam/London: North-Holland, 1970), 7, 21, 23, 45.

38. Fa-hien (Fa-xian), *A Record of Buddhistic Kingdoms*, trans. James Legge (New York: Dover Publications, 1965; originally published Oxford, 1886), 44–47. Fa-xian saw many stūpas of the two great disciples during his long journey through India early in the fifth century B.C.E., and witnessed many festivals held at their stūpas in their honor. See also Schopen, "Ritual Rights and Bones of Contention," 57.

39. Schopen, "Ritual Rights and Bones of Contention," 53–55.

40. Schopen, "Ritual Rights and Bones of Contention," 53–55. The Sonari and Andher stūpas that contain these same monks' relics are also situated at a distance from the principal stūpas at those sites: Cunningham, *The Bhilsa Topes*, 315–19, 345–50, and Plate V.

41. Schopen, "Burial *Ad Sanctos*," *Bones*, 118–20; "The *Stūpa* Cult and the Extant Pali Vinaya," *Bones*, 92–93; "An Old Inscription from Amarāvatī," *Bones*, 182ff.

42. Schopen, "Ritual Rights and Bones of Contention," 41; "The Suppression of Nuns and the Ritual Murder of Their Special Dead in Two Buddhist Monastic Texts," *Journal of Indian Philosophy* 24 (1996): 583 and note 66.

43. Schopen, "Suppression of Nuns," 563–92, especially 564–65. Another story is told in the *Mūlasarvāstivāda Vinaya* about the similar fate of a stūpa erected by nuns over the remains of a monk they especially revered: an angry senior monk destroys it. In that case, too, the Buddha formulates a new rule governing the conduct of nuns (op. cit., 575–76). The texts in which these stories are found, and also the account of Mahāpajāpatī's funeral, date in their present form to no earlier than the fourth or fifth century B.C.E., although the views they express could be older.

44. There are other important collections of inscriptions that have not yet been studied, to the best of my knowledge. Cunningham mentions that he found about three hundred inscriptions at Sonari, for example: *Bhilsa Topes*, 313. Those inscriptions were discovered 150 years ago and have received almost no attention from scholars. New sites with inscriptions are being discovered all the time. Perhaps in the near future it will be possible to write more definitively about early Indian Buddhism.
45. Majumdar 22, 341, 370, 372, and 780.
46. Majumdar 215.
47. Majumdar 60 and 728.
48. Schopen, "Monks, Nuns, and 'Vulgar' Practices," *Bones*, 238–57.
49. Schopen, "Monks, Nuns, and 'Vulgar' Practices," *Bones*, 238–57

WOMEN IN BETWEEN:

Becoming Religious Persons in Thailand

Monica Lindberg Falk

Introduction

Thai women are among Buddhism's most devoted faith keepers. Traditionally, however, they have not been associated with the Buddhist monastic world. Despite the fact that women have never been admitted into the Thai Buddhist Sangha,[1] there have long been female ascetics in Thai society. The role of Thai women renunciants is ambiguous, since they are formally considered to be lay women, but are also concurrently treated as religious persons. In Thailand the difference between the categories of religious and lay persons rests upon the number of Buddhist precepts the person is following, and the boundary is between the eighth and the tenth precepts. Thai nuns generally follow eight precepts, while novice monks receive ten precepts at their ordination.

This essay aims to illustrate how the category of contemporary Thai Buddhist nuns *(mae chis)*[2] is being formed in relation to the Thai Sangha and to lay people. Further, I offer a more varied picture of the *mae chis* who have previously been perceived as destitute women burdened with a "broken heart," illness, poverty, old age, and troubled minds as the result of bad kamma. The paper is based upon findings from fifteen months of anthropological fieldwork, which was completed in June 1998.[3] The research was carried out primarily at nunneries in central Thailand, and focused on the changes for *mae chis* as a social group and a cultural category, changes which are significant for Thai gender constructs.

An ideal Buddhist society consists of *bhikkhus* (monks), *bhikkhunīs* (nuns), *upāsakas* (lay men) and *upāsikās* (lay women), with a distinct boundary between the mundane and lay realms. Thailand has never lived up to this ideal since the category of *bhikkhunīs* has always been missing, for it has never been possible for women there to receive full ordination as *bhikkhunīs*. In my opinion, the lack of fully ordained nuns in Thai society has to be understood in the light of Thai gender roles, which tie women to the lay domain. In Thai society, women acquire maturity through marriage and childbirth, while men attain maturity through renouncing the world and becoming novice monks for a period of time. These assumptions concerning maturity prevent women from developing their potential to enter into the Thai religious realm, which lacks a prescribed role for women. In this essay, I will show how women who renounce the world are questioning expected gender roles and are obscuring the boundary between lay and religious realms, and how their ambiguous status reflects the dynamics of categorization in Thai society.

Mae chis do not constitute a homogeneous group. Their age, social background, educational level, aspirations, and motives for receiving nuns' ordination vary significantly and inform the differences that characterize *mae chis* as a group. It is also important where *mae chis* live in Thailand, since there are local variations in Buddhist teachings and forms of practice. There is a meaningful distinction between the lives of the *mae chis* who live in temples and those who live in nunneries. At temples, *mae chis'* activities are centered around the domestic realm, even though they have left the worldly life. Their responsibilities do not include religious tasks such as officiating at ceremonies and going on alms rounds, which are considered the monks' assignments. At nunneries, the role of the *mae chis* has been broadened and is more analogous to the monks' role. However, it is only in recent decades that Buddhist nunneries governed by the nuns themselves are starting to be established. Nunneries have proved to be an appropriate platform for *mae chis* who strive to fulfill their spiritual potential as Thai Buddhist nuns.

Presentation of a Thai Nunnery in Context

My principal research site is located in central Thailand, in a province south of Bangkok. About 7,500 persons live in the *tambon* (commune) where the nunnery is situated. Most of the villagers engage in vegetable gardening and pig breeding. At Ratburi Nunnery,[4] there are about fifty *mae chis*, a varying number of *chi phrams* (temporary nuns), and forty-seven school girls, called *thammacāriṇīs*. The *thammacāriṇīs* study secondary education and Buddhism at Thammacāriṇī School, which is situated at the nunnery.[5] The nunnery was established twenty years ago on land donated by lay supporters for the express purpose of setting up a nunnery, and has expanded over the years. In 1990, the nunnery opened the first school ever established by *mae chis* for girls in Thailand. In contrast, boys have always been able to get free education at the temple schools. The students come from many different parts of the country, mostly from poor villages in the northeastern and central provinces, and they stay at the nunnery for two or four years. The school also provides an opportunity for *mae chis* to acquire a higher education and nuns from all over the country come to live and study here. Ratburi Nunnery is a branch of the national organization, the Thai Nuns' Institute, and some of the *mae chis* find out about the nunnery through the institute. Head monks at temples are also concerned about the lack of educational opportunities for *mae chis,* and several nuns go to the nunneries at the suggestion of their temples' abbots.

The sālā *at Ratburi Nunnery (photo by Monica Lindberg Falk)*

At nunneries, the residents can be divided into two distinct categories. One is the *mae chi,* whose status varies according to how long she has been ordained. The other, the *chi phram,* also follows the eight precepts, but keeps her hair and eyebrows and only stays temporarily at the nunnery. *Chi phrams* are named after the Brahmin devotees who converted to Buddhism and wore white without shaving.[6] There are differences in the dress of the two *chis. Mae chis* wear a white blouse, a white *phasin* (long skirt), and a white cloth draped over the left shoulder. The *chi phrams* also wear a white blouse and *phasin,* but they are sewn differently, and *chi phrams'* outer robes are shorter than those of the *mae chis.* Spatial arrangements also betray the hierarchy and status differences at the nunneries. At ceremonies at Ratburi Nunnery, *mae chis* sit on a raised platform with the highest ranking nuns closest to the Buddha statues and the newly ordained *mae chis* furthest from the statues. The *chi phrams* and *thammacāriṇīs* sit behind the *mae chis* and beneath the platform, thus displaying their lower status.

Mae chis observe eight precepts on a permanent basis, as do *chi phrams* and *thammacāriṇīs.* Lay people may also follow the eight precepts during special occasions like the Buddhist holy day, *wan phra.* Otherwise, Buddhist lay people are expected to follow five precepts.[7] The eight precepts constitute a more ascetic regimen and include the first five precepts followed by the lay—with the exception that the third precept requires the *mae chis* to abstain from sexual activity altogether. The additional three precepts are to abstain from eating after noontime, using beautification or entertainment, and sleeping on a thick mattress. The novice monks observe ten precepts, of which eight are the same as those observed by the *mae chis.* However the seventh precept, dealing with abstinence from beautification or entertainment, is divided into two precepts in the monks' case. The tenth precept is to abstain from using gold or silver (that is, money) and is important in separating the mundane realm from the religious; it is often violated by the monks, however, as they sometimes have to handle money.

At many temples in Thailand, the *mae chis* live in separate communities *(samnak chi)* within the temple complex. This is in accordance with the traditional Theravāda practice where the living quarters of male and female renunciants are separated from one another. Today, nuns have various reasons for choosing to live at a nunnery instead of a temple. Most of the nuns at the nunneries have been ordained at temples and have experienced living at both temples and nunneries. *Mae chis* who have been ordained at Ratburi Nunnery say they find living in a *mae chi* community more appropriate than living in a temple where monks also reside. In their opinion, monks and nuns should practice separately. Another motive cited for choosing to live at this particular nunnery is a *mae chi's* desire to study.

During the last two decades nunneries, independent of temples, have increased in number. According to the Thai Nuns' Institute's statistics, there are about 850 nunneries in Thailand today. Because Thai nuns do not fall under traditional Sangha administration, it is much easier for *mae chis* to establish their own communities than it would be if they had more official status. Some nunneries are established on land owned by the *mae chis* themselves or by their families. Generally, the foundation of nunneries is instigated by lay people who give land and financial support, and who often assist in erecting the buildings. Nunneries are generally modeled on the structure of a Buddhist temple, but do not contain all the constructions usually found at temples. Temples *(wat)* in Thailand may differ substantially in terms of architectural features, style, and size, but inside each temple's boundaries there are usually the same basic structures. There is, for example, a *sālā,* open to both laity and renunciants, where ceremonies and other gatherings take place; a *vihāra,* which is used by the monks for various religious services and where laity may also congregate; and an *ubosoth,* which is used primarily by the monks for ordination ceremonies and other strictly monastic ceremonies. This building is erected on consecrated ground and surrounded by *sīmā* or boundary stones. There is also a *chedi,* or stūpa, which is a bell-shaped tower containing relics, as well as lodgings for monks and nuns, which may be dormitory-style buildings or individual huts, known as *kuṭis.* The main building at a nunnery is usually the *sālā,* where ceremonies and many other activities take place. Nunneries do not have *vihāras* or *ubosoths.* Some nunneries have *chedis,* and all nunneries have huts or dormitory-style buildings for the nuns. Temples usually have crematoria but nunneries do not. Both temples and nunneries usually have a special showcase holding the many volumes of the *Tipiṭaka,* the Buddhist canon. Likewise, a Bodhi tree is usually found on temple grounds but seldom at nunneries. While temples usually have a school building, it is only recently that a few nunneries have built schools.

The daily life of the *mae chis* at nunneries does not differ significantly from the life of the monks. *Mae chis* at the independent nunneries I have visited follow the religious tradition of morning and evening chants, meditation practice, and studies of the Dhamma. The nuns also go on daily alms rounds, an activity that has become more widespread in recent times among *mae chis* from village nunneries. To support the monastic community has always been highly valued and continues to be seen as an important and meritorious deed in Thai society. *Mae chis* have traditionally not been perceived as merit-producing alms persons and have not been in the habit of practicing alms rounds. The villagers have therefore not previously supported *mae chis* directly. Instead they have been in the habit of giving alms to the monks who would later distribute food to the *mae chis.* Research in Theravāda countries like Burma and Sri Lanka has shown that many women renunciants were dependent upon their relatives for their daily sustenance.[8] Thai nuns as well have been used to assistance from their relatives or to living on private means, but today *mae chis* are, to a great extent and like their male colleagues, supported by the laity.

As a *mae chi,* a woman chooses to live a single and celibate life. By choosing the nunnery, she chooses as well a life in a female community that has little male influence. *Mae chis* who come to live at a nunnery have usually selected this life over the option of living at a temple. The *mae chis* express their understanding of the advantages of living at a nunnery as having greater freedom *(isālā)* and more time and opportunity to study and meditate. In actual fact, however, the *mae chis* at nunneries have to work fairly hard, as they cannot rely on the laity to the same extent as monks and *mae chis* at temples usually can.

Life at nunneries differs in several respects from the life of *mae chis* at temples where monks also reside. Both monks and *mae chis* are expected to study and practice meditation, but the government only supports monks' education, and meditation has usually been perceived as most suitable for *mae chis.* Nuns at temples do not have the authority to officiate at ceremonies. However, nuns at nunneries conduct ceremonies similar to those of the monks. At temples, *mae chis* are usually responsible for the kitchen, while the monks alone perform the alms round. At nunneries, *mae chis* cook food as well, but they also go on alms rounds in the morning, which has been found to have an important, positive impact on *mae chis'* identity as ordained persons.

The Mae Chis' Ambiguous Position

There are a variety of sub-categories within Thai notions of "femaleness" *(phety-ing),* and *mae chi* is one that challenges the traditional order. The somewhat negative attitude towards *mae chis,* together with their ambiguous position as renunciants, has made the role of *mae chi* vague and questionable. Generally, Thai people are ambivalent about women who abandon traditionally accepted social roles, and they do not encourage women to renounce the world. The ideal Thai woman is expected to fulfill the role of wife and mother. Thus, *mae chis* violate cultural norms of gender by abandoning their home life and renouncing the world, even though they are not admitted into the Thai Sangha. In spite of the social pressures to keep women from living a religious life as nuns and the fact that the Sangha door is closed to them, *mae chis* have started to create and refine religious roles and communities for themselves. *Mae chis'* daily activities at nunneries parallel those of the monks with meditation, alms rounds, religious practice and ceremonies, and this often blurs the distinction between their status as either lay or religious persons. This is further expressed in the terms of address used by lay people, who sometimes refer to the *mae chis* as laity and sometimes as religious persons by using the classifiers *rup* or even *ong,* which are normally used for monks. People in positions of authority also treat the *mae chis* in ambiguous ways. The government gives support to the monks with free education, free medical care, and free or reduced fares for buses and trains. Nuns do not receive such support from the government because of their official status as laity. However, the same government denies *mae chis* the right to vote in public elections, citing their ascetic status and renunciation of worldly matters.

Women's secondary status in Thai Buddhism is demonstrated by the fact that men who receive the ten Buddhist precepts are considered religious persons and members of the Sangha, whereas women who observe the same ten precepts are referred to as lay people.[9] The social background of the *mae chi* has significance for their lives as religious practitioners. Wealth and high status can sometimes enhance an individual *mae chi's* position, but are not enough to assure acceptance as a religious person, which requires a combination of religious knowledge and practice. Thus, education and sincere religious practice are crucial for *mae chis* in their roles as ordained persons. During the last two decades the *mae chis'* role has started to change. *Mae chis* at nunneries are invited by their supporters, and also by monks, to chant at various ceremonies. Most *mae chis* who live at nunneries develop an identity as monastics rather than as laity, and this corresponds with the view of most lay supporters who accept and encourage this identity. However, the situation is not the same for all *mae chis,* and some *mae chis* report experiences of not being met with respect while visiting places like Bangkok or areas without nunneries.

Recognizing the inequity and difficulties for *mae chis* in gaining acceptance as renunciants, a well known and respected former lawyer, Mae Chi Khunying Kanithaa Wichiencharoen, has proposed a law that would give *mae chis* formal status as ordained persons. This issue has been discussed in detail at the Thai Nuns' Institute's meetings for several years. In 1998, the institute finally agreed to send the proposed bill to the authorities for approval. If the bill is passed, it would give legal recognition to nuns as Buddhist clerics and enable them to receive educational and other state benefits similar to those of monks. The proposed bill clearly states that the women are seeking recognition as *mae chis,* and not as fully ordained nuns; thus their position relative to the monks will not change.

Reasons Thai Women Renounce the World

Mae chis have been stereotyped as either destitute or broken-hearted women who are viewed more or less as housekeepers for the monks at the temples. In spite of both the lack of a role model for female spirituality and the dubious status *mae chis* possess, tens of thousands of Thai women have chosen to become nuns. From living with *mae chis* at nunneries in Thailand for almost a year, I have learned that those who have received ordination as *mae chis* are often strong, talented women of all ages who have chosen a religious life not because of destitution or failure in lay life, but to develop themselves spiritually.

Women's reasons for choosing to live as Buddhist nuns vary. Experience or anticipation of suffering is sometimes involved, but often there is a combination of reasons. A survey, carried out about ten years ago, showed that a frequent motivation for becoming a *mae chi* was to study and practice Dhamma. Other common reasons included the desire to fulfill vows and to help other people. Only a small percentage stated that they became *mae chis* in order to reach *nibbāna,* the ultimate Buddhist goal.[10] *Mae chis* cite the same reasons today but, in my research, the order of the motives seems to have changed. The most frequent reason given is to live a pure life *(chiwit borisot)* in order to attain *nibbāna.* This might be seen as a shift in women's motives for ordination, but might equally reflect the fact that I interviewed nuns mainly at nunneries outside Bangkok, whereas Suwanbubbha's research was carried out solely at temples in the Bangkok area.

It is important to note that men also have various motives for becoming ordained. Some of the reasons men offer for becoming monks are to study and practice Dhamma, to fulfill a vow, to flee from sorrows, and to escape poverty.[11] The number of young men who are ordained as novice monks for the period of the rainy season *(vassa)* has decreased in recent decades, although parents often wish that their sons would keep up the tradition and become novice monks for a limited period of time. Young women are usually not subjected to this demand and are not expected to renounce the world. If they do, their action suggests the need to leave behind some kind of misfortune. Several young *mae chis* I have interviewed claim that their families were initially against their ordination.

Women who become ordained as *mae chis* abandon their families and all the social expectations of lay life. Because traditional Thai cultural values hold that daughters should care for their parents in all ways possible, a woman violates society's sense of order when she becomes an ascetic.[12] A daughter's ordination is therefore often experienced by her parents as a loss, and young girls are generally discouraged by their families from becoming nuns. In general, *mae chis* maintain some contact with their natal families and, among my own informants, it was quite common for head nuns to take care of their aging mothers at their nunneries. This could be seen as fulfillment of the duty of the nun-daughter, but it should be noted that even famous monks like Ajahn Chah have taken care of their elderly mothers in the *samnak chi* (nuns' department) of their temples, which implies that taking care of aging mothers is as important to monks as it is to nuns.

Those *mae chis* who were ordained at a young age usually state that they had previously longed to become nuns and to live a spiritual life. They declare that they wanted to become ordained as soon as they realized it was possible for women to live a religious life and thus, for them, lay life held no attraction at all. Prior to their ordination, these young women had often developed a deep faith through listening to Buddhist radio programs, reading Dhamma books, and attending sermons by monks at the temples. *Mae chis* who became ordained later in life, usually after having their own families, routinely describe how boring and empty they found the life of the householder. Often, for a long time before being ordained, these same women gave material support to Buddhist clergy. Because support from lay people is not the norm for nuns as it is for monks, some women who become *mae chis* report that they planned their ordination and worked for years to save up money for their ordained lives. The *mae chis* who become nuns in order to fulfill a vow *(boat khae bon),* however, generally stay for a limited period of time and make no permanent commitment. At Ratburi Nunnery, these women more often become *chi phrams* instead *mae chis.*

At temples and nunneries in Thailand, the number of *chi phrams* is increasing, and at some temples the *chi phrams* even outnumber the *mae chis.*[13] Generally *chi phrams* come to temples and *samnaks* in order to practice meditation and to learn

***A* chi phram *meditating with* thammacāriṇīs**
(photo by Monica Lindberg Falk)

about Buddhism, with the goal of obtaining a peaceful mind through Buddhist training. But fulfilling a vow or making merit for family members or relatives are also motives given for their temporary ordination. The *chi phrams* have created a new category of "lay ordained" women who are under the guidance of and subordinate to the *mae chis;* this new development has put the *mae chis* in the role of religious instructors.

Creating Space for Women in Thai Buddhism

Despite the lack of a Thai nuns' order, female renunciants have a long history in Thailand. The first written records of *mae chis* in Thailand are from the Ayutthaya period (1350–1767), and it was a French missionary who first described the elderly, white-robed women who lived at the temples. There is no description of the nuns' lives or who they were—they are pictured simply as old women with shaved heads who dressed in white. *Mae* means "mother" in Thai, and the word has extremely positive connotations for Thai people, implying a sense of high regard and honor.[14] It is not clear, however, where the term *chi* comes from, though it probably connotes the nuns' ascetic way of life.[15] The treatment of *mae chis,* however, does not follow from the traditional role of the Thai mother. As "mothers in white," *mae chis* have not enjoyed the high esteem normally given to mothers, nor have they generally attracted much public or scholarly interest. However, there are a few exceptions, and some individual *mae chis* are earning public recognition for their activities, most particularly for their meditation skills. There are also examples of nuns who were well known before they became ordained as nuns, and who continue to gain respect even in their new role as *mae chis*. These "public" nuns are generally well educated, and often appear in television programs as well as in newspapers and magazines. To some extent, they have helped to broaden the picture of *mae chis* as it has become stereotyped in Thai history.

Sri Lanka is the only Theravāda country other than India that has had an official *bhikkhunī* order. The order flourished there from the third to eleventh centuries C.E., after which both the monks' and the nuns' Sanghas broke down. The monks' order was later restored with help from Thai and Burmese monastic lineages. The nuns' order, however, has still not been reestablished, though it has been a controversial issue in Sri Lanka for decades.[16] The main objection to the revival of the nuns' order is that the Theravāda *bhikkhunī* lineage has been broken and, once broken, it cannot be restored. For the ordination of nuns, representatives of both the female and male Sanghas are required but since the female lineage is considered irretrievably severed, it is impossible to fulfill this requirement.[17] It is true that the *bhikkhunī* Sangha does not exist in any Theravāda country today. However, Sri Lankan nuns introduced full ordination of nuns into China in 433 C.E., and it is argued that it would be possible to let those Mahāyāna *bhikkhunīs* from China ordain Theravāda nuns since both groups originate from the same lineage. The opponents argue that China belongs to the Mahāyāna tradition, and the validity of the lineage is questionable because it has not been transmitted continuously.[18]

In Sri Lanka there are nuns (*dāsā sīl mātās;* "ten-precept mothers") who follow the ten Buddhist precepts. In their struggle to reestablish the nuns' order in Sri Lanka, they have noted the importance of getting the approval of the Sri Lankan monks' Sangha. According to Goonatilake, monks as well as lay people are becoming increasingly sympathetic to the issue of higher ordination for women.[19] There are also groups of ten-precept nuns in Thailand, but they have not received the same recognition as the *dāsā sīl mātās* in Sri Lanka. Neither has the *bhikkhunī* issue been as popular in Thailand as it has been in Sri Lanka. There are some who advocate the establishment of the *bhikkhunī* order in Thailand. The best-known is Dr. Chatsumarn Kabilsingh, who has long advocated the reestablishment of the nuns' Sangha. However, the Thai monks' Sangha stands firm in its refusal to recognize *bhikkhunīs* in Thailand, although a few individual Thai monks are favorable to a nuns' order in Thailand. *Mae chis* in general, however, are not struggling for full ordination. Although a few of the *mae chis* I have interviewed state that they would be interested in receiving full ordination if it were possible in Thailand, most report that they would rather develop themselves spiritually as *mae chis*. The fact that the *mae chis,* who strongly identify with the Theravāda tradition, would be ordained by Mahāyāna monks and nuns if they were to receive full ordination, makes them hesitant. They are uncertain about whether such an ordination would imply that they have renounced the Theravāda practice. Most Thai nuns are scrupulous about following the precepts and they anticipate difficulties in maintaining the more than three hundred precepts needed for full ordination, some of which are outmoded and therefore hard to follow today. The *bhikkhunī* ordination would also subordinate the nuns to monks because of the eight chief rules for nuns *(garudhamma)*, which are generally believed to have been established by the Buddha.[20]

Thai nuns' low educational level and ambiguous position in society have contributed to the *mae chis'* low status, though there are many examples of individual women renunciants in local Thai Buddhism who are well respected for their wisdom and knowledge by both monks and laity.[21] These nuns are, nevertheless, exceptions and not representative of the general pattern of the *mae chi* career. New directions in Thai Buddhism, however, have given rise to new opportunities for women. In recent decades, the shift from *mae chis'* marginal position at temples to their governing roles at nunneries has made it possible to expand the options for the *mae chi.* Twenty years ago it was rare to find nunneries in Thailand; now, the number of nunneries is increasing every year. Through the nunneries, *mae chis* have become visible in the local communities, and their interaction with the lay people has often come to resemble the relationship between the monks and the laity. In daily religious practice, then, *mae chis* have increasingly gained recognition as religious persons.

The activities of the *mae chis* at nunneries include a wide range of religious duties, and it is clear that the new identities of the *mae chis* are becoming conceptualized through their new roles and practices. The nuns do not have many female ascetic role models and are often inspired instead by famous Thai monks. One of these is the well-known and highly respected monk Buddhadāsa Bhikkhu (1906–1993), whose teaching has been an important source of inspiration for many *mae chis.* Buddhadāsa is known as the first "middle-class monk." He reconceptualizes fundamental Buddhist concepts and explains Buddhist cosmological ideas by defining heaven and hell as mental states. He describes central Buddhist concepts differently from traditional Thai understanding and sees kamma, merit, rebirth, and *nibbāna* as things of the present, thus making past and future lives less relevant. He places the "free mind," a mind free of self-centeredness, at the core of his philosophy and argues that, with a state of mental calmness and mindfulness in every action, we can all achieve *nibbāna* in this world. Jackson points out how important it is to Buddhadāsa's thinking that all men and women have access to the same spiritual insights as monks have.[22] Thus, his teaching can be seen as a legitimation of *mae chis* as religious persons, and of women's capability to attain *nibbāna*.

Most *mae chis* come from a rural background and, among them, the older ones usually only have four years of primary education. Today, the primary level *(prathom suksa)* of school consists of six grades, which are compulsory for all Thai youths. Education is seen as one of the key factors for uplifting the status of *mae chis*, for *mae chis* need education in order to fulfill their role as ordained persons.[23] Young *mae chis*, in particular, are keen to study, and there are more educational possibilities for nuns today than there were ten years ago. In 1990, secondary education was made available to *mae chis* through Thammacāriṇī School and is now accessible at two nunneries in central and north Thailand. It is also possible for them to study at the open universities, and for this they are able to obtain financial support from Ratburi Nunnery. The two Buddhist universities situated in Bangkok have also started programs for *mae chis* and, beginning in recent times, it is also possible for monks and nuns to study at the public university, Mahidol, where their expenses are covered by donations from the laity. Another new project is the building of the first *mae chi* college, supported by private donations of land in Korat. Not all Thai nuns, however, are interested in education. As with monks, there are nuns who prefer to dedicate themselves solely to the practice of meditation. Nevertheless, access to education will almost certainly affect the social and religious status of *mae chis* and influence their identity as ascetic women.

Approximating the Religious Realm

Ordination is the first step a person has to take in order to progress from the secular realm of the lay to the spiritual realm of monastics, and thus to become a member of the religious community, the Sangha. The ordained person in Thailand collects alms, has Buddhist knowledge, officiates at ceremonies, and practices meditation, among other activities. Not all men fulfill the conditions necessary for becoming a monk. The person must be a male[24] and have reached the age of twenty years. The candidate must be a "whole man," not a eunuch or physically crippled. Furthermore, he must not have a criminal record and must not have committed any offense against the Sangha if previously ordained as a Buddhist monk.[25] Monks' ordination procedures are an elaborate and often costly event at which family, relatives, and friends gather. When a poor village man wishes to be ordained, he must either find a wealthy sponsor or pool resources from kin and neighbors. In general, people are happy to contribute to an ordination ceremony since it is seen as an auspicious occasion from which all participants, especially donors, gain merit. However, the ordination of *mae chis* is not very expensive, and usually just a small group of people gather at the temple or nunnery. While still a meritorious act, it is conceived to be a secular event.

Traditionally, *mae chis* have not belonged to a religious community like the Sangha. The role of the *mae chis* has not involved going on alms rounds, studying Buddhist philosophy, or officiating at ceremonies, but has instead been associated with meditation. However, growing numbers of nuns today have tasks similar to those of the monks but, to achieve any kind of parity, nuns have to overcome several obstacles. Nuns are scattered all over the country. Their religious practices are not uniform, and there are variations in their ordination procedures and in their daily regulations. Until 1969, Thai nuns lacked a national network and, consequently, a public representative. In the late sixties, this lack was recognized at an International Buddhist Association meeting, which later led the Supreme Patriarch to order the secretary of the Mahamakut Education Council to coordinate the *mae chi* population.[26] In 1969, the Thai Nuns' Institute *(Sathaban Mae Chi Thai)* was founded and, in 1972, came under the patronage of the Thai queen.

The Thai Nuns' Institute's headquarters are located in a small office at the prestigious royal temple, Wat Bowonniwet in Bangkok. The central goal of the institute is to help the *mae chis* develop intellectually and spiritually. Training courses in practical and religious education and various meetings are all organized at this office. Books, clothes, and other necessities for *mae chis* and *chi phrams* are sold here also. Membership in the institute is voluntary and free of charge, and the number of members varies between four and nine thousand. The institute emphasizes the importance of the community in which *mae chis* live and practice. Nunneries run by the *mae chis* themselves have proved to be suitable, and today the institute has more than twenty branches in the country which operate as self-governing dwellings for *mae chis.* The institute is hierarchically organized with offices and heads *(hua na)* at regional, provincial, and district levels. The structure of this nationwide organization is modeled upon the monks' Sangha. The head, *Hua na,* of the institute parallels the supreme leader of the monks' Sangha. The institute has been significant in uniting the nuns and in forming a *mae chi* identity distinct from lay practice.

During the first two decades of the institute's existence, the *mae chis* experienced trouble with many "false nuns," especially in urban areas. These women shave and dress as *mae chis* in order to attract donations from people.[27] Their behavior has become a threat to the reputation of serious *mae chis,* and the problem has not been easy to solve. It is the institute's efforts to shape the *mae chis* into a special category that has proved to be instrumental in controlling false nuns. Proper ordination procedure, appropriate conduct, religious practice, and education make it easier to distinguish serious *mae chis* from false ones. The special *mae chi* identification card that the institute issues has also been helpful in identifying *mae chis.* They are available to *mae chis* who are members of the institute and who have been ordained for at least one year. There is also a test to prove the *mae chi* knows the *mae chi* rules as stipulated by the institute. The rules are printed in the nuns' disciplinary handbook, which, among other things, also contains ordination procedures and careful descriptions of how to dress as a *mae chi* and as *chi phram.*

According to the Department of Religious Affairs' 1996 annual report on monastery dwellers, there are more than fifteen thousand registered *mae chis* at temples in Thailand. Registration is voluntary and not all temples register the *mae chis* who reside there. The *mae chis* at nunneries, however, are not listed anywhere in the Department of Religious Affairs' statistics. The Thai Nuns' Institute, however, recorded about five thousand members in 1998. Both the nuns who stay at temples and those who stay at separate nunneries can enroll as members of the institute. There are also *mae chis* living in Thailand who choose to stay at nunneries or private places without being members of the institute, and these women are not included in any statistics. This means it is difficult to know the actual number of nuns in Thailand. There are, however, *mae chis* in all the five regions of Thailand, with the largest percentage living in the central area, although this does not indicate that the nuns living there are actually from the central region. At my field site in central Thailand, in fact, many of the nuns originated from the northeastern provinces. The northeastern region is considered to be a highly religious part of Thailand, with many venerated monks; it is not, however, a region considered to have a large number of *mae chis.*[28]

A *mae chi's* ordination is regarded as a lay ordination, although it has a deep impact on the ordained women's identity. It is usual for a woman before ordination as a *mae chi* to follow the eight precepts as a *chi phram* for a period of time. It could be argued that the statuses of *chi phram* and *mae chi* are equal, since they follow the same precepts and are both formally perceived as lay women. However, a clear difference in status is experienced by both *mae chi* and *chi phram,* and a hierarchical order is explicitly displayed at nunneries. The *mae chis* I interviewed stressed the great difference ordination makes to their individual identity as religious persons. They claim their religious practice has deepened and become more sincere since ordination and that, by shaving their heads, they experience a complete break with their old lay life. *Chi phrams,* who usually stay at temples or nunneries for a short period of time, do not experience this break with lay life. The *mae chis,* especially if they follow the Thai Nuns' Institute's recommendations, also have special sets of rules modeled after the monks, Pāṭimokkha,[29] which regulate *mae chis'* behavior as ordained persons and also separate them from the category of *chi phrams.*

The Thai Nuns' Institute has also formulated a list of requirements for ordination as a *mae chi,* and these are modeled on the rules for the monks. The candidate must be a woman, not pregnant or caring for a baby, of good behavior and in good health, free from debt, and have no addiction to drugs. She must not be escaping from home or from governmental duties, and must not have a criminal record or suffer from an infectious disease. Moreover, she must not be disabled or too old to perform religious duties, and must have permission from her parents or her husband for her ordination.[30]

At Ratburi Nunnery, five monks and five nuns usually officiate at the *mae chi* ordination ceremony. Monks are ordinarily invited from the nearby temple but, if the aspirant wishes, the head nun *(khun mae)* at the nunnery can be the preceptor and, in that case, no monks are invited. In a traditional ceremony, once the novice is shaved and dressed in the *mae chi* robe, the ceremony starts with "taking refuge in the triple gem": the Buddha, the Dhamma, and the Sangha. Then the aspirant asks, in Pali, for the eight precepts from the *upacha* (a monk qualified to be in charge of ordinations), after which the monks are presented with candles, incense, flowers, and envelopes with money. Thereafter the monks end their part of the ceremony with chanting. When the monks have finished, the aspirant receives ordination from a chapter of five *mae chis.* These too receive a donation, though the sum of money is smaller than for the monks. Following this, the *mae chis* end the ceremony with chanting. This ceremony is a form of dual ordination almost certainly inspired by the *bhikkhunī* (fully ordained nuns') ordination. At other temples and nunneries, women are usually ordained only by the monks.

In Thailand and in other Theravāda Buddhist countries, merit-making or acts of generosity play a central role in village religious practices. The word *thambun* (to make merit) is generally used to refer to a wide range of good deeds and acts of generosity. It is important for most Thai people to seek to improve their kammic status through meritorious activities. There are ample opportunities for people to make *thambun*—for example, through various kinds of donations, often administered by temples. The most oft-cited form of merit-making is offering food to the monks on their alms rounds, just before noon each day.

Since most of the *mae chis* live at temples where nuns do not perform the alms round, it is still quite unusual for *mae chis* to collect food in the mornings. At Ratburi Nunnery, the nuns initiated alms rounds at the request of the lay people in the nearby village. Every morning at 5:30 A.M., fifteen nuns walk barefoot, carrying their white alms bowls in front of them, collecting rice and side dishes from about fifty households in the neighborhood. They walk in silence, and the interaction between the donor and receiver has a ritual pattern that defines it is a religious act. When the nuns come to a house, they stand quietly with their eyes downcast. Before giving the rice, the lay people remove their shoes as a sign of respect, lift the rice bowl above their heads, and put a spoonful of rice in each *mae chi's* bowl. Upon completing this, they usually kneel down and raise their hands in a gesture called *wai.* During the offering the nuns are completely silent. They do not look directly at the donor and they walk away quietly.

A lay woman offers alms to **mae chis** *in northeast Thailand (photo by Monica Lindberg Falk)*

While interviewing *mae chis* about what it means to them personally to collect alms, *mae chis* declare that it makes them feel proud to be ordained. They say this interaction with the laity is important for their practice. They feel a greater sense of responsibility towards lay people and they say it deepens their practice and their identity as religious persons. They also claim that the alms round demands that they practice Buddhism seriously and maintain excellent behavior in order to be worthy recipients of alms.

Often, lay people who give alms in the morning to the nuns also give to the monks. When I asked villagers whether they believe giving to the monks makes more merit than giving to the *mae chis,* they usually replied that the two are equally meritorious. They state that the important thing is how well the *mae chis* and the monks keep their precepts and practice Buddhism. Thus, *mae chis'* new role also comprises officiating at ceremonies and assisting the laity in various ways. The importance of Buddhist education is emphasized, and more nuns today are studying Pali in order to be able to read the original Buddhist scriptures and pronounce the Pali words correctly. Through their more elaborate ordination ceremonies, the practice of alms rounds, and the task of officiating at ceremonies, *mae chis* are approximating the full religious realm in their daily practice.

Gendered Ways to Maturity

Thai women are traditionally thought to belong to the mundane world, and they are expected to be dutiful daughters, caring wives, and self-sacrificing mothers. If a woman fails to fulfill her role expectations, she could lose her inheritance, create demerits *(bap),* and cause her husband to seek a "minor wife."[31] According to Thai cultural values, the evaluation of women as "good" or "bad" depends upon the way they enact their primary duty to the family. A "good" woman's place is in the home.[32] Kinship in Thailand is conventionally characterized as cognatic, with a preference for uxorilocal residence. Thai women have authority in the household but are socialized to behave submissively in public.[33] Thus, a Thai woman's sexuality must be confined to the environment of the family and the home. For "good" Thai women, monogamy is the only acceptable practice, and Thai girls are taught that virginity is of crucial importance. In Thai history, there are warrior heroines[34] who can be seen to represent a contrasting model, although ultimately these women sacrificed themselves in order to protect their family and the nation.[35] There has been no marked preference for boys over girls, and families have largely been organized around women.[36]

Motherhood is highly esteemed in Thai society. The mother symbolizes virtue, selflessness, sacrifice, goodness, and forgiveness. Mothers have given life to their children and have suffered, loved, and cared for them. Therefore children are always in debt to their parents and especially to their mothers. Young men are expected to become novice monks for at least one period of their lives out of gratitude to their parents. Through ordination, a young man's parents are perceived to acquire merit, and this is particularly important to the mother, who gains high merit primarily through her son's ordination. I have met *mae chis* who have received ordination on request of their families, but this is unusual. Usually daughters fulfill the traditional expectations of womanhood by being dutiful and lifelong caretakers of their parents. The rite of passage through ordination as a novice monk is also the traditional way for a man to become socially mature and ready to take on the adult male role. In contrast, young women are seen to mature through marriage. Progression through the different stages in a girl's life as she approaches adulthood is more gradual than for boys. Marriage marks one change in her status. The birth of the first child and the custom of "lying by the fire" *(yu fai)* after the delivery later reinforce her adult role.[37] Despite women's strong position in the family, patriarchal values dominate legal codes. Thus, it is not illegal for a man to have more than one wife, and adultery is grounds for divorce only for the husband, while rape is legally defined as a crime only when it is committed against a woman other than his wife.[38] Many Thai women no longer passively accept these discriminatory laws and male-biased notions. Indeed, the choice made today by increasing numbers of women not to marry but to become educated and economically independent may be a protest against them.[39]

In Thailand, women have always worked alongside men and even today play an important role in the economic field. Scholars have debated whether Thai women should be regarded as having high status because of their traditional involvement in economic activities, or low status because of the notion that they are "karmically" inferior to men. Thai women, however, seem to have internalized the notions that the female gender is both inferior to the male and polluting to the monastic order.[40] Gender polarization is evident in the attitudes towards men and women who search for spiritual fulfillment, attitudes manifested in the veneration of married men who leave their familial duties and become monks, compared to the perception of women who would like to be ordained as eccentric or selfish.[41] As we have seen, young men gain maturity through ordination as novice monks into a religious life which constrains their behavior and detaches them from the secular life. In contrast, women are assumed to gain maturity by becoming mothers, tied to the mundane reality. The elevated role of the mother, perceived as the highest priority of women's roles, has indirectly undermined women's other needs and aspirations.

Conclusion

Thailand has been a Theravāda country since the twelfth century, and more than ninety percent of Thai people call themselves Buddhists. Although the rapid changes in Thailand resulting from new socio-economic conditions have affected the pivotal position of the monks and the temples in society, Buddhism still continues to play a central role in Thai people's daily lives. Thai Buddhism is also being reconceptualized by the influential, educated middle class, which feels a growing disenchantment with the traditional civic religion.[42] Jackson has noted that during the last two decades there has been a weakening in Thai politicians' interest in controlling forms of Buddhist religiosity.[43] However, the decline in interest in regulating institutional Buddhism does not signal a decay of religiosity. On the contrary, many Thai people are shifting their association to new religious movements at the margins of state control. It is not only new Theravāda Buddhist movements that attract many Thai people, but also cults such as those associated with the Mahāyāna bodhisattva Kuan Yin (goddess of compassion) and the former Thai king Chulalongkorn. With the emergence of new Buddhist religious trends, the number of nunneries is growing, and *mae chis* are gaining increasing support from the laity.

In this paper I have portrayed *mae chis* at nunneries and their changing roles in Thai society. I have tried to show that the widespread notions of *mae chis* as elderly, brokenhearted, or destitute women are no longer fully valid. Besides searching for spiritual fulfillment, women as well as men have various reasons for renouncing the world. The status of *mae chis* is inferior to the monks' and provides them with neither state benefits nor social prestige. In contrast to women, the benefits of men's ordination as monks are manifold. They are supported in various ways by the government. Men also play an important role in transferring merit to their parents, especially to their mothers, who are prevented from becoming members of the Thai Sangha and achieving high-quality merit by themselves. Thus, sons are able to repay their moral debt to their parents, which daughters cannot do through renouncing the world.

The Thai Nuns' Institute is a national umbrella organization for the *mae chis,* and its ambition is to assist and unite *mae chis* from all over the country. The institute promotes the foundation of *mae chi* communities and the streamlining of their practice and rules, and this has strengthened the *mae chi* as a distinct category. The *mae chi* rules and regulations are modeled upon the monks' rules, and the national organization of the institute has also copied the organization of the monks Sangha. Access to education for *mae chis* is an important issue that the institute emphasizes. There are ascetic women in Thailand with profound knowledge of Buddhism and meditation skills, but they have seldom had scholastic training.[44] Thus, education is necessary for nuns' spiritual advancement, and a higher level of secular as well as Buddhist education will surely improve the lives of Thai nuns.

It is no longer possible for any woman to be ordained as a female Theravāda monastic or *bhikkhunī* as it was in the distant past. All women who become *bhikkhunīs* today receive ordination from Mahāyāna monks and nuns. As far as I know, there are only two Thai *bhikkhunīs* in Thailand today. One was ordained in Taiwan more than twenty-five years ago, and the other in 1998 in India. Neither is recognized by the Thai Sangha. There has never been a *bhikkhunī* order in Thailand, which could explain why the issue of installing the order there has received so little attention. The majority of the nuns I have interviewed declare that they would not be interested in being ordained as a *bhikkhunī* even if it were possible. In the first place they are reluctant to receive ordination from the Mahāyāna order, even though it originates from the Theravāda lineage. The *mae chis* are also aware of the difficulties of observing the 311 or 348 *bhikkhunī* precepts. They argue, further, that membership in the monastic order is not a prerequisite for leading a monastic life, and being a member of the Sangha would mean institutionalized subordination to the monks.

The notions of kamma and *dāna*, donation, are important features in Thai Buddhism, and their traditional interpretation has reinforced Thai women's secondary status. Conventionally, men are seen as having "better" kamma than women; it has therefore been essential for women to give donations to the monkhood and gain religious merit in order to improve their kamma. The reinterpretations of these and other central Buddhist concepts by monks such as Buddhadāsa Bhikkhu have aimed at moving lay people, women and men, increasingly into the center of religious life, which many *mae chis* view sympathetically.

The category of *mae chi* is being formed in relation both to the Thai monks and to the lay people. The role of the *mae chi* is in many respects modeled upon the role of the monks. Although women ascetics do not fit with traditional Thai women's gender roles, in areas where nunneries are situated *mae chis* are gaining increasing acceptance by and support from the laity. Formally, *mae chis* have been treated as lay persons by the authorities, but at the same time as religious persons by their lay supporters. This ambiguous position has allowed space for ascetic women to found their own communities. Women's roles in Thai society are augmented by the new possibilities that women create as religious persons—possibilities in which a novel religious autonomy is made possible.

Notes

1. Sangha: the collectivity of people who have been ordained as Buddhist monks and novices; nuns *(mae chi)* are not part of the Sangha.
2. I shall use the word *mae chi* interchangeably with nun. Thai terms are romanized according to the *Romanization Guide for Thai Script* devised by the Royal Institute, Bangkok, Thailand (1968) 1982. The spelling of personal names follows the individual's preference.
3. The research was conducted with the permission of the National Research Council of Thailand and is supported by the Swedish Humanities Research Council, the Swedish Council for Planning and Coordination of Research, and the Vega Foundation.
4. The name is fictitious.
5. See Monica Lindberg Falk, "Thammacāriṇī Witthaya: The First Buddhist School for Girls in Thailand" in *Swimming Against the Stream: Innovative Buddhist Women*, ed. Karma Lekshe Tsomo (Curzon Press, forthcoming).
6. Cook (1981), 44.
7. The five precepts are to abstain from: killing, stealing, sexual misconduct, lying, and taking intoxicants.
8. H. Kawanami, "Economic Position of Buddhist Nuns in Burma," Paper given at Sakyadhītā Fourth International Conference on Buddhist Women, Ladakh, 1995; Bartholomeusz (1994).
9. Kabilsingh (1988), 145.
10. Suwanbubbha (1987).
11. Terweil (1994), 88–98.
12. Douglas (1994).
13. Yongyuth (1997).
14. Komin (1991).
15. Kabilsingh (1991).
16. Goonatilake (1997), 31.
17. The nuns' Sangha is not ordinarily involved in monks' ordination.
18. Goonatilake (1977), 32–35.
19. Goonatilake (1977), 38.
20. The eight special chief rules, or *garudhamma:* (1) A nun must always bow down before a monk no matter how long she has been a nun. (2) A nun is not to spend the rainy season in a district where there is no monk. (3) In order to perform the Uposatha ceremony (days for special meetings of the Sangha and for recitations of the Pāṭimokkha rules) the nuns must wait for the monks to come and deliver the teaching. (4) After

the rains retreat the nuns are to hold Pavāraṇā (to inquire whether the nuns have committed any fault) to both the monks and the nuns. (5) A nun who is guilty of a serious offense must undergo the Mānatta discipline before both Sanghas. (6) When a novice has trained for two years in the six precepts, she should seek ordination from both Sanghas. (7) A nun is not to revile or abuse a monk under any circumstances (8) Admonition of monks by nuns is forbidden; admonition of nuns by monks is not forbidden (Horner [1989], 118–20).

21. Tiyavanich (1997).
22. Jackson (1988).
23. Kabilsingh (1991), 41.
24. This question goes beyond the differentiations of male and female sex. It carries an implication of being human.
25. Vajirananavarorasa (1989).
26. Cook (1981), 195.
27. Cook (1981), 205.
28. Kabilsingh (1991), 65.
29. Pāṭimokkha: monks disciplinary code of 227 precepts.
30. Rules of Practice of the Thai Nuns' Institute, Bangkok 1979.
31. Tantiwiramanond and Pandey (1987).
32. Van Esterik (1982 (b)), Hantrakul (1988), Komin (1991).
33. Soonthorndhada (1992).
34. In Thai classical literature of the Rāmāyaṇa and Inao.
35. Klausner (1997), 74.
36. Tantiwiramanond and Pandey (1996).
37. Yoddumnern-Attig (1992).
38. Klausner (1997).
39. Klausner (1997); Daorueng (1998).
40. Tantiwiramanond and Pandey (1987), 140; Terwiel (1994).
41. Tantiwiramanond and Pandey (1987), 140; Terwiel (1994).
42. Taylor (1993).
43. Jackson (1997).
44. Tiyavanich (1997).

VORAMAI KABILSINGH:

The First Thai Bhikkhunī

Voramai Kabilsingh is one of the few fully ordained nuns in Thailand. She went to Hong Kong to receive full bhikkhunī *ordination. She wears yellow. When she came back from being ordained, monks wanted her to stop wearing yellow. Someone pointed out that since monks wear only orange and ochre, why could not she wear yellow? Since then she has been left in peace by the higher council of monks. After a very active and engaged spiritual life, she is now very old and ill. People come from far and wide just to see her and pay their respects.*

I PRACTICED various techniques of meditation according to circumstance: watching the breath, single-pointedness on the breath, visualization, and so on. Meditation is to concentrate the mind so that we can apply it wisely. Compassion comes from the heart. When I help, I do not help just one person because that would be preferential: I help everyone. I wanted to help people for a very long time.

I did not really need to be a *bhikkhunī* to do this. However, I wanted to set an example, as there were no *bhikkhunīs* and many obstacles to becoming one. I was able to show that a woman could become fully ordained. Nowadays, many people come just to see me, as a living example of a *bhikkhunī* in Thailand.

When I became ill, the bodhisattvas came to protect and help me. If you fulfill your spiritual goal, you will see and understand many things.

Compiled by Martine Batchelor and translated by Chatsumarn Kabilsingh

CHATSUMARN KABILSINGH:

Advocate for a Bhikkhunī Sangha in Thailand

Chatsumarn Kabilsingh is the daughter of Voramai Kabilsingh. She is a professor of Religion and Philosophy at Thammasat University in Bangkok, and an active feminist. She teaches meditation and organizes retreats for women in Thailand.

MY MOTHER WAS ORDAINED as a *mae chi* [nun] when I was ten, thirty-six years ago. She transformed our house into a temple. Slowly other *mae chis* came to stay with her. By the end of the first year we had about twenty. They wore light yellow.

Her decision to become a nun was the culmination of different things. When my father was still an M.P., she used to follow him. She was a journalist. While reporting on his activities in the countryside she saw some very poor children. They were the future of our country, but they had no help at all. She decided to form an orphanage. She was also interested in meditation. She gained certain heights of meditational achievements. She thought that becoming a nun would help, and enable her to help others in a better manner.

I was too young to like or dislike the fact that my mother had become a nun and turned the house into a temple. But I remember feeling uncomfortable when my mother came to my school, as I did not know how to explain this to my friends. She had always been the kind of person whose word was the law in the house, and we just followed whatever she said. I participated in the chanting and all the activities of the temple. I was brought up very much in that kind of atmosphere.

When we moved to this place, my mother started a school, and my elder sister took care of it. It was a day school open to the general public. At the beginning we had very few children, only about thirty. Now there are four hundred. When the students are on vacation, we can use the school for women's retreats.

We used to have an orphanage. One year we had to take care of eighty people, both nuns and orphans. After thirty-five years we have entered a period of decline because my mother is old. She used to be very active, but three years ago she took a step back from all the activities in which she was once involved. She published a monthly magazine for thirty-two years. She became ill last year and could not get up anymore. The orphanage came to an end ten years ago. It had become too big a responsibility for my mother, and I am not in a position yet to take over her work.

When she was active, she was like a supervisor cum advisor for the orphanage and the school. The nuns were actually teaching at the school and also taking care of the orphans. We also did farming ourselves. A large area of the temple grounds was rice fields, and we grew enough rice for our own needs. I am trying to reflect on the temple decline. Where did we go wrong? This is why I put the emphasis more on retreats, on training to understand and develop in the Dhamma and the practice.

My mother was like a spiritual leader who walked so fast that she left her followers far behind. Very few people understood what she was doing. People would do the manual work with her without sharing in the mind and in the heart. This is what I saw was lacking in this organization. We have to work closely together; whatever I do, my students must understand it and walk together with me.

I am slowly taking over, keeping the flame burning, but going in a slightly different direction. In traditional Buddhism, to make merit one builds temples. I told my mother that when my time came, I was going to build people instead. We have enough buildings here; she spent a lot of money on them. She was so capable, so successful, in providing all these funds to build all these houses for us. Now that we have them, our only responsibility is to maintain them, keep them in good shape, but we have to fill these buildings with people, Dhamma people. I intend not to be so involved in social activities and social welfare. We are going to give people strength so that they can walk on their own feet.

Many times I have felt I wanted to become a nun. When the time comes, I must be very certain. Once I am ordained I should not leave it; it should be a lifelong commitment. I could not step back because I would be setting an example. One has to be a good example, otherwise one might as well not become a nun in the first place. I am waiting for the right time when the foundation of my life is strong enough, and when I have a solid financial and social foundation. I feel my life is like a triangle. I also want my children to be strong enough on their own. My husband knew this from the beginning. When he asked to marry me, I told him that being a nun was my goal.

Recently I have been traveling a great deal. On each trip I have been asked to lead meditations. I do not see myself yet as a meditation teacher, but people get so much from just sitting together. At first these requests came only from Westerners, and I started to think I was not being beneficial to my own people. Last year I gave some lectures. Some of the people asked for meditation, and it seemed to help them tremendously. This gave me more confidence, so I started to think about leading some retreats.

We had the facilities here, and people offered to do the catering for us. Everything just seemed to fit. For the first retreat we had a hundred and eight people. It was not as successful as the standards I had set in my mind, but many people were happy with it, and some of them gained something. It seemed to help them become more confident and happy afterwards, and that was very rewarding. In the first retreat I set out three different days: the first day was to let go, the second day was to build up compassion, the last day was to learn to forgive.

What I teach is so basic that we do not need to go in any details yet. We are doing two things at the same time; training people and letting them go. We will have group meetings together often enough to build people up so they will become trainers. In turn they can teach in their neighborhoods all over the country.

We want to ignite sparks here and there, and hope to give strength to women. The training here is how to become a better Buddhist with an understanding of the teaching and the practice. They will become strong Dhamma practitioners with a tint of feminism. I hope that the trainees will do social work. The training is learning to understand. We have to know our own problems and the suffering we have unknowingly caused others. Generally we only know part of ourselves, so we are trying to get people to know themselves better and to improve themselves in order to serve society better. It is not for ourselves only; this training is to enable us to serve others better.

Compiled by Martine Batchelor

BUDDHIST ACTION:
Lay Women and Thai Monks[1]

H. Leedom Lefferts, Jr.

Our view of the place and role of gender in Thai Theravāda Buddhism has much to do with where we locate our questions and perspectives. Often, discussions about Thai Buddhism appear to be positioned in a Theravāda abstracted from the cultural framework of which it is a part. While it must be granted that Theravāda Buddhism carries statements of morality and action, the student of Thai culture must also acknowledge that these statements exist within a more comprehensive framework; Buddhism cannot be abstracted from its cultural context as if it existed alone.

Tambiah, in *Buddhism and the Spirit Cults of Northeast Thailand*,[2] established that Buddhism and spirit cults exist within a framework of interpenetrating relationships. The same thesis pervades this essay: that gender roles and relations exist within a comprehensive framework of morality and action and that, while we may try to isolate one aspect of this framework from the others, we must think of these as elements belonging to a total institution.

Thus, this paper follows Tambiah's approach by relating how lay women act in relationship with Theravāda Buddhism, schematically outlining the contexts of their actions in reference to each other, to men, and to monks. It posits that a more comprehensive view of Thai culture permits us to see the fully active role women take in shaping Theravāda Buddhist activities. This view has often been obscured by observers who focus exclusively on those people who are seen, and are seen by the actors themselves, as "adepts" in this religion's belief systems, its articles of knowledge, and its rituals. After close observation in a rural community where continuous Theravāda Buddhist and related ritual action occurs, I have come to the conclusion that women play significant and formative roles in defining this behavior and in bringing it to fruition. This is so much the case that, following Tambiah, I believes separation of these actions from their total context is arbitrary and counter-productive in terms of understanding the roles of both genders in forming and perpetuating the contexts of their tradition.

Western descriptions of Thai Buddhism place women in an ambiguous relationship with regard to the triple gems: the Buddha, the Dhamma, and the Sangha. However, while depicted as a part of the social universe within which Theravāda Buddhism operates, women are characterized as subordinate and fundamentally powerless participants in the religion's social universe. In this role, women are often seen as supportive or nurturing and thus not directive.

On the other hand, women are acknowledged to have once been placed on an equivalent footing with monks by the Buddha, who instituted a co-ordinate order of nuns, following the establishment of an order of monks.[3] For reasons inadequately understood, lineages of nuns did not survive in South and Southeast Asian cultural systems. This ambiguity highlights the problem faced by commentators on women in Theravāda Buddhism, for in previous times women possessed recognized power in the context of the religious system. Today, however, women do not appear to have this power. The question arises, then, about the nature and extent of the power women might exercise in Buddhism, for usually, the power women have is seen to be inadequate and diminished.

This paper is divided into three parts. Following a brief description of Thai-Lao communities in Northeast Thailand, the first part considers the background of Western understandings of Thai Buddhism, with special attention to domains of action that have not normally been included in such analyses. Most particularly, this paper holds that material culture and the exchange of things and words between women, men, monks, and ancestors plays essential and significant roles in these actions.

The paper's second section depicts the exchange of things, words, and people, especially women, that takes place in some salient Thai-Lao Buddhist rituals. Of particular importance are the exchanges that currently take place, initiated and sustained by women with the cooperation of monks, that bring about transformations in people and things to perpetuate the cyclical universe at the heart of Theravāda Buddhism and of Thai-Lao life. These exchanges determine the roles of monks and bring about changes in the results of past actions which affect the future actions of everyone.

Finally, the essay's third section attempts to understand how contemporary changes in Thai society alienate women from the system of exchange described in section two. In particular, the paper contends that modernization, stemming from the West and carrying with it particular patterns of gender relations, undercuts the cyclical system that forms the foundation of Thai-Lao Theravāda Buddhist culture. The paper ends by suggesting how the perpetuation of the intricate system of exchanges in Thai-Lao Buddhist culture might take place, given the changing roles of women.[4] The paper concludes by noting the directions in which Thai Buddhism might evolve and how women might come to exercise a degree of power similar to that which they have had for several hundred years.

The Settings, in Thailand and the West

This paper comes after thirty years of research in northeast Thai-Lao Theravāda Buddhist communities. The research was initiated not to study Buddhism and its role in the life of the people, but the course of development in communities subjected to intensive input by the Thai government, international agencies and, more recently, non-government organizations.

Northeast Thailand is ambiguously incorporated into the Thai Kingdom.[5] The northeast as a direction is enigmatic in South and East Asian culture. It is the direction from which unknowns may come: the city of Mandalay was consciously positioned so that Mandalay Hill is to its northeast, for example; the mountains to the northeast of Kyoto, Japan, are seen to have special powers. Thailand's northeast, colloquially named *Isan*,[6] echoes this ambiguity. This is the direction from which the last major military threat to central Thailand, then Siam, originated.[7] The region is considered intemperate due to its dryness, and this is seen to contribute to its poverty in relation to the kingdom as a whole.

Moreover, Thailand's northeast, which contains a third of the kingdom's population and area, is inhabited primarily by people who are not considered part of mainstream Thai culture. The Thai-Lao, the largest single ethnic community in the kingdom,[8] reside for the most part in villages and engage in rain-fed, wet-rice paddy agriculture. The "Laoness" of this population has meant that it has been subjected to intensive colonization efforts by central Thais. These efforts include an educational system that uses a form of the Thai language and favors a view of history as perceived and written by the Central Thai elite while overlooking certain areas of local history. Central Thais often note, however, that many if not most of the Theravāda Buddhist monks and novices who inhabit Bangkok's *wats* (monasteries) are Thai-Lao; this phenomenon has been termed "Wat Isan."[9] However, this increased religiosity of the Thai-Lao is often construed by Central Thai to be a result of the poverty of the region, with education through the monastic tradition providing the primary vehicle of upward mobility.

Concerned over the past fifty years with separatist movements, the Thai government has undertaken intensive development efforts, often with the assistance of bi- and multi-lateral support from foreign nations and institutions.[10] Even more recently, as a result of the Vietnam War, which led to the training of locals in mechanical and technical skills, Isan's men and women have provided a substantial portion of the kingdom's foreign remittances and tourist and manufacturing income.

The Thai-Lao village in which the major amount of research has been undertaken was founded in 1922. The oral reconstitution of over a hundred family and household demographic, structural, and land tenure histories established a comprehensive history of the community.[11] A secondary result of this work was to highlight the roles of women in household and village social organization.

Households are, fundamentally, lineages of women of different generations into which men marry. Rice land tends to be inherited by women; rice land bought by a couple is usually inherited by their daughters. Sons' inheritances are usually paid off at or about the time of marriage. Women tend to control a household's finances; household production that results in monetary return is handed over to the woman of the household for keeping and dispensing for household needs.

An unanticipated byproduct of this research was an understanding of the role of textiles, produced by women, in manifesting household and village roles. This, in turn, gave rise to a pan-mainland Southeast Asian study concerning the varied meanings and import of textiles in Tai populations.[12] The result of this was the conclusion that women are active agents in constructing and perpetuating the system of which they are a part.

The complex cycle of village life and the ways women symbolize their roles in this cycle reflect the ways in which women exercise power and express it among themselves and to others. This symbolization occurs with special emphasis not only in the organization and perpetuation of households, but also on the provision of material evidence reflecting the transformations undertaken in the perpetuation of Theravāda Buddhism. Prestations of cloth are particularly important in establishing occasions that move young men to become members of the Sangha.[13] This transformation is initiated by women as they raise their children, whereby they instill in their children the obligation, *thaup taen bun khun*, of offspring to compensate their parents for the sacrifices they made in raising them. In part, with regard to sons, this transformation reaches fulfillment in a mother's dressing her son as a *naak*, or serpent, with textiles she and other members of her lineage have woven, and then in his ordination as a monk, in robes made of cloth produced or donated by his mother.

Stemming from this research, this paper contends that Thai—especially village-based Thai-Lao—Buddhist action is insufficiently captured by the actions and written and spoken words of only monks and men. It holds that the division between material and spiritual domains that permeates Western-based cultures is inapplicable in Thai Buddhism.[14] Moreover, understanding such a system of interaction requires that attention be paid to the complex exchange and cycling of things and people through the system. In particular, the use of divisions concerning who is adept and who is not deprives observers of understanding the active role one gender has in constructing this religion.

Following Tambiah, current statements depicting systems of action, such as those included in the "anthropology of technical systems,"[15] the study of gender,[16] and of exchange theory,[17] lead to the possibility of a new synthesis of action in Theravāda Buddhist cultures. These studies lead to analyses of continuing action-as-meaning in systems such as Theravāda Buddhism, in which objects and people are presented and moved in constant exchange. Thus, material culture includes not only the objects themselves, but also meanings involved in the production of these objects, as well as in the results of such production as they are exchanged between different members of the social system. This also relates to Theravāda Buddhist ritual events for which contexts must be arranged so that the events themselves can take place.

Coordinate with this approach is the idea that much of what is expressed in many cultures may not be voiced in the way and to the extent we believe salient aspects of Western cultures are articulated.[18] Many actions, even those in Western cultures, may be non-verbal. However, in Western cultures, because we do not voice these actions and things, we tend to ignore them. In Thai-Lao villages, whose inhabitants may have known each other since birth, many—perhaps most—significant actions are unvoiced. However, just because words are not used does not necessarily mean actions are not valued. Actions without words may be more valued, as they express deeply held values that participants recognize as given.[19]

Drawing on the theoretical orientations and the research noted above, this paper sees women playing important, productive, and essential roles that carry positive connotations in Thai Buddhist terms. Moreover, this paper holds that the exchange and prestation of things and sons between monks and (lay) women (rather than lay men) defines and reinforces the contexts for Thai-Lao Buddhist actions.

This is not to say that women in Thai-Lao villages act in ways akin to men or monks in order to be positively valued. (If this were so, one form of the argument would be that the order of *bhikkhunīs* must be reestablished so that women could have their own channel to salvation.) Rather, significant here is Sahlins's discussion of Schieffelin's depiction of the Kaluli: that women, men, and monks may be "constituted as complementary and interdependent factions...involved in reciprocal exchanges that assist in the resolution of their opposition."[20] Because observers tend to pay little attention to women's actions as part of Theravāda Buddhist systems, we tend to ignore women as constituting an opposition that is complementary, interdependent, valued, and determinative of the direction of religious discourse.

Ritual Exchange in Thai-Lao Culture

Tambiah's charting of Theravāda Buddhism and the spirit cults in which the Thai-Lao participate provides a landmark synthesis of the inseparable interrelationships between the two. By showing that these beliefs and actions exist and operate together in the lives of the people, he provides a way to see Thai-Lao in a holistic, comprehensive, and contemporary field of action. However, while this synthesis provides a means of access to people's lives, emphasis in follow-on studies has tended to be placed on the Theravāda Buddhist segment of this ritual action. This has probably happened for a number of reasons too complex to be discussed here.[21] However, the emphasis on ritual action in Theravāda Buddhism has led to a neglect of the possible role of those people who are not considered "adept" at Buddhism itself. Tambiah's own study rarely mentions women; it focuses on men and monks as actors and does not consider the crucial roles women play in propelling men into ritual action and in undertaking important ritual actions themselves.[22]

The Buddha established the Sangha in ways to be necessarily dependent on exchanges with a lay population.[23] Fundamental to this dependence, in addition to the very beings/bodies of the members of the Sangha themselves (a subject to which we will return), are the requisites for these members' survival, including food and clothing, from their initiation into the order throughout their existence in it. Through the establishment of "The Middle Way" with orders of monks and nuns, the Buddha declared that they should be moderately and appropriately attired and that they should eat regularly.

However, the Buddha established a conundrum by prescribing that monks and nuns could neither cook nor make their own clothes. To satisfy this, he provided ways for monks and nuns to be clothed and fed. He specified where and how cloth could be acquired—initially from discarded cloth in cemeteries and forests and, later, from lay people—and how it could be made into appropriately respectable yet devalued garments.[24] He also specified how food could be secured—with an alms bowl—and eaten modestly.

In establishing these requirements, the Buddha constructed a system of requisite exchanges between lay people and the members of the Sangha. Additionally, in part because gender differences lay at the foundation of South Asian culture of the period, the Buddha constructed slightly different rules for the male and female orders of the Sangha. He also established different ways by which lay men and women could relate to these orders. On the one hand, women may have provided a substantial core of patronage to early Buddhism. On the other, however, monks followed heightened prohibitions in their association with women, including not touching them and not sitting on the same bench or being alone with them.[25]

As Theravāda Buddhism migrated to Southeast Asia, the organization of a Sangha consisting of orders of both monks and nuns disappeared. This resulted in an order of monks in which men could participate, while women assumed foundational lay roles that set them in complementary and reciprocal opposition to the order of monks. Women became the owners of houses and productive land from whom donations would come. Additionally, because children are the product of women, women became the providers of monks, their sons. Thus, Buddhism evolved in the Thai-Lao context, and more generally in Southeast Asia,[26] into a complex of exchanges by which women and their symbols represented one pole, and monks and their symbols the other.

The Double Renunciation of Bun Buat Naak

While much work—in both anthropology and religion—has focused on the social organization and the moral ethos of Buddhist monks and men in Thai and Lao culture, little has been done to specify the direction and extent of exchanges that underlie this system.[27] The series of exchanges involve women as mothers clothing and presenting their sons for ordination, first as novices and then as monks. The rituals surrounding these exchanges involve the renunciation by the mother of her offspring, even as he renounces himself and his family of birth. The son's part in this double renunciation, his ordination as a monk, signifies his obligation, *thaup taen bun khun*, to his parents, and especially to his mother.

The festival of ordination, Bun Buat Naak, takes place before the beginning of the rains retreat in late April, May, or early June. At this time sons move from representations of fertility and procreation (*naak*, serpents), that is, exemplifications of women, to the symbolic death embodied by monks, who cannot materially contribute to the continuation of the social system.[28] Symbolizing this transition is the interim adoption by the ordinands of clothing that sets them apart from their roles as sons. For this ritual, sons of Thai-Lao women are usually dressed in the many hues of the rainbow, thus participating in the pan-Southeast Asian notion of protection and power through color.[29] Sons of Thai women are customarily attired in white, which represents not only relative purity, but also Brahmanism, *Satsana Phraam*. Thai Buddhists conceptualize Brahman religion as the religious era immediately preceding Buddhism and usually symbolize it by white cloth.[30]

The complex meanings of this ritual have yet to be adequately explored, especially in terms of "the total social phenomena," the "entire system of exchanges,"[31] of which the Bun Buat Naak is an integral part. This cannot be done in this short paper, but some further elucidation of these exchanges is appropriate.

The double renunciation begun in the Bun Buat Naak creates for individual women and their sons a close connection within the larger cycle of exchange by which Buddhism in Thai-Lao society is perpetuated.[32] This larger cycle consists of a series of exchanges, usually but not always mediated by monks, but initiated by households—noted earlier as fundamentally consisting of lineages of women—between the present and deceased ancestors. These exchanges consist of water, cloth, and ancillary objects. By sending these objects to ancestors, women ensure the continuation of the social system of which they are the center so that, after death, they and their relations can be assured of the prestation of cloth, water, and other objects needed for their life away from this world and for re-entrance into it at a future date in a heightened state of merit.

Exchanges with Ancestors

Others have remarked on the obligation owed by children, both sons and daughters, to their parents for raising them, signified by the phrase *thaup taen bun khun.*[33] This obligation can be repaid in several ways, the most traditional being that sons become monks while daughters marry and remain in their mother's household to continue the household line.[34] Sons who had been monks but who have returned to lay status take on the duties first of son-in-law in their bride's parental household and then, either by establishing their own household or taking over that of their parents'-in-law upon their deaths, become householders themselves.

It must be emphasized, however, that the Thai-Lao cycle of exchange not only encompasses this life, but also the lives of those who have preceded them and, consequently, those who will follow. Moreover, the responsibility for the perpetuation of these exchanges rests primarily with women, since women traditionally hold the resources of land and house, which connote wealth. Hence members of neither gender fulfill and dispense with their obligations to their parents, their relatives, or distant ancestors simply by becoming a monk or by marrying and continuing an ancestral line. Over the span of a person's life, exchanges continue to occur often, but not solely, within a Theravāda Buddhist framework.

The pouring of consecrated water, *yaat nam*, during the daily but especially weekly *wan phra* (Buddha Day) ceremonies in the *sala wat* (meeting hall on the grounds of a Buddhist temple) is a major event for the transference of merit to ancestors.[35] On these occasions, while monks chant a specific blessing (Isan, Lao: *suat yaat nam;* Thai: *kham kruat nam*), members of the congregation pour water from a small container into a dish or other receptacle. After the service, this water is taken outside and poured down the lower trunk of a tree or bush in the *wat* onto the ground while the offerer whispers another prayer, conveying the water to Phra Mae Thoranee, the keeper of the earth. People say that they do this to transfer merit to their ancestors as well as to other living things, animals and plants.

The major offering of *yaat nam* occurs during the mainland Southeast Asian New Year in mid-April, called Songkran in Thai and Lao. In tourist literature, much is made of the throwing of water on passing motorists, bicyclists, and pedestrians at this time. This is normally explained as a way to cool off, since this is usually the hottest time of the year. However, this water has not been blessed and therefore is not part of the water that is poured to ensure the transfer of merit.

During Songkran much more takes place than the throwing of water on passing tourists. Two events involving water are of particular importance in understanding the roles of women in Theravāda Buddhism, as well as in household and village continuity that focus on this holiday: (1) the request for blessings that descendants ask of the eldest generation in the family line, and (2) the washing of ancestors' ashes and the presentation of gifts.

Within each household or group of extended households descendants gather at a private ceremony and request a blessing, *pon*, from the eldest generation of both men and women. Descendants on both the male and female side, including their spouses and children, come from some distance for this blessing. However, the local families formed by the continuity of women who have inherited these households are sure to be there and form the core of the requesters. The eldest male descendant asks for the blessing, while the respondent is usually the eldest person, male or female, in the line. Then water, *nam hom*, previously sacralized by the eldest male of the represented households, is poured by the descendants respectfully (at least at first) over the ancestors' hands. Later these ancestors pour water over the descendants. Finally, the women of the households give gifts, especially new clothing, such as a blouse and a *phaa sin*, a woman's tubular skirt, to each of the elder women, while elder men receive a shirt and a pair of pants or *phaa sarong*, a man's tubular skirt.

This ritual and the pouring of water during the weekly *wan phra* blessing are extended to deceased ancestors on the third day of Songkran, *wan ruam yaat*, by a ritual at the *wat* involving the washing of their ashes. With this ceremony the living have fulfilled their obligations toward the dead. This forms the culmination of Songkran at the household and village level[36] and signifies the continuity of household and village as enacted through reciprocal obligations.

During *wan ruam yaat* (the day for bringing together close and distant relatives), family representatives and all members of descendants' households gather at the *sala wat* (meeting hall of the village monastery) bringing gifts, such as uncooked rice, fish sauce, and cloth.[37] These items are for deceased ancestors to be placed in their domain once they have been blessed by the monks in a ceremony similar to *suat yaat nam*, in which blessed water is passed on to ancestors. Villagers inscribe on pieces of paper the names of deceased ancestors and other deceased villagers known to them who may not have descendants living in the village. These pieces of paper are collected in a tray, and the abbot of the *wat* or another designated monk sets them on fire.[38]

The monks then perform the usual ceremony for a *wan phra*, including the blessing of *yaat nam*. While the monks chant the *suat yaat nam*, some women of the congregation, rather than pouring water into dishes for later pouring outside, pour their water into the tray containing the ashes of inscribed names. Later, this tray and water are taken out and poured at the base of the *wat's bodhi* tree. Other water poured during the *suat yaat nam* is poured on the bases of trees and plants, as usual.

Later, in a significant expansion of the usual *wan phra* ritual, household members gather at the stūpa[39] of deceased ancestors in which their ashes (often including fragments of charred bones) are kept in reliquaries. These stūpas are opened,[40] the reliquaries removed and opened, and pleasant-smelling water, *nam hom*, or, in some cases, *suat nam yaat*, is poured over the ashes and bones. Even the ashes of people who have no living descendants are so anointed; anyone can wash ashes contained in opened reliquaries.

This description of the core rituals of Bun Buat Naak and Songkran conveys the importance of present household members, especially the women of that household, in instituting and continuing the series of prestations by which Theravāda Buddhism exists. Women give their sons in an act of double renunciation and they give merit to their ancestors during Songkran. Monks, as their mothers' sons and as descendants of their households, sacralize water and goods, which are then conveyed to the earth to be distributed to the ancestors. Without the active purposefulness of women to convey their resources for these actions and to participate in them, these rituals would not take place.

Theravāda Buddhist Exchange in the Village

Discussion so far has focused on ritual exchange in the *wat*, the locus of activities of the Sangha, but it is only a portion of the total social space in which lay people as well as monks operate. The *wat* is not the only locus of ritual exchange between ancestors and their household descendants. When requested by members of households or villages as a whole, monks also perform rituals outside the *wat*, especially at funerals (which can take place inside or outside the *wat* grounds) and at ceremonies in which immediate ancestors are commemorated with the pouring of sacralized water through *suat mon*, which takes place in the household.

Another cycle of rituals, coordinate with *wat* rituals, that focuses on the lay center of the village (as well as the governmental center), takes place at the *sala klang baan*, the meeting hall in the village center. Many of these involve monks and, equally important, the village as a locus for women's power. In these ceremonies, the men fade into the background somewhat in their roles as ritual intermediaries, as women assert their concern with the welfare and prosperity of their houses and wealth.

The Bun Buak Baan, usually held at the beginning of the sixth lunar month (mid-April to early May), is the first ritual to follow the New Year celebration, of which Songkran is the core. During the Bun Buak Baan, monks come to the *sala klang baan* for three evenings to conduct the usual ceremony and to perform special chants for the protection of the village. This ceremony pays special attention to the spirits that exist within the village. This aspect becomes especially important on the morning of the fourth day when, in addition to the usual ceremony that includes *suat yaat nam*, the monks conduct a ritual in which they pour water collected from all houses over small triangular banana-stalk vessels containing representations of bad things or things that should be protected, such as animals, people, fingernail clippings, and different kinds of cooked rice from each house. The monks then take other *nam mon*, water that is especially powerful and thought to bring good health, representations of things meant to appeal to spirits, such as cigarettes, betel, and flags, as well as decorated banana leaf containers and the banana-stalk vessels previously washed, and deposit them in auspicious locations around the village perimeter. As they do this, the monks and novices perform chants and throw stones, sand, the *nam mon*, and shredded money in the various directions to ensure that bad spirits will not enter.[41] This part of the ceremony is performed only in the living area of the village, not in the *wat*.

Women are especially prominent during this ceremony because they come representing their households, bringing items that exemplify them. Moreover, they are responsible for erecting money trees and collecting money during each ceremony, and they alone place rice in the alms bowls of the monks (the rice to be blessed being the product of their own lands). In recognition of the importance of their roles, only women have *nam mon* and shredded money thrown at their heads, sacralizing them and bringing them assurances of prosperity.

Similar ceremonies, also celebrated in the household section of the village, take place during the dry season, from the end of the harvest in January until the beginning of the rains in June. An important one is the *Bun Bang Fay*, the Rocket Festival, also centering on the *sala klang baan*, in which rockets, designated as *naak* (serpents), are fired into the air in order to initiate the rains on which household prosperity depends for the coming agricultural year.[42]

Finally, each household has its own ceremony conducted by women on *wan phra*. On the morning of *wan phra*, usually before she goes to the *wat* as part of the *wan phra* ceremony there, the woman who is head of the household presents candles, incense, rice, and water, *nam hom*, to the Buddha shrine in her house. Women are their own ritual specialists in ways that men are not. The knowledge of appropriate behavior and prestations as well as the chants spoken on these occasions are handed down from mother to daughter and are meant to be undertaken in the privacy of these ceremonies.

This schematic rendering of these rituals in both the *wat* and the domestic areas describes the ways in which current members of Thai-Lao households and villages are embedded in a total system of exchange, through Theravāda Buddhism, with ancestors and future descendants. Recognition of this cycle of prestations, from past through present to future, makes apparent the importance of women in Thai Buddhism. In this system, women form the core and continuity of households: men move to their bride's house at the time of marriage, not the other way around; men move from their mothers to their statuses as monks in Theravāda Buddhism; it is women who hold property, rice, and rice fields; and it is women who renounce their sons as the means for the continuity of their households by giving them to the monkhood. In short, women and monks are the poles between which material things and blessings for past, present, and future are exchanged, and in this system men too are exchangeables.[43]

The Future of the Cycle

Northeast Thai-Lao rural women have the potential to live full and fulfilling ritual lives. Women and monks together have constructed a complementary opposition by which women, men, and monks together achieve their soteriological goals. The question for the contemporary period is the extent to which Thai and Thai-Lao women may be allowed to continue to pursue their goals in this arrangement. The impetus for modernization, coming from Western cultures, is a male one. In Western developmental processes, women tend to be assigned subordinate roles, which women in the West have recognized and struggled to break.

As Western culture intrudes into Theravāda Buddhist ritual culture, the ways in which women can achieve success in traditional forms could be lost. The image of the successful woman, advertised and perpetuated through movies and television, promises freedom, yet contains its own chains. This image is aggressively promoted by the Thai state as well as by industry and capitalism; it induces women to move to cities and engage in employment. But in moving from villages to cities, young women are cut off from the ritual cycle of success in which their mothers participated. These women attempt to continue to participate in both worlds—the urban and the rural—by sending remittances to their parents, by returning to the village for major festivals, and, most importantly, by returning to the house of their mothers for their wedding, all the while showing off their success by wearing fancy clothes and using expensive cosmetics.

However, in increasing numbers they find they are unable to meet these obligations, especially as their labor, both rural and urban, becomes devalued under the stress of the recent economic downturn. The avenues of success in both worlds become closed to them as a male-oriented and dominated world becomes important in their lives.

Other articles in this volume chart the course of Thai women as they move into meditation and other exercises that attempt to satisfy goals of soteriological success. However, their new roles in no way replace the central role that women have in Thai-Lao rural Theravāda Buddhism. Moreover, involvement in these activities requires a middle-class freedom that many rural women do not have. In effect, many women are deprived of appropriate ways to satisfy their goals.

The extent to which this urban syndrome penetrates into the rural environment is unclear at this point. Today, most rural villages provide only a partial subsistence base for their inhabitants; the Thai government has done nothing to promote the possible benefits of modernity for rural life, and nothing to insure that villagers become involved in a cash economy. Thus, many villagers I know now depend on remittances from relatives living in more prosperous situations. Other villagers may provide income for their village families by commuting to cities for work on a daily or weekly basis.

Even with such pressures to become modern and discard the cycle of household and village rituals by which Theravāda Buddhism provides a framework for success, many young women continue to assert their involvement in such activities. Major and minor occasions to make merit are important to them, from giving rice to monks as they complete their morning rounds (before these women leave for work), to representing their households in Bun Buak Baan, to participating in the major festivals of Songkran and Bun Buat Naak.

While the cycle of rituals by which ancestors and descendants are connected, as perpetuated through Theravāda Buddhism, continues, it is unclear how significant it is and how many may want it to be discontinued. Individualism, including a lack of concern with ancestors and obligations, is a paramount product of modernization. How long young Thai and Thai-Lao women can live between the world of modernization and the world of ancestral and parental obligations remains to be seen.

Notes

1. This paper was completed while I was resident in a village with which I have been involved for some thirty years. If I have not adequately acknowledged in previous publications the invaluable, caring help the people of this village have given to this work, I wish to do so now. Without their forbearance and generosity in letting me enter, observe, participate, and ask numerous questions on this paper's topic and many other subjects, I would have nothing to write. I hope that, in some small measure, this paper adequately reflects the lives and drives of these people. I also wish to thank the Department of Anthropology, Smithsonian Institution, for giving me the honorary rank of research associate so that I could have the privilege of working with the librarians of the John Wesley Powell Library, who provided invaluable assistance in tracking down obscure publications by interlibrary loan.
2. Stanley J. Tambiah, *Buddhism and the Spirit Cults of Northeast Thailand* (Cambridge: Cambridge University Press, 1970).
3. The extent to which the order of nuns was of a status equivalent to monks is itself a matter of contention. Kabilsingh (1982), 67, states, "When the Buddha eventually allowed the organization of Buddhist nuns, or bhikkhunis, he proclaimed many rules which made it clear that the bhikkhuni Sangha must always be under the spiritual guidance and protection of the male bhikkhu Sangha." However, Gunawardana (1988), 5, notes that even though the Buddha prescribed that the ordination of a nun must be approved by both Sangha of monks and nuns,

    > The greater importance attached to participation of nuns in the ordination of a new nun is also evident from the stipulation that a monk who advises a nun who has been ordained only by the order of nuns would be committing an offence by the *dukkata* category while if he advises a nun ordained only by the order of monks, he would be guilty of a more serious offence of the *pācittiya* category.

    In short, "in Sri Lanka...women could not be admitted into the order in the absence of nuns."
4. This statement brings to mind the aphorism of Professor Robert Hackenberg of the University of Colorado, "People survive, cultures change."
5. Keyes (1967).
6. Sanskrit for "northeast."
7. Wyatt (1984).
8. This includes even the Central Thai, who consider themselves the dominant ethnic community in the kingdom.
9. Klausner (1993).
10. Moore et al. (1980).
11. Lefferts (1974).
12. Gittinger and Lefferts (1992).
13. Lefferts (1994).

14. While anthropological discussions of Thai Theravāda Buddhism have been somewhat broader than the characterization by Asad (1993) of Western discussions of non-Western religions in general, none unseats the dualistic tension between mind and body stemming from the folk anthropology of "Western" civilization (Sahlins [1996]). Additionally, these studies tend not to deal with the complex systems of exchange present in Thai Theravāda Buddhism. (For a partial initial step in this direction, see Bowie [1998].) See Cort (1996) for a discussion of the importance of material culture in understanding the South Asian Jain religion.
15. Lemonnier (1986).
16. Van Esterik (1996).
17. Mauss (1989), and Barraud et al. (1994).
18. Bloch (1991).
19. Geertz (1980), 130, quoting T. S. Eliot, sees the Balinese king as the "still point of the moving world," whose non-actions exemplify the immobile center around which chaos rotates.
20. Sahlins (1996: 403). Schieffelin states "resolve." I have amended this to reflect, more accurately I think, the disposition of such opposition in complex cultures such as the Thai-Lao.
21. I have previously noted that since most research in anthropology and religion in Thailand has been undertaken by men, we have tended to talk with men and monks. Similarly, few intensive village studies have been undertaken, so that the thesis propounded by Tambiah has not been intensively examined in the Thai or Thai-Lao contexts. Finally, attention to Theravāda Buddhism resonates with studies of other religions, while studies of the spirit cults would be seen as parochial. I believe that with the heightened attention now paid to exchange theory, such a reexamination may now prove to be of potentially great import. Of course, the emphasis on women's studies and the detailed examination of women in religion plays a central role in this paper.
22. I have written a number of studies on aspects of women's participation in ritual action, of which this is an extension and elaboration of some important points; see, especially, Lefferts (1992 (a)) and (1994).
23. While this paper does not hold that the exchange relationships seen today are meaningful in precisely the same ways as those established by the Buddha over 2,500 years ago, it means to say that establishing the possibilities for these relationships permits contemporary constructions of meaning that are fundamental to Theravāda Buddhism today in northeast Thailand. In a previous paper (1993), I have proposed a "history" of how these exchanges could have become constructed; regardless of the veracity of that construction, central to its thesis is that in their adoption of this religion, pre-Theravāda Buddhist Tai women and today's Thai-Lao and Thai women could and do see themselves becoming active agents, a role which may have been denied under previous conditions.
24. Lefferts (1992 (b)).
25. Willis (1985).

26. The processes proposed in this paper have yet to be tested among other Southeast Asian populations, such as the Burmans, Central and North Thai, Shan, and the Dai of Sip Song Panna in southwestern China. It would seem, however, that with minor variations, the formulations proposed here would hold for these populations also.
27. It is peculiarly interesting that even with the current emphasis on exchange theory in anthropology and gender studies, this approach has yet to find its way into studies of Thai, Lao, or other forms of Southeast Asian Theravāda Buddhism. Bowie's recent article (1998) treats merit-making as a way to initiate and reinforce relationships between elites and the less fortunate in the context of Theravāda Buddhism. The essay presented here, however, delves into the foundations of reciprocity and obligation throughout the system, showing how it may be subject to the twists and asymmetries of contemporary life.
28. Lefferts (1994).
29. Hamilton (1998).
30. Lefferts (1996).
31. Barraud et al. (1994: 4).
32. The exchanges schematically highlighted here are not the only exchanges that take place between ancestors and people living in the present. See the following section.
33. Mills (1998) and Mulder (1979). Often this phrase is shortened to *bun khun*, but the inclusion of *thaup taen* makes clear the reciprocity involved in *bun khun*, the merit owed by children to their parents: *thaup* means to answer, *taen* means to take the place of.
34. This is an extraordinarily schematic presentation of a complex of actions. See Lefferts (1974) and Lux (1969) for more general descriptions and statistical statements.
35. Water of various kinds plays important roles in Theravāda Buddhism in Thai-Lao communities. This essay focuses on *yaat nam*, but also considers water with special potential for health, *nam mon*, which is also blessed by monks. Finally, *nam hom*, pleasant-smelling water, is also produced on certain ritual occasions, by either lay men or monks.
36. To my knowledge, this ceremony has not been previously reported. Its bearing on issues of household continuity and the structural importance of women is apparent. However, that other researchers have either not observed or paid attention to it is a puzzle.
37. Individual households, in bringing together widely dispersed descendants, may hold their ritual on another day of Songkran. Additionally, the abbot of a monastery may change the date on which this ritual would take place and Songkran would end for that village.
38. This is a near replication of the cremation that marks nearly everyone's death. In some important senses, the weekly water pouring and this and the other Songkran rituals discussed here recapitulate the Theravāda Buddhist funeral ceremony. Thus, even as ancestors die, their descendants continue to commemorate them through annual and more frequent celebrations. This makes a powerful statement about the continuing circle of life and death in which these people see themselves.

39. I use "stūpa" as a proxy for a number of places in which these ashes might be kept. Many reliquaries, which may simply be glass jars in which something has been bought and used, such as instant coffee, are kept either at home or in the *wat* along with other such containers from other households. (This depends on whether another ritual has taken place, conveying these ashes to the *wat.*) Or, these reliquaries might be kept in the wall of the *wat,* in special caches made for the purpose. In some villages monks have decreed that too many ashes are exposed during Songkran and have mandated that stūpas and fence caches should be sealed. In these cases, household members pour water over the stūpa or portion of the fence where the ashes are contained. Often a sign and, in contemporary usage, even a photograph, might be in place to identify the ashes of the person placed there.
40. Surprisingly few stūpas are cemented shut. Reliquaries containing ashes can also be placed in niches in the cement posts of *wat* walls, which can either be cemented shut or not. Whether ashes are available or not seems to depend partly on the number of present and past inhabitants. Thus, there can be a certain amount of confusion of people and reliquaries during this period of heightened awareness of the past in the present.
41. Now that Thailand celebrates a second New Year, in agreement with the international New Year of 1 January, some villages celebrate Bun Buak Baan twice, once for each New Year. The earlier Bun has absorbed the Bun Sukhwaan Khaaw, in which the rice was blessed and its increase requested. Before this ritual takes place, a household's rice barn containing rice just harvested is not opened.
42. It is no coincidence that just as the rains begin some weeks later, these serpents, which have initiated the rainy season, are converted, in Bun Buat Naak, into monks and novices, restricted to their *wat* during the period of the Rains Retreat.
43. Keyes (1986).

WESTERN BUDDHIST NUNS:

A New Phenomenon in an Ancient Tradition

Bhikṣuṇī Thubten Chodron

Years ago, at an interfaith conference in Europe, I was asked to speak about the lives of Western nuns. Thinking that people would not be interested in what was ordinary life for me, I gave a Dharma talk instead, about how we trained our minds in love and compassion. Afterwards, several people came up to me and said, "Your talk was very nice, but we really wanted to hear about the lives of the Western nuns! How do you live? What are your problems and joys?" Sometimes it is difficult to discuss this. When speaking about the problems, we risk complaining or having others think we are complaining; when speaking about the joys, we risk being too buoyant or having others perceive us as arrogant. In any case, this essay is written from the viewpoint of being ordained in the Tibetan tradition and is not universal to all Western Buddhist nuns.[1]

The Dharma has spoken deeply to the hearts of those of us from the West who have chosen to become Western Buddhist nuns. Thus, counter to all expectations of our cultures and our families, we quit our jobs, part from our loved ones, are ordained as Buddhist nuns and, in many cases, go to live in other countries. Who takes such radical steps in order to practice the Dharma? How are we unlike Asian women who are ordained?

In general, Asian women receive ordination when they are young, malleable girls with little life experience, or when, elderly and with their families grown, they are seeking life in a monastery for its spiritual or physical comforts. Most Western nuns, however, are ordained as adults. Many are highly educated, have careers, and often have families and children. While they bring their talents and skills to the monastery, they also bring habits and expectations that have been well polished through years of interactions in the world. When Asian women are ordained, their families and communities support them, and becoming a nun is socially acceptable and respectable. In addition, Asian cultures focus more on group than on individual identity, so it is comparatively easy for the newly ordained to adapt to community life in a monastery. As children, they shared bedrooms with their siblings, and were taught to place the welfare of their families above their own and to respect and defer to their parents and teachers. Western nuns, however, grew up in a culture that stressed the individual over the group, and this leads them to be more individualistic. Western women have to have strong personalities to become Buddhist nuns: their families reproach them for relinquishing a well-paying job and not having children; Western society brands them as lazy parasites who don't want to work; and Western culture accuses them of repressing their sexuality and of avoiding intimate relationships. A Western woman who cares about what others think about her is not going to become a Buddhist nun. A woman who becomes a Buddhist nun is more likely to be self-sufficient and self-motivated. These qualities, which in general are valuable, can be carried to an extreme, sometimes making it difficult for highly individualistic women to live together in a Sangha community. That is, if there is a community to live in.

As first-generation Western Buddhist nuns, we indeed lead the homeless life. Few monasteries exist in the West and, if we want to stay in one, we generally have to pay to do so because the community has no money. This presents some challenges: how does someone with monastic precepts, which include wearing robes, shaving one's head, not handling money, and not doing business, earn money?

Many Westerners assume that there is an umbrella institution, similar to the Catholic Church, that looks after us. This is not the case. Our Tibetan teachers do not provide for us financially and, in many cases, ask us to raise money to support their Tibetan monk disciples who are refugees in India. Some Western nuns have savings that are rapidly consumed. Others have kind friends and family who sponsor them. Still others are forced by conditions to put on lay clothes and get a job in the city. This makes keeping the ordination precepts difficult and prevents Western nuns from studying and practicing intensely—the main purpose for which they were ordained.

How, then, does one receive monastic training and education? Some Western nuns opt to stay in Asia for as long as they can. But there they face visa and language problems. Tibetan nunneries are generally overcrowded, and there is no room for foreigners unless one wants to pay to live in a guest room. Tibetan nuns do rituals and receive teachings in the Tibetan language, their education beginning with memorizing texts. The majority of Western nuns, however, do not speak Tibetan and need an English translation to receive teachings. In addition, memorizing texts in Tibetan is generally not meaningful to them. They seek to learn the meaning of the teachings and how to practice them. They want to learn meditation and to experience the Dharma. While Tibetan nuns grew up with Buddhism in their families and cultural environment since childhood, Western nuns are learning a new faith and thus have different questions and issues. For example, while a Tibetan nun takes the existence of the Three Jewels for granted, a Western nun wants to know exactly what the Buddha, Dharma, and Sangha are and how to know they in fact exist. Therefore, even in India, Western nuns do not fit into established Tibetan religious institutions.

Offering water bowls at a stūpa (photo provided by Venerable Thubten Chodron)

Many Western nuns are sent to work in Dharma centers in the West, where they receive room, board, and a tiny stipend for personal needs in return for working for the center. Although they can receive teachings in their own language there, life in Dharma centers can be difficult for the newly ordained because they must live among lay people. The curriculum in the center is designed for the lay students, and the resident lama, if there is one, is usually too busy with the lay community to train the one or two Western monastics who live there.

Transforming Difficulties into the Path

Difficulties such as those described above are also challenges for practice. A nun needs to focus on the Buddha's teachings in order to maintain serenity in whatever circumstances she finds herself. She has to meditate deeply on impermanence and death so that she can be comfortable with financial insecurity. She has to contemplate the disadvantages of attachment to the eight worldly concerns[2] so that praise and blame from others do not affect her. She must reflect on karma and its effects to accept the difficulties she encounters in receiving an education. And she needs to generate an altruistic heart that wishes to remedy these situations so that others do not have to encounter them in the future. Thus, her difficulties are the catalyst for her practice and, through practice, her mind is transformed and becomes peaceful.

One of the biggest challenges is to live as a celibate in the West, where sexuality spills from all the media. How can one be happy when Western culture pronounces romantic intimacy to be the summum bonum of life? Again, practice is the secret. To keep our precepts, we have to look beyond superficial appearances. We have to understand how deeply ingrained are the emotional and sexual patterns of attachment that keep us imprisoned in cyclical existence. We must understand the nature of our emotions and learn to deal with them in constructive ways without depending on others to comfort us or make us feel good about ourselves.

People wonder if we see our families and old friends and if we miss them. Buddhist nuns are not cloistered. We can visit our families and friends. We do not stop caring for others simply because we are ordained. However, we do try to transform the type of affection we have for them. For ordinary people in worldly life, affection leads to clinging attachment, an emotion that exaggerates someone's qualities and that encourages us to wish not to be separated from him or her. This attitude breeds partiality—the wish to help our dear ones, to harm the people we don't like, and to ignore the multitudes of beings we don't know.

As monastics, we have to work hard against this tendency, using the meditations on love, compassion, joy, and equanimity to expand our hearts so that we see all beings as loveable. The more we train our mind in this way, the less we miss our dear ones and the more we feel close to all others simply because they, like us, are sentient beings who want happiness and do not want suffering. This open-hearted feeling does not mean we don't cherish our parents. On the contrary, meditation on the kindness of our parents opens our eyes to all that they did for us. However, rather than be attached only to them, we endeavor to extend the feeling of love to all others as well. Great internal satisfaction arises as we develop more equanimity and open our hearts to cherish all other beings. Here, too, we perceive something that seems to be a difficulty—not living in close contact with our family and old friends—to be a factor that stimulates spiritual growth when we apply our Dharma practice to it.

Some conditions that may initially seem detrimental can also be advantageous. For example, Western nuns are not an integral part of the Tibetan religious establishment, whose hierarchy consists of Tibetan monks. Although this has its disadvantages, it also gives us greater freedom in guiding our practice. For example, the *bhikṣuṇī* or full ordination for women never spread to Tibet due to the difficulties of having the required number of ordained nuns travel across the Himalayan Mountains in previous centuries.[3] The novice ordination for women does exist in the Tibetan tradition and is given by the monks. Although several Tibetan monks, including the Dalai Lama, approve of nuns in the Tibetan tradition receiving *bhikṣuṇī* ordination from Chinese monastics, the Tibetan religious establishment has not officially sanctioned this. In recent years, several Western women have gone to receive the *bhikṣuṇī* ordination in the Chinese and Vietnamese traditions, where it is extant. Because they are part of the Tibetan community and more liable to its social pressures, Tibetan nuns at present face greater difficulties if they were to do this. In this way, not being an integral part of the system has its advantages for Western nuns.

Receiving Ordination

To receive ordination as a Buddhist nun, a woman must have a good general understanding of the Buddha's teachings and a strong, stable motivation to be free from cyclic existence and to attain liberation. She must, then, request ordination from her teacher. In the Tibetan tradition, most teachers are monks, although some are lay men. There are very few women teachers in our tradition at present. If the teacher agrees, he will arrange the ordination ceremony, which in the case of the *śramaṇerikā* or novice ordination, lasts a few hours. If a novice nun in the Tibetan tradition later wants to receive the *bhikṣuṇī* ordination, she must find a preceptor in the Chinese, Korean, or Vietnamese traditions. She must then travel to the place where the ordination ceremony will be held, and go through a training program which lasts from one week to one month, before the actual ceremony. I received the novice ordination in Dharamsala, India, in 1977, and nine years later went to Taiwan to receive the *bhikṣuṇī* ordination. Going through the one-month training program in Chinese was a challenge and, after two weeks, the other Western nun and I were delighted when the preceptor allowed another nun to translate for us during some of the classes. However, the experience of training as a nun in both the Tibetan and Chinese traditions has enriched my practice and helped me to see the Dharma in all the Buddhist traditions, despite the externally diverse and culturally conditioned forms each uses.

After ordination, we need to receive training in the precepts if we are to keep them well. A new nun should request one of her teachers to give her teachings on the meaning of each precept, what constitutes a transgression, and how to purify transgressions should they occur. Although a Western nun can usually receive teachings on the precepts without too much difficulty, the lack of monasteries for Western nuns means she often misses out on the practical training that comes through living with other nuns in community.

On a picnic (photo provided by Venerable Thubten Chodron)

As nuns, our first responsibility is to live according to our precepts as best as we can. Precepts are not a heavy burden, but a joy. In other words, we adopt them voluntarily because we know they will help us in our spiritual pursuit. Precepts liberate us from acting in harmful, dysfunctional, and inconsiderate ways. Novice nuns have ten precepts, which can be subdivided to make thirty-six;[4] probationary nuns have six precepts in addition to these;[5] and fully ordained nuns *(bhikṣuṇīs)* have 348 precepts as listed in the Dharmagupta school of Vinaya,[6] which has the only extant *bhikṣuṇī* lineage today. The precepts are divided into various categories, each with its corresponding method to deal with transgressions. The root precepts are the most serious and must be kept purely in order to remain as a nun. These include avoiding killing, stealing, sexual contact, lying about spiritual attainments, and so forth. If these are broken completely, one is no longer a nun. Other precepts deal with the nuns' relationships with each other, with monks, and with the lay community. Still others address how we should conduct ourselves in daily activities such as eating, walking, dressing, and residing in a place. Infractions of these are purified in various ways according to their severity: purification may entail confession to another *bhikṣuṇī*, confession in the presence of the assembly of *bhikṣuṇīs*, or relinquishing of a possession obtained in excess or in an inappropriate way.

Keeping these precepts in the West in the twentieth century can be a challenge. The precepts were established by the Buddha during his life in India in the sixth century B.C.E. While nuns in some Buddhist traditions, such as Theravāda, try to keep the precepts literally, other nuns come from traditions that allow more leeway. By studying the Vinaya and knowing the stories of the specific events that prompted the Buddha to establish each precept, nuns come to understand the purpose of each precept. Then, they will know how to adhere to its purpose even though they may not be able to follow it literally. For example, one of the *bhikṣuṇī* precepts forbids nuns from riding in a vehicle. If we followed that literally, going to receive or to give teachings would be difficult. In ancient India, vehicles were drawn by animals or human beings, and riding in them was reserved for the wealthy. The Buddha's concern when he made this precept was for nuns to avoid causing suffering to others or cultivating arrogance. To adapt this precept to modern societies, nuns should try not to ride in expensive vehicles and to avoid becoming proud if someone drives them somewhere in a nice car. In this way, nuns must adapt themselves to the conditions in which they live today.

Of course, there will be differences of interpretation and implementation among traditions, among monasteries within the same tradition, and among individuals within a monastery. We need to be tolerant of these differences and to use them to motivate us to reflect on the precepts more deeply. For example, Asian nuns generally do not shake hands with men, while most Western nuns in the Tibetan tradition do. If nuns do this simply to conform to Western customs, I do not see a problem. However, each nun must be fully mindful so that attraction and attachment do not arise when she shakes hands. Such variations in observing the precepts can be accepted due to cultural differences in various places.

Daily Life

The precepts form a framework for further Dharma practice. As nuns, we want to study and practice the Buddha's teachings and share them with others as much as possible. Western nuns live in a variety of circumstances: sometimes in community—a monastery or a Dharma center—and sometimes alone. In all of these situations, our day begins with prayers and meditation before breakfast. We also do practical work to sustain ourselves and benefit others, and this includes daily chores. In the evening, we again meditate and do our spiritual practices. Sometimes fitting several hours of meditation practice into a busy schedule is challenging, but since meditation and prayers are what sustain us, we make a great effort to navigate the demands made upon our time. When the work at a Dharma center is especially intense or many people need our help, it is tempting to take time out of our practice. Doing this, however, exacts a toll and, if done for too long, can make keeping ordination difficult. Thus, each year we try to take a few weeks—or months if possible—out of our busy lives to do a meditation retreat in order to deepen our practice.

As Western nuns we encounter a variety of unusual situations in daily life. Some people recognize the robes and know we are Buddhist nuns, while others do not. Wearing my robes in the city, I have had people come up to me and compliment me on my "outfit." Once a flight attendant on a plane leaned over and said, "Not everyone can wear her hair like that, but that cut looks great on you!" A child in a park opened his eyes wide in amazement and said to his mother, "Look Mommy, that lady doesn't have any hair!" In a store, a stranger approached a nun and in a conciliatory way said, "Don't worry, dear. After the chemo is finished your hair will grow back again."

When we walk on the street, occasionally someone will say, "Hare Krishna." I have also had people come up and say, "Have faith in Jesus!" Some people look delighted and ask if I know the Dalai Lama, how they can learn to meditate, or where a Buddhist center is in the town. In the frenzy of American life, they are inspired to see someone who represents spiritual life. After a series of glitches on an airline trip, a fellow passenger approached me and said, "Your calmness and smile me helped me get through these hassles. Thank you for your meditation practice."

Even in Buddhist communities, we are treated in a variety of ways because Buddhism is new in the West and people do not know how to relate to monastics. Some people are very respectful to Asian monastics and eager to serve them, but they see Western monastics as unpaid labor for the Dharma center and immediately set us to work running errands, cooking, and cleaning for the lay community. Other people appreciate all monastics and are very courteous. As Western nuns, we never know when we go somewhere how others will treat us. At times this can be disquieting, but in the long run it makes us more flexible and helps us to overcome attachment to reputation. We use such situations to let go of our attachment to being treated well and aversion to being treated poorly. Yet, for the sake of the Dharma and the Sangha, we sometimes have to instruct people politely on the proper way to act around monastics. For example, I had to remind members of a Dharma center who invited me to their city to teach that it is not appropriate to put me up at the home of a single man—especially since he had a large poster of a Playboy bunny in his bathroom! In another instance, a young couple was traveling with a group of nuns, and we had to remind them that it is not appropriate to embrace and kiss each other on the bus with us. As a young nun, such events annoyed me but now, due to the benefits of Dharma practice, I am able to react with humor and patience.

The Role of the Sangha in the West

The word "Sangha" is used in a variety of ways. When we speak of the Sangha as one of the Three Jewels of refuge, we are referring to any individual—lay or monastic—who has realized emptiness of inherent existence directly. This unmistaken realization of reality renders such a person a reliable object of refuge. In traditional Buddhist societies, the term "Sangha" refers to a group of four or more fully ordained monastics, and an individual monastic is a Sangha member. The Sangha members and the Sangha community are respected not because the individuals are special in and of themselves, but because they hold the precepts given by the Buddha. Their primary objective in life is to tame their minds by applying these precepts and the Buddha's teachings.

In the West, people often use the word "Sangha" loosely to refer to anyone who frequents a Buddhist center. This person may or may not have taken even the five lay precepts, to abandon killing, stealing, unwise sexual behavior, lying, and intoxicants. Using "Sangha" in this all-encompassing way can lead to misinterpretation and confusion. I myself believe it is better to stick to the traditional usage.

Individual nuns vary considerably, and any discussion of the role of the Sangha has to take this into account. Because Buddhism is new in the West, some people receive ordination without sufficient preparation. Others later find that the monastic lifestyle is not suitable for them, give up their vows, and return to lay life. Some nuns cannot observe the precepts well because their mindfulness is not well developed and they fall prey to strong, disturbing thoughts. In discussing the role of the Sangha, therefore, we are considering those who are happy as monastics, who work hard to apply the Dharma to counteract their disturbing attitudes and negative behavior, and who are likely to remain monastics for the duration of their lives.

Some Westerners doubt the usefulness of the Sangha. Historically, although individual Sangha members often came from all social classes, everyone received a religious education once he or she was ordained, because it was the Sangha's role to preserve the Buddha's teachings for future generations. Now, in the West almost everyone is literate and can study the Dharma outside the Sangha or hear scholars give lectures on Buddhism. Moreover, in earlier times, only the Sangha had the time to do long meditation retreats to actualize the meaning of the Dharma. Now in the West, some lay people can take months or years off from work in order to do long meditation retreats. Given these changes in society, lay people might now wonder, "What is the use of monastics? Why can't we be considered the modern Sangha?"

My experience as both a lay woman and a nun tells me, however, that there is a difference between the two. Even though some lay people do the traditional work of the Sangha—and some may do it better than some monastics—there is nevertheless a difference between a person who lives according to ethical precepts (a fully ordained nun, or *bhikṣuṇī,* has 348 precepts) and another who does not. The precepts put us right up against our old habits and emotional patterns. A lay retreatant who tires of the austerity of retreat may bring her retreat to a close, get a job, and resume a comfortable lifestyle surrounded by beautiful possessions. A university professor may make herself attractive. She may find part of her identity by being in a relationship with her husband or partner. If she does not have a partner who gives her emotional support, that option is open to her. She can teach Buddhist principles but she blends into society, and no one recognizes her as a Buddhist or as a religious person. She does not represent the Dharma in public and, thus, it is easier for her to behave in a less than exemplary fashion. If she has many possessions—an expensive car, or attractive clothes—and lies on the beach to get a tan, no one thinks twice about it. If she boasts about her successes and blames others when her plans do not work out, her behavior does not stand out. In other words, her attachment to sense pleasures, praise, and reputation are seen as normal and may easily go unchallenged either by herself or by others.

For a nun, however, the situation is quite different. She wears robes and shaves her head so that she and all around her know that she aspires to live according to certain precepts. This aids her tremendously in dealing with attachments and aversions as they arise in daily life. Men know that she is celibate and relate to her differently. Both she and the men she meets do not become involved in the subtle flirting games and self-conscious behavior that people engage in when sexually attracted to one another. A nun does not have to think about what to wear or how she looks. The robes and shaved head help her to cut through such attachments and bring a certain anonymity and equality when she lives together with other monastics, for no one can draw special attention to herself due to her appearance. The robes and the precepts make her much more aware of her actions, or karma, and their results. She has put much time and energy into reflecting on her potential and aspiring to think, feel, speak, and act in ways that benefit herself and others. Thus, even when she is alone, the power of the precepts makes her more mindful not to act in unethical or impulsive ways. If she acts inappropriately with others, her teacher, other nuns, and lay people immediately comment on it. Holding monastic precepts has a pervasive, beneficial effect on one's life that may not be easily comprehensible to those who have not had the experience. Thus, there is a significant difference between the lifestyles of Buddhist scholars and lay retreatants on the one hand, and monastics on the other. A new nun, who had been a dedicated and knowledgeable lay practitioner for years, told me that before ordination she did not understand how she could feel or act differently simply by being a nun. However, after ordination she was surprised at the power of the ordination: her internal sense of being a practitioner and her awareness of her behavior had changed considerably because of it.

Some people associate monasticism with austerity and self-centered spiritual practice. Contrasting this with the bodhisattva practice of benefiting other beings, they say that monastic life is unnecessary because the bodhisattva path, which can be followed as a lay practitioner, is higher. In fact, there is not a split between being a monastic and being a bodhisattva—they can easily go together. By regulating our physical and verbal actions, monastic precepts increase our mindfulness of what we say and do. This, in turn, makes us look at the attitudes and emotions that motivate us to speak and act. In doing this, our gross misbehaviors are curbed as are the attachment, anger, and confusion that motivate them. With this as a basis, we can cultivate the heart that cherishes others, wishes to work for their benefit, and aspires to be able to do so most effectively. Thus, the monastic lifestyle is a helpful foundation for the bodhisattva path.

The Contributions of Western Nuns

Many people in the West, particularly those from Protestant cultures, have preconceived ideas of monastics as people who withdraw from society and do not contribute to its betterment. They think monastics are escapists who cannot face the difficulties of ordinary life. I have found such preconceptions to be untrue. The fundamental cause of our problems is not external circumstances, but our internal mental states—the disturbing attitudes of clinging attachment, anger, and confusion. These do not vanish when we shave our head, put on monastic robes, and go to live in a monastery. Until we eliminate them through spiritual practice, these attitudes accompany us wherever we go. Thus, living as a nun is not a way to avoid or escape problems. Rather, it makes us look at ourselves because we can no longer engage in distractions, such as alcohol, intoxicants, shopping, and entertainment. Monastics are committed to eliminating the root causes of suffering in their own minds and also to show others how to do the same.

Although they try to spend the majority of their time in study and practice, monastics do make valuable contributions to society. First, like monastics of all spiritual traditions, Western Buddhist nuns live a life of simplicity and purity that is available for all to see. By avoiding consumerism—both the clutter of many possessions and the mentality of greed that consumerism fosters—nuns show that it is indeed possible to live simply and to be content with what one has. Second, in curtailing their consumerist tendencies, monastics safeguard the environment for future generations. And, third, as celibates, they practice birth control (as well as rebirth control) and thus help stop overpopulation!

By taming their own "monkey minds," nuns can show other people the methods to do so. As others practice, their lives will be happier, their relationships better, and their minds less stressful and angry. Teaching the Buddha's techniques for subduing disturbing emotions within oneself and for resolving conflicts with others is an invaluable contribution that the nuns can make to society.

Western nuns are cultural bridges between East and West. Often they have lived in many cultures and can translate not only from one language to another but also from one set of cultural concepts and norms to another. In bringing Buddhism to the West and engaging in the ongoing process of differentiating the Dharma from its Asian cultural forms, they provide invaluable help along the path to those interested in the Buddha's teachings. They can also help Westerners recognize their own cultural preconceptions that block correct understanding or practicing of the Dharma. They are able to speak to diverse audiences—from American high school students to Asian senior citizens—and communicate well with all of them.

Western nuns are not bound by certain pressures within Asian societies. For example, we can easily receive teachings from a variety of masters of different Buddhist traditions. We are not bound by centuries-old misconceptions about other traditions, nor do we face social pressure to be loyal to the Buddhist tradition of our own country in the same way that many Asian nuns are. This gives us tremendous latitude in our education and enables us to adopt the best from various Buddhist traditions. It also enhances our ability to teach others and promote dialogue and harmony among various Buddhist traditions.

Western nuns offer many skills to the Buddhist community. Some are Dharma teachers, others translate oral and written teachings, and still others engage in long meditation retreats, providing examples of dedicated Buddhist practice. Some nuns are counselors who help Dharma students work through difficulties that arise in practice. Many people, particularly women, feel more comfortable discussing emotional or personal issues with a nun rather than a monk. Other nuns work in day-care centers, in hospices with the terminally ill, or in refugee communities in their own countries and abroad. Some nuns are artists, others writers, therapists, or professors at universities. Many nuns work in the background; they are the crucial but unseen workers whose selfless labor enables Dharma centers and their resident teachers to serve the public.

Nuns also offer an alternative version of women's liberation. Nowadays some Buddhist women say that associating women with sexuality, the body, sensuality, and the earth denigrates women. Their remedy is to say that the body, sensuality, and the ability to give birth to children are good. They offer the example of Tantric Buddhism in support of this, which trains one to transform sense pleasures into the path. But regardless of whether these women are actually able to transform sensuality into the path, they nevertheless perpetuate the association between women and sensuality. Nuns offer a different view. We nuns do not exalt the body and sensuality, nor do we disparage them. For us, the human body is simply a vehicle with which we practice the Dharma. It doesn't have to be judged as good or bad.

Human beings are sexual beings, but we are also much more than that. In essence, nuns stop making a big deal out of sex.

Western nuns have the opportunity to be very creative in their practice and to set up institutions that reflect an effective way to live the Dharma in the West. As Westerners, they are not subject to many of the social pressures that many Asian nuns must deal with. Thus, they are better able to separate the essence of the Dharma (to bring to the West) from Asian cultural practices that do not apply to Western practitioners. Western nuns do not seek to change Buddhism, however, but to be changed by Buddhism. While the essence of the Dharma cannot be changed, Buddhist institutions are created by human beings and reflect the cultures in which they are found. As Western nuns, we can change the form these Buddhist institutions take in our society.

Prejudice and Pride

People often ask if we face discrimination because we are women. Of course! Most societies in our world are male-oriented, and Buddhist ones are no exception. To avoid the distraction of sexual attraction, for example, monks and nuns are housed and seated separately. Since males have traditionally been the leaders in most societies and because monks are more numerous than nuns, monks generally receive the preferable seats and living quarters. In Tibetan society, monks receive a better education than nuns and also more respect from society. Moreover, female religious role models are scarce. Furthermore, the public—including many Western women—generally give larger donations to monks than to nuns. Since the Sangha has traditionally received its material requisites—food, shelter, clothing, and medicine—in the form of donations from the public, nuns face more difficulties in receiving proper training and education because they cannot cover their costs and must spend their time, not in study and practice, but in finding alternative means of income.

While Western nuns face the same circumstances, they are generally more self-confident and assertive and are apt to take advantage of situations that present themselves. Due to the relatively small number of Western monks and nuns, we are trained and receive teachings together and thus our teachers give us equal responsibilities. Nevertheless, when participating in Asian Dharma events, Western nuns are not treated the same way as Western monks. Interestingly, Asians often do not notice this, as privilege for monks is so much the norm that it is rarely questioned. Sometimes people ask me to discuss how nuns in general, and Western nuns in particular, face discrimination. I do not find this particularly useful. For me it is sufficient to be aware of the habits of discrimination and to understand its cultural roots, and thus to not let it undermine my self-confidence. Then I try to deal with the situation in a beneficial way. Sometimes I may ask a polite question; other times I must first win someone's trust and respect and later point out the difficulty. However, all situations require that I have a kind mental attitude.

Many years ago, I would become angry when encountering gender prejudice, particularly in Asian Buddhist institutions. For example, I was once attending a large *tsog* offering ceremony in Dharamsala, India. I watched three Tibetan monks stand up and present a large food offering to His Holiness the Dalai Lama and other monks distribute offerings to the entire congregation. Inside I fumed, "The monks always perform these important functions and we nuns have to sit here! It's not fair." Then I considered that if we nuns had to get up to make the offering to His Holiness and distribute offerings to the crowd, I would complain that we had to do all the work while the monks remained seated. Noticing this, I saw that both the problem and the solution to it lay in my attitude, not in the external situation.

Being a Dharma practitioner, I could not escape the fact that anger is a defilement that misconstrues a situation and is therefore a cause of suffering. I had to face my anger and my arrogance, and apply Dharma antidotes to deal with them. Now it is actually intriguing for me to deal with feeling offended. I observe the sense of "I" that is offended and the "I" who wants to retaliate. I pause and examine, "Who is this I?" Or I stop and reflect, "How is my mind viewing this situation and creating my experience according to the way I interpret it?" Some people think that if a woman relinquishes her anger and pride in such circumstances, she must see herself as inferior and will not work to remedy the situation. This is not a correct understanding of the Dharma, however, for only when our own mind is peaceful can we clearly see methods to improve bad circumstances.

Some people claim that the fact that fully ordained nuns have more precepts than monks indicates gender discrimination.[7] They disapprove of the fact that some precepts that are minor transgressions for monks are major ones for nuns. Understanding the evolution of the precepts puts this in proper perspective. When the Sangha was initially formed, there were no precepts. After several years, some monks acted in ways that provoked criticism either from other monastics or from the general public. In response to each situation, the Buddha established a precept to guide the behavior of the Sangha in the future. While *bhikṣus* (fully ordained monks) follow precepts that were established due to unwise behavior of the monks only, *bhikṣuṇīs* (fully ordained nuns) follow the precepts that arose due to inappropriate behavior of both monks and nuns. Also, some of the additional precepts relate only to female practitioners. It would be meaningless, for example, for a monk to have a precept to avoid promising a nun a menses garment but not giving it!

Personally speaking, as a nun, having more precepts than a monk does not bother me. The more numerous and strict the precepts, the more my mindfulness improves. This increased mindfulness aids my practice and helps me progress on the path.

In short, while Western nuns face certain difficulties, these very same situations can propel them toward internal transformation. Women who have the inclination and ability to receive and keep the monastic precepts experience a special fortune and joy through their spiritual practice. Through their practice in overcoming attachment, developing a kind heart, and realizing the ultimate nature of phenomena, nuns can benefit many people.

Notes

1. I do not know of any reliable statistics about the number of Western Buddhist nuns in the various Buddhist traditions and where they live. However, several hundred women from North America, Europe, Australia, and New Zealand are nuns. Discussing the differences in practice and living conditions for nuns of the various Buddhist traditions is beyond the scope of this paper. Please see Thubten Chodron, ed., *Blossoms of the Dharma: Living as a Buddhist Nun* (Berkeley, CA: North Atlantic Books, 2000). Also see Martine Batchelor, *Walking on Lotus Flowers* (San Francisco: Thorsons/HarperCollins, 1996).
2. These eight come in four pairs: being pleased (and therefore attached to) receiving money and material possessions and being adverse to not receiving or losing them; being pleased by receiving praise and approval from others and being adverse to receiving criticism, blame, and disapproval; being pleased by having a good reputation and image in society and being adverse to having a bad reputation and image; being pleased to experience pleasures of the senses (pleasant sights, sounds, smells, tastes, and tactile sensations) and being adverse to experiencing unpleasant ones. While most people value these eight, they are, in fact, major obstacles to spiritual practice.
3. Discussing the ordination procedure and the issue of the *bhikṣuṇī* ordination in the Tibetan tradition are beyond the scope of this paper. Please see Thubten Chodron, ed., "Preparing for Ordination: Reflections for Westerners Considering Monastic Ordination in the Tibetan Buddhist Tradition" in *Life as a Western Buddhist Nun* (Seattle, 1997). For free distribution, write to: Dharma Friendship Foundation, P.O. Box 30011, Seattle, WA 98103, U.S.A. Also see: Karma Lekshe Tsomo, *Sisters in Solitude: Two Traditions of Monastic Ethics for Women* (Albany, New York: State University of New York Press, 1996). See the review of the above book at: http://www.kalavinka.org.
4. For the precepts of a *śramaṇerikā,* or novice, see Thubten Chodron, ed., "Preparing for Ordination: Reflections for Westerners Considering Monastic Ordination in the Tibetan Buddhist Tradition."

5. In the Dharmagupta Vinaya, these six are to avoid: killing, stealing, sexual contact, lying, taking intoxicants, and eating at improper times, that is, after noon. The six are listed differently in the *Mūlasarvāstivāda Vinaya.*
6. For the precepts of a *bhikṣuṇī,* see Karma Lekshe Tsomo, *Sisters in Solitude: Two Traditions of Monastic Ethics for Women.*
7. For the vows of a *bhikṣu* according to the *Mūlasarvāstivāda Vinaya* followed in the Tibetan tradition, see Tenzin Gyatso, *Advice from Buddha Shakyamuni Concerning a Monk's Discipline* (Dharamsala: Library of Tibetan Works and Archives, 1982).

SAKYADHĪTĀ IN WESTERN EUROPE:

A Personal Perspective

Rotraut Wurst

I worked for Sakyadhītā, the International Network of Buddhist Women, as executive member responsible for Sakyadhītā Europe from 1995 to 1997. In that office, I received countless inquiries. Women wrote and asked for information about Buddhist centers in Europe and for addresses of Buddhist nunneries where they could stay for a while. They wanted to know which Buddhist tradition they should choose, what possibilities existed in the West to make a retreat and, finally, how they could become Buddhist nuns. The substantial interest in Buddhism shown by European women raises a number of questions for me: Why are Western women interested in Buddhism? Don't they feel at home in their own tradition? Why do some women want to become ordained as Buddhist nuns? How do they come to this decision? What do women expect from Buddhism? And, finally, does life as a Buddhist woman correspond to the expectations they had prior to their entrance into the Dharma path? While I can't begin to answer these questions here, I believe it's imperative to have a centralized office where information about women and Buddhism in Europe is easily accessible.

There are many prejudices and stereotypes about Buddhism in the West, and reports in the media often don't probe deeply enough to examine them fully. In the West, especially in Germany, the media depicts a Buddhism that is spilling over onto Western shores like a giant ocean wave. Buddhism is mentioned in the same sentence with obscure sects and esoteric practices and, as this superficial attitude has become the media norm, a more serious discussion of the phenomenon has become necessary, especially as it highlights the phenomenon of Buddhism and women in Europe.

With misinformation or no information at all, many Westerners assume that anyone who gives a course in meditation or in techniques of stress removal is a Buddhist. Most don't know the differences between the various Buddhist traditions and, more unfortunately, they are not really interested in learning anything about them, preferring instead to engage in anything "esoteric," anything that makes them different from what other Westerners do. The great ignorance about

Buddhism is evident, for example, on television talk shows where people pretend to be interested in Tantric Buddhism, but are only so because they think it is about sex orgies. This ignorance obscures the real interest some Europeans may have in Buddhism. Here, then, I will explore the important resources that the bureau of Sakyadhītā Europe can provide in response to legitimate questions about Buddhism.

Western Women

Women, especially, are disillusioned with the Christian tradition because of the misogyny and patriarchy they experience in its thought and practice. Because of this, they are searching for something new, better, more satisfying. As Buddhism spreads to Europe and to the United States, it allows Western women to come in contact with different cultures. European interest in Buddhism focuses on its practice and its way of life. Especially appealing is the individuality involved, for one must make a decision to become a Buddhist, and that decision is one's own, not that of one's parents or of others.

Buddhism is changing in its transmission to the West. Although it may be too early to talk about an all-inclusive "Western Buddhism," the movement towards self-determination and democracy in Western Buddhism is a significant sign that a solid foundation is being established. Some American Buddhist teachers speak about an "American Buddhism." It appears that women are able to hold a more significant position in American Buddhism.[1] Venerable Ayya Khema envisioned a German or European Buddhism along similar lines. In their practice, Western women are pragmatic with regard to Buddhist doctrine for, as Karma Lekshe Tsomo notes, women "take the best and leave the rest."[2] While many Western women don't normally retain many Asian elements in their Buddhist practice, it is important to be able to borrow from earlier Buddhist traditions where appropriate. "We have the option of studying with many great teachers, experiencing a wide variety of techniques, corroborating our understanding with studies of the textual tradition, and verifying it through our own inner experience," Tsomo argues.[3] Women don't have to *believe* to be a Buddhist, as they do in Christian tradition but, rather, they can test spiritual practice and try it out for themselves. And, as Tsomo says, women don't have to "accept anything.... American women, having broken with [the] patriarchal path, are creating their [own] direction, incorporating wisdom wherever they may find it."[4] American Buddhist women have thus carved out a unique and forward-moving path that will also come about, one hopes, for Buddhist women in Europe. It is especially important that these changes happen for German Buddhist women, who appear to be very strict with Asian traditional practice, perhaps even stricter than Asian Buddhist women themselves. His Holiness the Fourteenth Dalai Lama, said in an interview while in

Germany in 1998, "Germans are so conservative, so earnest." American women have found a more pragmatic form, an easier way, for being Buddhist women "Western style."

For many Westerners, the main form of Buddhist practice, that is, meditation, is an alternative to other recreational activities. Such people go to Buddhist temples or Buddhist centers to learn meditation, saying "I like meditation, but I am not a Buddhist." Serious Buddhist women in the West, however, ask questions such as "How does our meditation practice influence the interactions we have with people and help us deal with everyday situations, such as an angry bus driver or a domineering boss? How does it make us more congenial and more constructive members of society? How does it help us develop patience while driving on the freeway, raising our children, or resolving difficulties with partners?"[5]

Sakyadhītā, International Network of Buddhist Women

The International Network of Buddhist Women, Sakyadhītā, was founded in 1987 in Bodhgaya at the First Conference on Buddhist Nuns by Venerable Karma Lekshe Tsomo, Venerable Jampa Tsedroen, Dr. Chatsumarn Kabilsingh, and Venerable Ayya Khema. Although there were some councils after the death of the Buddha, this was the first recorded conference on Buddhist women and, in particular, on Buddhist nuns.

Under the patronage of His Holiness the Fourteenth Dalai Lama, the conference was organized as the first time women from different Buddhist traditions and different countries could come together and exchange their opinions about monastic and lay life in modern society in both Buddhist and non-Buddhist countries. Since the first conference, four other conferences, now called Conferences on Buddhist Women, have been organized: 1991 in Bangkok, Thailand: 1993 in Colombo, Sri Lanka; 1995 in Leh, Ladakh; and 1997/98 in Phnom Penh, Cambodia.

In the West, the work of Sakyadhītā is to facilitate networking by fax, phone, and letter. One of the main functions of the Sakyadhītā network is to encourage contact among Buddhist women, especially Buddhist women in the West. Because it's so difficult to live as a Buddhist in a non-Buddhist country, Western women ask about women's groups that are based on a common meditation practice, search for retreat centers that offer retreats for lay women, and ask about Buddhist nunneries in the West, places where one can live a disciplined life of calm and equanimity. Very important is the search for Buddhist counselors who can help respond to life crises; the need for these is exacerbated by such things as single motherhood, female unemployment, and domestic violence. It has become clear that a Buddhist advisory board is needed to administer Buddhist responses to such issues and to monitor available Buddhist support.

According to Tsomo, the old and new general secretary of Sakyadhītā International, there are more than six thousand Buddhist nuns worldwide, with only a few hundred in the West. Most Buddhist women worldwide are lay women, and for them Buddhism has to be continually responsive to their social milieu. To maintain this responsiveness, Buddhist women must engage themselves in different women's projects or network services.

The International Network of Buddhist Women aims to support ordained and non-ordained Buddhist women. It does this by giving financial support to projects in Asia and by building up nunneries and educational establishments. It also provides instruction about the situation of women in Asian society, about the status of ordained women in the Sangha, and about any possible improvements being made on their behalf.[6]

In this way, then, Sakyadhītā needs to take on the responsibility of providing women worldwide, but especially in Europe, the opportunity to share and exchange their experiences with different Buddhist schools. The organization should, in addition, give support when there are problems within meditation practices. A big priority is finding or establishing nunneries and retreat centers where women can live and meditate together. These are critical issues for, while no longer an executive member of Sakyadhītā International, I still receive calls from European women asking me about such opportunities for women. Currently, women-only meditation groups are very few. Because of this, seminars like those of Sylvia Wetzel are overbooked. More such seminars are needed because women in the West who are interested in a spiritual life are not confident with what can be provided by the Christian church.

During the various conferences on Buddhist women, questions about being ordained as an *upāsikā* or as a *śramaṇerikā* routinely come up.[7] For the first steps in establishing *bhikṣuṇī* ordination, we have to thank Ranjani de Silva, president of Sakyadhītā International, who made it possible at the end of 1996 for ten women to receive *bhikṣuṇī* ordination from Korean *bhikṣus* and *bhikṣuṇīs* of the Dharmagupta lineage, with the support of Singhalese *bhikkhus.* This took place in Sarnath, India. The next *bhikṣuṇī* ordination took place in Bodhgaya, India, in February of 1998. Women from Sri Lanka and from the Tibetan Buddhist tradition took ordination supported by Chinese *bhikṣus* and *bhikṣuṇīs* from Taiwan. On March 12, 1998, the *bhikkhunī* order in Sima Malaka (Chapter House) in Dambulla Raja Maha Vihara, Sri Lanka, was newly established by the ordination of Singhalese *bhikkhunīs.* The interest among the Sri Lankan public was immense. Soon, after a preparation time of about ten months, there will be other ordinations of Singhalese "ten-precept nuns" as they become *bhikkhunīs.* This means that "re-evaluating the role of Buddhist women which tends to become invisible or ignored by so-called 'history'"[8] is truly happening on a regular basis. To see that the low status of Buddhist nuns can be improved by the new support of a tradition that has an unbroken *bhikṣuṇī* lineage will be a tremendous encouragement for Buddhist women worldwide. It's an encouragement not only for nuns but for lay women as well.

Visions for Sakyadhītā Europe

During my tenure at Sakyadhītā Europe, the office was a place for inquiries about Buddhism, and in this capacity the organization served as a networking conduit, as an advisory board, and as an information bureau. This organization, however, was only a small, private bureau with a fax, a telephone, and a computer—and, more than that, it was a bureau staffed by only one person. Out of this, however, has come a vision to build up a European "ecumenical" Buddhist educational establishment and an information center, an institute that would have a substantial library and that would sponsor conferences where teachers from different Buddhist traditions could give papers. This institute would also offer the daughters of the Buddha and their different traditions in Europe a counseling and resource center, and would provide a room for Buddhist practice and meditation, with special emphasis on promoting Buddhist women's studies. As Sakyadhītā International continues to respond to Buddhist women worldwide, the vision for a vital Sakyadhītā in Europe remains, and it is a hope of many European Buddhist women that this vision will come to greater fruition in the years ahead.

Notes

1. Leonore Friedman, *Meetings with Remarkable Women: Buddhist Teachers in America* (Boston: Shambhala, 1987).
2. Karma Lekshe Tsomo, *Buddhism through American Women's Eyes* (Ithaca, New York: Snow Lion Publications, 1995), 156.
3. Tsomo, *Buddhism*, 157.
4. Tsomo, *Buddhism*, 158.
5. Tsomo, *Buddhism*, 156.
6. Kulcharee Tansubhapol, "The Silent Nunhood Finds a Voice," in *Newsletter on International Buddhist Women's Activities* 11.2 (no. 42): 7–9.
7. For example, in 1993, during the Conference on Buddhist Women in Colombo, Sri Lanka, we had one ordination to *an thai mae ji* and some ordinations to *upāsikā*.
8. Rajani De Silva and Hiroko Kawanami, "Women in Buddhism: Unity and Diversity," in *Sakyadhītā Newsletter* 1.1 (summer 1998): 1.

NOVICE ORDINATION FOR NUNS:

The Rhetoric and Reality of Female Monasticism in Northwest India

Kim Gutschow

Early one morning, three humble nuns appeared on the doorstep of a young monk, Ngawang Tharpa, after traveling several thousand kilometers from his and their homeland of Zangskar, a region high in the valleys of Buddhist Kashmir on the western edge of the Tibetan plateau.[1] The tradition of pilgrimage from the Indian Himalaya to Tibet had been established centuries earlier by Indian saints like Atiśa who had come this way in the eleventh century.[2] Women, however, rarely undertook these dangerous and lengthy journeys, and the young monk greeted his Zangskari compatriots who waited at his door with a mixture of surprise and recognition. The women, with dusty robes and emaciated faces, were overjoyed to find one of their countrymen at the famous Tibetan monastery known as Ganden. In time, Ngawang told them how Tsongkhapa, the fifteenth-century monk who founded their own Gelugpa order, had established Ganden monastery on Consecration Hill *(dbang skur ri)* soon after founding the Great Prayer Festival in Lhasa.[3] He also told them that this year's prayer festival was to begin shortly. The nuns were relieved to hear that they had arrived just in time.

As Ngawang told the nuns how he came to Ganden, they were unaware of how closely entwined their futures would become. They could not foresee that he would facilitate their ordination as novices *(dge tshul ma)* and that he would become the abbot of their nunnery thirty years later in the village they had left behind months earlier. Instead, the nuns and Ngawang shared their stories and then decided to seek an audience with the Ganden Throne Holder. Paying no attention to the nuns' lack of self-confidence, Ngawang took his guests to meet the venerable head of the monastic complex. After leading them through many chapels brimming with sacra such as Tsongkhapa's throne and the stūpa that held his remains, the group proceeded to the Throne Holder's residence. Before they could flee, the women were called into his chambers. The Throne Holder graciously received their meager gift, the ubiquitous white blessing scarf, and inquired about their background and religious education. After a brief consultation, he invited them to participate in a novice ordination ceremony to be held in Lhasa during the course of the Great Prayer Festival. This ceremony would prove to be a turning point for each of them, in different ways.

These humble nuns participated in an event beyond the wildest dreams of their countrymen. They could not have known that they would be some of the last Zangskari monastics to be ordained in Lhasa by the Ganden Throne Holder, whose leadership of the Gelugpa order made him the third highest ecclesiastic hierarch in Tibet after the Dalai and Panchen Lamas. A few years later, the Chinese troops who had already arrived in Lhasa would force the Dalai Lama and the Ganden Throne Holder to flee to neighboring India along with thousands of Tibetans. Within a decade, the Red Guards would shell the monastery relentlessly. Eventually, Tibetan citizens would be forced to do the unthinkable as they were urged by Chinese authorities to dismantle the temple and destroy religious antiquities their ancestors had venerated for centuries.

The curiously entwined fates of several nuns and one monk serve as a starting point for an examination of monastic life in the Indian Himalaya. Although their paths may occasionally converge, the lives of nuns and monks are demarcated by gender more than any other social fact. After their joint initiation as novices, and despite their shared commitment to celibacy and asceticism, monks and nuns do not enjoy the same opportunities or privileges of the monastic life.

An Ordination in Lhasa

When the Zangskari women arrived at the Great Prayer Festival in Lhasa, their proposed ordination under the Ganden Throne Holder caused a stir among their fellow pilgrims. In due course, three other Zangskari nuns who also held the five precepts decided to be ordained as well. These nuns and their fellow pilgrims were spellbound by the arrival of the Dalai Lama—the incarnation of the bodhisattva Avalokiteśvara and the newly enthroned political and spiritual leader of Tibet. Every day, they joined other pilgrims from throughout Tibet and Central Asia in making merit by circumambulating the congregation of over twenty thousand monks from many monasteries seated at the foot of the Dalai Lama.

When the nun Yeshe told me the story of her ordination some forty years later, she recalled several key moments clearly.[4] On the morning of the ordination ceremony, the six nuns rose before dawn to wash their bodies and shave each other's heads in preparation for the ritual. Their freshly shorn heads signaled a lifelong intention to renounce sex and fertility.[5] From this day onward, they would bear new names and wear sacred robes *(stod thung, sham thabs, zang gos, chos gos)* to signal their commitment to the Buddha's teachings. While the five Buddhist precepts they had held thus far may be followed even by lay people and then abandoned without much shame, novice ordination represents an irreversible step. In the Mahāyāna tradition, taking monastic precepts represents a fundamental shift in one's karmic condition that can never be erased, even though it may come undone.[6]

Arriving at the ceremony, the Zangskari nuns saw that most of the participants were men. They were shocked to find only three other nuns, shyly clustered in the rearmost corner close to the door. Although they had come from afar, the Zangskari contingent was twice as large as the local contingent of Tibetan nuns. Indeed, the pilgrims told me later that they had been surprised to find relatively few nuns in Tibet compared with their homeland.[7] The Ganden Throne Holder sat on a raised dais above the sea of monks as a head officiant for the ritual. In front of him, a proper quorum of monks was assembled to conduct the joint ordination ceremony for both male and female novices.[8] Dazzled by the crowd, the candidates prostrated themselves three times and found a spot in the rear of the crowded hall to lay down the square seating mat *(lding nga)* that they would now be entitled to use.

The head officiant began his discourse on the virtues and pitfalls of the monastic life, urging the ordinands to take their precepts seriously. He reminded the candidates before him that they would now be examples of the Buddha's noble discipline, which had been carried in an unbroken lineage up to this day. After the officiant explained the necessary preconditions for adopting the sacred Buddhist precepts, the initiates were asked to repent the innumerable transgressions they had committed in the present and previous lifetimes. They were obliged to admit to countless faults of body, speech, and mind generated by the three mental poisons—greed, hatred, and ignorance. After completing a perfunctory repentance, the candidates recited the novice precepts that they would keep from this day onward.[9] Although they recited the same thirty-six precepts, the male and female novices present at the ceremony were destined for very different ritual roles.

After the head officiant called the monks up before him, one by one, the tiny group of nuns were called to be consecrated into their new status. The experience of being a separate and unequal group of monastics who necessarily deferred to their male brethren would become a familiar one for the nuns ordained that day. When they were finally called forward, the candidates each offered a blessing scarf and placed a bit of sweetened barley dough *(phye mar)* or sweet rice *('bras sil)* into the replica of the Buddha's begging bowl before the officiant. Each candidate placed her two hands around the ritual staff *(mkhar gsil)* held by the head officiant. The officiant then consecrated their new robes by pinching them between his fingers, reciting a brief prayer, and blowing his blessing upon them. The ceremony came to a close as the newly initiated novices were dismissed.

When the venerable officiant and other teachers had departed from the hall, the Zangskari nuns sat contemplating the extraordinary blessing they had received from the last Ganden Throne Holder to sit on Tsongkhapa's throne in Tibet. They would now be among the "homeless ones" who pledged themselves to celibacy, detachment, and compassion towards all other sentient beings. They wondered how they would fulfill the physical and mental challenges that the doctrine demanded. Even today, Yeshe still regrets that she was unable to maintain the initial practice of fasting after noon. Since she was on pilgrimage thousands of kilometers from home, she had to rely on sporadic meals given at any time during the day. While many novices fast after noon for a few weeks after their ordination, most later abandon this precept due to health constraints.[10]

The decision of how to practice the novice precepts and the broader bodhisattva vow they had just taken was less their own than they imagined. While novice ordination represents the highest ordination possible for women in the Tibetan tradition, it provides them scant opportunity for ritual or scholastic advancement. Although male and female novices following the Mūlasarvāstivāda canon may receive the same precepts, wear the same robes, and can easily be mistaken for each other, their spiritual paths are radically different.

The History of Female Ordination

The Buddha's initial ambivalence about instituting the female order was primarily due to the perceived social threat women would pose to the male order. While admitting that women had the same capacity for enlightenment as men, the Buddha showed extreme reluctance to found a female order. Initially intransigent when hounded by his aunt, Mahāprajāpatī, the Buddha showed a rare display of changed heart when Ānanda interceded on the behalf of women.[11] After relenting, the Buddha admitted women into the religious order he had founded just a few years earlier. He is supposed to have predicted that the monastic order would last only half as long as the result of admitting women, equating women in the order with the blight of mildew on a rice crop or red rust on sugar cane. In addition, the Buddha only agreed to ordain women on one condition: that they accept the so-called "eight chief rules" *(garudhammas)*.[12] These rules require nuns to defer to male monastic authority for both discipline and punishment. Monks are required to conduct the ordination, the bi-monthly confession, and the annual rainy season confession rituals. While it was forbidden for nuns to admonish or rebuke monks, they were forced to perform their penances in front of both the monks' and nuns' assemblies. The Buddha's aunt objected, but only to the rule making nuns categorically inferior to monks. This rule specified that even a nun who has been ordained for one hundred years must bow down to a monk who has been ordained only one day. While these baneful rules may never have been spoken by the Buddha, and while their authenticity has come under question by some scholars, their lasting legacy is undeniable.[13]

Nuns from Karsha Nunnery in Zangskar bow to the departing Tibetan rinpoche *who has graced their nunnery with a rare visit (photo by Kim Gutschow)*

Confined to an asymmetrical position of subservience relative to monks, nuns have seen the condemnation and eventual dissolution of their monastic profession. Although the Buddha preached that his disciples agree to disagree and forgo sectarian divisions, the issue of who can ordain or be ordained, and in what manner, nonetheless led to the formation and demise of countless sects. Falk (1980) argues convincingly that as popular and devotional forms of Hinduism grew in the first millennium throughout the Gangetic basin, the newly formed Buddhist orders had to compete for a shrinking base of donors. During periods of declining economic support, nunneries suffered more than monasteries because they could not command the same institutional prestige and scholarship that monasteries could. As monasteries continued to receive most of the available patronage, female ordination lineages disappeared one by one throughout South and Southeast Asia. While the arrival of Islam completed the rout of monastic Buddhism in India, elsewhere the monks' order fared far better that the nuns' order did. In Sri Lanka, for example, efforts were made to reinstate the monks' order from neighboring regions. When full ordination for monks died out in the eleventh century and was severely compromised in the sixteenth and seventeenth centuries, Burmese monks were brought to revive the lineage. Similarly, while Tibet lost its ordination lineage in the ninth century, it was later revived by a quorum of monks who had fled to the peripheries of the collapsed empire. By contrast, no effort was made to revive the nuns' order after its demise in many parts of Asia.

By the eleventh century, women could no longer seek full ordination in most of South and Southeast Asia. Even today, most women in Sri Lanka, Burma, Thailand, Cambodia, and Laos who wish to renounce lay life can only hold between eight and ten precepts, living as de facto but not de jure nuns.[14] In the Tibetan cultural sphere—including Bhutan, Sikkhim, Ladakh, and Zangskar—the historic record offers no evidence of a lineage of fully ordained nuns, although exceptionally gifted women may have received full ordination solely from monks.[15] At present, an unbroken lineage of fully ordained nuns following the Dharmagupta canon survives only in China, Japan, Korea, Taiwan, and Vietnam. More recently, Buddhist women have sought to reinstate full ordination lineages in South Asia and elsewhere with the assistance of Dharmagupta nuns from East Asia.[16] Although it was Sinhalese nuns who first introduced the order of nuns into China in the fifth century, Sinhalese monastic authorities reject the authority of latter day Dharmagupta lineage holders from China, arguing that their doctrine has diverged from the canon current in Sri Lanka. With the Dalai Lama and others on record in support of reviving female ordination lineages, many Theravāda authorities and some feminists remain opposed, albeit for distinctly different reasons. While the religious authorities contend that there are not enough disciplinary structures in place to ensure the purity of the lineage being transmitted, the feminists argue that women are better off as precept holders, free from the disciplinary gaze of monastic authorities.

The Scholastic and Ritual Inferiority of Nuns

The Buddha's unfortunate stance has left nuns in a difficult position. They cannot administer their own ordinations or confessionals, and the proscription against admonishing monks gave them little chance to become public teachers or ritual professionals. In the Tibetan realm, the inability of nuns to seek higher ordination may have proved the single most damaging fact to their status. Paraphrasing Bourdieu (1991), one might note that the most significant boundary that rituals create is not between those who have been initiated and those who are yet to be initiated, but between those who have or will be initiated and those who will never be initiated. Put another way, male initiation rites are significant not because they separate the men from the boys, but because they reify a more obvious distinction between men and women, as the latter remain permanently ineligible for certain rites.

Analogously, full ordination is significant in the Tibetan Buddhist context not so much because it separates fully ordained monks from novices, but because it separates monks from nuns, since only the former were eligible for full ordination until recently. In Zangskar, for instance, there are fewer distinctions in status and function between fully ordained monks *(dge slong)* and novices *(dge tshul)* than there are between monks and nuns. The collective inferiority of nuns is usually enforced in public contexts by segregated seating and by the different roles held by monks and nuns in those contexts. In contrast, novices are not clearly distinguished from fully ordained monks in most public assemblies and many private ritual performances. Tantric prowess or seniority may be more important than full ordination for conducting or participating in many rituals, although classic Vinaya rites such as the bi-monthly confessions admit only fully ordained monks.[17] In sum, both novices and fully ordained monks cooperate in many ritual settings that have been categorically closed to nuns. Until recently, none of the four orders of Tibetan Buddhism encouraged nuns to learn sacred practices such as making sand *maṇḍalas*, performing fire sacrifices *(sbyin sreg)*, or holding ritual dances *('chams)*.[18] In Zangskar, only monks conduct the periodic fire sacrifices and make the elaborate effigies *(glud, be le)* required for household expiatory rites.

As monks monopolized esoteric practices, nuns were excluded from the training and transmission of sacred knowledge. Exclusion and inferiority proved mutually reinforcing as nuns were left stranded on the margins of an intellectual and ritual hierarchy. Over time, nuns became dependent on monastic scholarship for instructions and initiations. While nuns might study meditation and esoteric subjects at the feet of great masters, they were not given the necessary authority to transmit that knowledge on to their own disciples.[19] Overall, nuns were made increasingly dependent on monks for whom they would always be second-rate students. In the Gelugpa order, for example, nuns were taught neither dialectics nor the highest forms of ritual practice studied in the upper and lower Tantric colleges. While monks became virtuoso meditators, philosophers, or bureaucrats, nuns were confined to retreat centers where they might make merit quietly for the benefit of other suffering beings.

The Efficacy of Monks

As a result of their monopoly on certain forms of ritual knowledge and practice, monks wield considerable symbolic capital in the Zangskari religious economy. Monks are considered to have greater ritual efficacy than nuns and to be more successful in warding off noxious spirits, apologizing to offended deities, and luring the countless demons and sprites of the six realms of existence *('gro ba rigs drug)* into cooperation with the human realm. In short, monks are preferred for most rituals of exorcism, expiation, and benediction, while nuns are left to perform the most basic merit-making tasks such as reading ritual texts, fasting, or doing prostrations on behalf of the sponsor. While nuns may be quite capable of performing Tantric rituals, they are usually summoned only when monks are unavailable. Even at rituals such as funerals and weddings, where local custom demands that both orders of nuns and monks are called to chant, monks are given exclusive right to perform the cremation rite and the customary blessing *(g.yang 'gugs)* held at the bride's house.

> By oneself is evil done and by oneself is one defiled.
> By oneself is evil left undone and by oneself is one purified.
> Purity and impurity depend on oneself. No one can purify another.[20]

While the Buddha clearly disavowed the role of the priest in purifying others, Zangskari and Tibetan monks regularly perform rituals of purification in order to maintain a state of harmony between the human and divine worlds. Monks have a prerogative to perform these rituals since nuns are handicapped within a Brahmanical world view that claims that women are innately impure.[21] Indeed, the Tibetan word for woman is "lower rebirth" *(skyed dman).* All women—and by extension, nuns—are excluded from highly charged ritual spaces such as the protective shrines *(mgon khang)* for monastic protectors *(chos skyong)* and the most exalted spaces on certain pilgrimage routes. Nuns cannot attend the propitiation of local village gods *(yul lha)* or underworld spirits *(klu)* for fear that their impurity might offend the deity being worshipped.[22] Since nuns are excluded from many spaces and practices where ritual purity is emphasized, only monks are authorized to perform many local rituals in Zangskar. Only monks can perform juniper fumigation ceremonies *(bsangs)* held at village shrines to purify the village of inadvertent ritual pollution *(grib),* although nuns may be called to perform a household *bsang* when no monks are available. Ordinarily it is monks who perform rites of expiation and appeasement *(gtor rgyab, bskang gsol)* as well as ritual ablutions *(khrus)* to cleanse individuals and entire villages suffering from unknown afflictions. Last but not least, only monks officiate the annual circumambulation of the fields *('bum skor),* although nuns may assist in this "spring cleaning" of village space. Because monks maintain exclusive command of the most subtle Tantric practices, they reserve the right to mollify the demonic agents whose obscurations *(sgrib)* and harmful thoughts *(gnod pa)* continually threaten to disrupt the human realm.

Monks and Merit: Education and Subsistence

The monastic monopoly on ritual practices and scholastic knowledge enabled monasteries to amass considerable economic and political power. Whether stationed at the monastery or serving a three year rotation in an outlying village as a sacristan *(mchod gnas),* monks are deeply embedded in a cycle of ceremonies that provides a meaningful exchange for both donor and officiant. Because the monks' order is considered to be a higher "field of merit" than the nuns' order, villagers tend to channel most of their donations and alms to the monastery and its monks.[23] By giving to monks rather than nuns, donors both make merit and fulfill more prosaic goals. Monks enable a pragmatic type of merit-making that secures health, prosperity, and good fortune, while nuns tend to perform unfocused types of merit-making that have fewer practical effects.[24]

Within the Zangskari "economy of merit," nunneries have remained impoverished while monasteries have combined the wealth and power of the Church, the Bank, and the University all in one.[25] As kings and nobles gave land grants to monasteries and charismatic monks, the monasteries consolidated their economic holdings and political power. By 1908, Zangskari monasteries owned nearly one-tenth of the cultivated land in the region. At the close of the twentieth century, Zangskar's largest monastery owned roughly ninety times the average private holding of 2.8 acres per household.[26] Roughly a quarter of all households in Zangskar lease one or more fields from a monastery and pay annual rents in grain. Besides these farflung holdings, every monastery is supported by a dedicated group of full-time sharecroppers who pay exorbitant rents for the dubious privilege of tilling monastic estates. Customary tithes and voluntary donations, as well as vast endowments in land and livestock, provide the monastic incomes of grain and butter, which are rationed out to the resident monks throughout the year.

While sharecroppers till monastic estates and local villagers flock to the monastery bearing loads of firewood, dung, grain, and butter, nunneries collect neither rents nor tithes. Zangskari nunneries have paltry estates if any. Five of Zangskar's nine nunneries have no fields at all, and the remaining four own a handful of fields from which they harvest a pittance. For example, Karsha Nunnery owns two small fields, yielding an annual crop of less than one hundred kilograms of grain (barley, wheat, or peas). After the cost of seed and other expenses have been subtracted, each nun receives a symbolic handout (eight kilograms) of grain every three years.[27] Because nunneries have so little endowment, they cannot afford to feed their members on a daily basis, nor can they sponsor the extensive rituals the monastery performs. Institutional poverty forces most nuns in Zangskar to seek their own subsistence through domestic and agrarian work. Many live at home with their parents, working on family farms in exchange for their daily bread.

In contrast to monastic rituals, which are underwritten by special tithes or local labor obligations, the nunnery's rituals are sponsored on a rotational basis by stewards who solicit local donations of butter, flour, and other staples. While some nunneries have recently begun to receive foreign sponsorship, they cannot buy the three most critical resources in the Zangskari economy—land, water, and fuel. Ownership and communal access to these resources is based on centuries of patronage, which has been the exclusive privilege of male monasteries.

Sending a daughter to the nunnery is something like placing her in an impoverished public university. She may have access to knowledge and peers, which take her far beyond the provincial village life, but she or her parents must pay her way. Sending a son to the monastery, however, is like enrolling him in an Ivy League or Oxbridge college. A monastic education will secure a comfortable livelihood in cash and kind as well as ample opportunities for privilege and private profit. The most senior monks at monasteries graduate into more obscure offices for which the duties are less understood but the remuneration becomes ever more handsome. While renunciation is a full-time occupation for monks, it is merely an unpaid vocation for nuns.

It is no surprise that nuns in Zangskar are less concerned with full ordination than they are with the necessities of daily subsistence. Even as nuns elsewhere in South Asia are pushing for full ordination or less regulation by monastic authorities, Zangskari and Ladakhi nuns have sought far more modest goals.[28] When Yeshe and her companions returned from Tibet, they spent two decades developing a small community of renunciants and slowly building up their ritual calendar. The next decade was spent building a place to worship. Soliciting donations on foot from all over Zangskar and the neighboring district of Ladakh, they built an assembly hall complex where they could conduct their monthly rituals in seclusion. Their efforts have come to fruition as Karsha Nunnery now boasts one of the most elaborate ritual calendars in the Zangskar region as well as a Great Prayer Festival lasting longer than any held at Zangskar's other monasteries or nunneries.

For the time being, nuns in the Indian Himalaya are concentrating on educating the next generation by building classrooms and bringing teachers willing to live in inhospitable climes. Overall, nunneries still lack the mixed education taught at monasteries and most suited to a changing economy. While monks may learn arithmetic, science, and Hindi at local monasteries throughout Ladakh and Zangskar, nunneries remain intellectual backwaters. With the help of foreign patronage and local initiatives, however, scholastic programs have been instituted at nunneries throughout Ladakh and Zangskar.[29] While some of these projects include ambitious programs to train nuns as local nurses and midwives, or as traditional practitioners of Tibetan medicine, they remain in their early stages. Attempts to teach advanced philosophical topics have been hampered by student absenteeism and a lack of infrastructure. Without sufficient teachers and textbooks, these training programs can offer only the barest introduction to the classic curricula taught only at select Tibetan monasteries. In recent decades, over two dozen nuns have left Zangskar to seek admission to Tibetan institutes in Dharamsala and South India to study dialectics and other subjects. Yet these exile nunneries can hardly keep pace with the growing interest, and many reserve most of their places for newly arrived refugees from Tibet. In the meantime, Ladakhi and Zangskari nunneries are expanding rapidly while monasteries face declining membership. As Zangskari monks increasingly make their way to Tibetan monastic colleges by paying their own way, nuns still lack basic options for educational advancement.

How Nuns Practice Customary Compassion

> Women are amputated of the purpose of their action, forced to be disinterested, self-sacrificing, without ever having chosen or wanted this. The path of renunciation described by certain mystics is women's daily lot...[30]

Nuns are poor not by choice but by necessity. They live out the dual roles of dutiful daughters and sacrosanct celibates. For monks, renunciation is synonymous with abandoning the duties of a householder. Nuns, however, are expected to adopt the ideals of selfless detachment while devoting their labor to the household economy. Out of customary compassion, nuns do not shirk the persistent clamor of relatives asking for help in this agrarian economy. In recent decades, women and the older generation have been left behind to run the farms, as young men seek cash wages in government or military service beyond Zangskar. With many households in desperate need of labor, the growing population of nuns represents a critical resource in the household economy.[31] Nuns usually stay close to their natal villages and can be called home for daily chores. Furthermore, since they are not burdened with husbands or children, they are expected to be "on call" to take care of their relatives' children and households. By contrast, daughters who marry out cease to work in their natal homes after the first few years of marriage. Zangskari nuns do not have much time for study or for religious practice, because they are too busy ploughing, weeding, irrigating, and harvesting. Although compassion is idealized as universal, in practice it is exacted along precise lines of kinship.

Just as nuns learn to transmute polluted substances like blood and excrement into divine nectar during their visualizations, so too they may transform petty domestic demands into the endless play of compassion. Worldly duties as cook and washerwoman, or irrigator and baby-sitter, may serve as a forum for advanced spiritual practice. When nuns practice selflessness and detachment, these roles are rarely glorified or even recognized. By contrast when Tantric adepts *(siddha)* take up mundane occupations, these serve to teach a hidden message about selflessness and saintliness. Although Tilopa and his colleagues appear in texts as fishmongers or wine sellers in order to teach the equivalence of conventional and absolute reality, nuns appear rarely, if at all. In both the Mahāsiddha's and the Buddha's life stories, women often appear as courtesans or prostitutes offering teachings on desire rather than domesticity. Household drudgery rarely appears as a means for gaining ultimate realization.

Nuns and Non-Attachment

Self-sacrifice and voluntary poverty were some of the most radical aspects of the Buddha's doctrine. When the Vedic ritual of sacrifice was internalized by the Buddha, an entire class of priests in India was supposed to become obsolete. Directly contradicting the Brahmin's role in purification, the Buddha urged his followers to abandon their houses and use their bodies as ritual vessels of purification. By offering his own body for renunciation and thereby fusing the position of patron and priest, the Buddha became the means and the beneficiant of the sacrifice.[32] While the Buddhist monk may have internalized the Vedic sacrifice through fasting, meditation, and other asceticism, priestly prerogative and social hierarchy crept into the Buddhist context over time. The peripatetic and penniless disciples who followed the Buddha's example have given way to a sedentary lot of officiants and bureaucrats. The monastery, which began as a temporary way station for monks during the rainy season, has become a vast corporation managed by a staff of monastic stewards and treasurers. By contrast, it is the nuns who still practice the profound material poverty and non-attachment that the Buddha taught.

Zangskari nuns embody the Buddhist ideal of self-sacrifice because they live a daily regimen of detachment and service. They live out the doctrine that their monastic brethren so skillfully debate, teach, and transmit. While most nuns live in simple, barren rooms with only a handful of possessions to call their own, monks live in splendor at the top of the social and spiritual hierarchy. By closely pursuing humility and detachment from material things, nuns approach Buddhist ideals, yet at the same time lose the respect and attentions of the villagers. Villagers rarely give more than a passing thought to conditions at the nunnery, unless they have a daughter residing there. Monks may enjoy the wealth and luxury that their ritual duties afford them, while disdaining the nun's tedious participation in the daily drama of subsistence. Of course a monk's rebirth is the most desirable one, according to most of my Zangskari informants. The monk's life is thought to afford the best chance at making merit or even escaping the wheel of *saṃsāra* all together. While monks race onwards toward the Buddha fields in their fancy vehicles, nuns seem to be left struggling on the dusty roadside. Yet it is far too early to know who will reach the distant shore first.

Acknowledgments

Thanks above all to the Karsha nuns and all other Zangskari nuns for hosting me with infinite compassion and patience, and for endless cups of butter tea, which I can never hope to repay in this lifetime. Thanks to Michael Aris, Arthur Kleinman, Nur Yalman, Sarah Levine, Elli Findly, and Rebecca Norman for helpful conversations along the way. Funding for my research between 1991 and 1997 came from the Jacob Javits and the Mellon foundations and Harvard's Department of Anthropology.

Notes

1. Zangskar is a subdistrict within the Indian state of Jammu and Kashmir on the western end of the Greater Himalayan range. Covering an area of seven thousand square kilometers, it is twice the size of Rhode Island, but only supports a population of twelve thousand people, making it one of the least populated regions on the Indian subcontinent.
2. Atīśa's journey is described in Chattopadhyaya (1981), while Vitali (1996) offers some correctives about the Guge King Yeshe 'Od's supposed invitation.
3. Founded in 1408, the Great Prayer Festival *(smon lam chen mo)* was held annually every year until 1959 when the Dalai Lama fled to India. The Gelugpa (*dGe lugs pa*, literally "virtuous ones") order held the political leadership of Tibet after the Mongol chieftain Altan Khan first conferred the title of Dalai Lama upon the third incarnation of Tsongkhapa's main disciple in 1578.
4. Ani Yeshe is one of the founding members of Karsha Nunnery. Two of her companions hailed from Karsha, and the other three came from Pishu Nunnery.
5. The symbolic significance of women shaving their head is discussed by Lang (1995), Eilberg-Schwartz and Doniger (1995), Cixous (1981), Gutschow (1998), Leach (1958), and Obeyesekere (1981), among others.
6. A monastic who commits one of the four root (Pali *pārājika*) offenses is like a man who has lost his head, a tree without roots, a needle without an eye, or a rock that has been broken in two, according to an ordination manual from Guang Xiao Si and Wu Ju An Monasteries in China. Thanks to Sarah Levine for supplying a copy of this manuscript.
7. The ratio of nuns to monks resident in Zangskar in 1997 was 2:5, whereas the corresponding ratio for pre-1959 Tibet was 1:9, according to Shakabpa (1984). While

Shakabpa may have overestimated the number of monks, he did the same for nuns. His calculation of 120,000 nuns far outpaces Havnevik's (1990) and Tsomo's (1989) estimates (27,180 and 18,828, respectively), which are based on information supplied by the Dalai Lama's Council for Religious and Cultural Affairs.

8. Yeshe did not recall the number of monks who constituted the quorum that day in Lhasa, but Gombrich (1988, 107) reports that the standard quorum of monks in the Theravāda tradition is usually ten monks, although five monks are sufficient in a border region like Tibet.
9. The thirty-six novice precepts of the Mūlasarvāstivāda canon can be abbreviated to ten precepts, which involve abstention from killing, stealing, lying, sexual activity, intoxicants, eating after noontime, dancing and singing, wearing garlands or perfume, sleeping or sitting on high beds or seats, and handling gold or silver.
10. The Buddha forbade fasting if it would endanger the health and thus well-being of a monk or nun due to illness or the severity of the climate. Tibetan monastics use the same argument to justify eating meat in Tibet, where vegetables are relatively scarce, although this argument holds less for exiles in India.
11. The origin of the nun's order is described in Horner (1930).
12. The "eight chief rules" *(garudhammas)* are found in Cullavagga X of the Pali canon and in the eleventh *(da)* volume of the Tibetan canon *(bKa' 'gyur)* as part of the Vinaya *('dul ba)* literature. The Pali and Tibetan versions of the Buddha's prophecy and the order of the eight rules vary slightly. Translations of the eight rules are found in Horner (1930) and Paul (1985).
13. Horner (1930) and Paul (1985) question the authenticity of the eight rules, while Barnes (1994), Falk (1980), Gross (1993), Tsomo (1988, 1996), and Willis (1985) discuss the status and eventual disappearance of the nuns' order.
14. Tsomo (1988) notes that 60,000 women hold Buddhist precepts throughout the world: 15,000 are fully ordained nuns, 5,000 are novices or probationers, and 40,000 hold a varying number of precepts (five, eight, or ten). Bartholomeusz (1992, 1994), Gombrich and Obeyesekere (1988), Jordt (1988), Kabilsingh (1991), Kawanami (1990), Keyes (1984), Kirsch (1985), and Salgado (1996) report on female renunciates in Burma, Thailand, and Sri Lanka.
15. Tsering and Russell (1986) indicate that between the twelfth and the sixteenth century, several Tibetan women may have been ordained as nuns by monks alone, without the benefit of a quorum of fully ordained nuns.
16. The debate about reestablishing the full ordination tradition in South Asia is discussed in Bartholomeusz (1992, 1994), Gombrich and Obeyesekere (1988), and Tsomo (1988, 1996). S. Levine observed roughly 140 nuns taking full ordination in Bodhgaya, India, in 1998, of which 30 were from Taiwan, 20 from Sri Lanka, 12 from Nepal, 29 from India (of which 5 came from Ladakh), 11 from Europe, 8 from Australia and North America, and the rest from various countries such as Korea, Vietnam, Japan, China, and Malaysia. Tsomo (1996) reports that there are over 100 Western women who have taken ordination from Dharmagupta lineage holders in the last decade.

17. Novice monks are excluded from the recital of the monastic vows (Skt. *pratimokṣa*), yet in Zangskar this rite opens with a joint tea service for both novices and ordained monks.
18. The recent developments at nunneries in Nepal and India, such as Kyirong Thukche Choling, Kopan, Jamyang Choling, and Ganden Choling, where nuns have begun to study dialectics, *maṇḍala* making, and fire sacrifices, represent an exciting new trend in female monastic education. The Dalai Lama has expressed tenuous support for these efforts, while cautioning that rigor and discipline are essential to underpin these modest advances. See Melissa Kerin (this volume).
19. I only consider monastic nuns and not female consorts, *yoginīs*, and enlightened beings like Yeshe Tsogyal and Machig Labdron, who founded ritual practices and lineages.
20. Dhammapada, verse 165. Translated in Rahula (1974), 130. For a Tibetan version, see dGe 'dun Chos 'phel (1995).
21. The idioms of purity and pollution in the Tibetan context are summarized in Ortner (1973), Daniels (1994), and Gutschow (1998), while Huber (1994) describes woman's exclusion from pilgrimage routes.
22. Exceptions are made in villages where there are only nuns and no resident monks; yet even here nuns perform only simple textual recitations and not the more complex rites of expiation or propitiation.
23. Although Buddhist discipline actually forbids monastics from handling money, most Zangskari monastics accept payment for their ritual services, and some serve the monastic treasury, which loans cash to local villagers, in addition to managing other endowments.
24. Gutschow (1997) describes the distinction between focused and unfocused merit-making by monks and nuns.
25. Gutschow (1998, 1997) describes the historical origins of the economy of merit that enfolds the monastery, nunnery, and village households in Zangskari society.
26. The statistics on land ownership in Zangskar are compiled from Muhammad (1909) and the *District Census Handbook: Kargil (Village and Town Directory), 1981.* For a discussion of monastic and private land holding in Zangskar, see Crook and Osmaston (1994), Gutschow (1998), and Riaboff (1997).
27. By comparison, a Karsha monk receives roughly sixty kilograms of raw grain per year from the monastic coffers. Führer-Haimendorf (1976) and Aziz (1976) describe a nunnery in Nepal that provided each of its twenty-three nuns with eighty-four kilograms of grain per year, or one fifth of a nun's annual consumption.
28. Education has been a priority for nuns in much of South Asia. In Kathmandu, a charismatic Theravāda nun, Dhammawati, has encouraged her urban novices to complete their secular education even after they take ordination, and actively promotes foreign study in Burma and Sri Lanka. Her rigorous program of study, meditation, and ritual recitation at Dharmakirti Vihar has drawn patrons and practitioners from throughout the Kathmandu valley, as noted by S. Levine.
29. In the last decade, study programs have been instituted at Wakkha, Lingshed,

Julichen, Tia, Timosgam, Karsha, Zangla, and Pishu Nunneries. After Sakyadhītā sponsored its Fifth International Conference on Buddhist Women in Leh, Ladakh, foreign sponsors rushed to support these fledgling projects. However, many projects still lack the landed endowments and local support critical for success in the traditional economy.

30. See Irigaray (1987), 120.
31. Most Zangskari households are self sufficient in basic foodstuffs such as grain, dairy, and meat products, for heavy snows block vehicular traffic for seven to eight months of each year. The three staple crops—barley, peas, and wheat—along with small plots of hardy vegetables and herds of yak, cows, goats, and sheep are all maintained at a mean altitude of 3,500 meters.
32. Collins (1982) provides an excellent discussion of how the Buddha intended to usurp the position of the Vedic priest in the social hierarchy.

AN EMPOWERMENT RITUAL FOR NUNS IN CONTEMPORARY JAPAN

Paula K. R. Arai

Japanese Buddhist history is filled with women who have devoted themselves to a Buddhist way of life, requiring courage, creativity, and ritual expertise. Illustrations of Japanese Buddhist women's activities from various time periods reveal that women have found ways to empower themselves in diverse circumstances. They have established precedents in Buddhist practice and have accomplished many of their goals, even when there was systematic institutional resistance. Analysis of Japanese Buddhist women's accomplishments show that rituals played a key role in their strategy. After a brief overview of key moments in Japanese Buddhist women's history, I will explore in greater detail the historical and social context of a ritual of gratitude, performed by Sōtō Zen nuns and dedicated to Ānanda, called the *Anan Kōshiki.*

Overview of Japanese Buddhist Nuns' History

The first major recorded Buddhist ritual act in Japan was performed by a Japanese woman in 584 C.E. As the ordination of the first Japanese Buddhist, it was a ground-breaking act. In the ordination ritual she received the Buddhist name Zenshin-ni, establishing her identity as a Buddhist renunciant.[1] Women and men have followed in her footsteps ever since. Today Japanese Buddhist nuns still derive empowerment from the knowledge that it was a woman who inaugurated the Buddhist monastic path in Japan. Between that initial act and today, however, currents in the society shifted many times, forcing women to find innovative ways to continue on the path of Buddhist renunciation.

Despite the fact that women laid the foundation for Japanese Buddhist monasticism, by the Heian Period (794–1185), androcentric encroachments threatened to truncate women's official status. The male-dominated institutions that controlled the official ordination ceremony would not authorize women to receive ordination. Curtailing women's opportunities in this way, however, did not result in women abandoning the lifestyle or values of Buddhist nuns. Instead, this became a catalyst for women to fortify their own devotion to Buddhist renunciant life. Their actions demonstrate that these women of ancient Japan saw themselves as having the capacity to live according to the Dharma, regardless of what the male-dominated institutions of the day did. They apparently understood that the power of ritual could not be exclusively controlled by men and, with this in mind, created a new ordination ritual with a new category of renunciation called *bosatsukai-ni* (bodhisattva vow nun). Since this ritual did not depend upon any male-headed institutions,[2] they were able to use it to continue on the path they had started.

Although obstacles occurred along the way, in general, in the inclusive spirit of the Kamakura Period (1186–1333), women received significant support for their commitment to the Dharma. Sōtō Zen nuns today celebrate the sect's recognized founder, Dōgen (1200–1253), for his teachings affirming women's practice and ability to live according to Buddhist ideals.[3] Dōgen's writings indicate that nuns could perform the same rituals and practices as monks. Dōgen was not alone in his positive attitude towards women as Buddhist practitioners; indeed every founder of each of the major new sects that emerged during this period offered specific teachings in support of women.[4] This support buttressed women's commitment to the path of practicing as Buddhist nuns, but it did not eliminate the discrimination against them.

The perspicacity and determination of nuns was again put to the test during the Tokugawa Period (1603–1868). Every sector of society was put under the restrictions and regulations of the Tokugawa feudal government, but especially women's activities, which were narrowly circumscribed in this climate of male authoritarianism. There is more than one story from this period of a woman who, when informed that she was not "allowed" to undergo the monastic ordination ceremony, burned her face in a *hibachi* stove. Subsequently she was granted permission to become a nun.[5] Such events expose the tyranny of male chauvinism with which women had to wrestle and reveal the depth of women's resolve to become Buddhist nuns.

Despite Dōgen's egalitarian teachings about gender, Sōtō Zen nuns moved into the twentieth century living under institutional regulations that deemed them inferior to monks. Unlike monks, they received almost no support from the main sect for practice facilities and educational opportunities, and they received only minimal recognition for their efforts and accomplishments. The highest rank a nun could attain was lower than the lowest monk's rank, no matter how hard a nun practiced or studied. In addition to this unequal treatment, nuns also experienced tremendous financial difficulties. Nuns were systematically restricted from access to the avenues of income (via donations) available to monks. In short, since nuns could not attain the rank necessary to head a full-fledged temple, they had no official lay followers.[6] During this century, however, Sōtō nuns have directed the course of their lives with the specific understanding that Dōgen supported women. Documents testify to the fact that traditional Sōtō Zen nuns were undaunted by the male-dominated sectarian administration. They led their sect through educational and institutional reforms that reflected their ideas of Dōgen's egalitarian teachings.

Through the mode of ceremonial ritual, nuns have found a powerful way to express their emotional and political concerns. Focusing upon one particular ritual, the *Anan Kōshiki*, I will illustrate how the ritual, cloaked in the non-contentious expression of gratitude, functions to legitimize and empower the nuns.

Sōtō nuns perform the *Anan Kōshiki* ceremony to thank Ānanda for what they maintain was his act of wisdom in entreating Śākyamuni to allow women to enter the path of renunciation. The *Anan Kōshiki* can be seen as an act that catalyzed Sōtō nuns to fight for and, by the 1960s, win equal rights in the institutional records of the Sōtō Sect administration. The *Anan Kōshiki's* power lies in its affirmation of nuns. The ritual ends with a declaration that all women can attain enlightenment, and from this vantage point, the erroneous ways of the male-dominated institution seem glaring, yet inherently surmountable. In effect, the *Anan Kōshiki* authorizes nuns to demand that Buddhist ideals be practiced despite sexism in society.

Historical Background of the Anan Kōshiki Ritual

The *Anan Kōshiki* is one of a number in a genre of ritual ceremonies called *kōshiki*. *Kōshiki* are performed on special occasions, and they are particularly designed for praising and offering gratitude to an important Buddhist figure, such as Śākyamuni Buddha, Bodhidharma, Jizō Bosatsu, and the *rakan (arhats)*.[7] Cultivating awareness of one's indebtedness to these figures and expressing gratitude for one's own practice is the impetus and core of this type of ceremony.

The minimal historical information currently available gives us some clues to the circumstances that gave rise to the *Anan Kōshiki* ritual performed by Sōtō Zen nuns today. The earliest record of a sighting of this type of ceremony is found in Fa Hsien's *Record of the Buddhistic Kingdoms* (394–414 C.E.),[8] in which he mentions seeing nuns in India perform a ceremony to Ānanda. More research, however, is needed in order to give a full history of this early ritual form. Where the trail clears is in Japan, where the ritual takes the form of a *kōshiki*, a type of ceremony performed largely in the Heian and Kamakura periods. For example, Genshin (942–1017) wrote a number of *kōshiki*, including the *Eikan Ōjō Kōshiki*. Myōe

Shōnin (1173–1289) wrote *kōshiki,* which are found in his *Shiza Kōshiki.*[9] The *Anan Kōshiki* is one of them. In the possession of Kōzan Temple's sūtra pavilion are three texts: *Anan Sonja Kōshiki, Anan Sonja Santan,* and *Ananda Sonja Kōshiki.* The *Anan Sonja Kōshiki* was probably copied during the middle of the Edo period (1603–1867).[10] The *Kōzanji Engi* (the history of Kōzan temple) mentions that on April 21, 1224, at the nuns' temple Hiraoka Zenmyō-ji,[11] the nuns had a ritual ceremony for opening the eyes of sixteen *rakan (arhats)* and Anan Sonja statues. A nun, Kaikō, founded the temple after her husband, Nakamikado Chūnagon Muneyukikyō (clearly of aristocratic stock), died in the battle of Shōkyū no Ran. Her articulated intention for establishing this nuns' temple was to pray for her husband. Kaikō was the disciple of Myōe. Many widows from this war gathered at her temple. It is likely that the *Anan Kōshiki* was reconstituted for the nuns at this temple and performed by them there.[12]

In July of 1829, the Sōtō Zen nun Jakushū Kankō-ni (1785–1868) of Owari no kuni, present-day Nagoya, copied the *Anan Kōshiki* text from Kōzan Temple. She recreated the ceremony and asked for permission to use it. Kōsen, the twenty-eighth-generation head of a Nagoya temple, Manshō-ji, wrote the *saimon* (formally chanted explanation of ritual) for it. A woodblock carving was made, and the ritual text was passed around for nuns to use.[13] Kankō-ni was Mizuno Jōrin's (1848–1927) teacher. With the assistance of three other nuns, Mizuno Jōrin was the leading founder of the Sōtō Zen Monastery for women in Nagoya in 1903. It is currently called the Aichi Senmon Nisōdō. The nuns who trained at this monastery were the prime movers in establishing egalitarian regulations for the Sōtō Zen sect.

With the advantage of historical perspective, we can see that the revitalization of this nuns' ritual occurred on the eve of nuns launching a public and institutional effort to bring egalitarian practices to bear on twentieth-century Sōtō regulations. Not only was the timing important here, but the actors were as well. The teacher (Kankō-ni) of the nun (Mizuno Jōrin) who led the movement to establish an official Sōtō Zen monastery for woman is the one who revived the ceremony. This relationship of events and people, then, strongly suggests that performing a ritual that acknowledges the legitimacy and importance of being Buddhist monastic women helped cultivate a community of women who were not dissuaded by the male-dominated institutional attempt to treat nuns as though they were subordinate to monks.

The *Anan Kōshiki,* however, is not included in the *Sōtōshū Zensho* (eighteen volumes) or the *Zoku Sōtōshūzensho* (ten volumes), texts that collectively purport to include all Sōtō Zen rituals. The one article in Japanese that describes this ritual says that it is no longer performed today. Therefore, field research was essential to learn about the performance of this ritual, its importance to Sōtō Zen nuns, and its emerging place in contemporary Japanese Buddhism.

Description of the Anan Kōshiki *Ritual*

The *Anan Kōshiki* is still performed at Aichi Senmon Nisōdō in Nagoya. Due to the complexity of the ritual, the nuns perform it only every six to eight years, or when they are celebrating a major event.[14] It takes several hours of group practice to refine the exact motions demanded by the ritual, and additional hours to learn individually the complicated chants. A ceremony called the *Anantan* is performed at the end of the *kōshiki.* The entire ritual, with both the *Anan Kōshiki* and the *Anantan,* takes about one hour and forty-five minutes. The *Anantan,* when performed alone, takes about fifteen minutes. The *Anantan* is performed at the Nisōdō on the evening of the seventh of every month, unless there are extenuating circumstances.

The *Anan Kōshiki* ritual begins when the lead celebrant *(shikishi)* enters with bells, and bows. As in all *kōshiki,* the first major section is the *sangege,* a verse chanted while three nuns process around the worship hall. The first carries an incense burner *(shōkō),* the second sprinkles pure water about with a pine branch *(seisui),* and the third scatters lotus blossom petals *(sange)*—actually, lotus blossoms printed on cardboard cut in the shape of petals—throughout the worship hall.

The next major section of the ritual is found in all *kōshiki.* It is the recitation of the *shichisan* or four wisdoms (Skt. *catvārijñānāni).* The four wisdoms are as follows: 1. the great perfect mirror wisdom (Jap. *daienkyōchi*; Skt. *ādarśajñāna*) reflects all phenomena in the three worlds in their true state, with no distortions; 2. the wisdom of equality (Jap. *byōdōshōchi*; Skt. *samatājñāna*) perceives the underlying identity of all dharmas and works to overcome separating oneself from others; bodhisattva compassion draws on this wisdom; 3. the wisdom of wondrous perception (Jap. *myōken zacchi*; Skt. *pratyavekṣaṇājñāna*) enables one to see the truth/Dharma clearly, so one can preach free from error and doubt; and 4. the wisdom of accomplishing metamorphoses (Jap. *jōshosachi*; Skt. *kṛtyānuṣṭhānajñāna*) takes on various forms to act in the world for the benefit of others' advancement toward enlightenment.

The third section of the ceremony, the *nyōhachizu,* is also typical of all *kōshiki.* This part of the ceremony is a cymbal performance, which serves as a musical offering and helps raise the intensity of the ritual proceedings.

The fourth section involves making offerings to Ānanda at the main altar. Although the offerings—candles, flowers, incense, tea, rice, and cakes—are typical, the utensils are refined and the method of handling them is extremely formal and elaborate. The lead celebrant makes the formal offerings while five nuns assist. Each food item is placed elegantly on tall red lacquer trays. The angle of the fingers and the placement of the thumbs on the tray are carefully practiced to achieve an elegant appearance, a gesture of respect. After each nun handles an item to be offered on the altar, she places her hands together as in prayer and slowly bows to a ninety-degree angle and maintains this posture for about five seconds. Those about to receive the offering to pass to the altar simultaneously bow at a ninety-degree angle. Slowly and respectfully, each offering to Ānanda is placed on the altar.

The fifth section is the *saimon*—again, a standard feature of all *kōshiki.* This is where the background and purpose of the ritual are chanted. Therefore the contents of each *kōshiki's saimon* vary accordingly. The *saimon* of the *Anan Kōshiki* explains Ānanda's activities and merits, including his great virtue in resisting the temptations of a woman who wanted to marry him and compassion in helping Mahāprajāpatī with her request to become a renunciant.

The sixth section of the ceremony is the *bonbai* or "Sanskrit chanting."[15] Two nuns enter the worship hall and do three full prostrations before the altar. Then, before the esoteric chanting begins, the text is brought into the main worship hall very dramatically, thus preparing people for something significant: with dynamic and exacting motion, a nun carries in the formal, red ornamented stand upon which the text lies and places it before the two nuns who will perform the chanting. The *bonbai* chant is more melodic than most chants done in Zen rituals, and there is a sense of gravity to its slow tempo. This chant lasts about five minutes. The text of the chant is short: *"Nyorai myō shikishinze,"* that is, "The miraculous form, body, and world of the Thus Come One." Most of the chant's emphasis is on the word *myō,* which, in this context, seems to mean miraculous. Aoyama Rōshi, the current abbess of Aichi Senmon Nisōdō, speculates that this verse may have been written by Mahāprajāpatī to express her profound joy on having first seen the enlightened Buddha. Even if this is not the case, it is significant that the abbess believes it is possible and presents it this way to her disciples and trainees in modern Japan.

The seventh section of the ritual is called the *sanbonshaku.* Three nuns process around the main worship area and stop directly in front of the altar to chant. Each of them carries a tray adorned with trailing ribbons that has "lotus petals" arranged on them as well as the text of the chant. The first nun in the line chants the Sanskrit *(bonnon)* chant; the second nun chants the blossom *(sange)* chant; and the third nun carries a Buddhist mendicant's traveling staff *(shakujō)* and chants the *shakujō* chant. These chants are of a distinctly lighter style than the *bonbai* chant. The chants include phrases like: "All together we advance on the Buddha's path," and "We make offerings of incense and flowers to the Buddha." This section ends with the three nuns chanting in unison, making a request that the merit from this ceremony go to help all sentient beings.

The eighth section is called the *shikimon.* This is the main section of the ritual, and it is divided into five parts. The first part praises Ānanda for practicing hard and renouncing the world. The second part expresses the nuns' indebtedness *(hōon)* to him for their renunciation. It mentions the legend in which Ānanda asked Śākyamuni three times to allow women to follow in his path of renunciation. They then chant that Ānanda is their *"nyonin tokudo no daishi,"* or "great teacher of women's ordination."

The third part of the *shikimon* highlights some of Ānanda's merits. These chants praise Ānanda for his countenance, presence, and appearance; for having been Śākyamuni's personal attendant for twenty-five years; and for having heard many of the Buddha's teachings.

Part four of this section expresses profound gratitude to Śākyamuni. It recounts the legend that Ānanda reasoned with Śākyamuni on behalf of the women whom Mahāprajāpatī led to become renunciants on the Buddha's path. Ānanda first used an argument based on sociological categories, but when that did not work, he offered an argument based on soteriological categories to persuade Śākyamuni. When the Buddha heard this, he granted the request. As recounted in this ritual, when the women led by Mahāprajāpatī themselves heard this, they became ecstatic. Following this section, the nuns make prostrations and chant praise and gratitude to Śākyamuni. The current abbess of the Nisōdō, Aoyama Rōshi, stressed to me in an interview[16] that Śākyamuni came to understand that he had to treat Mahāprajāpatī with at least the same compassion she had shown him.

The fifth part is an offering of prayers *(ekō)* to transfer merit to all sentient beings. The lead chanter *(ino)* chants in a loud and clear voice, "We sentient beings all together realize the Buddhist way." This is followed by the climax of the ceremony when the lead chanter announces, "Now all women, like Queen Vaidehi, transform their bodies with five limitations and attain buddhahood."

The *Anantan* is performed at the end of the *Anan Kōshiki* and also independently on the evening of the seventh day of the month. Special offerings *(kenshuku)* and chanting dedicated to Ānanda are done on the eighth day of the month during the regular morning worship service. The chanting for this ceremony is reminiscent of Indian music, creating an atmosphere that ritually transports one back to the era in which Śākyamuni, Ānanda, and Mahāprajāpatī lived. The lead chanter begins the ceremony with the phrase "*Namu daihi Anan son*" ("Praise to the great compassion of Anan"). All participants, nuns and laity, stand with hands held in *gasshō* (as in prayer) and repeat this phrase after each of the ten praises chanted by the lead chanter. After a praise and refrain chant is completed, all do a full prostration. The first praise is to Śākyamuni's enlightenment and birthday. The second praises Ānanda by describing how all experience the bliss of five heavens just by looking at him. The third is praise for those in the three realms who are near the Buddha. The fourth is praise for Ānanda's having ears to hear the wonderful Dharma. Fifth, nuns praise women's ordination and their eight special vows. Sixth is praise for receiving a spiritual mountain of gratitude. Seventh is praise for having compiled the scriptures in one generation. Eighth is an expression of praising with beautiful gold brocade that hangs on a pillar. Ninth is praise for manifesting the light of three types of gods. The tenth is praise for entering *nirvāṇa.*

After the *Anantan* is completed, the entire ceremony ends with a memorial service *(kuyō)* for the ancestors of those present at the ceremony.

Analysis of the Ritual

An examination of the *Anan Kōshiki* using categories of ritual analysis offered by Catherine Bell in *Ritual Theory, Ritual Practice*[17] reveals a number of things accomplished by the ritual.[18] These accomplishments are not immediately obvious in the performance of the ritual itself, but are best seen when placed in a social and historical context, for rituals are dynamic aspects of a culture, and both shape and are shaped by it.

The goals of the *Anan Kōshiki* include praising and thanking Ānanda, Śākyamuni, and Mahāprajāpatī; cultivating virtues like respect and gratitude; affirming the women's self-identity as legitimate Buddhist nuns; confirming that being a Buddhist nun is a positive thing; eliciting recognition from the community as disciples of the Buddha; gathering donations; verifying the nuns' ability to attain buddhahood; and winning status equal with men in the Sōtō Zen sect regulations.

As Bell shows, rituals are strategic actions that use culturally specific tactics to achieve particular ends. The fundamental strategy employed by this ritual is the use of a ceremonial format that is firmly established in the Japanese Buddhist repertoire of ceremonial rituals. The use of the *kōshiki* format, for example, puts the nuns ritually on the same plane as men, who are the normative performers of *kōshiki.* By using this format, nuns do not have to fight for the right to this ritual, and the ritual's performance signals to monks and laity alike that nuns and monks are not fundamentally different. It is a non-combative method, which makes the act of performance itself an actualization of the nuns' goal of equality with monks. It confirms for the laity attending the ritual that the nuns' acts are authoritative. In attending, laity are then brought into the drama of bringing about gender parity among renunciants, thereby acting as witnesses to the legitimation of contemporary nuns as Dharma heirs.

As is typical of ceremonies in Buddhist temples, the hierarchical relations among people are clear. The nuns perform the various ritual acts in front of the altar at the center of the worship hall. Lay people sit along the side. Even among monastics, hierarchy is delineated by who and how one moves in the prescribed space and what color robe one wears. The shaven heads and monastic robes, however, make it easy to distinguish monastics from laity.

The use of Sanskrit and classical Japanese also establishes the nuns' authority. Through the use of esoteric chants, they are seen by the laity to have special, and hence empowering, knowledge. Moreover, that nuns know how to handle sacred ritual implements and make elaborate offerings further establishes their authority and high rank in the community. The ornamentation around the altar area and the ritual acts of scattering "lotus blossoms," sprinkling spiritually pure water, and burning incense cultivate a sensory experience that distinguishes the place and time of the ritual, and the nuns' performance of it as authoritative. While all is done explicitly to thank Ānanda, implicitly the nuns are demonstrating their spiritual power and status.

The ritual performed on behalf of the ancestors of the laity in attendance establishes a reciprocal relationship between laity and nuns. Nuns offer the ritual to benefit the lay people, and the lay people offer donations for this service, which help the nuns pay the bills. Tacitly, the very presence of the laity empowers the nuns, for it shows that they recognize the nuns as legitimate, efficacious, and authorized to perform the rituals. In return, the nuns bestow on the laity the confirmation that they are devout lay Buddhists.

The practice of *kōshiki* in Zen contrasts with the iconoclastic impulse common in popular Western representations of Zen. *Kōshiki* are ritualized, communal reifications of individuals and formal expressions of gratitude to them. The values that are manifested and inculcated in the ceremony include respect, gratitude, remembrance, and compassion. Through all the ways in which Ānanda is praised, the ritual teaches people, both lay and monastic, what being an exemplary Buddhist entails. The ritual also creates and enforces the patterns of human relations hoped for outside the performance of the ritual.

The actual practice of being grateful is one of the ways nuns are empowered through this ritual. Being a grateful person, especially in the gift-giving culture of Japan, facilitates one's agency with other members of the community, for having strong reciprocal relationships, then, makes one a more effective actor in society. The nuns' public display of gratitude to a person who lived nearly 2,500 years earlier effectively suggests to the people in attendance that these nuns are people with whom one would want to have close relationships, because one can be assured of being respected and appreciated. In order for the nuns to build their monastery facilities, large donations from laity were required. Indeed, in part through the effectiveness of the Ānanda ritual, these nuns continue to receive support from donors of all backgrounds.

Moreover, cultivating the virtues found in this ritual probably increased the nuns' effectiveness during the first half of the twentieth century, when they challenged the sectarian authorities who were in charge of the monastic regulations. My research on Zen nuns reveals that nuns have been and continue to be highly respected in Japanese society because of their adherence to traditional Buddhist virtues as exemplified in the *Anan Kōshiki*.[19] In these ways, the *Anan Kōshiki* contributes to establishing the meaning and content of being a Zen Buddhist using nuns as exemplars. Moreover, through the *Anan Kōshiki*, it becomes apparent that the power of Zen is not in "self," but in community.

The act of jointly praising and offering gratitude to Ānanda makes the nuns a distinct group. First, it gives identity to the nuns themselves: these women belong to a long line of other women committed to living their lives fully in accordance with the Buddha's teachings. The ritual also highlights the merits of the monastic life, making it explicitly clear that those who enter this path are dedicated and serious disciples of the Buddha, dispelling the misinformed image that they are trying to escape to the nunnery because they could not succeed at anything else.

The *kōshiki* format also helps the nuns accomplish their goal of legitimizing themselves, effectively yet tacitly. Because a *kōshiki* is a ceremony of gratitude, it humbles the performers before the exalted figure being singled out for appreciation, but the very act of exalting also in fact exalts the nuns. To praise Ānanda for having served Śākyamuni for twenty-five years also establishes that Ānanda knew Śākyamuni intimately, which legitimizes Ānanda's request on the part of the women renunciants. By praising Ānanda for his vast knowledge of the Buddha's teachings, it establishes Ānanda as having the authority to recognize that the women's request was in accord with those teachings. So, in short, to praise Ānanda exalts the nuns doing the praising.

At the end of the ceremony the abbess stresses to the audience that Ānanda is responsible for the scriptures based on the Buddha's original teachings, and that his contributions, therefore, lie at the very foundation of Buddhism. By noting that the "I" of the "Thus have I heard" at the beginning of many sūtras refers to Ānanda, she implies that all Buddhists are indebted to Ānanda and, thus, that nuns are not exceptional.

The *Anan Kōshiki* was revived in Japan at the time when Sōtō nuns were beginning to work towards receiving the treatment they deemed consonant with Dōgen's teachings. The nun who went on to teach the ritual to many others was the same nun who took the lead in establishing officially sanctioned training facilities for nuns. Her disciples were the ones who fought for and won equal regulations in monastic training and in teaching ranks. In this context, it is no small thing that the Ānanda ritual climaxes at the point where it is announced that women are able to attain buddhahood. Thus, through expressions of gratitude, these nuns find empowerment for their spiritual goals.

Notes

1. *Nihongi*, trans. W. G. Aston (Rutland, VT: Charles E. Tuttle, 1972), 2: 101. Two more women became nuns shortly thereafter, as is recorded in the *Nihongi* (2: 101) and the *Gangōji Garan Engi* in *Jisha Engi*, comp. Sakurai Tokutarō, Hagiwara Tatsuo, and Miyata Noboru (Tokyo: Iwanami Shoten, 1975), 11. See chapter 2 of Paula Arai, *Women Living Zen: Japanese Sōtō Buddhist Nuns* (New York: Oxford University Press, 1999) for a more complete explication of this event.
2. Nishiguchi Junko, *Ama to Amadera* (Tokyo: Heibonsha, 1989), 288. See also Ishida Zuikō, "Bikuni Kaidan" in *Nihon Bukkyō Shisō Kenkyū* 2 (Kyoto: Hōzōkan, 1986). For further development of this issue, see Paula Arai, "Zen Nuns: Living Treasures of Japanese Buddhism" (Ph.D. dissertation, Harvard University, 1993), 72–76.
3. For more detailed information on Dōgen's teachings about women and his female disciples, see chapter 2 of Arai, *Women Living Zen: Japanese Sōtō Buddhist Nuns.*
4. For more information on this, see Arai, "Zen Nuns: Living Treasures of Japanese Buddhism," 78–81.
5. Arai, "Zen Nuns: Living Treasures of Japanese Buddhism," 98–99. Ueda Yoshie, *Chōmon Nisō Monogatari* (Tokyo: Kokusho Kankōkai, 1979), 67. Stephen Addiss, *The Art of Zen* (New York: Abrams, 1989), 94–99.
6. Feudal regulations had required families to officially register as members of a full-fledged temple. So, it is to that temple that people turn for various Buddhist services, especially funeral, burial, and memorial rites. Laity provide donations for these services. Even though people are currently free to choose whether or not to be affiliated with a temple, most people are loathe to "move" their ancestors.
7. Others include: *Hōon Kōshiki, Dentō Kōshiki, Nehan Kōshiki, Yakushiji Kōshiki, Hokke Kōshiki, Daihannya Kōshiki, Shari Kōshiki, Aizen Kōshiki,* and *Fudō Kōshiki.*
8. The Japanese pronunciation of Fa-Hsien is Hokken (339?–420? C.E.). The title of the book is *Bukkokuki* in Japanese.
9. Ebie Gimyō, "Anan Kōshiki" in *Sōtō-shū Jissen Sōsho* vol. 8, ed. Sōtō-shū Jissen Sōsho Hensan Iinkai (Kiyomizu-shi, Shizouka Prefecture: Daizōsha, 1985), 291.
10. Ebie, 291.
11. No longer standing.
12. Ebie, 292.
13. Ebie, 293.
14. The following description is based on my numerous observations of a video recording of the ritual performed in 1987. I have also observed live performances of other *kōshiki* performed by these nuns at Aichi Senmon Nisōdō, including the *Daruma Daishi Kōshiki* and the *Jizō Kōshiki.*
15. Use of *bonbai* in Zen derives from the influence from the Ōhara sect of Tendai Buddhism. It is especially used in *kōshiki.*
16. Interview with Aoyama Shundō Rōshi held at Kōrinji Temple on August 15, 1998.
17. Catherine Bell, *Ritual Theory, Ritual Practice* (New York: Oxford University Press, 1992).

18. I wish to thank Brian Kerins for his assistance in discussing the analysis of this ritual.
19. This conclusion is drawn from the results of the survey I conducted of seventy-five lay people who attended events held at Aichi Senmon Nisōdō in the spring of 1990.

PART II

Teachers, Teaching, and Lineages

WOMEN TEACHERS OF WOMEN:

Early Nuns "Worthy of My Confidence"

Ellison Banks Findly

The many faces of contemporary Buddhism reflect the interplay between the tradition's rich history and the complex forces of modern life. New, ad hoc Buddhist communities spring up and call themselves Sanghas, for example. Buddhist images, texts, and news materials proliferate electronically, visually, and in print. And Buddhist renunciants are involved, as they have been historically, in ambiguously interpreted practices of donation, social engagement, and political protest. One new focus of Buddhism is the heightened role of contemporary women, which has raised a number of questions of practice. The most centrally debated is that of full ordination for nuns, with special concerns about the authenticity of ordination lineages, cross-sectarian transmission, and the legitimizing role of the male religious community.

A part of these concerns is the role of education for religious women. Canonical dictates provide for male, as well as female, instructors for nuns, especially while they are in training, and for male presence and supervision at critical moments in the lives of Buddhist nuns—such as during the rain retreat, at the fortnightly confession meeting of Uposatha and the annual meeting of Pavāraṇā to establish harmony before leaving the rains retreat, for disciplinary matters and, of course, for ordination. Contemporary movements, however, strive for greater parity between the rules of the male and female communities and seek to reinterpret these traditional guidelines. New efforts are being made to develop advanced monastic education for Tibetan nuns,[1] for example, as well as institutional structures that would provide places and opportunities for these nuns worldwide to meet and give instruction in their religious specialities to other nuns.

Keeping true to tradition, in doctrine and in discipline, and at the same time allowing Buddhist practice to accommodate itself to new circumstances is a task perpetually present in Buddhist history, but one that seems especially pressing today. The tension between the need to preserve a faithful spirit and the need to respond to current demands and conditions has become particularly prominent in the current context of the issue of gender. Because early Buddhism makes clear that soteriologically women and men are equally able to become enlightened as women and men—as the eldress *(therī)* Somā suggests in the Therīgātha, in enlightenment there is no gender[2]—the disparities found in traditional arenas have arisen instead out of particular sociological valuations.

Four areas predominate as historical venues for discrimination against renunciant Buddhist women. First, the teachings and practices that guide male and female religious development have been applied inconsistently through the centuries, often unfavorably toward women, and women have had fewer opportunities to cultivate higher levels of spirituality even when their tradition offers a great range of possibilities. Second, the application of disciplinary rules to renunciant women has been stricter than for renunciant men. Third, the recognition of spiritual achievement through the use of titles and honorifics has been sharply curtailed for women but not for men. And, finally, women—known in the early Pali canon as *kicchalābha* (or *dullabha*), "obtaining [things only] with difficulty"[3]—have received far fewer material resources from donors with which to meet their individual and community needs than have men.[4]

There is no doubt that the Pali canon shares some of the negative views on women prevalent in the surrounding Vedic and Hindu cultures during the centuries of its compilation, and that these views, once canonized, became somewhat normative for the future tradition in practices regarding women.[5] There is no doubt, as well, that these views resulted in special accommodations made for nuns as they pursued their daily routines, viz., extra allowances in clothing during times of menstruation,[6] and rules against traveling alone during training[7] and against going unprotected on almstour through dangerous areas.[8] It is also true that in the early canon a great measure of independence is given to women, lay and renunciant: lay women, for example, have enormous freedom in the area of donation, being able to choose to whom and how much to give entirely on their own,[9] and renunciant women have freedom almost equal to that of men to shape the details of their monastic lives through the trial and error process of community interaction.

In contemporary times, the earlier freedoms of religious women are being recovered as Buddhist nuns become increasingly concerned about institutional disparities in the training and education available for new nuns, and in their options for full ordination. Although the alternatives available for nuns the world over differ according to geographical area and to tradition, the need for improvement in their educational opportunities and in their chances for full ordination in general are widespread. This essay will focus on early Pali materials by and about nun teachers of nuns, with a view to recovering elements in the tradition in which instruction only by women is a possible interpretation. As a part of this discussion we will also assess the canonical requirements for female teachers, compare them to those for male teachers, and make a case that the rules of strict seniority so often a part of nunnery life in contemporary times be tempered by a return to the original standards of leadership: experience, competence, and the ability to inspire confidence.

Self-Governance versus the Legitimizing Agency of Monks: Instruction and Ordination

The initial "going forth" of Buddhist women under the intervention and advocacy of the monk Ānanda is significant because it distinguishes between two perspectives on women's place in Buddhism. In the first, the soteriological perspective, women are thought to be as able as men to experience complete enlightenment, in terms of both technical achievement and experiential fullness. In the second, however, the sociological perspective, the rules, institutions, and practices under which religious women live out the Buddhist life limit the involvement of women according to the valuations of both the cultural context of canonical compilation and the local traditions of evolving practice—both of which are often restrictive for women.[10] The central canonical dictates that are seen to determine and to symbolize the subservience of nuns *(bhikkhunī)* to monks *(bhikkhu)* are the eight principal rules *(aṭṭha garudhamma)* said to have been lifetime-enduring preconditions laid down by the Buddha for the acceptance of the first Buddhist women into the renunciant life:

1. A nun must always pay proper homage to a monk, no matter what the age or seniority of each.
2. A nun must spend the rain retreat where a monk is present.
3. A nun must ask the monks' order *(bhikkhusaṅgha)* every two weeks about the date of the Uposatha and about the instruction *(ovāda)* of nuns by monks at this time.
4. At the conclusion of the rain retreat, a nun must participate in Pavāraṇā before both Sanghas.
5. A grievously offending nun must be disciplined before both Sanghas.
6. After two years of training in the six rules, a female probationer *(sikkhamānā)* must seek ordination from both Sanghas.
7. A nun may not abuse or criticize a monk in any way.
8. While nuns may not reprimand monks, monks may reprimand nuns.[11]

The two rules of major importance for the teaching of and by nuns are numbers three and six. Relevant to number three, the giving of *ovāda*, "exhortation or instruction," by a monk or monks to nuns at the time of Uposatha (the fortnightly ritual in the life of a Sangha when Dhamma is expounded and the precepts of the Pāṭimokkha are recited for the purpose of confession) are four rules that pertain to proper instruction of nuns by monks. Of these, the first is most significant for our discussion. Here, the monk chosen at the time to be the instructor of nuns is generally an elder *(thera)* who has been agreed upon by the monks' order according to the exhibition of eight qualities: he must be virtuous; he must abide by the rules of the Pāṭimokkha; he must behave well and according to law; he must acknowledge the danger of even the smallest fault; he must be trained in the rules of training; and he must be learned, know the learning by heart, and be a storehouse of learning.[12] The Aṅguttara Nikāya adds to these several other qualities: a monk instructor of nuns must also have a pleasant voice, good enunciation, and speech that is refined, clear, and informative, and he must be able to inspire nuns with his instruction and be pleasant and liked by the nuns.[13] Thus, the male instructor of nuns must be agreeable and friendly, of good reputation and learning, and never have been punished for habitual quarreling, excessive stupidity, breaches of discipline, and improper association with women.[14]

Several instances in the Vinaya demonstrate, however, that not all monk teachers of nuns perform as they should. Two cases are illustrative. The first, a narrative about the establishing of an office for qualified instructors of nuns, describes a group of six monks teaching the nuns with an inferior Dhamma talk. When the nuns complain, they hear an excellent one from the Buddha himself.[15] In the second, the monk Cūḷapanthaka is accused of simply asking about the eight important rules rather than discussing them fully in his instruction as he should,[16] and of simply repeating the same verse over and over again without explication. The monk then appeases the complaining nuns' with a display of supernatural powers *(iddhi)*.[17] These instances are tangible evidence not only that early nuns are determined to get the best spiritual training, but also that at their instigation parts of traditional practice are reshaped and modified.

Horner nevertheless draws our attention to the "implicit impossibility of the almswomen's giving the Exhortation to [other] almswomen" that is pre-eminent throughout early Buddhist practice, and their concomitant dependence on monks for it.[18] She does point out, however, that another part of the Uposatha, the recitation of the Pāṭimokkha, comes under the sole jurisdiction of the nuns. Originally the Pāṭimokkha is recited by monks to nuns, but early on the nuns get to questioning who really should be reciting the confessional dictates to them and, after consultation with the Buddha (says the *Cullavagga*), it is agreed that the nuns themselves will be the ones to recite the Pāṭimokkha to other nuns,[19] with additional instruction from the monks only if necessary.

This readjustment parallels, early on, other liberating shifts that take place in the lives of nuns. At the request of Mahāpajāpatī, for example, the Buddha is said to allow nuns themselves, rather than monks, to train probationary nuns.[20] Again, this time at the instigation of the general public, the rules are changed so that nuns, not monks, acknowledge any offenses committed by nuns and presumably, set the punishments for them when appropriate.[21] Finally, at the instigation of the monks, formal acts on behalf of nuns come to be carried out by the nuns themselves, not by monks[22]—although instruction by monks may be given if nuns do not know the proper procedure. Thus, as Horner notes, "all these concessions...show a growing tendency among the almswomen to be as dissociated as possible in their internal government from the Chapter of Almsmen."[23]

Rule number six of the original eight set down by the Buddha—covering the full ordination *(upasampadā)* of nuns[24]—represents an important exception to the growing focus on self-governance for the nuns' order *(bhikkhunī)*. In the developed tradition, full ordination takes place when a female probationer has finished her two years of training as a *sikkhamānā* in the six rules: the five moral precepts of non-violence, not stealing, chastity, truth-speaking, and abstention from liquor, plus abstention from eating at the wrong time.[25] It appears that one reason for this probationary period is the possibility that the candidate may be pregnant—the extra time allows for full gestation and delivery and for proper arrangements to be made.[26] Just as for monks, the decision to admit (and then later to ordain) a woman into the Sangha is not a matter for a single individual, but for the whole monastic community. Moreover, even though one of the most important tasks is choosing a woman preceptor[27] who will be responsible for the candidate's formal monastic education. The choice of a preceptor takes place early on, beginning with the nun's admission, and her instructional presence carries through the training period, the ordination, and the nun's first two years as a *bhikkhunī*.

When a female candidate is ready for ordination, she is approached by her preceptor to rehearse the answering of the requisite twenty-four questions to be posed during ordination. These include eleven on gynecological issues and five on diseases, and as a whole they are comparable to those questions asked of a male candidate at his ordination.[28] No questions are asked, however, about the kind or amount of education the candidate has as yet received, as this has presumably been covered during her training under the preceptor. The woman candidate is also required at this time to give the name of the senior nun *(pavattinī)* who will propose her reception as a fully ordained nun. For the actual ordination, the nuns' order is informed that the woman candidate wishes ordination. She is then brought before them dressed in the proper arrangement of robes, her five robes and bowl having just been conferred upon her as she again chooses her preceptor to guide her through ordination and her first two years as a new nun. In the presence of the

Sangha, then, she honors the feet of the senior nuns, sits on her haunches with hands in the *añjali* position, and asks for ordination. The nuns' order hears the candidate's answers to the twenty-four questions, and is consulted for their agreement to her ordination by her proposer.[29]

If the woman candidate is found acceptable to the nuns' order—as indicated by their silence when asked three times—the candidate is then taken to the monks' order by her proposer and, through a designated monk, is agreed upon in the same way. Her ordination in front of the monks' Sangha does not, however, require answering the twenty-four questions, as that has already been done; the monks' Sangha, thus, accepts this establishing act of the nuns' Sangha in full. At the end of the ordination process, the nun is then given other instructions relating to her new life, and with this the ordination process is finished.[30]

From this array of rules, several observations can be made. First, nuns do receive full ordination in the early Pali Buddhist tradition, even if they receive full legitimation only with the final sanction of the monks' order. Second, ordination for nuns more or less parallels, point by point, that for monks: a formal going forth; a choosing of a preceptor (f. *upajjhā*, m. *upajjhāya*); a period of training within a set curriculum; special preparation in answering questions during ordination; and a formal ordination by the Sangha under the advocacy of a specially designated senior renunciant. What differences there are in procedure or in content may be accounted for by the Buddhist tradition's regular policy of accommodation to particulars of biology, background, training, and temperament, which have always governed the shaping of Vinaya rules. The specific case of women's ordination reflects the tradition's own ambivalence: on the one hand, women can attain enlightenment as women but, on the other hand, they need some special attention to do so (an added probationary period to their novitiate, for example). At work here is the assumption that differences stemming from culture or biology brought to the renunciant life can be evened out through the structured institutions of the training and ordination process.

Third, the monks' order accepts the nuns' order's testing of the appropriateness and preparedness of the candidate, meaning that the monks' involvement is really only to give a formal stamp of approval. Although "the final decision of allowing a candidate to become a senior rested" with the monks, it appears that the monks do not ever reject a nun offered up for ordination.[31] It is important to note here that self-governance for nuns has thus already been partially established in the ordination context, where it is the nuns' order alone that witnesses and testifies to the absence of stumbling blocks to ordination through its own asking of the twenty-four questions. While I argue that the need for a woman candidate to go before the men's Sangha is important in terms of the tradition's view of legitimacy, I also argue that this final ceremonial moment is superfluous, for the real work of the ordination has already been done in the training and questioning of the candidate by the nuns themselves.

If the letter of the law does not necessarily demonstrate parity between the nuns' and the monks' ordination process, it is possible that the spirit is more persuasive. Since I have already argued that the monks' final legitimation of nuns' ordination is, for all intents and purposes, a pro forma act not involving any of the real work, the only other setting in which the heavy hand of male authority seems most critical is in the teaching of women candidates. In this matter, we have seen that in time a great deal of self-governance is allowed the nuns' Sangha but that, whenever information or proper training is found to be lacking, the nuns are required to make recourse to the monks. For the teaching and guidance of male renunciants, however, the only recourse advocated in the Vinaya texts is to other more experienced and competent men. That only nuns are to be instructed by both men and women may not be an issue of gender but rather of merit—with personal qualities rather than male authority being the critical element. That is, during the time of the formation and compilation of canonical texts there is not yet a strong, broad tradition of experienced and properly trained women teachers who are able to give definitive teachings in Vinaya. But, in fact, as the Dhamma spreads, women as well as men teach lay people, and it may well be that Sangha instructional procedures in the monastic area lag some distance behind the reality of day-to-day Buddhist practice.

Life in the nunnery with regards to education is, for the most part, self-governing and self-correcting. Nuns can speak to other nuns concerning their bad habits,[32] they can admonish other nuns[33] and, if necessary, they can complain about senior nuns, Thullanandā being the most obvious example.[34] The individual nun's most important education, however, takes place under the preceptor who is central in the instruction of the female candidate from admission through the two years after full ordination, but is also important in guiding nuns at other seasonal times such as during the rain retreat.[35] The preceptor is responsible for sharing her living quarters *(vihāra)* with her probationer student during times of study and for making sure that when the student needs help, she is given it.[36] Moreover, during the period of her training prior to full ordination, the probationer is required to wait on her teacher and to attend to certain of her teacher's needs. As we saw, one of the most important formal roles of the preceptor is to train the probationer in how to answer the twenty-four questions that will be asked at the time of full ordination. And, since spiritual training continues beyond ordination up to the experience of *nibbāna*, preceptors play important ongoing roles in nuns' careers for at least the two years after the more formal roles have come to an end.

As argued elsewhere,[37] evidence abounds in early texts testifying to the full and complete experience of *nibbāna* by early Buddhist women as women. We add to this, then, the above observations that a great deal of independence is given to nuns and to the nuns' order for self-governance and for adjudicating the spiritual progress of their own community members. What is of importance now are the criteria for designating a female teacher of women, as well as the degree of parity between these criteria and those used for a male teacher.

Standards for Women Teachers

In sections on the ordination procedure for novice women, the Pali canon gives considerable attention to whether the preceptor and the proposer are not only adequate for the task, but represent the highest standard for personnel the nuns' order can offer. These discussions consistently focus on two criteria that must be present before the community can put its full trust in the chosen nun: she must be experienced *(vyattā)* and competent *(paṭibalā)*. While the use of these two standards is so frequent whenever nuns (and monks) are deliberating the choice of a leader to oversee the successful settlement of an issue pertaining to an individual member or to the community as a whole, they are in fact quite serious and meaningful as traditional standards.

The term *vyatta*, like the related Pāli term *viyatta* meaning "of settled opinion, learned, accomplished,"[38] is normally translated as "experienced, accomplished, learned, wise, prudent, clever."[39] Horner routinely takes *vyatta* as "experienced," focusing on the many practical precedents such a person might bring to a case to help shape the most appropriate and useful response—thus underscoring the Buddhist position that accommodation to the unique array of particular moments in human history provides the flexibility and adaptability so central to a consistent cleaving to the middle way. The term *paṭibala* is normally translated as "able, adequate, competent."[40] Here Horner takes *paṭibala* as "competent," drawing upon the community expectation that whomever is chosen to oversee and adjudicate a situation will not only have lived thoughtfully and sensibly through many related circumstances, but will be skilled in training and be of such high mental and temperamental fiber that trust from the community is unquestioned.

The terms *vyatta* and *paṭibala* are used consistently in the context of monastic activity for men. The normative standard for a monk who demonstrates proper Buddhist posture in his behavior is that he be modest, contented, conscientious, scrupulous, and desirous of training.[41] When it comes to monks taking leadership positions, however, experience and competence are the two single-most traits to be looked for above and beyond the normative five. Only experienced and competent monks can be preceptors and proposers.[42] Only experienced and competent monks can inform the Sangha of Uposatha, where it is to be held, or what the boundaries of the community are that determine eligibility. Only they can inform the Sangha of Pavāraṇā, or that it has fallen into a collective offense; only they can invite monks to tell what has been seen, heard, or suspected, or can inform it that monks are quarreling.[43] Only experienced and competent monks can inform the Sangha of decisions on allowable lodgings, of the accruing of the yearly donation of *kaṭhina* cloth and of its proper disposal, of the allocation of a room as a storeroom, and of the disposal of the effects of a monk who has died.[44] Only experienced and competent monks adjudicate the process of appointing a selector of robe material, an assigner of meals, an assigner of lodgings, an assigner of bowls, and an exhorter of nuns.[45] And only experienced and competent monks can inform the Sangha of misdeeds by members of its community and adjudicate a reasonable solution.[46]

These two qualifications for monastic leadership have clear equivalents in the running of early Buddhist nunneries. Although the examples are not as numerous for the women's communities as they are for the men's, it is well established that experience and competence are among the two critical criteria for any nun managing and overseeing institutional procedures. In this way, then, only experienced and competent nuns can: act as preceptors or ordain through messengership;[47] assign a companion to a nun who has to raise a child within its boundaries and inform the Sangha of this;[48] and tell the Sangha of an offense by one of its women members and adjudicate a reasonable solution.[49] In these and other ways, the experienced and competent nuns in a Sangha—for example, those exhibiting these two qualities above and beyond those of the well-postured nun who, like her male colleagues, is modest, contented, conscientious, scrupulous, and desirous of training—[50] speak forth as representatives of and guides to their community sisters on a host of important matters, dealing not only with the technicalities of appointment to office but also the rectification of spiritual careers.

Nowhere is leadership more important than in the education of members of the community, however, and we have already seen that women preceptors of the early canon have to be experienced and competent. From texts like the Therīgāthā we learn that there are other qualifications as well, and that in many ways women teachers of women have (and are required to have) full parity with their male counterparts. There is no doubt that women routinely teach other women. The Therīgāthā uses words like *dhamma* (doctrine), *vacana* (utterance), *sāsana* (teaching), *anusāsana* (advice), *ovāda* (exhortation), *anusiṭṭhi* (instruction), and *vinīta* (instructed)[51] to describe the extended work of women teachers and the instruments of transformation they use with their students. Many women hear other women's preaching and, as a consequence, go forth from the home into the homeless life, and many find their women teachers to be such brilliant speakers *(cittakathika)*[52] and of such great learning *(bahussuta)*[53] that they choose monastic training and lifelong guidance under them and, supported by their supervision, go on to experience *nibbāna*. The names of some of these early teachers have been preserved in the text, and women like Paṭācārā, Uppalavaṇṇā, Isidāsī, Jinadattā, and Sumedhā continue to be models for women educators in all traditions of Buddhism. Women teachers, like their male counterparts, are also known to specialize, and two in particular, Paṭācārā and Jinadattā, are famous as *vinayadharīs* "mistresses of the discipline."[54] The use of the term *ovāda* in Therīgāthā numbers 125 and 126, moreover, suggests that while monks normally deliver the instruction at Uposatha times to nuns, women teachers like Paṭācārā may also deliver it then, though in the Therīgāthā, *ovāda* appears to be one of many general glosses on teaching.

There is one standard for women teachers, however, that seems to be used exclusively in the case of nuns. In the Therīgāthā, a phrase appears twice to describe a nun approached by a woman for teaching: *yā me saddhāyikā ahu* "who is fit to be trusted by me," or better "who is worthy of my confidence."[55] This phrase does not appear in the Theragāthā, though other forms of *saddhā* do, and its use in the Therīgāthā is as an added criterion by which women can identify an empathic and qualified teacher for instruction. I have argued elsewhere[56] that although most translate *saddhā* as "faith," a better choice would be "confidence" or "trust," since these shift the emphasis away from a blind belief in the saving power of a religious tradition toward sure mental knowledge that certain religious views are true but have yet to be experienced by an individual as lived wisdom. Use of the term in the Theragāthā confirms this perspective. Many elders note that they go forth from the home into the homeless life out of *saddhā*,[57] and that this *saddhā* is *saddhā* in Buddhist doctrine that arises in them during the beginning of their Buddhist careers.[58] As maturation towards *nibbāna* takes place, *saddhā* or confidence that Buddhist doctrine is valid is replaced by experienced wisdom as personally realized truth.

This process is assumed as well in the Therīgāthā, where women go forth from the home into the homeless life out of *saddhā*[59] and move toward *nibbāna* as the experienced culmination of that confidence. While normally confidence or trust is placed in Buddhist doctrine, it is occasionally placed in a person—the person of the Tathāgata or Buddha.[60] That the Therīgāthā, seemingly uniquely, requires that confidence and trust be placed in certain women teachers (unnamed in the text) not only adds an additional qualification to instructional leadership in the nuns' order but also adds a qualification that specifically focuses on the evolution of individual personal experience rather than the technicalities of Sangha life—a singular dimension of the Therīgāthā's depiction of women's spiritual careers we have noted elsewhere.[61]

After the application of these three criteria, the *Cullavagga* makes clear that the appointment of a nun preceptor, who has either volunteered herself for the job or has been nominated for it by another, has to be agreed upon by the Sangha.[62] And we may infer from the text, then, that Sangha agreement to an appointment comes, as all agreements do, with being asked three times and three times remaining in silence.

We come, finally, to the last criterion at work in the Sangha related to leadership issues, that of seniority. The choice of a leader in certain cases is not always based on honor and veneration—in which questions of merit and personal qualifications are key—but often on seniority, that is, on the appointee's length of time as a renunciant (rather than absolute age). Once a monk (or nun) is ordained and becomes eligible for the title of *bhikkhu* (or *bhikkhunī*), he (or she) moves through three levels of status within the Sangha: *nava*, a newly ordained renunciant; *majjhima*, a mid-level renunciant; and *thera*, a senior or elder renunciant.[63] Among monks, elders are: first to be greeted;[64] honored by juniors touching their feet;[65] consulted about the settling of questions;[66] the first to be asked (and sometimes the only ones to be asked) to a meal at a householder's home;[67] and the first to assemble on Uposatha day.[68] They take the lead in certain behavioral customs related, for example, to the wearing of sandals,[69] in agreeing to the disposition of a dead monk's effects,[70] and in leading others in walking (and during that time are not to have another's outer robe touch them).[71] Moreover, they should be given adequate sitting and sleeping space by others,[72] and should be given preference in relieving their bodies in the morning (although this rule is amended early on in favor of bathroom time assigned on the basis of arrival time).[73] In an interesting ritual highlighting the importance of seniority, any monk who receives a new bowl outside regulation procedure has to forfeit that bowl to the Sangha, and the bowl is then passed from the senior-most monk to the junior-most, each choosing to keep the new bowl or the one currently in use and passing the rejected bowl on to the next in line who makes the same choice. The offending monk is last in line to make a choice.[74]

Again, these procedures to honor seniority are at work in the nuns' Sangha as well, though again the examples are not as numerous. Here, for instance, junior nuns have to honor the feet of senior nuns[75]—although at ordination time the new nun honors all the nuns, not just the senior ones. Again, nuns eating in the refectory are seated according to seniority up to a specified number of nuns, while the others sit as they come in.[76] An interesting twist on the seniority issue for nuns is found in the narrative of the first going forth of women. After having been given the eight chief rules by the Buddha by which nuns must practice their tradition, Mahāpajāpatī asks the Buddha through Ānanda if the first rule can be emended: instead of all nuns honoring all monks regardless of length of time as a renunciant, can the question of who is to honor whom be based on seniority rather than gender? The Buddha declines, citing current cultural standards among other sects.[77]

Now let us focus on the issue of seniority vis-à-vis merit. In assessing the examples where seniority guides monastic behavior, it is clear that most actions that confer honor on a senior member in no way signal that length of time spent in the renunciant life can be equated with spiritual achievement. In fact, it is clear at least twice in the case of seniority issues among monks that elders, qua elder, routinely lapse in the performance of a duty. While it is the prerogative of elders to settle questions, for example, it is not unheard of for elders to encounter displeasure from others at their decision.[78] Again, the Mahāvagga records that a certain elder who is to announce Uposatha continues to forget to do it even with several reprieves from the Buddha.[79] No such implied or stated criticism, however, appears in the text when the nun or monk in charge is in place because of experience and competence.

I am not arguing here the demerits of a seniority system in Buddhist communities, for there are often good and sound reasons for resorting to seniority in given situations, as it provides an easy, unambiguous structure for order when questions of etiquette and some monastic procedures and allocations are involved. I am arguing, however, that in the early Pali canon another system is at work for both nuns and monks that might be seen to be in conflict with seniority, but in fact is more attuned to the operating Buddhist posture of flexibility and accommodation. A system of allocating leadership, community responsibilities, and even places of honor based on merit rather than seniority would encourage a more vital and active group of women as well as one that more thoughtfully and carefully attends to what the Buddhist life is all about. Highlighting the original Pāli criteria of experience and competence, then, would be a significant direction for contemporary communities to move in today, preventing them from reverting to stagnant traditionalism. Moreover, a further recovery of that unique criterion of early nuns in choosing teachers "worthy of my confidence" would markedly underscore the high standards present in the Therīgāthā and the authentic Buddhist nature of its grounding in personal experience.

Men Teachers of Women

As Horner has noted, "women shared with men the privilege of hearing the dhamma preached to them in exactly similar terms," and both women and men are, because of this, expected to "be prepared to hand on the torch, and spread the teaching wide in the land."[80] This conclusion moves beyond the often negative views expressed in the Pali canon on women to focus instead on the substantial teaching efforts made on behalf of both genders and the general decision to spread teaching among and by them both.

Religious instruction of women moves beyond the substantial denigration that is expressed of them in canonical texts. This denigration appears in many forms but is of particular significance in prescribing the behavior of monks. Ānanda, the Buddha's faithful companion, for example, asks the Buddha just before the latter's death how Sangha members are to conduct themselves around women, and the

Buddha says to "keep wide awake."[81] Sight of a woman, and especially physical contact with one,[82] are thought to bring considerable distraction from the monastic life, and the Buddha is normally depicted as quite concerned when a monk ventures too far in this direction. When the monk Moliyaphagguna, for example, is asked by the Buddha if it is true that he is associating closely with the nuns, he answers "yes," and is then reminded by the Buddha that he has "gone forth" into the homeless life precisely to curtail such diversion and is given a discourse on stringent mental training.[83] And when the monk Udāyin privately teaches Dhamma to a housewife and her daughter-in-law in their home, other monks worry about the propriety of this and tell the Buddha, who rules that no monk should teach Dhamma to women.[84]

Establishing an office of an instructor of nuns under the supervision of an experienced and competent monk reflects, then, the general ambivalence of the canon towards women. Harmonizing judiciously with the prevailing view that, soteriologically, women can achieve enlightenment but that, sociologically, they need extra support structures, the office of the instructor of nuns is bolstered, first, by the delineation of strict requirements for the monk(s) who hold it.[85] Focusing on characteristics of moral fiber and expert training, the tradition adds requirements in elocution and personality,[86] realizing that the teaching cannot be effective unless the presenter can make a workable connection with his audience. The office then gains authority, second, by getting full agreement from the Sangha,[87] an act that, fitting neatly into the regular legal activity of Sangha business, thus institutionalizes a certain vision of Buddhist religious women. While legitimizing disparity between the genders (nuns do not give regular instruction to monks), the office nevertheless recognizes that nuns need to be guaranteed the instruction necessary to the quest for *nibbāna* already guaranteed fully to monks.

The final component to the office of instructor of nuns is that holders of the office take turns.[88] This means that we frequently find textual references to monks by name who happen at the time to find themselves agreed upon by the order to give instruction to the nuns. Monks are not always happy to do it, and are especially not always conscientious in their performance of these duties—we have already noted the haphazard instruction by Cūḷapanthaka, who, the compilers of the Vinaya say, overcomes the nuns' criticism of his instruction with a display of supernatural powers.[89] Other instructors of nuns include the great *iddhi* master Mahāmoggallāna.

The monk known as the "foremost among instructors of nuns"[90] is Nandaka who, contrary to his title, is one of those monks famously *unwilling* to take his turn in instructing the nuns. One narrative from the Majjhima Nikāya describes his unwillingness to instruct five hundred nuns; Ānanda's subsequent report of this unwillingness to the Buddha then elicits the latter's personal intervention, which obliges Nandaka to do his job. Nandaka's decision to instruct the nuns by putting them through a process of formulaic questions and answers[91] has been described by Horner as "a kind of catechism...a series of stereotyped questions...[given] as though he were bored by the whole proceedings."[92] After he finishes his instruction, Nandaka dismisses the nuns, who leave reluctantly as the Buddha watches. Aware that the instruction is adequate but not fulfilling, the Buddha asks Nandaka to give another instruction to the nuns the next day—and this he does with better results.

The most supportive and sympathetic male teacher of women is the monk Ānanda, the Buddha's cousin and personal companion for the last twenty-five years of his life. Ānanda is depicted in the canon very ambivalently and in such a way that one of his great characteristics—his powerful and attuning emotion—can be seen as either a great flaw or a great strength. Seeing it as a great strength, we can interpret Ānanda's famed empathic compassion, directed especially towards the downcast, the disenfranchised, and the forgotten, as an early model for the later posture of the Mahāyāna bodhisattva. Many narratives featuring Ānanda connect him to the instruction of women, and there is a consistent tendency to use him didactically. Once, for example, Ānanda gives a Dhamma talk to King Udena's concubines, who are so pleased that they give Ānanda five hundred robes. When Udena questions, critically, Ānanda's acceptance of so many robes, Ānanda persuades him of the expert use to be made of every little scrap, and Udena responds by giving him five hundred more.[93]

Ānanda's general reputation is that he is much beloved among the lay and among women, lay as well as renunciant. In this spirit, Ānanda is often depicted instructing women: he visits a settlement of nuns and talks on mindfulness;[94] he speaks to the nun Jaṭilāgāha on concentration;[95] and he goes to the dwelling of the lay woman Migasālā, whose questions to Ānanda cause her to be criticized by the Buddha when Ānanda passes them on.[96] Women often do extraordinary things to receive his teaching. In one case, Ānanda is called to the bedside of a "sick" nun who, seeing him coming, quickly lies down and covers her head. Not knowing the true state of things, Ānanda proceeds to give her a Dhamma talk on the frailties of the body. Halfway through the talk, the nun jumps out of bed, and confesses her deception, which is then acknowledged compassionately by Ānanda, who urges restraint on her in the future.[97] In another case, Ānanda asks Mahā Kassapa to accompany him to the nuns' quarters and, although Mahā Kassapa urges Ānanda to go alone several times, he eventually does go with him. There Mahā Kassapa gives a successful Dhamma talk but, after he leaves, a nun named Thullatissā complains loudly and vociferously as to why it isn't Ānanda giving the talk. "It is as if the needle-peddler were to deem he could sell a needle to the needlemaker."[98]

Mahā Kassapa overhears this remark, turns on Ānanda, and mockingly compares their spiritual prowess. Ānanda is cowed, Thullatissā falls away from religious life,[99] and hints remain of the possibility of affection between Ānanda and certain nuns. Despite disparaging narratives such as these and others, Ānanda remains in tradition, even more than the Buddha himself, the monk most concerned about the spiritual well-being of the nuns in particular, and women in general, and is the one who most successfully promotes it.

Women Teachers of Women

The range of personalities found in the array of men teachers of women is found as well in that of women teachers, and the human weaknesses and frailties that lead to straying from the Buddhist path are no less evident among early women teachers than among men. Human frailties acknowledged, they end up being part of the lessons learned by novice and ordained women as community life evolves, and it appears that education for Buddhist women is a combination of memorization, travel to learn from distant teachers, and service to teachers at their dwellings. The memorization of texts and the oral transmission of canonical materials seem to be at the heart of a nun's education with the focus, perhaps, less on doctrine than on discipline.[100] Although it is true that both Paṭācārā and Jinadattā are mistresses of the discipline, there is much evidence that women hear the Dhamma, convert because of it, and then convert others using it.

As hearers of the Dhamma, early women excel. The great lay matron Visākhā often hears talks on doctrine that are long and complicated.[101] Sumanā and Cundī, both princesses, engage the Buddha in talks on the alms giver and the merits of the Buddhist way, respectively.[102] During a Dhamma visit by the Buddha to her house, the lay woman Kāḍigodhā experiences the fruits of streamwinning *(sotāpatti-phala)*.[103] Visiting nuns at their lodgings, Ānanda instructs them on mindfulness.[104] The canon also contains stories of the instruction of "wayward" women: the monk Udāyin cannot preach to a Brahmin woman until she, at long last, realizes she must take off her sandals, unveil her head, and sit on a low seat,[105] and the woman who tries to seduce the monk Anuruddha during his visit to her is converted by his ensuing Dhamma talk.[106]

Lay women are also a powerful force in the conversion of others to the Buddhist path. Although it can be a husband who converts first and then turns his wife to the tradition,[107] it is often the other way around, with Visākhā's conversion of her father-in-law being the most famous example. The Brahmin woman Dhānañjānī, for instance, now a follower of the Buddha, is instrumental in converting the Brahmin youth Saṅgārava, as well as her husband, to the path.[108] And the anonymous mother who successfully urges her only daughter to become a nun uses four nuns as standards of the excellence of the monastic life: Khujjuttarā, Veḍukaṇṭakiyā, Khemā, and Uppalavaṇṇā.[109]

As with men teachers, not all women teachers of lay and renunciant women are first-rate. A nun student of the nun Uppalavaṇṇā, after studying discipline with her for seven years, remains confused and forgetful. She tells the nuns, who tell the monks, who tell the Buddha, who then allows nuns to be taught the discipline by monks.[110] Uppalavaṇṇā's reputation, however, does not suffer much as she is known in tradition as the nun most proficient in supernatural powers.[111] The nun Thullanandā, with whom fault is found on many issues in the Vinaya, is also a respected teacher of student nuns and she is known to be a repeater *(bhāṇikā)* of great learning *(bahussutā)*, wise *(visāradā)*, and skilled at giving Dhamma talks *(paṭṭhā dhammiṃ kathaṃ kātuṃ)*.[112] She is often caught out, however, doing reprehensible things such as exchanging one gift of medicine for another, asking a donor for a woolen garment, and bargaining with lay people inappropriately. Perhaps her greatest breach is based in her jealousy of another nun teacher, Bhaddā Kāpilānī, whom she makes extremely uncomfortable in the residence and whom she eventually throws out of the rain retreat quarters they share. Thullanandā is then punished accordingly.

Bhaddā Kāpilānī herself, like Thullanandā, is known as a teacher who is a repeater, learned, wise, skilled in giving Dhamma talks, and, additionally, esteemed for her eminence.[113] She is also attended upon respectfully by her nun pupil[114] and is known as the nun most able to remember past rebirths.[115] Khemā, the nun of greatest wisdom,[116] and Uppalavaṇṇā are mentioned as being the two nuns most worthy of emulation.[117] As a teacher, Khemā is known as being wise, experienced, intelligent, widely learned, a brilliant speaker, and of sharp wit, and her most famous pupil is King Pasenadi with whom she discusses the existence (or not) of the Tathāgata after death. The king's pleasure in her talk is compounded when he learns that the Buddha's talk on this topic would have been exactly the same.[118] The nun Dhammadinnā is known as the first among Dhamma teachers *(dhammakathikā)*,[119] and her most famous pupil is the great woman donor Visākhā to whom she gives a long sermon on basic Buddhist teachings—including desire, the nature of the body, the eightfold way, meditation, and perceptions.[120] Again, when the Buddha hears of Dhammadinnā's sermon, he tells Visākhā he would say exactly the same thing were he giving the sermon.

The greatest early teacher, however, is Paṭācārā, known to tradition as an expert in the Vinaya[121] and as the women's teacher par excellence. She is as persuasive a speaker as the Buddha, fully available at every instance to students who need her and especially attuned, because of her own painful experiences, to the particular problems of women. The Therīgāthā commentary provides a narrative of her life prior to becoming a nun that details the deaths of her husband, her two children, her parents, and her brother.[122] Her own dealing with these losses and grief becomes a model for younger women who, struggling with their own individual bereavements so beautifully characterized in the Therīgāthā, find in Paṭācārā an empathic and compassionate guide. Because of her ability to identify with the pain and sufferings of other women, Paṭācārā is exceedingly effective in bringing female novices into the Buddhist renunciant community and in guiding them on to enlightenment. These women specifically include the thirty anonymous nuns of the Therīgāthā, as well as Candā and Uttarā;[123] in addition there are commentarial lists of Paṭācārā's female students, one of which notes the standard hyperbolic number of five hundred. Because Paṭācārā's teaching springs from her own extraordinary experiences of loss, the focus of her sermons is often on impermanence and the need to accept it fully for attainment of the highest knowledge. Perfectly suited to the female audience of her time, Paṭācārā connects easily with the widespread experience of losing family and friends to death, which, in the Therīgāthā, brings so many women into Buddhism.

Final Thoughts

Many of the initiatives of early Buddhism are instigated by women. Among the lay, the new Buddhist role for women donors in the fifth century B.C.E. represents substantial change from the older Vedic model, allowing women at the household door to choose to give or not based on the worthiness of the renunciant, as well as to choose on their own to pursue a specific religious affiliation.[124] Two initiatives undertaken by early women donors stand out. In the first case, Visākhā decides she wants to give eight types of donations (foods and textiles) to the Sangha as lifetime gifts. Since this is a new and unusual request, she has to go to great lengths to persuade the Buddha of the value in each instance of this request. Because of her significance as a supporter and her vigorous argument, she is eventually successful.[125] In the second, the courtesan Ambapālī is foremost among other courtesans like Aḍḍhakāsī and Vimalā whose devotion to the Buddhist tradition is strong. Her own initiative to give substantially of her earnings to the Sangha helps to rework the image of courtesans in society, especially when the gift is as considerable as the mango grove she gives to the Sangha when the Buddha is on a teaching tour in Vesāli.[126]

Initiatives by lay Buddhist women are also evident in the ongoing shaping of monastic behavior. Women are prominent among the groups of people who complain about issues of aberrant dress (such as fancy robe ties), bodily ornamentation (such as earrings or beards), and improper conduct (such as lust-driven behavior). With their complaints to the Buddha, women donors are able to help create a renunciant posture that suits certain ideals prevalent among the non-renunciant populace. (No change in or addition to the rules is made by the Buddha, however, unless it supports in principle the perspectives of the middle way.) Interesting here is the early criticism of nuns for the robe decorations they wear and the body massages they give; the complaint, probably made by lay women donors themselves, is that they are acting like women householders who enjoy the pleasures of senses.[127]

Initiatives by early Buddhist nuns are equally significant. Most obvious is the initiative led by Mahāpajāpatī and a group of Sakyan women to go forth from the home into the homeless life in the first place. The struggle is monumental physically and emotionally, but is decidedly a woman's struggle (with a little help from Ānanda), for neither the Buddha nor any other monk (even Ānanda) would have initiated the nuns' order on his own. Second are the initiatives—some by "the people," some by monks, but many by nuns—to further explicate the application of the eight chief rules to be followed by the nuns. For example, Mahāpajāpatī gets the rules of training to be presided over only by nuns; nuns instigate the recitation of the Pāṭimokkha for the nuns only by the nuns; nuns instigate their practice of the confession of offenses; and nuns are responsible for the fact that only nuns can adjudicate legal acts in the Sangha for themselves.[128] These changes move the nuns' order, as we note above, closer to full self-governance and provide for them a greater measure of independence than they have with the original formulation of the eight chief rules. Finally, nuns urge that teaching be of the highest quality when one particular instructor of nuns, Cūḷapanthaka, does not do his job well. Even though the narrative presents the complaining nuns as satisfied by Cūḷapanthaka's display of supernatural powers as recompense for a less than stellar Dhamma talk,[129] it is a significant canonical precedent for female activism within Buddhist practice that they do complain hoping for a higher standard of instruction, and get some results even though they are not the most desirable.

The initiatives by early Buddhist women are important not only because they are precedent-setting for later Buddhist women, regardless of sectarian tradition, but also because they set the stage for two Sangha issues: institutional parity with monks, and the elevation of standards of merit over those of seniority within the nuns' order itself. Movement toward parity with monks in the instructional arena is evident from the Pali canon involving at least three issues. First, while the monks' order must ordain all women into full nunhood, that act is a pro forma one, as all the real work of instruction and final questioning takes place on the nuns' side. Second, while instruction at the biweekly Uposatha is given by the monks to the nuns, there is ample additional evidence that much instruction of the nuns is given by the nuns themselves—who are required to seek help from the monks only if initial coaching is needed. In fact, the evidence of the Therīgāthā is that if nuns are not receiving instruction from the Buddha himself, they are receiving it from other highly qualified nuns, rather than from monks. Third, a cursory examination of some of the early teachers of nuns, male and female, reveals that teachers of each gender show frailties and weaknesses, (for example, Cūḷapanthaka and Thullanandā), as well as learning and compassion (for example, Ānanda and Paṭācārā). While there is not strict canonical precedence, I argue that the canonical movement toward self-governance and institutional independence already evidenced in early times, coupled with the three issues noted above, may lead in the contemporary setting to the full instruction of nuns by nuns alone. This is possible, provided that substantial measures can be taken for the broad education of nuns in religious and secular topics, which would result in highly qualified women willing to bring Buddhist nuns into the complex international setting of today while at the same time preserving the essentials of traditional Buddhist doctrine and practice.

Finally, the Sanghas of both genders have two systems by which rank and honor are given: one based on seniority, and the other on merit. The seniority system (of three levels—newly ordained, middle ranking, and elder) functions to honor those nuns who have been renunciants for the longest time, and focuses primarily on an etiquette that expresses this honor and provides greater comfort and ease in such things as eating, sitting, and sleeping. The other system, that of merit, parallels, for the most part, the system of monks, and in it nuns as a group agree on an experienced and competent nun to preside over important decisions and transactions and to facilitate the resolution of problems and questions. These are clearly the (temporary) offices of rank that have the greatest impact on Sangha life, and it is fortunately significant that the founders of Buddhism highlight merit as considerably more important than seniority in allocating positions of rank to those who would oversee key business in the ongoing life of the Sangha. While both Sanghas routinely refer to meritorious leadership being exercised by those who are "experienced" and "competent," there is an added criterion among nuns, evident in the Therīgāthā, which highlights even more the individual qualities of personal character and spiritual achievement at the same time as it focuses on the effectiveness of personal connection: *yā me saddhāyikā ahu.* To be able to be led and taught by a nun "who is worthy of my confidence" is a profound testament not only of the high quality of women teachers already present in early Buddhist tradition, but also of a young nun's opportunity personally to choose the most trusted teacher for her.

Notes

1. The commonly used term for Tibetan nuns is *ani* in central Tibet (*jomo* is used in western Tibet, Ladakh, and Amdo, while *gema* is used in northeastern Kham).

Because there is some discrepancy about the exact designation of *ani*—whether it refers to "a woman who has taken the novice ordination" only or can refer as well to "unordained women dressing and living like the ordained ones"—and because *ani* designating "aunt" may carry impolite connotations, the general term "nun" will be used here. See Havnevik, p. 44–46.

2. Therīgāthā (hereafter referred to as Therī), no. 61.
3. Vinaya (hereafter referred to as Vin) 3.208; 4.175 (references given to volume and page in Pali texts). See also Vin 2.270.
4. See Findly in *The Nuns' Circle,* p. 3. The fourth of the eight rules of the Mahāsāṅghika-Bhikṣuṇī-Vinaya states explicitly that nuns are not to receive any donations until after monks have been offered. If nuns are offered first, they automatically ask that the donation go first to monks. Hirakawa, pp. 83–85.
5. See Findly, "Women and the *arahant* Issue."
6. Vin 2.270–71; 4.303.
7. Vin 4.227–30.
8. Vin 4.295.
9. See Findly, "Women and the Practice of Giving."
10. See Findly, "Ānanda's Case for Women."
11. Vin 2.255; 4.52–53.
12. Vin 4.51.
13. Aṅguttara Nikāya (AN) 4.279–80.
14. See Vin 2.5, 261–65; Vin 4.49–53. For a discussion see Horner, *Women,* pp. 126–28.
15. Vin 4.50.
16. Vin 4.315.
17. Vin 4.54–55.
18. Horner, *Women,* p. 133.
19. Vin 2.259–60: *anujānāmi... bhikkhunīhi bhikkhunīnaṃ pāṭimokkhaṃ uddisitabban ti.*
20. Vin 2.258: *yathā bhikkhū sikkhanti tathā tesu sikkhāpadesu sikkhathā 'ti.*
21. Vin 2.260: *anujānāmi...bhikkhunīhi bhikkhunīnaṃ āpattiṃ paṭiggahetun ti.*
22. Vin 2.260: *anujānāmi...bhikkhunīhi bhikkhunīnaṃ kammaṃ kātun ti.*
23. Horner, *Women,* p. 137.
24. The definition of a *bhikkhunī* is a woman who has been fully ordained by both Sanghas. See Vin 3.206, 209, 235, etc.
25. Vin 4.318–20.
26. The Mahāsāṅghika text deals at length with a woman's *sikkhamānā* stage and, while it does not differ substantially from the Pali text, it does make more specific the ongoing role of the preceptor from the beginning of renunciation well into the lives women have as *bhikkhunīs.* See Hirakawa, pp. 35–37.
27. Vin 2.272; Vin 1.44–55.
28. Vin 2.271–73; Vin 1.71–79.
29. Vin 1.56; see Vin 2.272–73; Vin 1.94–95. The more detailed Mahāsāṅghika text identifies fully the officials taking part in the ordination. Since the ordination is a legal act (karma) of the Sangha, the proceedings are conducted by a karma master nun *(karma-*

kāraka-bhikṣuṇī). The preceptor is present as sponsor of and advocate for the candidate and is the one who, at ordination, provides the requisite five robes and bowl for the new nun; the preceptor also has to be legally reinstated, agreeing at this time to take on the new nun as her disciple. Of the other officials present, one of the most important is the *rahonuśāsanācāryā/rahonuśāsaka bhikṣuṇī,* or the instructor nun who is responsible for finding out if the candidate fulfills all the conditions necessary for receiving ordination (in a session conducted by the instructor nun in an open and quiet place). Hence this instructor is often called the one who imparts the esoteric teaching. This is a departure from the Pali tradition where the questions are asked in front of the whole Sangha.

The Mahāsāṅghika ordination takes place within a small enclosure, which "might be either inside or outside of the boundaries of the uposatha-sīmā" (*sīmā* means "boundary"). The boundary for ordination is called "the precepts platform or upasampadā-sīmā-maṇḍala" (Hirakawa, pp. 34–35), and in it ten nuns, including the preceptor, perform the ordination for the candidate with the whole nuns' order in attendance. Hirakawa, pp. 34–35, 50–62. The Mūlasarvāstivāda text, which acts as the Vinaya for the Tibetan Buddhist tradition, describes both the ordination of "going forth" and full ordination and includes the ritual whereby the candidate first chooses a preceptor at the time of admission. See Banerjee, pp. 107–25.

30. Vin 2.271–74. For the role of the preceptors and other teachers *(ācāryas)* in the final stages of the Mahāsāṅghika ordination, see Hirakawa, pp. 62–76 and, for the Mūlasarvāstivāda tradition, see Banerjee, pp. 124–47.
31. Horner, *Women,* pp. 143–44.
32. Vin 4.239–40.
33. Vin 4.240–42.
34. Vin 4.249–50.
35. Vin 2.272; 3.35.
36. Vin 4.324–25.
37. Findly, "Women and the *arahant* Issue."
38. T.W. Rhys Davids and Stede, pp. 632–33.
39. T.W. Rhys Davids and Stede, p. 653.
40. T.W. Rhys Davids and Stede, p. 397.
41. Vin 1.44, etc.
42. Vin 1.56, 57, 60, 62, 80, 83, 94, 95.
43. Vin 1.102, 107, 109, 110, 127, 159, 162, 168, 169.
44. Vin 1.239, 254, 284, 304.
45. Vin 1.283; Vin 2.75, 167; Vin 3.246–47; Vin 4.50.
46. Vin 2.18; Vin 3.238, 246; Vin 4.136.
47. Vin 2.272, 273, 277.
48. Vin 2.279.
49. Vin 4.219, 236, 244, 294.
50. Vin 4.213.
51. Therī. nos. 103, 119, 126, 170, 172, 178, 211, 363, 404, 449.

52. Therī. no. 449.
53. Therī. nos. 427, 449.
54. Therī. nos. 427.
55. Therī. nos. 43, 69.
56. Findly, "Ānanda's Hindrance."
57. Theragāthā (Thera.) nos. 46, 59, 195, 249, 250, 251, 789.
58. Thera. nos. 311, 509, 745, 1019, 1090, 1254.
59. Therī. nos. 90, 92, 341, 363.
60. Thera. no. 507; Therī. no. 286.
61. Findly, "Women and the *arahant* Issue."
62. Vin 2.272.
63. Dīgha Nikāya (DN) 3.123–24.
64. Vin 1.339; Vin 2.16.
65. Vin 3.199, 238, 243.
66. Vin 2.98.
67. Vin 2.16.
68. Vin 1.108.
69. Vin 1.187.
70. Vin 1.304.
71. Vin 2.220.
72. Vin 2.224; Vin 4.42–43.
73. Vin 2.221.
74. Vin 3.246–48.
75. Vin 4.244, 330.
76. Vin 2.274.
77. Vin 2.257–58.
78. Vin 2.98.
79. Vin 1.117.
80. Horner, *Women*, p. 281.
81. DN 2.141.
82. See Vin 3.119–27.
83. *bhikkhunīhi saddhiṃ ativelaṃ saṃsaṭṭho viharasi.* Majjhima Nikāya (MN) 1.123.
84. Vin 4.20–23.
85. See Vin 4.51.
86. AN 4.279–80.
87. Vin 2.263–65; Vin 4.49–53.
88. MN 3.270–77.
89. Vin 4.54–55.
90. *bhikkhun' ovādakānaṃ.* AN 1.25.
91. MN 3.270–77.
92. Horner, *Women*, p. 278.
93. Vin 2.290–92.
94. Saṃyutta Nikāya (SN) 5.154–58.

95. AN 4.426–28.
96. AN 5.137–44.
97. AN 2.144–46.
98. C.A.F. Rhys Davids, *Kindred Sayings* 2.145.
99. SN 2.214–15.
100. Horner, *Women*, pp. 238–39, 247.
101. AN 1.205–15.
102. AN 3.32–36.
103. SN 5.396–97.
104. SN 5.154–55.
105. SN 4.121–24; see AN 2.144–46.
106. Vin 4.17–20.
107. Vin 1.242–43; see Vin 1.15–20.
108. MN 2.209–13; SN 1.160–61.
109. SN 2.236.
110. Vin 2.261.
111. AN 1.25.
112. Vin 4.239, 254, 255, 256, 290, 292.
113. Vin 4.290. *bhikkhunī bahussutā hoti bhāṇikā visāradā paṭṭhā dhammakathaṃ kātuṃ.*
114. Vin 4.275–76.
115. AN 1.25.
116. AN 1.25.
117. SN 2.236; AN 1.88; AN 2.164.
118. SN 4.374–80.
119. AN 1.25.
120. MN 1.299–305.
121. AN 1.25; TA 560.
122. PD 108–17.
123. Therī. nos. 117–21, 125–26, 178.
124. See Findly, "Women and the Practice of Giving."
125. Vin 1.291–94.
126. Vin 1.231–33.
127. Vin 2.266–67.
128. Vin 2.258–61.
129. Vin 4.54–55.

ACHAAN RANJUAN:
A Thai Lay Woman as Master Teacher

Achaan Ranjuan is a Thai woman who became a nun late in life but mastered meditation very quickly. She was encouraged to teach early on by her own teacher, Venerable Buddhadāsa. When I met her, she was teaching a retreat for a hundred people but gave me all her time as if she had nothing else to do. Her eyes radiate an amused kindness, and she seems like the epitome of compassion and attentiveness. Her status is ambiguous: she has a shaved head and wears black and white instead of all-white as Thai "nuns" do. Though she says she is more like a lay woman, she seemed to me more like a nun.

FIFTEEN YEARS AGO I went to the northeastern part of Thailand for a weekend. Driving past a village, my friend told me that nearby there was a very interesting forest monastery. I was keen to visit monasteries, so we went. The road was very bad and muddy, so it took us a long time to reach the monastery, and we had to stay overnight. The abbot was kind, gentle, and very old. That night he gave a Dhamma talk, and listening to him, I woke up. I learned that a good Buddhist has to practice to understand the nature of mind, especially the deluded mind. I started to meditate to calm the mind. Then I contemplated the three common characteristics of impermanence, suffering, and not-self.

For a time I was still teaching library science in the university. After five years of meditating while working, I became convinced that meditation was the path I should take. Everything I should have done, I had done already. I had fulfilled my function and duty as a citizen of this society. I felt free, and decided to quit everything to study and practice under Achaan Chah. He was my first master, but I did not study under him very long. During my first summer retreat, Achaan Chah became sick and paralyzed, and he could not teach anymore. It was eleven years ago, and at that time I felt very young on the path, so I decided to find a new master. Some friends took me to Wat Suan Mok to meet Venerable Buddhadāsa. I thought I would try his method for a while. It was quite different, and I wanted to check if it worked for me or not. It worked, and I stayed. I liked its practical slant.

Venerable Buddhadāsa emphasized that all of us should have fun in work. We needed to practice Dhamma while working. It was important to be aware all the time. We were to develop concentration and wisdom in action instead of just sitting quietly with closed eyes. He insisted that we should practice right in the midst of difficulties. Venerable Buddhadāsa encouraged me to teach. The first year he left me alone to be by myself. When I had some questions, I would go to him, and he was very willing to explain anything. Most of the time I would just study and meditate. After a year he sent a group of students, teachers, and lay people to me to be taught Dhamma. In this first request he just wrote that I should tell them what I knew. I complained to him that I did not know much, but he suggested that I could tell people just what I knew, no more than that.

I am an *upāsikā* [lay woman]. I have taken eight precepts like the *mae chis*. The only difference is the black skirt that I wear with the white top. Why don't I ordain as a *mae chi*? When I was still working and began to be interested in the Dhamma, I went to a woman teacher who was blind due to cataracts, and she dressed like this. She was not a nun formally, but her behavior, the way she practiced, was the same as a good nun. I decided that if I were to take up this kind of life, I would dress like her. I do not care for the form or the uniform. To ordain in the heart is what is important. This is convenient. I just shave my head and wear black and white (*mae chis* wear all white).

I do not have any special feeling about the position of nuns in Thailand. Many Westerners and Thai women reporters ask me about this. When we come to this life, we want to cultivate the mind to lessen greed, anger, and delusion. If we ask for this or that, we are leaning towards increasing these delusions. This is not the aim of Dhamma practice. If everybody tried to cultivate mindfulness and relinquish all defilements, there would be no problems. We could live together harmoniously. People who ask about this generally do not feel happy about my answer.

It might be true in some ways that it is more difficult for a Thai woman than a man, financially and educationally, to be a monastic. The problem might originate in the way of teaching Dhamma and Buddhism in this country. If the essence of Buddhism were taught directly, there would be no problems for nuns or monks, no need to feel superior or inferior. Some women might think they have less opportunity because they expect something out of leading the monastic life, but if they come without expectation and just learn to meditate, I do not think there is any problem at all.

In Achaan Chah's monastery there are more than sixty nuns. Not all of them are educated, and he tried to help them because he had a lot of sympathy for those who have fewer opportunities in society. His idea was for them to stay in a monastery to learn to meditate and to learn to help themselves by developing a pure heart and benefiting others.

For me, to be an *upāsikā* means to be an ordained person. I do not see any difference between being an *upāsikā* or a nun. To be ordained helps me to be aware. Away from the place I call home, away from the people whom I call relatives, away from work or the worldly life, I have more free time to practice and study the Dharma.

Compiled by Martine Batchelor

PATTERNS OF RENUNCIATION:
The Changing World of Burmese Nuns

HIROKO KAWANAMI

BURMESE NUNS are the most numerous among nuns in the Theravāda Buddhist world.[1] Although they have not been ordained and their official religious status remains ambiguous, they have initiated many changes in their own lives and produced a remarkable network of scholarly nuns in the last hundred years. Now they pride themselves on their high standards of Buddhist learning, and attract student nuns from many countries abroad. In this chapter I explore how the improvements in their religious standing were brought about by their single-minded determination and yearning for spiritual progress. It is important to acknowledge that their most urgent task is not to seek a religious status equal to the monks, but to enhance the standards of their religious education, maintain their influence in the monastic community, and achieve social recognition and respect. I also examine the significance of renunciation for Buddhist women whose patterns may be varied, but who all aspire to improve their present spiritual position.

Virgin Nuns and the Elevation of Female Scholarship in Myanmar

In general, Buddhist nuns in Myanmar are classified into two categories according to their previous marital status. The first category comprises those who have become nuns while young and unmarried and, thus, sexually inexperienced. They are trained to become professional nuns by vocation. The other comprises those who were previously married or widowed, or who have left their homes to become nuns through changes of lifestyle. The former are referred to as *ngebyu*, meaning "ones who are young and pure," and the latter are known as *tàwdwet*, "ones who have left for the forest." *Ngebyu* monks and nuns are generally regarded as spiritually more accomplished than *tàwdwet* renunciants and occupy more significant positions in the monastic hierarchy. Having joined the order earlier in their lifetime than *tàwdwet* nuns, virgin nuns are more educated in the Buddhist scriptures and hence command greater respect from the lay congregation. In fact, almost all monk scholars and nun teachers and those who have influential positions in official religious committees are in the former category. The primary mark of the *tàwdwet* nuns is that they spend much of their time in meditation.

In Burmese society today, becoming a nun is increasingly seen as an opportunity for village girls to acquire an education and a religious career. In this context, the importance of virginity in the training of the nuns has assumed renewed significance because of the purity and single-minded commitment it symbolizes. Many nunnery schools with good reputations and high educational standards require virginity as one condition for admission. However, meditation centers, which are occupied by older nuns as well as by the laity who come for weekend retreats, are not concerned about such criteria. Here we observe the difference in status between those who study (for whom virginity means additional spiritual value) and those who meditate.

As an indication of this, scholarly nuns generally receive far more donations and are well looked after by their lay donors, compared to the meditating nuns, who generally suffer from a lack of patronage. As a result, a wide gap has developed between the standing of the two groups in the monastic community. This trend was set in the post-war period when nuns increasingly started to show their aptitude in Buddhist education, passing the state exams with high marks and winning the admiration of the lay society. Ninety percent of these cases were virgin nuns, the fact of which helped gradually to replace the prevalent negative images of nuns.

As King states, "traditionally, most religions have excluded women from advanced learning and teaching."[2] In the recent history of Buddhist nuns, however, religious education has become significantly more important as nuns hope to enhance their social and religious status. To confirm this, the data I collected in the last decade in Myanmar suggest there is a strong correlation between the tendency for younger girls (between the age of twelve and sixteen) to aspire to become nuns and the rising standards of the nuns' education. After completing the compulsory education offered in state schools, many young girls perceive nunhood as a valid and appealing option, as a meaningful career that will provide them with an alternative to a life of reproduction and domesticity.

One such woman is Daw Malayi (1880–1984), who was born in Nyaundon district in Lower Myanmar into a wealthy and religious family. Her family grew wealthy through buying paddy fields and investing in the rice, oil, and salt trades, and was very religious—spending the annual Buddhist Lent taking the precepts, abstaining from business transactions, and going on pilgrimages.

From an early age, Daw Malayi was interested in the life story of the Buddha and wanted to learn his teachings. She was also attracted to the idea of becoming a nun, but her father discouraged her by saying that nuns were so poor that they had nothing to eat but rice and salt. By the time she reached the fourth standard in school at the age of twelve, Daw Malayi's family had accumulated a fair amount of wealth, and her father had became increasingly active as a patron to the monks. Being a sensitive teenager, she often thought about death and hell, and became more and more convinced that the only future for her lay in becoming a nun. Hearing this, her family objected firmly by telling her that a girl from a good family did not lead the life of "a beggar." Daw Malayi remained adamant and went to study Buddhist philosophy under a learned monk who was visiting the village. During this time, she became friendly with the nuns who accompanied him; she even went to stay with them for many nights to show her parents how strongly she felt. In spite of all kinds of threat and cajolery by her family and relatives, Daw Malayi did not falter in her determination. When a relative of theirs who was a monk told her parents that it was bad kamma for them to keep obstructing their daughter from acquiring spiritual merit, they finally relented and gave her their consent. She became a nun at the age of seventeen, accompanied by her younger sister.

Obstacles remained for Daw Malayi, however, even after becoming a nun. One of her major motives in becoming a nun was to study the Buddhist scriptures, but there were few monks at that time who were open-minded enough to give tuition to the nuns. She searched more widely for sympathetic monks, and finally found a learned ex-monk who was willing to help. Htayanga Hsaya-gyì had been a respected scholar monk, but he had disrobed due to political problems following the deposal of King Thibaw in 1885. Daw Malayi and her sister went to live temporarily in a remote village where the former monk had settled to receive his tuition. When they set up their own nunnery, they invited him to come and stay in Sagaing. He taught them, and other nuns, and many of these nuns later went on to become important nun teachers. Due to his contribution, this former monk later came to be known as "the father of nuns' education." Daw Malayi's nunnery, Thameikdàw Gyaùng, was officially founded in 1911. She imposed discipline and diligence on her students. Many students from her nunnery sat for the government Buddhist exams and passed with distinction, increasing the reputation of her nunnery. Her branch nunneries have spread all over the country, playing a central role in nuns' education in Myanmar.

Another example of the academically minded nun is the celebrated Daw Damásari (1878–1971). She was born into a middle-class merchant's family in Mandalay, Upper Myanmar, in the late nineteenth century. After being educated up to the compulsory fourth standard, she entered the family trade and became trained as a silk merchant. She was "fair, had a good figure, and became one of the most popular vendor maids among the silk stalls at Mandalay Zeigyo market at that time."[3]

Her family was very religious and used to visit the monastery regularly, so Daw

Damásari acquired a basic understanding of Buddhism quite early in her childhood. She learned the prayers, observed abstinence on holy days, and went to listen to monks' sermons. She was comfortably well-off, but subsequently became bored with her mundane business dealings. She dreamed of becoming a nun, but when she told her family about her decision, everyone was appalled. Her brother said he would rather die than be referred to as a brother of a Buddhist nun.[4] When she was sixteen, Daw Damásari's desire became so strong that she could bear it no longer. So, she took drastic measures: she cut off her hair and ran away from home with a close friend. The two went to hide in a nunnery in Mingun where her friend's mother-in-law lived as a nun. She was found by her angry parents, but refused to go home. The nunnery, however, refused to grant her permission to stay as it had received threats from her angry father, who declared that he would take whomever made his daughter a nun to court.[5] It took another year of negotiation between her parents and the nunnery before consent was given. Thus, when she became seventeen, Daw Damásari's parents, realizing how firm her decision was, finally consented, and she officially became initiated as a nun in Mingun. Later, she became one of the most learned nun-scholars of the twentieth century, being highly respected for her standards of scholarship even by the senior monks.

This respect was not always evident, however, for Daw Damásari was once asked by the Rice Distribution Association in Mandalay to conduct a ceremony. When this was announced to the community, there was an uproar of opposition. The disapproval did not come from the learned monks with whom she closely associated, however, but mostly from the lay devotees and ordinary monks. They disapproved of her role at the ceremony on the grounds, first, that it would not be acceptable to place a nun higher than the monks, who would be sitting on the floor, and second, that it would not be acceptable to seat a woman on the golden seat, which was traditionally reserved for kings and principal monks, and third, that a woman sitting on the golden seat would anger the ancestral spirits. Eventually, however, Daw Damásari decided not to cause any offense and declined their offer.

Motives for Becoming a Nun in Myanmar

It may generally be assumed that nuns are women from poor and disadvantaged backgrounds; however, Burmese nuns traditionally come from families of all walks of life. In practice, nuns have to rely on the material support of their families early on in their career since it is difficult to find a sufficient number of lay donors to support them, and most poor families simply cannot afford to sustain a non-productive member. On the other hand, Burmese parents tend to discourage their daughters from becoming nuns since, compared to a monk who has a fair chance of moving upwards on the social scale, joining the nunnery does not guarantee a nun security or prestige. It is more likely that she will confront hardship and discrimination in society; within the nunnery, moreover, she will find it harder to succeed in the hierarchy of the monastic institution itself unless she has the determination and commitment to persevere. When asked why they have become Buddhist nuns, women monastics usually have a standard answer: "In order to accumulate spiritual merit." This may be an appropriate religious answer, but it allows them to disguise the real motives, which may be private and delicate in nature.

The most common motivations for women becoming nuns are the experiences of suffering preached about by Buddhism: ill health, old age, and the death of close family members. Grief and frustration over social or economic misfortune can also bring the realization of *dukkha* "suffering" and can, likewise, be a direct or indirect incentive to renunciation. A few women I interviewed said that they became nuns in order to avoid being forced into an arranged marriage by their parents. The notion of marriage elicits strong reactions among Burmese women, who perceive it as an obligatory undertaking requiring much mental and physical strength. In a country where infant mortality is high and contraceptives expensive, marriage for women may imply frequent pregnancies, painful childbirth, infant deaths, and the burden of raising many children. They also talk about philandering husbands, bad relationships with mothers-in-law, exhaustion, illnesses, and becoming confined to the family arena with no time for their own spiritual development. Thus, bolstered by Buddhist ideology, which teaches that reproduction is the beginning of *saṃsāra* and the perpetuation of suffering on into the next generation, fear of marriage has become a strong underlying motive for many teenage girls.

One nun I interviewed, Daw P. (b. 1952), said she had been scared of getting married from a very young age, as she had heard many horrible stories about it. She heard that husbands beat their wives, drink, and are not faithful. She also didn't want to become pregnant because she had seen how terribly painful childbirth was when she held her sister's knees in the middle of a difficult labor at home. She was so shaken to see her sister screaming out in pain that she made up her mind on the spot to become a nun. She had also seen her uncle cry out in agony due to kidney stones. This was enough to confirm her decision. When she was seventeen, her father died, so it was finally possible for her to leave home and become a nun.

In recent years, an increasing number of nuns are joining the order for a reason that was relatively unknown in the past, that is, to join their relatives already established in the Buddhist community. This tendency has become more prevalent in the last twenty years as government restrictions and regulations governing entrance into the monastic community have become increasingly rigid in order to keep insurgents and anti-government elements out. It is easier for those who already have contacts in the monastic community to obtain relevant documents and reference letters required for entry. Moreover, due to the unstable political situation in recent years, people are generally more wary of accepting complete strangers. More than a quarter of those who recently entered monastic communities may have used the reason of joining their kin to enter, though prior to the 1980s this proportion was much smaller.

Another tendency, also more popular in the last twenty years, is the rising number of girls who enter the nunnery temporarily. They spend a certain amount of time in the nunnery as designated by their vows, and then go back to secular life after fulfilling their promise. This trend is, interestingly, an urban phenomenon that was uncommon in the past. Interviews with temporary nuns indicate that some of them have taken the precepts for a specific reason, for example, to recover from illness, to pass exams, to regain their husbands from a mistress, or to recover from financial problems. Others have become temporary nuns to accumulate spiritual merit or to learn the Buddhist prayers, or simply because "my friends have done it too." Some girls become temporary nuns not only for their own sake but also to accumulate merit on behalf of their parents. Furthermore, many temporary nuns, who are usually girls from middle-class educated families, have spoken about their admiration for professional nuns who do well in the Buddhist exams. Learned nuns in their colorful pink robes seem to have caught the imagination of the urban population, providing the younger generation of girls with a new type of role model. This, in itself, indicates the changing position of Buddhist nuns in Burmese society today.

Old Women, Widows, and Social Prejudice

It was more common in the past for older women to become nuns in Myanmar. These were women who had left their domestic roles as wives and mothers in order to spend their remaining lives in solitude and quiet retrospection. Since a woman's management of the household and any spiritual development she might aspire to were considered to be incompatible, leaving home implied her actual retirement from domestic duties and the delegation of any authority she had to her daughter or daughter-in-law.

We also need to note that traditional renunciation for women was not always based on personal aspiration and private faith. Unattached women such as virgins and widows were a social liability and, in most cases, it was family pressure that encouraged a young widow to shave off her hair and retire into an ascetic life lest she attract men and bring disgrace upon a family's honor. It may have been that, traditionally, widows found solace as nuns, for otherwise their status was practically one of "social death." This is very different from the present-day situation of

Burmese nuns, who are actively involved in society and are becoming more and more indispensable in the monastic community.

A well-known Burmese proverb states, "Buddhist nuns are those women whose sons are dead, who are widowed, bankrupt, in debt, and broken-hearted." These stereotypes depict women who have left their ordinary, secular roles as those who are either disgraced or have some reproachable quality. Careful observation of social reality, nevertheless, shows that such images are not based on current facts, and do not coincide with the actual life of contemporary nuns. Furthermore, taking sanctuary as a nun does not necessarily guarantee a woman a quiet retreat where she can escape her problems or retire peacefully in old age. Once a woman becomes a nun, the expectations placed upon her and the actual roles she is required to play in the monastic community are demanding and strenuous. So, unless she considers it a full-time commitment, it is difficult to live as a nun. Moreover, since there is no stigma attached to those who leave the order, a nun can leave at any time and go back to her previous life. In most instances, those who have become a nun in order to escape their problems do not stay for more than a few months at most. Therefore, as the social and religious positions of nuns rise in contemporary times, nunhood has become equated less and less with lonely widowhood and dysfunctionality, and more and more with fulfilling personal potentials and making active contributions to society.

Daw Z., in her later forties, and her thirty-year-old daughter Ma K. are two nuns who exemplify the distinction between generationally different monastic adepts. The mother, Daw Z., became a nun when she was twenty-seven years old, taking her young daughter with her after having confronted the hardships and miseries of a householder life. She had been very religious, and became a nun in a Buddhist community near the ancient capital of Mandalay. Daw Z. first lived with an old nun friend who took her and her young daughter into her home. However, Daw Z. was ambitious for the future of her daughter and wanted her to receive a good education in Buddhist scriptures. In order to do this, she affiliated her daughter with a nunnery in Rangoon, famous for its teachers and the academic results of its students in the state Buddhist exams. Entry into the school at this nunnery was strictly limited to virgins, which permitted only her daughter to join. Wanting the best for her daughter, the mother nun sent her daughter to this nunnery school, but she was not able to continue to live with her. However, the daughter's health was often poor, and the mother became extremely concerned. She pleaded with the head nun of the nunnery school to allow her to stay and look after her daughter until she regained health. Although this was against regulations, the mother was allowed to stay with her daughter, since Ma K. was a very bright student and the teachers didn't want to lose her.

The mother nun then took on various responsibilities around the complex, helping to run the nunnery administration and look after the medical dispensary. She didn't neglect her studies, however, and having memorized Buddhist scriptures at night while her daughter slept, she successfully sat for the state exams. In spite of the rules, Daw Z. stayed at the nunnery school for the next twenty years. The mother nun would occasionally mention that she felt embarrassed for once being married, but she was treated by all there as an exception. In time, she made herself indispensable to the running of the nunnery, and she was especially welcome since her daughter continued to be recognized as an outstanding student. However, when the daughter passed the final level of state exams and was awarded the title of *Dhammasarīyā* ("teacher of the Dhamma"), the mother nun finally decided to leave. Her daughter's qualification allowed them to branch out and start their own nunnery school. Currently, they have been donated a plot of land and are in the process of starting their own nunnery school. When asked about her new nunnery's entry qualifications, the mother nun says that she only wants to accept young girls who are *ngebyu* because they are easier to discipline. She says, "Their brains are still young and fresh" and they have a better chance of becoming trained as vocational nuns.

Religious Roles for Nuns in Myanmar

Certain religious roles and functions have traditionally been closed to women. Officiating at a public ceremony is one of them. It is taken for granted that monks officiate at religious ceremonies because of their superior religious status in the Sangha. However, it is not technically impossible for a nun to officiate at a ceremony, such as one that involves the giving out of the five and eight precepts and the recitation of major prayers. It is conceded that those who keep a large number of precepts are able to confer precepts on those who keep fewer precepts, but it is not socially acceptable for a nun to take up such a significant religious role that puts her in so public a domain. In theory, the problem does not concern the ability of the officiant, but her religious status and qualifications.

I have witnessed, for example, a young male novice who observes ten precepts officiate and confer the five precepts upon a lay congregation. If such a procedure is acceptable, then it should be possible for a nun who observes eight precepts to perform the same role. However, because the issue concerns social approval for granting religious authority to women, its acceptance depends on whether the monks, the laity, and even the nuns themselves are willing to abide by such a precedent. When asked, Burmese people expressed apprehension about allowing important ceremonies to be handled by nuns who observe only eight precepts. Monks displayed obvious displeasure at such a suggestion, and nuns themselves seemed rather hesitant about such a possibility, although among them were very competent ritual specialists who were equipped with knowledge in regard to every ritual procedure.

Preaching is another area of religious importance that is exclusively monopolized by monks in contemporary Myanmar. In spite of the presence of famous female preachers in ancient Buddhism,[6] Burmese nuns have not continued this legacy. In a country where mass media are not highly developed, preaching is a powerful method of communication, and eloquent preachers attract thousands of devotees far and wide. There are even monk preachers who are more popular than film stars or politicians, for example, and they are often feared for their ability to easily mobilize the populace. Buddhist nuns seem to be obstructed from preaching because of social pressure, and incidents of them preaching in public are rare. In Sri Lanka, however, it is reported that there are many nuns who are acknowledged preachers, and an increasing numbers of nuns in many places have taken up the role of public speaking.[7]

In practice, Burmese nuns do preach and teach people about Buddhist ideas and philosophy, but mostly in informal and private settings. They preach inside nunneries, for example, as well as in peoples' houses. They preach to villagers whenever they visit for alms and, as a consequence of these Dhamma talks, village girls are persuaded to join the nunnery. Nun preachers also visit prisons and preach to female inmates or go to hospitals to console the patients, but these are limited activities performed in restricted circumstances. Learned nuns are experienced at public speaking since oration is part of their education and, being enthusiastic audiences at the monks' sermons, they usually have a good number of Buddhist anecdotes in their repertoires.

However, most of my learned nun informants visibly shrank from the idea of preaching in public. They were worried about what their prospective donors would think and what their public image might be. Some said, "Nuns should be modest and reserved. It is bad to do things that are too bold, such as preaching in public." Others said, "It is the role of monks to preach, not nuns." They anticipated that audiences would not like them to talk in public; besides, they explained there was no tradition for them to preach. Daw Yūsanda, however, one of the few to break out of the customary pattern, preaches regularly during the rain retreat (July to October) at one of the most important pagodas in Rangoon. Most of her themes concern ethics and moral behavior for Buddhist women, and for that reason she may be tolerated. Nevertheless, it still requires much courage on the part of nuns to break out of the traditional mold and to have the confidence to speak out in public at all. In this context, it is significant that Daw Yūsanda has set such a precedent.

Daw Yūsanda was born in 1943 in a small village in Pandaóng township. She accompanied her renunciant mother into the nunnery and became a nun herself at the age of seven. She received a formal Buddhist education at Daw Nyanāsari's nunnery school in Rangoon and passed the state Buddhist exams up to the fourth level. When I met her, she had passed two subjects of the *Dhammasarīyā* exam and was studying for the third. She was also a keen meditator and had been practicing meditation for six years. Influenced by a senior monk who taught her how to deliver sermons, she started preaching at the main Shweidagon pagoda in 1976 on every full and new moon day during the Buddhist Lent. She also traveled around the country delivering sermons and preaching in a variety of public venues. Her topics concerned the social behavior of women, the moral deterioration of society, and other ethical and religious topics. Today, she continues to administer and teach at her nunnery school in Rangoon, which has more than sixty students and five teacher-nuns. In spite of general worries on the part of the nuns for their director, Daw Yūsanda has been fairly well accepted by the general public, and a large audience, composed mostly of women, goes to listen to her sermons. Daw Yūsanda manifests confidence and humor, and is beautifully eloquent. Her popularity derives, in part, from her sermon topics, which support the traditional values and morality of Buddhist women; in this way neither the general audience nor the monks are threatened by her presence. She is not a radical or a liberal but, on the contrary, is a suitable conveyer of conservative values as transmitted to lay women. And this task is clearly regarded as more easily done by a nun than by a monk.

Finally, one of the essential religious roles expected of monks in Myanmar is to chant magical prayers called *paritta.* Traditionally, people invite monks to their homes on special occasions to chant one or two of the eleven *paritta* believed to bring them protection from evil spirits. Such ritual chantings are conducted for newborn babies at the time of childbirth, or at a son's initiation ceremony. Other occasions for recitation are certain life crises and life transitions such as at weddings, funerals, and serious illnesses or injuries, as well as during the Burmese New Year in April. These days, nuns are increasingly invited to peoples' homes to chant *paritta* prayers because of the growing reputation of their beautiful recitation and their increasingly strong voices. They are also popular for their accessibility and friendly, easy manners. Nuns are invited to Buddhist functions such as funerals and boys' initiations to assist and complement the monks. Their presence as ritual specialists has come to be acknowledged and supported because of their intricate knowledge of the details of all manner of ceremonial procedure. Moreover, they give practical advice to lay donors on such things as how to conduct a ceremony according to the donor's budget, what to buy and prepare, which monks to invite, and how to address them. In such roles they have come to be indispensable for the lay donors who no longer have the expertise traditionally associated with village elders. These events and religious occasions also provide the nuns with important donation income, which is essential for their daily upkeep.

Buddhist Precepts and the Position of Women in Myanmar

Since Burmese nuns observe only eight precepts, they are not subject to, for example, prohibitions against cash transactions. In contrast, however, monks and novices have achieved a state of detachment in this regard, the result of traditional canonical rules and regulations prohibiting them from handling money. Nuns, who often find themselves in a position to handle money on behalf of the monks, are routinely needed as treasurers or caretakers of monastery administrations. In recent times, nevertheless, more nuns have aspired to ten-precept status, which allows them renunciation of money. This position is regarded as akin to that of novice monks, and would allow them to spend more time on meditation and their spiritual development.

Some nuns have attempted to become part-time ten-precept observers—on abstinence days or even for half-days in the afternoons. They often combine this state of tranquil purity with vegetarianism or eating one meal a day in order to further enhance their perceived religious position. The move towards a purer, more enhanced practice of Buddhist precepts, although still within the limited confines of their current religious setting, reveals the strong aspiration on the part of nuns for whatever higher spiritual life is available to them. Burmese nuns may consider it infeasible to become a *bhikkhunī* under present circumstances, but even without the security of such religious status, their yearning for higher spirituality has never been thwarted. Becoming a ten-precept observer provides them with an ideal environment to concentrate fully on their own spiritual progress.

There are several nuns who observe the ten precept rules in Myanmar. Daw N. is one of them. For a scholarly nun, she became a nun fairly late—after graduating from Rangoon University—although previously she had been very religious and had meditated during the holidays for many years. She was determined to become a nun, but her family was very much against it. Her father was very angry at first, but because of her determination he gave her his consent on the condition that she not go out on alms-round. He was a very wealthy gold merchant and, in order to provide her with a comfortable lifestyle as a nun, he decided to give her full material backing. Her mother and six brothers and sisters also gave her much support, and, because of their efforts, she was able to take her vocation very seriously, studying the Buddhist scriptures earnestly and passing all the state exams with high marks. By the time she completed her studies and became qualified as a Buddhist teacher, her scholarly reputation was well established. She became known as a skilled meditator, and her reputation was further enhanced when she became known as a rare ten-precept nun who did not receive any cash from her donors. People spoke of her good kamma to have such a wealthy and supportive family. Ironically, her reputation of purity and detachment intensified the fervor of donors wanting to give to her through her lay assistants.

As noted, however, in order to become and stay a ten-precept nun, a nun must have either a wealthy family background, or a highly successful academic career so as to be able to attract numerous benefactors who can give her solid financial backing. It may be paradoxical, but in order to maintain the position of detachment suitable to following the ten precepts, a nun must have sufficient resources and stable material support to be able to afford the luxury of this high status. Such a nun must also have a reliable secretary or a nun-assistant to attend to her daily needs, especially when money is donated. But nuns of such high status are rarely in a position to be looked after as much as monks are, since they usually cannot attract sufficient attention from the laity to be attended to on a full-time basis. Furthermore, such nuns themselves frequently act as financial and treasury assistants to ten-precept monks, and having assistants of their own would be an odd fit in normative Burmese monastic structure.

In contemporary Myanmar, there is another useful category for women who wish to leave the householder's life without becoming fully committed to a life as a monastic, and that is to become a yogi. The position of yogi is normally for a lay practitioner, male or female, who observes the eight precepts and practices meditation in a religious compound, a meditation center, or a monastery or nunnery, for a temporary or semi-temporary period. Becoming a yogi provides one with a quiet religious life that affords more time and freedom to concentrate on personal spiritual advancement. Old women in Burma who become freed from their responsibilities as mothers and wives generally choose to spend their time as yogis rather than become nuns. In this respect, the old stereotype of Buddhist nuns being "widowed old ladies" is less and less based on fact. The appeal of the yogi lifestyle is due, firstly, to the fact that, as the educational standards of nuns continue to rise, being a nun is increasingly regarded as a "professional" religious career, something older women may be less inclined to pursue. It is due, secondly, to the difficulty women have in deciding to renounce fully so late in their lives, and to adapt to the lifestyle of full-time alms-women. Thirdly, some of the older yogis find fasting in the afternoon strenuous, as they cannot consume the large amounts of food in the morning that professional nuns are used to consuming from an early age. And finally, being a yogi allows a woman to maintain her normal relationships with her family and, at the same time, gives her a pretext to stay away from family conflicts, as she routinely moves between meditation centers and home, meditating for certain periods of time and then returning home to rest. Theoretically, the religious status of a yogi is equivalent to that of a nun who observes the same eight precepts, for example, refraining from sex, food after midday, and worldly pleasures and secular matters. Nuns, however, regard yogis as mere lay women, not as proper renouncers like themselves, since "yogis are still attached to their hair." Nuns regard the hair as an important symbolic demarcation between themselves and yogis, between those who are true members of the monastic community and those who are not. Having said that, many monasteries and nunneries accommodate old and infirm parents of monks and nuns who live as yogis. Nuns also acknowledge that this provides a leeway for those who cannot endure in old age the rigorous religious commitment expected of mendicants. The yogis expressed a totally different point of view. The majority of those interviewed said that they never considered becoming a nun because the business of a nun's life detracted from the time and energy needed for meditation and spiritual training. From their point of view, nuns were too occupied with cooking and looking after the monks and monastic community, and, as a consequence, neglected their own spiritual growth. One yogi said she never considered becoming a nun because she enjoyed her financial independence and wanted to keep her resources in order to be able to give to the monks. In fact, this notion of becoming materially dependent upon others seems to have ultimately discouraged many yogis from becoming nuns.

In spite of these positions, however, the majority admitted that the religious position of a nun is spiritually higher than that of a yogi. Perhaps it can be said that the distinction between yogis and nuns was less clear in the past, but as the religious importance, ritual skills, and educational standards of nuns have become more appreciated today, differences in motives and lifestyle have become increasingly emphasized.

Notes

1. There are presently more than thirty thousand Buddhist nuns in Myanmar, making it one of the largest concentrations of nuns in a single country.
2. King (1987).
3. Ludu Daw Ama (1982), 354.
4. Ibid., 345.
5. Ibid., 356.
6. Altekar (1978), 209.
7. Gombrich and Obeyesekere (1988), 285.

AN AMERICAN ZEN TEACHER

Trudy Goodman

> A priest is chosen by a bureaucracy in a dominant city, but a mystic, a shaman, is chosen by spirits in the wilderness.
>
> William Irwin Thompson, *Annals,* vol. XV, no. 2, 1997

I WAS "MADE" A TEACHER by the experiences of my life each time life pulled me toward an initiation into the mystery of who we really are. Several powerful experiences occurred before I ever practiced the way or Dharma. I figured everyone was like this and never spoke of it. Yet I began to seek a teacher and a path to follow, a path that would express and reveal the truth and show me how to live from a truthful place. For me, the fact that these experiences happened in the course of ordinary embodied mother-life—conception, childbirth, tending a critically ill little daughter—gave me great reverence, huge awe, for being female, for female being. This is my understanding of feminism.

I also learned trust in our ever-present buddha nature, the unborn, the innate great perfection. For I did nothing to induce or deserve what was revealed. We see simply because it is so. My life and teaching are informed by these two things: an immense love for life in female form as well as male, and knowledge that this sacred, mystical life is already here.

My first conscious sense of clear, bright awareness came as a very young woman, moments after the conception of my daughter. My mind and the whole world fell silent. Luminous presence glowed through everything, with a peace I had never known before. I lay wide awake, present, open, complete, knowing without knowing anything, while my young husband slept soundly. Nine months later, giving birth at twenty-one, I labored in a white-tiled hospital room, alone and unprepared for the immensity and intensity of giving birth. As the tiles turned blue at twilight, my suffering and fear suddenly gave way to a great amazement, my awareness merging with all women, all female creatures, birthing, being born *this* way—a beginningless, endless chain of beings, infinite, universal life in all directions, past, present, future. And I was no longer separate, or alone.

A couple of years later I was living overseas. My little two-and-a-half-year-old girl lay in a coma between life and death for a week, followed by months of uncertainty in the hospital. Standing behind a glass door during one emergency, while six doctors and nurses worked to save her life, I saw god. And god was all of us, in the form of this living moment, this place, this very activity of pure, empty compassion.

Buddhist meditation practices offered a way to let go and make room for these moments of presence, of grace. These early experiences cultivated faith and respect for the Buddha, the Dharma and the Sangha. By consciously, mindfully offering the heart of attention to what actually is, trust and confidence in our power of presence grows, as does gratitude for the teachings and teachers that recognize and point the way. This is my refuge.

There is a longing in each one of us to turn to another to find answers in our life. Many of us women have been specially conditioned to the old tropism of a female sunflower facing east towards a male sun. One recent summer I saw that sunflowers do in fact turn east, and then bloom, and go to seed still facing the sunrise. This turning shapes my own relationship to authority, to teachers and students. As experienced women practitioners and teachers, we express inner authority by working to change the ways of power and leadership in the Buddhist world; we sit and stand and walk at each other's backs, offering support and solidarity.

The reticence I battle within myself about assuming a leadership role may be rooted in simple unfamiliarity or in old self-doubts. It is not a bad thing, this reticence. It brings more level communication and dialogue, more circles and councils. There is more truth-telling of the kind girls are bolder at. I try to find a balance in my own work between wise voicing of truth, of inner authority, and genuine openness, unapologetic, strong vulnerability. This combination feels like an authentic female voice. As women we need to feel our own power and mastery, not power over something, but the surge of trust and confidence in our own inner authority, in the wisdom of practice and experience. We also need to acknowledge our particularly female vulnerability, in sexuality, in mothering, and in aging. I celebrate women's lives and perceptions so that we can inhabit our rightful place as leaders, as buddhas and bodhisattvas in the practice lineages of our traditions. And if any of those lineages are not able to include and accept the particularly female expression of life, then we need to find a way to work outside of such structures while respecting and protecting the essence, the core of the spiritual practice.

TEACHING LINEAGES AND LAND:
Renunciation and Domestication Among Buddhist Nuns in Sri Lanka[1]

Nirmala S. Salgado

Introduction

The tension between Buddhist monasticism's ascetic ideal of "renunciation" and its practical accommodation with the world or "domestication"[2] has been explored in both ancient and more contemporary monastic contexts.[3] Most studies of this tension in Buddhism, however, have centered on male monastics.[4] While recent investigations of Buddhist nuns have focused on how renunciation factors in the lifestyles of Buddhist women,[5] these studies do not fully explore the concomitant process of routinization and domestication whose dynamics can radically redefine the lives of female renouncers.

As evidenced in these studies, female renunciants in the Theravāda Buddhist tradition, unlike their male counterparts, rarely own the land on which they live. This lack of land entitlement reflects a necessarily transient lifestyle—there is the soteriological notion that land ownership represents an expendable attachment and encumbrance to the pursuit of the renunciant life—but is also attributable to a reluctance of women to own land. The nuns' hesitation to own land might be traced to the fact that women in Sri Lanka are generally not accustomed to doing so. Further, as I will demonstrate, the attitude of nuns to land ownership is related to particular definitions of "lineage" among contemporary nuns.[6] Overall, I show how the lives of contemporary Buddhist nuns in Sri Lanka entail an ongoing process of domestication, thereby bringing into question the notion that domestication, ipso facto, represents an aberration from the monastic ideal.

Renunciation and Domestication Among Male Monastics

According to Strenski, "domestication of the *sangha* occurs whenever certain relations are established between the *sangha* and laity."[7] Domestication includes five main areas: the residential, ritual, social, political, and economic areas[8] in which "the *sangha* and laity enter into a complex variety of relationships."[9] Strenski, following Weber, defines residential domestication as a process whereby the Sangha takes up a common residence instead of leading a life of homeless wandering.[10] He refers to social domestication as the Sangha's "social relations with the outside world—kinship, status, caste," which have a direct impact on the male renouncer living within the monastery who also maintains an identity or special relationship to caste and kin.[11] He demonstrates that the most evident element of domestication is "the economic relations between *sangha* and society.... Domesticated *sangha*... often possess property, the most problematic of which is land."[12] While maintaining the importance of all five areas mentioned, in this paper I focus specifically on the differential effects of residential, economic, and social factors on monks and nuns in Sri Lanka.

Strenski views domestication as an inevitable and natural process. However, some scholars consider the ownership of property by monks and the process of domestication itself as a deviation from the ideal of Buddhist monasticism.[13] More recently, Schopen has shown that such a conclusion represents a "reading" attributable to mistaking the living tradition of Buddhism for the world represented by its texts.[14]

While notions of monastic lineage in Theravāda Buddhism have been conditioned either by ordination practices[15] or by pupillary succession,[16] or both,[17] it is clear that caste and kinship have often become central in determining rights over temple lands among the more established male monastic institutions in Sri Lanka.[18] In fact, in the Theravāda tradition, the "success" of the establishment of a hermitage has often been gauged by the amount of land that accrues to the hermitage and its branches, as well as by the number of junior monks who owe allegiance to a particular preceptor.[19]

Incidences of land ownership by monasteries are legitimate with reference to the line of pupillary succession among Buddhist monks. The monastic land ownership system, originally referred to as "monastic landlordism,"[20] validated the "appropriation of monastic property by individual monks and the transmission of property from pupil to pupil within the same family along the ordination lineage."[21] This system is still in place among many monastic lineages in Sri Lanka. Interestingly, a close relationship between lineage traditions and land ownership holds true for both the older temples in Sri Lanka that have been associated with "monastic landlordism,"[22] as well as more recent forest reform movements in Theravāda societies.[23]

Renunciation and Domestication among Female Monastics

Social, historical, and cultural factors contribute to nuns' tenuous hold on hermitage lands. Unlike most male Buddhist monastics, nuns in Sri Lanka, whose lineages date to the late nineteenth century at the earliest,[24] have fewer historical precedents on which to draw, and are still often struggling to establish themselves. Moreover, nuns tend to view renunciation differently from monks. Sri Lankan nuns state that their purpose in becoming nuns is to achieve the goal of *nibbāna* or shorten the suffering in *saṃsāra*.[25] For women, renunciation also entails a certain freedom that is associated with leaving the traditional life in a family, for example, marriage and children.[26] A man who renounces is implicitly more likely to leave the household life because of the benefits provided by well-established monasteries and the state. Further, as Carrithers mentions, a monk joining the established Sangha associates himself with "a professional class of land-owning clerics."[27] Because educational privileges, inheritance, and land rights favor males, men, whether lay or ordained, are socially and culturally better prepared to handle real estate issues than are women.

Kinship studies have shown the close relationship between patterns of land inheritance and the clustering of male kin in a particular area.[28] In the traditional patriarchal and patrilineal family, the share of land controlled by women, if any, is comparatively restricted.[29] Furthermore, female kin are generally more dispersed than male kin who belong to a clearly defined network over successive generations.[30] Changes wrought during and since colonial times have been ineffective in bringing increased landownership and control to women.[31]

I suggest that the gender-differentiated kinship patterns evidenced among lay inheritance lineages have implications for female monastic systems. Clearly, succession within established male monastic lineages is not uninfluenced by caste and kinship patterns outside the monastery. Since inheritance and succession lineages among laity favor males, it is perhaps not surprising that nuns express more ambivalent attitudes to land ownership and control than monks.

Women entering the renunciant life often have not graduated from high school.[32] Even those from a farming background would generally not be trained in supervising work on farms or in the management of land. Their renunciation of the household has implications for their attitude to domestication, as they consider land ownership an obstruction to their lives as religious persons. The nuns are generally unfamiliar with role models of lay women who control land,[33] as they are with female renunciants who might do so. The physical and social confinement of women in South Asia also discourages them from entering a traditional male sphere in addressing land issues.[34] While nuns might explain their hesitation to accept ownership of land with reference to the ideal of Buddhist renunciation, there are probably, in fact, a variety of interrelated factors that determine their attitude. Most nuns I have interviewed characteristically take up residence in places which male monastics and laity consider uninhabitable. When nuns are in a position to improve their dwellings over time, male monastics or laity often lay claim to their residences, which in turn prompts the nuns and their supporters to assert their rights. Since most nuns lack land deeds, they usually fail in defending their claims.

Another issue confronting a typical head nun is the problem of establishing and preserving the lineage of a nunnery. In Sri Lanka the definitions of male monastic lineages, while not always clearly demarcated, are usually determined by the character of the higher ordination, which might in turn overlap with a pupillage tradition *(śiṣyānuśiṣyaparamparāva)* and a kinship tradition *(ñātiśiṣyaparamparāva).*[35] In contrast, among nuns, higher ordination or *upasampadā* is not widely established or recognized in Sri Lanka, and women may be ordained in a variety of ways.[36] In recent years, there have been efforts to reintroduce higher ordination for Theravāda Buddhist women in Sri Lanka. The first such ordination took place in March 1998, when Sri Lankan women who had received full ordination in a ceremony conducted in India conferred the *upasampadā* on ten-precept mothers in Sri Lanka.

Despite the recent introduction of the *upasampadā* for women in Sri Lanka, currently ordination lineages are not as clearly demarcated among female renunciants as they are among Buddhist monks, who have an established ordination tradition and can trace their lineages back several generations. Additionally, the paucity of educational facilities and the absence of an established tradition of education (whether meditational or textual) among the nuns,[37] as well as the lack of normatively strong female kinship ties, characteristically inhibit nuns from forming the lineage traditions comparable to those created by monks.

Nuns' tenuous hold on their hermitage lands has further contributed to the weakness of their lineages. Temple land ownership, monastic lineage, and inheritance rights are closely linked for male monastics,[38] a state of affairs seldom obtaining among female renunciants. While a direct causal connection between weak lineages and lack of land ownership has yet to be confirmed, a nunnery with a secure title deed cannot endure in the absence of young nuns who will assume the mantle of leadership. In 1997, I interviewed a government official who had twenty years of experience working among Buddhist nuns. She maintained that the main issue facing the nuns was "the problem of a dwelling place *(nēvāsika praśnayak)* and leading their lives in a suitable environment without troubles."[39] Confirming the putative relationship of residence to lineage, she further explained that this problem was a consequence of junior nuns being ordained in different places and by more than one head nun. The problem of residence and land ownership is exacerbated in a predominantly agricultural country such as Sri Lanka, where the rapid rise in population has increased the competition for land.[40]

Currently, a junior nun who is ordained in the ten precepts and lives under the tutelage of a senior nun is expected to abide by the rules laid down by the senior nun in addition to the ten precepts. These rules may vary from one hermitage to another, as may the interpretation of the ten precepts themselves. Further, in the absence of universally established regulations, the relationship of the junior nun and her *guru māniyo* (teacher-nun, preceptor) is determined to a large extent by the individual personalities of the two nuns. It is not uncommon for junior nuns who cannot adapt to a particular hermitage to leave that hermitage in search of another where the expectations and personality of a head nun might be more amenable to them. This would not be possible if the female renunciants received the traditional *upasampadā* of the Pali canon. In the canonical ordination, the junior renunciant accepts a particular senior *bhikkhunī* as a mentor and also agrees to accept 311 rules that are recognized by all *bhikkhunīs.* Arbitrarily rejecting the mentorship of her assigned preceptor and hermitage would entail her abandonment of her status as a *bhikkhunī.* She could not choose to reassume her renunciant status unconditionally. Hence, the strength of the canonical lineage tradition can be traced to the nature of the *upasampadā* ritual itself.

Another factor that accounts for the weak lineages among nuns is that junior nuns often refuse to remain with their *guru māniyo*, preferring instead to found their own hermitages. The government official explained that after the age of thirty or forty, most nuns had difficulties in subordinating themselves to a preceptor. This did not surprise me. The nuns I know, many of whom tend to be very independent individuals, have made a conscious decision to question certain cultural norms by renouncing. In her 1987 thesis, Kusuma Devendra also underscores the connection between a stable residence and the preceptor and lineage:

> The average DSM [ten-precept mother, nun] comes under the tutelage of the DSM who initiated her, but there is no binding rule that the teacher should hold responsibility or that the pupil should continue to live with the teacher. Therefore the community [of nuns] functions for the most part as fissiparous autonomous groups of individuals.[41]

Interestingly, in leaving the tutelage of their head nun, junior nuns often renounce a potentially secure residence for a more uncertain future.

In my case studies, I will demonstrate how attitudes to renunciation, land, and lineage are inevitably intertwined. While a hermitage that owns its land might be in a better position to establish and maintain a recognizable lineage, the renunciant attitude of the nuns living there and the lack of a good training facility can interfere with the process of routinization and domestication.

The Story of Nandā Māniyo[42]

Nandā Māniyo's story is inseparable from her many peregrinations. Ordained in 1957, at age twenty-two, Nandā Māniyo has experienced a rather nomadic existence, living in five different residences. During this time she has provided guidance to twenty-seven junior nuns, sixteen of whom she ordained, and has also started a Buddhist Sunday school, which was at one time attended by some one hundred children. Although she confronted several problems in establishing and maintaining her various abodes, she eventually succeeded in obtaining the title to a piece of land that now houses a spacious hermitage as well as a *caitya* (stūpa, relic house). However, since none of her junior nuns remained with her, she currently lives alone and is considering donating her present hermitage to a Buddhist monk.

Below is a brief chronological sketch of select events of importance in Nandā Māniyo's life.

1952–1957: underwent probation in rented place with teacher
1957: was ordained, age 22
1957–1958: lived with *guru māniyo* and three other junior nuns in same rented dwelling place as before
1958–1962: lived in Uduwa
1962–1964: lived in Digalla with two of her junior nuns
1965–1967: lived with a woman doctor and took classes in the city
1967: moved to Lonuwara (lived there till 1988)
1980: refused government offer of land at Sinipitiya
1980: founded a Sunday school in Lonuwara
1983: began negotiations to accept land offer at Sinipitiya
1988: moved to Sinipitiya
1992: obtained title deed for Sinipitiya

(At the time of our last interview in 1997, she was still living in Sinipitiya.)

Relocating

Between 1957 and 1967 Nandā Māniyo lived in three different dwelling places. At the first two residences, she lived under the tutelage of her head nun. Some years after her own ordination, Nandā Māniyo moved to a residence in Uduwa. This relocation turned out to be unsatisfactory because some of the owners disagreed over how the land should be used and were unwilling to allow the nuns to live there. Further, relations with local monks had posed difficulties. After her *guru māniyo* died in 1964, a monk offered some land and buildings to Nandā Māniyo and the junior nuns she was then training. The buildings had been inhabited previously by monks, but the absence of running water encouraged the monks to move elsewhere. However, a problem arose after the nuns' relocation. A neighboring monk with a "bad reputation" insisted on visiting the nuns frequently and began sending his junior monks to the nuns, despite the objections of the head nun. The nuns continued to live there for about four years. Nandā Māniyo eventually refused the offer of the deed, partly because the monks' visitations disturbed her but also because of the lack of access to water. Moreover, she expressed reluctance in accepting *saṅghika* land.[43] She made plans to relocate.

For a few years Nandā Māniyo was sponsored by a woman doctor with whom she lived while attending classes in the city. Later, in 1967, Nandā Māniyo relocated again. This time the government offered her a piece of land in Lonuwara, not far from Uduwa. This land was augmented by the acquisition of some adjoining land whose purchase was made possible by pooling her own resources with those of the junior nuns. Nandā Māniyo ensured that the deed was written to the six nuns then under her tutelage. When I asked her why she refused to have the title deed written in her name she responded: "I have no use for land, my intention is to remove the suffering of *saṃsāra* and realize *nibbāna*." She continued to develop the Lonuwara hermitage, relying upon her own funds and the assistance volunteered by lay people in the area. She opened a Sunday school, which was eventually attended by over one hundred children. However, after a neighboring monk began complaining to lay people for sending their children to her Sunday school rather than his, the Lonuwara hermitage suffered a drop in attendance. There were other difficulties. For example, the nunnery, was located on top of a steep hill and lacked access to water; this entailed fetching water in buckets from the bottom of the hill.

Nandā Māniyo was willing to remain there regardless of such difficulties. When a more suitable piece of land nearby became vacant, the government offered it to Nandā Māniyo. Despite the protests of her junior nuns, she initially refused. "Why does one want so much land and property? ...what we have here is enough" was her response to her junior nuns. The junior nuns, considering her attitude "crazy," urged her to accept the new offer. She eventually did so, resolving to donate the land they had bought collectively at Lonuwara to a monk who had previously made several requests for it.[44] When asked why she did not sell the land that she had developed with considerable difficulty, she responded that doing this would "then mean that I would be selling the *śāsana* [Buddhist dispensation]."

In 1988, Nandā Māniyo, who by now had accepted the government offer, founded a new hermitage at Sinipitiya. Since her relocation to Sinipitiya in 1988, she has worked hard to renovate and improve the buildings there, a task which has required considerable work. In addition to making the building habitable, Nandā Māniyo had also raised funds for a fine *caitya* and separate shrines for the Buddha and the gods to be built. Yet, several rooms, which could be used to house junior nuns, remain empty. However, just as the land in Sinipitiya was being deeded to her, a monk requested Nandā Māniyo's permission to use it as a center for social and religious programs, while she continued to dwell there. Acceding to his request, she signed a document the monk gave her thereby effectively transferring her land to him.[45] In 1989, she was surprised to receive notification from the prime minister's office stating the government's intentions to deed the land to the monk in question.[46] However, the monk was forestalled in his actions by Nandā Māniyo, who by then had asserted her proprietary rights over the land and buildings at Sinipitiya.[47]

Lineage

Nandā Māniyo, one of four nuns ordained by her *guru māniyo*, was unable to give me the name of the teacher-nun of her own *guru māniyo*. Of the three other sisters ordained by her own teacher, one disrobed, one died, and only one remains in robes. Today the latter lives in another district and contacts Nandā Māniyo intermittently, about once in two years. She has ordained some ten junior nuns, but few of them remain with her at the hermitage because, according to Nandā Māniyo, she is too strict. Nandā Māniyo has ordained sixteen junior nuns, two of whom have subsequently disrobed. She is in touch with nine of them, several of whom visit her about twice a year, either on special ritual occasions or when she falls ill. Five of the nuns she ordained teach at Sunday schools in the region, while two others assist at meditation centers attached to their hermitages.

Considering the relatively spacious two-and-a-half-acre area of land and the respect enjoyed by Nandā Māniyo, I was puzzled as to why no junior nuns still lived with her. She maintained that the parents of her junior nuns encouraged them to establish their own hermitages, for junior nuns too, after all, "wish to establish hermitages and be the head...rather than be under someone." She added that the nine nuns with whom she is still in touch have founded hermitages. These nuns, in turn, have themselves ordained about twelve junior nuns, none of whom tends to visit or even know her.

Domestication and Lineage

Although Nandā Māniyo has trained twenty-seven junior nuns and ordained several nuns in the past forty years in her vocation as a nun, she now lives alone and without a suitable junior nun to whom she might eventually leave the hermitage. Nandā Māniyo's predicament typifies that of the nun who reluctantly comes into possession of an abandoned piece of property, develops it, and then is inclined to renounce it once again.

Currently, several monks from temples in the area have requested that she eventually deed them the land on which she lives. When asked why she does not consider leaving the land to a nun, she hints that nuns "would not be able to live here... because of the surroundings." Lowering her voice, she adds that the house adjoining the hermitage is the home of a rapist and murderer who has not been convicted. Young nuns are reluctant to stay there because of him.

Still puzzled by her apparent inability to attract a more permanent following of junior nuns, I chanced upon two young junior nuns whom she had ordained. One of them was living and training at a government study center for nuns not far from Sinipitiya. In the presence of other junior nuns, she mentioned that she had no desire to live at Sinipitiya because she felt that the hermitage was too close to the village and lacked privacy. Moreover, her family lived closer to the hermitage than was desirable. The second nun I met lived at a different training center, in a more remote area. When I spoke with her privately, she informed me that the real problem for Nandā Māniyo centered upon considerations of caste. In a lowered voice she explained that the villagers in the areas of Lonuwara as well as Sinipitiya were dominated by members of a caste "higher" than that of the head nun. Most of the junior nuns under the tutelage of Nandā Māniyo belonged to this "higher" caste. The lay people who gave donations to the hermitage objected to their caste members, the junior nuns (who in some cases were their own relatives), paying their respects to the head nun in a gesture of worshipful prostration. The relatives of the junior nuns felt this was inappropriate, especially as the head nun belonged to a caste that traditionally provided services to the "higher" caste from which the junior nuns came. It was evident that the establishment of Nandā Māniyo and her nuns in their new location at Lonuwara led to a domestication of the nuns that eventually augured the disintegration of the hermitage as an institution. I recalled that Nandā Māniyo, while omitting the caste issue, had indeed mentioned that the parents of the nuns wanted them to seek a higher status and become head nuns at their own hermitages. The inter-caste tension was undoubtedly a major factor in Nandā Māniyo's current isolation.

Caste was not an issue at the next two hermitages I surveyed, perhaps because all the nuns there were of a single caste. (The head nuns of both hermitages did assure me that women of all castes were welcome to join them.) These two hermitages faced similar problems in coming to terms with the interrelated issues of land ownership and lineage.

The Story of Mettikā Māniyo[48]

Mettikā Māniyo, like Nandā Māniyo, belongs to an attenuated lineage, a development exacerbated by problematic land issues and competition from monks in the area. Mettikā Māniyo however, can trace her lineage back five generations of nuns, to the time when one of the earliest hermitages for women was founded on the island. Today, Mettikā Māniyo (unlike Nandā Māniyo) continues to live with other sister nuns who were ordained by her own teacher. In exploring the relationship between land and lineage at Mettikā Māniyo's hermitage, I trace the lineage to which Mettikā Māniyo belongs and examine how attitudes to land have influenced her current situation.

Lineage

In the diagram below I indicate the lineage of nuns to which Mettikā Māniyo belongs. It is noteworthy, and indeed rare among nuns, that the identities of individual head nuns can be traced back several generations.

Selā Māniyo
|
Talwatta Māniyo (age 83 in 1953)
|
Randeniya Māniyo (age 67 in 1953)
|
Kirigama Māniyo (age about 37 in 1953)
|
Nuwara Māniyo (age 58 in 1953)
|
Ordained fourteen nuns including Mettikā Māniyo (one of whom has disrobed, and several of whom have died)

Mettikā Māniyo, who was ordained in the fifties, has a vague recollection of Talwatta Māniyo. Although Talwatta Māniyo ordained other nuns, Mettikā Māniyo does not know them. Although knowledgeable of her direct lineage and the sister nuns ordained by Nuwara Māniyo, Mettikā Māniyo was unable to provide information on other nuns ordained by members of this lineage. Nuwara Māniyo ordained several nuns. All but one of these nuns have remained in robes permanently and have chosen to live at the Gedige hermitage she founded. Of these two have gone on to ordain a total of five other nuns. Of the five, one seventeen-year-old nun continues to live at the Gedige hermitage with her preceptor. The other four were all ordained by the same nun (who chose to move away from Gedige), but only two of them continue to live with their preceptor (one disrobed and the other left for another hermitage). Mettikā Māniyo, the current head nun of the hermitage, has neither trained nor ordained any junior nuns. Currently, the five surviving *gōlayas* (junior nuns) of the late Nuwara Māniyo who still live at this hermitage are all in their forties or older. Consequently the only young nun at this hermitage is a third-generation seventeen-year-old. This is a cause of some concern for Mettikā Māniyo, who realizes that the nuns at the hermitage might have to endure the hardships of old age with little assistance from within the hermitage.

The fact that nuns can identify several generations of their forbears suggests that there is a loose sense of lineage at this hermitage. Since Nuwara Māniyo's move to Gedige, these nuns have for the most part shared a communal residence. However, their lineage appears to be threatened. This is partly because of the problems relating to residence and land issues, to which I now turn.

Establishing and Maintaining a Hermitage

When Nuwara Māniyo was invited to found a hermitage at Gedige in 1953, there were only two *kuṭis* (huts, cells) there, used by lay people for meditation on *pōya* (full-moon holy days). The Perera family that invited her was socially prominent and also distantly related to her. Mettikā Māniyo (also a distant relation of Nuwara Māniyo) was ordained at the Gedige hermitage in 1955 when she was still in her teens and has lived there since. The hermitage is located on a steep hill, where the water required for drinking, bathing, and washing robes is difficult to obtain. Water is currently conveyed to the hermitage in large vats by helpful lay people. Sometimes the closest well, located about ten minutes walk away, supplies water. However, in times of drought this well is often dry, prompting the nuns to trudge for half an hour (one way) to another remote well.

According to Mettikā Māniyo, when Nuwara Māniyo moved to Gedige, Perera senior offered a deed of four acres to the hermitage. This land included about half an acre on a hill and a flatter expanse suitable for growing fruit and vegetables. Nuwara Māniyo, however, did not see any point in such a formalized transaction. Mettikā Māniyo mentioned that Nuwara Māniyo had said to Perera senior, "If it is donated land, just donate it." Contemplating this view, Nuwara Māniyo added, "Our *guru māniyo* did not think ahead, then, did she?" When Perera senior died, his son, Perera junior, inherited the land. Initially he offered to give Nuwara Māniyo a deed of three acres of land, and she reluctantly agreed to accept this. However, Perera junior changed his mind and decided to sell off all but half an acre of the most inhospitable land on the hill that was included in the land originally offered to the nunnery. This sale contributed towards the dowries of his two daughters. Currently the half-acre of land used by the nunnery forms about two-thirds of the total land at the Gedige hermitage, the remainder (upon which a small school has been erected) belonging to a temple that was abandoned in the eighties. The hermitage still has no title deed to its name and effectively remains in the hands of Kanthi (a daughter of Perera junior) and her husband who live in the area.

Mettikā Māniyo mentioned that the Perera family descendants had initially wanted to write the deed in her name. However, Mettikā Māniyo felt uncomfortable accepting property in her name and suggested that the deed be written to another nun—"I refused partly because I had not trained any *gōlayas*," she explains. The Pereras, not favoring Mettikā Māniyo's choice, were prepared to compromise by giving it to another nun, but there was never any further discussion on the topic. When I asked Mettikā Māniyo why she did not probe further into the matter, she said, " We do not encourage them after all [to write the deed], but really...I am not happy to ask them. If they are giving [the land], they should just give it." In 1995, I asked about the possibility of problems arising with the land since it had no deed, and she responded, "No, this [land] will not be sold to anyone.... [Kanthi's family] is a respectable family in the area, they are all relatives of mine and of Nuwara Māniyo." Possibly, Mettikā Māniyo feared that insistence on a legal contract could compromise relations of trust between nuns and their lay supporters.

When Mettikā Māniyo and I visited Kanthi and her husband in 1997, they both assured us (much to the surprise of Mettikā Māniyo) that a deed for half an acre of land had already been prepared. On our return, Mettikā Māniyo expressed misgivings that a deed had ever been written. Despite their promises to show us copies of the deed, no evidence of its existence was forthcoming, corroborating the nun's suspicion that they had probably not written out a deed at all.[49]

An ongoing "feud" with a nearby temple has exacerbated the predicament of the Gedige hermitage. The temple owned several acres of land and at one time had two water tanks and a well that supplied it with adequate water. Earlier, a dirt road leading up the hill to the temple had been graded and fortuitously led most of the way to the hermitage. However, as the elderly head monk at the temple viewed the nuns as competitors for lay support, he closed a section of the road leading to the hermitage, thus forcing the nuns and their supporters to build and use another, much steeper dirt road to their hermitage. (This road, which is still in use by the nuns, was not improved until 1996.) Later, when a younger monk assumed leadership of the temple in 1976, relations with the hermitage improved. However, an increasing scarcity of water at the temple would ultimately leave it defunct and abandoned by 1980. Before leaving the temple, the new head monk invited the nuns to manage and continue the Sunday school that had begun at the temple. The Sunday school moved to a building that was erected by the hermitage. However, due to a lack of water and toilet facilities at the hermitage, school attendance dropped by about two-thirds.

Since the land on which the Gedige hermitage is built is private and not part of a *pūjā oppuwa* or "deed of gift," the state is under no obligation to assist in renovating the hermitage.[50] The abandoned temple is accorded a *pūjā oppuwa*. If the temple land was transferred to the nuns, they would acquire a water supply and a more habitable dwelling place. Since the temple occupies lower ground, it would allow the nuns easier access to water than the hermitage. When I suggested that the nuns consider using the temple lands, Mettikā Māniyo agreed, "Either they [the government] should make arrangements to give the temple to the monks or they should make the decision to give it to a nun. This land, this property should be given in a suitable manner, is that not so?"

Domestication and Lineage

Unlike Nandā Māniyo, the nuns at the Gedige hermitage can readily trace their lineage back several generations. This might be attributed to a few different factors. First, the ordination of several preceptor nuns occurred within a short span of time (Nuwara Māniyo was ordained at the age of fifty-eight, only two years before Mettikā Māniyo was ordained). Second, since these nuns placed an emphasis on education within their community, the importance of pupillage, and hence lineage, was probably enhanced. Finally, most of the nuns ordained by Nuwara Māniyo continue to live together, thus consolidating their identity as *gōlayas* of a single head nun. When I visited the hermitage in 1997, there were six nuns living there, five of whom had been ordained by Nuwara Māniyo. Of three of her ordinands not dwelling there, one lives in the vicinity, another disrobed, and a third, who was sickly, left the Gedige hermitage because she was unable to tolerate the hardship of not having adequate water.

Today, Mettikā Māniyo appears to belong to a dying lineage. I asked her why she had not trained or ordained junior nuns. She responded, "It is like this: if I were to train *gōlayas*...I would be very sad. Here I am, a *gōlaya* of [my] *loku māniyo* [ordaining nun] and I have suffered so much. If I were to have *gōlayas*, I would want a place with water and a good place to live.... So I don't have the inclination to train *gōlayas*." She explained that there was no dearth of nuns awaiting the ordination: "There are nuns who are waiting to be ordained here, but because of the water problem, they went to find another place." I suggested that the hermitage where they had been living might be appropriated by others, simply because of a lack of junior nuns to continue the lineage. She agreed: "If, for example, the nuns who are here trained young *gōlayas*...if a young *māniyo* came here to learn...we could continue in the future....Once the nuns are no more, then even a monk could take over...one cannot say [what will happen]." Here she has clearly expressed how the integrity of her lineage may be undercut by her inability to acquire a more amenable dwelling place. She obviously believed the predicament to be irremediable.

While the nuns at the Gedige hermitage share difficulties similar to those endured by Nandā Māniyo (lack of access to water, competition from monks, a weak lineage), they have succeeded in living together and maintaining a communal identity and a stable residence for several decades. However, their success is only partial, since the nuns cannot effectively exert control and demonstrate full legal ownership over the land on which they live.

The Aligoda Hermitage[51]

Like the Gedige hermitage, the Aligoda hermitage was founded in the mid-1950s. Since then, the hermitage has expanded and now consists of a total of five plots of land, only two of which have secure title deeds. In the following account I briefly discuss the history of this hermitage and identify the various plots of land associated with it as well as their legal owners. I then elaborate on the interrelationship of land and lineage.

LAND OWNERSHIP AND LAND ISSUES

The hermitage has the use of five pieces of land. Barring one, all of these adjoin each other.

a) Plot no. 1: A small paddy field. (In 1997 this was filled, and a *caitya* was built here.) Twenty members of the extended Silva family legally own this land.
b) Plot no. 2: One lot of land and a house, which were given as a pūjā oppuwa, or "deed of offering," to the founding nun and her successors in office in 1974 for the purpose of educating the junior nuns. At that time, the land was worth two thousand rupees.
c) Plot no. 3: A parcel of land on which were erected a bodhi tree (tree of enlightenment), a *budugē* (shrine for the Buddha statue), *sālāva* (hall; demolished in 1997), and a living area for the junior nuns. The latter includes about four individual *kuṭis* as well as a kitchen and eating area. Originally this land consisted of a family cemetery as well as a *billāva*.[52] Currently the land is legally owned by several descendants of the Silva family.
d) Plot no. 4: A smaller piece of land adjoining plot no. 3, which includes about seven coconut trees and a separate two-room hut in which the senior nuns reside. This land had no deed and is owned by neighbors.
e) Plot no. 5: A spacious piece of land that makes up about half the area of the entire hermitage (excluding the land mentioned in 2 above), which has been written over to the current head nun and her successors. The title for this land, which was made to the nuns in the early 1990s, valued it at nine thousand rupees. A large meditation hall, which includes about fifteen *kuṭis*, was erected here in 1994. In 1997, when the old *sālāva* was demolished, a new one was built adjacent to the meditation hall and is now used by nuns for such purposes as teaching children at the Sunday school and conducting meditation classes for the laity.

I visited the son (Silva senior) and grandson (Silva junior) of the lay founder of the family that currently owns most of the land used by the hermitage. They explained that in the mid-fifties, a clearing was made in the jungle (on plot no.3) on which a *kuṭi* of coconut palm leaves and thatch was erected. Different groups of monks temporarily made use of the *kuṭi* as they passed through the area. According to Silva senior, "The first monks were *piṇḍapāta* [mendicant monks], but that did not last long." Eventually laity brought alms to the monks.

The father of Silva senior built a more enduring structure, hoping the monks would live there permanently. However, the resident monks of the area, fearing competition, objected. "Monks are against monks, not just the nuns," said Silva senior. Much to the disappointment of the father of Silva senior, the monks were reluctant to remain there permanently. They would say the dwelling was "not appropriate" and leave. Silva senior explained that the facilities for the monks were inadequate; they could not be guaranteed lay support or assistance in case of sickness. According to him: "We did our best, but it was not good enough for the honorable monks. We could not give them the facilities that a temple would provide."

Eventually the father of Silva senior, identifying a nun who could be persuaded to live there, promised to construct new and better buildings if she agreed to relocate. Yet, before the nun, Utterā Māniyo, could settle there, the Silva family had to ensure that the monks would vacate the premises. One monk (who had been alienated from his home temple) kept returning. Silva senior explained: "We told him that he could not have the land. Years after he left it, he came back ...because this place was being improved. We explained that we wanted the nuns to stay here permanently.... We reminded him that we had not given the place to him...we wanted someone who would stay here permanently." The monk left reluctantly, and Utterā Māniyo moved in together with another nun, Vimalā Māniyo. When I interviewed her in 1985, Utterā Māniyo explained that she was initially hesitant to move there, especially when apprised of the villagers' expectation that she found a Sunday school. She felt that such a social involvement might compromise her commitment to renunciant life.

Although Vimalā Māniyo left, Utterā Māniyo eventually established a very successful Sunday school by the late sixties. At the time of my first visit to the hermitage in 1985, there were about three hundred students attending this school, and the attendance has since remained stable. I learned that monks had contributed towards the construction of the hermitage (for example, the Buddha statue, and more recently the *caitya* and the new *sālāva*). Land that was gradually acquired during the tenure of Utterā Māniyo as head nun was, during the next three decades, generally "given" informally except for plot no. 2. Utterā Māniyo spoke to me of her plans to build a study center for her junior nuns and other female renunciants in the area. At that time, a title for the land intended for this use had not yet been deeded to the nuns. Utterā Māniyo was unable to complete her project before she died in 1985. Lay people later invited Vimalā Māniyo to take her place as head nun.

The Silva family and other supportive lay people assisted in arranging the deed for plot no. 2, but not without some difficulty. The lay people who owned that land agreed to donate it to the nuns after the government had consented to confer on them land of equivalent value in the area. However, after the government deeded them this land, the lay people, reneging on their promise, continued to occupy the land promised to the nuns. Only after considerable persuasion did they agree to abide by their part of the bargain. Although a school for nuns was not established on the land (despite the hopes of Utterā Māniyo), the new buildings erected there are now used primarily for meditation. The junior nuns lead the meditation for a handful of lay women during most of the month. Once a month on *pōya* days, about two hundred lay people visit the hermitage to attend meditation classes conducted by monks.

Today the Sunday school and the meditation center continue to attract the support and attention of lay people. The building on plot no.2, which was temporarily rented for a minimal amount to enable the government to conduct sewing classes there, has now fallen into disuse. Interestingly, the plots on which the nuns themselves live (plot nos. 1 and 3) are owned by others, while the lands with title deeds are either neglected or are used both by monks and lay people. Silva senior mentioned that it would be too difficult to draw up a title deed for plots nos. 1 and 3 for the nuns at this point. Since his own father did not draft a will, the land that the latter owned reverted automatically to his three sons and their descendants, who are now widely dispersed. The brothers of Silva senior are now deceased, so their share of the land has been inherited by their children. Now the land is jointly owned by about fifteen or twenty members of the Silva family, many of whom are difficult to locate and contact. In the mid-eighties, Silva senior had attempted to contact these relatives and make arrangements for a deed to be written donating the land to the nuns, but the undertaking did not prove feasible since the total expenses incurred in obtaining the approval of all parties involved would have far exceeded the value of the land itself.

During my visits in 1995 and 1997, I asked Vimalā Māniyo, the current head nun, about the recent changes at the hermitage and the possibility of writing a deed for the hermitage. She seemed to know little about the land to which the hermitage was legally entitled. When I queried her about the only paddy field that the nuns "owned" (plot no. 1.), which enabled the Silvas to provide rice for the nuns, she responded, "Since people give alms, what is the point of [owning] paddy?" She seemed confident of the continued support of the lay people. In discussing the rationale for acquiring a title deed, I explained that I was acquainted with nuns who often had to fight for their land once they had established themselves, and that the Aligoda hermitage could potentially be taken over by others. Her response was, "Who would take [this land}?...When one dies...this land, the coconut trees, the buildings...whatever there is here...there is no one who would take it, is there? ... One leaves everything behind and dies and is reborn elsewhere." However, when I raised land issues with Silva senior and the junior nuns, they expressed misgivings about the nuns' prospects for remaining at the Aligoda hermitage.

Lineage

Utterā Māniyo, who was ordained in 1942 when she was thirteen years old, ordained and trained nine junior nuns, four of whom were residing at the Aligoda hermitage when I last visited in 1997. Of the five others, two live together at another hermitage, one resided at still another hermitage until her death in 1988, a fourth teaches at a Sunday school, while the fifth lives in a *kuṭi*, rather than a hermitage. Some of these nuns are not head nuns at their hermitages, thus indicating a possible discontinuation of lineage. They would visit Utterā Māniyo about four times a year before she died. Now they visit the Aligoda hermitage only once every year or two, showing a further weakening of any sense of lineage they may have had. I was unable to obtain information concerning the *guru māniyo* of Utterā Māniyo's own preceptor, or of the nuns the latter had ordained. Vimalā Māniyo and Utterā Māniyo were not ordained by the same nun. Vimalā Māniyo could not identify the teacher of her own *guru māniyo*. She herself became a nun in 1939 when she was fifteen years old, and later ordained two junior nuns. One of these is a head nun and has in turn conferred ordination on three nuns. Although the two *gōlayas* of Vimalā Māniyo visit her once or twice a year, the ties between them are not strong. All four junior nuns currently living at Aligoda were ordained in the early 1980s, since which time no young junior nuns have received the ordination here. Although Utterā Māniyo and Vimalā Māniyo had lived together for several years both before and after moving to Aligoda, the junior nuns mentioned that there had been a disagreement between the two, whereupon Vimalā Māniyo had left Aligoda. After Utterā Māniyo's death, Vimalā Māniyo was invited by lay people to take the place of head nun at Aligoda. Initially, there was some dissension between Vimalā Māniyo and the four junior nuns, still fiercely loyal to Utterā Māniyo. However, over time their relations apparently became more amiable. It is clear that if no new ordinations occur or if no young nuns join the hermitage, it will be in a position similar to that of the Gedige hermitage, where an aging population of nuns faces the prospect of an insecure future.

Land and Lineage

At this moment, the Aligoda hermitage is thriving and well supported. However, the long-term prospects of this nunnery are far from certain. The only secure parcels of land that have *pūjā oppuwas* and belong to the hermitage are where the meditation classes and the Sunday school classes are held. The nuns do not exercise full control of this land, since a monk leads the most popular meditation sessions held on *pōya* days, and since the assistance of volunteer lay teachers is indispensable for the continuance of the Sunday school. Given their apparently moribund lineage, this hermitage may either come under the control of others or fall into disuse. It is possible that the meditation classes and the Sunday school will endure whether or not nuns continue to reside at Aligoda. It is not unlikely that the story of the Aligoda hermitage will come full circle, since the secure land with the *pūjā oppuwas* will necessarily at some point legally revert to monastics of some sort, most probably monks.

Comments

The three case studies all relate to nuns who were ordained in the 1940s and 1950s and established and maintained religious institutions whose roots date back about four decades. All the three "founding" nuns (Nandā Māniyo, Nuwara Māniyo, and Utterā Māniyo) were invited to take up residence in various dwelling places either by laity or, as was evident in one instance for Nandā Māniyo, by monks. Initially they engaged in a "residential" domestication[53] by agreeing to live together with other monastics. They resided in places or on land considered inhospitable or undesirable by others. They persevered, and eventually succeeded in gaining the support that enabled them to improve their hermitages, thereby maintaining the ritual area of domestication in which they become the "ritual receiver of gifts"[54] while also providing "preachers, teachers [and] scholars."[55] Nevertheless, all the nuns have shown some initial reluctance to own and manage the land on which they live. Both Nandā Māniyo (initially) and Mettikā Māniyo balked at having title deeds made in their name. Interestingly, Mettikā Māniyo, in stating, "We do not encourage them [the lay people] after all [to write the deed].... If they are giving [the land], they should just give it," echoes the words of her own head nun, despite Mettikā Māniyo's recognition that this nun had made a mistake in refusing the offer of a title deed in the first place.

All the head nuns I have interviewed appeared indifferent, or at best ambivalent, with respect to seriously addressing land issues. Mettikā Māniyo is still uncertain about who actually owns the land on which her hermitage is built. The current head nun at Aligoda, apparently oblivious to the intricacies of land issues, seems proud to point out a *caitya* rising from a plot of land that was once a paddy field. Nandā Māniyo, who was initially reluctant to accept a title deed in her name, eventually acquiesced. However, unversed in handling land issues, she almost lost the deed to a monk. Perhaps one source of the nuns' resistance to ownership of land is related to the doctrinal view of *anatta* (no self). Ontologically, this notion has philosophical implications for interpreting the uniquely Buddhist understanding of human existence. From a soteriological perspective, notions of self might be interpreted as a "conceptual manifestation of desire and attachment, [which] as such need not so much philosophical refutation as a change of character in those who hold them. This change of character will issue ultimately in the attainment of enlightened status," a status the nuns clearly strive to achieve.[56]

As improvements were made to their hermitages, all the nuns had to confront problems threatening their livelihood and their title to land. Monks living near Nandā Māniyo undermined the success of her Sunday school. Additionally, neighboring monks attempted to acquire the land on which she resided at various points in her career. Initially, certain monks who were reluctant to leave Aligoda posed a problem for the Silvas. However, after Utterā Māniyo took up residence there, she was assisted by other neighboring monks (one of whom was her younger brother). However, plot no. 5 at Aligoda was threatened by lay people, which in turn impeded the expansion of the hermitage. The land associated with the Gedige hermitage might have been larger, had the family that originally offered it not divided and sold off a section. Like Nandā Māniyo, the nuns at the Gedige hermitage faced some difficulties caused by neighboring monks. These monks refused to share a road and valuable well water with the nuns. Yet when the monks decided to leave the area, they appealed to the nuns for assistance in continuing the Sunday school they had begun. Given the growing scarcity of land as well as the monks' resistance to new monastics (male or female) who set up residence in their *godurugama* (neighborhood that supports them), it is not surprising that monks feared competition from nuns. Traditionally, monastics are not allowed to participate in religious activities in the *godurugama* of another temple without the permission of the head monk of that temple.[57] The nuns' acceptance of their domestication in the face of their continued renunciatory attitude toward land ownership indicates an interesting tension among Buddhist monastics, which has often been inappropriately dichotomized and romanticized by scholars.[58]

It is likely that the founders of the hermitages I discuss have been more successful than several in their generation in establishing themselves because of their religiosity, individual charisma, and interpersonal skills. Nandā Māniyo and Utterā Māniyo were recognized by the laity for the services they offered in educating children at a Sunday school. Also, both were given recognition by the state in the form of assistance in contributing title deeds to their hermitages: Nandā Māniyo's title deed has provided her with a place to live, whereas the deed offered to Utterā Māniyo (plot no. 5) is now a facility used for training lay meditators. Although the state has given some help to Mettikā Māniyo in installing electricity in the Gedige hermitage, most of the assistance to her hermitage has come from neighboring lay people.

Another thing these three hermitages have in common is the moribund status of their lineages. The current head nuns in this study do not maintain strong links with the junior nuns they ordained. Nandā Māniyo lives alone and is seldom visited by her junior nuns, some of whom wished to avoid conflicts with neighboring kin over the caste issue, and some of whom desired to strike out on their own. Vimalā Māniyo at Aligoda maintains some contact with the nuns she ordained, but no young junior nuns have been ordained at Aligoda since the early eighties. The Gedige hermitage similarly lacks young junior nuns to perpetuate the lineage. Today, all but one of the nuns there are over forty years of age. It is likely that the strength of the training programs for junior nuns at the three hermitages were an initial attraction for them. Nandā Māniyo and Nuwara Māniyo focused on familiarizing their junior nuns with Buddhist texts and encouraged them to teach children. However, Nandā Māniyo is now too old to mentor junior nuns and has no one to replace her. Nuwara Māniyo is deceased, but some of the nuns at the Gedige hermitage continue their education at state-sponsored classes in the area. Utterā Māniyo, who is now also deceased, provided textual training for her junior nuns. After her death, her junior nuns either chose to train at a government-sponsored class or attended meditation classes at various meditation centers where they were instructed by monks.

While a tradition of pupillage is one means of determining monastic lineage among Buddhist monks, the lack of clear notions of such a tradition at the three hermitages I discuss has led to a weakened definition of their respective lineages. It is probable that just as a landed temple attracts and contributes to the identification of lineage that might be based on pupillage or kinship, nuns who resist owning land have less incentive for recognizing, let alone respecting, lineage patterns. Evidently, the most junior nuns associated with the three hermitages who have chosen to leave those hermitages will be in situations similar to those of their preceptors. They too will, in all likelihood, encounter land problems and conflicts with monks or lay people and, like their preceptors, might not know how best to address them, thus perpetuating the cycle of renunciation and domestication that began generations ago. The case studies I have examined confirm that while a charismatic figure may contribute initially towards creating a monastic community, "for charisma to be transformed into a permanent routine structure, it is necessary that its anti-economic character should be altered."[59]

Overall, I have demonstrated that in regard to renunciation and the process of domestication, communities of nuns are very different from those of most Buddhist monks in Sri Lanka. Monks, whose roles are defined in terms of adherence to patrilineal kinship patterns and caste affiliations, often participate in lineage networks that enable them to inherit and control land more easily than nuns. Additionally, their lineages, which are also based on a well-established system of ordination and education, help consolidate their relationships with senior monks.

Nuns, whose leadership tends to be more charismatic and less institutionalized, currently do not observe these lineage patterns and consequently form communities that are significantly different from those of Buddhist monks.

The type of hermitage that I have chosen to study here may represent a dying breed in more ways than one. Since the 1980s there have been several attempts to provide nuns with an education comparable to that of monks.[60] Increasing numbers of female Buddhist renunciants from Sri Lanka are finding opportunities for advanced education in local universities and in study and monastic centers abroad in Taiwan and in India. It is likely that the new generation of female renunciants who seek initiation today are attracted to centers with strong programs rather than to a charismatic head nun alone. Additionally, since the late eighties there have been attempts to confer higher ordination on Sri Lankan women, both within and outside the country. The educational centers for female renunciants and the training women receive for higher ordination are now primarily in the hands of monks and lay people, a development that de facto precludes the foundation of a female religious lineage per se. While it is possible that enduring lineages of female renunciants will eventually form, it is still too early to assess fully the implications for lineage formation of the study centers that were initiated in the eighties and the recent higher ordinations.

Conclusion

In the past fifteen years, discussions on the prospects of Buddhist nuns have become increasingly prominent in the public discourse in Sri Lanka.[61] During this time both governmental and non-governmental organizations have taken a special interest in addressing the perceived needs of female renunciants. Endeavors to meet these needs have focused on education and ordination,[62] rather than land issues. Agarwal, in her study of land rights among South Asian women, has demonstrated that a major oversight among developmental theorists and scholars studying women's needs is their focus on employment, education, and health, in which gender is treated as an "additive category"[63] rather than "as a lens through which the approach to development should be examined."[64] She argues that the examination of land issues in relation to gender is central, as is the importance of women's ownership and effective control of land.[65] I suggest that it is possible to make a similar argument for female renunciants. While facilities for education, health, and higher ordination might enhance their status, their exclusion from land ownership and control will preclude their long-term social sanction and empowerment.

Although one should not derive generalizations about all Sri Lankan nuns from an investigation of three case studies, I suggest that the case studies I have examined are probably fairly representative of a type of hermitage that arose in Sri Lanka in the 1940s and 1950s. Some such hermitages may cease to exist because of the demise of the head nun, the loss of lay support, or the lack of junior nuns willing to reside there and train others. The findings of my case studies indicate the reasons nuns are reluctant to lay claim to the land on which they live and the consequences of their attitudes, which lead to various hardships and a possibly transient lifestyle. The lack of secure land is one factor in the weak lineages among Buddhist nuns. The junior nuns who continue to live at their preceptors' hermitages may continue to endure the hardships freed by latter (as is well illustrated at the Gedige hermitage). Those junior nuns who leave to found their own hermitages in the same manner as their preceptors may also be forced to confront land problems similar to those of their preceptors. In either case, it is clear that this type of nun, unlike the typical Buddhist monk, does not belong to a strong lineage and cannot inherit land easily. She continues to perpetuate a cycle whereby her ambivalence to land ownership entails a continued tension between renunciation and accommodation with the powers that be. This results in an ascetic livelihood that contrasts sharply with that of most monks.

Acknowledgments

I am thankful for a 1995 Augustana College faculty research grant as well as grants from the American Academy of Religion (1996) and the Augustana College Research Foundation (1997) that enabled me to conduct the research for this paper in 1995 and 1997. In Sri Lanka I am deeply indebted to the assistance given by Indira Salgado, as well as Ananda and Rukmini Kulasuriya. I am also very grateful to Paul Westman for reading and commenting insightfully on drafts of this essay and to Elli Findly for her helpful suggestions. Different aspects of this essay were presented at the following conferences: the Great Plains Regional Conference of the American Academy of Religion (Utah, 1997), the Sixth Sri Lanka Studies Conference (Sri Lanka, 1997) and the Midwest Conference of Asian Affairs (Illinois, 1997). Names of places and nuns in this paper have been changed.

Notes

1. By "nuns" I refer to the ten-precept mothers also known as *dāsa sīl manīyo,* or simply *manīyo.* I do not refer to fully ordained women or *bhikkhunīs* as nuns in this paper.
2. See M. Wijayaratna, *Buddhist Monastic Life According to the Texts of the Theravāda Tradition,* trans. C. Grangier and S. Collins (Cambridge: Cambridge University Press, 1990) 24.
3. See Heinz Bechert, *Buddhismus, Staat und Gesellshcaft in den Landern des Theravada Buddhismus,* 3 vols., 1966–1973 (Frankfurt: A. Metzner; Wiesbaden: O. Harrassowitz); Bechert, "Theravada Buddhist Sangha: Some General Observations on Historical and Political Factors in Its Development," *Journal of Asian Studies* 29 (1970): 761–78; Steven Kemper "The Buddhist Monkhood, the Law and the State in Colonial Sri Lanka," *Comparative Studies in Society and History* 26 (1984): 401–27; Hans-Deiter Evers, "'Monastic Landlordism' in Ceylon: A Traditional System in a Modern Setting," *Journal of Asian Studies* 28.4 (1969): 685–92; Kitsiri Malalgoda, *Buddhism in Sinhalese Society, 1750–1900* (Berkeley: University of California Press, 1976); Gregory Schopen, *Bones, Stones, and Buddhist Monks: Collected Papers on the Archaeology, Epigraphy, and Texts of Monastic Buddhism in India* (Honolulu: University of Hawai'i Press, 1997); Max Weber, *The Religion of India,* trans. H. Gerth and D. Martindale (New York: Free Press, 1958); R.A.L.H. Gunawardene, *Robe and Plough: Monasticism and Economic Interest in Early and Medieval Sri Lanka.* (Tucson: University of Arizona Press, 1979).
4. See George D. Bond, *The Buddhist Revival in Sri Lanka: Religious Tradition, Reinterpretation and Response.* (Columbia: University of South Carolina Press, 1988); Michael Carrithers, *The Forest Monks of Sri Lanka: An Anthropological and Historical Study* (Delhi: Oxford University Press, 1983); Carrithers, "The Modern Ascetics of Lanka and the Pattern of Change in Buddhism" *Man* 14 (1979): 294–310; Richard Gombrich and Gananath Obeyesekere, *Buddhism Transformed: Religious Change in Sri Lanka* (Delhi: Motilal Banarsidass, 1988); Ivan Strenski, "On Generalized Exchange and the Domestication of the Sangha" *Man* 18 (1983): 463–77; S.J.Tambiah, *World Conqueror and World Renouncer* (Cambridge: Cambridge University Press, 1976); N. Yalman, "The Ascetic Buddhist Monks of Ceylon" *Ethnology* 1 (1962): 315–28; J.L.Taylor, *Forest Monks and Nation-State: An Anthropological and Historical Study of Northeastern Thailand.* (Singapore: Institute of South East Asian Studies, 1993); Kamala Tiyanivich, *Forest Recollections: Wandering Monks in Twentieth-Century Thailand.* (Honolulu: University of Hawai'i Press, 1997).
5. See Tessa J. Bartholomeusz, *Women Under the Bo Tree: Buddhist Nuns in Sri Lanka.* (Cambridge: Cambridge University Press, 1994); Kusuma Devendra, "The Dasa Sil Nun: A Study of Women's Buddhist Religious Movement in Sri Lanka with an Outline of Its Historical Antecedents" (privately owned manuscript) 1987; K.M. Lily Beatrice Thamel, "A Study of the Dasa-Sil Maniyo (Consecrated Women) in the Buddhist Society of Sri Lanka" (M.A. dissertation, University of the Philippines, 1983).

6. I use the term "lineage" in a fairly loose sense in relation to female renunciants who themselves seldom recognize an affinity with more than one generation of nuns. Among Buddhist monks, lineage is a functional concept of monastic life. Whereas the ability to name one's predecessors or take over after a predecessor dies might indicate a sense of lineage among nuns, they do not appear to perceive it as a concept that defines their relationship to their neighborhood or land ownership.
7. Strenski, 464.
8. Strenski, 465.
9. Strenski, 466.
10. Strenski, 465.
11. Strenski, 465.
12. Strenski, 466.
13. Weber, *Religion of India,* 242–43; Warnasuriya, 71.
14. Schopen, 7.
15. Taylor, 59.
16. Taylor, 6, 124–25; Lawrie, 111, 412, 968.
17. Lawrie, 361–64.
18. Kemper, "Buddhist Monkhood," 408–9; Bechert, "Theravāda Buddhist Saṅgha," 768; Lawrie, 133, 457, 749.
19. Taylor, 35, 83, 124, 199; Carrithers, *Forest Monks,* 84, 104–5, 112.
20. Weber, *Religion of India,* 257.
21. Evers, "Monastic Landlordism," 686.
22. Gunawardene, *Robe and Plough,* and Hans Dieter Evers, *Monks, Priests and Peasants: A Study of Buddhism and Social Structure in Central Ceylon* (Leiden: E.J. Brill, 1972).
23. Taylor, 125; Carrithers, *Forest Monks,* 83–84.
24. Bartholomeusz, 92–108.
25. Devendra, 150–57 and 163–64; Thamel, 75–77.
26. Bartholomeusz, 132–36.
27. Carrithers, *Forest Monks,* 106.
28. Tambiah, "Structure of Kinship," 24, 35–36.
29. Bina Agarwal, *A Field of One's Own: Gender and Land Rights in South Asia* (Cambridge: Cambridge University Press, 1994), 188–91.
30. Tambiah, "Structure of Kinship," 25–33.
31. Agarwal, 180–93.
32. Thamel, 86.
33. For exceptions to this and further information, see S. Goonesekera, "Status of Women in the Family Law of Sri Lanka," *Women at the Crossroads: A Sri Lankan Perspective* (New Delhi: Vikas, 1990), 153–81.
34. Agarwal, 298–300.
35. Bechert, "Theravāda Buddhist Saṅgha," 768.
36. Salgado, forthcoming.
37. Salgado, "Ways of Knowing and Transmitting Religious Knowledge."

38. Kemper, "Buddhist Monkhood," 408–9, 419.
39. Interview conducted in August 1997 with Manik Dissanayaka, assistant director of cultural affairs, Kandy.
40. Gombrich and Obeyesekere, 68; Obeyesekere, 137.
41. Devendra, 269.
42. I first met and talked with Nandā Māniyo in December 1984 and then again in April 1985. I was out of touch with her until November 1995, when I was able to continue our conversations. My account of her story is primarily drawn from discussions with her during my stays at her hermitage in 1995 and 1997.
43. She said this was an issue because *saṅghika* land (land belonging to fully ordained monastics, which traditionally excludes women) would someday be returned to the monks since this was a part of their heritage.
44. This was a monk from a nearby temple who had shown some hostility to the nuns' presence in the area. After gaining possession of the property in Lonuwara, he then went on to request the newly acquired property of the nuns in Sinipitiya.
45. Nānda Māniyo admitted that she had fully trusted the monk and therefore had not read the document that she signed.
46. Letter to the additional government agent *(atireka disapatituma)* from the district member of parliament, dated 30 December, 1989.
47. Nānda Māniyo later discovered that this monk had previously attempted to acquire land in a like manner and was known to government officials for his activities.
48. I first met Mettikā Māniyo in 1995 and have continued communications with her since then, in particular during several visits to her hermitage in 1997. Although I was unable to interview the junior nuns at this hermitage, I met and interviewed members of the Perera family on two consecutive occasions in 1997.
49. Tracing land deeds at the local office in Sri Lanka is impossible unless one has the identification number of the deed in question. I was unable to obtain such a number and could not search for the putative deed without further assistance.
50. I questioned officers at the Department of Buddhist Affairs concerning providing some assistance to the Gedige hermitage, but they informed me that this was impossible since the hermitage was built on private land.
51. I had the opportunity of visiting this hermitage several times. During my 1985 visit I interviewed the founding head nun, Utterā Māniyo, as well as all the junior nuns there. In later visits to this hermitage in 1994, 1995, and 1997 I continued discussions with the junior nuns and also talked with the new head nun and members of the Silva family, who are important lay supporters of the Aligoda hermitage. My account of this hermitage includes information drawn from several repeat interviews culled from my communications with this nunnery since 1985.
52. A *billāva* is a small piece of land that is connected to a paddy field. Whoever owns the paddy-field also owns the *billāva.* In this case, the *billāva* is owned by members of the Silva family.
53. Strenski, 365.

54. Strenski, 465.
55. Strenski, 465.
56. Steven Collins, *Selfless Persons: Imagery and Thought in Theravada Buddhism* (1982; Cambridge, Cambridge University Press, 1990), 119–20.
57. Weerakoon, 18.
58. Schopen, 1–55.
59. Weber, *Max Weber on Charisma,* 61
60. Salgado, "Ways of Knowing and Transmitting Religious Knowledge."
61. Salgado, "Buddhist Nuns."
62. Salgado, "Ways of Knowing and Transmitting Religious Knowledge."
63. Agarwal, 4.
64. Agarwal, 4.
65. Agarwal, 10–19 and 44.

TRANSFORMATION OF A HOUSEWIFE: *Dipa Ma Barua and Her Teachings to Theravāda Women*

AMY SCHMIDT

As a practicing Buddhist, I have often wondered how much transformation is possible within this life. Am I fooling myself to hope that my deepest habits can be eradicated, especially in me, a lay person? Could my daily experiences of fear, anger, frustration, and envy really begin to dissipate?

The story to follow, of a formerly anxious, pudgy, middle-aged housewife named Dipa Ma, is about a woman who cracked open under the blows of repeated loss and grief. It is about a woman who in some ways was not so different than me, a woman who began as a lay person and made it her mission to teach ordinary people. She became a Buddhist saint who influenced the future of vipassanā *meditation by touching the hearts of the foremost American teachers. She became a living example that "anything is possible."*

Dipa Ma's story has inspired me to keep practicing moment after moment, year after year, with the ember of hope that I, too, can find such peace and loving-kindness.

DIPA MA was born as Nani Bala Barua in a tiny village in the plains district of Chittagong, Pakistan, now Bangladesh. The year was 1911, and she was the first child born into Purnachandra Barua's family, part of a Bengali clan whose members trace their lineage back to the time of the Buddha.[1]

Nani was close to her parents and the six siblings who followed. Her parents found her an unusual child, for from a very young age she was fascinated with Buddhist rituals. Contrary to the custom of keeping small children away from monks, her parents allowed Nani to offer food, wash the monks' feet, and sit with them while they ate. Instead of pretend-cooking like most little girls her age, Nani seemed solely interested in creating miniature altars and offering flowers to the Buddha. Nani also loved going to school. Although it was not traditional for village girls to attend school, she could not be kept away. Even if she was sick, she would sneak off to the classroom, and often sat up late in the evenings with her father discussing lessons.

According to the laws of Bengali culture, Nani was to be married before the onset of menstruation, thus, despite her love of school, her education ended abruptly during the fifth grade. At twelve, she was offered in marriage to Rajani Barua, a man of twenty-five, and sent from her small village and family to live with his parents. Within two weeks of the marriage, Rajani left for an engineering job in Myanmar. Nani was left behind to suffer two long years with her demanding in-laws. At fourteen, she was put on a boat to Rangoon to begin a life in a new country with a man she had known for only two weeks.

Stepping off the boat was quite a shock to this timid country girl. Rangoon was a loud, strange place with unfamiliar faces and a language she could not understand. Married life, too, presented new territory for young Nani. Although she had been carefully instructed by her mother and aunts about how to run a household, no one had ever said a word about sex. Her husband was the first to tell her. Nani recalls that she was "very shocked, very nervous, and terribly ashamed." For the first year of married life she felt quite terrified of her husband. During that year, Rajani remained unfailingly gentle and supportive of his new wife. Nani came to see him as a "rare human being," and a trust developed between them. She considered Rajani her "first teacher" and, over the next few years, the two of them fell deeply in love. Despite their happy relationship, Nani became increasingly anxious as the years went by: to fulfill her commitment as wife, she should have borne a child, preferably a son, during the first year of marriage. But year after year went by with no pregnancies. Nani tried going to doctors and healers, but no one could find the reason for her infertility.

Meanwhile, Rajani's family and village, concerned that Nani was disgracing their reputation, lured Rajani back to Pakistan under the guise of family illness. Once home, Rajani was informed that a new wife was waiting and he was to marry her immediately. Rajani refused to participate, asserting that this would be unfair to Nani. He then returned to Myanmar and told Nani never to worry about having children. He offered her some advice she used the rest of her life: "Why don't you just make every person your own? Adopt each person you meet and treat them as if they were your only child." These words unfolded for Nani in her later years. She lovingly addressed each person with "You are my son," "You are my daughter." A student, Dipak Chowdhury, recalls, "She was not only a teacher, but also a mother. She taught each one of us with as much care as her own children. I will always be just a little boy of 'mother.'"

At age eighteen, Nani's wish for a child was ironically granted when her beloved mother died suddenly and left behind an eighteen-month-old baby boy, her youngest brother Bijoy, in need of a home. Nani and Rajani offered to raise the child as their own.

Family portrait of Dipa Ma with Bijoy and husband Rajani, Rangoon, 1937 (photographer unknown); Bijoy is 10, Dipa Ma is 26

As a family they were actively involved in the Buddhist community. They followed the precepts, maintained daily rituals, and often sponsored feast days for the monks. Frequently Nani asked Rajani if she could learn meditation. He refused each request, always suggesting that she wait until she was older, in accord with the Indian custom of pursuing the spiritual life, as a *sādhu,* in later years after one has dispensed with one's householder responsibilities.

At age thirty-five, with Bijoy now out of the house and her father deceased from old age, Nani thought that the time to learn meditation was near. Suddenly, however, a miracle happened. After over twenty years of trying to bear a child, Nani discovered she was pregnant, and happily gave birth to a girl. Three months later, the child became ill and died. Overwhelmed with grief, Nani developed heart disease. Four years later, she was blessed with another pregnancy. Again it was a girl, whom she named Dipa, thus the origin of her name Dipa Ma, mother of Dipa. Dipa was a healthy child who was growing into a toddler when Ma became pregnant yet again, this time with the all-important boy child. This infant died at birth, again causing Ma tremendous grief. In desperation, she demanded the right to learn meditation to relieve her sorrow. Again, Rajani insisted this was not the time. Ma boldly persisted, claiming she could sneak away if necessary, prompting Rajani to ask a neighbor to keep watch over her.

This vigil soon became unnecessary since Ma was stricken with high blood pressure and hypertension and couldn't leave her bed, much less the house, for the next five years. She was expected to die at any time. Rajani nursed Ma and took charge of toddler, Dipa, himself while he continued to work full-time as an engineer. The stress of this situation eventually became overwhelming. Rajani arrived home from work one night, feeling ill, and was dead within hours of a heart attack.

Dipa Ma was overwhelmed with grief and confusion. "I couldn't find any way to see what to do, where to go, or how to live. I had nothing." Both her parents, two of her children, and her husband were dead. India was far away. She was a forty-four-year-old invalid, with a six-year-old daughter, and no one to help her. Months went by, and all Ma would do was cry and hold a photo of Rajani in her lap. Ma's health continued to worsen, and her doctor suggested that her only hope of survival was to learn meditation. Ma reflected on the irony of this: When she had been healthy and eager to practice, she was prevented; now, totally exhausted and facing death, she was encouraged to work with a teacher.

> I looked around me. I looked at my dowry—my silk saris and gold jewelry—and I knew I couldn't take them. I looked at my daughter, and as much as I loved her, I knew I couldn't take her. So what could I take? I said, "Let me go to the meditation center. Maybe I can find something there I can take with me when I die."[2]

The Buddha appeared before her in a dream one night, his presence luminous. He looked at Ma and chanted softly his lesson for her:

> Clinging to what is dear brings sorrow.
> Clinging to what is dear brings fear.
> For one who is entirely free from endearment
> There is no sorrow or fear.[3]

When Ma awoke, she felt clear and calm. She knew she must meditate no matter what her state of health. She understood the Buddha's advice. If she wanted true peace, she must practice until she was free from all attachment. Ma knew of the Kamayut Meditation Center in Rangoon and she immediately made arrangements to go there. Though she had performed Buddhist rituals all her life, Ma didn't have a clue what meditation was or how to practice it. She gave all her property and jewelry to a neighbor saying, "Please take whatever I have, and take care of Dipa." She expected never to return.

At the center, Ma was given her first practice instructions at one in the morning. The rest of the night and the next day Ma spent meditating. Ma became astonishingly focused and entered a state of *samādhi.* Late in the afternoon, she began her slow, mindful walk to the teacher interview. About halfway there, she noticed a heaviness in her leg. Puzzled, she tried to lift her foot but was unable. She stood there quietly for several minutes noticing heaviness and trying again to move her foot. Ma finally turned her gaze downward and saw, to her horror, that a large dog had clamped its teeth around her leg. Jolted from her concentration, she screamed for help. She tried to shake off the offender, but the dog, with an equal display of concentration, would not let go. The dog was finally pried loose by some monks. Afterwards, Ma traveled upriver to the hospital for daily rabies injections. She eventually became too weak from this ordeal and had to return home.

Once home, the nine-year-old Dipa, traumatized by the earlier departure, would not let her mother out of her sight. Ma felt that her one opportunity for enlightenment had passed and out of frustration she wept frequently. She didn't give up the practice, however. With her initial instructions, she patiently practiced at home whenever she was able for several years. Fortuitously, her life events once again provided her with the opportunity for retreat. Ma learned that a Bengalese family friend, Munindraji, was living at a nearby monastery. She invited him to her home and related her meditation experience over tea. Munindraji encouraged her to come to Thathana Yeiktha, the meditation center where he was studying under Mahasi Sayadaw. This rare opportunity to learn from such an eminent teacher became a reality as her sister Hema arrived in Rangoon with her family. Dipa could feel safe with her aunt, uncle, and many favorite cousins.

So off Ma went, for the second time. She had been an insomniac since Rajani died, and was baffled to find that no matter how hard she tried, now she couldn't stay awake. Quickly though, by the third day, Ma had shifted into deep concentration again, and the need for sleep vanished, along with the desire to eat. Munindraji, concerned that her concentration was out of balance, requested that she attend Mahasi Sayadaw's weekly talk, even though she wouldn't understand a word of his Burmese. Ma didn't want to go, but he encouraged her.

> She got there with a lot of difficulty. She experienced heart palpitations on the way, and ended up actually crawling into the hall on her hands and knees, feeling very weak. She didn't understand the talk and just continued her practice. When Sayadaw finished his talk, he checked some students' practice and left. Ma found she couldn't get up. She felt stuck to her seat. Her body was stiff, immobilized by the depth of her *samādhi*. Some friends stayed with her and looked after her until she could leave.[4]

In the following days, Ma's practice went through the classical phases of the progress of insight. She experienced a brilliant light, followed by the feeling that everything around her was dissolving. Her body, the floor—"everything was in pieces, empty, broken." This gave way to intense mental and physical pain. The physical pain manifested as a sense of sudden burning and constricting in her body, which became unbearable. She was ready to burst with pressure when something happened. She describes the next moment as "I did not know"—a simple moment, wherein everything ceased. Such a delicately quick and quiet moment, it seemed as if nothing had happened at all. Yet, Ma realized, "a change had come in my life."

After three decades of searching for freedom, in six days she had reached first-stage enlightenment. And change indeed came into her life. Almost immediately Ma's blood pressure returned to normal. Her heart palpitations decreased dramatically; Ma recalls that "in one sitting my heartbeat went down by seventy-five percent." Previously unable to climb even the monastery stairs, now this ascent was effortless, and she could walk at any pace, anywhere. As the Buddha had predicted in her dream, the grief she felt day and night vanished. And with fear also gone, Ma felt a prevailing sense of equanimity.

For the rest of the year, Ma went back and forth between home and the meditation center. She practiced for another stage of insight, and experienced a breakthrough after only five days of meditation. The progress leading to this insight was similar to the first, except that it entailed even more pain and suffering. After this second stage of enlightenment, her physical and mental condition was transformed yet again, with a diminishment in irritation and restlessness and an increase in physical stamina.

Ma's friends and family, fascinated by her transformation, began to trickle into the meditation center. The first to arrive were friend Khuki Ma and sister Hema. Later Ma's daughter Dipa and several of Hema's daughters joined them. They were quite a sight to behold: two middle-aged mothers with their covey of teenage daughters in a sea of saffron-robed monks. Since women rarely came to the monastery, their accommodations were rustic. Ma's niece Daw Than Myint remembers laughingly that "we had to climb through the bushes to get to our teacher interviews."

Hema, as adept as Ma, progressed rapidly to a level equal to her sister's. Although neither Ma nor Hema would reveal the extent of their spiritual progress, both sisters liberated their minds of craving and ill will to an unusual degree. Dr. Jack Engler, during his research with Ma, did get her, circuitously, to reveal her progress:

> *Jack Engler:* Very often in most people's practice, sense-desire comes up. Does this come up in your own meditation?
>
> *Dipa Ma:* Sense-desire comes up for everyone. It came up for me also. When it arose, I knew it. Through knowing when it occurs, you can overcome it. I don't feel sense-desires anymore now.
>
> *JE:* You are never bothered by them any more?
>
> *DM:* No. After the "third path" they are no longer there. The five "lower fetters" have been removed. [She names them in Pali, translated in English as: belief in permanent self, attachment to rites and rituals, skeptical doubt, sense-desire, and anger.]
>
> *JE:* Just to clarify, could I ask again if you yourself experience sense-desires?

DM: Yes, I did.
JE: You do?
DM: I did.
JE: You did, but now you don't?
DM: Now I don't.
JE: Has your basic understanding of life changed?
DM: My outlook has changed greatly. Before I was too attached to everything. I was possessive. I wanted things. But now it feels like I'm floating, detached. I am here, but I don't want things, I don't want to possess anything. *I'm living—that's all. That's enough.*

Ma also revealed an absence of anger: "It comes and it dies right out." This, she said, created particular difficulties for her as a mother. Though she realized the need to guide Dipa in what was appropriate behavior, no matter how mischievous her daughter got, Ma never felt angry. Ma finally decided to "pretend" to be angry, something she remembered being quite hard.

In addition to the rewards of enlightenment, Ma became involved in a new dimension of practice. Nineteen sixty-five was also a year of fun and magic. Mahasi Sayadaw advised his student Munindraji, before he returned to India, "You are going to go back to the land of *siddhis* [powers] and teach. You should know something about them." Munindraji had been too busy with his Bengali students to train himself personally in the access of psychic powers. So, as an experiment, he chose his most devoted students (Ma and her family) and trained them directly out of a book.[5] Since Munindraji knew that psychic powers were in essence amoral, he carefully selected students who were at least at first-stage enlightenment, so that they would not be seduced or swayed by the use of their new-found powers.

Ma, Hema, and their three daughters were introduced to the realms of dematerialization, doubling the body, cooking food without fire, mind-reading, visiting the heaven and hell realms, time travel, and more. Ma was the most adept of all Munindraji's students and was also very playful. She would arrive at her interview by nonchalantly walking through the wall or by appearing spontaneously out of the air. On one occasion Munindraji looked out his window and saw Ma sitting in the sky in a room she had created, playing happily. Ma and her sister once used their psychic powers in combination. At the time they were traveling by bus to an appointment some distance away. The bus was behind schedule and, so as not to miss their appointment, they picked up the crowded vehicle, and moved it through time and space. Much to the surprise of fellow passengers, they arrived "on time" at their destination.

Munindraji enjoyed using Ma in psychic power "experiments" that he could verify. At the time, a Burmese diplomat, U Thant, was to become the new secretary general of the United Nations. Munindraji, knowing that U Thant would give an acceptance speech, asked Ma to go into the future and remember its contents. Ma recited the speech, and while Munindraji recorded it, sure enough, a month later U Thant gave the exact same speech, word for word.

Munindraji's most notable experiment involved third-party verification and occurred much later after they both had returned to India. Munindraji's friend, a professor of ancient Indian history at Magadha University, said he did not believe in psychic powers. Munindraji told him that they were true and he could prove it. The two of them set up the following situation: the professor posted a trusted graduate student in a room at the Gandhi Ashram where Ma was meditating. The student watched Ma continually. While the student was doing this, Ma walked into the professor's office ten miles away and had a conversation with him.

Despite an incredible year, the magic ended when Munindraji returned to India in 1966. Ma, Dipa, Hema, and Hema's two daughters continued to practice meditation, but eventually chose to discontinue the *siddhis.* Ma never demonstrated these powers again, except when Munindraji made a special request. She always insisted that these powers were "nothing" and "did not lead to freedom, which is the true goal of practice."

After Munindraji's departure, Dipa Ma became sought after as a guide in meditation. Her first formal student was Malati Barua. Malati was trying to raise six very young children. She was quite eager to meditate but unable to leave her house. Dipa Ma devised home practices for her new student. She taught Malati to be steadfastly mindful every time she held and nursed her infant son. As Ma had hoped, Malati attained insight without ever leaving her home. This was the beginning of Ma's long career of leading householders, and especially women householders, to wisdom in the midst of their daily lives.

In 1967, the Myanmar government ordered all foreigners to leave the country. The monks pleaded with Ma: "Don't go from here. You can remain here forever as a teacher, and your daughter can remain here forever." This was an unprecedented honor for a woman, a foreigner, and a single mother. But Ma decided it would be best to return to India where Dipa could pursue a higher education in Bengali. They moved to a relative's house in the suburbs of Calcutta. Ma felt isolated in her new surroundings. She recalled that whenever she mentioned meditation, the local women "would get annoyed."

After a year, Ma and Dipa moved to a tiny apartment in an old building above a metal grinding shop in the center of the city. It had a closet-sized kitchen with one charcoal burner on the floor, no running water, and a communal toilet for two families. Ma's bed was a thin straw mat. This was her choice, because "too much luxury can become a hindrance to practice."

Slowly, over the course of years, word spread throughout the Bengali community that an accomplished meditation teacher had come from Myanmar. There was a certain hesitancy in the beginning. Although many families observed the Buddhist rituals, meditation was still foreign to the average lay person. Ma represented a new and different direction for the community. Word spread, however, that this was a teacher who could "bring results." One by one, Calcutta housewives began to arrive.

Dipa Ma taught them to make every moment of their lives a meditation. She emphasized bringing mindfulness into talking, ironing, cooking—every activity. She frequently stated, "The whole path of mindfulness is whatever you are doing. Be aware of it." Student Michele Levey recalled, "She believed you could become enlightened ironing your clothes...she felt that every activity should have that much mindfulness! And the care should be there too, the care for whoever you were ironing the clothes for."

Ma also demanded that her students closely follow the five precepts, something she herself did until the day she died. She requested students to sleep only four hours a night, despite full working lives. They were to meditate several hours a day, report to her twice or more a week, and undertake self-guided retreats for periods of time when she deemed them "ready." Jack Kornfield, *vipassanā* teacher and author, remembers Ma's unique home-style teachings: "She didn't want people to come and live in India forever or be monks or join the ashram; she said, 'Live your life, do the dishes, do the laundry, take your kid to kindergarten, raise your children or your grandchildren, take care of the community in which you live, and make all of that your path, follow your path with heart.'"

Ma had so much faith in the power of everyday practice amid the hubbub of home life that one admirer dubbed her "the patron saint of the householder."[6] When asked about the difference between formal meditation practice and daily life, she adamantly advised, "You cannot separate meditation from life."

Because she believed so deeply in these middle-aged Calcutta housewives, and because they had such incredible faith in her, one by one, simply from meditating within the context of daily life, a remarkable percentage of them experienced deep insight. Similar to the stories of the Buddha, wherein he uttered just a few words, and the listener would become fully enlightened, Dipa Ma affected her students in profound and sudden ways. Engler relates the story of one particular student, Madhuri Lata:

> Since Madhuri was a semi-retarded woman, perhaps with an IQ of 80 or so, Ma gave her the basic instructions [to follow her breath at her abdomen and note] "rising, falling, rising, falling." Madhuri said "right," and started to go home. She had to go down four flights of stairs and across the alley to her apartment. She didn't get halfway down the flights of stairs before she forgot the instructions. So, back she came.

"What was I supposed to do?"

"Rising, falling, rising, falling," said Dipa Ma.

"Right."

Four times she forgot the instructions and had to come back, and Ma was very patient with her. And it took her almost a year to understand the basic instructions. But once she got them she was like a tiger. Before she began practice she was bent over at a ninety-degree angle, she had arthritis, rheumatism, and intestinal problems. When I met her, after meditation, she walked with a straight back. There were no more intestinal problems. She was the simplest, sweetest, gentlest woman. And she attained enlightenment. After she told me her enlightenment story, she said, "All this time I've wanted to tell someone this wonderful thing that happened to me and I've never been able to share this before. This is the most precious thing in my life."

In a tradition of mostly male teachers, male roles, and male buddhas, Ma was a powerful reminder that women can find freedom too. Michele McDonald-Smith, a *vipassanā* teacher, recalls, "For me to meet a woman who was that enlightened, it was more powerful than I can ever put into words. She embodied what I deeply wanted to be like. She is like a lighthouse...a light I can orient to so I can do it myself. I've never needed anything else in terms of inspiration!"

Ma announced to her women students, "You can go more quickly and deeper in the practice than men because your minds are softer," adding, "Women's tendency to be more emotional is *not* a hindrance to practice." Softness of mind, she explained, is what brings more emotion, more movement. This is something to be witnessed, not identified with. Ma was also not afraid to challenge the traditional Theravāda doctrine that claims only men can be buddhas. Her feminist stance, normally just an undercurrent, could sometimes surprise her students:

On this particular day we were all sitting on the floor of Ma's room. Dipa was also there. It was very crowded, and very hot. Munindraji was sitting on a chair in the corner talking to Ma's students about the Dhamma and about their practice. He and I were the only men in the room. While he talked, Ma was sitting on her wooden bed leaning back against the wall, with her eyes closed. It looked like she dozed off. She hadn't been well and no one took any notice. The conversation was about rebirth. Somehow it got on to the rebirths of the Buddha. Obviously not thinking much about it, since it was part of the tradition, Munindraji happened to mention that only men could become buddhas—to become a buddha, you had to have taken rebirth in a male body. Suddenly, Ma bolted upright, eyes wide open, and said in a tone of spontaneous and utter conviction, "I can do anything a man can do!" Our reaction was equally spontaneous—we all laughed, Munindraji included. I think we all knew it was absolutely true![7]

Ma's support of women had a deep and lasting impact. One woman recalls: "What she said was shocking. Coming from a tradition where women are treated as inferiors, just to talk about equality was a big deal. Then to have Ma say, 'Well, actually women have an edge on the practice,' now that was revolutionary!" Ma also dared to challenge the Indian cultural norms for women. Dipaka Barua, along with many other housewives, was continually chided by Ma to "get an education and become economically independent." Ma would not accept any excuses or objections. If a woman expressed doubt in this regard, Ma would firmly assert, "Never think that women are helpless."

Ma pushed each person to go further, to practice harder, to make use of every moment as if it were his or her last. She continually reminded students: "Human life is most precious. You should not waste it." In a caring way, but with eagle eyes, she looked for the slack in her students' practice—where they were being lazy, what could be improved. Kate Wheeler described Dipa Ma as someone who "had seen her mind go through every kind of suffering and was able to sit through it. Later, when she came out of that fire there was something very determined, almost frightening, about how she could look at you because she had seen herself. There was nowhere to hide."

Ma wasn't interested in helping students "move the furniture around."[8] She wanted real change, and real change meant diligence. When a student, Sudipti Barua, insisted that managing a demanding bakery business and large family left no spare time for meditation, Ma adeptly asked, "Well, can you sit with me for just five minutes now?" After five minutes, Ma said, "Let's do this again tomorrow." Within a few months Sudipti was

Dipa Ma, 1984
(photo by Janice Rubin)

meditating late into the night, sacrificing sleep for many hours of practice. Ma didn't believe in "time off." She wanted students to make meditation and mindfulness a first priority. Bob Ray recalls:

> When Dipa Ma asked me about my practice, and I told her that I meditated in the morning and the evening every day, and the rest of the day I worked at my job. Then she inquired, "Well...what do you do on weekends?" I don't remember my answer but her response was, "There are two days. You should be practicing all day Saturday and Sunday."

And Joseph Goldstein recounts:

> The last time I saw her before she died, Dipa Ma turned to me and said, "You know, you should sit for two days." She did not mean a two-day retreat; she meant I should sit for two days straight! Just sit, for two days! When she said this, I started to laugh because it seemed so beyond my capacity. She looked at me with deep compassion and said, "Don't be lazy."

The ultimate magic of Ma, however, was her ferocity combined with an outpouring of motherly love. She bathed students in blessings, which brought rapture from head to toe. She doted, gave gifts, caressed hearts, hand-fed students with curries, and soothed and cooed over each person as if she or he were a newborn. Once, she playfully conducted a group interview with her grandson's plastic toy dump-truck turned upside down upon her head. During the course of a day nothing escaped her love. In the morning she might be tapping good wishes to every fish in the aquarium, at noon blessing a friend's dog, and in the afternoon chanting to the airplane before boarding. Her delight was like that of a child's, and it was contagious.

She taught a *metta* (loving-kindness) meditation, emphasizing over and over again "the first thing is to love yourself." She advised, "You cannot progress by self-doubt and self-hatred; only by self-love. This is the fuel. Our mind is our friend. It is our own source of help. It is our refuge. Unless you have respect for yourself, you can't proceed." She encouraged students to discover where tiger-like effort arises from the heart. For her, love and mindfulness were one.

Ma's teachings began to draw record numbers to her tiny tenement apartment. The daily fare included a melange of parents, children, grandparents, curious neighbors, devout relatives, and studious monks. One senior monk and scholar, Dr. Rastrapal Mahathera, pursued Ma's advice despite colleagues who wondered,

"After doing your doctorate how could you practice meditation under a woman?"[9] Sometimes Ma had so many visitors that every space in her room was filled, and students had to stand out on the balcony. Students came from early in the morning until eleven at night. Ma took very little sleep and was tirelessly available to anyone seeking the Dhamma.

Ma's caring presence changed not only her students but all those around her:

> When she first moved into her apartment complex it was a pretty noisy and contentious place, with a lot of bickering, arguing and yelling among the tenants, amplified by the open courtyard. Everyone knew everyone else's business because it was being shouted back and forth all the time. Within six months of her moving in, the whole place had quieted down and people were starting to get along with each other for the first time. Her presence, and the way she dealt with people—quietly, calmly, gently, treating them with kindness and respect, setting limits and challenging their behavior when necessary but out of concern for everyone's welfare, not out of anger or simple desire for her personal comfort—set an example and made it impossible to carry on in the angry, contentious way they had before.... It was the simple force of her presence: you couldn't act like that around her. You just didn't.[10]

Gradually Ma's popularity filtered into the American meditation community. Joseph Goldstein was the first to arrive and later brought his friend Sharon Salzberg. Sharon and Joseph adored Ma and continued to seek her guidance until the day she died. Each of them described Ma as "the most loving person I have ever met." Ma took a very motherly stance towards young Sharon, offering advice and sometimes interesting premonitions:

> In 1974, when I went to Calcutta to say good-bye, I told her, "I'm going back to America for a short time, to get my health together, to get some more money, and then I'll be back." She shook her head and asserted, "No, when you go back to America you'll be teaching meditation with Joseph." And I said, "No, I won't," and she said, "Yes, you will," and I said, "No, I won't..." Finally she just looked me in the eye and declared, "You know, you can do anything you want to do.... It's only your thinking that you can't do it that's stopping you." This was a great blessing with which she sent me off, back to America. And that was twenty-one years ago. She was right!

Sharon and Joseph told other friends about Ma, including Jack Kornfield, who met Ma in the late 1970s. Each teacher told their students about Ma, and they in turn told others, who told still others. Ma was a curious entity to Westerners. Physically, she was almost invisible—a frail, old woman poking from her white sari like "a little bug wrapped up in cotton."[11] Yet in terms of sheer energy, she was a giant. Entering her presence was like "walking into a force field" where magical shifts happened. Sometimes these shifts included the experiences of mind-to-mind communication and changes in perception and concentration states. Other times the shifts were calming, as though one were merging into her "unshakable peace" or finding a place to "rest in her silence, like resting under a large shade tree."[12]

Dipa Ma developed an even greater following of Americans when she helped teach the three-month retreat at Insight Meditation Society in 1980 and again in 1984. Even though Ma was sixty-nine and experiencing heart problems, she agreed to make the long journey to America, bringing her daughter and toddler grandson.

The cultural stretch was immense. With Ma around, one could not take for granted anything that Americans normally take for granted, for example, that corn flakes and milk are best eaten with a spoon, that a shower has a spigot and faucets through which water is dispensed, that large dogs actually live in houses and are fed off plates, or that boxes manned by empty machines spit money when you push buttons. Steven Schwartz, whose house she lived in that first month, spent a lot of time trying to make her comfortable, until he finally realized that, like the Buddha, she had no actual preferences.

The power of Ma's presence was profound. In a group interview Jack Kornfield innocently asked Ma, "Just what is it like in your mind?" Ma smiled, closed her eyes, and quietly answered, "In my mind there are three things, concentration, loving-kindness, and peace." Jack, not sure he was hearing right, said, "Is that all?" Ma calmly replied, "Yes...that's all." The room was silent. There were a few sighs and laughs, then Jack's barely audible whisper "Ah, how wonderful." Although health problems prevented her return to America, she continued to teach from her Calcutta apartment until her death five years later.

Dipa Ma died on the evening of September 1, 1989. She was seventy-eight years old. Her death came quite unexpectedly and entailed little suffering. According to her daughter, it only took Ma about ten to twenty minutes to die. Sandip Mutsuddi, neighbor and devoted student for years, had prayed, "Please let me be by Ma's side when she dies." Miraculously, given the sudden onset of her death, his wish was granted. Sandip relates the story of her death:

> When Dipa came back from the office that evening, Ma told her she was feeling uneasy. Dipa asked her, "Should I call the doctor?" She was silent

for awhile and after some time she said, "Okay." Dipa asked me to go get the doctor. So I went, but the doctor was not at his chambers—he was at another patient's house. When I returned, I told her the doctor was out and would come as soon as possible. Then I went and sat down next to Dipa Ma, and Dipa and I massaged her. Then Ma asked me to touch her head. So I touched her head and I started chanting the suttas she taught me. When she heard me chanting, she bowed with her hands in prayer. She bowed toward the Buddha and did not get up. So we both lifted her off the floor and found that her breathing had stopped. She had died in her bow to the Buddha! Her face was very calm and at peace.

Three to four hundred people, including monks, attended Dipa Ma's funeral several days later. She was on an open cot. One by one, students filed past and laid a flower on her body, until she was completely covered in flowers.

Notes

1. Throughout this chapter, almost all of the historical information and direct quotations are from Jack Engler, Ph.D. These are his personal, unpublished writings provided for a book in progress about Dipa Ma. Jack graciously gleaned through voluminous amounts of research notes and personal memories to provide the body of this story.

   Other information was provided by Venerable Rastrapala Bhikkhu, Ph.D., in his writing of the 1989 Indian biography of Nani Bala, and by Sukomal Chowdhury, Ph.D., in his 1997 English translation of this biography. And many thanks to Ma's daughter Dipa Barua for her many additions.
2. Jack Engler, personal writings.
3. Ananda Maitreya and Rose Kramer, ed., *The Dhammapada* (Novato, CA: Lotsawa, 1988), 4, 16.
4. Jack Engler, personal writings.
5. Bhadantācariya Buddhaghosa, *The Path of Purification: Visuddhi Magga* (3rd ed.; Kandy, Sri Lanka: Buddhist Publication Society, 1975).
6. Daeja Napier, interview, 1997.
7. Jack Engler, personal writings. A first version of this story is published in the following: M. McDonald, "Dipa Ma: A Memorial," *The Inquiring Mind* 6.2 (winter/spring 1990): 19.
8. Kate Wheeler, interview, 1997.
9. Fortunately Dr. Rastrapal's persistence paid off: after eighteen years of practice as a monk, within just a week Ma guided him to experience deep insight. In gratitude to

Ma, he built a meditation hall in her name (the Nani Bala Meditation Hall) at the International Meditation Center in Bodhgaya, India.

10. Jack Engler, personal writings. A first version of this story is published in the following: M. McDonald, op. cit.
11. Kate Wheeler, interview, 1997.
12. Alan Clements, interview, 1997.

MY DHARMA TEACHER DIED TOO SOON

James Whitehill

Miko (photo by James Whitehill)

My Japanese Dharma teacher died last year, too young and too soon. She was fifty-four, with no Dharma heirs and only five live-in students in recent years. I was her oldest student at fifty-six, but also her newest and only male student. I lived in her compact Midwestern group for only ten years, while her youngest female student already had fifteen years of close nurturing under her care. From their privileged position of "seniority-by-date-of-admission" in our little Sangha, the much younger female disciples feel free to make fun of my bald head and recent admission, often calling me "old stepfather." I don't mind at all, for I was happy from the beginning to be close to "my" *roshi*, trusting that daily physical, cellular proximity to her could bring me to a threshold of spiritual intimacy wherein my true nature could shine at last.

Living with her, I hoped to become a buddha or at least considerably wiser and more virtuous than I thought I was going into the arrangement. Since she died, I have thought much about her and, lately, she seems to visit me in dreams, where she tries to give me a message, written on paper. In the most recent dream, I glimpsed a corner of one side of the white sheet she was holding. I see my signature, and scribblings above it. The scribbling is not mine, I am sure, and I feel frustrated as I try to decipher it. Then she hugs me, and her face dissolves as I look down on her. As in real life, I am a foot taller than she is. I was never comfortable looking "down" on my *roshi*, but in the dream I like the close feeling.

Sometimes during the day I feel her voice inside me, interrupting my thoughts when they are about to screw me up or become too intellectually speculative. It feels like her voice, saying the typically surprising things to me, but I may be mistaken.

In truth, her voice became one of my voices through a very close ten-year absorption, of "taking her in," so much so that it is hard for me to distinguish between them sometimes, depending on my mood. She was very present to me, my *roshi*, and I "swallowed" her like every good student does with his or her Buddhist master. So her "voice" might be "her" voice as transmuted through me into one of "my" voices. But, as I said, she had no Dharma heirs, so I can't really speak for her. Only about her, from the standpoint of a special intimacy, perhaps rare, perhaps not so rare at all. But not ordinary, I am certain.

Nevertheless, the sense of her being here, of her compact, intensely physical presence, ebbs irreversibly. I am losing her, as my grief works at its own pace. Daily, I observe my reactions to absence and loss as they take on different, but steadily fading, weights, colors, and sharpness. She dims, and I seem to evaporate with her, losing myself, my sticking points. Where can I anchor myself, in this mist-blinded grief time, on these darkened waters? Which way, to glimpse buddha nature again? What should I do now? These are very jagged questions, once your teacher dies. With a living teacher you know where to orient yourself: simply dance around the *roshi*. But, a dead teacher is gone and yet still going, so I ghost after her, wanting to dance. "Please come back, my teacher," I cry.

That is a temptation, I know. Not the crying, but the longing to invent the reality that suits me, to retie our karmic knots. Neurotic. A hindrance. A delusion. I am discovering that only three things keep my attention focused on important matters these days: pain, the other four disciples, and the bright world around me. The pain is grief, of course, a natural wrenching pain or oozing sadness that works according to its own rules and sense of time and place. I let it happen, maybe even push it along. Watching it. Moving my body with it sometimes, and sometimes being very still with it on my *zazen* cushion. I respect my grieving: it reveals to me, bit by bit, moan by moan, the extent and nature of my losses. These losses add up to my feeling lost myself, since the death of my *roshi* has left me without my old center, my aim, a direction felt to be true. My grief also makes me quiet. I find myself not breathing. I become the moment before waiting begins. I pause and almost freeze. At this point, some little thing in the world usually presents itself and brings me back on track: a flash of light through the trees as a breeze turns the leaves, Cleo the cat entering the room looking for someone, one of the women disciples banging the front door closed (it sticks and it's my job to fix it—but not now). I know only what my direction is not: I have entered a stream, and I cannot get back up it to the past. I drift downward.

I am still connected with the four disciples of my *roshi*, who are orphaned even more than I. We try to take care of each other. I am becoming "old stepfather *roshi*" in my own mind, if not in theirs. My role seems to be: "Just be there." This is easy: I will just hang around, do my chores, keep in touch. I can't be the nourishing *roshi,* but I can cook, see the bills are paid, and make sure the endowment is not squandered. I lock the doors at night. Easy. Like a father.

But a *roshi* is a mother, using skillful and varied means to advance each and all. Patiently, not pushing too often or too hard. Generously, dwelling with ignorant animals, infant buddhas, quarreling bodhisattvas, hopelessly hungry ghosts. Courageously, for it takes courage to give birth to buddhas. I'm having a hard time here with the young disciples (although they are more senior than me and the *roshi* "raised" them to be independent, as if she knew she would not be around for them). One is depressed and confused. One weeps frequently. Two say little at all to me about our beloved teacher and friend. I don't know how to be their *roshi,* to mother them—and our *roshi* left no Dharma heirs to whom we can attach ourselves. The two oldest have gone out on their own into the world—in search of whomever will become their next teacher.

Roshi loved to garden and cook. Gardening in season was morning work, and cooking was afternoon work. To supplement the Sangha income, I had to work an outside job four or five days a week. But our *roshi,* following tradition, stayed on the home ground, working for the Sangha and also continuing her work on herself in her own special ways. While I worked late afternoons in the world, she trained the other disciples to cook the evening meal in a Buddhist manner, focusing first on recipes and technique, then moving on to the kind of spiritual attitude found in Dogen's instructions to the cook of his monastery, essentially, "Pay attention to this wonderful work!" I think the two older female disciples received Roshi's final blessing or seal as "good cooks." I envy them a little their authentication as worthy ones. Even though Roshi had tried to support me by saying, "You are a good handyman, a good writer, and so forth," I knew I had not finished or perfected anything yet, much less my self.

Almost every day, our *roshi* started a one-hour "cooking meditation" at 5 P.M. and served us a delicious, healthy meal at 6 P.M. sharp. In the year before her cancer was diagnosed, I noticed that 6 P.M. was not always achieved sharply, that evening meal came at 6:05 or even 6:15—but I thought only that she was getting older. Her "kitchen ceremony" year after year was paced in a special way: much preparation, followed by a burst of action. She would take thirty minutes or more scanning, finding, touching, and squeezing what was at hand, the "leftovers" often, preparing in her mind several recipes so that we would have more than one main dish to savor as we brought our different moods to the meal. The last fifteen minutes of the hour were spent in an effortless whirling about the kitchen, bringing all parts of the meal together into a harmony of taste and color at the stroke of six. Sometimes we would sit in the kitchen and watch, and try to talk, but clearly she was absorbed in her activity and preferred to be alone. The feeling in the kitchen was casual and natural, yet precise and true. Like a Japanese tea ceremony.

Perhaps her cooking drew upon her training in tea ceremony, but the same principles of action were evident in other areas of her life. Either the tea spirit had come to pervade everything or she had reached a point beyond the forms of tea and all arts. I think it was the latter: her actions came from some cool fountainhead of natural inspiration in almost all things, from the Zen source itself. Her refreshing Zen spirit and teachings were displayed in action, rarely in words. If I could summarize the teaching, it would rest in three aspirations for herself and for us. She reminded us, above all, to "try to pay attention." Be alert and mindful in the moment. Concentrate on one thing in one time. Her second aspiration was virtue-oriented: "Try to do your best at what you choose to do." There was no hint that this aim meant winning in contests against others, but rather working with yourself to improve your skill, spurred by friendly and helpful competition if appropriate.

Her third and final aspiration was to "try to be natural, in harmony with yourself." We could see her "naturalness" and self-content in different ways. She insisted on wearing comfortable clothes. She especially loved to have children as guests, playing with them and bringing them special gifts of sea shells or paper toys she always kept ready. A calm, quiet woman, she laughed easily, readily, happily, sometimes in a way that I can only hint at by saying it was ecstatically joyful. These epiphanies of laughter were, at first eruption, rather surprising, but within seconds infected us all irresistibly. The humor of something mysterious exploding from the depths of our teacher would rush over her face, bring tears to her eyes, and come cascading over us as inspiring, divine mirth. I remember a couple of times trying to hold myself back, so I could look into this whirlwind of giggles, tears, guffaws, and roiling bodies, which seemed to be far out of proportion to the meager stimulus of a pun or slip-of-tongue. Her laughter was too deep and overwhelming for me to sustain an objective distance: I always caved in to her glee.

Most of the incidents of laughter came at supper time, at the table. Her tea training or Zen aspirations radiated most clearly at this meal. Without a doubt, supper was the supreme moment for Dharma training and confrontation, in her view. Although she had the dining room set up in the Western manner, with chairs around a large, oval-shaped oak table, the atmosphere for eating was sifted through the subtle filters of tea culture. The detailed panoply of precisely practiced form and ancient gestures were not important here. She distilled from tea ritual its spirit, and what was minimally needed to give body and recognition to that spirit.

We were, after all, a tiny group of American-born disciples, with few resources. She was not going to impose Japanese culture upon us, except where it was the best tool she had in helping us undertake the way of wisdom and compassion. She had come to the U.S. as early as 1966, and preferred living here, because Japan was difficult for women like her. Our *roshi,* who said she refused to bow, was never ordained and never sought a lineage certification, of which she was as suspicious as she was of Ph.D.s. An almost infallible judge of character, she never gave undue weight to certificates because she could see into our true nature and our false ego-posturing. We didn't even call her "Roshi." I am doing that in retrospect and respect rather freely, but she preferred a more modest, feminine title, drawn from the Shinto tradition of shrine priestesses called Miko-san. We called her Miko. Most friends and neighbors thought it was her name, but it was her title, her pseudonym, her twist on the notion of *roshi*.

Our Miko, our *roshi*, would gather us at six for evening meals. It was not acceptable to miss the meal or be late. Our meal combined delicious food (another break from monastery tradition) and subtle practice in paying attention to what we were doing so that we could do it right and naturally. "Just eating." Talking was not encouraged, but allowed. The less mature disciples (including me on a bad day) would sometimes break out in binges of complaining or everyday storytelling: "Guess what happened today?" Roshi would not stop this, but would minimally reply or go on eating. She might ask, "How do you like the food?" to get our attention back to eating. Once focused on eating, she would now and then give us hints about "right eating." Many of the hints came from the way she ate herself, night after night, thousands and thousands of lessons performed before us: deliberately, quietly (we used chopsticks, being quieter than silverware can ever be), smoothly, and steadily.

From my point of view, she was totally focused on her own eating and enjoyed food with an appreciation and intensity I have never seen anywhere else. And yet, she was also fully, simultaneously, and precisely aware of what we were doing, and especially how we did it. This wide awareness, which included herself, was a great mystery to me. Years of Zen practice had given me an ability to focus on one thing with some stability, but not to have a more generalized, flexible openness at the same time. She knew this, of course, and I suspect my lack of "wide awareness" explains why I was the only disciple judged not ready for Roshi's teachings for cooks. She focused, rather, on my eating habits as the platform where she would struggle to instruct me about Buddha, Dharma, and Sangha, about awakening, truth, and the family of beings.

One evening meal, in an excited mood, I was eating and drinking quickly, talking to the group about something I now forget, and topping off my rice bowl at every opportunity. This was too much for our Miko, who usually let us talk a little, refill our bowls ourselves, and even become slightly restless or argumentative while eating. As I reached across the table toward the shallow bowl of bright green broccoli with the chopsticks in my right hand, with my left hand I also raised my water glass and started drinking. Hands suspended in two different grasping positions, I paused to say something to one of the others when—"Crack!"—Miko whacked my broccoli-seeking fingers with her chopsticks, and shouted, "Don't do that!" I froze, since she never had yelled at me. It felt as if I had tumbled into a hole, an abyss colder than ice. My loins tightened in fear. No idea came to my rescue to tell me why I had fallen or how to save myself. The small boy in me tried to stand up, as if to brace stubbornly against his mother's correction—but that effort collapsed. This was not my mother, but my wise and compassionate teacher—catching me in a nameless sin in front of the whole wide world.

Miko held me in suspension: I couldn't speak, and her slap had frozen my mind and body. Seeing that I was frozen and in danger, she eased off her hold on my spirit, saying, "In every moment, do only one thing. Don't reach for food, prepare to drink, and talk at the same time."

The lessons poured out in an uncharacteristic flood of advice. "Don't reach across the table with your chopsticks for the broccoli pieces. First, bring the broccoli bowl to your side plate and then use the chopsticks. Pay full attention to what you're doing! Don't divide your mind with many things, because you will never do them as well as they deserve and so degrade them." She demonstrated how to do these things rightly, quickly, beautifully, respectfully, decisively.

Breathless, I watched her and, as she closed off her just-right movements and brought her advice to an end, a great mass of shame rose up in me. I felt dizzy. In my great shame there was a corner, a little niche, of no-shame. From this little open corner I could see how fortunate I was to have such a teacher, even as my breath contracted against a storm of guilt and failure. "I know you can do this better," she said, as she turned to one of the female disciples and changed the subject.

Looking back on this meal, the slap, the teaching, the shame, I am tempted to smirk or stick out my tongue and say, "Oh, it was only a Japanese etiquette thing." But that doesn't ring true. What was very clear, in the mirror of that moment, was how far I had yet to go: I lacked mastery of myself—my diffused focus, my sloppy expressiveness, and my gluttony were evidence. I had insulted her, the disciples, the broccoli, and the moment, by not respecting each enough to give them my widest, deepest, most transparent attention. She was angry, but maybe at herself, too, for I had been her closest student, her intimate attendant, for at least six years. Had she failed me? Would she ever find a Dharma son or daughter?

If supper table was a special inner zone, where our *roshi* could observe our states of mind by watching such things as the coordination of our chopsticks and our hearts, garden work was a more open, wild arena where she invited us to train differently to become awakened beings. She liked active, physical means of training, although she could sit quietly for many hours, and appreciated that I could sit in *zazen* very comfortably, even with my temperamental back. She also valued quiet hours of scholarship and would not interrupt us when we were studying our books. For the younger minds in the Sangha, she would say, "Young minds should mainly study." I guess she felt I was smart enough already, because she never advised me to study more. Instead, she advised me to study less, and to study one thing at a time, until I mastered it to a useful degree, no further. She knew I liked studying books and concepts too much.

I never attempted to master her meditative style of gardening, stubbornly resisting her calls to enter the flower world. Gardening, developing a conversation among plants, soils, water, sun, and your self, hurt my back. "Stoop, lift and twist—throw out my back" was what gardening meant to me. The younger disciples tried gardening, but failed, too, each in her own way, to start a conversation with flowers. Our master was puzzled and sometimes visibly frustrated by our failures. She died too young to carry us any distance into her garden teachings. I feel sad about that. I felt then, and feel now, that her biggest teachings are in the garden, because she wanted so much for us to look and see. What we needed to learn in the garden was what I call the "flower pilgrimage," a journey in a circular path around the grounds through different gardens, that is, four or five different ecological textures of soil and plants, shifting shadows and sunlight. A journey with flowers, compost, vegetables, boundaries, herbs, and breath to the nameless origin.

The path of the flower pilgrimage is outwardly the simple, uneven footpath around the main building, running from vegetable beds, to cutting flowers, to the herb garden, past the compost bin, down into the woods and wildflowers, and back around through the "orphanage," where Miko gave a home to solitary, unloved, wilted, leftover refugees of June and July plant sales. Maybe 150 paces would take you around the full circuit. Less than two minutes will do it—if you don't pay any attention to the beans and cucumbers, the exuberant peonies and day lilies, the compost bin's dark bottom soil, the spring beauties and may apples crowding the small *kyudo* platform set in between the tall, thin oaks and advancing maples, or, as you come out of the woods, the countless orphan flowers of forgotten names who shyly appear in random patterns as you walk the path aiming west toward the civilized street. The thick iris bed at the curb marks the end, but not the goal.

The goal of the path of flowers is becoming a buddha, naturally, slowly, practicing every day one little bit or one small thing, with a purpose so reduced in your mind it doesn't feel like a purpose. A day's flower practice might take ten minutes or two hours, to an outside observer like myself, but that misses the point entirely, as even I could see. At the end of her too-short life, before going off to radiation or chemotherapy sessions, Miko would always walk the path, do the pilgrimage, before I took her in the car to the white cancer center with black windows squatting on a hill that overlooked the city. A few weeks before she died, when she was very weak, she would still stand in the garden, among the vegetables, at the beginning of the path. My last photos of her are there.

The photos are discolored by a yellowish haze on her and the plants. I can't decide yet if the effect reminds me of jaundice or of gold. I do know it pains me to see these images, so I have hidden them away. I wonder what I will be able to see and how I will feel, looking at those pictures next year or twenty years from now. Perhaps I will see only the unshakable calm in her face, the irony in her smile. Perhaps, then, suddenly, I will see her as Buddha, and her image will strike so deep I will awaken, all at once from myself. But it won't happen all at once, if my teacher is to be believed. Becoming a buddha is slow work, so that we can learn patience with ourselves and others, give ourselves a break from schedules and missions that pull at our guilt tendons, and take enough time, as long as we need, to practice doing "one moment, one thing."

This slow work is easily done in a garden, she believed, and she wanted us to get started. The first step was to learn the names of the flowers along the flowery path, all of them. Not their Latinized botanical names, but their common names. All of us resisted. Miko would lead us along the path, asking us a flower's name or telling us. This would take ten to twenty minutes. It was clear on this pilgrimage that we were undergoing a test, that we were at the first of the flowery gates through which she wanted us to pass. We were quizzed always—immediately on the path, or at the end near the iris bed, or six hours later, when an arrangement of flowers would dominate the center of the supper table. "Well, now, what is this?"

All of us disciples would fail, for less than a perfect score was unacceptable. Why did we have to know every name? Why did we even have to know one name? These questions she would not answer, beyond declaring, "To know it, you must start with a name." We challenged her: "You often confuse the names of your disciples, even calling us by the cat's name sometimes! Why should we be perfectly accurate in naming these dumb flowers? And besides, you keep adding new ones, those orphans you plant, and from the woods come volunteers that seed themselves. We don't have a chance," we whined.

"I already know you, so I don't have to remember your names," she said. "And you know your names very well and defend them loudly, even when you don't have to do it. The flowers are defenseless, weak, and silent—unlike us. So, we start by naming them. It's not their real name, but when we name them, we feel more friendly toward them, they become more specific and stand out. It helps us pay attention to them so that, over time, we will get to know them so well we won't need to call them by a name. Then, they will come to us without our calling. They will come to us even in our dreams. But first you must name them."

For myself, I made a few less-than-half-hearted attempts to remember the flowers' names. That not working, I thought I would create my own names, as in "the tall, blue flower that looks like a tulip but isn't" or "the orange flowers growing next to the peonies every year." This helped me remember, but something was missing, namely, a name. I rationalized to Miko that my descriptions were very Buddhist, because they were contextual or relational identifications, not analytical names suggesting singularity and isolation. This clever dogma went nowhere. I want to speculate at this point. The name, I'm guessing, was essential to paying attention to "one moment, one thing." I think now she saw what the tea master Sen no Rikyu saw when he displayed a single flower in a plain vase in his sixteenth-century tea ceremony hut. Until you know something well, until you can approach it as a buddha, you need its name to "single it out" and respect it. Respect is carried by the name until our familiarity matures to the point where names dissolve and things present themselves to us like the air we breathe, as something both inside and outside us, yet neither inside nor outside. At this point, the name fades, and the thing itself is seen. We relax and smile—or even become wonderful.

I glimpsed this "wonderfulness" along the flower path only after my teacher's death. One quiet morning a few weeks after her early October passing, I scuffled half-alert along the path around our home. At a certain point in the garden of orphan flowers, halfway around the pilgrimage, I stopped for no particular reason. As I saw Miko do many times, I squatted low, very low, on the path and found myself looking in a relaxed way at a single plant, with tiny, blue petals. A thought came, "This is not me seeing this."

I felt something in me was expanding outward, meeting the solitary flower with an easy, alert openness. As my eyes focused, more clearly than they usually do for some reason, the blue petals and thin stem revealed themselves to me in a crisp, absolute way. "To me," yet not to "me." I felt the flower "presenting itself" before my face in a very intimate, bold way. It was before "my face," but yet not "my" face.

I am struggling and failing to describe the experience. But I knew clearly, and in a strangely calm way, that the flower was showing itself to Miko. Miko, my beloved wife. She was seeing through my eyes what she wanted me to see in the years of many fine mornings when she tugged at my hand, eagerly pulling me along the flowery path—to meet a small, quietly radiant, very beautiful orphan—and all the other wonderful buddhas.

PART III

Political and Social Change

WOMEN CHANGING TIBET, ACTIVISM CHANGING WOMEN

Serinity Young

Tibet, Real and Imagined

Despite a recent slight increase in Western news coverage of Tibet, it still remains more a land of imagination than of reality in many Western minds.[1] Most Westerners have a very idealized notion of Tibet under the rule of the Dalai Lamas,[2] and few are clear about the historical shiftings of its geographical boundaries.[3] When the Chinese government speaks of Tibet, it means the Tibetan Autonomous Region (TAR), defined as the area that was actually under the authority of His Holiness the Fourteenth Dalai Lama's government in 1950, stretching from the western half of the province of Kham in the east to the borders of Kashmir and Ladakh in the west. The Peoples' Republic of China considers the rest of Kham and Amdo as Chinese provinces. Supporters of Tibetan independence, on the other hand, speak of Tibet as including all of Kham and Amdo as well as the TAR.[4]

In 1950, three years after the withdrawal of British colonial power in South and Southeast Asia, and one year after the revolution in China, the army of the newly founded People's Republic of China advanced into Tibet in order to liberate the Tibetan people from feudalism and foreign imperialists. Including Tibet in the Maoist revolution, as the Chinese destroyed monasteries and imposed collectivization the situation there deteriorated steadily. In 1959, the people of Lhasa rose up against the Chinese, and the Fourteenth Dalai Lama fled to India along with several thousand other Tibetans, beginning a stream of refugees that continues to this day. The Chinese then systematically expanded the destruction of Tibetan culture, especially its religious life, by demolishing more monasteries, plundering their wealth of manuscripts and art, and either imprisoning or executing both lay and monastic Tibetans or sending them to work in labor camps.[5] Difficult as this period was, it was only the beginning, for in the Cultural Revolution of the 1960s and 1970s additional monasteries and nunneries were blown up, and the remaining walls of these buildings were taken apart brick by brick. Nuns and monks were forced to disrobe and many were imprisoned, tortured, and killed. Though the Chinese government has relaxed its policies somewhat since that time—for example, by allowing foreigners back into the country and reopening some monasteries and nunneries—it has pursued a course of plundering the natural environment, destroying wildlife, and allowing the immigration of Han Chinese people into Tibet to such an extent that Tibetans are rapidly becoming a minority in their own homeland. This is apparent to even the most superficial visitor to Lhasa and other Tibetan cities where signs have Chinese characters at least twice as large as the Tibetan script under them. Moreover, it is astonishing to see the extent of the Chinese military presence in Tibet beyond the capital as well.[6]

In 1987, a fresh round of pro-independence demonstrations began. On September 27, twenty-one monks were arrested for leading a pro-independence demonstration in Lhasa. The demonstration spread, and on October 1, 1987, the police fired upon two to three thousand demonstrators. In the next few years, hundreds of Tibetans were killed and thousands imprisoned. On March 7, 1989, the Chinese declared martial law and expelled all foreign journalists, diplomats, and tourists. In 1990 martial law was lifted, but the situation was still tense during my visit in 1997. This essay, then, will focus on the role of monastics, especially nuns, in ongoing demonstrations in Tibet and the consequences they face for their activities.

The situation in Tibet is part of a larger policy the Chinese government pursued quite vigorously until fairly recently—to bring about the destruction of all religion among its own people.[7] For the revolutionary government of China, liberation meant abandoning ideologies of other traditions like Buddhism, Daoism, and Confucianism, a policy that was carried to its extremes during the Cultural Revolution.[8] Warren Smith quotes from a government document that states, "Since religion is harmful to the socialist construction of the mother country, it will inevitably prove harmful to the progress and development of the minority nationalities [for example, the Tibetans]."[9] While I do not want to minimize the destruction that went on and continues to go on in Tibet, it is important to bear in mind that the Chinese government treats dissident or religious Han Chinese in similar ways. Tibetans are generally quick to make the point that it is the Chinese government, not the Chinese people, that is the cause of their suffering.

Tibetan Nuns, Then and Now

Tibetan nuns have always been a monastic minority.[10] Tsepon Shakpa estimates monks made up 18 percent of Tibet's pre-1950 population while nuns comprised only 2 percent.[11] Nevertheless, nuns have had such a significant presence in political demonstrations for the liberation of Tibet that a larger percentage of nuns appears to be involved in political activities than monks.[12] A Tibet Information Network report entitled "Timing of Incidents: Nuns as the Leading Edge" states, for example:

> Protests by nuns have been noticeable as initiating a series of incidents which have become more and more frequent until culminating, after one to two months, in a major confrontation with police.
>
> Recent activity in Tibet divides clearly into four phases, each one ending in a new attempt by police to shoot on demonstrators and intern dissidents. In each case the period of rigid police control which has followed these major incidents has been broken by nuns after a period of from one to six months—after the October 1, 1987, crackdown there was no incident (apart from an October 6th demonstration) till Garu nuns demonstrated on December 19, 1987. Police control after the March 5th incident, which allegedly involved some 10,000 lay people, was absolute until the 17th April demonstration by Garu nuns; after the shooting on December 10, 1988, there was no demonstration (except for a semi-official student demonstration on December 30, 1988) till the nuns took to the streets on February 22, 1989. The first incidents after the imposition of martial law on March 7/8, 1989, were the nuns' demonstrations on September 2nd and September 22nd.
>
> In this sense the nuns are clearly spearheading the fight against the Chinese authorities, being the first each time to test or goad police control.[13]

During the spring of 1997, in fact, I was repeatedly told that monks were increasingly leaving it up to the nuns to organize demonstrations.

Interestingly, nuns traditionally have much lower status than monks. One manifestation of their low status and of the lack of interest paid to them by lay and monastic Tibetans and, until recently, by Western scholars, is an almost complete lack of historical information about Tibetan nuns. Most significantly, it is doubtful whether a traditional ordination lineage for nuns ever came to Tibet. If it did, it has been lost for centuries. This is reflected in Tibetan texts that translate the Indian term *bhikṣuṇī,* meaning ordained nun, as *gelongma.* In Tibetan, this term is used in Buddhist texts to refer only to ordained nuns from the Indian past; all Tibetan nuns, by contrast, whether they live in nunneries or remain at home, are called *ani,* a respectful term also used for aunts. Traditionally, Tibetan nuns have remained permanently in the novice *(dGe tshul ma)* state, living in nunneries, which were generally poorer than monasteries and where educational opportunities were severely limited. In recent years, the Dalai Lama has advocated the full ordination of women, but Western and Tibetan women who were ordained have yet to be officially recognized by the Tibetan government-in-exile.[14] Of course, this has not directly influenced the lives of Buddhist nuns in Tibet either way; it appears that, for all intents and purposes, they remain in the novice stage. For them, full ordination is not an immediate issue of concern; political liberation is.

Political Activity among Nuns

According to the most recent figures available from Amnesty International, the number of political prisoners in Tibet known by name as of December 1994 was 628. Over ninety percent of these are monastics; 176 are women.[15] It is of critical importance to have the names of prisoners in order for Amnesty International to monitor their treatment and attempt to procure their release. More recent figures from the Tibetan Centre for Human Rights and Democracy list 921 male, 295 female, and 39 juvenile prisoners in 1997.[16]

Life in a Chinese prison is unimaginably brutal. After the Tiananmen Square massacre, many Tibetans said to me, "If this is what they do to their own people, what do you think they are doing to us?" According to the Amnesty International report of June 1995 on women in China, the treatment of Han Chinese women prisoners appears to be as brutal and sexually humiliating as it is for Tibetan nuns. Being stripped naked before male guards and male prisoners is common practice, and beatings are savage, with electric batons used freely and often inserted into vaginas. Other forms of rape are not unknown, and sometimes this is accomplished by incarcerating female prisoners in cells with male prisoners. Prisoners often die, usually shortly after they are released to their families for medical attention, as the recent film *Windhorse* depicts (prisoners are released to undermine any criticism of the prison system for bringing about the deaths of inmates). Phuntsok Yangkyi, for instance, a twenty-year-old nun from Michungri Nunnery, died in June of 1994 at the police hospital in Lhasa due to severe beatings and possible medical mistreatment in the hospital.[17] Another nun, fifteen-year-old Sherab Ngawang, died in April of 1995 from internal injuries received from repeated beatings, two months after she was released from prison.[18] Little or no medical attention appears to be available to prisoners, and medicine must be procured from family visitors who generally get to see the prisoner only once a month for ten minutes and in the presence of several guards. These prisoners are the lucky ones. Many prisoners are held incommunicado and are thus beyond help from their families or from having their names put on the Amnesty International list. Sentences for nuns are harsh and usually include several years of hard labor; moreover, the sentences can and are increased for infractions while in prison. For instance,

> Phuntsog Nyidron, a twenty-eight-year-old nun from Michungri Nunnery, is serving the longest known sentence for a female prisoner in Tibet. On 14 October 1989, three days after Tibetans heard that their exiled spiritual leader, the Dalai Lama, would receive the Nobel Peace Prize, Phuntsog Nyidron and five other nuns staged a peaceful demonstration in Lhasa chanting pro-independence slogans. They marched for only a few minutes and were arrested. All the nuns were reportedly tortured during interrogation in police custody.
>
> Phuntsog Nyidron was considered the ringleader and so was given the harshest sentence of nine years' imprisonment. On 8 October 1993 her prison sentence was increased to 17 years. Thirteen other nuns faced a trial with her at which their sentences were increased up to nine years. The nuns had used a tape recorder smuggled into the prison to record pro-independence songs which were then circulated secretly in Tibet. On the tape each announced their name and dedicated a song or poem to supporters, reaffirming their commitment to Tibetan independence and demonstrating they were in good spirits. One nun sang, "To all of you outside who have done all you can for us in prison, we are deeply grateful and will never forget you." Another spoke of prison life: "Our food is like pig food, we are beaten and treated brutally. But this will never change the Tibetan people's perseverance. It will remain unfaltering."[19]

The use of leg and hand shackles is common, but the worst is called the "tiger bed" or the shackle board, which "consists of a wooden door laid flat on short legs with handcuffs at the four corners. Prisoners are attached to the board for long periods with their arms and legs spread out and handcuffed at the corners. A hole in the centre of the board allows evacuation of urine and excrement."[20]

Not surprisingly, attempted suicide rates are high among women prisoners, so much so that it has been discussed as a major problem in academic articles published in China.[21] One documented case of the prison experiences of a Tibetan nun is as follows:

> Upon arrival at Gutsa prison, the nun was stripped of all clothing and placed in a room with two trained dogs and two policemen. The dogs were trained to attack whenever she moved. The policemen proceeded to hit her with rods until she tried to move away, at which time dogs would attack, biting and lacerating her arms and legs. During this torture, they continually asked her about her involvement in the demonstrations as well as the involvement of others.[22]

Generally, nuns conduct political demonstrations while circumambulating the Jokhang Temple, the most sacred center of Tibetan Buddhism, in the heart of Old Lhasa, sometimes by shouting out, "Independence for Tibet." There is an almost never-ending stream of pilgrims circumambulating this site, and a police presence is common, both in and out of uniform. When nuns demonstrate, they do so knowing what awaits them, yet Chinese prison officials cannot accept the nuns as independent agents. Almost all the testimonies of imprisoned nuns "detail the interrogators' relentless pursuit of an 'admission' that men or others aside from the nuns are behind the protests."[23] The self-representations of nuns in these accounts are a significant part of their story, and I will explore their meanings below.

Spring, 1997

Much of what follows, which is based on my two-month visit in the spring of 1997, is highly impressionistic; people took chances talking to me, and I tried to listen on all levels. Direct questions were inappropriate, as the monks and nuns who spoke to me were already in jeopardy—I could not push them any further than I did. I do not use the real names of people or of monasteries and nunneries, for even though they have asked me to speak and write of what I saw and what they told me, the need to protect the identities of all persons and places is obvious.

The Tibetans are marginalized in their own country and subjected to invasive tourism.[24] Many monastics are directly coopted into the tourist trade as monastery guides, ticket takers, and guesthouse workers, while others have their routine continually interrupted by tourists stumbling into their spaces and their ceremonies at any hour of the day. Young lay people are under the conflicting pressures of being loyal to their own culture and Chinese efforts to change them, and many young men have turned to alcohol and drugs for comfort.

Young Tibetan lay women appear to be the backbone of Tibetan society: they work hard, smile often, and aim to please. On the other hand, young Tibetan lay men, while attempting to be agreeable, cannot hide their deep dissatisfaction: a clearly evident sense of alienation and hopelessness, which is sharpened by their exposure to Westerners who freely travel their world reeking of unspent opportunities and, no matter how scruffily dressed, appearing unimaginably rich to Tibetan eyes. Moreover, I was shocked to find that many of the young Tibetans I met in Lhasa were illiterate. Throughout the TAR, educational opportunities for Tibetans are severely limited by the scarcity of schools, by their cost, and by the fact that better schools have a curriculum based on Chinese language proficiency. Additionally, many new schools are open only to ethnic Chinese.[25]

All foreigners in Tibet must stay only in certain hotels and never in private houses. Any foreigners with a residency permit must register any guests they have with the police. If the police find pictures of His Holiness the Dalai Lama on tourists, they rip them up and step on them. Tibetans found with them are at minimum roughed up and berated.[26] Tour guides who say too much or the wrong thing are denied work.

There is an overt and a covert police presence in nunneries and monasteries. I witnessed an overt example at a medium-sized monastery while traveling northeast of Lhasa. When we arrived, all the monks were assembled in the courtyard where a Chinese lay man was conducting a roll call. Some Tibetan nomads were sitting on the edge of the courtyard, watching the proceedings. It seemed friendly enough, but it also had a sinister edge. I found that I was witnessing part of an ongoing "re-education" process, in which monks are required, once a month, to say publicly that they don't believe the Dalai Lama is the reincarnation of Avalokiteśvara and that the Panchen Lama supported by the Chinese (as opposed to the Panchen Lama supported by the Tibetans) is the real reincarnation of Amitābha Buddha. Such statements are in direct contradiction to central Tibetan Buddhist beliefs about the two most important spiritual offices in the land. Moreover, the six-year-old candidate for Panchen Lama approved by the Dalai Lama disappeared from Tibet along with his immediate family in 1995, and their whereabouts are still unknown.[27] The Chinese lay man in the courtyard calls out a monk's name, the monk answers, and then the lay man asks him about the Dalai and Panchen Lamas. Each answer is noted down, and a wrong answer gets the monk expelled from the monastery. According to the Tibetan Centre for Human Rights and Democracy, there have been 3,993 expulsions, 294 arrests, and 14 deaths between April of 1996 and February of 1998 in connection with this policy.[28]

Even more problematic is the covert infiltration of police who live in the nunneries and monasteries disguised as nuns and monks, undermining monastic solidarity. As there are travel restrictions on such visitors as scholars and journalists, foreigners are also under surveillance, although I was more amused than annoyed by repeated attempts to question me informally. Most commonly, these contacts occurred in restaurants frequented by Westerners. Usually two young Tibetan men, the only ones dressed in suits, would appear at my table and say, "I understand you can speak Tibetan" and not so subtly question me about why I was in Tibet.

Consequently, a lot of my communication with monastics was oblique. One instance occurred at a major monastery on the outskirts of Lhasa where I spoke with a monk who took some chances in speaking with me after we exchanged a few pleasantries in Tibetan: he subtly drew my attention to certain visual cues rather than making explicit statements. For example, as he spoke lightly of Chinese violence against some of the monks at his monastery, he slowly turned his face away from me, revealing an ugly scar across his forehead and down over his eye. Later, when I commented that there were so few monks in sight, he merely said the police had come that morning and asked for sixty monks to do work, and then he looked off into the distance where at first I saw only a cloud of dust, but then saw that it was a road crew of monks breaking rocks.

Dolkar: The Experiences of One Buddhist Nun

My primary guide to life in Tibet was a young Buddhist nun who had been arrested in 1987 when she was fifteen years old. Her experiences and their continuing aftereffects are typical. After serving four months, she was released during a general amnesty but was not allowed to return to her nunnery, as political activity of any sort leads to expulsion from the community. For the past ten years, she has maintained her robes and vows in a hand-to-mouth existence in Lhasa, even though maintaining her robes precludes her finding any work, as her employers would be subjected to close police surveillance. Her pseudonym is Dolkar, meaning White Tārā, a female Buddhist deity. I met Dolkar through an American psychologist staying at my hotel who told me about her imprisonment, but I have never directly questioned Dolkar about her arrest or her incarceration. By giving me such information, she would not only jeopardize her already precarious freedom, but also have to relive traumatic experiences. I did notice, however, that she walks as if her pelvis is badly damaged, and I assumed that this was from torture while in prison. We traded language lessons each morning I was in Lhasa—she teaching me Tibetan, and me teaching her English—and we made several day trips outside Lhasa, although she was reluctant to join me on longer journeys.

Dolkar's courage has something transcendent about it. In spite of, or perhaps because of, her own prison experiences, she visits friends who are in prison. I asked her if Westerners can visit prisoners, and she replied that only relatives are allowed visitation rights; she can visit one of the nuns because, being from the same village, they are considered cousins. Visits last ten minutes, occur once a month, and are conducted in the presence of two or three policeman the whole time. The involvement of nuns in political activity can be evidenced in the fact that twenty-two nuns from Dolkar's convent are in prison. Dolkar is not allowed to see them and can only find out about their condition from their relatives. When she has something extra (medicine or food, for example) she gives it to one of the imprisoned nuns' family members who can take it to them. This is usually the only decent food and medicine inmates receive.

Dolkar is cheerful, full of life, curious about the world, devoted to the Dalai Lama, and determined to stay in Tibet. She wants very much to return to her nunnery, and she was ecstatic when we ran into her former abbess while following the pilgrimage route around Old Lhasa. I walked away to a tea stall while they talked so that they would attract less attention. I'm not sure what the consequences are for such a meeting. After about a half hour Dolkar joined me again. I could tell she was very moved by this meeting, and I asked if she could give some money to the abbess for me. Dolkar brightened up immediately, said yes, and ran after her while I remained where I was. The abbess and I nodded across several hundred yards of pilgrims, and Dolkar returned in high spirits. It is not only that she wants to return to her nunnery, but that she wants to return to productive membership in it. As far as I can see, though, she is doomed to live out her life on its fringes because one day ten years ago she said out loud, "Freedom for Tibet."

Conclusion

One of the central tenets of Buddhism is the doctrine of no-self—that there is no empirical proof of an abiding entity that defines who we are.[29] Through careful analysis, the notion of an enduring and isolated self is shown to be a grave misreading of reality. For Buddhists, the self and the world it occupies possess only a conditional reality, which is to say that they participate in a reality that is *conditioned* by other factors, all of which are themselves conditioned. Consequently, the Buddhist journey toward enlightenment emphasizes abandoning the personal and the individual and, instead, embracing patterns of selfless giving established by the Buddha and maintained by other Buddhist saints.[30] Correspondingly, Buddhists postulate an ultimate reality versus a conditional reality wherein we act "as if" this world were real but know that ultimately everything, ourselves and our world, is empty of enduring reality. Through this analysis, the dichotomous separation between self and others breaks down. In the Buddhist world, then, patterns of selfless giving are paramount and range from forbearance in the face of disrespect and even cruelty from those who do not know better to legends of great saints who have cut away their own flesh to feed starving animals. One's body, feelings, and thoughts are understood to be impermanent and thus easily sacrificed if they will benefit other beings. By sacrificing their freedom and enduring torture in prison, Tibetan nuns and monks are following an ancient Buddhist tradition of selfless giving designed, at least in part, to win over their tormentors, to get the Chinese to rethink the values that encourage them to oppress and punish the Tibetan people.

Needless to say, ideas of selflessness and selfless giving are hard to maintain in the context of ordinary life.[31] While living their lives within the understanding of the self as conditioned, like other traditional people, South Asian Buddhists experience the self situationally, as intrinsically part of family, clan, and other cultural constructs—including past lives and many different kinds of beings, both visible and invisible.[32] As Anne Klein has said, "Persons do not spring to life in one individual form only, but are embedded in a series of lives, as well as in the social, spirit, and natural networks."[33] Hence, the Buddhist sense of self is expanded, first, by its acceptance of the idea that we have had past lives and will have future lives, all of which affect our present life, second, by including relationships with spiritual and natural beings of many different sorts and, third, by social arrangements that include family and clan members as an essential part of oneself.[34]

Belief in the doctrine of no-self has obvious relevance to the sacrifices of freedom, comfort, and even life itself by Tibetan monastics in Tibet for the benefit of Buddhism. Behind the call for Tibetan independence is the desire for independence in order to practice Buddhism. As monastics, though, they have also loosened their ties to and identities with family and clan members. This has been characterized by a former nun in the film *Satya*, Tsultrim Dolma, who says that as a nun she had no family and thus could act more freely than a lay person.

Gender is significant here, however. As mentioned at the beginning of this essay, nuns are becoming increasingly prominent in demonstrations for Tibetan independence, and this prominence is a problem for the Chinese. Despite decades of rhetoric about gender equality, Chinese officials cannot accept women as autonomous agents, and interrogators constantly want to know who—that is, which man—is behind their actions. Questioning can go on for hours, days, and weeks and is often accompanied by acts of terrible humiliation and torture. It is always the official hope that the nun being questioned will implicate others who can be arrested, but behind the questioning is the assumption that women do not, indeed cannot, act on their own volition and are instead following the instructions of men. While it is very important to Chinese ideology to insist on gender equality ("Women hold up half the sky"), it is a point of fact that traditional Chinese gender roles have undergone only superficial modifications.

In another context of gendered Tibetan resistance to Chinese rule, Charlene Makley has analyzed the role of Tibetan lay women who adhere to traditional taboos against women's presence in certain sacred spaces even as those spaces are frequently violated by Chinese and Western female tourists. Tibetan women, at the Labrang Monastery in the Amdo region for example, dress in traditional Tibetan clothes and observe restrictions on where they can go within the monastery, in spite of the fact that, perhaps only moments earlier, Chinese and other tourists of both sexes occupied those spaces. Like tourists everywhere, Chinese and foreign tourists in Tibet often dress and behave inappropriately, and the monks have to put up with it. By dressing properly, behaving demurely, and respecting traditional gender limitations, Tibetan lay women signal their independence from Chinese ideology and from Chinese rule, and mostly escape censure.

Tibetan nuns, however, behave more boldly, and, as Dolkar's story shows, they do this at a great personal cost to their own physical and emotional health and by embracing a lesser social and religious status. Chinese officials find it difficult to comprehend the nun's resistance partly because they believe that Tibetan nuns have nothing to gain from Buddhism—that they will never have the status accorded to learned or spiritually advanced monks, and they are losing the supposed opportunities afforded them by Chinese gender policies.

As monastics, Tibetan nuns have less status than monks do[35] and they not only accept this but assert it as part of their identity to both the Tibetans and the Chinese. Indeed, one reason for the increase of nuns in political demonstrations and the decrease of monks may be to allow monks to continue their advanced studies of Buddhism, studies in which nuns do not participate.[36] My argument here is that a defeated people often looks to the women of its community to uphold its communal values, and that these values are often expressed more conservatively during crises than in other periods.[37] Consequently, when Tibetan nuns assert their traditional identity, it is highly nuanced: they are asserting their Buddhist identity of selfless sacrifice as well as their gendered identity of having a lower status than monks, and they do so in the full understanding that the consequences will be a severe incarceration experience involving torture that is specifically gendered. Tibetan nuns who demonstrate in Tibet are being punished not only for political insurrection but also for revealing the ambiguities in Chinese policies about the equality of the sexes. Their demonstrations are a rejection of the Chinese as benevolent rulers and of Chinese promotion of the advancement of women, especially ethnic women. Because they touch many sensitive nerves in the now dominant Chinese culture, Tibetan nuns cannot help but bring upon themselves a vicious response.

Notes

1. See, for instance, Tsering Shakya's essay "The Development of Modern Tibetan Studies," in *Resistance and Reform in Tibet*, ed. Robert Barnett and Shirin Akiner (1994; Delhi: Motilal Banarsidass, 1996), pp. 1–14; Charlene E. Makley, "Gendered Practices and the Inner Sanctum: The Reconstruction of Tibetan Sacred Space in 'China's Tibet,'" *The Tibet Journal*, vol. xix, no. 2 (summer, 1994): 61–94; and Donald S. Lopez, Jr., *Prisoners of Shangri-la: Tibetan Buddhism and the West* (Chicago: University of Chicago Press, 1998).
2. The present Dalai Lama, Tenzin Gyatso, has frequently referred to the mistakes that were made by the Tibetan government and has deplored its conservative tendencies. Of course, Tibet's status as a pawn between England and Russia in the late nineteenth and early twentieth centuries created additional problems. See Peter

Hopkirk, *The Great Game: On Secret Service in High Asia* (London: Murray, 1990).

3. See Premen Addy's essay on some of this history, "British and Indian Strategic Perceptions of Tibet," in *Resistance and Reform*, ed. Barnett and Akiner, pp. 15–50.
4. This is to simplify a more complex situation. See, for example, the map in *Resistance and Reform*, ed. Barnett and Akiner, pp. xvi–xvii.
5. A detailed and moving story of these and later years of the Chinese occupation is contained in Adhe Tapontsang as told to Joy Blakeslee, *Ama Adhe, The Voice That Remembers: The Heroic Story of a Woman's Fight to Free Tibet* (Boston: Wisdom Publications, 1997).
6. These impressions are based on my visit to Tibet in the spring of 1997.
7. See Miriam Levering, "Women, the State, and Religion Today in the People's Republic of China," in *Today's Woman in World Religions*, ed. Arvind Sharma (Albany: The State University of New York Press, 1994), pp. 171–224, and Warren W. Smith, "The Nationalities Policy of the Chinese Communist Party and the Socialist Transformation of Tibet," in *Resistance and Reform*, especially pp. 61 and 67.
8. On this point in China see Levering, "Women, the State, and Religion," in *Today's Woman in World Religions*, pp. 171–224.
9. Smith, "The Nationalities Policy," in *Resistance and Reform*, p. 61, quoting from Ling Nai-min, ed., *Tibet 1950–1967*, "Communists Are Complete Atheists," (Hong Kong: Union Research Institute, 1968), p. 246.
10. See, for example, Hanna Havnevik, "The Role of Nuns in Contemporary Tibet," in *Resistance and Reform*, pp. 259–66. The history of Tibetan nuns can be found in Hanna Havnevik, *Tibetan Buddhist Nuns: History, Cultural Norms and Social Reality* (Oslo: Norwegian University Press, 1989); Nancy J. Barnes, "Buddhist Women and the Nuns' Order in Asia," in *Engaged Buddhism: Buddhist Liberation Movements in Asia*, ed. Christopher S. Queen and Sallie B. King (Albany: State University of New York Press, 1996), pp. 259–94; and two works by Karma Lekshe Tsomo, ed., *Sakyadhita: Daughters of the Buddha* (Ithaca, NY: Snow Lion Publications, 1988), and "Tibetan Nuns and Nunneries," in *Feminine Ground: Essays on Women and Tibet*, ed. Janice D. Willis (Ithaca, NY: Snow Lion Publications, 1989), pp. 118–34; and Janice D. Willis, "Tibetan Ani-s: The Nun's Life in Tibet," in *Feminine Ground: Essays on Women and Tibet*, pp. 96–117.
11. Tsepon W. D. Shakapa, *Tibet: A Political History* (New Haven, CT: Yale University Press, 1967), p. 6.
12. See Barnett and Akiner, eds., *Resistance and Reform*, p. 265, for a brief discussion of one nun, Thinley Choedon, who was executed in 1969. She is also discussed in the same book by Smith, "The Nationalities Policy," pp. 70–71; and Robbie Barnett, "The Role of Nuns in Tibetan Protest—Preliminary Notes," (London: Tibet Information Network, 1989); and various issues of "Human Rights Update" from the Tibetan Centre for Human Rights and Democracy, such as May 5, 1998, April 14, 1998, March 15, 1998, and December 30, 1997. For a useful essay on the Dalai Lama's philosophy of liberation, see José Ignacio Cabezón, "Buddhist Principles in the Tibetan Liberation Movement," in *Engaged Buddhism*, pp. 295–320; see also in the

same volume the introduction by Christopher Queen (pp. 1–44) and the conclusion by Sallie King (pp. 401–35) for the larger background of Buddhist liberation movements throughout Asia.

13. Barnett, "The Role of Nuns in Tibetan Protest," p. 3.
14. Barnes, "Buddhist Women," p. 274. Indeed, a double message seems to be going around about the Dalai Lama's position. For instance, in 1996 when I questioned monks in Buriyata, Russia, where a great revival of Buddhism was in full swing, about bringing back the order of nuns, they said they were not going to do that because the Dalai Lama (whom they consider their spiritual leader) was against the ordination of women. I am sure my protests to the contrary fell on deaf ears.
15. "People's Republic of China: Persistent Human Rights Violations in Tibet," Amnesty International, May 1995, pp. 40–52. I have relied on this report for much of what follows.
16. "Human Rights Update," December 30, 1997, vol. 2, no. 24.
17. "Human Rights Update," April 15, 1998, vol. 3, no. 7, p. 3.
18. "Human Rights Update," March 15, 1998, vol. 3, no. 5, p. 3.
19. "Women in China," Amnesty International, June 1995, p. 15.
20. "Women in China," p. 16.
21. "Women in China," p. 16.
22. John Ackerly and Blake Kerr, "The Suppression of a People: Accounts of Torture and Imprisonment in Tibet" (Somerville, MA: Physicians for Human Rights, November 1989), p. 40.
23. Ackerly and Kerr, "The Suppression of a People," p. 40, and "Women in China," June 1995, p. 16.
24. Makley, "Gendered Practices and the Inner Sanctum," pp. 61–94.
25. United States State Department, "Human Rights Report on China," 1997, pp. 50–51.
26. The most recent ban on possessing the Dalai Lama's picture is part of China's Strike Hard campaign in Tibet inaugurated in April of 1996. For more on this campaign, see "Closing the Doors: Religious Repression in Tibet" and "Human Rights Update," December 30, 1997, vol. 2, no. 24, both published in Dharamsala by the Tibetan Centre for Human Rights and Democracy, n.d., pp. 6–8. These reports are available through the U.S. Tibet Committee in New York City.
27. For some details on this case, see ibid., pp. 57–58, and the 1997 United States State Department's "Human Rights Report on China," p. 49.
28. This is also part of China's Strike Hard campaign in Tibet. See note no. 26.
29. This doctrine is perhaps most famously formulated in Nāgasena's simile of the chariot in the *Milindapañho*, ed. V. Trenckner (London: Williams and Norgate, 1880), pp. 25–28.
30. Reginald A. Ray, *Buddhist Saints in India: A Study in Buddhist Values and Orientations* (New York: Oxford University Press, 1994), pp. 6 and 61, contains brief but stimulating discussions of the Buddhist idea of the self in relation to Buddhist saints, part of which argues for their sharing "the same core of personality."
31. This is perhaps seen most clearly in Buddhism's involvement in the death anniversary

ceremonies of South and East Asia. See Donald K. Swearer, "Folk Buddhism," *The Encyclopedia of Religion*, ed. Mircea Eliade (New York: Macmillan Publishing Company, 1987), vol. 5, p. 376. See also Schopen, "Archaeology and Protestant Presuppositions," pp. 13–15, for archaeological and epigraphic evidence of Buddhist belief in a continuing self after death.

32. Sudhir Kakar has wonderfully captured the East-West distinction when he says, "The Indian injunction 'Know Thyself' *(atmanamvidhi)* is related to a Self other than the one referred to by Socrates. It is a self uncontaminated by time and space and thus without the life-historical dimension which is the focus of psychoanalysis and of Western romantic literature." *Shamans, Mystics and Doctors: A Psychological Inquiry into India and Its Healing Traditions* (1982; Delhi: Oxford University Press, 1990), pp. 7–8. See also Alan Roland, *In Search of Self in India and Japan: Toward a Cross-Cultural Psychology* (Princeton, NJ: Princeton University Press, 1988), pp. 7–10 and passim, who distinguishes between the "I-self" of the West and the "we-self" of Asia.
33. Anne Carolyn Klein, *Meeting the Great Bliss Queen: Buddhists, Feminists and the Art of the Self* (Boston: Beacon Press, 1995), p. 44. In chapter 2 Klein offers an interesting comparative discussion of the notions of the self in Western and Buddhist thought. See also the dialogue between His Holiness the Dalai Lama and the philosopher Charles Taylor in *Sleeping, Dreaming, and Dying: An Exploration of Consciousness with The Dalai Lama*, ed. and narrated by Francisco J. Varela (Boston: Wisdom Publications, 1997), pp. 11–21.
34. Steven Collins arrives at similar conclusions, but his analysis is based on what he sees as the dichotomous discourses about the self of the little and great traditions. See Steven Collins, *Selfless Persons: Imagery and Thought in Theravāda Buddhism* (Cambridge: Cambridge University Press, 1990), especially pp. 147–54 and passim.
35. See, for instance, Barbara Aziz's discussion of the generally low status of Tibetan women, "Moving Towards a Sociology of Tibet," in Willis, *Feminine Ground*, pp. 76–95.
36. See Melvyn Goldstein's discussion of this tension in "The Revival of Monastic Life in Drepung Monastery," in Melvyn C. Goldstein and Matthew T. Kapstein, eds., *Buddhism in Contemporary Tibet: Religious Revival and Cultural Identity* (Berkeley: University of California Press, 1998).
37. See Makley, passim, and Cynthia Enloe, *Bananas, Beaches and Bases: Making Feminist Sense of International Politics* (Berkeley: University of California Press, 1989), passim.

THE WOMEN'S ALLIANCE:
Catalyzing Change in Ladakh

Helena Norberg-Hodge

When I first visited Ladakh in 1975, life in the villages was still based on the same foundations it had been for centuries, evolving in its own environments, according to its own traditional Buddhist principles. In the past, the region was protected from both colonialism and Western-style "development" by its lack of resources, inhospitable climate, and inaccessibility. Change came slowly, allowing for adaptation from within.

One of the first things that struck me about Ladakh was the wide, uninhibited smiles of the women, who moved about freely, joking and speaking with men in an open and unselfconscious way. Though young girls may have appeared shy, women generally exhibited great self-confidence, strength of character, and dignity. Almost all early travelers to Ladakh commented on the exceptionally strong cultural place of women.

Anthropologists looking from a Western perspective at formal, external structures might have been misled by the fact that men tended to hold the public positions and often sat separately from women at social functions. However, from my experience of several industrial societies, I would say that women in traditional Ladakh actually had a stronger position than in any other culture I know.

Traditionally, most significant for the status of women in Ladakh was the fact that the informal sector of society, with women at the center, played a much larger role than the formal sector. The focus of the economy was the household; almost all important decisions had to do with basic needs and were settled at this level. Thus women were never forced to choose between being with their children and playing an active part in social and economic life. The public sphere, in which men tended to be leaders, had far less significance than it does in the industrialized world.

Since about 1974, however, external economic, political and cultural forces have descended on the Ladakhis like an avalanche, bringing massive and rapid disruption of all aspects of the traditional culture. Like so many other cultures exposed to the centralized global economy, Ladakh has become ever more dependent on distant centers of production and consumption. As local economic and political ties have been broken, Ladakhis have become estranged from one another; as the speed of life and mobility have increased, so familiar relationships have become more superficial and transient. In this situation, the connections between people have been reduced largely to externals. Villagers have come to be identified with what they have rather than with who they are, and thus are hidden behind their clothes and other belongings.

As a result of these changes, I have seen the strong, outgoing women of Ladakh being replaced by a new, alienated generation, unsure of themselves and extremely concerned with their appearance. Traditionally, the way a woman looked was important, but her capabilities, including tolerance and social skills, were much more appreciated. I experienced this alienation directly when I stopped off one day to see my friend Deskit. I found her sitting alone in front of the television at ten o'clock in the morning: her children were at school, her husband was at work. I had known her in the village when she was a bit shy, but pretty and sparkling. She was still pretty, but the sparkle had gone. Now she was clearly unhappy and had become quite withdrawn. I had come to see her because an aunt of hers had told me she was unwell. Neither her aunt nor Deskit herself knew why she was so unhappy. Her husband had a good job as a doctor, her children were in the best schools in Leh, and their house was modern, clean, and comfortable. But the process of development had isolated Deskit, imprisoning her in a nuclear family, removing her from the larger community, and leaving her without meaningful work. It had also separated her from her children. It was heartbreaking to see a scene that is played out endlessly in the West repeated over and over again in Ladakh.

In opposition to these trends, there is now a growing movement at work to restore and promote traditional culture in Ladakh. The vital lesson that the so-called "developed world" can learn from Ladakh is this: self-reliance, frugality, social harmony, environmental sustainability, and spiritual sophistication are possible and are being recognized as such. We at the International Society for Ecology and Culture (ISEC) have been working with a growing number of non-governmental organizations and Ladakhi leaders to restore respect for Ladakhi culture and to counter the avalanche of forces that have led to a loss of self-respect among Ladakhis.

Since its formation in the early 1990s, the Women's Alliance of Ladakh (WAL), now with four thousand members and a presence in every village, has gained a growing reputation for its work in promoting and preserving the cultural and spiritual foundations of Ladakhi culture. The organization has won the genuine respect of the government as an authentic force for positive change in the region. Thubstan Chhewarg, the head of the local government, stated that the founding of the

WAL was a historic turning point for Ladakh because of its concern for maintaining Ladakhi culture and values. The WAL encourages members to retain their cultural identity by challenging the claims of "progress." Groups of women from different regions of Ladakh come together to discuss the impact of "development," their feelings about current trends, and their ideas about Ladakh's future. They talk about how communities and families are being broken down by the psychological pressures of advertising, television, and tourism; about the greed and envy that are now separating people; and about the women who have stopped spinning because it has come to be seen as "backward." Ladakhi women have been greatly strengthened by the opportunity to join with others to discuss these issues. Many now have renewed pride in being farmers, and in providing for their families.

The WAL also encourages women to continue wearing the unique Ladakhi dress. The rejection of Ladakhi clothing, particularly by the younger generation, is a disturbing symptom of the embarrassment and sense of inferiority Ladakhis feel about themselves and their culture. The WAL has reminded the community about the importance of wearing Ladakhi dress with pride.

The WAL plays an important role in celebrating Ladakhi dance, songs, and other artistic traditions at meetings and social events. Such celebrations are a vital way of maintaining community and protecting Ladakhi culture and centuries-old tradition in the face of Western pop music and video games. The organization also arranges educational programs for both Westerners and Ladakhis, and has gone so far as to sponsor six Ladakhi women on "reality tours" to the West, enabling them to experience directly the negative aspects of Western-style economic development.

The women of Ladakh are both willing and able to take direct, collective action to resist the forces that beset Ladakhi culture. A "No TV Day" has been organized, as well as a demonstration that managed to reverse a rule prohibiting the sale of the women's vegetables in the central bazaar. In 1998, the WAL organized a tour of twelve villages in order to discuss the kind of future Ladakhi women wanted for their children, and to speak as a collective voice to influence more effectively the policies of both village leadership and the government. A further objective of the tour was to exchange local goods and to raise awareness about the need for the continued replanting of local crop varieties in the face of persistent government pressure to use "green revolution" technologies. As the tour moved from village to village, the group steadily grew in size, as women in each village responded to its message.

All of these efforts, we believe, have had much positive impact on different sectors of Ladakhi society. The efforts of the WAL have helped fuel a growing dialogue among members of the community about appropriate paths toward the future and have had, at their core, women working for change for women.

SUJĀTĀ'S ARMY:
Dalit Buddhist Women and Self-Emancipation

Owen M. Lynch

Madhumaya in "Sujātā's Army" uniform (photo by Owen Lynch)

In India today, one rarely picks up a daily newspaper without some mention of Dalits (the oppressed, downtrodden, depressed).[1] Since independence, India's has been a parliamentary system of government whose constitution declares all citizens—men, women, educated or illiterate, Dalit or non-Dalit—free and equally possessing the precious right to vote. Formerly known as Untouchables, Dalits, using their new rights and freedoms, have become important and increasingly assertive participants in India's vibrant, rough-and-tumble political democracy. One result of this is that they suffer from more and greater atrocities on the part of those who resent Dalits' increasing self-emancipation and assertiveness. This essay concerns another less noticed, less assertive, and less widespread movement, that of Dalit female self-emancipation. In particular, it is about a small but significant group of Dalit Buddhist women living in Agra city, India, who are organizing an "army" *(vāhinī)* to set in motion their emancipation from patriarchy, caste hierarchy, and gendered ignorance. All of them, along with their extraordinary leader, Madhumaya Jayant, are members of the Dalit community known in Agra as Jatav.[2] Madhumaya and her sisters seek their emancipation by entering public spaces and the public sphere, which have been traditionally denied to them by the patriarchal customs of their own community and because of their Dalit status.

The Soldiers

The movement of which Madhumaya is the founder, the National Indian Women's Union, is otherwise known as "Sujātā's Army." Madhumaya is now the president of its Uttar Pradesh state branch. Madhumaya named her army after Sujātā, because it was Sujātā, who, according to one legend, was the first to offer the Buddha food when he reached enlightenment. Madhumaya explains that in another legend about the Buddha he was apprehensive during his search for enlightenment about what to do, so he set the silver bowl in which Sujātā had given him food in the river. When he saw it float upstream against the current, he took courage and knew he would receive enlightenment. Thus, the symbolism in Madhumaya's choice of name is that women had and still have an important role in bringing Buddhist enlightenment into the world. Sujātā's army's mission is to bring enlightenment to Dalit women so as to improve the social condition of their lives in the contemporary world, as Ambedkar wished.

Madhumaya is in her late forties or early fifties, a grandmother relieved of household chores by her daughter-in-law and, most important, happily married to an educated husband fluent in both French and English and employed in a local tourist emporium. Madhumaya's husband, like some of her followers' husbands, supports her in her endeavors and travels in and beyond Agra. That crucial support makes these women unlike many of their less fortunate Dalit sisters. Most important, Madhumaya, having an eighth-standard education, is literate, as are some of her followers. Literacy enables her to carry on a widespread correspondence and to read books and newspapers to which she occasionally submits press releases. Literacy also enables her and some of her sisters to read such things as government regulations so that they can assist illiterate widows and others in need. Unlike their community's few college-educated women, who most often work in public sector jobs and, therefore, are forbidden to engage in political or politically tinged activities, Madhumaya and her followers remain based in the domestic sphere but are free to enter the public sphere where they quietly seek to influence their community's less fortunate and/or less enlightened sisters as well as patriarchal brothers. In short, they are grassroots activists.

The ideal upon which Madhumaya models herself is Mother Theresa. Despite the handicap of diabetes, her most endearing characteristic is humor, which she uses with a marksman's precision to disarm opponents or defuse tense situations, while hitting home her point. She can also laugh at herself, as when, with a chuckle, she said to me, "Men! When you are young, they admire your long, black tresses, but when you are old, all they can do is complain about a string of grey hair in their food."

Dr. Ambedkar's Legitimating Teachings

In pre-independence India, members of Madhumaya's community were known as Untouchables. Untouchables were among the lowest castes in India's hierarchical caste system. Because many Untouchables worked with polluting substances such as leather, soiled clothes needing to be washed, cut hair and nails, dead animals, human waste, and garbage, they and their touch were seen as polluting to upper-caste people. Consequently they were despised and avoided, forced to live in their own hamlets and drink water only from their own wells, denied full participation in many religious rituals and entry into temples of the upper castes, subject to corvée labor and atrocities, relegated to the least remunerative jobs, and excluded from schools and education. Their lot was a miserable one. Orthodox, upper-caste people believed that their own higher status, like Untouchable status, was religiously ordained. Untouchables, therefore, were regarded as inherently polluted and polluting as well as condemned to do polluting occupations.

Madhumaya and her supporters are followers of Dr. B. R. Ambedkar.[3] Ambedkar was a Dalit who, through a series of unusual circumstances, rose to become the first minister for law in independent India. Dalits revere him as the father of the Indian constitution, which made them equal citizens. Most important, it was he who, against great opposition, fought to include in the constitution the universal franchise that has empowered them to fight for their rights, to speak with their own voice, and to participate in India's parliamentary democracy using the power of their votes. Just before his death in 1956, Ambedkar converted to Buddhism as a rejection of Brahmanical Hinduism, which in his eyes made him and his fellow Dalits "untouchable." Ambedkar wrote his own well-researched and scholarly interpretation of Buddhism called *The Buddha and His Dhamma*[4] and has himself become a bodhisattva for Dalit Buddhists. In Ambedkar's interpretation, the Buddha gave women rights to knowledge and to the realization of their own potential equal to those of men. He once wrote:

> Ever since I began to work among the Dalit classes, I made it a point to carry women along with men. That's why you will see that our conferences are always mixed conferences. I measure the progress of the community by the degree of progress which women have achieved.... Above all let each girl who marries stand up to her husband, claim to be his friend and equal and refuse to be his slave. I am sure that if you follow this advice, you will bring honor and glory to yourself and the depressed classes.[5]

Almost all of Madhumaya's community's members in and around Agra are avid Ambedkarites who follow his political and other teachings. Every day more and more Ambedkarites are following Ambedkar's example and advice by converting to Buddhism, which, they believe, is the "true" religion of their ancestors. Conversion, then, is really reconversion back to, and a rediscovery of, their real Buddhist identity, religion, and culture, all rooted in the ancient soil of India itself. In her struggles Madhumaya uses, just as she no less sincerely believes in, Ambedkar's counsel to "educate, organize, agitate." That counsel and his other teachings legitimate her and her sisters' efforts to overcome the patriarchal ways of their own community's males and to empower themselves and their sisters to change their lives. They do so in a variety of ways.

Liberate Bodh Gaya Movement

Dr. Ambedkar's birthday *(Ambedkar Jayantī)* is celebrated annually in Agra on April 14 with a huge parade through the city's streets. It begins around 8:00 P.M. in the evening and ends about 9:00 A.M. the next morning. Nineteen ninety-one was special; it was Dr. Ambedkar's one hundredth birth anniversary. A year earlier, Madhumaya and her sisters prepared for the coming event by organizing the "Foot Pilgrimage [Carrying] the Torch of the [Buddha's] Law *(Dhamma Jyotī Pad Yātrā)*" to all of Agra's Dalit Buddhist neighborhoods. Madhumaya described the pilgrimage in her own words:

> That parade [marched] through all Agra. For example, every Sunday, it might start from the Buddhist temple of this neighborhood, Chakki Path, and march to Jagdishpura. Along the way, wherever a Buddhist temple stood, sermons were given. They [the women] would march to a place where they lit a flame of the Law and after lighting a wax candle from the Torch of the Law they left that place.... They marched on to another place where hymns were sung, sermons were given, and the women were garlanded. My strict instruction was that the women should march in their white *pañcaśīl* [five precepts] uniforms bearing *pañcaśīl* epaulets. They carried in their hands *pañcaśīl* flags. I spread my message, and my message was that women would make a special contribution in connection with the 100 anniversary of Dr. Ambedkar's birthday. Beginning on 6 December [1990] and ending on 14 April 1991, they would make a journey through all of Agra. And on 14 April, when the [annual] celebratory parade set out, for the first time my women accompanied it.[6]

Before 1991, the parade had been an all-male, public affair. On that historic day Dalit women in Agra moved onto the public stage *with* Dalit men. Their action overtly announced Ambedkar to be their leader and implicitly declared him to be their Buddhist emancipator whose teaching legitimated and facilitated their participation in the parade.

A Dalit female participant in the foot pilgrimage writes of it in these words: "The pilgrimage's onlookers were amazed to see the new consciousness of the female devotees, their enlightenment and their efforts to spread the Buddhist religion."[7] Under Madhumaya's leadership, the women openly entered a public space. More importantly, they simultaneously entered the public sphere of social and religious life to spread the Buddhist message and their feminist interpretation of it. Symbolically all of Agra's Jatav neighborhoods, not just the Buddhist ones, were encircled and united. They were also at least symbolically incorporated into the Buddhist Sangha through the lighting of the wax candles from the same torch of the Law, just as occurs in the Olympic games. At the same time the foot pilgrimage was also a major feminist event. The female marchers asserted and revealed organizational skills independent of men and despite the hitherto male monopoly of them. In effect, the Buddhist women sought to change the culture of Agra's Dalit women by bringing them into the public sphere and showing their more timid sisters that emancipation is possible and there is a road to it, at least for some.

Agra's Dalit women have also stepped into the nationwide public sphere through their participation in the Liberate Bodh Gaya Movement (hereafter LBGM). Since 1992 Buddhist Dalits from many parts of India have engaged in this liberation movement to gain control of the Mahabodhi Temple, the site of the Buddha's enlightenment in Bodh Gaya. For Buddhist Dalits, Bodh Gaya is the main center of their religion, which, unlike the religious centers of other religions in India, is not under the control of the people to whom it is sacred.[8] Rather, it was until recently under a managing committee in which Hindus were the majority. In 1993 the movement escalated into a nationwide agitation of Dalit Buddhists to *regain* control of the temple at Bodh Gaya. It is a *regaining* because Dalit Buddhists following Ambedkar's teaching believe that they were originally Buddhists, but had been deprived of their religion and cultural patrimony through the deceit and trickery of those who espoused Brahmanic Hinduism, the religion of caste and inequality in Ambedkar's view.[9]

In 1994 I attended a third agitation to liberate Bodh Gaya. Agra's Dalit female Buddhists, again under Madhumaya's leadership, organized another foot pilgrimage and took the torch of the Buddha's Law to Bodh Gaya, where thousands of male and female Dalit Buddhists had assembled. Agra's women distinguished themselves by marching to the stage, where Ganga Devi, the oldest "soldier" of the army, presented the torch to the assembled dignitaries. All wore the uniforms of Sujātā's Army: white saris with five colored epaulets symbolizing the Buddhist *pañcaśīl* (five precepts). The uniforms symbolically assert the unspoken Buddhist, feminist subtext of feminist emancipation. Thereafter, Arati Baudh, a "soldier" in Agra's Sujātā's Army, gave her first public speech from the stage. Other Buddhist Dalit women, especially those from Maharashtra State, also gave speeches and asked both for the return of the temple to Buddhist management and for further emancipation of women.

Agra's Dalit Buddhist men proudly told me that the participation of so many women in the agitation showed how much change there has been in their community and its women. Many of the women traveled together in public to Bodh Gaya. Many did so without being chaperoned by male relatives, who at the time of the agitation urgently needed to return to work in Agra's shoe factories after the long and unpaid Hindu Divali holidays. None of the marching women veiled their faces, a custom that was prevalent back in 1962 when I first met them and is still expected of Agra's Dalit women when in public. The participation of so many women in the movement is not completely innocent, insofar as women are less likely to be attacked by the police trying to control a mob, and their actions are more likely to be understood as peaceful.[10] On the part of the Dalit women, participation enables them to develop their public presence, to meet and hear women from elsewhere, to develop the independence to travel without men chaperoning them, and even to enjoy themselves. These are not small gains in a conservative community where women are by and large controlled by men who have always claimed the right to speak publicly for their women and to "protect" them. Ironically, the women don't exactly welcome the men's pride over the extent of the change of "their" women, as we shall see, since they are not necessarily proud for the right reasons. Male Buddhists see the women as a resource to do much of the work for which the men can take the credit. Female Buddhist activists, however, see the men as a problem and the Buddhist movement as a means for their emancipation from it.

Ban the Lottery Campaign

In another, more dramatic encounter Dalit Buddhist women independent of Madhumaya marched on January 21, 1995, in a demonstration against the lottery ticket sellers at Agra's Jaipur House. According to a local newspaper, the lottery ticket sellers had become a problem "after hundreds of people had been ruined [by buying lottery tickets]."[11] Many Dalit men have become addicted to buying lottery tickets and spend almost all their earnings in search of the pot of gold, while their families languish for want of a pot of rice to eat. When the Dalit women entered the marketplace of the ticket sellers, the women set foot not only in a place morally abhorrent to them but also in a profoundly male, public place, where resentment against Agra's Ambedkarite Dalits has been long standing. The lottery ticket sellers angrily reacted by stoning and beating with sticks the Buddhist female protestors. According to a local newspaper:

> Eight [Dalit women] were wounded and three seriously enough to be admitted to the hospital; the rest fled in fear from the place. When the news of the attack reached neighbors and friends they…in a rage began to wreck that area and attack stores.… Charges were filed against the [women's] attackers and…only after the enraged mob [of the women's neighbors and friends] surrounded the local police station did the police promise that the perpetrators would be jailed within 12 hours.[12]

Thereafter, women from all castes high and low joined in and virtually coopted the movement. This was perhaps the first time in Agra's history that Dalit women had successfully initiated an intercaste and multi-party movement in the public sphere. Despite its ultimate failure, the protest was a radical emergence in Agra's culture where Dalits have been traditionally discriminated against and their women barred from the public sphere, particularly when acting on their own initiative, as in this case. A local newspaper reported on a meeting in which Dalit women optimistically interpreted the atrocity's consequences:

> Women were not despondent about the Jaipur House incident; rather they have been awakened by it. In Agra city a great movement against the lottery will begin. Nowhere will lottery selling be allowed. Speakers appealed for women to take part immediately in the picketing.[13]

The subtext of the Dalit Buddhist women's campaign, however, was the heretofore unheard of public critique of their own husbands and sons who had become irresponsible addicts of the lottery and who had failed to live up to the teachings of Ambedkar and the Buddha.

Subvert Hierarchy Campaign

Sometimes against their best conscious intentions, Dalit men throw up the greatest obstacles to their women's self-upliftment and emancipation. Early in my field work I attended a meeting of Agra's Indian Buddhist Society. The meeting was held on a platform in front of the Buddhist temple in the Chakki Path neighborhood. I arrived in the middle of an argument about the date for the 1994 protest at Bodh Gaya. At one point Madhumaya, as is her wont, interjected, while holding up in her hand for all to see a piece of paper on which was written, "If it [the protest] were not taking place, then how could I have this flyer stating the date on which it begins."* Later in the discussion she stood up and lectured to men about the women's difficulties in trying to organize for the Mahabodhi agitation when the men could not decide when it would take place. Men from the audience then tried to silence her by shouting her down with cries that she was wasting time with petty women's problems, which had no place at such a meeting. Before sitting down Madhumaya steadfastly defended herself by saying, "A right attitude will do the work, the Buddhist Women's Union will endure." This was an implicit criticism of the men for not having the right attitude taught by the Buddha.

Madhumaya and her followers had affiliated themselves with the male-dominated Indian Buddhist Society only at the men's request. After that meeting she said to me, as she began to choke up with tears of disappointment and anger, "These tears, these tears, why haven't they been shed? Why are these tears being shed now—because of grief. From each and every side they are doing such things [causing her grief]." She felt that the men were making all sorts of unfair accusations against her. But, then, as she always seemed to do, she regained her courage and at one time said to me, "Treat me as a wise guy *(cālāk)*, and soon I will become a wise guy too."*

Why were some of the men so angry and annoyed with Madhumaya? It was not merely because of the issues that she raised. If a man had raised those same issues, he would not have caused such a furor. Rather, she had twice transgressed. First, she had publicly entered a heretofore specifically Dalit male public space, the platform in front of the temple, and even sat down among the men. Second, and even more daring, she had gotten up in that space and not only spoken directly to the men, but had also challenged them to make a decision on the basis of the printed announcement from the LBGM's central office that she had held up. Although Indian women, including Madhumaya, do speak publicly in other forums, women of her community are perceived to have no right to do so in the community's spaces reserved for men, particularly those spaces having to do with public decisions, power, and representation. "Sujātā's Army" is, then, a name well chosen by Madhumaya. The battle is a religious one; it is also a difficult, emancipative, and feminist one in which social landmines lurk everywhere its soldiers tread.

At public Buddhist and non-Buddhist meetings around the city, Dalit men often rail against Ambedkar's' three enemies of mankind: blind faith, superstition, and traditionalism or adherence to outdated customs. By blind faith they mean faith not founded on reason, such as belief in gods and goddesses and in inherited caste status; by superstition they mean belief in such things as the evil eye and pollution by touch; and outdated practices include such things as face veiling, the dowry system, and untouchability. Both males and females speak of these evils in the discourse of Buddhism, but women speak of them with additional connotations, which include the kinds of male behavior I have described, as well as things such as alcoholism, gambling, wife beating, and neglect of female education. As the Dalit political scientist Gopal Guru perceptively writes, "The whole situation compels us to defend the claim of [D]alit women to talk differently."[14]

Madhumaya admitted that she had to use some of the men's own weapons against them. One tactic was to start a new and separate organization and take her followers along with her whenever the men tried to coopt the present organization by putting in charge their own female candidates who lacked the necessary skills. Unfortunately for the men, they often now find themselves dependent upon Madhumaya and some of her sisters for organizing the women to provide essential services for events such as the LBGM movement.

Literacy is the weapon of the underdog. Just as Madhumaya and her sisters use their literacy to help themselves and their sisters, so too Madhumaya is quick to use it in defense of Buddhism. In 1992 it was rumored that Mira Nair, the maker of the film *Salaam Bombay*, was going to make a film in which the Buddha would appear as an incarnation of a Hindu god. Madhumaya immediately sent a statement to the local newspapers, which then published it. In it, she threatened an agitation against the film if the Buddha were portrayed in that way. Likewise, in 1995 Mayavati was briefly installed as the chief minister of the state of Uttar Pradesh. Mayavati was the first Dalit, who also happened to be a woman, to hold that post. On that occasion Madhumaya and some male Buddhists published the following press release in the local newspapers:

> Years ago a Buddhist emperor [Aśoka] sat on the seat of government. After a long hiatus Ms. Mayavati's assumption of the Chief Ministership has restored that ancient age. The hope [then] has become manifest that through Ms. Mayavati's running Uttar Pradesh's ship of state in a Buddhist way, Bodhisattva Baba Saheb Ambedkar's dream of social reformation and social unity will be realized.[15]

Aśoka is the ideal ruler with whom Agra's Buddhists compare present-day government officials. The incidents of Mira Nair's movie and Mayavati's appointment, however, illustrate both how well tuned into public events Madhumaya is and how quickly she, with only an eighth-grade education, turns them to Buddhist *and* female advantage.

Summary

The meaning and impact of Buddhism in the lives of these extraordinary women is deep and significant. Enlightened and legitimated by Dr. Ambedkar's Buddhist teachings, Dalit women have begun the task of their own empowerment. In that process, the soldiers of Sujātā's Army battle on three fronts. The first is Agra's public sphere, where they battle against some evils shared by all communities, such as the lottery ticket sellers. On the second front they battle for their religious rights, their sacred monuments, and recognition of their Buddhist identity. At the same time, they are opening a wedge to participate in the nationwide feminist movement, even if they do so with a different voice. And finally, they have entered a battle in the public sphere of their own community's profoundly gendered and patriarchal social spaces, customs, and beliefs. They are creating an emerging feminist Buddhist culture of emancipation from, rather than of resistance to, their own patriarchal men. On all those fronts they are showing how some of India's most discriminated against people, Dalits, and some of its most marginal members, women, may be leaders and innovators. With the relatively rare support of their husbands they fight not with guns and bombs, but with the powerful weapons of literacy and the legitimating and emancipative message of Dr. Ambedkar's interpretation of the Buddha's enlightenment.

Epilogue

In 1999, I returned to Agra for a short trip to observe the April 14 annual parade in honor of Dr. Ambedkar's birthday. On that day the men of the Indian Buddhist Society struck. They boycotted Madhumaya by installing her former follower, Usha Baudh, in her place to carry the torch of the Buddha's Law in the parade. They also told others not to speak to her and, she said, warned her to leave Agra for her own safety. Madhumaya was outmaneuvered and isolated. The reasons circulated for the boycott were her excessive self-promotion and her ignoring, if not defying, the men's sentiments. The commander of Sujātā's Army had lost the battle, but it is by no means clear that she has lost the war.

Acknowledgments

The nine months of research upon which this essay is based was carried out during academic year 1994–95. It was supported by a grant from the National Endowment for the Humanities given through the American Institute of Indian Studies as well as by a sabbatical year given by New York University. Earlier versions of this paper were given in the 1996 American Anthropological Association Meeting's session, "'Fight the Power': Critical Reflections on Changing Forms of Consciousness" in honor of Dr. Constance Sutton; at the 1998 "Women Changing Contemporary Buddhism" session of the Trinity College conference, The Nun's Circle; and at the 1998 Association for Asian Studies Meeting's session "Ideologies and Strategies in Dalit and Black Movements." I am grateful to all the participants in those sessions who offered me helpful comments not all of which I have been able to follow.

All quotes followed by an asterisk are from my remembered notes of what was said to me. All other quotes are verbatim translations from taped interviews.

Notes

1. "Dalit" is the term by which today's enlightened, former "Untouchables" refer to themselves and by which they prefer others to refer to them.
2. For further information on the Jatavs and their relationship to Buddhism, see Lynch (1969), (1972), and (1998). For further information on Dalits in other parts of India, see the articles and extensive bibliographies in Mahar (1972) and Zelliot (1992).
3. A standard bibliography of Ambedkar is Keer (1962). For other biographies, see the select bibliography in Zelliot (1992).
4. Ambedkar (1957).
5. Ambedkar (1969).
6. The *pañcaśīla* are the five principals of ethical action; "*pañcaśīl* epaulets" are five colored epaulets that symbolize the five principals.
7. Sohni (1992).
8. For an enlightening history and description of contemporary pilgrimage practice in Bodh Gaya, see Doyle (1997). Doyle reveals how current Dalit Buddhist contestation over, and religious practice in, Bodh Gaya and the Mahabodhi Temple is part of a long history of similar controversies.
9. See Ambedkar (1948); Lynch (1972). It is important to note that Ambedkar did not see this in racial or purely class terms. Rather, for him it was a primarily ideological issue in which the religion of caste, Brahmanism, was used to deprive Untouchables and others of their Buddhist religion and their basic right to equality. See Omvedt (1995), 43–52.
10. This is a not a new tactic used by women in India since they used it also during the independence movement. I am grateful to Dr. Anne Waters who informed me of this and other historical precedents that women have used especially since the fight for independence.
11. *Dainik Sainik* (*Daily Soldier;* Agra newspaper), 22 January, 1995.
12. *Dainik Sainik,* 22 January, 1995.
13. *Amar Ujala* (*Eternal Light;* Agra newspaper), 23 January, 1995.
14. Guru (1995).
15. *Amar Ujala,* 26 June, 1995.

RELIGIOUS LEADERSHIP AMONG MAHARASHTRIAN WOMEN

Eleanor Zelliot

There are two strands of the Buddhist movement in Maharashtra, both known for strong leadership by women. One movement is the Trilokya Bauddha Mahasangha Sahayaka Gana ("Friends of the Great Worldwide Buddhist Order," hereafter TBMSG), an organization with ties to the Friends of the Western Buddhist Order in England. The other is the Buddhist activity initiated by individual Buddhist women, chiefly in Mumbai (Bombay), Pune, Nagpur, Aurangabad, and New Delhi. While there is much material in print about the dynamic TBMSG, little has been published about individual Buddhist women's activity. Information about it must come from visits and from the small amount of literature that is published by these women themselves. Except for those in the TBMSG and the beginnings of an ordained Sangha, women Buddhist leaders are not organized in any specific way; local activity, however, is of an extraordinary sort and is quite common. Some of these women are organized in Dalit women's groups, which are not specifically Buddhist in practice but are based on the empowerment afforded by Buddhist conversion. When Buddhist teaching is expressed in social action, however, its effectiveness depends on the power and charisma of the individual Buddhist women involved, and it is the lives and backgrounds of some of these women that I will focus on here.

The women of the Buddhist movement in Maharashtra are different, I would claim, from any other group of Buddhist women. First, the word Dalit means "ground down or oppressed," and it is the word now used by politically aware groups of Untouchables in India in place of earlier terms such as Depressed Classes, Gandhi's term Harijan or "people of god," the government term Scheduled Castes, indicating castes on a list or schedule to receive affirmative action benefits,[1] and the word Untouchable itself, which indicates pollution by birth. The word "Dalit" became current in Maharashtra in the early 1970s, and is now used widely across India. It is a proud word, indicating oppression rather than personal fault. Ex-Untouchable is another word often used, since the practice of untouchability is now illegal in India, much as the practice of racism is illegal in the United States. The terms "Dalit Buddhist," "Neo-Buddhist," or "ex-Untouchable Buddhist," however, are not used by the Buddhists of Maharashtra; members of this group use no other designation than the simple term "Buddhist." Although the claim to be Buddhist obliterates any other caste designation, the Buddhists of Maharashtra must still be seen in some contexts as belonging to those groups that designate themselves proudly as "Dalit," such as writers in the "Dalit Sahitya (Literature)" movement or women in Dalit women's organizations, both of which include members other than Buddhists.

While there are many highly educated Buddhist women in the middle class, the majority of Buddhist women in Maharashtra are poor, not well educated, and are still at the mercy of the inequalities of their former status as Untouchables. Specifically, rural Buddhists may be the victims of physical and psychological atrocities, and women all over India may suffer the indignities of low caste. Under these circumstances, then, contemporary Buddhism in India has a very strong social agenda, which must be seen as an implicit part of its religious content.

The activity sustained by all groups of contemporary Buddhist women in Maharashtra is based in the Buddhist conversion movement begun by Dr. B. R. Ambedkar in 1956. Bhimrao Ramji Ambedkar, known affectionately and respectfully as "Babasaheb," was a highly educated Untouchable Mahar from Maharashtra. He attended school in Bombay, and went to Columbia and London Universities under the auspices of a reform movement that offered the aid of non-Brahmin princes from the principalities of Baroda and Kolhapur. Ambedkar's degrees include a B.A., M.A., Ph.D., D.D.s, and Bar-at-Law,[2] and he used this education to "educate, agitate, and organize" his fellow Untouchables. After vain attempts to penetrate the social and religious citadels of Hinduism, Ambedkar declared publicly he "would not die a Hindu" and turned to a long held interest, the ancient and egalitarian religion of Buddhism. Two months before his death in 1956 at the age of sixty-five, he converted to Buddhism in the Maharashtrian city of Nagpur at the hands of Chandramani, the oldest *bhikkhu* (fully ordained monk) in India.[3] He invited the masses who attended the ceremony to convert, and after his death, conversion ceremonies were held all over Maharashtra as well as in other cities in greater India.

Dr. Ambedkar left no structure or trained leadership for the conversion movement, and there were no Buddhists left in India, the land of its birth, save marginal groups in the east, Tibetan refugees, and a few converts from high-caste Hinduism. There was a strong intellectual interest, however, and Ambedkar himself was deeply influenced by the work of D. D. Kosambi and of other Brahmin scholars. He reprinted, for example, a 1908 piece by Lakshman Narasu entitled *The Essence of Buddhism*, a classic statement by a low-caste convert from Tamilnadu still in print today (though without Ambedkar's introduction).[4] In addition, Ambedkar left an interpretation of Buddhist stories and teachings called *The Buddha and His Dhamma*, which continues to inspire a large group of followers who feel not only that he can do no wrong, but also that Hinduism is a religion that they must disavow if they want dignity and equality. Many of Ambedkar's early followers were from the large Mahar caste of Untouchables, a group with a heritage of village servitude but no specific craft or especially polluting duty. It was a caste already eager for education, on the march to a more respectable place in society, and bent on securing rights and recognition of worth. Ambedkar's work helped channel that energy, especially that of women.

One of the Buddhists Ambedkar was in touch with before his conversion was the Venerable Sangharakshita, an English convert to Buddhism who had been in India for twenty years. Venerable Sangharakshita toured Maharashtra immediately after Ambedkar's conversion and death in 1956, and again several years later before returning to England. There he established the Friends of the Western Buddhist Order and, as a corollary of that in India, the Trilokya Bauddha Mahasangha Sahayaka Gana, which now has centers in Pune, Mumbai, Nagpur, and Ahmedabad, as well as in smaller towns. It also maintains a retreat center at Bhaja, across the valley from first-century B.C.E. Buddhist cave temples.[5]

The Trilokya Bauddha Mahasangha Sahayaka Gana (TBMSG)

In contrast to other women in the Ambedkar conversion movement who act independently in their own localities, the women who are ordained *dhammacāriṇī*[6] in the Trilokya Bauddha Mahasangha Sahayaka Gana are well organized, highly trained, and part of a centralized institution. They do share, for the most part, the same Dalit background, and are equally part of the Ambedkar movement. The dozen or so women who have undergone the rigorous ordination procedures of this group, the same that men in the movement must undergo, do not become robed or cloistered nuns but hold very responsible positions working among non-ordained girls and women in various localities. They do return to the TBMSG retreat center at Bhaja for lengthy meditation and Dhamma sessions, but otherwise they are very much out in the world.

One of the most important duties of four of the *dhammacāriṇīs* is the directorship of hostels for girls. Pune was the site of the first hostel, founded in 1990, followed by two in 1994, one in Nagpur and one in Latur, the site of the massive 1994 earthquake in Maharashtra. The most recent hostel was established in 1997 in Goa,

Bhikkhunī Mataji Rupananda of Nagpur with a statue of the walking Buddha and a portrait of Dr. B. R. Ambedkar (photo by Christopher S. Queen)

an area in which the Buddhist conversion movement has hardly made itself felt. The girls in the hostels all come from villages or from homes that do not support their desire to learn or at times even their personal well-being. The hostels provide supplementary classes, meditation sessions, recreational activities, and much intellectual and physical support, as well good food and lodging. The girls go to local schools and colleges for their basic education.

Three *dhammacāriṇīs* at the hostel for girls at Mohanwadi, on the edge of Pune, illustrate the experiences and backgrounds of many in the movement. All three happened to be at the hostel when I was there because they had just attended a TBMSG retreat at Bhaja, near Pune, and were exchanging information informally for a day or two afterwards. The hostel in Mohanwadi is an elegant building, a gift of concerned Buddhists outside Maharashtra, which houses seventy-seven female students, most but not all of them of Buddhist or Untouchable background. Other Buddhist women serve as officials in this hostel: there are four wardens, all Buddhists, and a hostel cook who participates in meditation sessions with the other adepts. It is the *dhammacāriṇīs,* however, who have the most responsible positions.

Dhammacāriṇī Alokashri has been the chair of the Mohanwadi hostel since 1990. She supervises all hostel activities and, in vacation periods, goes out to villages to find girls who might need a hostel life in order to be educated. Even though the students are not all Buddhists, all are exposed to a meditation session in the evening and to Buddhist celebrations, such as Buddha Jayanti, the celebration of the Buddha's birthday. Many of the girls come from very poor backgrounds and need special classes in order to meet the requirements of Pune schools. Alokashri hopes to write about the problems of Dalit and Buddhist women, but at the moment is totally involved in her work. The hostel offers participation in Girl Guides, the British term for Girl Scouts, and the possibility of learning karate, as well as more conventional help for its chiefly rural students.

Dhammacāriṇī Vijaya, who is married and has a child, is head of the women's work in Nagpur, which includes a kindergarten, a hostel for fifty girls, and sewing classes. The ordination of both men and women in the TBMSG does not require a reclusive or celibate life, but is in recognition of special religious gifts. The retreat at Bhaja that brought her to Pune in the first place was an intense period of meditation and Dhamma lectures for ten women, including four *dhammacāriṇī* from England. Vijaya comes from a millworker's family and has an M.A. in social work. Her husband is a *dhammacārī* and chairman of all the TBSMG work in Nagpur.

A third *dhammacāriṇī*, Vimalasuri, has a husband (whom she married at age fifteen) and three children and, with the help of the husband, has been doing Dhamma work for ten years. Too poor to go beyond the ninth standard, she has become a lively and articulate Buddhist of considerable experience and a very effective spokesperson for Buddhism in the city slums where the majority of urban Buddhists live. She was born in a village in Satara district but came to Bombay in her teens. Her father had become a Buddhist during the early days of the conversion movement, so she is grounded in the Ambedkar vision. With her village and urban backgrounds, she understands thoroughly the problems of Buddhist women.[7]

The English *dhammacāriṇī* Padmasuri, who wrote *But Little Dust* about Dalit life, developed a close friendship with Vimalasuri during her time in India. Padmasuri came from England in 1987 to help with the first ordination of Indian women into the TBMSG at the then new retreat center of Bhaja. Padmasuri describes the ordination ceremony, held after days of meditation, in this way:

> The ordination ceremony comes in two parts, the "private" ceremony, followed the next day by the "public" ceremony. The former symbolizes your intention to put the ideals and practices of Buddhism at the center of your life even if nobody else in the world is doing likewise; it is an individual commitment which nobody else can do for you. The ceremony is performed privately, on your own with just your preceptor. The public ceremony is with the Sangha, the gathering of other individuals who have also Gone for Refuge, welcoming you into its fellowship.

Padmasuri continues with a description of the public ceremony:

> An awning...had been set up outside where the ceremonies were to take place, giving a bit of shade. Final touches were being put to the mass of flowers on the shrine as the first trickle of people were arriving in a snake-like procession over the fields, not only from nearby Pune, but

people from Bombay, Aurangabad, and as far away as Nagpur, a day and a half's journey away. Ratnasuri led the ceremony with great joy, and a mighty shout of "SADHU" reverberated around the valley. She placed white kesas [a kind of robe adopted from the Japanese tradition] around their necks, and their new names were announced.[8]

At this time, Nirmala Kharat from the Bombay slums became Vimalasuri. Vimal means "pure, stainless, clean, or bright." Suri is a title for a religious teacher, indicating wisdom. Padmasuri's description of Vimalasuri indicates that Vimal is a suitable name for this sparkling personality. A friend told Padmasuri before the ordination, "You must meet Nirmala. You'll love her. She's so full of positivity. She just bubbles with life and energy." These qualities belie a very difficult life, but one not atypical of Buddhist women in the Ambedkar movement. Nirmala was born in a Mahar family; her father rarely worked, but her mother worked on the roads, and Nirmala would help her during holidays. She was encouraged to go to school, and was the only ex-Untouchable in a class of twenty in their village. Nirmala remembers her mother's mourning when Dr. Ambedkar died on December 6, 1956, and her father's taking down the household pictures of deities and hanging ones of Dr. Ambedkar and the Buddha in their place.

Nirmala's marriage was a "love marriage," not an arranged one, but her husband's family, except for her father-in-law, did not welcome her. In her effort to spend time outside the house, now in Bombay, she met a Buddhist monk in a local temple and through her ties with him discovered political work. In the end, it was a retreat of the TBMSG that brought her a sense of place in the Buddhist world. In spite of having three children in her slum home, she has, with the help of her husband, been able to study a great deal and travel widely in India, espousing the causes of Buddhist teaching and of the improvement of slum life. She is at home in the slums, and her own experience makes her wise in the ways of the women with whom she talks.

There are nuns in the Maharashtrian Buddhist world who have taken ordination in the traditional Buddhist way, but there is little information about them. I met one sweet-faced older woman who took the vows of a Buddhist nun after raising her family and was traveling to Buddhist families in Nagpur and Mumbai. However, there may soon be a genuine movement toward *bhikkhunī* status. At a recent ordination ceremony held at Bodh Gaya by the Foguangshan Monastery in Taiwan, twenty-eight women from Maharashtra took their vows. Nine of these walked for five days to Bodh Gaya, arriving footsore and with ragged clothes, but determined to become *bhikkhunīs*. The Taiwanese order is the largest and most active of any in Asia, and their commitment to bringing ordination to India (where the tradition died out), will aid in the bringing of Indian, Tibetan, and Sri Lankan women into full status. It remains to be seen how the women's order will be sustained in Maharashtra, who will support the women, and what sort of duties they will be able to perform. It should be noted, however, that many women outside the circle of the TBSMG support the organization by going to its meditation retreats. Others, often with their entire families, go to the *vipassanā* meditation retreats at Igatpuri in Maharashtra or to other *vipassanā* centers in Delhi, Hyderabad, Madras, and Jaipur.

Three Buddhist Women's Circles

A small apartment in the Government Colony in Bandra for first-class officers[9] is a center for Buddhist women's activities in Bombay. The government officer is Vasant Moon, permitted by the Maharashtra government to spend his time editing a multi-volume series called *Dr. Babasaheb Ambedkar: Writings and Speeches*, which now numbers sixteen volumes. His wife, Meenakshi Moon, is a powerful leader for Buddhist women in her own right. She began *Maitrani*, a Marathi bimonthly magazine with an occasional English article, in 1992 and has published it faithfully ever since. The name tells us something of her aim—it means "woman friend" in village Marathi. Articles on Buddhism written by women appear as often as possible, and, in the second issue for example, Vibhavari Sontakke contributed an article on the *Dhammapada* as a guide to life. In addition, *Maitrani* publishes considerable Buddhist art and poetry, as well as a variety of articles on Dalit problems, Buddhism, and the work of Babasaheb Ambedkar.

Because of her editorial work, as well as out of personal interest, Meenakshi Moon keeps track of many Buddhist women living and working in Maharashtra. Among them are Kirtibai Patil, a writer on Buddhist Dhamma; Sushila Mool, a professor of Pali at Milind College (established by Dr. Ambedkar) and creator of a fictional life of Siddhartha; Aruna Lokhande, an activist and a professor of sociology; Shantabai Dhani, the best-known woman in the political parties of Ambedkar, who has not only founded educational institutions for girls in Nasik but more recently built a Buddhist center or *vihāra;* Kusum Gangode, a labor leader and Buddhist; Sanghamitra Khobragade, a writer on Buddhism in *Maitrani;* and Kusum Pawde, a retired teacher of Sanskrit who conducts classes in Buddhist religion.[10] The list of such women is very long, and it is only through contact with activists like Meenakshi Moon that the full network of Maharashtrian Buddhist women becomes clear.

Some Maharashtrian Buddhist women have entered into the campaign to free Bodh Gaya from Hindu influence. As Owen Lynch's article in this volume indicates, the chief drive for the reclaiming of Bodh Gaya for Buddhists comes from the Buddhist women of Agra, but some Maharashtrian women have joined this effort as well, and Saraswati Kamble and Meenakshi Moon are among those who went to Agra for a conference on the Bodh Gaya situation. Meenakshi Moon has also attended meditation retreats at the TBMSG center in Bhaja but, like other independent Buddhist women, she has an active Buddhist life outside that organization.

The Bandra apartment of the Moons is not only the home of the publication *Maitrani*, but also a place for women activists to gather and plan strategies. Among those who come is Bharati Meshram, who has been to twenty-five different slums, often establishing an "Ambapālī *mahila mandal*," or women's organization,[11] or encouraging the building of the small *vihāras* that are almost always to be found in the slums of Bombay. Meenakshi Moon estimates there may be as many as two hundred of these women's organizations in the Buddhist areas of Bombay. Bharati Meshram qualifies for a government job but prefers to spend her time doing social work among Dalit women. Kusum Gangurde does have a regular government job but is able to work outside of it in order to help Moon with *Maitrani;* she also writes poetry, some of it Buddhist, and has developed a credit cooperative for women. As is the case with most Buddhist women, social and economic aid to other women is a major part of their Buddhist commitment.

Although Mumbai and Nagpur are the most important centers for Buddhist women, there are other areas of the state where there is additional activity. Women's activism also takes place, for example, in the old British section of the Maharashtrian city of Pune. Here, two women's organizations are especially interesting. Modi Khana consists of rows of single or double story row houses situated around several central open areas. This complex was built for those servants of the British who took care of the donkeys and mules in the army and thus most of those allowed to live here were Mahars, traditionally the grooms of horses. Over the years, the proximity of this area to the main center of the "camp" in the booming city of Pune has made it an open area of prime housing. Several apartment houses within Modi Khana and many just on the fringe, as well as numerous small businesses and non-Buddhist residences, give it a multi-cultural look. One of the women's organizations here dates almost from the time of the 1956 conversion and has, at the center of its practice, the teaching of Pali chanting and Buddhist scriptures. There is a small Buddhist *vihāra* in the middle of the area, built by local people but linked to the TBMSG through their teachers. Although women are not always present during the weekly Buddhist service at the Modi Khana *vihāra*, they do appear regularly on important occasions, such as Buddha Jayanti, the Buddha's birthday.

The other women's organization in Modi Khana illustrates the contemporary integration of religion and social service suggested by Ambedkar's writings on early Buddhism. The story of its founding is as follows. In Ramabai Nagar, a slum in

Bombay named after Ambedkar's first wife—four hours away by train and over the Ghats, two low mountain ranges, from Pune—Buddhists awoke one day to find Dr. Ambedkar's statue garlanded with shoes, which is the ultimate insult in India because of their association with the most polluting part of the body, the foot. As they gathered around the statue in huge numbers, the police arrived and, although the Ramabai Nagar inhabitants claim they did not initiate any violence, police fired into the crowd, killing ten people. In the aftermath of the shooting, tens of thousands of Dalits, from Ramabai Nagar and elsewhere, shut down Mumbai—stopping even the trains into the city. Word of the deaths incensed Buddhists and Dalits everywhere. Realizing the vulnerability of the Buddhist and Dalit communities, a Modi Khana Buddhist woman responded to this incident by founding a women's organization, which emphasizes the improvement of women's lives through the learning of skills. Sewing, typing, and literacy are now taught by volunteers in the slum. Those who have been encouraged to become educated are, for the first time in an organized way in this locality, teaching those left behind. Buddhism in this case has made women very aware of the needs of other women around them, and although the action was spawned by violence far away, a sense of the need to reach out to others has become a major part of the contemporary Buddhist message. In this way, the activist women create a sense of sisterhood that is quite different from a simpler, patronizing sense of helping others.

In another example, several years ago I was invited by an educated young Buddhist woman I had met at a conference to speak on Buddhism to the dock workers in their *chawl*—a large two-story cement structure, usually built in British days, which houses workers in apartments of one room plus a kitchen. Upon arrival I found that water comes into the common outlet at the *chawl* only a few hours a day. The Buddhist women had left their children with their husbands to go fill their water vessels before coming to the meeting. Ten or twelve women at last entered the tiny room, and I spoke very simply in Marathi about the meaning of Buddhism for me. When one woman began accusing others of continuing their Hindu practice and not being real Buddhists, attention shifted from me to the women themselves. As they argued, some of what it means to be a Buddhist in the hard-working, lower-class areas of Mumbai emerged. It became clear that illiterate women found it difficult to give up their Hindu gods and the possibility of praying to them for various benefits and successes for their husbands and children. The Buddhism that Ambedkar brought to these groups is, by contrast, an austere Theravāda Buddhism, a rational and humanistic religion that emphasizes equality and justice. What was eventually understood by even the least educated present, however, is that freedom from caste inferiority, a belief in the power of the mind, and the need for compassion and justice in all lives is at the heart of the Buddhist tradition they now espouse.

Creative Forms of Spreading Buddhism

In contrast to the experiences of urban Buddhist women, which stress forms of social organization, the activities of rural women represent especially unusual efforts as they are dependent, more so than the programs in the cities, on the dedication of single individuals. In Akola, for example, a district in northern Maharashtra in which Mahars have been active in reform for a hundred years and in which Buddhists continue to be active today, a woman organized a drama group, which presented the story of the Buddha first in a number of local villages. Their presentation became so popular and well known that the women involved were asked to perform their drama on Bombay television.[12] The women of Akola District also began to create Buddhist songs in the traditional patterns of folk rhythms, and the work of their women's organizations began to involve a wide-ranging song repertoire.

There is an old Maharashtrian saying: "In the Brahmin home, books; in the Maratha[13] home, grain; in the Mahar home, song." The musical tradition of the area has been continued in the folk drama called Tamasha as well as in the singing groups that are part of every local and citywide Buddhist celebration. Together with this tradition-based creativity has come, in the last thirty years, the phenomenon of Dalit literature, a powerful movement of self-expression. In Maharashtra, the chief symbol of education and culture is literature—having, as its basis, the ability to write—which until recently was the prerogative of Brahmins. In the early 1970s, Dalits began to challenge Brahmin domination of the field of literature with poetry and stories of their own that revealed the life of the poor in very realistic ways, and with previously unheard examples of Dalit language. The established doyens of Marathi literature have had to accept the new talent, and Dalit literature has become a vital element of all important Marathi cultural scenes. Women who enter the field of this new writing are, like men, fulfilling the concept of Dalits as creative and contributing people, and are providing an added and unusual dimension to the literary movement.

Dalit women writers who are also Buddhist began to be published about twenty years ago and have become increasingly prominent. These women have often become spokespeople for the Buddhist community, writing as they do about the needs and aspirations, as well as the talents, of their people. However, while perhaps as many as ten Dalit women are known and honored as published writers, little of their work seems to speak directly of the doctrines of Buddhism. Indirectly, every one of the women would say, "I have been freed to be creative by my commitment to Buddhism." For them, the inferiority enforced by untouchability is gone, the place of women in Buddhism has become known, and what is published is often a very moving and unusual contribution to "Buddhist literature."

Urmilla Pawar, for example, is a short story writer who has been widely pub-

International full ordination ceremony, Bodhgaya, 1998, sponsored by Foguangshan Monastery, Taiwan (photo by Venerable Karma Lekshe Tsomo)

lished and appears as a leading Marathi writer at international conferences. Her story entitled "Mukti" is about the early Buddhist disciple Śāriputra.[14] She has also written a profound Buddhist credo.[15] Another writer, Hira Bansode, ends her long and very unusual poem on Yaśodharā, the wife of the Buddha, with comfort for the woman whose husband left her to "brighten the world":

> But history doesn't talk about the great story of your sacrifice.
> If Siddhārtha had gone through the charade of *samādhi*
> A great epic would have been written about you!
> You would have become famous in *purāṇa* and palm leaf like
> Sītā and Sāvitrī.
> O, Yaśodharā!
> I am ashamed of the injustice.
> You are not to be found in a single Buddhist *vihāra.*
> Were you really of no account?
> But wait—don't suffer so.
> I have seen your beautiful face.
> You are between the closed eyelids of Siddhārtha
> Yaśu, just you.[16]

There are two other poems about Yaśodharā, one of which is by Pradnya Lohande, the daughter of the late Buddhist poet Daya Pawar, whose book cover shows an abstract female figure holding a *bodhi* leaf and a Buddhist wheel. Like that of Hira

Bansode, Lohande's poem is from the viewpoint of Yaśodharā, recognizing that while the Buddha "effortlessly cast off the garments of early desire," her life was barren. When he returned, "as vast and fathomless as sky" and stood in front of her, "spreading arms of boundless compassion," she wondered if he could see the "thirst in her radiant eyes."[17] Such poems seems to indicate a very personal view of the Buddha, appreciative of his bringing truth to the world but wondering about the sacrifice his wife made for the sake of others.

A very touching reference to the Dalit conversion movement comes from the pen of Jyoti Lanjewar, whose poetry is filled with images and very moving. Her poem entitled "Mother" makes an "everywoman" out of the poor working women who wash clothes and clean pots in different households, who carry fruit and vegetables for shoppers in baskets on their heads, who scavenge, or who move earth on construction sites. This composite woman is proud, self-sacrificing, determined to educate her children and control her drunken husband, and devoted to being in the thick of all the marches and demonstrations of the Dalit movement. There is nothing specific about her being a Buddhist, but Lanjewar refers to the *dīkṣā bhūmi*, the field in Nagpur on which Dr. Ambedkar and half a million followers converted to Buddhism in 1956, at the very end of this paean of praise to the dignity and courage of the poor:

> I have seen you on your deathbed
> giving that money you earned rag picking
> to the *dīkṣā bhūmi*
> saying with your dying breath
> "Live in unity...fight for Baba...don't forget him..."
> and with your very last breath
> "Jai Bhim."[18]

The importance of Bhimrao Ramji Ambedkar (here called simply "Bhim") is also illustrated by a Maharashtrian village woman's folk song:

> I am the daughter of Bhim
> And the granddaughter of Gautama

And while the song might be heresy (if there is such a thing in Buddhism) for the scripturally orthodox, it reflects the fact that the religion of Gautama Buddha came to the village through the fatherly figure of Babasaheb Ambedkar.

Meenakshi Moon has linked the conversion ceremony at Nagpur in 1956 itself to the best-known and most beloved religious site in Maharashtra, Pandharpur. Center of the *bhakti* devotional tradition, hundreds of thousands of pilgrims travel to Pandharpur every year to share the joy of their devotion and to take the *darśana* (holy sight) of the god Vithoba, all the while singing the songs of the saint-poets. While some think that the original religion of the Pandharpur site was Buddhist, Moon extends her tradition even more by including among its holy places the *caitya bhūmi* in Bombay. This was the last resting place of Dr. Ambedkar and is now a site of a great pilgrimage on December 6, the day of his death. Along with these newer places of sacred geography, her poem also includes the traditional holy places of Buddhist pilgrimage.

> On the fourteenth of October in 1956
> Baba chose the Buddhist religion in Nagpur
> And so created for Buddhism another Pandharpur.
> Now that is our ground of karma,
> That is the holy pilgrimage ground of Buddhism.
> Baba gave birth to a new form of Buddhism,
> He gave us a new religion
> Authentic Buddhism, scientific Buddhism.
> A Buddhism of freedom, equality, compassion and justice
> No more four *varṇas,* no more caste division, no more paternalism.
> Now our holy places are
> Nagpur, Sarnath, Bodhgaya
> Kashinagar, Lumbini, and the *caitya bhūmi....*[19]

A very different poem is by Mina Gajbhiye, whose tight, spare poetry is often critical of the outside world and also of the world of Dalits. The only Buddhist poem I have of hers suggests, however, hope for the condition of humankind in Buddhism. Her poem on the *bodhi* tree criticizes the seemingly hopeless and engrained orthodoxy of the middle class, but ends:

> I am satisfied that
> I have sown the seeds.
> They have already started the preparation for resistance...
> I am doubtful:
> Will at least one seed sprout?
> Bodhi tree.[20]

Buddhists in the Dalit Women's Movement

As the line between the Buddhist Dhamma and social activism is blurred among the women of the Ambedkar movement, so is at times the relationship of Buddhist to Dalit. There are three women's organizations, two of them nationwide, in which

Buddhist women play a predominant part. They are not limited to Buddhists, however, nor do they carry the Buddhist name. The oldest is the National Federation of Dalit Women, founded by Ruth Manorama, a Christian, in Bangalore. Two others emerged in 1995. The first is the Maharashtra Dalit Mahila Sanghatna organized by a Buddhist woman, Archana Hatekar, with meetings held in Dhule and Nagpur. It is open only to women who are Dalit by birth. Finally, the All India Dalit Women's Forum, established with Nanda Kamble (a Buddhist and a teacher of Marathi at Fergusson College in Pune, Maharashtra) as president, is open to any woman who wishes to be identified with Dalit activities. All three organizations serve chiefly as centers of education. The conferences they hold promote the exchange of ideas, confirmation of the validity of programs undertaken individually, and ways to travel and see something of the world. The National Federation, for example, sent some of its members to the Beijing conference of women. The Maharashtra Dalit Mahila Sanghatna went to Mahad, a town south of Bombay, on December 25, 1998, and burned those passages of the classic Hindu text the *Manusmṛti* that restrict the place of women and treat them with contempt. This repeats the 1927 gesture of Dr. Ambedkar whereby he burned those passages of the *Manusmṛti* that restricted Untouchables and prescribed harsh punishment for any action that led them out of an inferior place. These organizations cannot be specifically called Buddhist, but they allow Buddhist women a place of leadership, contact with other Buddhist as well as Christian women (Hindu women seem not to be involved, except as close friends and supporters of Buddhists), and a forum for discussing their problems and increasing action for equality and respect.

It is quite clear that Ambedkar saw potential for women's equality in the Buddhist religion. In *The Rise and Fall of the Hindu Woman* written in 1950 and published later as a pamphlet, he notes the restrictions on women that Manu, a legendary Brahmin lawgiver, details. He then lists the women of early Buddhism: Visākhā, the chief of alms-givers and one of eighty chief disciples; Ambapālī of Vesali, a courtesan in whose home the Buddha and his disciples ate; the one hundred women whom Mahāpajāpatī Gotamī brought to the Buddha for instruction; and Kokanadā and Queen Mallikā, who received substantial religious instruction. He also quotes the *bhikkhunīs* Muttā ("O gloriously free am I") and Mallikā ("Over my spirit sweeps the breath of liberty"). Further, he explains the rule of *bhikkhunīs* being placed under *bhikkhus* as a concern for the rule of celibacy, and the need to put "raw women under the instruction of trained *bhikkhus,*" and adds, correctly, that women were considered fully capable of realizing the Buddhist doctrine and of attaining enlightenment. Finally, he points out that in early Buddhism it was positively revolutionary for women to adopt the renunciant life of religion as opposed to the householder life and to be educated in any way. The Buddhist women of Maharashtra today follow the lead of Dr. Ambedkar in using their Buddhist-born freedom of spirit to promote not only their religion but a just and compassionate society.

Notes

1. Buddhists receive the same government affirmative action measures as scheduled castes, that is, reservations in legislatures, institutions of higher education, and government jobs.
2. Dr. Ambedkar returned from his overseas education in 1924 probably the most highly educated man in the state, and the first Untouchable to go beyond a B.A. degree. The Maharaja of Kolhapur and the Gaikwad of Baroda were both interested in promoting non-Brahmin education, and saw in Ambedkar an opportunity to make a statement about the intelligence of the lower classes. For Ambedkar's life, see Dhananjay Keer, *Dr. Ambedkar: Life and Mission* (Bombay: Popular Prakashan, third edition, 1991), and Eleanor Zelliot, *From Untouchable to Dalit: Essays on the Ambedkar Movement* (New Delhi: Manohar Publications, second edition, 1998).
3. Chandramani was a Burmese *bhikkhu,* head of a small Buddhist center in Kushinara, Gorakhpur District, in the hills of Uttar Pradesh. The center had been established by an Indian who converted to Buddhism in Sri Lanka in the nineteenth century, but by the time of Ambedkar's conversion the center was maintained by Burmese.
4. See my "The Indian Rediscovery of Buddhism, 1855–1956," in *Studies in Pali and Buddhism,* ed. A.K. Narain (New Delhi: D.K. Publishers' Distributors, 1978).
5. See Alan Sponberg, "TBMSG: A Dhamma Revolution in Contemporary India," in *Engaged Buddhism: Buddhist Liberation Movements in Asia,* ed. Christopher S. Queen and Sallie B. King (Albany: State University of New York, 1996) for details on Sangharakshita's life and the work of the TBMSG.
6. Sponberg, op.cit., p. 87, notes that *dhammacāriṇī* and the masculine *dhammacārī* are ancient non-technical terms that mean "Dhamma-farer." The TBMSG uses these terms to avoid the complete separation of *upāsaka* (lay person) and *bhikkhu* (ordained clergy).
7. For an interesting life history of Vimalachari and other *dhammacāriṇī,* see Hilary Blakiston (Padmasuri), *But Little Dust: Life amongst the "Ex-Untouchables"* (Birmingham: Windhorse, second edition, 1997).
8. Ibid., pp. 169, 172. This ordination is clearly not that described in the Pali canon, which advises ten *bhikkhunīs'* and ten *bhikkhus'* involvement. Having rejected the traditional Sangha, Sangharakshita has devised a very modern ceremony, meaningful in the context of the values of the Friends of the Western Buddhist Order and the TBMSG. Interestingly, Sangharakshita's name means "Protector of the Sangha."
9. Government Colony is a collection of apartments for government officials. Reserva-

tions in government jobs has been the chief way up for most ex-Untouchables, and so government-sponsored housing finds many Buddhists clustered in one place.

10. Kusum Pawade has described the difficulty she encountered as a Dalit in her pursuit of a degree in Sanskrit, India's holy language, and a subsequent teaching job, in *Poisoned Bread: Translations from Modern Marathi Dalit Literature,* ed. Arjun Dangle (Bombay: Orient Longman, 1992).
11. Ambapālī was a courtesan in whose home the Buddha ate, and who later became a *bhikkhunī. Mahila mandal* simply means "women's organization."
12. Gopal Guru, *Dalit Cultural Movement and Dialectics of Dalit Politics in Maharashtra* (Mumbai: Vikas Adhyayan Kendra, 1997), p. 29.
13. Marathas are the dominant land-owning Śudra caste. The proverb reflects on the Mahars' poverty as well as on their musical ability.
14. In her collection of stories in Marathi in *Chauti Binta (Four Walls)* (Bombay: Sambodhi Prakashan, 1990). Veena Deo, a professor of English at Hamline University, St. Paul, Minnesota, has given several papers on Urmilla Pawar at academic conferences and will soon publish an article on her writing.
15. Urmilla Pawar's statement on her Buddhist concepts as well as that of Meenakshi Moon appear in my "Buddhist Women of the Contemporary Maharashtrian Conversion Movement," in *Buddhism, Sexuality and Gender*, ed. Jose Cabezon (Albany: State University of New York Press, 1992).
16. See my article above. Sītā and Sāvitrī, committed to serving their husbands, serve as models for orthodox Hindu women. The Buddhist temples in Maharashtra are generally known as *vihāras*, although classically the term refers to the living quarters of monks and nuns.
17. Pradnya Lokhande, *Antahstha* (Pune: Mansanman Prakashan, 1996).
18. See "Stri Dalit Sahitya: The New Voice of Women Poets" in *Images of Women in Maharashtrian Literature and Religion,* ed. Anne Feldhaus (Albany: State University of New York Press, 1996). Baba refers to Babasaheb Ambedkar, the fond name by which he is known to his people. "Jai Bhim" refers to Bhimrao Ramji Ambedkar and is used as a greeting and a cheer.
19. *Maitrani* 2.5 (1994): 37. Translated from the Marathi by Eleanor Zelliot and Vimal Thorat. *Varṇas* are the traditional four-fold caste divisions of Brahmin, Kṣatriya, Vaiśya, and Śudra. Untouchables are outside the traditional *varṇa* system. The phrase "caste divisions" refers to the thousands of *jatis* that are the endogamous units of daily life, often limited to one language area, often pursuing a specific occupation, and Untouchables are in various *jatis.* The English (from the Portuguese) word "caste" conflates the two concepts.
20. In "Stri Dalit Sahitya," op cit.

JAMIN SUNIM:
Prison Work for a Korean Nun

In Korea, full monastic ordination is available to nuns. They have their own nunneries, their own preceptresses, their own abbesses, and their own teachers. They are financially quite independent from the monks. For five hundred years, from 1400 to 1900, Buddhism was repressed by a Confucian regime, so monks had little power. Monks and nuns were equal in their having to survive against difficult odds. In Korea, there is also a very strong tradition of female shamans. All these various historical and social conditions explain why Korean nuns are among the most equal to the monks of all Buddhist traditions.

At the turn of the century, the Confucian regime collapsed, and a Buddhist revival occurred, which not only affected the monks but also the nuns. The nuns took advantage of this revival and went to settle in abandoned temples, rebuilding them and constructing meditation halls and sūtra halls where nuns could be trained thoroughly. Many accomplished Zen master nuns and eminent scholar nuns arose, and ordinary nuns too achieved much in their own individual and creative ways.

Jamin Sunim is a widely respected nun of sixty-some, belonging to the council of elder nuns in Korea who visit prisoners in jail. She is very kind and friendly, although quite busy.

AFTER BECOMING A NUN, I went to many Buddhist colleges to study the sūtras for thirteen years. Following this, I went to meditation halls and found meditation very beneficial. However, because of my studies, people kept asking me to teach them the sūtras because I had received transmission and was authorized to teach in the well-known *Pomosa Sūtra* lineage. I started teaching and also helped with translating the *Avataṃsaka Sūtra* [a large Mahāyāna text dealing with interdependence] into vernacular Korean. For thirteen years I taught monastics, but because of illness I had to stop teaching full-time, and started to give occasional lectures on Buddhism to lay people instead. About three years ago I was asked to visit people in jail.

I went to the prison without thinking much about it, as I had been asked to give only one Dharma talk. However, when I got there and saw the prisoners, my view changed. Though some are hardened criminals, most have acted accidentally or from necessity. They can assume the form of a criminal in a second, but it passes, disappears, and then they look and remain very ordinary. Those who gathered to listen to my talk did not have the appearance of criminals whatsoever.

When people enter jail, they often become defeated and broken. Although I try to inspire hope, it is difficult as we cannot find a state more sorrowful than being in jail. The environment seems designed to be grim, and one sees, hears, and learns about crimes. For many prisoners, it becomes a vicious circle. Thus, what we call crime has no true inherent existence—it is conditioned by many factors.

I try to teach the prisoners the law of cause and effect, karma and retribution. "All things made by me, I will receive in return." I ask them about themselves. Many of them feel depressed and wronged and ask, "Why have I come to this pass? Why have I ended up in this situation?" They answer themselves, "Because of love, money, or social conditions." Before they reflect on themselves, they think of everything else and they feel bitterness and resentment towards life, society, their parents, and siblings.

I tell them that they must let go of all this bitterness, and reflect on how they did something and in turn received something. Our thoughts are all produced and developed from a seed in ourselves, so we must first watch ourselves carefully. When I give this kind of Dharma talk, some people cry, and amidst this crying there is a lot of self-examination and reflection. If they reflect again and again, when they go back to society, even if an unbearably distressing event happens, they will be able to bear it and be patient. The strength to resist impulses is developed by these reflections. I feel that however small it might be, if what I say can help them to strengthen their character, it is enough for me.

I meet them individually for counselling if they ask to speak to me. Often they want to talk about the betrayal of a loved one. Others are worried about their families while they are in jail and ask me to look after them, so I try to find their families and see how they are doing. There are some long-timers who have no families at all. I establish friendly relationships between them and other people, and arrange special presents of food. I also find out about their birthdays and organize something for them.

I listen attentively to them and, based on their individual circumstances, I try to find appropriate Buddhist teachings. I refer to some passages in the sūtras and compare them to their situation. Because I am a Buddhist person, a nun, all I have learnt is the Buddha's teachings, though I might also use my own words, telling them of my own experiences, what I learnt from them and what I would suggest to others.

Through developing wisdom we can achieve awakening. The Buddhadharma [Buddha's teaching] is not about anything else; it is about accomplishing and perfecting one's own character. When one has perfected one's character, love and compassion will exist. Without them, we will suffer from resentment, unhappiness, and blame.

Compiled and translated by Martine Batchelor

MYOHI SUNIM:
A Korean Nun Teacher of Elderly Women

Myohi Sunim is a Korean nun who is the founder of a home for elderly nuns and women. Twice a day she leads these women in calisthenics following the instruction of a radio program.

I BECAME A NUN forty-three years ago when I was fourteen years old, just after elementary school graduation. Now I am fifty-seven. I grew up in a Buddhist family and often met Buddhist monks and nuns. Listening to them talk about the Dharma, my outlook on life changed. When I was twenty years old, only five or six years after the end of the Korean war, Korea was very poor. I thought, "If I wait to save people till after I am enlightened, when am I going to help them?" I decided it would be better to help poor people directly by transmitting the Buddha's teachings to them warmly.

A few years ago I became the abbess of a small temple in Seoul where I established a large kindergarten to help children and their families. I was also a Buddhist chaplain working especially with prisoners who were dying, trying to help them at this difficult time and making their passing easier and more peaceful. In the 1980s, I went to Taiwan where I met a nun who had built a hospital for poor people and had founded a charitable association to help people in need. I was so impressed by her sincerity and struck by her great vows of compassion that I decided to form a similar association. I established an affiliation with them and decided to devote my life even more to people in need.

For this reason I recently organized this home for elderly women. It is important that they can come here because they have no clothes, no food, and no place to live. My main aim is for them to live nearer to the Buddha and thus obtain buddhahood more easily. There are four nuns here with me: the manager, the director, the nurse, and the driver. There are three elderly nuns and eighteen elderly women currently, but in the future we hope to be able to accommodate more than thirty people. Everything is free of charge.

We cannot receive women who are too ill or handicapped because we do not have facilities for such cases yet. The people we receive are able at least to wash a little and put on their own clothes, though we have two nuns who can barely walk. These elderly nuns are staying here because there is no retirement home for nuns yet. It is my intention to build a separate building for elderly nuns. Right now there is only one building, so everyone has to live together, which is not ideal because the lives of nuns and secular women are a little different.

We nuns chant together and also recite sūtras on our own. We rise at 5 A.M., chant, and then clean a little. At 7 A.M. we have breakfast, at 9 A.M. a snack, at 12 noon lunch, at 3 P.M. a snack, and at 6 P.M. we have dinner. At 7 P.M. we do some more chanting. In between, there is a little time for exercises and meditation and recitation of the sūtras. Wisdom and compassion must be cultivated and applied together. This is why I am doing this, but it is not enough. I hope that, in the future, Korean nuns will create more places like this one; they will be working on themselves, on their awakening, but they will also help other people to do the same.

I plan to have another building for people who are very ill. It will be more functional, with more facilities, and baths and toilets specifically designed for severe handicaps. I would also like to build a house where people can come to die, in the hope that I could make them feel at home, like being with their own family, where there would be a warm feeling. I have visited other old people's homes and found them sterile and unfriendly, not family-like. For this reason I wanted this place to be different, to be warm and friendly like a real Korean family.

Compiled and translated by Martine Batchelor

POMYONG SUNIM: *Flower Arranging for the Korean Lay*

Pomyong Sunim lives in a Zen nunnery in Seoul, where she practices meditation and teaches flower arranging.

I WAS BROUGHT to the nunnery when I was five years old. I was very ill, and my family was afraid I would die. They believed that only by sending me to live in a Buddhist temple would I survive. I was cured and I have been living as a nun for the last thirty-two years. I remained after I was cured because I liked the nunnery life so much. I have no regret and I plan to stay a nun all my life. I started flower arranging in 1988 when the Olympics were in progress, as we were asked to show visiting Westerners the Buddhist way of flower arrangement. We started an association that year, which has continued successfully to this day. Every year, now, there is an exhibition of flower arrangements by nuns on the Buddha's birthday.

In this Zen nunnery, there is a space reserved for cultural activities. Every Friday lay women come to practice flower arranging with me. Since I have some gift in this, I wanted to offer my skills to the lay people who come to this temple. Through teaching flower arranging I hope to transmit Buddhism. People of other religions sometimes join us. At the beginning, I do not talk about Buddhism. Slowly, as we practice flower arranging, as it comes naturally, I introduce Buddhist ideas.

I like flowers. Flower arranging came from offering flowers to the Buddha. There are six kinds of offerings made to the Buddha, and flowers are one of them. This art was lost in Korea when Buddhism was suppressed by the Confucians for five hundred years. I want to rekindle this Buddhist art because people can benefit from learning it properly. Flower arranging is not only putting flowers together. While I arrange flowers I meditate, and my mind becomes very peaceful as I forget everything. Even though I am a nun, I have troubles too. When I arrange flowers, what I supervise, what I am researching, all the afflictions I might have in my heart, everything disappears. For me it is equivalent to meditation.

At the beginning of a class, we chant Buddhist songs, the three refuges [the Buddha, the Dharma, the Sangha], and the *Heart Sūtra* [a short Mahāyāna text dealing with emptiness]. Then for five minutes we sit quietly in meditation. I tell the students that our minds and hearts should be beautiful like flowers. However, it does not seem to be so as we live in a dark cloud and in confusion. I encourage them to meet their children and friends with a virtuous and beautiful mind like a flower. I try to talk about the Buddha and his teaching using various similes and metaphors through the flowers. It is a total training; how to put the flowers in the right place, how to hold the mind and body. People must be aware of the right posture when arranging flowers. Their back must be straight. They must be beautiful and wise, not only during the class but also in their daily life. When I say they must live wisely, I mean they must live intelligently. Whenever they are confronted with difficult circumstances, they must try to deal with them sagaciously.

The lay women who come are generally married. In their family life, they have all kinds of difficulties—with their husbands, families, mothers-in-law. Nowadays, family life is often complicated, and this can be very distressing. I encourage them to deal with these problems wisely. Sometimes they tell me of great sufferings, which they do not know how to solve or endure, so after the class we have a private chat where I counsel them. Buddha is high on his pedestal, but nuns are human beings, and people can talk to me freely about what is on their minds. By opening up to me about their problems, they feel fresher and lighter.

These lay women are generally over forty. They are at a turning point in their lives. They wonder what the meaning of their lives is. They married between twenty and thirty, now they are forty or fifty, their children have grown up and left home. For twenty years they were very busy taking care of their children and supporting their husbands. Upon reaching forty, they start asking themselves questions: "What have I been doing all these years?" and "What is the meaning of my life?" All these years they were not able to do what they wanted to do. Hearing about flower arranging at the temple, they come, and it is a small way forward for them. From then on they can turn their attention towards themselves.

Although they might have visited the nunnery for many years and listened to Dharma talks, they have not tried to practice meditation yet. What the nuns said about meditation and life did not really penetrate. But through the flower arranging class they relate to me more closely, and begin to reflect and try meditation. Some tell me how their mind is so much more peaceful and pacified since they came here.

Compiled and translated by Martine Batchelor

WOMEN, WAR, AND PEACE IN SRI LANKA

Tessa Bartholomeusz

Introduction: Women, Patriotism, and the Rhetoric of Peace

In contemporary Sri Lanka, politicians, religious leaders, and ordinary citizens debate a devolution package that would grant more powers to Tamils, a proposal that is inevitably viewed against the backdrop of the insurrection of the Sinhala terrorist group Janatha Vimukti Peramuna (JVP) in 1988–89 and contemporary ethnic strife between the majority Sinhalas and the minority Tamils. Not surprisingly, a variety of opinions about women and war have emerged, which range from assertions that women have no place in the arena of war, to the notion that women, like all citizens, have a duty to protect Sri Lanka as warriors. More surprisingly, perhaps, is how infrequently we find the idea that advocating for peace is laudatory in a straightforward or unqualified way. In this essay I shall explore the discourse of war and gender in Sri Lanka, and the way it shapes popular opinions about the relationship between women, peace, and Buddhism.

First we must understand exactly what it means to be an advocate for peace in contemporary Sri Lanka. According to the government's position, peace can only be secured by offering the Tamils a devolution package, a plan that President Chandrika Bandaranaike Kumaratunga has been promoting since 1995. This devolution package would permit a certain degree of autonomy to Tamils in the north, most of whom have been held hostage since 1983 by the separatist movement, the Liberation Tigers of Tamil Eelam (LTTE). From my own reading of the situation in Colombo during the summers of 1997 and 1998, it is doubtful that even if the government should agree on terms for a devolution package, ordinary citizens among Sri Lanka's ethnic majority, the predominantly Buddhist Sinhalas, would agree to granting Tamils semi-autonomy in the north. One reason for the resistance is that there is suspicion among some Sinhala people that Tamil semi-autonomy would be the first step toward the LTTE creating a separate state in the northern part of the island.[1] Here, regional politics appears to be the chief concern:

some Sinhalas oppose the devolution package because they fear that if autonomy were achieved in the north, Sri Lankan Tamils would soon unite with India's southern state of Tamilnadu in a move that would create instability in the region from the Sinhala perspective.

There are also, however, religious reasons for Sinhala resistance to the proposed devolution package. Many Sinhalas regard Sri Lanka as a sacred Buddhist island. As scholarship on Sri Lanka in recent times suggests, the notion of Sri Lanka as a Buddhist "promised land" and the Sinhalas as the Buddha's "chosen people" resonates loudly in contemporary politics.[2] From this point of view, the entire island is sacred, and its division, therefore, a sacrilege. Like those who oppose devolution for reasons having to do with regional politics, the Sinhalas who adhere to the promised-land ideology argue that devolution is the first step toward a separate state for Tamils,[3] a step that can have only perilous results: the desecration of Sri Lanka. A further element in Sinhala resistance to devolution is the common assumption that, given the violence of the LTTE's commitment to a separate state, devolution has no real practical chance of success.

Some Sinhala people, however, see devolution as the only hope for a peaceful solution to the ethnic problem. Writing in 1995, soon after the LTTE launched a bitter attack in the north, a Colombo suburbanite published an editorial in an English-language daily urging the government to push forward with its peace plan:

> We earnestly hope that violent activities will be ceased and a political solution to the ethnic problem will be found soon. We firmly believe that no solution can by found by resorting to violence.[4]

Continuing to advise, the Sinhala writer makes allusion to "a strong peace movement" in the south, which has to face the threat of "Sinhala chauvinism," that is, the force that promotes the promised-land ideology. This strong peace movement is, in fact, Women for Peace, an organization in which each of Sri Lanka's ethnic and religious groups is represented, but which is predominately Sinhala and Buddhist, reflecting the vast majority of Sri Lanka's population.

According to members of Women for Peace whom I interviewed in Colombo from June–August 1997 and to newspaper articles that have appeared about them, Women for Peace is one of the few organizations in Sri Lanka that is committed to calling for "non-racist, non-chauvinist and non-sexist people to raise their voice for peace."[5] As one of the members noted, the fact that the organization consists of and is controlled by women makes it vulnerable to harsh criticism, inasmuch as autonomous women in South Asian forms of patriarchy are not socially accepted.[6] Indeed, in the Sri Lankan context, autonomous female activity is inappropriate behavior for women and girls. Given this, in addition to serving as a watchdog organization of human rights abuses especially against women and children, Women for Peace is also an organization that poses a challenge to the patriarchal bias in Sri Lankan society.[7] Since its inception in 1984, Women for Peace has played an important role in the debate over devolution. And despite the trend in Sri Lanka to oppose devolution, Women for Peace has remained steadfast in its insistence on a political, rather than a military, solution to Sri Lanka's problems.[8]

Women, War, and Emancipation

We now turn to the intersection of women, peace, and Buddhism. In the Sinhala-Buddhist areas of the country, where ideas about Sri Lanka's sacred mission permeate all strata of society, it is considered un-Buddhist to be an advocate for peace. The reason for this is that advocating for peace is tantamount to supporting the government's devolution package, which many fear is the first step in the sacred Buddhist country's division. It is not unusual to hear Buddhist monks and lay people alike arguing that "the government must finish the war"[9] (for peace), which in their view means killing Prabakaran, the leader of the LTTE. Only by killing Prabakaran, many maintain, can Sri Lanka's integrity as a sacred Buddhist island be preserved. People who advocate peace, then, are cast as subversive, unpatriotic, and un-Buddhist, in short, as the enemy. This explains why it is not appropriate to be an advocate for peace in contemporary Buddhist Sri Lanka (where there is a dearth of peace organizations). The problematic situation of peace advocacy, then, has important consequences for the public's perception of Women for Peace, and the role of women in war in Sri Lanka.

Perceptions of Women for Peace illustrate the degree to which peace advocacy in Sri Lanka is linked to subversive activity. One writer calls Women for Peace a pro-LTTE organization—a serious insult in the present context, where the LTTE is known to have massacred thousands and is the paradigm of unpatriotic and irreligious behavior.[10] The following writer's editorial on Women for Peace links the organization to the LTTE, alludes to religion and country, and unambiguously constructs the female gender as subordinate:

> While these "goody-goody" ladies resort to their "peace-antics" in Colombo, what they are doing is giving a chance to the LTTE to re-arm and re-deploy and kill more of our soldiers, Buddhist monks and innocent villagers.... Meanwhile the country would very much like to know...[the] sources of local and foreign funding [of the organization]. ...[is one of them] the church?[11]

In short, pacifist women are described as oblivious to the true situation and complicit in supporting terrorist activities. While the word "lady" has a complex significance in Sri Lankan society, there can be no evading its subordinating purpose here: however laudatory the word's potential in certain contexts, it does not conjure up the image of independent, free-thinking women. Its purpose here, then, is to suggest that "ladies" remain aloof from serious matters, for otherwise they risk being ineffectual ("goody-goody") or, worse, patsies. In the editorial, women who are advocates for peace are seen as puppets in a larger drama, the controlling hands of which might even be Christian. The reference to Christianity is a thinly veiled allusion to the West, whereby Women for Peace is linked to what many perceive are anti-Sri Lankan elements. Since activist women of Women for Peace are emancipated from Sri Lankan ideas about appropriate behavior for females, the argument goes, they become subordinated to another agent, namely, the Christian West.

To advocate peace in Sri Lanka, therefore, is to involve oneself in a conspiracy, whether wittingly or unwittingly, against the country and against Buddhism. In general, the response to alleged conspiracies against Sri Lanka is dramatic. Indeed, according to Mangalika de Silva, one of the founders of Women for Peace, strong opposition to the organization, based on misplaced patriotism, has had violent overtones:

> We have received hundreds and thousands of death threats, written and on the phone, specially during the time when the [former] government, who was supposed to be the guardian of the people, was the perpetrator of the violence. During this time we had to operate underground, but with the situation improving [under Kumaratunga's government], we could surface. But this does not mean we are entirely safe now.[12]

Pacifist women are the object of suspicion and, in some cases, harassment. According to de Silva, their gender has not made them immune to violent attacks. (Women for Peace is not the only organization that takes gender into account as it surveys the Sri Lankan war: the National Peace Council of Sri Lanka has argued that women "should come out of their homes, and take up the task of challenging the mind set that gave priority to imposition by force rather than to dialogue and compromise."[13] Perpetuating the idea that women are naturally inclined toward nonviolent resolutions, while men are prone toward violence, the National Peace Council argues that much work remains for women in Sri Lanka.) For both sympathizers and detractors of Women for Peace, gender comes to the fore in the conflict over who has Sri Lanka's best interests at heart.[14]

To illustrate, in an advertisement for the Sri Lankan Air Force that appeared in the English and Sinhala newspapers in February 1997, female gender is represented by two symbols: a woman in a military uniform, itself more typically an instantiation of male power and authority, and a civilian woman's high-heeled shoe, an emblem of the Westernized female who, in Sri Lankan gender rhetoric, is the standard for all that is debased[15] and, politically, is a symbol of colonization. In a negative reference to the sexy, spiked-heel shoe, the advertisement informs the reader that "There's a better way to stand out and be recognized," namely, by donning the uniform to "stand above the rest," presumably in flat shoes. The message that a "lady officer" is a better citizen than the "woman" who wears high-heeled shoes is thus underscored by the use of feminine symbols. To add to the complexity of the discussion, it is worth noting that clothing normally associated with males, but worn by women, can be negatively viewed in the Sri Lankan context. In a recent example,[16] a writer to a Sri Lankan newspaper refers to Women for Peace as "those trousered women," creating a confusion in imagery, for the opponents of Women for Peace would also be trousered women, this time in uniform.

In its appeal to females, the caption under the photograph of the "lady officer" is framed by a Sri Lankan feminist discourse that offers women new opportunities while maintaining biases based on gender:

> Suddenly, it's a woman's world. Modern day women are right up there with men. If you are a smart young lady, there's no better way to be recognized than to be dressed in the prestigious and *fashionable* uniform of Sri Lanka Air Force. Join us as an officer and stand above the rest.[17]

Encouraging the emancipation of women from the dual constraints of (old) patriarchy and the West, the advertisement—here sponsored by the government in its "war for peace" as it promotes a devolution package—aligns the emancipated female with fashion. (This recalls an American army recruiting brochure with a photograph of a smiling female in combat fatigues and a caption that claims "Some of the best soldiers wear lipstick."[18]) Here, the government exploits and reinforces prevailing ideologies of femininity. At the same time, it encourages females to enter the arena of war, maintaining that being an officer in the air force and being a "lady" are not antithetical. (The contrast with Women for Peace can hardly be more marked, especially since one of the organization's commitments is to protest against the manipulation of gender to advance war and "the policy of conscription and recruitment drives."[19])

The primary beneficiary of this emancipation of the female both from patriarchy and from "the West," however, is not the female. Rather, it is the country, whose violent conflict with the LTTE has cost Sri Lanka so much manpower that it is now in short supply. So short, in fact, that the air force must call upon "ladies" to defend the country. According to a Reuter's report, "Sri Lanka's Air Force, facing an acute shortage of pilots, plans to bring in women [because] Sri Lanka's tiny air force has lost several warplanes and helicopter gun ships [and their men] this year in combat operations against the Liberation Tigers of Tamil Eelam (LTTE)."[20] In short, it is militarily expedient, and therefore in the country's best interests, to emancipate the female from patriarchy and from the West.

War and Gender

When discussing a country that can claim the first female prime minister in the modern world, namely Sirimavo Bandaranaike, however, it is important to note the extent to which patriarchy determines female choices. To begin, a report about Women for Peace reveals much about the intersection of patriarchy and emancipation in Sri Lanka:

> The formation of Women for Peace in 1984 heralded a new era in liberation of women who felt the dire need for some organization which would help women who were victims of war and other violent crimes.[21]

Aligning the organization with women's emancipation, the correspondent casts Women for Peace as a forum for female empowerment. At the same time, the correspondent perpetuates the dual idea that women both "help" and are "victims," traditional notions that subordinate women. In Sri Lanka "the ascription of particular virtues—compassion, patience, common sense, nonviolence" to women "has a long history in the peace movement."[22] Despite the correspondent's rhetoric of empowerment, the accompanying rhetoric of the victimization of women contains within it the seeds for making Women for Peace dependent upon its protectors, the very faction of society Women for Peace critiques, that is, male combatants. In positing a world with two distinctive cultures, the Sri Lankan correspondent perpetuates the notion of "a female world of love and ritual and a male world of getting and spending and killing."[23] (It is the case, however, that women have been actual victims of war and violence in Sri Lanka and that Women for Peace is one of the only groups to address their plight.)

In another article about women and their relationship to peace and war, a writer casts women in the role of the country's memory—the bearers of both a peace and a war culture—a memory essential to the country's future welfare. This alliance of women and culture challenges Sherry Ortner's theory (1972) that there is a cross-cultural tendency to align women with nature and men with culture. Though Ortner's later work (1994) situates the female as the *mediator* of nature and culture, she squarely positions women as cross-cultural symbols of the inferiority of nature. At the same time, Ortner invites us to find exceptions to the rule;[24] indeed, the rhetoric of women and war in Buddhist Sri Lanka provides such an exception. In a Sri Lankan example of the alliance of women and culture,[25] Sri Lanka's population tends to forget the uprising of the Sinhala terrorist organization, the JVP, against the government in 1988–89, when both sides lost thousands of lives. But women have not forgotten: "Not everybody forgets and lives happily ever after. There are women who remember"[26]—namely, those who lost their husbands, sons, and fathers in terrorist and counter-terrorist attacks. Their memory is so enduring, in fact, that the 1988–89 period of terror "has been frozen" in time. Bearing the burden of remembering the horrors of war, women are cast as wise and important, yet victims in need of help. Women are aligned with culture, with memory and, ultimately, with peace, while men are aligned with nature, with "wild boars,"[27] who fight and then forget.

The dominant discourse on war in Sri Lanka, however, does not always link women to peacemaking. In addition to the current tendency to appeal to women to join the armed forces, the current perception of the president of Sri Lanka, Chandrika Bandaranaike Kumaratunga, illuminates contemporary ideas about women and war. Although Kumaratunga's political rhetoric during the 1994 presidential campaign centered on Buddhism, peacemaking, and healing ethnic strife, the controversy over the devolution package that she has been promoting since the mid-1990s has produced two opposing responses, both of which hinge on religion, patriotism, and gender. On the one hand, Buddhist monks opposed to Kumaratunga's devolution package argue that it is un-Buddhist[28] and, therefore, in the context of Buddhist Sri Lanka, as an irreligious activity it is considered unpatriotic. On the other hand, however, one Buddhist monk, doubtless responding to this monastic rhetoric has argued that "the peace-proposals [that is, the devolution package] designed to save the situation did not betray the nation as some believed."[29] In spite of the venerable monk's opinions and his support of President Kumaratunga's proposals, though, the most vocal monks in Sri Lanka vehemently oppose devolution.

Monks are not the only public figures to voice an opinion on the devolution package. Politicians, too, assess Kumaratunga's proposals. Like monks, they view them through the lens of the Buddhist promised-land ideology. In the rhetoric of at least one of her political allies, Kumaratunga's work is reminiscent of Sri Lanka's greatest Buddhist female patriot and peacemaker of ancient days:

> Deputy Minister of Samurdhi Reginald Cooray said that President Chandrika Bandaranaike Kumaratunga's name will be recorded in history as a brave leader like Vihāra Mahādevī of yore, who would usher in peace and prosperity to Sri Lanka before long.[30]

Yet Vihāra Mahādevī, the mother of Sri Lanka's Buddhist hero-king Dutugemunu, whose own legend has provided Sri Lankan Buddhism with the foundation for Buddhist justifications for war, was anything but a pacifist. According to the fifth-century Sri Lankan chronicle, the Pali *Mahāvaṃsa*,[31] Vihāra Mahādevī led her son Dutugemunu into battle against the *damilas* (the Sinhala translates the Pali into "the Tamils") "for the glory" of Buddhism. Prior to the battle, Dutugemunu's father, King Kakavannatissa, protested his son's involvement in war. Incensed by his father's seemingly effeminate behavior, the young prince sent Kakavannatissa "a woman's ornament."[32] Using such a gendered view of war, the monk-author of the *Mahāvaṃsa* argues that advocating peace when there is just cause to go to war is unfitting behavior for a man.

It is unfitting behavior for a woman, too, given the situation. As the war begins, Vihāra Mahādevī, whose Buddhist piety is the subject of much reflection in the *Mahāvaṃsa*, becomes her son's "counsel" and "by her counsel [Dutugemunu] formed thirty-two bodies of troops" (25: 55–56). Soon thereafter, Dutugemunu wins his war against the *damilas*, and restores peace by unifying the island, ostensibly with the help of his mother. Yet, despite Vihāra Mahādevī's prominent role in the saga of Dutugemunu's war against the Tamils, women do not feature in the *Mahāvaṃsa's* war sagas, which occupy most of the text. Vihāra Mahādevī, then, is unique. Thus, in the *Mahāvaṃsa*, war and peace are portrayed as distinct: war is abnormal, peace is normal. In normal times, women remained aloof from soldiering; in abnormal times, women—at least one, namely Vihāra Mahādevī—helped defend the religion. Vihāra Mahādevī, without author comment, disappears from the *Mahāvaṃsa* soon after acting as her son's advisor, which suggests that female recruitment was only "for the duration," that is, that it signals a reversal of normal social convention.

Politicians are not the only citizens of Sri Lanka to invoke ancient images of the war-like Vihāra Mahādevī as they boast a proud Buddhist heritage. In a 1990 reminiscence of the glorious days of *Mahāvaṃsa* legend, a lay man, Noeyal Peiris, told the story of the queen who, according to him, "was responsible for saving the Sinhala race and Buddhist religion by giving birth to a noble warrior son—namely, Dutugemunu."[33] But Vihāra Mahādevī was more than the mother of a hero; she was a hero herself:

> She was instrumental in getting him [that is, Dutugemunu] trained to fight and even accompanied him into the battlefield. After handing over his father's sword to him and giving him her blessings and thereby the power to overcome the enemies and save the Sinhala people and the *Buddhaśāsana* [Buddhism] from the hands of the Tamils who had destroyed our temples, [she]...was with her son in all the battles in the

> battle-fields, advising, guiding and blessing him and enabling him to capture one by one the Tamil strongholds.[34]

Allusions to Vihāra Mahādevī in the present context, then, are meaningful inasmuch as she is considered *the* paradigm of the patriotic female who, in order to bring peace, helps wage a just war against forces inimical to the island and to Buddhism.

As we have seen, Vihāra Mahādevī's resorting to war with the Tamils to usher in peace is brought to life in one politician's reading of Kumaratunga's relationship with the Tamil separatist group. Indeed, one of Kumaratunga's ministers, Reginald Cooray, said that "before long [the] armed forces would crush separatist Tigers and bring victory to people. If there is one leader who has the guts to do this it is President Kumaratunga."[35] The actions of Kumaratunga, who in this "abnormal time" has attempted to make peace with Tamils (the LTTE) through war (while at the same time promoting a devolution package), are justified by the *Mahāvaṃsa's* legend of an ancient patriotic and pious Buddhist queen. (It is clear that the government's position, as well as support for it, carry complicated gender messages, owing to the gender of the president and her political party's skill in manipulating the public's perception of her gender.[36])

Women for Peace has noted that the *Mahāvaṃsa's* legend of Buddhists at war with Tamils resonates in popular discourse on war. Soon after the publication in a Sinhala-language daily of a government-sponsored advertisement for the navy—that beckoned patriotic males to be "brave sons of Dutugemunu"—Women for Peace issued a reply that critiqued the government's use of potent mythic symbols that align Buddhism with war. According to the pacifist organization:

> The reference to Dutugemunu requires analysis since it invokes a vision of history in Sri Lanka as the sacred place of Buddhism which must be protected from outsiders. It entails an imagined past in which all Sinhalese are Buddhist and the enemies who invade are Tamil-speaking Hindus. ...The story [of Dutugemunu] has been used to legitimize the use of violence to protect or further the cause of Sinhala-Buddhist nationalism.[37]

Suggesting that the government is advancing the notion of the Buddhist promised land, Women for Peace links Sinhala-Buddhist ideology to violence, war, and the promotion of a "macho," warlike male.[38] Moreover, in their critiques of the government's appeal to men and women[39] to join the armed forces, the organization seems to be suggesting that in Sri Lanka, patriotism—the highest form of which in the present context of war is entrance into the armed services—makes one a "legitimate" citizen. Sri Lanka is not unique in its equation of full citizenship with participation in the military. Compare the United States in 1992, where the presidential candidacy of Bill Clinton almost foundered on the fact that he was a draft-dodger.[40]

At the same time that the government promotes the image of gun-toting, patriotic males and females, destined to liberate Sri Lanka from the grip of the LTTE, Tamils and Sinhalas on the internet debate Sri Lanka's war and the instrumentalization of women in it. The debate is often fiery and obscene, with each side casting the other as effeminate, sexually frustrated, or sexually perverted; each represents for the other the furthest reaches of depravity. For instance, one Sinhala writer condemns Tamils for being a "race of Barbarians who have assassinated two heads of state and [who] sacrifice children and women for political gains as no race on this planet has ever done...not even animals."[41] Pointing to the use of women in war as a sign of the debased and effete Tamil, the (presumably) Sinhala writer refers to the LTTE's female suicide bombers, suspected of blowing up Indian and Sri Lankan politicians alike.[42] An instrument of Tamil terrorists, the Tamil female is a pawn in the LTTE's unjust war against the Sinhalas. Subordinate to the Tamil male, she is also subordinate to "the West," inasmuch as, from the internet writer's point of view, the LTTE is funded by Sri Lanka's United National Party (UNP), which serves its "foreign masters."[43] In this Sinhala rhetoric, Tamil female suicide bombers, then, not unlike one critique of members of Women for Peace, are dual instruments of patriarchy and of the West.

In another dialogue between a Sinhala and a Tamil on the internet,[44] the "reality of war" is debated as the two reflect on a recent headline in the Sri Lankan press about the rape and murder of a young Tamil girl in the north by Sinhala soldiers. According to the Tamil writer, a "women's group in the South forced the government to admit the incident." In the allusion to Women for Peace, the Tamil writer attaches importance to women who act as peace advocates. In doing so, he invokes the gendered stereotypes and symbolism so often encountered in Sri Lanka and elsewhere of the traditional association of war with masculinity and peace with femininity. Here, that stereotyped dimension of femininity is valorized whereas elsewhere, as we have seen, it is criticized.

In an effort to justify the war crime of rape, the Sinhala writer cites world history: "How many German/Japanese girls do you think were raped and killed by Allied soldiers during the war?" He or she adds that all is fair in "ensur[ing] that [Tamils] will never get an inch of Sinhaladwipa [the sacred island of the Sinhalas]." Reflecting the state-sponsored, Buddhist promised-land and chosen-people ideologies, the Sinhala writer proceeds by comparing Tamils to Sinhalas: "We love our country and we will sacrifice anything to ensure that you will never get an inch of Sinhaladwipa. For you, 'Tamil' comes first. For us, it is *rata, jathiya, agama* (country, people, religion).... Country comes first."[45] As the Sinhala writer's ideology unfolds, we learn that he or she deems human rights violations, such as the rape of women, acceptable in the protection of country. Yet, the writer adds that it is now expedient to "toe the line with human rights groups in the West" to enable Sinhalas "to have a clear, uninterrupted run with the war and bury the Tamil motherfuckers."

Sinhala military men are not unique in perpetrating violence against women as one tactic in war, however; the LTTE, too, has been accused by the United States of "us[ing] rape as a weapon of terror."[46] Indeed, on the internet, the use of women for political and military advantage—both as passive (raped) and active (warrior) participants—is a prominent theme in Sinhala and Tamil assessments of the quality and condition of culture in Sri Lanka. This suggests that the rhetoric of war in Sri Lanka follows a general South Asian pattern that links the condition of culture to the condition of the female.[47]

Conclusion

In a quasi-poetic reflection on patriarchal Tamil culture in Sri Lanka, one Sinhala contributor to the internet connects the Hindu religion with politics in an attempt to defame all Tamils:

> Tamils worship stone cocks...Tamils walk on fire to please the Gods... Tamil mothers kill female children, because they want males...Tamils sacrifice women for political gain...Tamils are mental and walk around with cyanide capsules and think its macho.[48]

The Sinhala writer refers to the worship of Śiva's phallus, the preference for boy children (even among women), the exploitation of females as warriors, and the ability to commit suicide with ease as evidence of the male character of Tamil culture. In this Sinhala estimation, Tamil culture is constructed as mercenary and masculine (yet emasculated), while Tamil women, though pawns of patriarchy, promote the virtues of manliness.

For some Sinhalas, the LTTE's use of women as warriors is a barometer for measuring the degraded condition of Tamil culture; other Sinhalas, however, promote the image of women as warriors, hence demonstrating the worth of Sinhala culture. Though in contemporary Buddhist Sri Lanka the positive association between women and war is not uniform—Women for Peace is a case in point—the public discourse on women, peace, and Buddhism is one in which the loudest and most influential voice, that is, the government's, advances the idea that the paradigmatic Buddhist female is she who protects Sri Lankan Buddhism from its enemies. Her primary duty, either as keeper of memory or as warrior, is to foster Buddhism in a battle-fatigued sacred island. As memory, she instantiates particular stereotyped female virtues; as warrior, she is partially liberated from patriarchal constructions of the female in order to liberate the island from the grip of the LTTE and, ultimately, from the West. Not unlike her Tamil sister, the new Sinhala Buddhist woman must face death to remind herself of her liberation.

Notes

1. Interview with Dr. Nalin de Silva (July 30, 1998), one of the most vocal opponents of the devolution package. He expresses his views weekly in a column in Sri Lanka's newspaper *The Island.*
2. Steven Kemper, *The Presence of the Past* (Ithaca: Cornell University Press, 1990); and Tessa J. Bartholomeusz and Chandra R. de Silva, *Buddhist Fundamentalism and Minority Identities in Sri Lanka* (Albany: State University of New York Press, 1998).
3. For more on the promised-land ideology, see Tessa Bartholomeusz, "First Among Equals: Buddhism and the Sri Lankan State," *Buddhism and Politics in Twentieth-Century Asia,* ed. Ian Harris (London: Pinter, 1999).
4. "War or Peace?" *The Island,* 7 June, 1995.
5. "Women Against War and Militarism: Women in Black Challenge Militarism, Violence of All Sorts," *Weekend Express* (Colombo), 29 September, 1996.
6. Tessa Bartholomeusz, *Women under the Bo Tree: Buddhist Nuns in Sri Lanka* (1994; Cambridge: Cambridge University Press, 1995), pp. 136–37.
7. Tessa Bartholomeusz, "Mothers of Buddhas, Mothers of Nations: Kumaratunga and Her Meteoric Rise to Power in Sri Lanka," *Journal of Feminist Studies* vol. 25, no. 1 (spring 1999): 211–25.
8. Interview with Ms. Amarasekera, an active member of Women for Peace, Colombo, 23 July, 1997.
9. See, for example, "Maha Nayakas Want Elections Postponed," *Daily News,* 20 June, 1998, which recounts a statement, signed by the leaders of the three monastic fraternities in Sri Lanka, that asks the government to finish the war before it holds elections.
10. "A Man-hunt, Not a War," *The Island,* 7 June, 1995.
11. Ibid.
12. "Fighting for the Rights of Victims of War: Vociferous Voices of Women," *The Sunday Leader,* 15 December, 1996.
13. "Women in Peace Work," *Sama Yamaya (Time of Peace),* no. 6 (April/July 1998), internet edition of the newsletter of the National Peace Council of Sri Lanka.
14. John P. Neelsen, "Gender, Caste and Power in a Transitional Society," in *Gender, Caste and Power in South Asia: Social Status and Mobility in a Transitional Society,* ed. John P. Neelsen (New Delhi: Manohar, 1991), p. xvii.
15. Kumari Jayawardena, "Some Aspects of Religious and Cultural Identity and the

Construction of Sinhala Buddhist Womanhood," in *Religion and Political Conflict in South Asia: India, Pakistan, and Sri Lanka*, ed. Douglas Allen (Delhi: Oxford University Press, 1993), pp. 165–67.

16. "'War' or 'Peace,'" *The Island*, 22 May, 1998.
17. Italics mine.
18. Cynthia Enlow, "Some of the Best Soldiers Wear Lipstick," in *Living with Contradictions: Controversies in Feminist Social Ethics*, ed. Alison M. Jaggar (Boulder: Westview, 1994), p. 599.
19. "Women in Black," *Samakali* [newsletter for Women for Peace],(January–February, 1997), p. 10.
20. "Air Force to Recruit Women Pilots," *The Island*, 21 August, 1997.
21. "Fighting for the Right of Victims of War: Vociferous Voices of Women," *The Sunday Leader*, 15 December, 1996.
22. Katha Pollitt, *Reasonable Creatures: Essays on Women and Feminism* (New York: Alfred A. Knopf, 1995), p. 43.
23. Ibid., p. 58.
24. Sherry Ortner, *Making Culture: The Politics and Erotics of Culture* (Boston: Beacon, 1996), pp. 40–41.
25. For another example of this alliance, see Joanne C. Watkins, *Spirited Women* (New York: Columbia University Press, 1996), especially pp. 109–44. In her work, Watkins discusses the degree to which Tibetan Buddhist women in Nepal are constructed as vehicles of culture.
26. "The Women Who Refuse to Forget," *The Sunday Leader*, 10 August, 1997.
27. Ibid.
28. The article, "Mahanayake on Why He Quit Council," *The Island*, 12 January, 1997, outlines the reasons for monks' opposition to devolution.
29. "President's Peace Proposals Will See End to War—Prelate," *The Island*, 4 October, 1995.
30. "Only Leader Who Has Guts to End War is the President," *Daily News*, 14 July, 1997.
31. *The Mahāvaṃsa*, trans. Wilhelm Geiger (Colombo: Government Press, 1986).
32. Ibid, vol. xxiv, p. 6. For a Chinese example of women's jewelry as a symbol of cowardice during war, see Lo Kuan-chung, *Three Kingdoms: China's Epic Drama*, trans. Moss Roberts (New York: Pantheon Books), pp. 292–95. I am indebted to Cutler Edwards for this example.
33. Noeyal Peiris, "The Romantic and Heroic Story of Vihara Maha Devi," *The Buddhist* vol. lv, no. 3 (September–October 1984), p. 25.
34. Ibid.
35. "Only Leader Who Has Guts to End War is the President," *Daily News*, 14 July, 1997.
36. Tessa Bartholomeusz, "Mothers of Buddhas, Mothers of Nations: Kumaratunga and Her Meteoric Rise to Power in Sri Lanka."
37. "Abusing History: Women for Peace on 'Racist Advertisements,'" *Sunday Leader*, 15 September, 1996.

38. "Mark of a Man," *Samakali* (January–February, 1997), p. 11.
39. Ibid.
40. For more on this, see Alison M. Jaggar, *Living with Contradictions*, p. 574.
41. Sri Lanka chat room, September 7, 1997.
42. Among them, Rajiv Gandhi of India and Gamini Dissanayake of Sri Lanka.
43. Sri Lanka chat room, August 29, 1997.
44. Sri Lanka chat room, August 25, 1997.
45. Ibid., parenthetical remark is in the original.
46. From the resolution passed by the U.S. House of Representatives in September, 1995; quoted on the internet, Sri Lanka chat room, August 25, 1997.
47. We find one of the oldest examples of this pattern in the *Bhagavad Gītā* I, 41–42: "And when lawlessness prevails, O Krishna, the women of the family are corrupted, and when women are corrupted...a mixture of caste arises. And this confusion brings the family itself to hell..." (*The Bhagavad Gita*, trans. and ed. Eliot Deutsch [New York: Holt, Rhinehart, and Winston, 1968], p. 34.)
48. Sri Lanka chat room, August 21, 1997.

MAE CHI BOONLIANG:
A Thai Nun Runs a Charitable Foundation

Mae Chi Boonliang is sixty-five years old and has been a nun for forty-six years. She is very lively, humble and open-minded. In the past she taught Dhamma but now she is in charge of a meditation nunnery and a charitable foundation in Bangkok.

I BECAME A NUN when I was nineteen. When I was sixteen I was very sick. In the north of Thailand there is a tradition that if a child is seriously ill, the parents will ask for the child to become a monk or a nun if he or she becomes better. So when I was nineteen, I went to be a nun for a year. I was still ill and I did not want to be a nun in these conditions. So I went to the Emerald Buddha in Bangkok and prayed that if the Buddha wanted me not to be a nun, to let me go free. If I were to be a lay woman, I would be one. If it was not to be, then he must make something happen. At that time my father got very ill and died. I felt that I had nobody to depend on, so I remained a nun.

I went to a temple and stayed there for fourteen years. I meditated, chanted, and performed services for funerals, and felt that I got nothing. I heard of another temple where they did more meditation. It was said that it was a good place for a nun to live and meditate. One did not need to do a lot of chanting or perform funeral services. I moved to that temple and stayed there for a year.

Eventually, I went to Ragburi to visit Mae Chi Ghee, where they just meditated and did not sleep. Mae Chi Ghee would tell the nuns that to practice meditation they should look at everything and blank out nothing, just as they would look at nature. One day as I was meditating, I saw a rusty gutter, and I suddenly felt sad and sorry that it was going bad and rusty. I experienced that life was impermanent. I learned Dhamma from that gutter. I decided then and there that I would remain a nun forever.

I came to this nunnery and charitable foundation in Bangkok because Mae Chi Prapit asked me to be the head nun here. I was of the right age and had been a nun for many years, so I would take good care of the place. I have been here for twenty-five years. I wanted to leave after three years to go and meditate with Mae Chi Ghee again, but I was asked to continue as head nun and to perform other essential functions here at the Thai Nuns' Institute.

This is a place for young women who want to be nuns, and who want to train and help poor villagers. At the beginning it was not working well, and I wondered how young Thai women could become good nuns. The monks suggested that the women be taught sewing. So they prayed and chanted, and learned how to sew and how to meditate as well. The young nuns made a promise to stay for two years after they finished the course. After two years they could stay here, go to another nunnery, or stop being nuns. There is no charge. They promised to go and teach poor villagers in the provinces during those two years.

The women who come here to train are from remote villages. Their parents are very poor. They come here to study and to learn how to sew. When they go back to their villages, they can have an occupation. But because we observe strict discipline here, some people cannot stay because they cannot obey the rules. If they want to stop before the end of the two years, they have to pay three hundred *bahts* per month for food, accommodation, and cost of living. If they are very stubborn or very naughty and do not listen, they may go without paying anything.

After they graduate, many of them stop being nuns. They can get good jobs in factories or in the flower making shops. They know how to behave well and are good workers, and employers are happy to have them. Other nuns leave to study further because they have come here with little education. The Asia Foundation will help them. We have many supporters like the Asia Foundation, some government departments, and several women's organizations.

This is social work and welfare, because these women normally have fewer opportunities. If they come here, they have the opportunity to learn and help others. In this institute, we only teach nuns, and these nuns will go to the villages and teach the lay people. In the morning you saw a group of villagers who came to say goodbye to the nuns who were their teachers.

I am just the administrator. I wake up at 4 A.M. and meditate. After that I manage the finances and supervise the teachings. I also take care of the guests when they come to visit. I am a little tired and would like to retire from being an administrator and let other nuns do this. But the nuns want me to stay even if I do nothing; they want me to stay as supervisor and head and they will do the rest. There are about forty people in the nunnery. There are three teachers: one teaches Dhamma, one sewing, and one flower making.

As a Thai person I have a responsibility to help my country. The country, the king, and the religion have to help each other. I am only sorry that I can only teach a few nuns because of the lack of funds. I have been a nun for many years and feel that everything is *anicca*, impermanent: everything changes. I am happy to be a nun and to be able to help myself and other people. I understand now what real happiness is. I do not think about the future, I stay with the present. I believe that if you do good things, you will bring good results. Once the queen said that we should spread happiness to others. If you are happy, you help others; then other people share your happiness. We must help each other.

Compiled by Martine Batchelor

MAE CHI SANSENEE:
A Thai Nun as Patroness

Mae Chi Sansenee is a Thai nun whose temple is situated in a park she created on the outskirts of Bangkok. Her garden is full of lotus flowers, ponds, and bridges, and is an oasis of calm in the heat of Bangkok's arid suburbs.

I BECAME A NUN thirteen years ago because I was tired of living. I wanted to stop for a while. To stop, you have to choose a new way to go, and I chose Buddhism. I do not know if I will stay a nun all my life, but right now being Buddhist is the most important thing I can do. I try to do my best as a Buddhist nun. I became a nun at a temple two kilometers away from here. My teacher, the head monk of that temple, suggested that I buy this large piece of land. After my teacher died, I decided to repay him by following in his footsteps. He used to help a lot of people. I thought that on this piece of land I could build a place to continue in his spirit of compassion.

There are seven projects altogether. I started off with a preschool for handicapped children at the main temple. The second project is a junior high school where we train students to understand the core of Buddhism, as well as other studies. They do not have to meditate as much as in retreat, but they have to understand what is meant by Buddhism. What does it mean not to be selfish? What does it mean to have compassion and understanding for other people?

We also help a group of young boxers who come from upcountry and earn money boxing. Being a boxer does not mean you have to be cruel. It would help boxers to practice Buddhism. I have been supporting them so that they can have a spiritual life too. Other ideas are to have university students come here and meditate, and for lay women, nuns, and young unmarried mothers to come and do retreats.

All of these programs are about applying the teachings of Buddhism. People who attend are not necessarily Buddhist—they may come from a Christian background. It does not matter. They do not have to be believers, because the Buddhist teaching is universal. There are many things that they can take with them and apply in their daily lives.

I use work as the focus of meditation. While I am working I follow my breath. I do a lot of breathing exercises and make sure that I am always aware of what I am doing. My mind is calm, my breathing is calm. This is the reason why I have been able to work so hard. As a nun, there are certain things that I have to be aware of as well. For instance, I wake up early in the morning and do formal meditation before I come out, and I meditate a lot before I go to bed. When there is a lull in my activities, I take time off for retreats. Then I stay alone and do a lot of intensive meditation.

When there is nothing going on, no activity, I live here alone, but when there is a large retreat, volunteers come to help. Some of the volunteers are nuns, but most are lay people. In Thai Buddhism, it is not a condition that nuns have to be together—we only have to belong to the Thai Nun's Institute. I do not have to be in a large nunnery if I can be financially independent. Most nuns cannot be financially independent so they choose to be in a temple. At first I stayed at my teacher's temple because I felt the need to study, but now I feel quite ready to be on my own and to help others. I have become very relaxed and happy, and feel that all the energy I've put in has been worthwhile. I would like to do more and more. I will be forty in a month.

At first finances came only from my family. My family had been very generous to other temples in the past. When I suggested that I wanted to set up this place, all the donations came together as a family fund and supported all these activities. No-one who comes here has to pay anything. However, people who practice around here see how their society can benefit from this place. Some of them come back and make donations, and for this reason these projects have been going on for some time.

Compiled by Martine Batchelor

DIVERSITY AND RACE:

New Koans for American Buddhism

JANICE D. WILLIS

ON A HOT SUMMER'S DAY in 1981, I stood in the inner courtyard of a large Buddhist monastery in central Bangkok. The courtyard, showcasing the "Thousand Buddhas," was ringed by hundreds of life-sized Buddha statues, each one gilded and lightly draped with a delicate saffron shawl. Yet, even amid so many Buddha figures I found myself gravitating, ever so slowly, toward the sole statue there that still sat awaiting its new gold-leaf. In its as yet unrefurbished state, it sat peacefully, peering out from a body as black as soot. I had spent the previous year and a half in Nepal and had studied and taught Buddhism back in America for more than a decade. Buddha statues were no novelty to me. But this one in particular drew my attention because of its blackness. I was irresistibly drawn to it, pulled forward, I believe, by the urge to see myself reflected there. I asked a friend to take a photo of me staring back into this black Buddha's face. It seemed obvious that this Buddha was for me. It spoke to me because it mirrored me, physically and viscerally. I hoped to find others along my way. And, upon my return to the United States, I hoped to find other Buddhists who shared not only my interest in Buddhism but my racial background, my color, as well.

For many years after that I did not find other African-Americans in the centers and circles of Buddhism in which I orbited back in the States. There seemed to be very few African-Americans with either the time for, or the interest in, matters Buddhist. Of course, I had occasions to teach African-Americans in my university classes on Buddhism, but in most Buddhist venues outside the classroom our numbers seemed almost inconsequential.

In 1996 I wrote an essay about Buddhism and race and about African-Americans and Buddhism for an anthology called *Buddhist Women on the Edge: Contemporary Perspectives from the Western Frontier.*[1] It was no accident that the anthology focused on Buddhism as experienced and perceived by women. For throughout Buddhism's time in the United States, it has been mainly women who have challenged, and raised questions about, Buddhism at the institutional level.[2] Virtually all other books published on the subject of Buddhism in America have focused almost exclusively on meditation and on the tradition(s) of Buddhism as a spiritual path and practice.[3]

From that day when I stood in the Wat of a Thousand Buddhas, more than seventeen years would pass before I picked up a Buddhist magazine and read the following advertisement:

> Why doesn't Buddhism attract more people of African-American, Latino, and other ethnic backgrounds? A group of practitioners in the Bay area have formed the Buddhism and Racism Working Group, and in November they'll host a conference to address this question. "It is our hope that by addressing issues of race and diversity, our sanghas may become more welcoming and responsive to people from all backgrounds," says Working Group member Rosa Zubizarreta...."Healing Racism in our Sanghas," November 7 in Berkeley, will provide an opportunity for Buddhists from a variety of cultures and traditions to explore how their attitudes toward people of other races affect both themselves and their communities. The conference is co-sponsored by the Buddhist Peace Fellowship.[4]

Yet, even before seeing this advertisement, I had managed—on my own—to find other African-American Buddhists. In this essay I aim to introduce some of them and allow readers to hear our views—as African-American students, teachers, and practitioners of Buddhism in America. Of course, this does not mean that we share a single view. Our experiences are as varied as we, as unique individuals, are ourselves. I must admit, however, that I chose these particular African-Americans on purpose because I knew them to be serious, thoughtful, and extremely articulate individuals. (I also knew that they were industrious and compassionate enough to respond in relative haste to my request for their views.) Aiming to represent diverse Buddhist traditions, I contacted five individuals, four of whom responded in full. One is a Zen practitioner, another a Tibetan Buddhist lama, another a Theravāda *vipassanā* practitioner, and the last is an academic student of Buddhism in America. I myself am a professor of Indic and Tibetan Buddhism.

For the most part, I have tried to let each speak for him- or herself. However, I first devised a questionnaire in order to give coherence to the project. I asked them questions about their respective backgrounds, their earliest encounters with Buddhism, and their teachers. I asked whether, in fact, they considered themselves to be Buddhists, and I asked them to speak about their own experiences at Buddhist centers here in America—whether they found them to be "open" and welcoming spaces, whether they had ever personally experienced any forms of discrimination in them. Lastly, I asked them if they had any specific advice for other African-Americans, or for persons of color in general, who might be considering beginning Buddhist practice, and I asked them to share any specific recommendations for improving the current situation.

Their Backgrounds

Lori Pierce comes from a comfortable, upper-middle-class religious family in Chicago where her father is a surgeon. She was raised in the Catholic schools and church of the area, and was active in the church through high school and Lake Forest College, where her interests broadened to include world and comparative religions. Her first exposure to Buddhism, she writes, was academic.

> Reading Herman Hesse's *Siddhartha* was probably my introduction.... Through classes and casual reading I eventually began to read Shunryu Suzuki, D.T. Suzuki, Philip Kapleau, Robert Aiken, Eido Shimano, Alan Watts, etc. Sometimes it came in a "new age" package, but I came to Buddhism like many Americans—by way of the dregs of the countercultural movement. There was nothing systematic about it; we knew next to nothing about the complex intercultural movements that distinguished Japanese Rinzai Zen from Tibetan Buddhism. We read what was available and, as newly mature adults, believed that we were free to believe what we liked and be what we wanted to be.

After college, Lori went to California and for a time worked in the poor Black neighborhood of West Oakland for the Jesuit Volunteer Corps, an organization she describes as "a kind of Catholic urban Peace Corps." Referring to that experience as her first prolonged exposure to Black people since leaving the mainly White surroundings of her Chicago life, Lori determined that the question of religion and the question of race ought not to be separated. After studying a bit about Buddhism in the Bay Area, she entered the World Religions program at Harvard Divinity School. Of her California ventures into Buddhism, Lori writes, "I was sitting randomly on my own, studying tai chi, and running. It didn't occur to me to go to find an organization with which to get involved. And in the Bay Area in the early 1980s, there was just too much choice." Lori now lives in Hawai'i with her husband and six-year-old daughter. She is currently completing her doctoral dissertation for the University of Hawai'i on the racial dynamic of the religious encounter between European Americans and Japanese Americans in Hawai'i during the years before World War II.

Lama Thupten Gyalsten Dorje (Jerry Gardner), writes of his early life, "I was born on Guam to a military couple and then adopted by a different military couple. I was raised as an only child." His family moved around a lot in the U.S., living in Alabama, Texas, Washington, North Carolina, New York City, and Oklahoma. It was in Alabama that, with his grandmother, he attended Baptist services. "I remember the preacher yelling and shouting. It seemed surrealistic to me as a young child." In his early years, Gardner became obsessed with death. "Even though I wasn't Catholic, I used to sleep with a rosary." When he was twelve years old, he began his lifelong practice of the martial arts. This practice included meditation and he found he liked the discipline of learning to discipline his mind. Martial arts also helped him to become less fearful of death.

In 1968, in New York City, he met his first Buddhist teacher, Master Ronald Takanashi, a Pure Land Buddhist priest. Takanashi was the first to introduce him to a more formal meditation practice—for example, how to practice, and how to set up a shrine. Jerry began to search out books and teachers to guide him "to the mastery of self," and then determined to go to the east. "In 1970 I sold my belongings and was ready to travel to India or Tibet to search for a teacher." However, a series of "seemingly unfortunate" events occurred that forced him to cancel his trip. As a result, he met Lama Sonam Kazi in New York, and was accepted as his student. Commenting upon this turn of events, he says, "I find it interesting that instead of going to the mountains of Tibet to find a teacher, I went to the high-rises of New York City!"

Then, while living again in Guam in 1988, the opportunity arose for Jerry to travel to Kathmandu, Nepal. He remarks, "I went there without having any knowledge of what might occur or who I might meet, but my goal was to have a direct experience of Buddhism in a place where it was lived as part of the ongoing fiber of the society." In Nepal, Jerry met Chokyi Nyima Rinpoche, who sent him to his father, Tulku Urgyen Rinpoche. The latter became his root teacher. In the past ten years, he has traveled to Nepal two or three times each year. Most recently, he has been receiving teachings from Khenpo Kunchok Molam Rinpoche and writes that "it was Khenpo Kunchok Molam Rinpoche who was so kind as to ordain me as Lama Thupten Gyalsten Dorje."

In 1994, after moving to Salt Lake City, Utah, Lama Dorje and his wife established the non-profit Urgyen Samten Ling Meditation Center, in the "Nyingma, Dzogchen, Long Chen Nying Thig" lineage. Lama Dorje is the center's resident teacher. He also continues, now as a teacher, his martial arts—in the form of tai chi, kung fu, and mime—at the Red Lotus School of Movement, which he owns and directs.

Lewis Woods describes himself as "an African-American man who has lived his whole life in the post-civil-rights-movement U.S.," and goes on to note:

> By the time I was five years old, my family had moved to Berkeley, CA. This was in 1968, the heyday of student activism and radical social change. Though I was relatively sheltered from the events taking place across town, the atmosphere of liberalism, openness to change, and the questioning of authority and tradition was my native cultural landscape, if you will, reaching me through my teachers and my parents who very much chose to live in Berkeley because of this atmosphere.

Commenting upon the religious life of his family, Lewis writes, "If our family had a religion, it was atheism. Both of my parents had rejected the religions of their youth by the time I was born.... At present I am the only person in my immediate family who is at all religious." At the age of eighteen, Lewis "became a born-again Christian and remained within that evangelical, mixed race, doctrinally conservative church for four years." But at the age of twenty-two, he "made a decisive break with Christianity and began studying Judaism." In fact, after a three-year period of study which included becoming conversant in modern Hebrew and two prolonged visits to Israel and the occupied territories, Lewis formally converted to orthodox Judaism.

Lewis first encountered Buddhism through the books of Alan Watts and Suzuki Roshi though, he confides, "initially, I was more interested in Taoism than Buddhism." In the end, it was the Buddhist Dharma that impressed Lewis most. "For so long the *only* Buddhists I knew were in books. I didn't meet a 'real' Buddhist until well after I had become convinced of the merits of Buddhism." Although Lewis began by mainly sitting Zen in the Bay Area, he later took Buddhist refuge and lay vows with Geshe Michael Roach. He describes his daily practice as being "pretty idiosyncratic," saying that he draws "most on Tibetan and Theravāda traditions, though his background in Zen is never far below the surface." Lewis remains one of the main anchors of the Berkeley headquarters of the Buddhist Peace Fellowship.

Ralph Steele was born on Pawleys Island, one of the sixteen islands along the coast of South Carolina that stretch out for 160 miles between Myrtle Beach and Charleston. When Ralph was five years old, his father died, and so he describes his mom as being a single parent. "I was raised mostly by my grandparents," Ralph says. "Everyone called my grandmother Sister Mary; and everybody called my grandfather Baba James. My great-grandfather was called, by everyone, simply Father." Ralph's family members were very religious, and strong supporters of the African Methodist Episcopal Church, "for more than 110 years supplying ministers, deacons, treasurers and bookkeepers to the Church."

When Ralph's mother remarried a military man, the family left Pawleys Island and began traveling, moving first to Montgomery, Alabama, then to Bakersfield,

California, and then on to Japan, where Ralph went to high school. There, he encountered a Japanese martial arts master and began studying seriously with him.

> Even though I was only thirteen or fourteen years old, eventually I ended up in his class, the only student who was not in the military. And I learned a lot from him. I began to understand the concepts of Buddhism from a practitioner's perspective through the eyes of martial arts. And I began to go into temples at an early age and to get some understanding of what was going on there.

Before entering college, Ralph enlisted in the military and served a tour in Vietnam. He found himself in "very heated situations" and he saw many of his friends die. "I had to call on my own deep, deep inner self and what my martial arts teacher and Sister Mary and Baba James had taught me in order to keep my sanity and survive."

After returning from Vietnam, Ralph became a student at the University of California, Santa Cruz, and later did graduate work at Santa Clara University. In both locations, and in other places, he found Buddhist teachers: Zen master Kobun Chino, eclectic Steven Levine, Tibetans Kalu Rinpoche and Sogyal Rinpoche among them. But, eventually, Ralph found his primary teacher in Jack Kornfield, and in Theravāda *vipassanā* meditation he found his main practice. Ralph is now a therapist living in Santa Fe, New Mexico. Specializing in combining psychotherapy and Dharma practice for pain and grief management, his office group is called Life Transition Therapy, Inc. Having led *vipassanā* groups himself, Ralph is in training to become a *vipassanā* teacher. He is currently doing intensive meditation retreats in Burma and Thailand. For some years, he has also been writing his memoir, which is entitled *Tending the Fire.*

Jan Willis was born in Birmingham, Alabama, and raised until college age in a coal mining camp just outside the city limits. Both my parents were active in the Baptist church, my father being one of the youngest deacons of his church. Although my own baptism was a wonderfully expansive and spiritually liberating experience, I was not much attracted to the Baptist faith. As a high school student, I took an active part in the civil rights movement and marched with King and others during the Birmingham campaign of 1963. Always good at mathematics, I won a number of scholarships for college and selected Cornell University where, initially, I majored in physics. It was at Cornell that I became interested in Buddhism, in large part because of observing Buddhist monks and nuns immolate themselves protesting against the Vietnam war. I read works mostly by Alan Watts and D.T. Suzuki and determined to study and meditate in Japan. I was able to spend my junior year in India on a University of Wisconsin Year in India program scholarship and, while studying in Banaras, I met Tibetans living in Sarnath. I was immediately captivated by the Tibetans and was warmly received by them. Consequently, I never got east of India. In 1969, in Nepal, I met Lama Thubten Yeshe, who became my main teacher for the next fifteen years until his death in 1984. Back in the United States, I finished a B.A. and an M.A. in philosophy at Cornell, and then enrolled at Columbia, where I earned my Ph.D. in Indic and Buddhist Studies in 1976. In 1996 I was asked to write about my own personal journey from the Jim Crow South to Tibetan Buddhism. I have now completed this memoir. The book, titled *Dreaming Me: An African American Baptist-Buddhist Journey,* will be published by Riverhead Books (Penguin and Putnam) in the spring of 2000.

Five African-Americans on Buddhism in America

In my 1996 essay on African-Americans and Buddhism, I described myself as a "Baptist-Buddhist," remarking that I found the hyphenated description most genuine. I wrote then:

> I've headed my essay this way simply because it is descriptive of who I am. Actually, I think of myself as being more "an African-American Buddhist" really; when I seek to make sense of things or to analyze a particular situation, I am more likely to draw on Buddhist principles than Baptist ones. But...if it seems as though the plane I'm on might actually go down (and such has been, frighteningly, the case), I call on both traditions! It is a deep response.[5]

Not surprisingly, then, the questionnaire I sent for the present essay included the following question: *Do you consider yourself to be a Buddhist? Do you ever find yourself qualifying or hyphenating this appellation?* The answers I received were straightforward and varied.

Lori: "I see [taking Buddhist refuge] as something akin to being rebaptized. I figured if you're going to take refuge, to take on a teacher, you had better be pretty ready, pretty committed to this path, at least committed to the teacher. I wasn't—still am not—sure enough to want to do that. When people ask me if I am a Buddhist, I assume...they mean: have you taken refuge? Do you have a teacher? What is your practice? This to me is not something to be taken lightly.... Maybe I'm like a divorced person after having left the Catholic church; I'm not that anxious to make the mistake again. I've been known to say that I would be willing to entertain returning to the liberal American Catholic Church when it breaks from Rome, ordains married people, accepts homosexuals, and acknowledges its role in the perpetuation of patriarchy, sexism, and racism. I don't want too much, do I?"

Lama Dorje: "I am Buddhist. I follow the Buddhadharma. For me, the mixing and matching [hyphenating] does not work. The Buddhist tradition is complete. If one has truly embraced the teachings of the Buddha, there is no need to add or mix anything else."

Lewis: "I definitely consider myself a Buddhist, especially now that I have taken the five lifetime lay vows. I seldom feel a need to hyphenate that appellation except under certain circumstances. Adding African-American to the term Buddhist is important at times, but it really doesn't modify the term Buddhist in the same way that calling myself a Theravāda Buddhist, Vajrāyana Buddhist, or an eclectic Buddhist does. Calling myself a Northern California Buddhist, or better, a Berkeley Buddhist probably says a bit more about my approach to the Dharma. But even that doesn't explain enough to make it worth mentioning....When I'm feeling confident enough to follow my own path, I think of myself as a 'critical Buddhist,' as one whose approach to the Dharma is rooted in an attempt to take seriously the problems posed for Buddhism by modern, pluralistic social conditions and by contemporary philosophy and science. It is also based on an endeavor to remain responsibly open to criticism regardless of the quarter from which it arises. I also like to call myself an Engaged Buddhist to make it clear that I do not think that attention to social problems is tangential to the practice of awakening."

Ralph: "Of course I'm a Buddhist, from head to toe! Also, I'm a Hindu, a big-time *bhakti* [devotional] man. It's pretty hard for an Afro-American to run around saying he's a Hindu in this culture...but, a Buddhist? Yes, I am. A Buddhist from head to toe. I've taken vows many, many, many times; and any time the string falls off, I put one on again. So, that's who I am. And—what can I say?—the practice keeps my sanity."

Jan: "In an odd way, I have always found myself feeling especially 'at home' when I am with Tibetans in Nepal or India. I attempted to comment upon this feeling of welcomeness in my 1996 essay by saying:

> The Tibetans took me in instantly and I saw in them a welcoming family of compassionate and skilled people who, as I viewed myself, were refugees. I soon learned that the Tibetans possessed a type of knowledge and wisdom I longed for—knowledge of methods for dealing with frustrations, disappointments, and anger, and of developing genuine compassion. Indeed, their very beings reflected this. They had suffered untold hardships, had even been forced to flee their country. We shared, it seemed to me, the experience of a profound historical trauma. Yet, they coped quite well, seeming to possess a sort of spiritual armor that I felt lacking in myself."[6]

When I asked whether, in their experiences, these four African-Americans had ever noticed or felt discrimination or prejudice toward them in Asia from Asians, most of them skipped the question, giving, on my subsequent inquiry, the uniform response "No." Like me, they found their Asia experience to be most welcoming. Lama Dorje was quite specific on this point, saying, "When I visit Nepal, I generate a fair amount of curiosity from Nepalese and Tibetans, as I truly am a stranger in a strange land. If anything, my differences tend to draw people to me. Personally, I feel more comfortable walking the streets of Kathmandu than the streets of America!"

However, when I asked, *Do you find Buddhist centers in the U.S. "open" places for you and other people of color? Do you see yourself represented in them?* all four respondents had comments.

Lori: "Going to the Cambridge Buddhist Association was my first experience with *zendo* culture, and I have to say I found it a bit off-putting. I liked Maurine;[7] she was like a stern but loving grandmother, but...what, I wondered, was the point of schlepping all the way over there (a forty-five minute walk from our house) if, after sitting, chanting, and walking, you just went home? Where was the fellowship? Where were the tea and cookies? What was the point of a Sangha if you didn't know anyone's name? The whole thing felt so formal and distant, I never really warmed up to it."

Lama Dorje: "The Buddhist centers I have visited have been accepting of me as a person of color. But, then again, I don't walk in the door with the concern, 'Am I going to be accepted?' My feeling is that the Buddha taught all people, and his teachings are for all persons. The Buddha, himself, was a person of color. At this point in time, people of color are not well represented in the American Buddhist tradition.... In general, Buddhism has limited exposure in the Black communities, so even if someone of color had an interest in Buddhism, the resources may not be as apparent. Obviously, Buddhist centers are not as common as mainstream American religious organizations. An individual really has to make an effort to seek the Buddhist resources out. But I think these same dynamics are also found in many communities, regardless of color."

Lewis: "I have found the predominantly White Buddhist centers that I have been involved with open but not especially welcoming. I've never been overtly discouraged from participating in a Buddhist event. However, I have felt marginalized, not seen, and at times not just misunderstood but written off as all but inscrutable. In just about every Buddhist setting I have ever found myself, my being African-American has meant that my concerns are second-class, my experience insofar as it is conditioned by my ethnic identity is seldom addressed directly, that I have to do a lot of translating in order to apply the teachings to the social situation in which I find myself, and not infrequently have to endure the ever so unpleasant experience of having to listen to a White person talk about how much further we have to go in this society towards achieving true equality for African-Americans."

Ralph: "All Buddhist centers are 'open,' as far as I know. It's just a question of whether you're bold enough to walk through the doors. Of course, for any person of color who walks through any Buddhist center's door, it's just like walking through the doors of any European church where people of color don't normally go: you will be on stage. People of color need to understand that. The main concept of Buddhism is seeing things as they are; but it's the human nature in those Buddhist centers that manifests. Some people will be surprised and they'll be taken aback. But, they won't close the doors on you. Still, until the people in those centers, the practitioners in this country, deal with the fire inside themselves—the rejection, the hate, the anger, the racism—there will always be a conditioning in the fabric of those places. So, don't walk through the doors of temples in this country without expecting some subtly unintentional action coming towards you. Don't be offended by that because the practitioners [at those centers] themselves are not totally enlightened people. Who is? It takes time. This is a big process; a big subject matter here."

Jan: "All too often I find myself one of only a handful of people of color in Buddhist venues, whether retreats or large public lectures by prominent Asian Buddhist teachers. Yet, there seems to be little open and frank discussion of either why this is the case or of how the situation might be changed. That is a discussion that needs to take place."

Ralph's response to the former question made it seem only natural to consider the last set of queries on my questionnaire at this point. I had asked respondents, *What advice would you give to African-Americans or other persons of color who are considering beginning Buddhist practice?* Ralph wanted to forewarn people of color not to expect Buddhist centers to be any different than other institutions in this country. How could they be? Lori chose not to give a more specific answer to this particular question. She had, after all, already given focused and quite serious attention to it in her essay "Outside In: Buddhism in America."[8] I give below the comments offered by Lama Dorje, Lewis Woods, Ralph Steele, and myself to this specific query.

Lama Dorje: "Typically, it's not part of the Buddhist tradition to proselytize, but rather to let people come to the teachings/teachers on their own. But as Buddhism progresses in America, it may be a good idea to take a more engaged approach and create a better means of visibility that would allow easier access to the Buddhist practice for individuals who are interested. Speaking directly to people of color, if they see that there are Buddhist practitioners and teachers of color, this might be encouragement that they, too, have a place in this age-old religion that was started in a land that was infused with people of color. I'm interested in being instrumental in broadening the base of Buddhism in America to include people of color. If there is any way I can assist in this goal, please let me know."

Lewis: "At this point in time I would probably caution African-Americans or other people of color who are considering beginning Buddhist practice at a predominantly White center to be prepared for racism. I would also make it clear that I think that, up to a point, the Dharma is worth it. I would also suggest that they join with others for support, and express the hope that we all take responsibility for those who will come after us and to do what we can to make sure that others will have an easier time in the future."

Ralph: "I'd say, 'I'm a person of color, and I hope to see you at some of my retreats.' Don't look to the practitioners at any center to teach you about racism. Don't expect the practitioners themselves not to be biased, at least unintentionally. One thing to remember is it's not the practitioners, nor the teacher—any teacher. It's the teachings, the Dharma itself, that is important. That doesn't change. That's what is over two thousand and five hundred years old. That doesn't change. And that's what has saved me and kept me in this practice. I'm sitting in this room with two hundred people, la-di-da, and I'm the only person of color. So what? It's no big thing. Because I know my practice. And I can sit here and do my practice and do my thing. And that's what's so wonderful about this practice: it's about direct experience. And you don't need anybody to hold your hand, or anything of that nature. That's why I'm still in this practice. Because, if I needed someone to hold my hand, or if I needed to believe in something, I wouldn't be in this practice."

Jan: "There are many valuable insights to be gleaned from Buddhist teachings. These insights are as meaningful, and as potentially healing, for persons of color as for any other human beings. Therefore, I would encourage all people of color who have a desire to learn more about Buddhism to do so, through books, lectures, and visits to Buddhist centers and retreats. A well-known saying among African-Americans is 'Keep your eyes on the prize.' After carefully investigating and choosing a Buddhist teacher and organization or center, people of color should be willing to give the teachings and the practice a try."

I asked these articulate African-American Buddhists, *Are there specific recommendations for helping to make Buddhist centers more receptive and accessible for people of color?* Both Lama Dorje and Ralph Steele suggested that when people of color could *see themselves* represented in centers, they might come. Both said that becoming teachers themselves in their respective Buddhist traditions was part of their personal attempt to help provide such representation. (As I read their responses, I felt myself back in that monastery in Thailand.)

Jan: "In this regard, I am in complete agreement with Lama Dorje and Ralph.

If we, as people of color, prepare ourselves to become and continue to be *teachers* in Buddhist venues, whether in Buddhist centers or in universities, we will have an impact. I also believe that Buddhist centers throughout America ought to mount more concerted efforts to make themselves more open and accessible places. Hosting 'open houses' is a good way of breaking down even invisible barriers. For longer retreats, center-sponsored scholarships and work-study programs may serve to help alleviate conflicts in choosing between one's job and time for meditation."

Lewis Woods and Lori Pierce had more theoretically based recommendations.

Lewis: "Because racism and White supremacy are not going to end within Buddhist centers very much before they end in society—and at the rate things are going many Buddhist communities are lagging behind even the corporate world—the Buddhist community as a whole has a Dharmic responsibility to take affirmative action. Such action should at least include supporting the creation of alternative pathways (separate retreats, classes, and even separate centers) to the Dharma for African-Americans and other people of color. For these alternatives to be truly Buddhist they must be based on a recognition of the impermanent, unsatisfactory, and not-self nature of racial and ethnic identity. In practice, this means not only that they must acknowledge that the day will come when such separate institutions are no longer necessary, but that they will actively look forward to it.

Secondly, such action should also include acknowledging the contradiction in speaking of 'American Buddhism' when so many Americans are under-represented, if not functionally un-welcome, in Buddhist communities.

Thirdly, I hope that Buddhist teachers and leaders will not just acknowledge the racism that plays a role in the culture of their centers, but take responsibility for it and make every effort to include outgrowing it as part of the practice of Buddhism."

Lori shares her analysis and recommendations with people interested in these issues, in the classroom and through her published works. Since 1995, she has been writing and lecturing about "how institutional racism works to undermine discussions of race in religious groups."

Race and Gender

Before concluding this multivocal discussion, it seems only appropriate, given the context of the present anthology, to ask one additional question, namely, *Would/Does gender make a difference?* Although my original questionnaire did not ask this specific query, Lori Pierce and I do have some comments to make on this important concern.

Jan: "Yes. Gender makes a profound difference. For most of my early life, it seemed that the specter and concomitant hindrances of racism far outweighed those of sexism, even though, of course, the two worked very closely together. The question was, how was I, as a Black girl, going to be able to succeed in the world? For Black boys, there were some avenues open; but for Black girls, the possibilities seemed much more limited. Today, as an adult woman Buddhist scholar, the links between racially based and gender-based discrimination seem all the more obvious. Although I have managed to forge a career in an academic field that I find personally very rewarding, it is still a field that is disproportionately dominated by men. While some women are now assuming leadership roles in Buddhist centers throughout America, very few of these women are persons of color. Even fewer women of color are instructors of Buddhism within academia. As long as this is the case, Buddhism in America will continue to mirror the hierarchical and patriarchal institutions it has maintained throughout its long history in Asia. If genuine progress is to be made, the issues of race, class, gender, and sexuality need to be addressed much more seriously than they have been thus far. Only then will the tantalizing promises of Buddhist philosophical notions like selflessness, interdependence, inclusiveness, and, ultimately, insight and compassion become real possibilities."

Describing the aftermath of a lecture she had delivered at a conference on Buddhist diversity, Lori remarked, "I left there thinking that the Buddhist community needs a forum for an extended discussion of all aspects of race and gender, diversity and discrimination. I was encouraged by Rosa[9] who suggested to me that we must somehow make diversity a central practice. We always wonder what is 'American' about 'American Buddhism,' and Rosa suggested to me that diversity might be it. What might make American Buddhism distinctive is the challenge to think through problems of racial ideologies. To sit with them. How would you make that not just part of your practice, but the center of your practice?"

And on this matter, I think that Lori's remarks should be the final word. In Rinzai Zen practice, for example, one makes a *koan* the center of one's practice. One "sits" with it. A *koan* is a riddle, a puzzle, a question that cannot be "solved" by linear, discursive reasoning. Yet, as countless generations of Zen practitioners have demonstrated, *koans* can be resolved. Again in Lori's words, "a *koan* is *unsolvable*, but *resolvable*." So, what if Buddhists in America made "diversity" and "race" and "gender" their *koans*? I say, go ahead, American Buddhists. Please try these new *koans* on!

Notes

1. See my "Buddhism and Race: An African American Baptist-Buddhist Perspective" in Marianne Dresser, ed., *Buddhist Women on the Edge: Contemporary Perspectives from the Western Frontier* (Berkeley: North Atlantic Books, 1996), pp. 81–91.
2. Lori Pierce makes this observation in her essay "Outside In: Buddhism in America,"

in Dresser, ed., *Buddhist Women on the Edge*, p. 98. She writes: "Most of the published material by, for, and about Buddhism in America is about Buddhism as a spiritual path and practice. Though this is certainly interesting and important (and necessary, if Buddhism is to be a tool in understanding and destroying discriminatory practices), this emphasis can distract us from questions concerning racism and sexism. Feminist scholars and female Sangha members have vociferously critiqued Buddhism at the institutional level and examined how through hierarchical structures or adherence to unsuitable cultural forms, it has exacerbated problems between male and female teachers and students and other Sangha members."

Jan Nattier, in an essay entitled "Visible and Invisible: The Politics of Representation in Buddhist America" in *Tricycle: The Buddhist Review* vol. 5, no. 1 (fall, 1995): 42-49), had earlier described those she termed "elite Buddhists" as having "redefined Buddhism as [being] synonymous with the practice of meditation."

3. One need only glance at the several publications devoted to the subject of Buddhism in America in the past decade to see that these works focus almost exclusively on the spiritual path and practice of the various traditions of Buddhism here. Besides Rick Fields' journalistic social history, *How the Swans Came to the Lake: The American Encounter with Buddhism* (Boston: Shambhala Publications, 1992), most other publications treat one or more Buddhist traditions but always emphasize meditation. In the 568-page 1998 book *Buddhism in America: Proceedings of the First Buddhism in America Conference*, edited by Brian Hotchkiss, conference organizer Al Rapaport left no doubt about it. In his introduction (p. xiii) he states, "I envisioned the Buddhism in America Conference as a forum at which modern-day meditation teachers could present, and attendees could experience, the essence of the Buddhist teachings on life, death, compassion, and enlightenment."
4. *Shambhala Sun* vol. 7, no. 2 (November, 1998): 11.
5. "Buddhism and Race: An African American Baptist-Buddhist Perspective" in Dresser, op.cit, p. 81.
6. Ibid., p. 87.
7. That is, Maureen Stuart Roshi, the head of the Cambridge Buddhist Association from the early 1980s until her death in 1991. Information about Stuart Roshi's life can be found in Helen Tworkov's *Zen in America* (San Francisco: North Point Press, 1989), pp. 153–97. Following her death, a series of lectures by Stuart Roshi were collected in the book *Subtle Sound: The Zen Teachings of Maurine Stuart*, ed. Roko Sherry Chayat (Boston: Shambhala Publications, 1996).
8. See Lori Pierce's "Outside In: Buddhism in America, in Dresser, op. cit., pp. 93–104.
9. That is, Rosa Zubizarreta, none other than the member of The Buddhism and Racism Working Group who was quoted in the November 1998 advertisement in *Shambhala Sun* for the one-day Bay Area conference, "Healing Racism in Our Sanghas."

PART IV

Art and Architecture

FROM PERIPHERY TO CENTER:

Tibetan Women's Journey to Sacred Artistry

Melissa Kerin

Introduction

> It is genuine bliss for me [to go] through the process of [creating a sand] *maṇḍala*. When lay people see a finished *maṇḍala*, I feel they...more or less have an idea of the meditative residential mansion of the deities. By creating, I collect the merit, which [is] the stepping stone to the ultimate goal of liberation.
>
> *Yangchen Dolkar, Tibetan Buddhist Nun from the Keydong Thuk-Che-Cho Ling Nunnery of Nepal.*[1]

Yangchen Dolkar's words may seem typical of a Tibetan Buddhist nun who hopes that her meritorious building of sand *maṇḍalas* will both benefit other sentient beings and lead her closer toward the Buddhist goal of liberation. However, her statement takes on new depth and meaning when read with the knowledge that Tibetan Buddhist nuns traditionally have not created sand *maṇḍalas*. Through the course of this paper I will explore the significance of women becoming sacred artists of sand *maṇḍala* and *thangka*, two sacred art forms that have been traditionally practiced by men, monks and lay men alike. My intention is that this essay will not only convey information about the contemporary state of Tibetan women as sacred artists, but will also assist in formulating questions that will guide us in better appreciating and understanding the impact that this change has had on Tibetan Buddhist communities.

My interest in the subject of women as sacred artists began in 1993 when I lived at the sKyid Grong Thugs rJe Chos gLing (Keydong Thuk-Che-Cho Ling) Nunnery[2] in Swayambhu, Nepal, and studied *thangka* painting with an artist, Karma Thubtin, who lived close by. At the time, I shared a room with a nun named Tenzin Sherab who was an aspiring *thangka* painter. During many evenings we spoke

Nuns with the Dalai Lama during the dismantling ritual of the maṇḍala, *Brandeis University, Waltham, MA (photo by Dear Batchelder)*

about her interest in *thangka* painting and the probability of her never receiving proper *thangka* instruction in her life, it being so rare for Tibetan women to study such work. Although Tenzin Sherab thought it nearly impossible to learn *thangka* properly, she continued to draw and show her beautiful renderings of Śākyamuni Buddha and Green Tārā to those who were interested.

A year later, I returned to India and Nepal[3] in order to research the role of Tibetan women as creators of *thangkas* and sand *maṇḍalas*. Returning to the nunnery in November 1994, I found that Tenzin Sherab and another nun were taking *thangka* painting lessons and several nuns had received instructions in making sand *maṇḍala* (they had, in fact, just completed their first sand *maṇḍala* that fall). I spent much of my time at the nunnery observing the progress of both the *thangka* lessons and *maṇḍala* making, trying to better understand what inspired such changes. During this time, the nuns answered my many questions and shared with me the process of and their reflections upon creating these pieces. This paper is the result of research I conducted while in India and Nepal (1994–96) as well as continued research conducted while a graduate student (1996–1999) and during the nuns' visit to the United States (1998).

A Brief Introduction to Sand Maṇḍala (dkyil 'khor) *and* Thangka (thang ka)

When we speak of sacred art in a Tibetan Buddhist context, we are discussing images that are used as vehicles to bring both the creator and the viewer closer to the "divine."[4] These images are not valued for aesthetic or financial reasons, but rather serve as inspirational tools for engaging in the sacred realm of Buddhism, as objects for meditation, for initiations into practices, and as offerings to deities. Because the sacred image not only signifies the divine realm, but is also thought to contain the very essence of the deity, when engaging a sacred image, the practitioner potentially encounters a moment of transformation. Physically positioned in front of a *thangka* or *maṇḍala*—both signifying and embodying the divine—the practitioner is inspired to reflect on the nature of self in relation to the nature of the sacred realm.[5] Ideally, all the processes involved in sacred art—patronizing, creating, and viewing—are, therefore, primarily religious experiences that focus on gaining merit[6] and entering into the divine realm.

The two art forms with which we are concerned are *thangka* painting and sand *maṇḍala* making. *Thangka* is a powerful visual tool usually conveying the image of a deity, bodhisattva, Buddhist teacher, lineage holder, or even a *maṇḍala*. Traditionally, these sacred images are precisely painted on a thin cotton canvas with natural pigments made from stone. Each image is drawn to specific measurements and iconography derived from authoritative Buddhist texts.[7] Given that *thangkas* are often used as meditational tools, they have to be perfectly rendered in order to ensure the integrity and efficacy of the practitioner's meditation.

The *maṇḍala* is an integral symbol and theme permeating all of Tantric Buddhism. The *maṇḍala* form pertinent to this paper is *dkyil 'khor*, a flat or two dimensional circular structure made of brilliantly colored sands that are carefully placed to form intricate and perfect geometric patterns. The Tibetan term *dkyil 'khor*, meaning center and periphery, or circle, appropriately reflects the creative process of the *maṇḍala* itself, for the practitioners start the creation of the sand *maṇḍala* at the center of the *maṇḍala* platform and move outward to the periphery. A sand *maṇḍala*, however, is but one of the multiple forms that *maṇḍala* can assume. As Luis Gomez writes, "A mandala may be produced mentally, drawn temporarily on the ground with colored sand, or represented in permanent form through painting or sculpture."[8] To this I would add that the *maṇḍala* can also be represented by a practitioner's hand gesture or *mudrā* as well as by a small three-dimensional image made from metal disks that are piled with rice or barley into a pyramid-like structure; these last two are referred to as *maṇḍa la*. All *maṇḍalic* forms, despite the physical differences, embody and express the same cosmological and ontological principles. Lokesh Chandra speaks of the *maṇḍala* as that which is "above all, a map of the cosmos. It is the whole universe in its essential plan, in its process of emanation and of reabsorption."[9]

Venerable Tenzin Yignyen, a monk from Namgyal Monastery who has been making sand *maṇḍalas* for over fifteen years, describes sand *maṇḍalas* as having multiple meanings, which unfold contemporaneously. During a conversation we had at Trinity College in Hartford, Connecticut, he said:

> There are many different levels of the *maṇḍala.* On the gross level, *maṇḍala* is a palace or a pure land where the pure beings reside. On another level, *maṇḍala* shows all the [Buddhist] teachings from the start to the end.... The *maṇḍala* [also]...shows the impure elements of our existence.... It also reveals our impure mind, speech, and body.... It shows how we [can] purify the inner and external worlds. And it shows what the result of purification will be.[10]

As Venerable Tenzin Yignyen notes, the *maṇḍala* has the primary purpose of revealing the mental obscurations and impurities while also presenting a method by which to transform these impurities into the positive qualities of an enlightened being. Consequently, the sand *maṇḍala* can be regarded not only as a "map of the cosmos," but also as a map that reveals the way for one to initiate transformative changes affecting the mind and body of a human being.

While I was researching Tibetan sacred art, I was struck by the seeming paucity of Tibetan woman as creators of sacred art such as *thangka* and sand *maṇḍala.* It seemed that the exclusion of Tibetan women from these art practices was not based on written injunctions prohibiting women from becoming sacred artists; rather, their exclusion is more subtle and complex. In fact, Venerable Tenzin Yignyen implied that women had *permission* to make (sand) *maṇḍalas* provided they were given proper initiation. He speculated, however, that they never actually became the creators of sand *maṇḍalas* even with proper initiations because it was not accepted within the cultural and monastic traditions.[11] It seems that women's exclusion occurs on a social level, whereby they are prohibited from creating some types of sacred images while still permitted other forms of participation. An interesting dichotomy surfaces here: Tibetan women have had extensive involvement, in varying degrees, with *thangka* and *maṇḍala,* but their involvement stops at the point of creation. Take the ritual settings, for example. Many nuns routinely go through the process of visualizing *maṇḍalas,* making the "offering *maṇḍa la,*" or hand *mudrā,* during daily meditation practices, but they never, however, created sand *maṇḍalas.* This same dichotomy exists within *thangka* painting: lay women have a certain peripheral involvement with the art form, insofar as they contribute to the process of *thangka* painting by creating the sacred, clean space in which the art is made and sometimes by assisting their husbands in painting the background of the *thangka*, but they rarely, if ever, engage in the creation of the main deity of the *thangka*.[12] In an interview with the late Gega Lama, a well-known *thangka* painter of the Karma sGar Bris (Karma Gadri) tradition, he affirmed that there were women artists and further that women were instrumental in bringing Buddhist sacred art to Tibet in the eighth century.[13] However, although a strong proponent of women's influence in the sphere of sacred art, he was unable to name any sacred women artists. He did, however, mention his wife as being a *thangka* painter. With a smile he said, "I married one." In subsequent conversations, it became clear that Gega Lama's wife assisted in painting the elaborate backgrounds and detail work on her husband's *thangkas*, but did not create the main deities in these *thangkas*.

The Keydong nuns' new role as creators of *thangkas* and sand *maṇḍalas* radically alters this dichotomy; women are no longer left on the periphery, but are now learning the texts and skills necessary to competently and skillfully create these sacred images. Given these changes, we are compelled to ask, What are the ramifications of these practices for Tibetan Buddhist women's relationship to the sacred? Does this radical shift in tradition affect only the women who create these art forms? How, if at all, have the sacred art practices been subsumed within the monastic community of the Keydong Nunnery?

The Import of Sacred Art Praxis for Tibetan Buddhist Nuns

Why were women refused participation in the creation of sacred art forms? To answer this, it is important to bear in mind that the sacred art forms of sand *maṇḍalas* and *thangkas* can be powerful mediums through which a practitioner, as creator and/or viewer, can access important teachings and meditative practices. Hence, Tibetan women, in their new role of sacred artist, are beginning to interact with the sacred realm in very untraditional ways, which require them to be in proximity to and, in certain cases, a conduit for the divine. I postulate that Tibetan Buddhist women's questionable state of purity significantly affects their relationship to the sacred, thereby restricting women to the periphery of the sacred world in general. That is, Tibetan women's complex and multifaceted relationship with the sacred realms (due to their perceived inherent impure state) is at the heart of their exclusion from these sacred art practices. I suggest that women's new involvement in sacred art practice allows women more significant interaction with sacred realms and spaces and consequently alters their socially imposed status of being inherently impure.

As previously mentioned, the exclusion of women from sand *maṇḍala* making and *thangka* painting is not predicated on authoritative or overt statements of prohibition. Even the Dalai Lama stated, during an audience with the Keydong nuns in January 1998, that there was no mention in the Buddhist texts of the Buddha forbidding or discouraging women from creating *maṇḍalas.*[14] Women's exclusion from sacred art practices has rather taken place at a social level.

An example of this is found in the pilgrimage rituals at Tsa Ri, a sacred mountain located in the southeastern part of Tibet. Toni Huber noticed that Tibetan women are thought to have a very complex and difficult relationship with this sacred pilgrimage site.[15] The uppermost region of the mountain is considered to be a *maṇḍala,* the palatial abode of a Tantric deity couple, Cakrasaṃvara and Vajravārāhī. There are three routes around the mountain. The first is the longest and includes women; the middle route is closer to the summit and allows only men; the last circuit, "peak summit," is generally restricted to male monastics, who can perform the correct rituals. This is considered the most dangerous and powerful area of the pilgrimage site because it is the actual seat of the two Tantric deities; it also contains a lake, which is believed to be the collection of the female deity's menstrual blood. Women are denied entry into these last two circuits of the pilgrimage primarily because the summit is considered to be a pure *maṇḍala.* As one monk said,

> Because it is such a pure abode, inside the *maṇḍala* palace [of the mountain], that is why women are not allowed.... They [the mountains] have *maṇḍalas* of the gods and goddesses within them and are supposed to be too pure for women to visit. Wherever there are *maṇḍalas* on the mountain women can't go.[16]

This quotation raises some questions about women and purity: Is the restriction of women at this site intended to protect women from harm, or is it to protect the space from women's impurity? A less ambiguous quotation reinforces the latter: "The only reason is that women are of inferior birth, and impure. There are many powerful *maṇḍalas* on the mountain that are divine and pure, and women are polluting."[17]

But what of the female deity on top of the mountain and her menstrual blood? Why are she and her menstruation considered pure and venerable? The presence and veneration of this menstrual blood reveals yet another dichotomy: the divine female body and bodily fluids are worshipped and yet real women are thought of as impure and polluting. Moreover, women are not allowed to be in proximity to the female deity's residence or her "blood."

Larry Epstein and Peng Wenbin, in their article on a *lurol* ritual in the Amdo region of Tibet, discuss the issue of women's menstrual blood and impurity. This ritual includes dancing, drumming, and singing as well as an offering of blood to the deities by the male elders of the community. They observe that the majority of the roles seem to be performed by men, but unmarried girls participate in several dances. Epstein and Wenbin explain that women who are married or parturient are excluded from participating, although they can watch. "Married women are not allowed to participate in either the *labdze* ritual or the dances because they menstruate. If they did participate, they would pollute the gods and disaster would befall the village."[18] Further, in writing about Tibetan women's mutable and unstable relationship to sacred space, Charlene Makley tells about her Tibetan friend who refused to enter a monastery in Labrang while menstruating. "She explained that there was not any written 'rule' about such taboos, but that it was one way that women could respect the Buddha by staying away from sacred places when unclean."[19]

Although these examples pertain to specific pilgrimages and rituals, the conspicuous exclusion of women sheds light on the restrictions imposed upon women in the practice of sand *maṇḍala* and *thangka.* While the issue of menstruation is complicated and only briefly touched upon here, it seems that it serves as one of the primary reasons Tibetan women are associated with pollution and impurity. Simply put, women cannot be the vehicles or vessels of the pure divine given the perceived polluted nature of their bodies. Yet, paradoxically, their recent practice of sacred art makes them conduits of the divine and places them in what traditionally would have been considered "dangerous" proximity to the divine.

All the materials used in creating *maṇḍalas* and *thangkas* are required to be pure, and several expiatory rituals are performed in order to ensure the sanctity of the materials. For instance, the five primary colors used in both art forms must first be emptied of any negative or harmful elements.[20] And rituals are performed to ensure that the space on which and in which the image is made is free of defilements.[21] The responsibility of purifying the space and ridding the materials of impurities would not be given to those considered innately impure and polluted. Thus, it seems reasonable to surmise that women were not allowed participation on the grounds of the inherent sanctity and purity of the materials, instruments, and rituals employed in the making of *maṇḍalas* and *thangkas.*

Another contributing factor of this complex situation concerns notions of perfection and the insistence upon perfection as an indispensable element of the ritually created images of *thangkas* and *maṇḍalas.* If the artist makes a mistake, he endangers not only himself but also the practitioner using the art object. This point was elucidated during a short interaction I had with a Keydong nun. In 1993, when I started learning *thangka,* a nun leaned over to me in the middle of *pūjā* (prayer ceremony) at the nunnery and said, "You learn *thangka*?" I nodded my head "yes." She shook her head "no" and said, "Dangerous." This short interaction made me realize that these sacred art forms are to be taken very seriously.

Although they have the potential to be extremely meritorious, they can also be very unmeritorious if executed improperly. There are severe ramifications if the artist makes mistakes on any part of the deity, especially the eyes. In his book *Principles of Tibetan Art,* Gega Lama translates (from different Tibetan Buddhist texts) all the punishments for an artist who makes mistakes on measurements. The measurements, which are derived from Buddhist texts, ensure not only the perfect ordering of a perfect, ritualized world, but also the perfection of each sacred image. These artistic renderings need to be flawless in order to adequately convey the perfection of the deities or bodhisattvas depicted. These measurements, therefore, are sacred because they provide a "skeleton," or underlying structure, for the venerable icon.

There is no *one* particular reason why women could not work with measurements. My contention is that it was not appropriate to put the pure and sacred measurements in the hands of those who were considered impure. Further, it is plausible that the inherent risk in creating these art forms made it too dangerous for women, that is, for people who were already in a "low birth" status[22] and, therefore, who could not afford to risk putting this life or their next lives in further jeopardy.

Another key notion underlying our discussion of women's relationship to the sacred concerns how *thangka* and *maṇḍala* function simultaneously not only as offerings to the deity, but also as dwelling places of the deity. Although the *thangka* or *maṇḍala* is meant to serve as a divine house, the essence of the deity resides therein only after the consecration ritual. Yangchen Dolkar mentions in her quotation at the beginning of this article that the *maṇḍala* is the "meditative residential mansion of the deities." Once consecrated, the *thangka* is considered to be the "shadow"[23] of the deity—the very essence of the deity is believed to reside on the canvas. Their creation requires extensive knowledge of the texts, use of consecrated materials and tools, and employment of accurate measurements.

The practice of sacred art radically places Tibetan Buddhist women in direct relation to the sacred sphere. Some would argue, however, that women's involvement in the "patriarchal" sphere of sacred art is, at best, token and not a deeply rooted alteration with significant social implications. From such a perspective this practice could be misinterpreted as women simply seeking to do "men's activities" and, by so doing, making the patriarchal sphere the standard by which their lives and achievements are judged. In talking and interacting with the nuns, however, I discovered that their primary intention for engaging in this praxis is rooted in issues of spiritual advancement and in hopes of cultivating more merit for their nunnery and community. The adoption of these two sacred art practices has resulted in much more than obtaining merit, however. These practices have unequivocally challenged socially constructed notions of Tibetan women's impurity by virtue of the nuns' interaction with the consecrated materials, sacred measurements, and expiatory rituals, all of which allow them a new and vital relationship with the sacred. The new practices have also deepened and expanded the nuns' knowledge of Buddhism, cultivated greater feelings of gratitude in them, developed their sense of capability, and provided them with the opportunities to meet with His Holiness the Dalai Lama and to travel to the West.

The abbess of Keydong, Ani Dolma Younden, regards these sacred art practices as important additions to the nunnery, which have expanded the nuns' knowledge and provided significant merit for the community. As the abbess noted, Keydong nuns, both in Tibet before 1959 and in Nepal, primarily performed *pūjā,* recited prayers, memorized a few texts, and participated in *sMyung gNas,*[24] a fasting retreat. Although these are important activities, the abbess feels that they were limiting. *Maṇḍala* making and *thangka* painting, however, are specific and powerful ways to generate good merit for the nunnery and the community at large. Through the process of creating these sacred images, the nuns are beginning to grasp the complicated concepts of *maṇḍala* and *thangka,* and to ask searching questions about iconography, symbols, and the basic tenets of Buddhism such as impermanence, non-attachment and, ultimately, the Buddhist notion of emptiness. Tenzin Sherab, one of the two *thangka* painters at the nunnery, said that although she is not a *maṇḍala* maker, she feels as though the *maṇḍala* creation at the nunnery has allowed her to visualize the *maṇḍala* clearly in her own meditation. This is one of the purposes of the sand *maṇḍala:* to be a tool with which one betters one's "inner" or visualized *maṇḍala.* Another nun, Ani Ngawang Tendol, who has not learned the art of sand *maṇḍala* but has benefited from its creation at the nunnery, writes:

> Those who receive initiation and have finished the necessary prayers and retreats can learn the art of *maṇḍala.* I have only some knowledge about its teaching and meditational aspects. For instance, before building a *maṇḍala* [the house of the deity], the individuals who are working on [it] must develop the presence of the deity within themselves. At this point, they experience the realization of a subtle mind on a higher level of consciousness in them. It is also believed that even a single, tiny grain from the *maṇḍala* helps gain thousands of virtuous merits and dissolves negativities of previous and present lives.[25]

This description vividly portrays the depth of understanding nuns have come to have in their study of the *maṇḍala.* Tenzin Sherab also said that since studying *thangka,* she has started to ask more questions about the deities she is learning. "Now," she says "I know why the Buddha's right hand touches the earth, why his hair is deep blue, and why he has a jewel on his top knot."[26] Understanding the iconography helps her to understand the nature of these deities and what they represent. Ani Dolma Tsering speaks for many of the nuns when she expresses gratitude for having access to these art forms. "We are so lucky," she said thoughtfully. "This [*maṇḍala* making] is so precious and helps all beings. When we nuns started learning this, I thought, 'How can we do this? It is so difficult and dangerous. If we make any mistakes, our next life is very bad so we must be very careful.'" When I asked her why Tibetan women did not engage in this practice before this point, she said, "I don't know... [but] we are so lucky that we can do this now."[27] Doing such serious and significant practices at auspicious times of the year marks a considerable difference from the kind of work the nuns were doing in Keydong before they were involved in *thangka* and *maṇḍala* making.

The nuns' movement from the periphery to the center of the sacred art world has proven to be extremely beneficial on a number of counts: they have had the chance to deepen their practice and understanding of Buddhism, and to see themselves as serious Buddhist practitioners and in a different relationship to the sacred. Another important development derived from this undertaking is the nuns' increased sense of capability. The nuns perceive themselves as capable agents in transforming their own beings (and others) through this focused and specific merit-making practice. Yangchen Dolkar hints at this very sentiment in her words that open this essay: "By creating *maṇḍalas*, I collect the merit which [is] the stepping stone to the ultimate goal of liberation." This sense of capability has seeped into other areas of their lives as well; nuns are now teaching other nuns the skills of *maṇḍala* and they have traveled to spread their knowledge of the Dharma and these sacred art forms. They are, therefore, functioning as competent sacred artists and effective teachers; this is a significant transition in their duties as nuns and one that deeply affects their sense of self and their role in Tibetan Buddhist society.

Once the nuns learned sand *maṇḍala* and *thangka*, they had the historic opportunity to travel to the United States, where they were invited to create a *maṇḍala* and *thangka* at Trinity College in Hartford, Connecticut. This journey to the West was significant because it was one of, if not the first formal delegation of Tibetan Buddhist nuns to the United States as teachers, meditation instructors, and sacred artists.[28] The nuns created a second *maṇḍala* at Brandeis University, and this marked the first time the Dalai Lama saw a *maṇḍala* created by Tibetan Buddhist nuns. He also participated in the dismantling ritual. The liminal space of the United States, where the religious and cultural traditions of Tibet are not securely in place, seemed like an appropriate place for this radical and nontraditional event to take place.

This was not just a historical moment for the Buddhist tradition, but a very powerful one for the nuns who participated in the dismantling process as well. As the essence of Avalokiteśvara resided in front of them in the *maṇḍala*, the essence of the deity was also present beside them, in the deity's earthly manifestation of His Holiness the Dalai Lama.[29] The nuns stood on either side of His Holiness and in front of the eastern gate of the *maṇḍala* so as to face Avalokiteśvara as they chanted the prayer requesting the deity's departure. His Holiness then commenced the dismantling by picking up the five seed syllables residing on the central lotus. When he finished collecting these syllables, he placed some of the sand on the top of his head and in his mouth, an act that signified that this material was imbued with great power. By virtue of its consumption, the consumer embodies the essence of the deity. He then handed the role of ritual master to Ani Dolma Tsering and stood back to watch as she cut the eight power lines of the *maṇḍala,* thereby collapsing the main pillars of Avalokiteśvara's palace. At the end of the dismantling process, he told the nuns how very proud he was of their work. His response to the *maṇḍala*, and his participation in the dismantling ritual, were extremely important to the nuns because they publicly legitimized and affirmed their work and all their endeavors. Furthermore, this experience was personally transformative for the nuns. Usually, when in the presence of the Dalai Lama, any Tibetan will bow and keep his or her head lower than the Dalai Lama's as a sign of respect. These women could not take on this normative and expected physical behavior because they were performing a significant ritual *with* him.

Their journey to the West was, for both the Westerners involved and the Tibetan nuns themselves, an influential experience not only because of the historical nature of the event, but because of the intimate, memorable, and pivotal interactions that took place between the nuns and Americans. Through the many questions the Westerners asked, the nuns started reassessing their roles as nuns and as sacred artists, and the effect these sacred art practices would have on their Buddhist practice. By answering the questions of American students and practitioners, the nuns have re-viewed their culture, their position as nuns, and their skills. Before the nuns left the U.S., they said they wanted to meet with their *maṇḍala* and *thangka* teachers again to discuss the new questions they now have. Venerable Tenzin Yignyen, a *maṇḍala* maker from Namgyal Monastery, said that this is the ideal way for students to learn the profound significance of the *maṇḍala,* one step at a time. *Maṇḍala* teachers, according to Yignyen, cannot teach the complete meaning of the *maṇḍala*, with all its symbolism and profound meaning, at one time. The depth and dimension of the *maṇḍala* unfolds layer by layer according to the students' interest and perseverance. The student is meant to keep a dialogue running between him- or herself and the teacher, inquiring about the meaning until he or she comes to a profoundly deep understanding of the *maṇḍala.*[30]

The Impetuses for Tibetan Women Becoming Sacred Artists of Maṇḍala and Thangka

Given the traditionally limited role Tibetan women have had in the creation of *thangka* and *maṇḍala*, one wonders what has spawned this significant change within Tibetan Buddhist nuns' practice. In reflecting on this question, an observation of Alan Sponberg's comes to mind: "Buddhist attitudes toward women were shaped, in part at least, in response to the social circumstances of the day."[31] I posit that Tibetan women's participation in sacred art practice has emerged from a matrix of cultural changes and social circumstances developing over the past forty years of exile. This paper isolates three significant and connected factors that have served as the main catalysts for the evolving artistry of women: the liminal state of exile, the increased dialogue between Westerners and Tibetans, and the active role taken by the Keydong nuns themselves.

Tibetan exile has thrown much, if not all, of Tibetan culture, religion, and tradition into a state of flux. The Tibetan communities are now existing in what Victor Turner would call the "betwixt and between" state of liminality.[32] As Turner explains, "liminality is now seen to apply to all phases of decisive cultural change, in which previous orderings of thought and behavior are subject to revision and criticism."[33] This is certainly the case for exiled Tibetan communities living in Western and Asian countries. These exiled peoples are constantly influenced by both Asian and Western sensibilities, cultures, and traditions. As a result, the social codes and traditions of Tibetan culture are changing in order for Tibetans to adapt to their shifting environments, which change, in turn, has provided a space for transition and potentiality.[34] One result is a change in social roles. The old social and cultural codes regarding gender have changed radically, thereby creating possibilities that heretofore were not available to Tibetan women. Such possibilities include academic scholarships to Western institutions, fewer arranged marriages, establishment of women's organizations such as the Tibetan Women's Association, and the involvement of Tibetan Buddhist nuns in such practices as philosophical debate, religious dance, fire sacrifice, and sacred art. I suggest that the state of exile is the basic underpinning of the progressive shifts in Tibetan women's involvement in religious activities, and that without exile there would be fewer, if any, of these radical changes.[35] I also suggest that there is a concomitant resistance to this structureless, liminal state among members of exiled Tibetan communities, a resistance that comes in the form of reestablishing traditional religious and cultural practices, with an emphasis upon such traditional Tibetan Buddhist activities as *maṇḍala* making and *thangka* painting. Thus, the liminality of the exile experience combines in a unique way with a basic concern for cultural survival to make these practices accessible now for women.

Ani Tenzin Sherab painting a thangka, *Bodha, Nepal (photo by Kanga Namgyal)*

Although the liminal space of exile contributes to the potential for change, it does not, however, create change itself. This leads us to the second factor, the growing interaction between Westerners and Tibetans since exile. The dialogue between Westerners and Tibetans has become a very fertile place for the exchange of ideas about religion, art, and tradition—and even nontraditional ideas about gender roles. In fact, it played a central role in the nuns' learning *maṇḍala* and *thangka* painting. The Dzongar monks of South India, from whom the nuns learned sand *maṇḍala* making, traveled extensively through Europe in the early 1990s, sharing Buddhist teachings and making sand *maṇḍalas.* During several visits to the West, the monks encountered the same question from Westerners, "Do women also create sand *maṇḍalas*?" The monks explained that, to their knowledge, women did not create sand *maṇḍalas.* This comment was always followed by the insistent "Why?" from Westerners. Unable to provide satisfying answers, the monks became sensitive to the obvious absence of Tibetan women as *maṇḍala* makers and raised this issue with their abbot. It was at this same time that the elder nuns from Keydong approached the Dzonkar monks about the prospect of having their young nuns learn different Buddhist practices to enhance and deepen their knowledge of Buddhism. The Dzongar monks' concern over the lack of women *maṇḍala* makers, prompted by their contact with Westerners, together with the nuns' interest in expanding their practice resulted in the nuns learning to create sand *maṇḍala.*

The physical location of the nunnery also has bearing on the interaction between

Westerners and Tibetans. The nunnery is located off a main thoroughfare that circles the Kathmandu Valley, making it easily accessible to visitors. Perhaps because of its accessibility, this nunnery has had a host of Westerners affiliated with it since it was first established in Swayambhu in the 1980s. This exposure has not only opened the nuns to different ideas and possibilities, but has also affected Westerners. When I lived with Ani Tenzin Sherab in 1993, an important exchange of ideas took place between us. I came to realize, for example, how few women sacred artists there were and, as a result, spent significant time in subsequent years studying women's relationship to sacred art. As for Tenzin Sherab, perhaps she felt her interest in *thankga* painting was validated, and not an impossibility. Tenzin Sherab continued to draw and show her work to people, and was thus prepared when a woman from Switzerland saw her drawings and decided to sponsor *thankga* painting lessons for her.

Last, and most essential, is the nuns' role in establishing this change in tradition. The decision for the nuns' radical change of practice came after several conversations the elder nuns had amongst themselves regarding ways to expand the nunnery's educational opportunities and religious practices. These conversations led to their initial contact with Dzongar Monastery and the beginning of the nuns learning sand *maṇḍala.* Shortly after the nuns began studying *maṇḍala,* several of the younger nuns between the ages of ten and twelve enrolled in grammar school. The nuns, with their shaved heads, would don their school uniforms and learn basic math, English, and history during the day, and return to the nunnery to take up their red robes and monastic duties in the evening. Although untraditional because it placed nuns in proximity to the laity on a daily basis, this practice of secular education for younger nuns was instigated by the elder nuns who felt it was necessary to have some of their younger nuns learn these basic skills.

The elder nuns support all the nunnery's new endeavors and feel that the nunnery's undertakings represent less a radical shift in Tibetan gender paradigms than an opportunity for the nuns to expand their learning and religious practice as well as to bring great merit to their institution and to the immediate lay community.[36] The nuns are not advocating that all nuns implement these radical changes within their monastic structure. Such a sudden transition, without clear and meaningful circumstances particular to the institution, would be suspicious and superficial. The Keydong Nunnery's shift from the periphery of the sacred art world to its center grew out of a firm foundation in rituals central to this nunnery's practice. Moreover, many Keydong nuns have had ongoing curiosity about traditional art. Thus, the Keydong nuns' involvement in sacred artistry was particular to them, for it grew out of an already existing context particular to the community of their nunnery.

The three catalysts—liminality, Tibetan and Western interaction, and the nuns' willingness to transform tradition—have worked together to set a significant change in motion. But we are now in the position to ask, What has been the impact on and the response from within the Tibetan communities? What does women's creation of sacred art mean in terms of the nuns' present-day standing within Tibetan communities?

Conclusion

It is evident that these changes in practice have been beneficial for the nuns, but one is left asking how these changes have affected the larger Tibetan Buddhist communities. In investigating this question I draw upon Arnold van Gennep's classic anthropological paradigm of the tripartite structure of the ritual agent's rite of passage: the separation (pre-liminal) from the societal framework, the journey to the margin (liminal), a place without specific social structure, and lastly the return home, back to the community (post-liminal). This paradigm serves as a window through which one can view and understand the social implications of the nuns' transition.[37] Thus far, this essay has considered the first two states of the nuns' journey; their pre-liminal state was the societal preconceptions and social conditions that precluded women from fully creating *thangka* and sand *maṇḍalas.* In next analyzing the liminal state I explored the nuns' journey toward becoming sacred artists and the impact this journey has had on their lives.

Anthropologist Victor Turner explains the third element of van Gennep's tripartite structure—the post-liminal state, the time of re-entry into the community—in the following way:

> In the third phase (reaggregation or reincorporation), the passage is consummated. The ritual subject, individual or corporate, is in a relatively stable state once more and, by virtue of this, has rights and obligations vis-à-vis others of a clearly defined and "structural" type; he is expected to behave in accordance with certain customary norms and ethical standards binding on incumbents of social position in a system of such positions.[38]

In returning "home" to the community—after having developed skills in and knowledge of sacred art—the nuns cannot not simply return to the status quo and behave according to established social customs. Such an expectation would imply that these changes are happening in isolation and do not impact the community. I suggest that the "customary norms and ethical standards" that are expected to reify certain social patterns of interaction are indeed altered because of the reciprocal relationship between community and individual(s). After performing these rituals and undertaking these practices, these nuns are perceived in a different light within the community, and as a result their relationship with society changes.

Tenzin Dagyon, a young Tibetan woman who graduated with a B.A. in English Literature at New Delhi University, exclaimed that she has a physical reaction when she sees these women in formal ritual costume performing dances and rituals that she solely associates with monks. "It is just something that we Tibetans have not seen before. I think it is quite good that they are doing these things...but it is still shocking. I am taken aback every time."[39] Tenzin thinks that these practices and this exposure will help the nuns' practice as well as their image within the Tibetan communities. Tenzin feels it is important that Tibetans have the chance to see these women acting in such powerful and new ways. The Tibetan community will not associate them with just prayers and *pūjās*, but will perceive them as serious practitioners.

Tenzin's reaction is positive, yet there have been other mixed responses. I have heard murmurs of discontent from people of the Tibetan lay and monastic communities saying that the nuns are engaged in a practice that they could not possibly understand. In general, it seems Tibetans are surprised at these drastic changes and may not know how to incorporate them into their own practice or how to respond to them. One is left asking how interested and supportive is the lay Tibetan community regarding women's work as sacred artists? Ideally, the changes need to be accepted and supported by the Tibetan community. There have to be people willing to commission these nuns to make *thangkas*. Will the Tibetan community support the *thangka*- and *maṇḍala*-making endeavors through donations, commission, or in other ways? Will Tibetans treat the finished *maṇḍala* and *thangka* as the container of the divine deity?

These questions point to areas of potential social change and development and thus iterate that one of the greatest impact of the nuns' transition into sacred artistry lies in their return to the collective. It is here, in the nuns' re-entry into society, that the potential for creating ripples of change within the structure of Tibetan Buddhist society lies. This subtle and yet essential "call and response" between these communities (the women's monastic community and the larger Tibetan Buddhist community) propels these vital social changes forward. Although we are left with several unanswered questions and while the full social ramifications remain to be seen, this whole journey to the "center" suggests that social change is on the horizon.

Notes

1. Quoted in *The Nuns' Circle: Global Re-Visioning of Women in Sacred Practice,* compiled by Ellison Banks Findly, Trinity College, Hartford, Connecticut.
2. This paper centers on a nunnery of the Gelug sect. The Keydong Nunnery was originally established as a Kagyu nunnery nearly 130 years ago in southeastern Tibet by a Bhutanese lama named Drukpa Lama Sherab Dorge. It became part of the Gelug lineage during the Thirteenth Dalai Lama's lifetime.
3. These sixteen months' of study were made possible by a fellowship from the Thomas J. Watson Foundation.
4. Giuseppe Tucci and Gega Lama express similar ideas about the artist as vehicle for the divine in their respective works, *Tibetan Painted Scrolls* (Bangkok: SDI Publications, 1999) and *The Principles of Tibetan Art: Illustrations and Explanations of Buddhist Iconography and Iconometry According to the Karma Gardri School* (Darjeeling, India: Jamyang Singe, 1983).
5. In a course on Buddhist ethics, Professor Charles Hallisey discussed the important work of philosopher Emmanuel Levinas and his notion of the ethical moment, a time when one is faced with a moment (usually in the encounter with the Other) that challenges the understanding of one's very existence. Sacred art can be such a tool for reflection of this kind; granted, this profound transformation does not happen regularly in relation to sacred art, but the potential is there.
6. The notion of gaining merit is an important one in Buddhism. Kim Gutschow writes in her essay "Unfocused Merit-Making in Zangskar," "Buddhism continually urges its adherents to increase their store of merit, because innumerable sins are committed (and have been committed) without one's conscious knowledge" (in *The Tibet Journal,* p. 46).
7. When discussing terms such as "Tibetan sacred art," "artist," "viewer," and cathartic "artistic experience," care must be taken to avoid the trappings of Western exoticism regarding Tibetan sacred art. Here, it would be helpful to turn to Donald Lopez's thought-provoking book *Prisoners of Shangri La,* and specifically his chapter on Tibetan art. He has carefully explicated the way in which Tibetan sacred images have been overlooked in the world of art history, and how those who have shed light on Tibetan Buddhist art have tended to do so in a romanticized manner. It is important to note that *thangkas* today are not created with meticulous attention to the ritual process.
8. Luis Gomez and Hiram W. Woodward, Jr., *Barabudur: History and Significance of a Buddhist Monument* (Berkeley: The Regents of the University of California, 1981), p. 238.
9. Lokesh Chandra, *Tibetan Mandalas* (New Delhi: Crescent Printing Works, 1995), p. 9.
10. Venerable Tenzin Yignyen, interview, March 21, 1998, Hartford, Connecticut.
11. Venerable Tenzin Yignyen, interview, March 21, 1998, Hartford, Connecticut.
12. These observations were made only in India and Nepal, and therefore I cannot speak about women's developing roles as sacred artists in Tibet.

13. He is referring to the critical role that the Nepali and Chinese princesses—who were betrothed to the Tibetan king Song Tsen Gampo—played in bringing the first pieces of Buddhist art to Tibet. Gega Lama, interview, winter, 1994, Bodha, Nepal.
14. Audience with the Dalai Lama, Dharamsala, India, January 13, 1998.
15. Toni Huber, "Why Can't Women Climb Pure Crystal Mountain? Remarks on Gender, Ritual, and Space at Tsa Ri" in *Tibetan Studies: Proceedings of the Sixth Seminar of the I.A.T.S.*, edited by P. Kvaerne (Oslo: Institute for Comparative Research in Human Culture, 1994), pp. 350–71.
16. Ibid., p. 356.
17. Ibid.
18. Larry Epstein and Peng Wenbin, "Ritual, Ethnicity, and Generational Identity" in *Buddhism in Contemporary Tibet Religious Revival and Cultural Identity*, ed. M.C. Goldstein and M.T. Kapstein (Berkeley: University of California Press, 1998), p. 134.
19. Charlene E. Makley, "Gendered Practices and the Inner Sanctum: The Reconstruction of Tibetan Sacred Space in 'China's Tibet,'" *The Tibet Journal* 19, no. 2 (summer 1994): 82.
20. This ritual is no longer performed as often in *thangka*, but it is still performed for *maṇḍala* by the nuns.
21. It is worthwhile to note that these sanctified materials are vastly different from the materials used by women in creating butter sculptures and *torma*, which come from the domestic sphere, such as barley flour, butter, water, and wax (and sometimes a pigment of oil or poster paint). These materials are not consecrated but they are still thought to be "pure" since they are offerings to the deity. The main difference, however, is that these art forms do not contain the deity while sand *maṇḍala* and *thangka* do. Furthermore, they do not require special tools; they are made entirely by the hands of the practitioner. Sand *maṇḍala* and *thangka*, however, require pure or consecrated substances, special instruments, tools, ceremonies, and ritualized movements with which to make them.
22. This is derived from Barbara Aziz's study of the popular Tibetan word for women: *sKye dMan*, which is translated as "born low."
23. This statement is from Sakya Ksorchen Tulku, a *thangka* painter based in Bodha, Nepal. I am aware that in some sense it may be idolatrous to refer to art as being merely a shadow of the deity, representing, therefore, a distorted and fallible image. Here, it was intended in a positive manner.
24. This austere fasting ritual has been and continues to be a very important practice to this nunnery. The abbess has participated in it scores of times, her longest retreat lasting over two years. Even now, it is common to visit the nunnery and find that several of the nuns have initiated their own *sMyung gNas* retreat, some extending for as long as 108 days. This practice is said to have originated from a fully ordained nun by the name of Gey Lungma Palmo (dGe sLong ma dPal Mo) in the tenth or eleventh century. Given the importance of this practice to this nunnery, it is not surprising that they learned to create the *maṇḍala* of compassion that is used in *the sMyung gNas* practice.

25. Venerable Ani Ngawang Tendol, 1997, written correspondence.
26. Venerable Ani Tenzin Sherab, interview, spring 1998, Hartford, Connecticut.
27. Venerable Ani Dolma Tsering, interview, spring 1995, Swayambhu, Nepal.
28. I know that the Kopan nuns traveled to Europe in 1997 to create a sand *maṇḍala*. It is fairly certain that these nuns also learned sand *maṇḍala* in either 1993 or 1994. I have also heard that several other nunneries in Dharamsala have learned this art form in recent years.
29. To have the essence of a deity manifest in several places at once is reminiscent of what Diana Eck calls the "multiplicity of god" in her book *Encountering God: A Spiritual Journey from Bozeman to Banares* (Boston: Beacon Press, 1993). God, and in this case Avalokiteśvara, can be in more than one place at one time, with no incongruity perceived by the adherent.
30. Venerable Tenzin Yignyen, interview, March, 1998, Hartford, Connecticut.
31. Alan Sponberg, "Attitudes toward Women and the Feminine in Early Buddhism" in *Buddhism, Sexuality, and Gender,* ed. Jose Cabezon (New York: State University of New York), p. 4.
32. Victor Turner, *Image and Pilgrimage in Christian Culture* (New York: Columbia University Press, 1978), p. 2.
33. Ibid, p. 3.
34. It is important to note that there are most likely differences in the amount of change occurring for Tibetans in Tibet as opposed to Tibetans in exile. There are obviously many different factors with which each community has to contend.
35. This is based on several interviews I had with the senior Keydong nuns in February 1998.
36. Tenzin Dagyon, interview, June 1998, Somerville, MA.
37. The possibility of using this anthropological paradigm came out of a conversation with a fellow Divinity School student, Dennis Hargiss. I was deeply inspired by the many conversations Dennis, Amelia Perkins (another fellow student), and I have had regarding the import of reciprocity between the ritual agent and the community.
38. Victor Turner, *The Ritual Process: Structure and Anti-Structure* (New York: Aldine, 1982), p. 95.
39. Tenzin Daygyon, interview, June 1998, Somerville, MA.

PERFORMING *MAṆḌALAS:*

Buddhist Practice in Transition

Judy Dworin

His Holiness the Dalai Lama, in talking about religious practice in his autobiography, *Freedom in Exile*, says,

> It is not sufficient for religious people to be involved with prayer. Rather they are morally obliged to contribute all they can in solving the world's problems.... For what is religion? As far as I am concerned, any deed done with good motivation is a religious act. On the other hand, a gathering of people in a temple or church who do not have good motivation are not performing a religious act when they pray together.[1]

What His Holiness is describing is a spiritual and moral consciousness in which we take responsibility not only for ourselves but for how we affect other beings and the earth. And many of the basic tenets of Buddhism, such as nonattachment, the transitory nature of life, the interconnectedness of all beings, karma and reincarnation, support this viewpoint. These ideas resonate in different forms in other traditions such as Native American spirituality and Taoist thought.

Buddhism's fundamental spiritual and moral consciousness and basic tenets offer a critical message to our survival as a world civilization. As a creative artist committed to making art that speaks to issues of our contemporary culture and celebrates a spirituality that can be expressed through performance, I feel a distinct connection with these Buddhist ideals. And it is with this in mind that I embarked on two diverse creative projects that had, at their foundation, these important Buddhist values. Several questions arose for me in this process: Can ideas be translated from a culturally specific context to encompass a more universal meaning while still retaining their cultural origins and identity? Can contemporary performance be an effective vehicle for such a translation? And how can performance be integrated into educational settings to communicate more effectively important cross-cultural understandings and to reinfuse a spiritual consciousness into the learning process?

In this paper I will discuss these questions as I describe the process of creating two works: *Wheel*, a large-scale dance-theater piece developed for an international performance weekend celebrating the creation of a *maṇḍala* of compassion by seven Tibetan nuns; and *Moving Maṇḍala*, a community-based performance piece involving 150 school children, my performance ensemble, an African-American a cappella group, a percussionist, and the seven Tibetan nuns.

In February of 1998, seven Tibetan nuns from Keydong Thuk-Che-Cho Ling Nunnery in Kathmandu, Nepal, arrived at Trinity College in Hartford where they were invited to create an Avalokiteśvara *maṇḍala* of compassion that same spring. These nuns, among the first women monastics ever to learn the sacred art practice of *maṇḍala*, were, for the first time, sharing this process outside of their home environment and with a largely Western audience. It was this sacred art symbol of the *maṇḍala*, contextualized in this historic moment in women's spirituality, that inspired my work on these two performance projects. Each project, in its own way, took the traditional Tibetan Buddhist sacred art process of *maṇḍala* and attempted to communicate its values in a contemporary, cross-cultural performance setting.

The process of creating a sand *maṇḍala* is an act of spiritual transformation. The viewer, if open to the experience, enters a meditative world, confronting personal and cosmological demons and moving beyond them. The *maṇḍala* is both microcosm and macrocosm and includes the individual and the universe in its transformative power. As Philip Rawson, in his discussion of sacred Buddhist art, states, "The many varied icons represented in Tibetan art are not meant to depict separate objective or imaginary human-shaped beings, or even particular spirit-beings, but states of being which the human viewer is meant inwardly to adopt."[2]

Performance in and of itself is a fitting medium through which to communicate the symbolic nature and essence of the *maṇḍala*. One of the key concepts that the *maṇḍala* teaches is the ephemerality of life: once this intricately detailed sacred art manifestation is completed, it is dismantled, and the sand is offered back to the earth. Performance too is transitory. The moment of performance happens and in an instant it is gone. Both the performer and the audience experience a lesson in nonattachment. Just as the *maṇḍala*, once created, is destroyed, the moment of performance vanishes. One cannot hold onto either experience, and this is the lesson.

As I began to work on the idea of translating the essence of the *maṇḍala* into performance, I researched its significance in terms of Tibetan Buddhist culture particularly and other cultures comparatively. In terms of the Tibetan Buddhist tradition, the sand *maṇḍala* houses important and powerful deities. They are "temporary dwellings for divine principles"[3]—created to represent diagramatically the cosmic order as it emanates out from the center in a coherent network of interconnections and interrelationships.[4] The *maṇḍala* is a fleeting symbol, which encourages and supports a meditative process of envisioning what the physical *maṇḍala* represents. Its intricate designs and iconography all have specific and layered cultural meanings. They trigger a meditative journey in both the creator and the viewer. The *maṇḍala* is a visual metaphor for the path to enlightenment. As Robert Thurman suggests,

> In Buddhist usage, a *maṇḍala* is a matrix or model of a perfected universe, the nurturing environment of the perfected self in ecstatic interconnection with perfected others. It is a blueprint for buddhahood conceived as attainment not only of an individual's ultimate liberation and supreme bliss, but also an attainment of such release and bliss *by an individual fully integrated with his or her environment and field of associates.*[5]

As I investigated the specific meanings of the iconography of the *maṇḍala,* I began to grapple with the problem of presenting its meaning in a context that would be relevant and accessible to a Western audience. In this regard Chögyam Trungpa's writings were enormously instructive and helpful. As I read his book *Orderly Chaos: The Mandala Principle,* I began to envision the piece as a portrayal of the *saṃsāric* condition into which Buddhists believe humans are born. I imagined people traveling through a land of shadows, being confronted with, stymied by, and sometimes able to pass through ignorance and confusion to reach a clearer vision. I saw this journey as a wheel, the Buddhist wheel of existence perhaps—a circular path, a *maṇḍala.* As Chögyam Trungpa states,

> Liberation and confusion are seen in terms of a *maṇḍala* pattern, but in that *maṇḍala* pattern, realization and confusion are still interdependent, still conditioned. Therefore, even freedom or spaciousness or goodness is also part of the saṃsāric *maṇḍala,* along with a wickedness (or whatever you want to call it). So we are not discussing a war between *saṃsāra* and *nirvāṇa* and considering how one of them could defeat or overcome the other. We are discussing the environment in which the energy of those two can exist and maintain itself. We are talking about the energy that gives birth and brings death at the same time, that totality on its own absolute level without watcher and without observer.[6]

I chose the emotional states associated with the *saṃsāric* condition—ignorance, aggression, pride, passion, and jealousy—to be the focus of the first part of this *maṇḍalic* journey. These are the temptations, the lure to attachment, which bind us to our ignorance. I saw the four principal performers in this piece as travelers through *saṃsāra*, passing through and utilizing their experience to reach a clearer vision, a sense of freedom, focus, and insight. From this focus on the personal, my intention was to suggest the universal, just as the body can be a map for the cosmos in Buddhist thought.

I chose several selections of reading to share with the ensemble of performers.[7] When I create work with my ensemble, we engage in a process of exploration and collaboration based on ideas, structures, and images that emerge from my initial visions for the work. It is a collaborative dialogue, a democratic forum in which the performers' identification and ability to play with the material at hand becomes critical to the way the piece evolves. In this case, because some of the initial reading about the *maṇḍala* was specific to Tibetan Buddhist iconography, the performers felt stymied. However, as we explored the *saṃsāric* condition, that is, the environmental and emotional field from which humans emanate and evolve, we began to make progress. The notion of *saṃsāra* as a state of ignorance and confusion was something with which each ensemble member could identify. A formative image for the piece emerged at this time when one of the performers simply closed her eyes and began to cautiously make her path through the space in the midst of the sighted movers in her way. This became a metaphor for *saṃsāra*—the blindness with which we approach life—that can evolve into clear vision and freedom with an adherence to method, meditation, and disciplined practice.

Spatial considerations for this piece were also critical in its evolution. The Avalokiteśvara *maṇḍala* has a center point and two axes that divide it into quadrants representing the four directions: east, south, west, and north. At each direction there is an entrance gate and a specific color associated with the direction itself. The east is blue, the south is yellow, the west is white, the north is green, and the center is red. I wanted in some way to integrate the spatial integrity of the *maṇḍala* with the design created on stage.

The piece was to be performed on a proscenium stage with the audience facing the stage. But this frontal focus seemed antithetical to the circularity of the *maṇḍala*/wheel concept. I began to include the entire hall as potential performance space so that the audience could have a sense of total immersion in the *saṃsāric* world being created and the eventual evolution out of it. Also, the use of the entire hall was an attempt to create circularity in a rectangular space.

The world of *saṃsāra* was created on stage with a grouping of panels made of cotton netting fabric. Each panel was approximately four feet wide and was with two layers of fabric from floor to ceiling, with three panels side by side in a row, and two panels in front. The five panels presented a metaphor for the five *saṃsāric* conditions. Panel no. 2 was the entrance point to the larger *maṇḍalic* universe.

The horizontal arrangement of the fabric was chosen in part to indicate the boundaries that *saṃsāra* presents; the circularity of the piece was created by the performers' movements—energy, or trace lines that disappeared at the moment they occurred. Just as the physical aspect of the *maṇḍala* disappears after it is made, so did the currents of the performers' energy.

In addition to the core members of the ensemble, I invited Korean shaman/artist Hi-ah Park to join the piece along with four ethnically diverse women's singing groups and solo vocalists. Hi-ah's role in the piece was to introduce the other side of *saṃsāra*—to invite the possibility of clear vision and insight at the opening and conclusion of the piece. She was the shamanic connection—the conduit between the spirit world and the mundane world, suggesting also Tibetan Buddhism's earliest roots in Bön-po shamanism. As Philip Rawson points out:

> Like other archaic peoples, the pre-Buddhist Tibetans interpreted the forces of the outer world in terms of their own spiritual life-energy. They saw the objects of nature—trees, rocks, mountains, lakes—not as inert but animate, and interpreted them as manifesting spirits of their own far more powerful than humans and capable of destroying them totally.... When Buddhism came to Tibet shamanic rituals did not vanish, though their bloody sacrifices were interpreted as metaphorical. Buddhist monks and nuns took over many of the shaman's rites, myths, and symbolisms, and adapted them to Buddhist ideas.[8]

Hi-ah Park's role in the piece was the shaman's role: healer of both the individual and the community—artist and spiritual messenger working to help the community and its inhabitants move to a more beneficial place.

The four women's singing groups were selected to represent the multiculturalism of the earth and its womanhood. They were Ulali, a Native American a cappella singing group; Women of the Cross, an African-American gospel group; Rozmarin, an Eastern European trio; and Dadon, an internationally known Tibetan rock singer. Both the context in which this piece was performed, a weekend celebrating the feminine sacred, and my own personal commitment to giving voice to women's spirituality, influenced the choice of these all-women groups. The singers introduced not only the confusion and dissonance, but also the particular sense of disconnection among women of this world: the feminine voice, the wisdom keepers of the *maṇḍala* displaced, struggling to be heard, and voicing the pain. My own role in the piece, along with composer/percussionist Ed Fast, was to give further voice, by way of my own singing, to the unfolding of *saṃsāra* throughout the course of the piece.

The nuns' participation in *Wheel* was a significant contribution and was pivotal to rooting it in its Tibetan Buddhist context. I invited the nuns (all between the ages of nineteen and twenty-four) to participate in the piece while they were still in Kathmandu. At the time they expressed their willingness to do so, but I knew the real test would be when they came to the States and actually saw the work. It was only then that they could ascertain whether it resonated with their own values and beliefs.

Although they had never seen modern dance and had not been exposed to Western presentations of Buddhist ideas in a performance medium, the nuns were both responsive to the direction the piece was going in and agreeable to having a role in it. This was the most positive confirmation I could have of the potential of the piece for cross-cultural communication. Throughout their entire stay I was continually impressed with the nuns' openness to new forms, ideas, and ways of doing things. At the same time they continuously demonstrated a clarity of purpose and vision in themselves as Tibetan Buddhist monastics; they were also able to engage fully in new experiences and relate them to their own belief system.

The following is a description of *Wheel* as it was performed on March 13 and 14, 1998:

> The piece opens with one of the nuns going to center stage and lighting a butter lamp and some incense. In the darkness of that one candle the voices of *saṃsāra*—callings by the four women's singing groups—are heard from various parts of the audience space. As their dissonant calls diminish, the nuns are heard chanting. Their chant is a prayer that invites the Buddha into the space.
>
> On stage a blue light fades up showing four panels of cloth. The fifth panel, the east gate (panel #2), is raised, leaving an opening through which to pass. Shaman artist Hi-ah Park enters through this opening, picks up the incense and butter lamp, and performs an invocation to the four directions. She is accompanied by the nuns' chanting as well as the sounding of their horns, bells, and drum. She exits through the opening, and as she does the fifth panel descends...the world of saṃsāra is before us.
>
> The four performers appear from the wings. They are shadow figures in a land of shadows—they become larger than life, then diminish in size. Sometimes we see only legs or heads, sometimes full bodies. They embody ignorance, the birth state of all humans. They are distortions of the clear path. The images crescendo in rhythm and synchrony—all of a sudden the bodies behind the panels emerge in a blast of light. They look at each other—suspiciously, curiously—separate, there is no sense of community, commonality.

"Pride" (photo by Damyan Popchristov)

The focus turns to one of the four performers—the sole male in the group (Sean Maloney). He starts to push at the downstage left panel (#5). His pushing gets more frenetic and aggressive: he uses his head, his legs, his full body to push against, to force, to dominate. He becomes the epitome of aggression as the tension and action in his body builds. Suddenly his attention is diverted from the panel to a woman facing him at the east gate (K.C. Chun). They back off stage from each other and then wind themselves into cocoon-like shapes in panels #1 and #3.

The next section begins with another performer (Debbie Goffe) lying downstage of panel #4. A small vibration goes through her body. The vibration builds as she discovers panel #3. The vibration can be seen as a shudder or as the burst of some undefined energy. She clings to the panel—tries to wrap herself in it to resemble the cocoon-like shapes that surround her. She doesn't fit however—she can't find a comfortable place. She travels through the space as though with a sense of ownership—the excessive pride of someone who is really, underneath it all, afraid.[9]

She tries to enter the east gate (panel #2) but with no success. She stumbles into one of the other performers (Lisa Matias Serrambana) who is tentatively unwrapping herself and reaching out to her. She cannot accept this gesture, and the section ends with a faceoff as she pushes the other dancer out, claiming the space as her domain—a domain shadowed by her own fear.

The next section examines passion as the two remaining dancers (one male, one female—Sean Maloney and K.C. Chun) cocooned in their panels slowly unwrap themselves. The woman, accompanied by sounds of female laughter that is sometimes giddy, sometimes sensual, sometimes hysterical, explores the panels rapturously in numerous ways: as clothing, adornments, possessions. There is an atmosphere of acquisitiveness as the male observes her, then eventually grabs the panel she is playing with. A game of domination takes place—he is physically stronger than she, but she is wily and seductive, using her powers to possess him as well. Finally he becomes a partner in this game, and the section ends with her gathering all of the panels in her arms as he lifts her and she lifts them to the sky. It is the ultimate possessiveness—phallic in its imagery as both male and female are in partnership in the upsurge of energy that takes place.

The piece next explores jealousy. The male enters with another dancer (Lisa Matias Serrambana). She is pregnant (actually eight-months pregnant during the run of the piece). Her very real pregnant state lends a vulnerability to this moment as she is seen traveling with her male partner, and also challenges the cultural stereotypes of the appropriateness of a pregnant woman dancing onstage. However, his gaze wanders as they move together through the space, and he connects with another dancer (K.C. Chun) to whom he is drawn. They move behind one of the panels and sensuously embrace each other. Their movements become more passionate and involved as the pregnant woman looks on as if through a window at this overt infidelity. She runs back and forth towards the panel with increasing freneticism and finally returns to her own panel (#5)—moving through her pain and gradually soothing herself with a softer swinging of the panel in rhythm with her body motion.

Thus, the piece paints fleeting portraits of the saṃsāric conditions that humans experience in life and can sometimes move through. The panels and the dancers' manipulation of them help to illustrate this sense of attachment to suffering as the dancers physically attach themselves and detach themselves from them in their interactions. The lights designed by Blu and the musical score composed by Ed Fast with vocals by me all work integrally to support the *saṃsāric* environment and the journey towards some higher dimension.

The next section is the emergence from this *saṃsāric* condition to find a directed path leading to clearer vision. The male dancer becomes the fulcrum to which two of the female dancers connect. They roll in a clockwise circle on the floor, creating a crescendo of energy, which raises them up to a standing and circling position while the pregnant woman circles upstage with the fabric of the east gate panel. There is a sense of freedom, of release, as the four dancers begin to circle in the space moving through the world of *saṃsāra*, moving along the wheel of life.

Shaman Hi-ah Park appears at the east gate. She takes a wide, low stance and, one after the other, two female dancers emerge, as though being born from her. They roll out and roll over each other in a synchronous rhythm of folding and unfolding as Hi-ah leaves the stage. There is a sense of harmony, synergy, but it is not sweet—rather it is a directed sense of connection, a flow of energy.[10]

As the two dancers leave the space, the pregnant woman and the male dancer again meet. There is a connection as their bodies merge. It is the joining of male and female energies—the male compassionate method or means joins with the female wisdom and intuitive power. They are seen inside the downstage right panel (#5, the home panel of the pregnant woman), the male and female energy now joined at the immanence of birth.

There is a rainbow of light cast on each panel as the four dancers each pass through a panel and then begin to circle throughout the entire space, creating fleeting *maṇḍalic* designs of interweaving circular energy. As the dancers run through the space they are joined by the four women's singing groups who travel from their positions in the audience to the stage singing harmonious vocalizations as they move.

Hi-ah Park appears a third time. As she does the east gate opens, and the panel disappears out of view. As Hi-ah enters, each dancer finds her place in front of a panel. One after the other the panels drop down to the floor, and the dancers drop to their knees in a posture of humility and meditation. Meditation in Buddhist philosophy is the method, the way out of *saṃsāra* indicated here by the dancers' kneeling position as the physical reality of the *saṃsāric maṇḍala* disappears. Just as the sand *maṇḍala* is dismantled, so too this dismantling on the stage reinforces the idea of the transitory nature of all things and the importance of nonattachment and adherence to method.

Hi-ah Park moves downstage to a circle of light—the sacred center of the *maṇḍala.* The nuns begin to chant again; this time it is a prayer in which they present incense and other sacred offerings to the Buddha and ask him to keep us from *saṃsāra,* the world of ignorance. Hi-ah spins and spins in the center of the light—the wisdom center, the other side of ignorance, the moment of insight and clarity. She stops, and with arms uplifted to the heavens the light slowly fades as the nuns finish their chanted prayer.

Wheel is a vehicle through which basic tenets of Buddhism are portrayed, contextualized universally and cross-culturally. The joining of the women's singing groups with the dancers, the seven nuns, the composer, and myself, speaks to the interconnection of all beings in the world and to the possibility of insight and clarity. Dialogues with the audience following each performance indicated that people were both moved and reflective. Individuals could place their own experiences into the visual imagery that was portrayed—it was personal and also went beyond the merely personal.

Hi-ah's presence in the piece suggested both the notion of the performer as shaman and performance itself as having shamanic or transformative possibilities. The earliest roots of performance can be found in the sacred rituals of indigenous cultures as performed by the shaman, rituals for the health and spiritual renewal of the community. The contemporary world, in its focus on technology and mass communication, gives rise to a sense of growing spiritual bankruptcy; to a world devoid of personal and communal ritual. Art and, in this case, performed art, can help to fill this void and present a sacred space in which to open channels of spiritual expression. *Wheel* was one such example of this. And the voices directing this focus on spiritual expression in the piece were women's voices, implying the important role that women can play in this regard in global culture.

The actual performance of *Wheel* was in and of itself a lesson in impermanence. Some time after the piece, the nuns departed for Kathmandu, Nepal; the male dancer left the ensemble to seek a performance career in New York City; and the pregnant woman gave birth her baby. No reviewer was available to see the performance that weekend so there is no written record and the videotape documentation was dark with an echo in the sound, which distorted its quality. The live performance, in and of itself, was, like the process of *maṇḍala*, to be experienced and then never to appear in the same way again.

The second performance project inspired by the *maṇḍala* involved a group of 150 school children from Parkville Community School in urban Hartford. At the time of this project, the Judy Dworin Performance Ensemble was in the second year of a residency working with the fourth- and sixth-grades to integrate movement into their language arts and social studies curriculum.

The purpose of the ensemble's residency at Parkville was to encourage learning development by introducing movement as another means of both affective and cognitive expression. Many of the school children at Parkville, a largely Hispanic population, have language skills considerably below grade level. Since language development is directly related to success in learning, this is a critical area for the school curriculum to address. In addition to improvement in language arts, the residency focused on building personal interactive skills and a sense of community in the classroom.

In the months before the nuns' arrival, we had been exploring topics such as direction, maps, and the notion of discovering new lands with the fourth grades. We had been investigating ideas of democracy and community with the sixth graders. When the nuns arrived, it seemed a particularly ripe opportunity to give the children a real cross-cultural and multi-arts experience that could extend out of what they already had been learning.

The children were introduced to the idea of the *maṇḍala* through a direct encounter with the nuns while they worked on it. On three mornings in early March, a different group of the children came to Trinity by bus to observe the nuns making the *maṇḍala.* They visited the *maṇḍala* site for about forty-five minutes, during which time several children were invited to use the *chakpus* (the funnels through which the sand flows to create the sacred designs) and design something with the sand. Then they went to a separate space where they were given pieces of brightly colored paper, magic markers, and glue sticks, a large poster-size piece of cardboard, and asked to design their own paper *maṇḍala.* They then watched a piece performed by the ensemble, a section of which they would later learn. Some of their reactions follow:

> I loved the trip. The *maṇḍala* was fantastic. The color they used a lot was green and white. Then when it was my turn to draw, my heart was in my throat. The nuns look really nice. Oh! How they did their morning prayer was fascinating, and was cool. I loved that because it looked like they are really into it.... It is true that the nuns say that you have to let go to things and go on with your lives. Also when you had to make your own *maṇḍala* it was exciting because I never made one. I felt like a nun, and I really enjoyed it.
>
> Rosa,[11] fourth grade

> The Buddhist nuns used sand and rocks. The rocks are crushed, washed, dried, and then painted. The first thing they have to do is design it (like a blue print), which is hard work because they have to use a lot of geometry skills. Then, they use a special tool to [make] the sand perfectly aligned. The nuns explained to us that once the *maṇḍala* is finished one nun destroys it while the others meditate. When we left, me, Sophia, Matt, and Ashley showed them our *maṇḍala.* They applauded our *maṇḍala.*
>
> Manuel, sixth grade

> I like the *maṇḍala* because it was very artistic and beautiful. It made me feel like soaring through the sky and making my own *maṇḍala.*
>
> Alfredo, sixth grade

I think the *maṇḍala* was pretty neat. I was wondering how the nuns made the center walls so stiff. I wonder how the sand stays in place. I like the colors of the *maṇḍala.* The colors reminded me of happiness. They reminded me of positive things, joy, compassion for others, love, and courage.

Carla, sixth grade

Learning new things is fun, and I learned a lot of new things. I learned that with team work you can do anything you want. I know it's hard to make a *maṇḍala* out of sand because if you breath too hard you could mess it up. So know that team work is very important to do things.

The *maṇḍala* to the nuns and even me is important because there are not a lot of people who show their religion and culture, and it's important to show who you are, and I like that.

María Elena, sixth grade

When we met with the children again after their experience with the nuns, we discussed ideas of *saṃsāra* with them, ideas about confusion and ignorance, pride, jealousy, possessiveness, and aggression. We assigned each class a particular *saṃsāric* emotion based on our perception of what might be most helpful for them to work with, that is, the more aggressive classes had to portray aggression and its opposite of peace. They were each to create their own world of shapes that would connote the initial *saṃsāric* condition. Gradually this led to a crescendo of movement, a field of chaos culminating in everyone collapsing to the ground. Composer and percussionist Ed Fast developed a score for *saṃsāra,* and each class used it as a structure around which to design their pieces.

The *Moving Maṇḍala* was site specific—it was conceived to take place at Elizabeth Park in a historic rose garden, which itself is a *maṇḍalic* landscape. It is configured with arbored pathways, which converge at a central gazebo. An open field is situated directly in front of the rose garden. Given that Tibetan Buddhists see *maṇḍalas* as existing in nature as sacred landscapes, the outdoor location seemed particularly appropriate. The piece was designed so that the *saṃsāra* section would be performed in the field in front of the rose garden, dividing the field into quadrants with two circles of students in each quadrant and one group in the sacred center. The nuns designed a *maṇḍala* logo for t-shirts, which were printed and purchased for the children.[12] Each class was given a t-shirt based on the color associated with their *saṃsāric* emotion, based on each of the five buddhas of the *maṇḍala,* east, south, west, north, and center. Likewise, their *saṃsāra maṇḍala* circle was placed in the field according to the actual direction to which it was linked.

After the chaotic collapse of *saṃsāra,* the children (150 in number) began to move from their positions on the ground to standing positions, and out of their pockets they pulled a *kata*—a silk scarf that Tibetans customarily place around someone's neck as a demonstration of honor, respect, and welcome. This section symbolized an emergence out of chaos into a more directed path, and was thus similar to *Wheel.*

Each class then proceeded to one of the arched gateways opening onto the rose garden, where a nun awaited them. The nuns placed the *katas* on the children as they proceeded along the pathway. When everyone had found their places, they performed ensemble a short segment of the piece entitled *Fields,* which they had seen at Trinity College. *Fields* is slow and meditative and largely circular, inspired by tai chi chuan. It is about centering, connection, and breath. At the conclusion of this segment the children exited from their pathways accompanied by the singing of an a cappella gospel group Women of the Cross's rendition of "Down by the Riverside." As they sang, "ain't gonna study war no more," many of the children spontaneously joined in. Each class then began to create a wheel configuration in their original *saṃsāra* circles in the field with the *katas* connecting a small central group of children to a larger outside circle, each turning slowly in a clockwise direction. As the "wheels of life" turned, the nuns chanted a prayer for world peace and trust.

"Moving Maṇḍala," Parkville Community School student, 1998 (photo by David DiGiacomo)

The children's *Moving Maṇḍala* was a deeply felt experience. When the children exited the rose garden, they certainly looked transformed, as did the audience who had moved to watch the dance around the central gazebo inside. The children's exuberance after the performance was contagious—their sense of fulfillment and their understanding of what they had done were both apparent. It was a remarkable feat that for twenty minutes, 150 ten- to twelve-year-olds sustained complete concentration and focus and performed all together with only one rehearsal directly before the performance.[13] The event was a meditation in the truest sense. A sacred event had taken place, and even the threatening clouds held off and were replaced by sunshine as the piece ended.

The piece was the talk of the school. By word of mouth, child to child, the story of the *maṇḍala* was told, along with other information such as who the nuns were, why they were living in exile, that they were the first women to make a *maṇḍala* in the U.S., and that the *maṇḍala* was about compassion, peace, community, and wisdom. Many children asked the nuns to autograph their t-shirts and *katas*.

In completing questionnaires after the experience, the children spoke to its significance in their own lives:

What does the maṇḍala *teach us?*

> This *maṇḍala* taught us that this moving *maṇḍala* is not to play around with. It's a very special thing.—Eduardo, sixth grade

> The *maṇḍala* teaches us to be more helpful, to love everyone when you can. It teaches us how to feel our movements and to be yourself. Also it teaches to feel compassion.—Marisol, sixth grade

> I think a *maṇḍala* teaches patience and how to work together.
> —Andrew, sixth grade

> The *maṇḍala* teaches us to be one. Something like a group or something like a community and to be together.—Julieta, sixth grade

> The *maṇḍala* teaches us that from being in a state of confusion you can go to clear vision and understand what is happening around you.
> —Gabriela, sixth grade

> It teach us that there should be peace.—Mónica, fourth grade

> Well, I think it will teach us how to get along with each other because when we made the wheel together, we did it in a team.
> —Rosa, fourth grade

What did you learn from creating the dance?

> I learned that being friendly is a fantastic thing to do.
> —Ana, fourth grade

> I learned that there is hope and that it does not matter in what stage you are in, there is always time to turn back.—María Elena, sixth grade

What did you learn from performing the dance?

> That peace, love, hope, compassion, and being trustworthy is better than anything in the world.—Lisa, fourth grade
>
> That when we all work together like in a dance it comes out nice. —Luis, fourth grade
>
> I've known how to perform but I feel very good about myself and everybody else.—Eduardo, sixth grade
>
> I learned that I could make peace all over the world. —Ana, fourth grade
>
> When I performed the dance I learned the points of greed, and of not being greedy. I like not being greedy.—María Elena, sixth grade

What is our dance about? How did it change from beginning to end?

> Our dance was about jealousy and being mean. How it changed from beginning to end was that at first we were all mean at each other, but at the end we all came together and formed a wheel and we were all happy. That's how it all changed from the beginning to the end. —Julio, sixth grade
>
> Our dance is about how everything is not forever and how things change over a period of time. It changed when every single circle did something different. It seemed like each circle was a different planet and they were going about their business. Then it's like the universe turns into chaos and all the planets go wild. Then everything is destroyed. After that the planet's life form grows into a new community. We explore. Then we all meet at a star, the sun.—Shakirrah, sixth grade

It is clear from these selected comments as well as from many others that this experience impacted the children in a number of important ways:

1) It introduced the children to cross-cultural exchange through direct experience. The fact that the children had the opportunity not only to meet the nuns, but to observe their work on the *maṇḍala* itself was significant. Additionally, they had a chance to work on their own visual *maṇḍalas* as a group

as well as to translate all of this learning into a creative performance project. And they had the chance to perform this project as a large-scale community event in Elizabeth Park, an environment that reinforced the basic values of the project itself—the interrelationship of all beings, the transitory nature of all things, the idea of honoring each other and the earth, and the affirmation of such values as peace, cooperation, community, sharing, and shedding of ego.

2) It enhanced the children's understanding of art, spirituality, and community. First and foremost, the students' sense of spiritual and moral consciousness was expanded. Also they enlarged their understanding of art as a sacred activity, as well as of what goes into the process of making and performing art.

3) It helped build the children's self-confidence and ability to work as a community. The children expressed an enormous sense of pride and accomplishment in their work as co-creators and performers in the project. They also expressed an understanding of the importance of working as a community to realize shared goals. They worked hard, overcame fears of performance, and understood the frustrations and the joys of working cooperatively to achieve a higher end.

In conclusion, in both of these performance projects I attempted to communicate and universalize the basic tenets of Buddhism, which are so vividly expressed in the process of creating a Tibetan Buddhist sand *maṇḍala,* in this case, the *maṇḍala* of compassion. The projects were designed to promote cross-cultural dialogue and exchange and to catalyze a sense of spiritual consciousness and awareness.

The systems that male-dominated cultures have created, which move us into the twenty-first century, have encouraged us to believe that more is better than less, that faster is better than slower, and that power is to be expressed in material possessions and control, not only of ourselves, but of others. It has a familiar ring with *saṃsāra.* The cross-fertilization and suggestion of both a global and a spiritual consciousness that these projects encourage are part of a growing challenge to these long-standing ideas of progress that influence many of the present world systems.

As women begin to be heard in both sacred and societal circles, they can bring alternatives to these realities—they can catalyze change. The creation of a sand *maṇḍala* by the seven young Tibetan nuns—among the first women ever to learn this traditional sacred art—and the experience of their collective process were striking examples of this. For me, as a woman and a creative artist, it was an inspiration that translated into another artistic form—a dance/theater performance. And that performance itself became a catalyst, shaping felt experience of spiritual and cultural phenomena into multi-layered images which reached the observers not only intellectually, but past intellect to a place of feeling, and perhaps action (or non-action, as the case may be). And all of this, from the creation of the *maṇḍala* to the performance of *Wheel*, embodied the Buddhist idea of the transitory nature of all things. The further expression of this was the *Moving Maṇḍala* piece performed by the children at Parkville Community School.

The children at Parkville learned about peace, sharing, compassion, and how to work as a collectivity, a community, through the direct experience of a process that had these values at its foundation. Their reactions indicate the potency of their experience. And their performance, too, allowed them to experience the fleeting nature of life from a Buddhist perspective. Their experience of movement itself was its own lesson in impermanence.

These are examples of ways in which women and artists can bring spiritual consciousness to a new level in the very complicated labyrinth of our contemporary existence. As the old ways become tired and begin to counter progress in its most holistic sense, the arts and performance can channel a resounding voice in the development of spiritual and global consciousness.[14]

Notes

1. Dalai Lama, *Freedom in Exile: The Autobiography of the Dalai Lama* (New York: Harper Collins, 1990), pp. 202–3.
2. Philip Rawson, *Sacred Tibet* (London: Thames and Hudson, 1991), p. 13.
3. Rawson, p. 90.
4. Rawson, p. 90.
5. Robert A. F. Thurman, *Mandala: The Architecture of Enlightenment* (New York: Asia Society, Tibet House, and Boston: Shambhala), p. 127. Thurman's italics.
6. Chögyam Trungpa, *Orderly Chaos: The Mandala Principle* (Boston: Shambhala, 1991), pp. 61–62.
7. The Judy Dworin Performance Ensemble has been in existence since 1989 and is a collaborative group of performers, designers, and musicians under my direction making work that addresses social, political, and cultural issues of our time.
8. Rawson, p. 8.
9. Trungpa, p. 31. As described by Chögyam Trungpa, the feeling of pride portrayed here is without dignity or confidence; it is simply self-assertive. It is arrogant in the sense that you are not willing to let yourself be regarded as needing to be rescued or saved. Not only that—you want to be acknowledged. You want people to acknowledge your richness or your potentiality for richness so that you can march into other people's territory. If necessary, you are willing to roll into their territory, expand into it.
10. Trungpa, pp. 154–55. As Chögyam Trungpa describes, "The discontinuity becomes

continuity and the flow sort of dances as it goes along. So that is the basic way to view the *maṇḍala* and the five Buddha principles. It is a positive world, not in the sense of a simpleminded love-and-light approach, but in the sense that the world is workable. One can relate with such a world because everything is visible and very vivid. That dispels hesitation and fear and you can remold things. You can reshape the clouds and ride on the rainbow. Impossibilities can be achieved by not achieving."

11. The real names of the children have been changed for this article.
12. Funding for this project was provided by the George A. and Grace L. Long Foundation.
13. We had been developing this piece with the individual classes for six weeks before the performance.
14. Special thanks to Pat and Phil Kennedy for their assistance in the preparation of this manuscript.

WOMEN, ART,
AND THE BUDDHIST SPIRIT

Ann W. Norton

This article evolved out of an exhibition of Buddhist art I curated, which focused on women and complemented a sand *maṇḍala* created by Tibetan Buddhist nuns.[1] The seven nuns who came to Trinity College, Hartford, shared their ritual arts and practices with a large Western community, all the while remaining true to their traditions except for the highly unusual fact that they were women. These same nuns, however, also showed a genuine interest in and acceptance of non-traditional Buddhist art generated in the West. They reflected the same openness that His Holiness the Fourteenth Dalai Lama had shown in his allowing nuns to produce traditional ritual arts and to bring these arts to the West. With such a permissive attitude prevailing, I feel more confident to explore new territories of Buddhist artistic expression.

Introduction

A new chapter in the arts of Buddhism has begun. Tibetan Buddhist nuns in exile are creating sand *maṇḍalas*, painting *thangkas*, and dancing as *ḍākinīs*, thus breaking a long, monk-dominated tradition. While women have played an important role as subject in Buddhist art from early times onward, traditional arts were ordinarily created by men. Only in the late twentieth–early twenty-first centuries do we see radically new developments as women become more active contributors to the traditional arts. In the realm of "non-traditional" art, however, we see endless possibilities for self-expression. Non-traditional Buddhist art is more difficult to categorize than the traditional, because it encompasses not only the globalization of "modern" art but also the expansion of Buddhism (to include non-Asian followers of Buddhism, Asians in diaspora who often turn back to the Buddhism of their roots years or even generations after their initial move from Asia, and non-Buddhists who have made an intellectual study of Buddhist philosophy and art).

Traditional Buddhist Art

For over two thousand years most Buddhist art has remained strongly traditional. Even as Buddhism spread to different lands, new ways of interpreting the faith developed and quickly became codified within each culture. Now, at the end of the twentieth century, there are again new and individual approaches to expressing Buddhism in art—changes that are often quite subtle but nevertheless quite substantial. This article will focus on some of these changes in the arts of Buddhism as interpreted by women, highlighting contemporary works, both traditional and non-traditional, and works by Western women as well as by Asians in diaspora.

Women appear in the earliest figural art of Buddhism, as evidenced by the many "tree goddesses" from such sites as Sanchi, Bharhut, and Nagarjunakonda.[2] By the second century B.C.E., the miraculous birth story of Siddhārtha Gautama, who later became the Buddha, emerged, and artworks showing a beautiful young woman in a dancing pose under a tree became identified with Queen Māyā, the mother of the Buddha. The tree goddess, after which Queen Māyā is patterned, is actually an ancient pre-Buddhist fertility motif from India, which can often be seen in the art of the Indus Valley culture, Hinduism, and Jainism as well.

As the Mahāyāna tradition of Buddhism developed, the iconography expanded to include personifications and divinities. Some of these figures had friendly, calm aspects, others angry and frightening. Over time and with different cultural contributions, the growing number of divinities and spiritual helpers would change in appearance. An example can be seen in the Hindu-Buddhist goddess Mārīcī. Popular in Bengal as early as the tenth century, she is shown as a lovely young woman in a chariot drawn by seven pigs (figure 1). Her name means "ray of light," in reference to her personifying the dawn, and originally she triumphed over illness, especially smallpox. In more complex Tibetan Buddhism, Mārīcī is seen in the form of a *ḍākinī* or "skygoer." As the *ḍākinī* Vajravārāhī, her pig connection can be seen in the tiny boar's head sprouting from the right side of her head (figure 2). The iconography of this image goes still further to express the terrifying nature of a *ḍākinī:* not only does she exhibit a scowling visage, but she also originally held a chopper and a skull cup filled with blood. Her jewelry is carved from human bones, a pointed message that one must detach oneself from life and from fear of death. The late Stella Kramrisch made clear the beneficial nature of these frightening females: "This liberatrix lives on the essence of life out of the skull-cup wherein there is no distinction of substance and non-substance.... Her ecstasy is the power of inspiration."[3]

The highly positive nature of these powerful deities has been understood by Tibetan monks, who for centuries have dressed and ritually danced as *ḍākinīs.* Only in the last few years have Tibetan Buddhist nuns been given permission to

Figure 1 (see p. 370)

Figure 2

dance as *ḍākinīs* as well. One of the nuns from Keydong Thuk-Che-Cho Ling Nunnery of Kathmandu reported that she "tried to become a *ḍākinī*," and that the object of the dance was to "benefit and protect His Holiness, the Dalai Lama."

A milder Buddhist goddess, Tārā is beloved as a personification of compassion. The white form of Tārā, who sits in the lotus position, helps devotees to find inner peace. As Green Tārā, she is Active Compassion, portrayed with her right leg pendant, prepared at a moment's notice to jump from her throne and come to a person's aid. During the Trinity College exhibit and making of the sand *maṇḍala*, Ani Tenzin Sherab painted a *thangka* of Green Tārā, thus providing another example of women becoming involved in creating artforms that had before been almost exclusively the domain of men.

The numerous Buddhist divinities, both peaceful and wrathful, exist on two levels. One level is in a richly decorated palace, whose ground plan is in the form of a *maṇḍala*. The other level is in the mind of the meditator. Through strenuous meditation and ritual practice, elaborate and ultimately ephemeral sand *maṇḍalas* can be created. Such a *maṇḍala* was made and then dismantled at

Figure 3

Trinity College in 1998 by the seven visiting nuns from the Keydong Thuk-Che-Cho Ling Nunnery.[4]

Western Contributions

The majority of pieces in the exhibition accompanying this important event were traditional Tibetan Buddhist works. One work, however, showed a radical break with tradition—the "Three-Dimensional *Maṇḍala*" by Suzanne Wind Greenbaum, an American artist who, while not a practicing Buddhist, studied in depth the form and meaning of the *maṇḍala.* The resulting mixed-media work is her own interpretation of this complex subject. The standing part of the artwork enables the viewer to walk fully around it, offering the possibility of performing *pradakṣiṇā,* or circumambulation. The accompanying four painted panels (of which figure 3 is one example) represent the four gateways through which a devotee can enter into the *maṇḍala.* Each is painted in the color of that direction, and includes designs and details relevant to its complex meanings. At the "innermost" and "highest" place in this sacred precinct is a crystal of highest wisdom, while around it are actual human finger bones, denoting the detachment heralded by the *ḍākinīs.*

In figure 3, Greenbaum shows the gate to the eastern quadrant. Red in color, it is her interpretation of the portal of entry into the *maṇḍala.* As the beginning, it refers also to the pregnancy of the Buddha's mother, Queen Māyā. The artist has used a logarithmic spiral for this panel's composition. She explains, "The Buddha, like the spiral, is without beginning and without end."[5] The fourth panel indicates the northern gateway into the *maṇḍala.* Mainly blue in color, it refers to both death and liberation. The panel echoes the three-dimensionality of the stūpa through the central mast, painted in a glowing blue-white of *bardo,* the intermediate state between lives. The small, glassed niche, placed like a reliquary, contains teeth, symbolizing impermanence and detachment. Also included here are parts of computer circuitry, which Greenbaum interprets as suggesting the Eightfold Path of the Buddha's teachings.

Figure 4

A forty-two-inch wooden base holds the actual *maṇḍala*, which consists of five glass discs with photoetched or silkscreened symbolic designs. The base itself is meant to refer to the Vedic sacrificial post. On the top disc are human hand bones, which not only reiterate the message of impermanence and detachment, but also make subtle reference to ritual hand gestures, or *mudrās.*

The last hundred years have brought not only a new wave of Western scholarship in Buddhism, but also an increasing number of Westerners who have been spiritually moved by Buddhist teachings. Carol Brighton and Mary Laird are two California artists whose works express the influence of Buddhism in their lives.

Mary Laird, whose degrees are from the University of Wisconsin, Madison, is the proprietor of Quelquefois Press in Berkeley. In her works, she often treats recognizably Buddhist elements in new ways. Laird is a member of a Sufi community that employs Buddhist meditation among its practices. The group's pilgrimage to Tibet in 1986 was particularly influential on her subsequent works. In *For Sustenance: a Tibetan Deity,* Laird has used the medium of a handpainted woodcut on silk to express a powerful goddess who reflects but does not exactly copy traditional forms (figure 4). Here we see the double *vajra* (thunderbolt), a small Buddha figure, and hand gestures usually connected with the goddess Uṣṇīṣavijayā, the "victorious goddess of the Uṣṇīṣa," or the buddha intelligence, who is popular in Tibetan Buddhism. The artist states that since she chose not to reverse the figure before making the woodcut, "the result was a mirror image of the correct and traditional view."[6]

In her *Prayer Flag Sculpture,* Laird again draws on a known Tibetan Buddhist practice but adds elements of her own. She relates that "the prayer flags were poems of praise and heart that I letterset and printed on sheeting that I dyed according to the colors of the *cakras.* I circumambulated the main pole…[and] concentrated on becoming one in the heart of Buddha when I did this."[7] This offering/installation was in Black Earth, Wisconsin, near the site of a Native American sweat lodge. Later, one of the flags was taken to Drepung Monastery in Lhasa.[8] Laird states of her work:

> In attempting to break down barriers, my work links opposites, suggesting the interconnectedness of all things, the energy that transpires behind that which appears.... Our hope lies in how we resolve... [these]...personal and collective conflicts and how we share our visions, as we continue to work and seek the beauty of that unlimited part of our collective being, the essences behind it all.[9]

Carol Brighton, who holds a degree from the University of California at Berkeley, is a papermaker and printmaker who uses handmade paper with engraving and collage. Working in small *editions varieé* and monoprints, she sees much of the inspiration for her art coming from her Asian travels and experiences, as well as from her Buddhist practice.[10] Brighton's work combines sensitive interaction of mixed-media techniques and esoteric, philosophical interpretations of Tibetan Buddhism.

In a piece called *For One Departure Only*, Brighton refers in part to reincarnation but also reflects a more Western approach to mortality through what appear to be tombs. She writes that

> the arched grottoes (sometimes seen as windows, or tombstones) are a simulacra form of the Buddhist caves in China, where hundreds of grottoes are carved with Buddhist images in honor of ancestors. The work is about time as a dynamic circumstance of our physical dimension, a marker for our impermanence, and for the momentariness of conventional phenomenon. This is a departure for one person, and once only, across the threshold of time.[11]

For an *editions varieé* entitled *Squaring the Circle*, Brighton created *The Watchman* (figure 5), reflecting her own interpretation of the *maṇḍala*, especially in relation to meditation. Describing the work, Brighton states:

> The work is about integration.... The ladder could be seen as a symbol of the process of ascent (or descent), the bird is a symbol for the timeless flight of the soul. The square and the circle have a tradition in *maṇḍalas* as symbolic images for the earth and the cosmos, and the "x" for the unknown. In the middle of all this is a meditating figure, sitting still, the observer.[12]

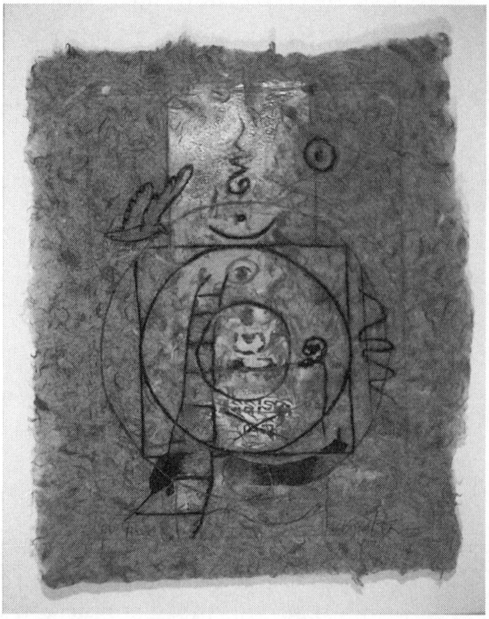

Figure 5

Asians in Diaspora

Unlike Westerners who have espoused a new religion, Asians in diaspora may turn to Buddhism either because they have an unbroken family tradition or because they are trying to return to their disrupted roots. The complexities of this issue can only multiply, since more Asians from many different countries are leaving their original homeland for a variety of reasons and settling in many different parts of the world. Compounding this, with each generation further away from the initial break from Asia, new problems, new revelations, and new attitudes will come.

Tibetans in exile have a compelling need to keep their culture alive. This is particularly clear in the case of the Tibetan Buddhist nuns now living in Nepal. Lay artists also follow traditional styles, however, as seen in the work of lay woman Tenzin Yewong, who escaped from Tibet in December, 1991 at the age of sixteen. Travelling mostly at night for nearly a month, she and twenty-five other young people braved cold, frostbite, and Chinese border guards, finally reaching Dharamsala, India. There she joined the School of Appliqué Thangka Art, run by Master Dorje Wangdue, and studied traditional appliqué for five years. She has recently settled in Nepal, where she is just establishing herself as a practicing artist, and is one of the first woman to work in this technique. Her appliqué *thangkas* include such traditional subjects as Amitābha, Green Tārā, and Śākyamuni.

The Tibetan appliqué medium was referred to in texts before the seventeenth century.[13] The fine fragments of silk cloth, generally Chinese in origin, contribute to both the preciousness and the fragility of such works. Most surviving examples date from no earlier than the mid-eighteenth century.[14] While earlier works might include embroidered inscriptions giving a dedication, a break with tradition can be seen with Tenzin Yewong's signature appearing on the lower right-hand side of her *thangkas.* (This is also true of Ani Tenzin Sherab, who signs her *thangkas* on the front, in the lower left- or right-hand corner.) It is remarkable that such a difficult and time-consuming technique continues in 1999. Appliqué *thangkas* tend

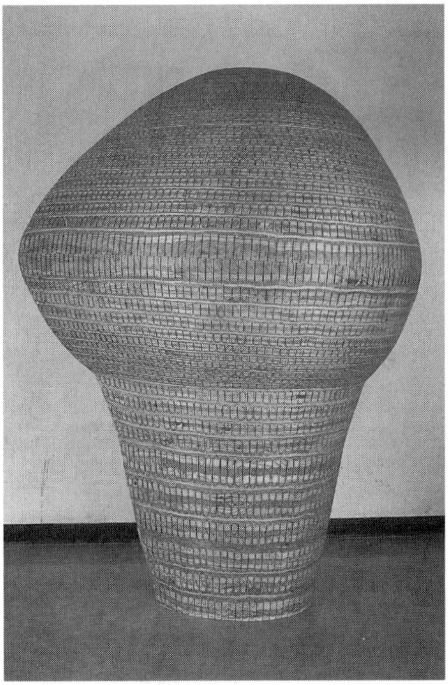

Figure 6

to cost more than painted ones, and the better customers are often foreigners, either visiting Nepal or ordering from abroad. But Tenzin Yewong is not discouraged by the hardships of publicizing and selling her work. She states,

> It is my sincere desire to establish a school of Tibetan appliqué *thangka* art where I can teach this unique art of Tibet to many young Tibetan girls and keep this great tradition alive.... I am determined to make this [my] career.[15]

I include Ken Takashi Horii in this article because of the special way women and Buddhism have influenced his art. A third-generation Japanese-American, Horii was originally trained in both painting and cabinetry. In 1983 he traveled to India on a research project. There he was deeply moved by the great sculptural monuments such as Karle, Ajanta, and Ellora, carved out of the "living rock," as well as by the Buddhist centers of Sarnath and Sanchi. By his second trip in 1987, he had turned to wood sculpture as his medium.[16]

Buddhism began to take on more importance for him during this time as well. His maternal grandfather had been associated with Shingon Buddhism in Japan, and his grandmother, who had been born in Gifu, Japan, maintained a strong connection to Buddhism despite the wrenching experience of internment during World War II. Horii's wood sculpture took a radical turn when in 1989 he created *Gifu Diary* as a memorial to his grandmother (figure 6). This marked the first time he was moved to incorporate his own Buddhist roots into his art. The work, using the craft of refined woodworking, combines Japanese and Indian iconography. *Gifu Diary*, no longer extant, was nearly nine feet high. It was made of hundreds of small pieces of laminated wood, and was Horii's own interpretation of a Buddhist stūpa, the original emblem of the "living Buddha" and a reminder of his experience of *nirvāṇa*, or final release.[17]

Gifu Diary was followed by a series of large, wooden sculptures dealing with aspects of Buddhist prayer. During this period Horii created *Unrevealed Truth*,

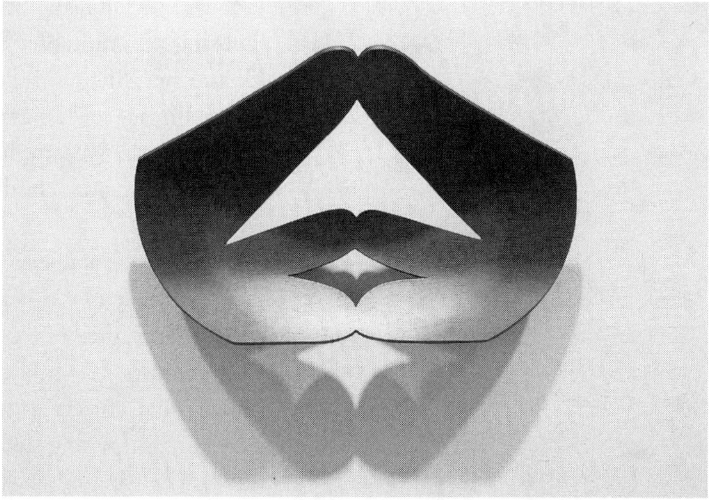

Figure 7

a work dedicated to his sister who died at the age of three, before he was born. Five feet high, the piece appears to be a giant scroll (or sūtra), bound in the middle by a wide, lead band. It is clear that it will never be opened. There is writing on the inside of the band, but the text, a message to his sister, is known only to the artist.

Most recently, Horii has created a vibrant series of twenty-four sculptures relating to his newly adopted daughter from China, Jina. In April, 1998, he and his wife, Harriet Pappas, went to China to bring Jina out of the orphanage where she had lived for her first year. Watching the baby in her crib, Horii observed how the one-year-old would calm herself for sleep by holding her hands in different ways, seeming to watch the patterns of shadows on the wall. He imagined Jina doing this in the orphanage—hundreds of times while confined to her crib—over the many months before he and his wife had met her. For Horii, the baby's hand movements suggested Buddhist *mudrās*, or sacred gestures, and he interpreted them on the level of Jina's and his shared Buddhist heritage (figure 7).[18]

Haruko Okano is a third-generation Japanese-Canadian artist from Vancouver, British Columbia. She is a mixed-media, interdisciplinary artist who in recent years has been involved in artistic collaborations among artists, in both the visual arts and other disciplines. Some of her strong artistic statements, including performances, installations, and works involving viewer participation, have produced both shock and admiration. Her works often address such subjects as Japanese attitudes, problems pertaining to Asians in a non-Asian culture, and women's issues. But Okano's own Buddhist practice can be felt—sometimes subtly, sometimes obviously—behind most of her work. Her family tradition belonged to the

Figure 8

Japanese Mahāyāna tradition focusing on Amitābha Buddha. Okano herself now follows the Sakya lineage of Tibetan Buddhism, with an emphasis on *guru-yoga* and bodhisattva vows.[19]

Okano's *Preciousness of Human Existence* is a 1995 installation, that invites the viewer into a shrine setting. It combines traditional ritual objects and images, as well as surprising details (figure 8). On the wall above a row of altars, each covered by a cloth printed with Buddhist symbols, is a row of small photographs, including one of the artist, a nude, and a Kannon painting. These images alternate with mirrors of the same size in order to "capture the face of the individual viewers as they walk across the installation."[20] The sacredness of the space is clear, however, so that even though a photograph of a nude has been placed near one of Kannon, there is such an integrity in the restrained atmosphere that there is no disruption of the total effect. In the foreground of the installation is a meditation bench, on top of which lie a *kata* (silk scarf) and *mālā* (meditation beads), and, underneath, a pair of worn Nike running shoes. "These," in the words of the artist, "are used Nike runners because the whole installation was inspired by a Nike advertisement aimed at women that implied women were never goddesses and would never be goddesses but that through trying out a pair of Nike runners the company could give women the experience of being goddesses."[21]

The Preciousness of Human Existence was created for an exhibition entitled "Art and Spirituality II" at the Richmond Art Gallery in British Columbia. "Based on the foundation of Buddhist understanding of human rebirth... [it] rejects the idea that women [like all human beings] are not divine."[22]

Laotian-American Ammala Douangsavanh is a junior at the University of Rhode Island. She and her parents came to the United States as refugees in 1981. Her parents are devout Buddhists, and while the Laotian community in Rhode Island has an active temple, Douangsavanh was not pressured to go. Her own relationship to the faith evolved through traditional Laotian dance. "Eventually," she states, "dancing and religion, which...[had been] separate entities for me, merged." Douangsavanh takes Lao dance seriously, and is now the cultural representative for the temple. But Douangsavanh is also a woman of the times and, as she researches Buddhism, she is questioning old viewpoints from a more feminist perspective. She is asking questions like, "Why did women have to be sinful beings? Why was it improper for a woman to touch a monk? Why couldn't women be as virtuous as men?" These questions, combined with such imagery as that of Queen Māyā and the story emphasizing the virtue and faith of Yaśodharā, wife of Prince Siddhārtha (later the Buddha), led to Douangsavanh's writing the following poem:[23]

"Reincarnation of a Woman"

Tell me I cannot reach enlightenment
    Because I am a woman
I am bound to the earth
My sole purpose is rebirth

Tell me I will continue to dwell in spiritual Hell
Reborn again and again
    Because I am a woman
Incapable of seeing the next level
My sole purpose is tied to the earth

Tell me I am Evil
    Because I am a woman
Because I am tied to the earth
A device of seduction, I cause wars
I move destruction, with the scent of my skin
I make fire with my lips
Evil temptress that I am

Tell me that I am all these things
And I will tell you this,
I reside in my glass palace
And drink Truth from a golden chalice

I am given infinite lives
To enlighten infinite minds

Release me from the cycle
And there will be no one to teach your disciples

Then you will die
Don't you know that it is I that keeps you alive?
I am your connection to the two planes
Yet you think me inferior

Blinded by your egoistic ways
Understand that we coexist
You could not have the universe that is this
If I was not the sun that showed you the earth
Now, simple man, you've become one with the universe
  Including me
I am bound to the earth
  Because I am a woman
My soul's purpose is rebirth.

Mayumi Oda, born in 1941 outside Tokyo, experienced early in her life the horrors of nuclear war. She grew up in a family rich in Buddhist philosophy and art appreciation. She was named in memory of her grandmother, a devout Nichiren Buddhist much admired for her compassion and social awareness. "Mayumi" means "sandalwood," the fragrant wood used for Buddhist rosaries and incense.[24]

After graduating from Tokyo University of Fine Arts in 1966, Oda moved with her American husband to New York, where she studied at the Pratt Graphic Center. Motherhood helped inspire her early silkscreen prints of colorfully exuberant women, including Buddhist male divinities transformed into goddesses (figure 9).[25] Samantabhadra, (male) bodhisattva of universal kindness, has an elephant as his vehicle. Oda has freely translated this traditional iconography to depict a meditative female, confident in her elephant vehicle before a rainbow of hope and renewal. Of her *Goddess*, Samantabhadra, Oda wrote,

> She turns meditation into action and dream into reality. We tend to think there is someone out there to help us do this, but unfolding the path completely depends on ourselves. When we become Samantabhadra herself we can freely ride this wheel of Dharma and receive wonderful support from people, friends, and teachers.[26]

Reflecting on her silkscreen prints of goddesses, Oda stated in a 1995 interview, "When I was pregnant in the late 1960s, I needed a vision that was very positive and could give me strength. For my talisman, the goddesses came to me. They became a guiding light—I drew my strength from them."[27]

Figure 9

A new phase in Mayumi Oda's work evolved in the late 1980s, when she painted large canvases of goddesses which could hang as inspirational banners in sacred spaces.[28] Turning away from the commercial aspect of art, she found that she could communicate to larger audiences with these portable hangings. Her *Mañjuśrī* (bodhisattva of transcendental wisdom), whose iconography is drawn from Tibetan Buddhist icons and who is traditionally male, appears in female form. But some aspects of her Mañjuśrī banner, such as the wisdom-guarding dragon and the ignorance-destroying flaming sword, refer to the more wrathful side of Buddhism sometimes needed for enlightenment and salvation. A work from the same series, *Ḍākinī, the Sky Goer*, shows a ferocious dark-blue female dancing in a pool of blood and surrounded by flames.[29]

Oda's banner series reflects her growing concern for world issues. In 1992 she was moved to action when reprocessed plutonium was to be shipped from France to Japan. She founded Plutonium Free Future, which, together with a related organization, Rainbow Serpent, is dedicated to demonstrating against and raising awareness about the hazards of nuclear energy.[30]

Oda breaks preconceived categories. Although she has lived in America for over thirty years, she refers to herself as a "Japanese living abroad."[31] In the last few years she has experienced a growing appreciation of her art in Japan, and in 1999 her *Goddesses* was translated into Japanese. She has in many ways returned to her own family and cultural roots, but her art and actions show her deep concern and compassion for the future of the earth, which goes beyond religion or nationality.[32]

Conclusions

At the beginning of the twenty-first century we see expressions of Buddhist art that reflect ancient traditions as well as new interpretations. Old molds and old iconographies are being broken or transformed. What remains is personal devotion, expressed individually. Will we need to emphasize gender in future studies of Buddhist arts? We need to remember that the princely bodhisattva Avalokiteśvara of Indian Buddhism gradually became transformed and feminized into the androgynous East Asian Guanyin and Kannon. Vajrayāna Buddhism makes clear the need for both genders in the many consort and *yab-yum* figures. And both nuns and monks of Tibetan Buddhism hold the feminine bell of wisdom *(ghaṇṭā)* together with the masculine thunderbolt of compassion *(vajra)* in all important rituals.

This paper has focused on a few examples of women contributing to or inspiring the transformation of Buddhism in the late twentieth century through the arts. Both women and men are becoming ever more free to validate their own spirituality through the arts, and these personal visions reflect a new vitality seen and felt in the contemporary Buddhist spirit.[33]

List of Illustrations

1. *Mārīcī*, Tibeto-Mongol, 18th century, xylograph book of "Three Hundred Icons." Ink on paper. 2 3/4." Private Collection, Providence, Rhode Island.
2. *Vajravārāhī*, Tibet, 16th century. Silver, with gold, turquoise insets, and pigments. 12 1/4." Collection of the Newark Museum. Purchased in 1970 by Mary Livingston Griggs and Mary Griggs Burke Foundation Fund.
3. East gate of *Three Dimensional Maṇḍala*, by Suzanne Wind Greenbaum, 1997. Oil on birch, silkscreened glass, and objects. 13" x 9."
4. *For Sustenance: A Tibetan Deity*, by Mary Laird, 1986. Hand-painted woodblock print mounted on silk. 3' x 4.'
5. *Squaring the Circle* #6/12 *The Watchman*, by Carol Brighton, 1996. Handmade paper with engraving and collage. 8" x 6."
6. *Gifu Diary*, by Ken Horii, 1989. Birch plywood. 9'5" x 7'5."
7. *One Thousand Confinements* (#22/24), by Ken Horii, 1998. Painted plywood. 23" x 15."
8. *Preciousness of Human Existence*, installation by Haruko Okano, 1995. Mixed media. Vancouver, British Columbia.
9. *Samantabhadra*, by Mayumi Oda, 1980. Silkscreen print. 29" x 40." ed. 48.

Notes

1. See articles by Ellison Banks Findly and Melissa Kerin in this volume.
2. Adrian Snodgrass, *The Symbolism of the Stūpa,* Studies in Southeast Asia (Ithaca: Cornell University Press, 1985), p. 44, fig. 15.
3. Stella Kramrisch, "The Art of Nepal and Tibet" in *Philadelphia Museum of Art Bulletin* 5, no. 265 (spring, 1960): 29.
4. It is important to view this "work" as both "installation" and "ritual process." The art objects in the gallery stood in place throughout the exhibition, while the sand *maṇḍala* was ever-evolving until its dismantling. At the same time, it was to be understood as a ground-plan for divine residence.
5. S. Greenbaum, "Dykil-Khor: Center and Periphery—Mapping the Spheres of the Buddha: A Three Dimensional *Maṇḍala*" (M.A. thesis, Wesleyan University, 1997), p. 24.
6. Artist's correspondence, November, 1998.
7. Ibid.
8. Artist's notation.
9. Artist's notation.
10. Artist's correspondence, November, 1998. I am grateful to Carol Brighton for her interest and great help in this study. She has been generous in sending slides of her own work, with explanations, as well as introducing me to the work of Mary Laird.
11. Ibid.
12. Ibid.
13. Marylin M. Rhie and Thurman, Robert, *Wisdom and Compassion: The Sacred Art of Tibet* (New York: Harry N. Abrams, 1991), p. 386.
14. Ibid., pp. 101, 386.
15. Information received in June, 1999, by email from Tenzin Yewong, translated by her uncle, Wangchuk Tsering.
16. I appreciate the time Ken Horii has taken to explain to me his work and its meaning.
17. According to Horii, it was clear to him, as he worked long and tedious hours on the *Gifu Diary,* that it was a sort of "meditation." He also was aware of the element of Buddhist "detachment" in his ultimately dismantling the piece.
18. Horii's series of painted wood sculptures entitled *One Thousand Confinements* was exhibited in the Providence College Art Gallery, October–November, 1998.
19. I am thankful to Haruko Okano for her generosity in corresponding with me about her own history as well as about the background and interpretation of her work. I am also indebted to California performance artist Canyon Sam for introducing me to Okano's work. (While performance art is beyond the scope of the present paper, it is important to acknowledge it as a valid and powerful artform. The nuns' *ḍākinī* dance can be interpreted as both ritual and performance.)
20. Information supplied by the artist.
21. Information supplied by the artist. It is interesting to note that "installation," a term so common for contemporary art, can be used not only for a number of

"modern" works shown here, but also in reference to the centuries-old sand *maṇḍala* tradition practiced by the nuns at Trinity College.

22. Information supplied by the artist.
23. This was first read at the Asian Students' Festival at Providence College in April, 1998. Douangsavanh has explained that she was first moved by the subject of women in early Buddhism when she read *Lady of the Lotus* by William E. Barrett (New York: Doubleday, 1975). The novel tells the story of early Buddhism through the life of Yaśodharā, wife of Prince Siddhārtha, who was destined to become the Buddha. I thank Douangsavanh for being so open and sharing with her genuinely personal expression.
24. Mayumi Oda, *Goddesses* (Volcano, CA: Volcano Press/Kazan Books, 1981).
25. Ibid., p. 63.
26. Ibid., p. 62.
27. Jacqueline Calayag, "Painting for Mother Earth and her Children" in *The Japan Times*, December 9 (1995): 15.
28. Mary-Ann Lutzker, "Mayumi Oda: Goddess Banners" in *Orientations* (February, 1990): 46–52.
29. Ibid., pp. 51, 52; fig. 10.
30. Jacqueline Calayag, "Painting." In 1994, Oda painted a frightening red *fudo*, a fierce Buddhist divinity that champions righteousness and combats evil, modeled after an eighth- to ninth-century Japanese esoteric Buddhist work. Like the original, Oda's glowering feminized Fudo is surrounded by flames and holds a fiery sword entwined by a dragon. This fierce goddess of the late twentieth century shows the results of nuclear war—a horrifying heap of skeletons at the base of her craggy rock seat. (Thanks to Mayumi Oda for sending me a slide of this remarkable work, as well as other images and texts used in this article.)
31. Jacqueline Calayag, "Painting."
32. Ibid. Speaking of the various religions that have influenced her work, Oda states, "They're different rivers, but they all run into the same ocean."
33. This paper only begins to touch upon the subject of contemporary Buddhist art. As I come upon more and more artists who are of the Asian diaspora as well as non-Asian practicing Buddhists, I am reminded of Jan Willis' paper read at Harvard University in 1992. There she asked, "Where are the American Buddhists of color?" Now she is answering her own question in this volume. A further study may reveal the artistic expressions of Western Buddhists of color.

SPACE AS MIND/*MAṆḌALA* PLACES:

Joan Halifax, Tsultrim Allione, and Yvonne Rand

Sarah D. Buie

Space and mind—or space as mind—exist in a dynamic and interdependent relationship. The spaces we make and inhabit both express and encourage qualities of mind, and it is from mind that spatial form emerges. Awareness of this relationship and its significance for the transformation of consciousness is apparent in spiritual traditions, ritual practices, and architecture worldwide, and has been long understood by Buddhist teachers in the siting and creation of stūpas, monasteries, shrine rooms, and practice environments. Among these teachers are some contemporary Buddhist women who bring heightened sensitivity to the creation of spaces for practice and living. In unprecedented ways, they integrate Dharmic, feminine, environmental, and traditional values and visions to create places that express and encourage a deep relatedness to the planet and the energies that govern it, while at the same time supporting a powerful level of practice. At different centers in New Mexico, Colorado, and California, teachers Joan Halifax, Tsultrim Allione, and Yvonne Rand are among those bringing into form a great deal of what they understand about the nature of mind and our oneness with the natural world. Each of their environments is unique in its history, its setting, and its direction, and each is an extraordinary example of the grounding of place-making in an awareness of the interdependence of all life—places that serve as and express the *maṇḍalic* condition in which we all exist.

Over the last six years, Joan Halifax has led in the development of Upaya, a residential and teaching center on the outskirts of Santa Fe on the site of earlier Buddhist communities. While proceeding in an organic and incremental way, integrating existing structures into the Upaya campus, Joan's vision for its present form has been comprehensive. It is based on her deep understanding of the consonance of mind and spatial expressions. She considers our condition of interrelatedness and interdependence (ties to ancestors and traditional uses of the land, natural cycles and resources, placing sites within the local topography of mountain and river, the interdependence of exterior and interior spaces, and relationships within the community itself) in the design choices she has made. Caring stewardship of the land and its resources has been a constant factor in development of the site. In its physical forms (buildings, materials, construction methods, rooms, shrines, works of art, gardens, location, etc.), Upaya expresses qualities of attentive and intimate dwelling, which Joan encourages as characteristics of mind and practice; it also embodies and allows for appreciation of the ceaseless flow of change and evolution, and the play of duality within the whole.

Tsultrim Allione first went to southern Colorado in 1993, and moved there to begin work on the newly purchased Tara Mandala in 1994. I visited and spoke with her there during her fifth summer on the land, at which time the community was still living in dwellings that resembled Tibetan summer encampments. In our discussions of space as it reflects program and practice here, she too emphasized interrelatedness—in the honoring of ancestors who lived on the land before, in a conscious exchange with the *maṇḍalic* topography of the land itself, in the play of inside/outside in the design of new buildings, and in the fundamental symbolism of both circle and *maṇḍala* as guiding images for their community. In the spirit of dharmic attention to the earth, the Tara Mandala community brings thoughtful and skillful awareness of the environmental implications of their settlement to the project, and intends to live as lightly as possible on the land, hoping to co-exist with the many animals who also live there. Their development plan includes the most progressive current thinking in the areas of energy, water, wastewater treatment, renewable materials, passive heating and cooling, as well as agricultural methods, preservation of natural wetlands and open space, and restoration of eroded hillsides and plantings. Their commitment to attentive and intimate modes of dwelling is being tested on a large scale, as they shape from scratch a complex human habitation within a landscape, and seek a natural balance within it. The *maṇḍalic* mountainside container in which they live physically reinforces an appreciation of the *maṇḍala* principle (our existence within an interdependent causal whole), which informs all of their work.

Joan and Tsultrim are relative newcomers to the places they now tend so thoughtfully. Yvonne Rand has lived in the same place for the last twenty-six years, slowly bringing into form the extraordinary compound of home, meditation hall, retreat kitchen, office, garden, and orchard that comprise the Redwood Creek Dharma Center. Located in northern California in the watershed of the western flank of Mount Tamalpais, this small Dharma center lies within an ecosystem Yvonne has known for nearly three decades. She describes the various local flowers and plants in her garden as though they were old friends. Her environment is on an intimate scale, in a constant state of evolution, and expressive of great care in the steady stream of small decisions that she has made, whether in the choice of materials for a floor or pathway, the siting of a bench, or the assembling of a shrine. One experiences a quality of harmony in the easy flow of these spaces, indoor and outdoor, in the constant cycle of birth and death and birth among her many plants and animals, and in the ways she attends to the oneness of mind, body, and spirit in her spaces, programs, and teachings. Her true and intimate dwelling in this place models how we might inhabit the larger *maṇḍala* of the earth.

Shrineroom in yurt, Tara Mandala (photo by Sarah D. Buie)

The *maṇḍala* is an all-encompassing spatial archetype; it maps in visual form the space of the whole, of all potential, and the interdependent quality of all form and activity arising within that space. At each of these three centers, one sees a conscious engagement with *maṇḍalic* principles and many other spatial archetypes as well—in response to the natural settings in which they live, and within the structures they create. These include awareness of location, relative to the energies of the land around and beneath them *(feng-shui)* and in regard to the four cardinal directions. Experiences of threshold are significant in both practice and living spaces; the unfolding of paths expresses interrelatedness, and serves as an environment for mindfulness practice. Cave, mountain, river, and tree are natural archetypes with significance in all of these environments. The *maṇḍala* arises in architectural forms, in ecologically sensitive ways of living, in the relationships of buildings to the natural environment, in the topography of the land, and in the forms and activities of the community.

Finally, these three teachers create numerous opportunities for the experience of emptiness, the ultimate spatial archetype, and the ground from which all form arises. Throughout, their skillful manifestations of and within archetypal space further our awareness of the universal conditions of energy and relationship, as well as of the space and mind which all living beings inhabit and share.

Joan Halifax and Upaya, Santa Fe, New Mexico

Joan Halifax trained as an anthropologist, and over the years of her remarkable career has integrated her understanding of shamanistic practices and indigenous healing systems with Buddhist practice and teaching. The author of several books, Joan does extensive work with death and dying (her book *Being with Dying* is forthcoming), and with engaged Buddhism, including environmental, prison, and health issues. She holds the Lamp Transmission from Thich Nhat Hanh, which she received in 1990, and belongs to the Tiep Hien Order. She is a founding teacher in the Zen Peacemaker Order, and was given Faka by Tetsugen Roshi in 1999.

In 1992, she founded Upaya on the outskirts of Santa Fe, in the valley through which the Santa Fe River flows down to the city from the Sangre de Christo mountains. The physical space of Upaya began with the main house, which Joan was given by Richard Brown Baker Roshi and Laurance S. Rockefeller. She has shepherded a steady organic expansion of the compound over the last six years, in order to meet the gradually expanding demands of program and community. She feels it is now nearly complete. Upaya includes a number of buildings on acreage between Cerro Gordo Mountain to the north and the Santa Fe River to the south, and there is ongoing work on the landscaping of the entire "campus." As a space, Upaya reflects (both in particulars and as a whole) Joan's heightened sensitivity to the way space shapes and expresses consciousness.

The compound is sited in an especially powerful location, in terms of geomantic energies as well as the historic use of the valley as a passageway.

> The building was given to me, I didn't choose it.... I really wanted to be in the countryside near wilderness...but it was given to me, and I was grateful for many reasons. It is in an east-west valley, very traditional, and a river runs through it—the Santa Fe River—which is the main

artery of this bioregion. Earlier inhabitants used this as a passage from area to area, so you feel the presence of ancestors here; also Hispanic peoples farmed and logged it. So it is the watershed, the main artery—all the water in Santa Fe comes from these mountains and drains through this valley. It is the perfect place for a Buddhist center because it is a liminal environment between civilization and the natural world.

The main building and the compound as a whole are sited such that the path of the sun both marks the cyclical passage of time and provides maximum heat and light. As spatial archetypes, mountain and river form a dynamic, synergistic pairing, and Upaya sits between them here, in the vital space of their coupling. This is auspicious from a *feng-shui* point of view, according to whose ancient principles the buildings are also sited:

> The sun throughout the year rides the eastern ridge, and it becomes a calendrical marker, a solar marker denoting the times of the year, the solstices and equinoxes. There is a fantastic view west. When I'm sitting in my office I can look all the way across to the Jemez Mountains. Just north of our main building is Cerro Gordo Mountain—it is a small mountain but from the top you can see Mount Taylor, the Jemez Mountains, Cataya—and south of our River House is the Santa Fe River. We have a strong mountain/river orientation, being on the south side of the mountain, and facing south, our accumulation of solar energy is very strong here.
>
> This is a classical temple space. In China, temples are given a specific form based on the human form, and [are placed] so that the buildings [relate well] to the natural environment and to each other. [Here] the head is the mountain [Cerro Gordo], the throat is the main building [Upaya House, meeting space, residence for students, and Joan's residence], the heart is the *zendo* [Cerro Gordo Zen Temple], and the kitchen and bathing functions are in the River House. The spine runs north to south, in terms of *feng-shui*—it is amazing how it spontaneously ended up perfect.

The *maṇḍala* is evoked in the ways that Joan uses the buildings, and in the rich assembling of cultural references, which coexist in satisfying harmonies:

> There are some really important aspects of the way [I use the space in teaching]...the space can be changed very easily, it is a container, and things within the space can be rearranged easily, and they are—so that

> there is a sense of open space, and constant movement within the space. The spaces themselves are very feminine, the adobe walls have a very soft sculpted feeling, with wooden vigas and latillas supporting the ceiling. The iconography from the four worlds is represented; it is very southwestern in feeling, and Buddhist (Tibetan, Zen), Hispanic Catholic, and native American [elements] are present...it is not subdued, there is a feeling of brightness and aliveness.

Loosening yet observing the boundaries between inside and outside is important to Joan, who has also given particular attention to the thresholds of the buildings, and marked them with wreaths, sculpture, and *ristras* (garlands of dried chili peppers):

> The interior space is different than the exterior space—the inside has [a] female feeling. Outside and inside...they are connected through many doors and many windows...there is a sense of transparency but containment. I think these are features we try to cultivate in our meditation practice. The plaster is like a living skin on the walls, something that covers the earth. Human touch is very apparent...this building is beautiful to live and practice in, soft and extremely sturdy, beautiful and solid, feminine and transparent. It works wonderfully environmentally—it is cool in summer, and holds heat in the winter.
>
> It is more than a home—it is a public space with many doors. The main building has ten doors, so it is very connected [to the outdoors] and River House also has ten doors. Non-inclusivity is very important... I added a lot of doors to this house, and to the other building as well....

As an environment, Upaya celebrates and expresses its location and makes careful use of natural resources, recycling whenever possible:

> I spent most of the spring working on the landscaping myself...I've had a lot of fun doing this.... When construction was finished around these buildings it was scorched earth, really awful, so that everything you see around the buildings we put in, and what I've tried to do is create a sense of wildness, with native grasses, [and] flowers that seed themselves through the seasons like flax, poppies, Mexican hats, and so on; we have a lot of native plants—juniper, chamisa, ponderosa, aspen, New Mexico privet, mountain madrone. There is a really incredible feeling of seasons here. In formal gardens one feels an attempt to fix something in

time and space, while here we really let things express change. We have worked hard to create a landscape that is natural, has its own life, that attracts wildlife, insects, birds, deer, bees, butterflies, that is low maintenance, that carries through the seasons in a beautiful way, and that uses little water, and provides shade for us when we go outside. We created a wetland...[using] waste water from the house, and cattails and other plants that purify the water—all the waste water from the house goes through the wetlands system. And then we have an underwater irrigation system [for] our fruit trees in the meadowlands. And on the north side of the house we have a beautiful vegetable garden, herbs, lettuces, and things.... It's a whole marvelous system.

The importance of scale, of the size of the space and the activities within them, relates to Joan's conviction that practice involves becoming intimate with ourselves, our minds, and with the world:

It does feel like a kind of village or a site for a big clan.... We can house about thirty-five people, including our staff, which is really just perfect. My main interest is not to create a big home Sangha. Our *zendo* cannot hold more than thirty people—this is small. This is a training center, where people come from all over the world, to study engaged Buddhism, and to learn how to practice in the world. [At this size] I don't feel I have committed myself physically or fiscally on a scale that is going to exhaust me, the people [who] work with me, or our resources. We're kind of like an inexhaustible source because we've kept the container small.

It's on an intimate scale, which is so important. I don't get a lot of pleasure standing before a thousand people and lecturing—my real nourishment [comes] from very deep, concentrated contact with a few people at a time. This is a limited environment—we can't have hundreds of people here. Intimacy is the key in having a practice that is true, because you are trying to become intimate with the world, abiding in ultimate closeness. Here we try to have a sense of Sangha, community, while at the same time living alone together. There is a great respect for people's individual spaces. There is often deep silence here. The rooms are quite insulated from each other because of the adobe, the deep walls, so its quite quiet, although we're not far from the center of the city. So it is a strong community with a great respect for solitude... transparency and containment....

The current common practice space is the Cerro Gordo Zen Temple, built over twenty years ago. It is a white, square building, with a white stūpa in its courtyard (the first Tibetan stūpa built in this country). Joan proposes that the last building project she will undertake at Upaya be a more feminine space, in its geometry, color, and in the ways it will be used. It will be dedicated to Jishu Glassman (Buddhist teacher and wife of Bernard Glassman), who died in the spring of 1998:

> I think we'll have one more building project here, one last project—a *kiva* dedicated to Jishu Glassman. We will call it a roundhouse...partially sunken in the ground, with no symbols at all. It will be a place where we will meet in council, where there will be music, dancing, meditation, and it will be intersectarian (Buddhist-wise), but also interfaith. It will be called Essence of Compassion (Jishu's name). On the south side of the building, we'll place a large red boulder, a stūpa for her, where others may also place ashes. I think we can build this as a community project. The current *zendo* is a square, and so is the white stūpa—they are more male in their energy...the roundhouse will be a feminine counterpart. The interior plaster of the roundhouse will be ochre-colored plaster, a gorgeous gold interior, and you will come in through a low door...it is good that people bow down, [as they do] in the current *zendo.*
>
> We do a lot of work with council, with the circle. We feel that it is a profound practice of deep listening and speaking, of right speech, very democratic, deeply allowing of differences. It is very important to hear from everybody.

Joan has and continues to create spaces in which movement is both possible and encouraged, in which multiplicities of view coexist and find voice; the Buddhist space of emptiness is present in both form and process at Upaya:

> In terms of emptiness, these are almost like cave dwellings with nothing in them. You can take all the furniture out. The principle of emptiness is strong here—the sky is important here, which is why we created a lot of outdoor space. This environment is beautiful all year round, and the sky is such an important element to the practice here, because you want to mix your mind with the sky. You see weather systems coming and going, and it's just weather. If we were just taking refuge inside these adobe buildings, inside the cave, I think it would be very restrictive. We create a lot of outdoor feeling here, people sit under the portals,

we meet in a lot of outdoor spaces as well as indoors. Sometimes we do walking meditation practice in the *zendo* courtyard, and also between the buildings...the making of paths has been really important, how worlds connect is relevant.

We have put a lot of time, energy, and money into pathmaking, connecting outdoor and indoor spaces. This area was used as a passageway before, and it still is.... This is a watering hole, people travel to it, are nourished [by] it. Only a few of us are here to give care to the pilgrims. It is an east-west path, a passageway for many people who have had catastrophic illnesses.... There is a feeling of a deep east-west travel, from awakening to dying.

Usually, when most women come into a center, [the creation of the space] has already been done...like in the San Francisco Zen Center, like what Blanche Hartman inherited, which was created by men. [Upaya] is really grounded in a female vision.

Tsultrim Allione and Tara Mandala: Pagosa Springs, Colorado

In alpine meadows and valleys between a small breast-shaped peak and the strong currents of the San Juan River, a remarkable process of place-making is underway. The Buddhist community of Tara Mandala is creating a center for study, practice, and environmentally conscious living within a landscape of a powerfully *maṇḍalic* character. One comes to Tara Mandala from Pagosa Springs—first down the valley of the San Juan River, then west into Burns Canyon. Climbing gradually up to the center itself, the land has a wild, fresh quality to it, opening to the vast sky and panoramas in all directions. Covered with wildflowers and a variety of trees (ponderosa pine, pinon, cedar, fir, and cottonwood), it is home to a great number of animals—hawks, ravens, eagles, owls, foxes, elk, deer, wildcats, bear, wild horses, among many others. One arrives at the center with glimpses of prayer flags catching the wind, and the white yurt, the original shrine structure, on the mountainside in the distance.

Tsultrim Allione is the founder and spiritual director at Tara Mandala, this unique retreat center on 850 acres of land between the San Juan National Forest and Ute tribal land in southwestern Colorado. She was first ordained as a nun by His Holiness the Karmapa in 1970, and studied with Kalu Rinpoche, Apho Rinpoche, Trungpa Rinpoche, and others. She gave up her vows to marry and raise three children, but returned to teaching when they were older. Her most recent study in Dzogchen practice has been with Namkhai Norbu Rinpoche, Gungteng Tulku, and Tulku Somgnag. She is the author of *Women of Wisdom*, an introduction to the role of enlightened women in Tibetan Buddhism. She intends for students at Tara Mandala to be supported so as to be able to enter the depths of meditation practice as was once possible in Tibet.

> I had several dreams about moving to the West and [about] land like this .... We had a circle at a retreat in California when I finally decided to really start looking, and everyone meditated and saw what they saw in terms of land.... In that vision I saw stripes of rock, different colors. When we came to look at this place I recognized those rock formations [at the entrance to the canyon where Tara Mandala now lies], but it wasn't until I climbed the breast-shaped peak and stood on top that I realized this really is a *maṇḍala*—it has a quality of receptivity and gentleness. This land has a very feminine quality; it holds you, and it has the feeling of center and fringe like a *maṇḍala*, and lots of different things can be happening on the land without disturbing each other, because of the way it's set, with ridges and separate valleys.... When I stood up on top of Ekajati Peak I said to Dave, [my husband], "This is it," and he said, "But we haven't looked at anything else," and I said, "I know, but this is it."

The five-hundred-acre property they purchased (plus surrounding private parcels now owned by community members) had been part of a very large ranch, which stretched almost to Pagosa Springs; it had been logged, homesteaded, and farmed in more recent years, but there is also evidence on the land of its earlier habitation by the native people, perhaps Anasazi or Ute. Pithouses, a metate (grinding stone), and arrowheads have been found here; Tsultrim speculates that the mountain may have been the site of vision quests. Having a relationship with those who lived here before is very important to Tsultrim, and she has sought connections from the beginning with the Utes, and especially Bertha Grove, one of the elders, who is supportive of Tara Mandala and has been doing ceremonies on the land since they came here:

> What you are trying to do here has the blessings of the land's guardian; in fact all that you are trying to do is already here, you must just bring it from the spirit world into the material world. So it will not be difficult, there will be a lot of support.

There was no known name, native or otherwise, for the small breast-shaped mountain, so they called it Ekajati Peak, after the protectress of Dzogchen, who has one breast, one eye, and one tooth. One feels the presence of the mountain and its nourishing energy at the center of the Tara Mandala, as it serves to center one wherever one moves on the land. From its eastern slope, one looks east toward the rising sun and the San Juan River, San Juan Mountains, and the Continental Divide in the distance. From its western face, one sees the setting sun, as well as Chimney Rock with its Great Kiva (one of the most northerly Anasazi sites) close by, and the Four Corners area, rich in sites sacred to native peoples.

Orienting the site to relate to major topographic features and to the movement of the sun is important in the community planning, as is building in such a way that the animals will continue to thrive, by leaving at least half the land undeveloped for "wildness, animals, and visions quests," and by developing in clusters, with as little impact on the natural landscape as possible. In its master plan, the community lays out its ecological design principles, which include careful attention to all aspects of their use of land and natural resources, including use of solar energy, a solar well pump, biological wastewater treatment, passive heating and cooling, and the use of renewable materials in construction. In siting, they will take advantage of the natural peaks and valleys that both separate and join spaces within the topographical *maṇḍala.*

> Essentially [development will be in] three different stages: this area [will contain] the more public, larger spaces for summer programs; the next valley over is the residential retreat center, and beyond that [lie] the hermitage cabins. [The original yurt] will always be here because this is the first [building], so it is sacred; it's been empowered by all the practice that we've done here already so [it] will always be maintained. The new part will be on the ridge—with a kitchen, dining room, our store, childcare.... We want to [build] an elders' home for people who want to go into retreat until they die, and to have a school, an institute, and a bigger meditation hall.... We are in the process now of working [on all of it] with an architect...
>
> We're living outside now. We live outside for five months a year in a tent. We eat outside and cook outside, and we want to try to maintain that feeling of outside in the buildings, with a lot of windows and open doorways, breezeways, outdoor cooking and eating areas...bancos and portals, things like that. [For the public area,] the idea is [to have a] summer encampment, which was traditional in Tibet. People come, receive teachings, and camp in the valleys, and they would go off to their caves and hermitages for the winter.

In many ways, Tsultrim and the Tara Mandala community are working to live out new models for relationship, to the land, to other living beings, to community, and to mind as they work with council and partnership models. Spatial archetypes, particularly those of the circle, the *maṇḍala* (with the four cardinal directions), and the tree, are central images and resources for them.

> You notice we have a round space and we have the shrine in the middle [of it] instead of at one end.... We're trying to move out of the dominator model into the partnership model, and we work with council—we have councils every day, small ones—so having the shrine in the middle means that everyone is facing the shrine and everyone is facing each other, instead of [being] in rows. Having the shrine in the middle creates the sense of the divinity facing each person, and each person facing each other, so there's a recognition of the awakened quality of each person. We [also] have this seat, the teacher's seat...the image is like a *mālā* with one bigger bead...[but still it's] a circle, with everyone connected.
>
> All the meeting and ceremonial spaces (like the outdoor dance platform) will be round; the housing and the kitchen will have straight walls, but the kitchen will be U-shaped, with a fire circle in a central courtyard looking out to the east. What I'd like to do when we build our meditation hall is to [model] it on the circle with the four directions—the *maṇḍala* principle—so there would be five shrines. Every year we do an event at Spirit Rock in California and set up five shrines of the five *ḍākinīs* on the *maṇḍala* principle, and work in that space. Everyone is always commenting how amazing it is to be in a space where every direction is sacred. Normally you just aim at one of them, but to have that experience of five shrines creates a very whole feeling.

Adjoining the outdoor kitchen space at Tara Mandala is their mother tree, a box elder, with a shrine of small offerings from the community—reminiscent of the tree shrines in India and Nepal where appreciation of the tree's role as tree of life and axis mundi is continually demonstrated.

> Another model we have used is that of the tree, with the trustees at the roots, the existing council as the trunk, the various functions and activities of the center as the limbs, and the retreatants as the leaves, coming and going.

Tsultrim has built a small retreat cabin on the ridge below the peak of Ekajati. It is built into the land on a promontory in such a way that it feels deeply rooted and protected, at the same time that it acts almost as the prow of a ship, its windows opening to views west, to the Four Corners area, Chimney Rock, and miles beyond. From this lofty place, one especially appreciates the remarkable natural container in which this community is rising, as well as the potential for structures to expand and support conscious awareness. Here, the balance of containment and expansiveness, safety and vulnerability, and the integration of natural given elements with architecture make a space that is both intimate and universal, a space for the transformation of mind.

> I chose that place, partly because of its strong relationship to Chimney Rock—it is a very powerful site, with a number of *kivas* below the peaks. [The cabin itself] has natural logs inside, like you are inside a tree, and one wall is the natural rock of the ridge. The stone acts as a solar mass and holds the heat, so that it doesn't freeze there in the winter [despite the elevation and exposure].
>
> A Nepali teacher who visited here often goes into a trance in places, and she did so here, and said a lot about the land. She said that everything would occur as we had planned, though a lot would take place after we'd died. She said that there were Tārās here, and that the Buddha had passed over here and dropped a bead from his *mālā*. She saw a Vajrayoginī *maṇḍala* in my retreat cabin, in the wall of stone.

Yvonne Rand and Redwood Creek Dharma Center, Northern California

Yvonne Rand is a Buddhist meditation teacher who holds retreats at Redwood Creek Dharma Center, and teaches all over the country as well. She was born in San Francisco, and has lived within a fifty-mile radius of the city all her life; she has lived and taught in her current center for twenty-six years. In the intimate space she uses to meet with students individually, she has pictures of her root teachers as well as images of some of the great practitioners in all of the schools of Buddhism, including Shunryu Suzuki Roshi, Dainin Katagiri Roshi, the Fourteenth Dalai Lama, the late Venerable Tara Tulku, and Harry Kellett Roberts. She is currently writing a book on her work with people as they are dying, as well as a book on right speech.

Yvonne is very knowledgeable about the ecology of the area of California where she lives and practices; she applies her experience with the plants and seasons of the bioregion to the development and tending of an extensive garden.

> We are located on the western flank of Mount Tamalpais in the watershed of Redwood Creek. We are at the opening of the valley, and Mount Tamalpais is the nearest high holy place. Harry Roberts, with whom I

studied for a number of years, worked as a cowboy in the adjacent valley where Green Gulch Farm Zen Center is now located. For a number of years a small group of us went out for a weekend once a month, year-round, criss-crossing the coast range from San Francisco to the Oregon border, studying plants and geology and all manner of things having to do with where we live.

Yvonne has created her retreat center over a number of years, slowly converting existing structures and adding others, so that now the compound is a rambling, comfortable mix of low buildings (home, meditation hall, retreat kitchen, small retreat huts, office and studio space) all with windows and doors opening out, encouraging a great deal of living outdoors in the abundant garden and orchard. The threshold to the compound is a gate house with a small shrine housing six figures of compassion, one for each of the six realms of existence; a gingko tree is planted nearby. A visitor enters here and follows the winding path through gardens to the *zendo;* the path itself is a golden orange—concrete colored with iron oxide.

Outside Tibetan temples you usually find incense burners. I found a clay Mexican fireplace, which is the same shape as those censers, and we have it here at the front porch and entry into the meditation hall.

The meditation space is at the heart of the compound and embodies much of what Yvonne speaks of in her teaching. A fluid, light-filled space, it houses an extensive collection of Buddhist art, especially from the Tibetan Buddhist traditions.

My main focus in teaching is on training the mind, aiming for cultivated awareness—awareness that can lead to the dissolving and transformation of our conditioning. On the Buddhist meditation path there is a clear description of the possibility of anything unwholesome being transformed into what is wholesome. The Tibetan sacred art tradition expresses the possibility of transformation well. We have many figures of wisdom and compassion, of male and female. Sarasvatī is at the front gate, Prajñāpāramitā is here, and in the meditation hall we have Vajrayoginī, Tārā—many, many buddhas and bodhisattvas.

The door of the meditation space faces east, and there are altars all around the sides of the room. There are many windows so there is a sense of being outside when we are inside, and we can see the great trees that stand at the west, north, and south. I wanted the room to be as open as possible. We have radiant heat so the room can actually be kept quite cool and still be comfortable, because the floor is warm. And the room has come to have quite an energy from all of the time people have spent doing practice here. I find this space calm and welcoming.

We use blue for the meditation cushions. Blue is the color associated with healing in Buddhism and for us Americans it is a welcoming and friendly color. People who come to practice here sometimes have to spend a long time learning to have ease in their practice. So I encourage people to explore all of the postures for practice and not just sitting meditation. I encourage an understanding of the mind/body relationship. You cannot practice meditation, really, without attention to the physical body. In Zen, coming from Japan, which is a body culture, much teaching is done nonverbally and by watching one's teacher closely. Learning in that way bypasses language. The physical body and breath body are the basis of meditation, if it is taught effectively. The body does not lie. I welcome practitioners, including adepts in yoga and tai chi or chi kung, when we do retreats. We need to pay attention to the details of sitting, posture, alignment, the physicalness of awareness, awareness of eating, with meditations on interdependence, on the food being eaten—being present with the texture and taste of the food, the physicalness of chewing and swallowing.

The meditation space is built on the site of an old painting studio, and in a serendipitous way, four trees around it mark the four cardinal directions—a dawn redwood to the south, a coast redwood to the west, a red alder to the north, and at the gate house to the east, a gingko. Dawn redwood and gingko are among the oldest species of trees known on the planet, while red alder has a relatively short life span. The gingko was planted recently, while the other three trees are the oldest living beings in the compound. Yvonne sees them all as embodying teachings on time, interdependence, change, and impermanence.

There are four trees, marking the directions. They stand as guardians around the meditation space. The dawn redwood does not make seed until it has been growing for seventy-five years, so one plants it for the next generation. It gives us the long view. Inside the meditation hall, we have an altar set up for reminding us about impermanence. That is the theme I decided to work on in my own practice for this year, but also for my teaching focus this year. We can all spend a long time with this focus.

Indoor and outdoor spaces here are linked by the flowing energy of windows, doors, paths, arbors, decks, and patios, which make the indoor and outdoor spaces truly interdependent and equally important to life in the compound.

> There is a deck all around the meditation hall for walking meditation. I encourage students to meditate out of doors, and we have a number of areas where people can walk or sit outside in the garden. Sometimes we sit outside and let our eyes rest on the sky, considering the vast, spacious sky-like quality of the mind.

In the extensive gardens of the compound, a large area with a serpentine path among plantings near the creek is dedicated to walking meditation. Several old tractor wheels have been mounted on posts and painted with mantras—American prayer wheels—and a rock garden of Jizō-like forms is located across from Yvonne's writing house, tucked away in the back of these gardens. The range of colorful flowers and their abundance is breathtaking and at the same time, very conducive to slowing down and paying close attention. There are some native flowers (lily, iris, currant, coffeeberry, manxantia, sorrel, thimble berry, ferns) and also medicinals like lemon balm, digitalis, mint, and lemon verbena.

In addition to the range of plant life, the garden attracts and sustains a wide variety of birds (forty-two species by one count), especially hummingbirds, mourning doves, and quail, with an occasional blue heron. Raccoons, opossums, skunks, foxes and rabbits also make their home here.

After our walk through the grounds, Yvonne and I spoke about what other Buddhist women here and abroad are doing in creating the places in which they live and work, to both express and nurture conscious awareness. Yvonne told me of her experience visiting a small nunnery being built in northern India.

> On a recent trip to India, I witnessed an extraordinary example of place-making. The nunnery at Dharamsala, Dolma Ling, is nonsectarian, and provides a classical education and training for young nuns. The land on which it is built has enormous black boulders. They looked to me like huge, slumbering beasts. There is a mountain behind the site and a significant stream, which the local Indian women use for doing their laundry. The buildings have been designed and placed in relation to the stones and stream; they are two stories high, made of concrete since wood is scarce. The nunnery is being built within the limits of its environment—placement of the road [has] not interfere[d] with the stream; the traditional washing area [has been replaced] with improved spaces for the women to do their laundry. The labor used to build the building has included the women of the nearby village—thereby giving these women some income they can control. This has helped to stabilize the local economy since the men often drink their money away.

The buildings, including individual rooms, library, infirmary, and dining room, are built in semi-circles, in relationship to the sleeping beast boulders. One hears the sound of water throughout. There is a water purifying system and solar electricity—the entire project has been built with a sensitivity to the environment. It was in such marked contrast to a monastic project I saw on the same trip, in which the emphasis was on building big, fast, and grand, with little attention to the environmental impact, natural or cultural. [The nunnery] is strongly relational—a good example of the best of feminist, environmental perspectives in touch with the Dharma.

Afterword

When visiting each of these teachers in their spaces, one experiences the consonance of their words and aspirations with the environments they are creating. The spaces themselves serve as teachings of an extraordinary order—to enter and inhabit them is to experience in a comprehensive, felt way, the actual conditions of the *maṇḍala*—abundance, interrelatedness of all aspects of the whole, a ceaseless flow of change and transformation, and expressions of clear attentive mind in action and in repose. Through them we can better see the relatedness of space and mind; through them we can move, in both practice and mind, toward the *maṇḍalic* awareness they embody.

PART V

Body and Health

SICKNESS AND HEALTH:
Becoming a Korean Buddhist Shaman

Hi-ah Park

Hi-ah Park was the first woman in modern times to be trained as a court musician in Korea. She was initiated as a Korean shaman in 1981, and has since translated the Korean shamanic tradition into vibrant, multi-cultural forms for a global context.

Shamanism is an ancient indigenous Korean spiritual tradition dating as far back as the Neolithic era, and has long been practiced as a way of life. During the Three Kingdom Period (57 b.c.e.–676 c.e.), the aristocrats abandoned shamanism and embraced religions imported from China, including Confucianism, Taoism, and Buddhism. However, the common people have continued to practice shamanism up to this day.

Shamanic Initiation

A female shaman is called a *mudang* in Korean. The word *mu* means "sacred dance," and *dang* means "altar." In this case we can translate the term as "sacred dancer," meaning the one who offers the sacred dance to the altar of the spirit or god. The *mudang* is called to her profession by a mystical illness, known as *sinbyong,* and is then initiated in a *naerim kut,* a Korean shamanic initiation ceremony, which resolves her suffering by enshrining the possessing god in her body.

Through her initiatory sickness, the *mudang* escapes from the ordinary world by withdrawing into darkness so as to be reborn into a purely creative realm. By surrendering, and thus dying in her own heart, the shaman starts to see streams of light and awakens to the possessing god. In "dying," however, the shaman does not wither away, but rather lets her heart become undivided and gathered into one with divinity. When her heart is fixed on one point with divinity, she finds that nothing is impossible. The shaman thus taps into the divine world with the intention to work for the benefit of all sentient beings and, as a result, starts to understand the meaning of their lives.

The *mudang* is a female shaman healer and ritual specialist. As such, she acts asan intermediary with other worlds, such as the world of the ancestors. She has the

Hi-ah Park performing in Italy, 1993 (photo provided by Hi-ah Park)

ability to transform a reality of problems into positive living energy by expelling "devils," that is, the projection of negative human emotions of bitterness and fear. Shamans understand that all problems arise because of an inability to change hidden emotions. By allowing herself to express those hidden negative emotions coming from the psychic unconscious and to purify them, she cures the sick and defends the psychic integrity of the community. Thus, the *mudang* is also a seer, mystic, poet, musician, and dancer—one who practices techniques of ecstasy to communicate with the divine world.

In Korea, when the female shaman has completed her initiation, she is immediately referred to as a *posal*, a bodhisattva. A bodhisattva is a "being destined for enlightenment" who in her compassion for humankind delays her entry into Buddhahood in order to help others. When one becomes a shaman in Korea, the initial and most important vow, that of the bodhisattva, is to work for the benefit of all sentient beings who, because of the suffering condition of their existence, are in need of help.

In Korea today, almost all shamans are women. In the distant past, there were male as well as female shamans but, over the centuries, male shamans have become much rarer. It may be that women have special access to the feminine principles of spirituality, which enable them to bridge the abyss between this world and multiple states of bliss. Or, it may be that Korean women have traditionally not had the same opportunities for education as men and, therefore, have become less alienated from their intuitive and psychic powers than those who have had years of over-intellectualization. I, for example, had to unlearn twenty years of education before I was ripe for initiation.

While living in southern California as a dancer, I received several requests to perform shamanic rites for the Korean community—even though I had not yet become a shaman. My first ritual performance was in June, 1980, at the Mingei International Folk Art Museum in La Jolla, California. Mr. Zozayong, the director of the Emile Museum in Seoul, Korea, asked me to perform a *kut*, a "Happiness and Guardian Spirit" dance. I was surprised when Mr. Zozayong respectfully introduced me as a *mudang*, particularly since *mudangs* are looked down upon in Korea. I was a little concerned about how I was going to perform the ritual, but when it came time to give the actual performance, I somehow knew how to do it.

During the next year, I performed two more *kut* in California. Each time, the spirits entered me in a most powerful way, guiding me to perform rituals whose meaning I only later learned. After these ceremonies, I sensed deeply that I could not treat these spirits who entered me lightly.

Every time I returned home from these performances, I felt oppressive aching in my shoulders and pelvic area. There was a great weight on my chest, and I felt as if someone or something were binding my body. Then I became completely incapacitated, unable to do even the simplest domestic chores. I was sick for two months, and I knew I needed help.

Since I'd had two similar illnesses prior to this one, I intuitively knew that this was not something a regular medical doctor could handle. The clarity, freedom, and heightened awareness I had experienced while performing the rituals conflicted with the rationalizations, anger, fear, and defensive feelings that plagued my normal state of consciousness. The conflict had given rise to a psychosomatic ailment.

During this illness, I had three consecutive visions. In my second vision, I saw Tan-Kun, the heroic founder of the Korean nation, sitting in a meditation posture inside a yurt and wearing a red hat and robe. As I gazed intensely at him, we became one; then I saw myself actually sitting as Tan-Kun. This clear vision of Tan-Kun convinced me to visit my homeland after an absence of fifteen years.

I didn't have any specific plan for my visit. However, from its start, everyone I met and everywhere I visited turned out to be connected somehow with shamanistic practices. Within a week, I was introduced by a friend, Professor Choi Jong-Min, to Kim Keum-Hwa, a well-known *hwang-haedo manshin* (a shaman from a western province of Korea).

When Kim Keum-Hwa came into the room in her house where I was waiting, we both shuddered. She told me she had the sensation that her spirits wanted to talk with me. She brought in her divination table and started to pronounce oracles:

"Double rainbows are surrounding in all directions. The fruit is fully ripe and can't wait anymore!" She told me I was very lucky to have surrendered to the spirits' orders and to have come to her. Otherwise, she said, I would have died, like an overripe fruit that falls onto the ground and rots.

My body started swaying uncontrollably in a circular motion. With tears running down my face, I tried to hold my knees still with both hands, but I couldn't stop the swaying. Kim Keum-Hwa continued to explain that I had disobeyed twice already and, consequently, I had to go through unbearable pain and loneliness and near-death experiences. She warned that if I were to resist a third time, there would be no forgiveness. It was absolutely essential that I undergo the *naerim kut* (initiation ceremony) without delay.

On a more positive note, Kim told me that she saw double rainbows stretched around my head, celestial gods surrounding and protecting me in four directions, and warrior spirits descending on me. She said that the warrior spirit in me was so strong that I would want to stand on the *chakdu* (sharp blades) of the initiation ceremony.

She predicted that, in the near future, I would be a famous shaman and I'd travel around the world as a global shaman. Then she set a date for the initiation—June 23, 1981, less than two weeks away.

My new godmother, Kim Keum-Hwa, asked me to eat no meat during the week before the ceremony. As in the previous rituals in the United States, I didn't know what would happen, but I was determined to find out what power had brought me here and what the meaning and purpose of my life were.

In the morning, I bathed in a cold mountain stream, then climbed Mt. Samgak (located to the north of Seoul) with my godmother. At one point, she asked me to climb up a steep cliff to get a branch from a pine tree. This task was the first test of the day. I did as she asked to receive *sanshin* (the mountain spirit), and we talked as little as possible.

At the mountain altar, I offered rice, rice cakes, three kinds of cooked vegetables, fruits, candles, incense, and *makgholi* (homemade rice wine). As my godmother chanted and beat a small gong, I held up the *sanshin dari,* a long piece of white cotton cloth called *minyong* (white cotton bridge) through which the shaman receives the mountain spirits.

My body started to quiver uncontrollably—a sign that the spirit was entering me. I completely surrendered to the spirit, turning off my internal dialogue and entering into inner silence. I sensed light coming from every direction, and I started to feel drunk with the spirit in me. It was the dramatic close encounter with the separated "lover" at long last. I felt the ultimate completion of my primordial self before separation. I knew that the spirit loved me and forgave my long resistance to accepting it. Bathed by the light of spirits, I felt clean and reborn. I practically flew down the mountain.

I joined the group of shamans and guests in my godmother's house at the foot of the mountain. I was the sole initiate. We began with a short ceremony invoking and greeting the spirits, followed by a *huhtun kut* (purification ritual). The *huhtun kut* is conducted to cleanse and humble the initiate, in order to dissolve the infantile image of her personal past and prepare her for transformation into a pure spirit of unlimited power.

The ritual started with drumming and chanting, while the shaman's assistants put a basket of cooked millet on my head. Then I danced in a circular motion toward each direction, ending the dance by throwing the basket. This process is repeated until the basket lands in an upright position—that is the sign that the evil spirits have been repelled. It wasn't easy in the beginning. The weather was very hot, and I was wearing a full Korean costume. Moreover, I felt self-conscious and a little ridiculous in front of all the onlookers. I kept failing until I couldn't bear the embarrassment anymore. Then, suddenly, something magical happened—all the onlookers disappeared from my view, I felt a point of true fire in my center, and I achieved complete tranquility. Finally, the basket landed correctly.

The initiation ceremony continued with an examination to test my psychic ability and to determine if I could identify the deities who had descended on me, by selecting the appropriately colored clothes. After I revealed all the spirits (sun/moon/stars, mountain spirits, high nobility, ancestors, and warriors) through dancing accompanied by drumming, my godmother nodded her head to signal my having made the correct choice and asked me, "Where are your bells and fan?" When I hesitated, she teased me for trying to figure it out. She said that "too much time in the university" was clouding my non-rational, intuitive, and all-knowing self. Then I moved into an ecstatic deep trance and found the bells and fan hidden under the big skirt of the drummer.

Next they put seven brass bowls with identical covers onto a table. My task was to uncover the bowls in the correct order. While dancing to the drummer's accompaniment, I started to feel and touch the covers. My hands followed the energy. Under the first cover that I removed I found clear water—which one is supposed to uncover first and symbolizes clear consciousness and face. I danced while holding that cover, then opened the rest of the bowls in this order: rice, ashes, white beans, straw, money, and filthy water.

My godmother interpreted the meaning of each. Rice is for helping people's lives. Ashes are a symbol of name and fame. Beans and straw feed the horse for the shaman's journey and are good omens for the successful growth of the new shaman. By picking the clear water first and the filthy water last, I showed a purity of consciousness and successfully passed the test. I saluted, with a big bow on the ground to my godmother and her assistant, and thus symbolized my rebirth as a new shaman.

The Korean shamanic initiation ceremony consists of many rituals, but I would like to describe in detail the *chaktu kori* (sharp blades ritual), the highlight of the *naerim kut*, the initiation ritual. This ritual takes place around a seven-foot tower of *chaktu* blades, which is made of seven layers that include drums, a table, a water jar, a rice pot, and boards.

My initiation ritual began when my godmother pulled me next to her. She started to sing a *mansubaji,* a shamanic invocation chant, and gave me two swords. Taking them, I began dancing and, connecting with my spirit body, I arose transformed as a spiritual warrior. I knew then that I had to contact my deep fear of death, to die completely, and to be reborn with the warrior spirit.

Initially, I was overwhelmed by my unconscious fear of death. When I started dancing with the swords, my normal awareness shifted into one of the primal spirit. As I increased my energy tremendously, I gained sufficient courage to enter the room where the two *chaktu* blades were kept wrapped in red cloth. Entering the room was like going into the underworld, some unknown distant place an eternal journey away.

The moment I brought the red cloth close to my eyes, I felt the unknown warrior in me smiling and I grabbed the *chaktu.* With this elation, a totally different person emerged who knew no fear or limitation. I unwrapped the red cloth and the big sharp *chaktu* blades revealed themselves—looking like large meat cleavers with handles on both ends.

I started pressing the heavy *chaktu* against my arms, legs, face, and mouth, but it didn't cut me. All around me the onlookers were very afraid and paid close attention to the ritual. After I proved nothing could harm me, I did the most vigorous dance I have ever done in my life and, at its peak, I flew up to the *chaktu.* People told me later that my eyes did not look human, but took on the luster of the eyes of a tiger.

When I stood barefoot on the sharp blades, I was freed from the constraints of being in time and space. People pleaded with me to come down to the ground but, as they told me later, I stayed up there nearly an hour. Everyone was breathless, and some wept from the sheer intensity of the experience.

When a *mudang* enters into a *mu-a*, the shamanic trance state, her body transforms into the apparitional body known in Buddhism as the *nirmāṇakāya.* She becomes one with the divine presence, and this union creates the pure pleasure of the *dharmakāya* or emptiness. I emphatically believe that the highest level of human evolution is experiencing this union with the divine presence, the mystical rapture of the shaman's ecstatic trance or the "empty" state of the Buddhist meditation. Preceded by the submission of the persona or ego, this is the key to the most creative processes. The shaman's journey of ecstasy, or profound Buddhist meditation, makes the human mind capable of exploring and discovering a higher state of being. It truly helps us to understand the art of divine energy.

Naerim kut, the Korean shaman's initiation with its sacred dance and music, provided me with a direct introduction to the primordial state through the unification of mind, body, and spirit. This ritual became my most significant personal rite of passage and it led me to self-empowerment. Fundamentally pure from the very beginning, there is nothing now for me to reject or accept. I experience myself as I am, as the center of the universe. Maintaining this utmost pure, primordial state, "the body of light" is achieved—the common ground of both the *mudang* and the bodhisattva.

On the Path to Shamanic Initiation

When I began studying shamanism in 1975, I had neither the wish nor the intention to become a shaman. I initially considered the process solely an artistic endeavor, and began my inquiry as a way for me to reach deeper into the core of my being and work. Yet everything I encountered along the shamanic path seemed to create a thirst in me for spiritual fulfillment.

My first experience of shamanism was in early childhood. A neighbor of ours had a severe case of hiccoughs that continued for several days. I remember that a *mudang* came to the man's house and waved her sword around his head—chanting, singing, and dancing with total integration. At that time I did not know what a *mudang* was, but I was literally entranced by the shaman's performance. I found it difficult to talk about this experience to anyone because of my staunch upbringing as a Christian. Shamanism and supernatural activities were viewed as superstition, so I kept this experience a separate reality deep in my heart.

It wasn't until I was a graduate student in the UCLA dance department in 1975 that I began to integrate that childhood experience. One day in class, Allegra Snyder, chairperson of the Dance Ethnology Department, asked us each to remember and then describe the most extraordinary experience in our lives. As I closed my eyes in the meditation process, I entered an altered state. My body started to shake uncontrollably, not from nervousness but, rather, as if someone were shaking me. As I talked about my experience of seeing the *mudang,* I felt as if someone else were speaking through me.

Later I experienced a similar physical sensation while watching a film called *Pomo Indian Sucking Doctor.* I immediately recognized that the Pomo Indian healing ceremony was related to the dancing and chanting I had observed as a child.

After those incidents, I began to experience frequent episodes of physical trembling and inner vibrations, which frightened me. Until then I had never thought it important to talk about my childhood experience, but I now found that it was necessary to do so if I were to understand myself. I began to explore who I was, where I came from, how I got here, and where I was going.

Although I wholeheartedly loved and respected traditional Korean music and dance, my real quest was to answer the questions "Who am I?" and "Where am I going from here?" Entertaining onlookers who were hungry for amusement was not enough of a reason for me to perform, and I started to feel that some very important element was missing. For a while the performances made me very happy, but I started to lose interest doing the performances just for their own sake. I realized I did not get any new information or insight from them. I needed to push my limited mind beyond what I saw as cultural conditioning. I needed to be free from any established religion or fixed cultural boundaries, and I wanted to know a deeper meaning of my life.

At this point, I suffered from about nine months of insomnia, tedium, and terrible paralysis. My interest in mundane affairs and domestic chores waned completely. I longed for the mountains, and spent many nights weeping endlessly or dreaming of impending death. In my dreams, I was imprisoned in the underworld and chased by wild animals who dismembered my body. I endured many sleepless nights until I had an incredible, lengthy dream about an ancient royal funeral procession. My insomnia stopped right after this mysterious dream. I was happy without any specific reason and felt elevated, as though somebody were lifting me into the air. After this dream, my dreams started to become lighter, more celestial ones.

In one unforgettable dream journey during this period, a white unicorn with wings appeared and rode with me through the galaxy and the almost endless Milky Way to an incredible, infinite space of dark indigo. In that space, I heard a deep and resonant voice ask me, "How are the people down there?" I still remember clearly the conversation I had with that voice, and the ecstatic feeling I had. The voice then told me I had to go back to earth to teach people. Without any sense of waking up from a dream I found myself in my bed.

For a while I was obsessed by this dream and felt very connected with another reality. Although I couldn't understand it, the other space was so clear that I now felt as if my waking state were the dream. I allowed myself to be completely lost, without knowing who I was and without the benefit of any spiritual map or specific form of guidance. The more I was lost, the more I began to improvise with sound and movement to create energy in my meditation. I started to experience the power of sound and movement as healing to my own wounded child, as personal transformation, and even as empowerment.

During this time, the fall of 1977, I was invited to perform with an avant-garde improvisation group called Kiva at the University of California at San Diego. The night before my first participation with Kiva, I had an extraordinary dream.

As I started to dance in the studio, the studio became an underwater place in the ocean. I started dancing in slow motion like an octopus, absolutely out of breath and time, and weightless. I still remember the luminous sensation. As I continued to dance, various kinds of light and forms passed, ending up with a radiant bright rainbow light. Then I saw Emilie Conrad D'aoud sitting, watching me dance—she is a founder of Continuum dance studio whom I met shortly after this dream and with whom I eventually studied movement meditation. She was smiling brightly and was nodding her head as a sign of special recognition. The wave forms were singing, and I was riding on their song. Each song lifted me higher; I was blissful, and radiant light came from every direction. I experienced "love's body" as the fluidity that can openly embrace the creative unknown—an experience I was later to have over and over with Kiva and Continuum.

The next morning, as I had promised Kiva, I went to the Center for Music Experiment. I saw some very strange instruments in the studio and seeing them, I felt a little crazy. I found myself drawn to this extraordinary environment. When I got there, I didn't have any idea what I was going to do, and yet I didn't have any fear. This trust gave me the courage to embrace the unknown music. Since I didn't know anything, I couldn't do anything, so I gave up "doing." As I surrendered to the situation, I gave up gravity. I felt the whole universe supporting me, and I was very comfortable and relaxed even though I knew nothing about the musicians and their new music. Without any idea or program, I gained freedom without choice. This strange freedom made me aloof, free from bad and good, beautiful and ugly, which I saw as my own beliefs. In other words, I didn't have a mind to interpret, so I couldn't give myself any identity by using language. I started to feel warm and safe, and the whole environment became loving and supportive. I kept breathing deeply and slowly, and moved on through deepening experiences. Since I had no self to be identified with, I became like a mirror, a witness to my inner being; things came and went, and I (the mirror) remained vacant and empty. I reflected together with my own being.

Then a wondrous thing happened. It actually felt like something touched my inner self—the divine infant—the spirit, the soul, the essence of who I am. I kept breathing. I sensed the presence of the divine. I experienced a blissful tingling sensation all over my body. Then suddenly the "I" that I thought was in control of my breath was gone, and my breath breathed me! As I made connection with my inner breath, I was actually connected with my inner self. I merged with my breath—flowing, glowing, soaring, awakening my inner being—and with the tranquil sounds of my soul. I relaxed more, I breathed fully and freely, and then just when I thought I was relaxed more than was humanly possible, I breathed more fully than on any day since my birth. Then came the breathing release, and then the energy release—a cosmic orgasm, the ecstasy. I'd been in touch with something or someone that was incredible—beautiful, moving, and real. The rebirthing process went on for over an hour and a half. I felt absolutely out of time and space, in a weightless continuum. That was my first experience with Kiva. I was born again, free from mind and body.

This helped me more than anything else to touch my true nature. I slowly melted away from my ordinary, rational, intellectual mind and developed a new sense of who I am at a cellular level. I went back to being an unborn child. I still remember the intense loneliness of the quest for self during this period. The only source of medicine I had was my own movement meditation. However, the unbearable loneliness of the search for my identity took me to the threshold of genuine death and touched the abyss of my unconscious fear.

Prior to my actual shamanic initiation, and in the wake of this terrible period of confusion, I met His Holiness the Sixteenth Karmapa at the Shrine Auditorium at Los Angeles in 1976. Here he hosted an occasion of the special "black hat ceremony" for Westerners for the first time in history. As part of the *pūjā*, or worship, he touched everyone's head one by one. When His Holiness touched my head, I was literally electrified, and I was "far gone" until after everybody left the auditorium. When I came back to normal consciousness, there wasn't a single person left in that large room, and I found myself lying on the ground, trembling with uncontrollable energy. This was my first encounter with the living Buddha, the embodiment of buddha nature.

Later, after teaching summer school in 1977 at UCLA, I retired to a ranch located deep in the mountains. I left all worldly affairs behind, obsessed like a lover longing for the mountains. In the mountains I could feel the presence of something indescribably different, an exotic apparition, the spirit of which one cannot find in a human: a beautiful, bewitching spirit embracing boundless joy. I journeyed to Yosemite, Mt. Rainier, Death Valley, and the Grand Canyon, among other places.

In Canyon de Chelly, I was led by endless double rainbows to the White House cliff dwelling, which had ancient *kivas*, subterranean ritual chambers. As I emerged from a ruined *kiva*, a sudden thunderstorm came down on me mercilessly. I fainted onto the sand and, in a total surrender, I offered myself to the presence of the spirit. I awoke with the most incredible orgasm I have ever known, basking in the most luxurious ecstasy. The sky was replete with rainbows and the reflections of rainbows reaching the horizon. The mountain breeze passing through the canyon seemed to be coming and going in time to an inaudible chant. As I followed that chant, my soul ascended as a flying unicorn, higher and higher into the sky. At last I was free and flying with such a feeling of exhilaration and joy that I wanted to cry, for I was experiencing the ecstasy for which I had been yearning for so long.

TOKWANG SUNIM:
A Korean Nun as Medical Practitioner

Tokwang Sunim is a dedicated young nun and an herbalist and traditional medical doctor. She has a small practice on a busy street in the middle of Seoul.

FROM AN EARLY AGE I was interested in Buddhism and studied quite a lot. I became a nun when I was twenty-three years old. I went to Unmunsa Nunnery to study the sūtras for four years. I was not able to go to a meditation hall because halfway through my study I became quite ill for a while, and this made me interested in diseases. I studied Asian medicine for six years. I wanted to become a doctor to diagnose, treat, and cure the physical illnesses of people. I wanted also to help relieve their mental suffering by teaching them Buddhism, guiding them towards a more peaceful state of mind.

I plan to do this for a few more years. At the same time I continue my medical studies, and I am learning counseling and Buddhist psychology. During the day I treat people, and in the evening I study. There are three nurses who help me. First, I see the patient and do a diagnosis. Afterwards, the nurses get the acupuncture needles ready, get the moxibustion, and prepare the herbal medicines I prescribe for the patient. I apply the needles and the moxa; they take the needles out and wipe the moxa off. They also disinfect and sterilize everything.

I treat women and men without discrimination. Although I am a nun and should not touch men, I have no problem treating men because I do it with the mind of a doctor who sees only a patient in pain. I do it out of compassion. There are many ways to practice Buddhism and meditation. The path I have chosen is that of the bodhisattva: helping other people by treating their illnesses, and by telling them how to take care of themselves properly so as to prevent illnesses.

If my patients have mental pain and are in distress, I indicate some passages to read repeatedly in the sūtras, which could be helpful. I encourage them to chant and pray to gain the strength to cure their illness quickly. I do a lot of praying and chanting myself, and try to be very sincere and wholehearted when I do my job. Faith is very important to healing. Because it is a nun who makes the diagnosis, my patients have even more faith that they will be cured. Because I prescribe the various herbs myself, they have great confidence they they will make them better. It is the same with acupuncture; because a Buddhist nun applies the needles, it gives them more faith that they will be cured, and that it is good for them. When I prescribe chanting, they believe in it more, and it seems to have a good effect. A lot of the cure comes from having faith in the doctor and the treatment.

People have all different tendencies and temperaments, and their bodies also have different characteristics. Someone will have a weakness in the stomach, someone else in the liver, someone else in the lungs, or in the eyes. If someone is stressed, it can produce pain in their stomach; another person may get pain in their heart. We have to tone ourselves according to our characteristics and build up our health. We must take care of our health daily and we can rid ourselves of stress by relaxing, meditating, or doing sports and exercises.

Many illnesses are cured by the patient themselves. The doctor only helps. Doctors give medicines, but people should help their body by exercising and taking care of their diet. I ask my patients what they do and what their eating pattern is like. I advise them about nutrition and tell them about the mind and what to do to relieve stress. The doctor can prescribe a course of treatment, but only the patient can take the medicine.

Compiled and translated by Martine Batchelor

HOW A BUDDHIST DECIDES WHETHER OR NOT TO HAVE CHILDREN

Kate Lila Wheeler

Introduction

Near my bed at home I keep an antique postcard. Dating from the turn of the century, it is a hand-tinted photograph, taken in Sri Lanka, of a typical country scene. At the edge of a smooth dirt road, a woman bows to an ocher-robed Theravāda Buddhist monk, offering him a pot of food. The pot lies on the ground between them. He is slender, solemn, dignified. Various lay men and boys stand about in relaxed attitudes, observing the exchange. Behind them is a thatched dwelling of open, tropical construction.

The lay woman is giving alms food to the monk, a daily ritual still performed in Theravāda Buddhist countries, as it has been for more than 2,500 years. Soon, the monk will pick up his alms bowl from the ground, tuck it under his arm, and return to his nearby monastery to eat his last meal of the day, no later than noon.

Then he will spend the rest of his day studying, meditating, and cultivating virtues: a calm and collected mind, a mind of penetrating insight unencumbered by delusions and attachments. Meanwhile, the woman will continue her own daily tasks. We assume she has a husband or children somewhere, for whom she also cooks and generally fulfills the traditional role of wife and mother. According to Buddhist doctrine, by her alms giving this morning, she too is cultivating positive qualities and moving toward enlightenment. Her generosity, by the inevitable functioning of karmic law, will redound to her own benefit sooner or later. Since a monk was the object of her gift, her enlightenment will come sooner than otherwise, though probably not as soon as his.

I choose this image as a way to begin focussing on the topic in question, namely how a Buddhist decides whether or not to have children, or, how Buddhist philosophy and world view impinge upon this important choice. This question may be difficult to answer, not least because there are so many varieties of Buddhism, each one lived and interpreted in almost as many ways as there are individual Buddhists. Not every aspect of childbearing is exactly philosophical either, or amenable to decision. Nor is the decision purely personal; rather, it is influenced by powerful external factors, including the wishes of other people, as well as many internal factors, which, even so, are beyond personal choice. These last include the physical limitations of fertility, mental qualities that seem intractable, and desires located so deep in the mind and body as to be inaccessible to so-called "rational self-knowledge." In my own case, I still sometimes wonder exactly why I feel and think all of the things I have felt and thought throughout the process of considering whether I should try to have a child myself.

> After twenty years of thinking of myself as more or less fitting into Buddhist philosophy by not wanting children, I started doing some therapy and in the course of that I realized that what had really kept me from wanting a child was my terrible relationship with my mother.
>
> *Woman Vajrayāna Buddhist practitioner, university professor, in her mid-forties; paraphrase from a conversation, 1998*

For several years now I have been speaking to many people, Buddhists and non-Buddhists, about how they decided to have children, or not. Invited to write this essay, I was glad for the chance to clarify my own thinking and to begin resolving my personal dilemma on the subject of motherhood. For several years my research was completely informal, since the topic of childbearing was a natural one for me to talk and think about. Now, I could imagine no greater reward than sifting through my thoughts and feelings and, for this purpose, I began to conduct my interviews in a slightly more directed fashion. For inclusion here, I selected some of my more formal interviews with dedicated Buddhists and one Advaita Hindu. They represent the three great schools: Vajrayāna, Mahāyāna, and Theravāda, and their teachers have been Tibetan, Korean, Southeast Asian, Nepali, Indian, and North American. Mostly, my interviews were with college-educated women, born in Europe and the United States. I spoke too with several North American men, one whose formal education had ended after high school, the others college graduates. I wrote letters to an old Burmese friend, now a *thilashin* nun in her early thirties. I conversed in person and by fax and letter with two middle-aged Bhutanese women, one of them a lama's wife, the other a lama's attendant and the mother of two grown sons. I chatted with a Bengali friend who teaches meditation, is the daughter of a saint, and the mother of a son. I corresponded with a Peruvian lay man who is a university professor and has spent three years meditating in a cave in Nepal. Lastly, I asked the advice of an elderly Tibetan-born lama, who performed a divination for me. Their statements, either in general or in detail, are in a few instances paraphrased from well-remembered conversations. I intersperse their words between my own analyses and ruminations. They inform what I wrote right from the beginning of the essay, and have informed what I think on the subject. I have not included their names, in order to protect their privacy and also to call attention to a kind of universality in what they say.

Myself

Buddhist philosophy has had a deep and undeniable impact upon me. I reached the age of thirty-nine without ever having felt the urge to procreate; I was quite consciously set against child-bearing in general. My attitude was conditioned by many factors, including a childhood in South America where the poverty of those around me, combined with prevailing anti-American attitudes, not only led me to feel guilty about my own existence, but also to consider the links between overpopulation and the sorry state of masses of people in this world. As a young adult, I became a Buddhist practitioner, attended many intensive retreats, and even ordained as a nun for a short time in Burma. Even though this stint of nunhood was relatively brief and was never intended to be permanent, it remains significant that I did that instead of, for instance, marrying and raising a family. By the time the question about motherhood arose, I had spent a sum total of about three years in formal retreats, and had reached a sense of satisfaction with my practice. Though I was short of full liberation or anything like it, I can say that I was no longer burning inwardly to quite the same degree.

It was then that I figuratively stuck my head out of my cave and began to look out at the world. I had the chance, but rather than automatically going to Asia in search of teachings, I decided to return to South America. There, I was suddenly struck by the image of motherhood as embodied in the families I observed and by the culture's love of children. Though I could also observe a great number of disadvantages, such as the prevalence of wife abuse and families having more children than they wanted or could afford to maintain, these were somehow not as influential. One could say any of a number of things to explain my reaction: that I had allowed myself to be "bitten" by a different religious ideology; that I had replaced one burning question with another; that I had reached some degree of mental health; that some hitherto unconscious process related to aging had been set off, the infamous and denigrating "biological clock" much bruited in popular culture; that, having become mature as a Buddhist practitioner, I also became capable of questioning certain of its tenets; that I had lost some part of my faith; or that all of these things had taken place simultaneously.

My experience at the time was that wherever I went in the world, I now noticed how most people were extremely interested in having children and how they raised the status of the parent-child relationship to near worship. I felt, rather than the slight ideological advantage that a non-parent enjoys in Buddhist settings, the suspicion, criticism, and mild fear that a non-parent, especially a woman, often feels in "ordinary" society, particularly in the Catholic countries where I had been brought up. Then, in my intimate relationship with a man who has a daughter, I tasted a little of a parent's passionate love for his or her offspring. Yet in their presence I also felt excluded, partly for my own complex reasons and partly because I had fallen into the shadow that commonly engulfs a step-parent. Furthermore, my partner was unwilling to have another child with me. There were many reasons, both positive and negative, why I sometimes felt acutely deprived of that connection with a child, and why the wish to have my own child became a burning issue.

The result was that I now questioned all of my long-held opinions about having children, and the real value of all those years in retreat. I wondered why I had never wanted a baby and why I now desired exactly the opposite of what I had desired before, to have a child and to be a mother. My Buddhist friends remarked that it was clear that merely becoming a parent was not equivalent to enlightenment, though the depth of love and unselfishness a mother feels for her child might be as close to enlightenment as a non-practitioner can come. My non-Buddhist friends who were mothers scoffed that enlightenment must only be a pale, exsanguinated version of the unconditional love and fascination they felt for their children. In my own case, I felt I could understand very well what each camp was saying, since I wavered between two very different and self-contained emotional realms. The Buddhist realm was spacious and unburdened; in that universe, one dealt with tormenting desires by seeing through them and letting go of them. The realm of motherhood was passionate and warm; here, one acted to fulfill desires, and to realize one's wishes. Surely a Zen master would have swatted me to abolish the distinction, but nonetheless to me they felt like contradictory experiences, alternating in time, each one internally consistent and somewhat exclusive of the other. Deep down, too, I still felt shocked and unready for such a radical change in who I thought I was, and how I had structured the life I had thought I wanted to continue living. When the desire for a child swept over me, it seemed so deep as to be coming from the earth itself—not from the "me" I recognized.

Rather comically, when I felt obsessed with the desire to have a baby, I would often consult a non-Buddhist or a parent in order to glean support, then rush to find a Buddhist when I wanted not to feel guilty for reveling in having a little time and money and choice to spare in my life, or if I needed to feel that I was not a coward for not overcoming the obstacles to having a child. Then, in turn, I would resist the Buddhist answers and feel incapable of acting on the encouragement of the motherhood supporters. Some of my heavy pro-parenthood rooters seemed to consider it insufficiently mentally healthy and proactive of me not to leave my "selfish" partner and seek a child by some other means. These people were more affirming of my personal desires, soothing of my fears, and enthusiastic about all the ways in which I could adapt to my new status. Meanwhile, the Buddhists were much more understanding of reasons why a person might choose not to be a parent, less pitying of the childless, more validating of what one might do with one's life in the absence of children. However, even with the consolations of philosophy, it was hard to think that I would leave such a powerful wish and curiosity unfulfilled.

Because I had already practiced quite a lot of Buddhism, becoming a mother seemed to be the only way of understanding all the points of view, and of finding out whether I could be a strong practitioner and a parent at the same time. Yet there were still universes of Buddhism left to explore, and what if I found it impossible to know them? Would a baby really be a sufficient substitute? My partner remained unwilling. The idea of leaving him in order to become a single mother, despite the cultural propaganda in favor of the heroism of such a choice, seemed too great a challenge for me. I began a process of investigation, wriggling, and rumination that lasted about four years. I went to a lawyer and had a paper drawn up promising to pay for every expense of a child, and presented this to my partner, who eventually agreed to it, albeit with so much fear and reluctance ("I'll never drive it to Little League, okay?") that I felt discouraged. I ordered a catalogue from a sperm bank listing the physical and intellectual characteristics of all the donors, their eye color, and their hobbies. An intellectual Buddhist friend did away with the queasiness I had felt about never meeting the father by saying, quite calmly, that perhaps that man and I only had the karma to be parents together, but not to meet.

As it turns out, I decided not to have a child, but it was not an easy decision to make. With it, my desires and feelings have not instantly subsided, nor has it been easy to endure the sadness, regret, and fear I have about how I will feel when I am old and alone, without reviving the whole question again of whether I should go ahead by any means.

In sum, it is clear that just as Buddhism supported my desire not to have children, once I had entered the ordinary world more fully, the general emphasis on having children also influenced different aspects of my sense of who I was. Personal, historical predispositions were in play as I went through every step of this process, and I can trace throughout the influence of generational forces, and changing fashions. In the end, I have watched myself over and over again *not* overcoming the various obstacles to motherhood that arise in my own case. Watching myself act this way gradually became a kind of posterior evidence of "decision" and "preference," and it seems to be the work of my "true nature," for better or for worse, whatever that is. When I think that I won't have a child after all, being nearly forty-four now, I take comfort in the idea that I can go on lots of retreats. I believe that there are too many people in the world anyway. If I believe that some people have got to start restraining their urges, where better to begin than with myself?

> One question I have about the baby thing is, do you think that when you mostly don't want a baby, it has something to do with some kind of brainwashing you've been doing to yourself? That's what I worry about. It looked to me as if [your partner] were actually considering saying "yes" to you, at least for a while there. Was there a turning point there, when you had the opportunity to say, "Okay, let's do this" and yet decided not to, as I did? It has to be a free choice, otherwise you are compromising just because you don't want to leave, or lose, [him] and you lose integrity within yourself. To arrive at clarity in this issue is so goddamn hard. You know it drove me nuts, and I know it's been driving you nuts. What a time to write an article about this. I wish you luck. The agony of it all might help you produce some really good stuff.
>
> *Advaita practitioner, childless,*
> *in her early forties; email message, 1999*

The Postcard

If we return to the postcard, we see that it is a black and white photograph hand-tinted by the artist and intended for a foreigner, presumably European, to send home to relatives or friends. For them, the scene depicted might seem lovely but somewhat exotic and illegible. Depending on temperament and degree of observation, the addressee might have enjoyed either the confounding or the confirmation of his or her own prejudices. Women ought to bow to men, for example, but why are they all wearing skirts?

We Westerners are spiritual people, honest and intelligent enough to admit that we've been deeply influenced by the religions we were born into, but also that these religions didn't satisfy us entirely. If we are not exactly Christians, Jews, or atheists any more, and if aspects of the postcard do seem alien to us, we nevertheless try to distill meaning and personal relevance from them, rather than simply relying on our immediate reactions, opinions, prejudices, and bewilderment.

> I am sad about not having a child, and now I question how I allowed Buddhism to indoctrinate me and deprive me of ordinary relationships, including children, although I have to take responsibility for having faith in their weird, mind-boggling notions of the universe.
>
> *Former Tibetan Buddhist lama's consort,British, writer, in her fifties; written communication, 1997*

Quite unlike us, to those people who were actually photographed one warm morning in Sri Lanka a hundred years ago, the scene would have been familiar. Since monks are not supposed to travel more than forty-five minutes from their monasteries, it is more than likely that this alms-giving was re-enacted in this very spot, by these same people, hundreds of times, hence, the look of bored attention of some of the lay men standing by. They might even be watching in the absence of anything better to do, as a break from work, or in hopes of witnessing some slight infraction or mistake that would constitute a variation in routine. Buddhism will happily tell us that human nature remains, in certain fundamental respects, unvarying—corrupt, but liable to improvement through the practice of morality, concentration, and wisdom. Even without grandiloquent explanations we can be fairly certain that there must have been a morning on which every one of the people in this postcard felt less than perfect piety at the moment of donation. But just as modern-day Buddhists enjoy the image of this card, I imagine that most of these country people, had they been given the opportunity to look at it, would have approved of the photographer's having chosen to shoot them at this moment (perhaps with the exception of one or two of the lay male onlookers, who may have wished they were better dressed or standing up a little straighter).

Given that contemporary Western Buddhists want to map themselves into this image, how do we do this? Although the moment of alms-giving may resonate with a kind of stillness, vibrant and pure, for Westerners of Christian, Jewish, and other religious heritages, it must be taken metaphorically. We practice a variety of Buddhist forms, and we tend to believe that our practices are largely based on, or at least homologous in their alterations to, Asian models. Yet no matter how hard we try, our imitation is perforce selective. Western society at large has not adopted Buddhist values, which makes it impossible for many of Buddhism's fundamental practices and traditions—such as alms-giving and celibate monasticism—to continue in their original form. These practices have not become widespread, while others—such as meditation retreats, chanting, or pilgrimages—have thrived far beyond their original proportions. And so, if we consider this postcard to depict a traditional range of social relationships, an encompassing world of spiritual choices and positions that are still widely available in the Asian Buddhist context, we may fail to recognize that we're not exactly reproducing the models we've adopted. Despite the fact that alms-giving is almost never practiced in a Western setting, most Western Buddhists of my acquaintance would find a way to project themselves into this postcard scene. Though the people arranged on this roadside are Sinhalese, and long dead, they are Buddhists like us. We feel or want to feel that we understand what they are doing and the values they're enacting, and we sense that we have a truly closer affinity with them.

The Monk

Despite the fact that we are lay people, we are likely to begin by identifying ourselves with the figure of the monk, rather than with the woman or with the lay men standing about. Certainly he is the figure most representative of Buddhism; he is also the focus of attention.

All of his "worldly" activities have been minimized. Just as he does not spend time farming and preparing his own food, or engaging in business activities, he also does not immerse himself in the entangling passions of sexual love with their burdensome results including, notably, children, who require their parents to engage in still more demanding and time-consuming levels of work or business, food preparation, and household chores. Moreover, he does not immerse himself in the attachment of a parent to its child. It is accepted by most Buddhists that enlightenment, or complete mental freedom, is a genuine human potential achieved only as a result of effort and cultivation. To develop the mind takes time and work, and if you have children, you cannot cultivate formal meditation practice as thoroughly.

Child is very lovely but I don't want too many [children in this world] and I don't want to born baby. I am afraid to born baby but I have always brought up baby. My youngest brother was brought up [by] me. I am 14 years older than him so I looked after him instead of my mother. Though I don't want baby I want to make children of other people to be clever, to know how to sit meditation very well. Now I am trying for babies of other people. If you have a baby to take care of you will even less be able to do retreats surely. Babies cause many trouble for mother. Mother's love is very big so I brought up my youngest brother for my mother. But I don't want to be mother.

Ordained nun, Burmese, early thirties; letter, December, 1998

Male Western Buddhists would almost certainly identify with the monk. Gender alone would surely lead a man not to wish to see himself in a subservient female role, bowing to a superior who is male. As for female Buddhist practitioners in the West, we are unlikely to be content with an old-fashioned female role, which relegates us to being mere cooks for, and sharers of merit with, the real heavy-duty male practitioners. Thus we too might identify with the monk, eliding the fact that he's male and that if we were to be magically transported to that roadside we would never be permitted to receive alms food, nor to ordain as he has done.

If we want to be mothers, then, identifying with a monk presents quite a significant conceptual obstacle.

I have been pondering the imponderables of how Buddhists have babies, or don't. I find myself reverting to what I said last time, but not very well, about women being naturally in a state of *saṃādhi*.... Because we're more concrete, less abstract, than men, because we're more verbal, more in touch with our emotions, I think we are naturally more mindful, more spiritual (in the sense of "being here now") than men. A gross generalization that will of course break down on an individual level. Men try to keep women out of the spirituality business for the same reasons they try to dominate everything else: power. So they categorize our biological concerns (relationships, childrearing) as too mundane to qualify. Also, I think men are more at the mercy of lust than women, so to follow their spiritual rules against sex, they have to keep women out. All that...stuff about how dark and smelly and painful the womb is seems to me to be pure misogyny, and I wish for all of us not to buy into it.

Man, I feel like I'm stumbling around in the cobwebs here—what I'm trying to get at is a feeling that it's not right to say that sitting on a cushion is spiritual but changing a diaper isn't. That if we let men make the definitions of what is spiritual, then we get defined out, so we have to make our own definitions that include our feminine reality.

Tibetan practitioner, United States, painter, fifties; email, spring 1999

Nowadays, teachings about meditation and enlightenment formerly reserved for celibate male practitioners are routinely offered to lay people of both sexes at retreats in Asia and in the West. Thus, it is not actually necessary to become a monk in order to identify with his figure; his life is like the one we experience on retreat. In the retreat context, there is one element of parenthood that all people are admonished to imitate, and that is boundless love. Buddhists should try to love all living beings with the same intensity as if all beings were their own children, but without a mother's personal attachment. Special meditation practices exist, in fact, to cultivate this finely calibrated love.

Moreover, Buddhist texts shock us with their widespread emphasis on the undesirability of rebirth, for example, birth and rebirth are negative events, except insofar as human birth provides an opportunity to escape from itself, by becoming enlightened during the life that follows. The womb itself is full of filth and discomforts and descriptions of it are discouraging: it is noisome, dark and cramped, and not a place to yearn to return to.

Inconceivable stench and filth,
constriction and darkness
To enter the mother's womb is like a hell...

Gampopa, Jewel Ornament of Liberation

Unpleasant as these descriptions may be, they may brutally force us to recognize that birth, for ordinary people, means bondage; once birth has occurred, death is inevitable. Death is one most obvious reason why birth is undesirable, along with sickness and old age. Added to this is the ubiquity of frustration: suffering is part of life, despite all of our ruses to avoid it, and Buddhism asks its practitioners to be honest in facing this fact, as an incentive to ardor in practice. Though Mahāyāna and Vajrayāna Buddhism present a view that is superficially more positive—for example, offering a possibility to be born in the human realm as an enlightened being—such an enlightened birth is quite difficult to achieve even in these schools, and it takes many years of meditation to achieve it. This kind of birth is a qualitatively different event from what has happened to most of us, for whom appearing in human form was more or less a surprise.

> A child is an eighteen-year prison sentence. No exceptions other than for the very, very rich or the very, very callous. One's daily life is changed in ways that are unimaginable from the childless perspective.... My expertise is...in the educational assessment of multi-handicapped children. I was working...in a federally funded unit...that was charged with locating and assessing every school-age child in New England who was eligible under a new education act for the deaf and blind.... A team of four of us drove all over...for three years, into all the institutions and state schools, assessing and testing kids. Saw problems in the back wards you would not believe if I described them. Every expectant mother's nightmare. Also found a reasonable number of children who were locked away but should not have been. It was an extraordinary education.
>
> *Lay woman, North American Buddhist practitioner, radio commentator and social activist, in her forties; written communication, October 14, 1998*

The Woman

In the nineteenth century, the roles of the postcard figures were not as fluid and interchangeable as they are now. A country woman gives alms to an ordained Buddhist monk, continuing an ancestral practice. She may never have heard teachings on meditation, these being reserved for monks; but she would have been encouraged to practice generosity, morality, and compassion in her daily life, and to support monks. By doing so, she shares the merit of those who are performing more important practices than hers. She could never ordain as a monk herself, and although there have been enlightened women throughout Buddhist history, the scriptures clearly state that the entanglements of household life make it nearly impossible for her to become enlightened sooner than the monk.

Let us assume, for now, that she enjoys alms-giving, believes in it, and is not simply submitting to social pressure. All day she will feel buoyed by her participation in this ritual; she trusts in the doctrine by which her alms-giving will bring her karmic benefits. If she is devout, perhaps she will try to practice more continuously and extend her generosity to all whom she encounters during this day. There are texts that tell her she need feel no shame about her relations with her husband and children. Though it is made clear that she occupies a lower position now, in some future life she may enjoy the freedom to be a monk. In this life, of course, it is unlikely she can find as much time to meditate as he does. Perhaps she is even glad of this, loves her children and her husband, and thinks a monk's life would be boring.

With all its emphasis on wombs, it becomes clear in Buddhist doctrine that conception and childbearing are considered women's province. Though the

Tantras speak of the union of male and female principles at conception, what we might call "the whole man's" participation in childrearing is not much spoken of, and male desire for offspring is not emphasized. The desire of women to bear children, however, is given space and tolerance, and even encouragement. In her own time, then, the woman in the postcard would have felt no shame whatsoever as a woman to become a wife and the mother of a family.

> [X] went to [her meditation teacher, a monk] to talk about her desire to have a baby, and he said it would be fine if she wanted to, she would be a great mother, she would bring up a Buddhist child, create the community of the future, but she decided that retreats were more important to her and so she didn't do it.
>
> *Lay woman, United States, forties*

Buddhism does contain the gratifying doctrine that there is no difference between women's and men's capacity for enlightenment. During and shortly after the time of the historical Buddha, when there was an order of nuns nearly as successful as the monks', many of the women's enlightenment poems speak of their relief at no longer having to inhabit traditional female roles, at escaping the drudgery and subjugation involved in serving a man and one's family. Many women, too, exulted in knowing they were no longer constrained to return to any womb, for there have always been women practitioners who have "reached the highest goal." Nowadays in most Buddhist centers I know of, no distinction is made between men and women's candidacy to participate in intensive meditation retreats. As a woman I have not been barred from any teaching but I do, like all practitioners, have to sift the teachings I've received for those best for me.

> I went into a long retreat before ordaining as a *bhikkhunī* [nun], and the idea of [having] daughters came up. And I worked with the grief of not having that, not just rationally but in the body. All these questions came up of what would be possible for me. It was clear that I wanted to dedicate my life to formal practice, and knowing many people in family life, I didn't have that many illusions about it.... If you could do [family life] well, I am sure enlightenment [would be] there. But for most people it seems it is a harder way. For me the practice has always been about a consistent effort, the effort of seeing into the nature of what's going on and the nature of my interest in it, and it seems that for me, my true nature is to move through [those kinds of desires.]
>
> *Nun, United States, thirties*

In general, it is undeniable that there has always been less official support for women's taking up the life of religion full-time than for men to do so. In some schools of Buddhism, practitioners take vows never to denigrate women; yet if one visits monasteries filled with beings who have taken those vows, and observes who is doing the cooking and cleaning, and who is representing the highest truth—and who is bowing to whom, and who is not bowing in return—one observes the gendered nature of the situation and sees that the arrangement is precisely the same as what is shown on the postcard.

> In my mid-thirties I went to see my sister give birth to a baby, and that desire, that pull, came. I went home and said to my...partner that I wanted to have a child, and my partner said, "No way." We had a year of couples' therapy. For a year the desire was there very strongly. I talked to my teacher, and [she] said, "Do you really want to bring more suffering into the world?" [She] really encouraged me to think about it carefully. And I talked to a lot of women, single mothers that I knew, and they all said, "It is so much more than I ever imagined," and I saw the financial struggles they had, and I felt I would not have the time or flexibility I needed. I think you have to look at the situation very carefully. We imagine in a relationship that the relationship will last, but in reality this is often not true. And in this sexist society, so many...mothers have told me this, the support is just not there for a woman with a child, and it is very hard. And after that I found myself just encountering the obstacles to having a child and not doing what was necessary to overcome them....
>
> *Lay woman, African, meditation teacher, forties*

In Buddhism, and in the world, women seem to be always halfway outside of the system. This may leave more space and function as an odd kind of encouragement for some women to think critically about the system, to develop alternative theories and opinions about doctrinal matters, and to decide that the doctrine is mistaken or inapplicable to them. Our Sinhalese woman may have been lucky not to be well educated in the Buddhist scriptures, thus being spared some of the worst excoriations, but it is likely that she heard that her being female meant that she was a "lower" rebirth. Buddhist texts on the household life are few, but one that describes her proper behavior toward her husband stipulates that she should get up before him and go to bed after him, working to keep him comfortable, making sure she answers him sweetly. If she had read such texts, would she have believed a little less in what she was told to do and instead have created her own independent philosophy?

At the very least, this woman donating food to the monk must have scrutinized him at least once, judging whether he seemed a worthy recipient of alms. She may have asked, "Does he seem more enlightened this month than last? Is he really making the best use of my support?" She may have wondered which of them was truly the more deserving of a day without worldly chores and drudgery. She may well have believed, for she had likely been told, perhaps by this very monk standing before her now, that as a result of her donation she would be reborn more auspiciously, in a male body next time. Quite possibly she looked forward to such a rebirth, as a time when she would have the option of ordaining as a monk, and thus no longer have to cook for so many people. Or perhaps she preferred her worldly role, and thought that being ordained would be boring, that the idle aren't holy, and that having children would be as fulfilling to her as any spiritual enlightenment she could imagine.

> So many Western practitioners don't understand Buddhism really. They only identify with monks and monastic practice. Intensive retreats—that's all they know. It's crazy because they're not monks and they can't be in retreat all the time, but they think that's all that Buddhism is. They don't see that Buddhism has teachings for a whole society. These [Westerners] feel that reproduction is just the reproduction of delusion. What if it were the reproduction, the cultivation, of awareness? If I teach my child to recognize that her anger is not her real self, is this not a valid practice of Buddhism? With a child every day is important, every moment is so important. You can't just say, "It doesn't matter," because you are forming a person. How is that not meditation, how is that not intensive practice?
>
> *Lay woman, Denmark, social scientist, forties; paraphrase from oral communication, October, 1998*

The most enlightened woman teacher I have ever met was Dipa Ma, a Bengali woman who practiced in the Burmese *vipassanā* tradition and was said to have attained the third of four degrees of enlightenment. She once told a group of students, of whom I was one, that very few factors were at work in her mind: she could identify awareness, intention, and compassion. Dipa Ma countered the common argument that children are a distraction by saying that, on the contrary, children build up mental strength and focus and are excellent practice for a meditator. A mother cannot wallow in ordinary, self-centered thoughts, according to Dipa Ma. A mother has to put her attention fully outside of herself, focusing here, there, and there, in very quick succession. The attention has to be not merely focused, but also soft and loving, aware of its own quality.

> She is my robes, she is my rule of discipline.
>
> *Buddhist woman, doctoral student, in her forties; watching her child across the room*

These observations of Dipa Ma's came out of her own experience and opinion-making. They are not to be found in any formal text. As mentioned above, for Buddhist women who are sincere and deep practitioners, motherhood nearly invariably seems to inspire a restatement of orthodox doctrine. These women feel, and say, that they are practicing like monks. They draw many parallels, including monks' short sleeping hours. Mothers' personal preferences are abandoned, just as after ordination. To be bound to the needs of children is the equivalent of having to follow 227 rules and regulations. Given the tendency of doctrine to discourage childbearing somewhat, these philosophizing women are committing a rather subversive act, rephrasing some of the most precious tenets of the religion in terms that would be seen as antithetical to what was intended, but which the women understand as a deep expression of truth, which they understand viscerally, and which they often wish to communicate and teach to others.

> Why avoid family life? If you can't practice love and generosity and mindfulness with those you love, where is that at? If you just make your life to avoid conflict and obligation, what does that mean? I believe in working with what is real, not in avoiding it. And so here is my practice—(laughs) to find myself right in the middle of fighting with my husband and my children, to ask how are we going to come through this, what is best for all of us, what is the path of wisdom in this case?
>
> *Buddhist lay woman, Swiss, retreat center supporter, mother of four, forties*

The Lay Men Bystanders

As identification with the two main figures in the postcard has proved only tentative, I now turn to an examination of the bystanders. I don't understand turn-of-the-century Sinhalese society well enough to know why so many other adult men are hanging around this spot in the road, unless they are harvesting coconuts, or the thatched house is also some kind of small store or roadside restaurant where they are waiting to be served after the monk. Perhaps the hut is a business, that the woman was forced to open after her son and husband were both ordained as monks. For now, and for the purposes of developing the discussion, let us take the bystanders to represent, in their freedom of posture, the "take it or leave it" part of the doctrine. Even the Buddha emphasized in one of his sermons that his followers should test his theories, take what they needed, and leave the rest.

After many years of practice, a certain maturity may come, in which women and men feel capable of judging Buddhist values in informal situations, and of making decisions for themselves. This is perhaps especially true in Western Buddhist retreat centers, where the doctrine has undergone inevitable, conscious adaptation to a new context.

> In the [North American] Buddhist community people are looked at as individuals, so the idea of maturation until you become a mom and so forth is not the only way to go. Those who say they want to have someone to love, though of course it is more complex than that, could find plenty of beings already in existence. They could use that Buddhist practice. On the other hand, if you want a baby and don't have one, you can't blame Buddhism. There's lots of room for working out one's relationship to the doctrine. If you want to have a kid, go off and do it. I'm not sure what kind of message I would have gotten if I'd had a baby, but I never had the sense that it would not have been one possible choice.
>
> *Theravāda lay woman practitioner, United States, acupuncturist, forties*

From all of the interviews I have learned several things. First, for the most devout of Buddhist women practitioners, having children "inattentively" smacked of a transgression, and those Buddhist women I spoke with who were also mothers defiantly compared their daily praxis, usually favorably, with that of an ordained monk or a person on retreat. Most Buddhist mothers rephrased texts and doctrine in order to equate the conditions of motherhood to the rules of discipline for celibates, and the formalities of meditation practice on retreat. With one exception—a mother of two who felt too frequently overwhelmed by the endless demands of family life, so that she said she could not find the time even to pause and reflect on her condition—mothers who were meditators compared their personal development as mothers with insights they had already attained, or which they might be attaining were they attending retreats instead of being parents. They sometimes reached the point of criticizing meditators who were non-parents as deluded about the unique value of formal practice.

> If you become a mother and remain a meditator, you will be an "M" squared. Now you are just an ordinary woman, but when you are a mother, you will have sensations similar to [reaching the first level of enlightenment].
>
> *Meditation teacher, Indian, mother, early forties*

Second, all Buddhist women and men whom I interviewed consciously took their spiritual commitments into account when deciding what to do about childbearing. The time-consuming nature of childrearing and retreat practice were seen, quite pragmatically, as somewhat mutually exclusive. Several women consulted celibate, male, Asian meditation practitioners or teachers as they worked out their decisions. When meditators chose not to have children, they often understood that they were making a sacrifice so as to preserve their commitments to formal practice. When they chose to have children, they adapted the language and attitudes of formal practice to childrearing, so that raising a child was seen on a global, spiritual plane as a "reproduction of wisdom," in the words of one informant, rather than as a reproduction of ignorance or of suffering. However, the degree of this adaptation varied considerably. Some parents, even meditation teachers, felt it was important and healthy to allow their children to absorb the culture around them and grow up in a more conventional fashion than their parents' lifestyle might have implied, and to allow them to choose to be Buddhists when they were mature enough to decide for themselves.

Perhaps most importantly of all, men and women who had matured in practice considered their decision whether or not to be parents in terms of spiritual development. Most valued parenthood as an experience that might cultivate positive qualities, such as kindness, responsibility, and "softness," thus becoming an extension of their formal meditation practice. But they also carefully considered their unique personalities and circumstances. Some described the ways in which childbearing was more likely to seem a frustration and a burden, thus leading to the cultivation of negative mental states and the eventual spiritual detriment not only of themselves but their child as well. The question of maturity in practice was often cited, by meditation students as well as teachers. A person who had meditated sufficiently was ripe for parenthood, while one who was not yet "stable" or mature was considered more likely to fall prey to difficult and problematical mental states that could often become intensified in parenthood, such as narcissism, worry, pride, grief, lack of concentration and, most of all, the delusion of considering anything or anyone, including oneself and one's children, fundamentally and inherently real, permanent, and self-existent.

> Generally in Asia it is believed that each child brings his own dose of fortune, karma in Buddhist language, and if, because of some affinity, you end up with an evil child, then you have to suffer the consequences of that affinity. Then again, all suffering is an opportunity to expand your awareness. Of course it could be that the karmic relationship is beneficial and that life becomes rich for both—for parent, father (or mother),

and child.... On the other hand there is the vision of the obsessive "practitioner." "If I have kids I won't have time to practice." Of course, if you believe that the only way of practicing is to sit on a cushion.... But since it's also indispensable, generally, to sit in order to have a certain clarity, it's also not untrue. Probably this question always has the same answer, yes and no. It depends on your karma, your level of practice, and the maturity of the practitioner—though we all think of ourselves as superman (or superwoman, sorry!)—how we see our needs in practice. In any case it seems an extremely important decision as much for the practitioner as for his or her future kids. That should be a conscious decision and it should lead to some kind of preparation, an attitude of taking the children's education as a practice.

Lay man, Peruvian, university professor, late fifties

One of the most striking things I noticed was the maturity with which so many Buddhist women, and men, approached their choices. Having spent hours, months, and years in practice, they could be very articulate about their motivations, thoughts, and mental states. Even in evaluating considerations that might be called "worldly" or concrete, most of the women I interviewed had considered in an honest and searching way what would be the best choice for them in terms of cultivating a practice of insight and wisdom. Those who decided to have children took the children's education and development as their spiritual practice, and saw the difficulties involved as constructive. I cannot help but think that these children benefited from their mothers' insight and sincerity, from the language they had developed to privilege and honor their interaction with their children.

When women were deepest in the throes of a dilemma about whether to start a family or not, some of them consulted their spiritual teachers for advice. In no case did a woman take advice that went contrary to her inclinations, though her inclinations were often strengthened or redirected slightly. When one friend spoke to a monk about her anguish at not having a baby, the monk said, "How *often* do you feel that way?" His question redirected her toward examining the nature, rather than the content, of her process; she eventually decided against having a child. In my own case, when I knew I was tired of my dilemma *qua* dilemma, I went to a Tibetan lama and asked him to perform a divination for me on the subject. He prayed and flipped a series of colored tassels, whose order he interpreted. The result of the divination was that in my case retreats were more auspicious. The lama further suggested that if I wanted children, I should have two rituals performed on my behalf and attend one more retreat. The old monk didn't know me well, and the language barrier was such that it was difficult to ask him specific questions or explain my situation. Yet his divination seemed similar to the answer my young Burmese nun friend had already offered. If my karma were to have children, children would have come easily to me, and my life would arrange itself so as to fit them in. On the contrary, my life contained all but perfect circumstances to continue attending retreats. Why fight my advantages? My circumstances were not considered to be full of deprivation, but of opportunity. Meanwhile my non-Buddhist friends were still cajoling me to rearrange my life so as to fit my desire for a child into it. But to me the divination made sense.

> [X] has softened so much from being a mom, and it is a gift not just to her but for everyone. It depends on the woman. I can see that early in practice it might not be possible to have a child and still practice, but a maturity can come where the child does not bring the practice to an end....
>
> *Meditation teacher, African, in her forties*

Conclusion

So am I going to have a baby or not? I really can't see it happening. Can I be happy about that? Yes. Although I'm still occasionally flooded with regrets that contain internal admonitions for action, I think these will fade over time. Would I have been happy with a baby? Yes, I am sure I would have, though I'm also convinced that in my current life circumstances the child and I, and my partner and his daughter, would have faced some profound emotional difficulties. I guess I prefer to rest without one.

And now, child or no, which figure on this roadside should I choose to identify with? The woman is the most obvious choice, since I am one myself. On the other hand, I have to admit that I've never cooked for an alms round, and I'd prefer not to bow to a monk I haven't met. Should I not identify with him instead, since I have no children and was ordained as a nun once myself? I became a Buddhist because I want to be enlightened. Though Buddhist practices have taught me to identify less and less with my body and gender, making it easier to identify with the monk, and though these same Buddhist practices are closer to those he is practicing than to alms giving, alas, I cannot fully identify with him either. I am living as a householder now, having nice sex, and am no longer ordained; moreover, it's also hard to get around the fact that I'm not a man and can't ordain in his manner. Why, then, don't I simply decide to identify with one of the postcard's onlookers, sympathetic but far less rigid in his engagement than either the monk or the woman? If I look at them closely and with an eye to making correspondences, they do remind me of my own attitudes, approving, and distanced, even faintly tinged with laziness, irony, and divergent personal judgments. Yet to identify with these lay men is the most artificial choice of all, the one that involves the biggest leap on my part. I haven't inherited the luxury of being a bystander in Buddhism while still considering myself included. I have no natural reason to identify with male, turn-of-the-century, Sinhalese peasants, except as the elaboration of a metaphor and in contrast to the dissatisfaction of the other two possibilities presented in this picture.

For a moment it seems that the complexities of my situation can only be addressed if I include myself in all of the positions and yet in no particular position; I can't get out of the dilemma except by saying that I'm everyone and no one at once. In some traditions, such as Zen, this non-positionality is ideal. To be utterly concrete about my relationship to the postcard image, I have to admit that I do not appear in it at all. My form is nowhere depicted! All of this discussion has been a pure invention and projection.

Is this the truth of Buddhism, which I must reinterpret for myself, today—that there is no existing image that corresponds to what I am? Buddhism does return us to our own experience; at its purest, that is no definable experience at all.

> My life story is consistent, in a way, without a child.
>
> *Lay woman, university professor, in her forties.*

THEANVY KUOCH: *Buddhism and Mental Health Among Cambodian Refugees*

THEANVY KUOCH

I AM THE DAUGHTER of Kim Tho and Bun Phao Kuoch. I was born in a town in western Cambodia where my family has lived for centuries. My mother's mother was the only daughter of my great-grandfather, the governor of our province, and my great-grandmother was his first wife. As governor, my great-grandfather had thirty concubines who came from families throughout the territory.

My great-grandfather was a Buddhist, and it is possible that my family was Buddhist from the time that the teachings of Buddha first came to Cambodia in the thirteenth century. My great-grandfather's name is over the entrance to the pagoda where my family still worships, and just as he was the source of our lives, Buddhism is the source of our identity as a family. The principles of Buddhism were taken very seriously by my parents, and I believe that these teachings helped us survive the greatest hardships our family has ever known. This was during the Khmer Rouge years, from 1975 to 1979.

For a time my family was very prosperous. As a child I helped my father collect rent on more than twenty-seven properties, and everywhere he went people treated him with great respect. But our prosperity was lost as simply as it came, and from the time I was eleven years old in 1957, my family had to struggle just to keep our family home. Even as we lost our material wealth, however, my father continued to hold the respect of the community.

I was encouraged to work hard at my studies so that I could make a good name for my family. My father believed that I would be the child who would take care of all the others. He also thought that I would travel far away, but as a young child that seemed impossible, as I couldn't bear to be far from my mother.

The first year I went to school, my mother taught me a lesson in patience, gratitude, and respect for family. She taught me not so much through her voice but through her manner, her face, and her actions. I still try to copy her in mind and spirit.

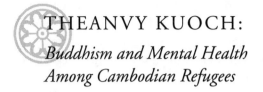

My mother took me to school the year my hand could reach over my head and touch my ear. She gave me over to the teacher, but I couldn't contain my fear and clung to her skirt begging her not to leave. For several weeks, my mother remained in school with me, at first sitting close to me in the classroom and then moving into the hallway where I could still see her. When I was ready, I told her to go home, and from that time on, school was a great joy for me because I felt that my teacher was the person whom I trusted and respected after my mother and my family.

My father also believed in the tenets of Buddhism, but he had to struggle more than my mother to accept the loss of material possessions. Patience and control of anger did not come easily for him. As a young man, he had once lost his temper and hit his horse. This was an event that would disturb him his whole life. Looking back, I think that he was quite depressed, and it was his worry that made him angry. But he practiced Buddhism every day of his life.

My mother and my grandmother taught us there was great joy in giving to others. Every morning we gave food to the monks who walked by our house. This meant that we had to get up very early to cook. My mother said that giving earned us merit for our next life, and she would not allow us to feed the monks unless we truly wanted to. She said that our attitude was very important and if we gave only because it looked good to give, we would lose our merit.

During my high school years, I had to leave our town and go live with a cousin in Battambang City some distance from my home. Life was changing quickly in our country, and war was spilling over from Vietnam. I understood little of what was happening, but as the country changed, Buddhism remained our link with a life that had seen little change in more than a thousand years. We made our offerings to the monks and enjoyed ceremonies and celebrations as we had always done.

By the time I went to the university, the unrest had turned into civil war. Still, this seemed unreal for me, perhaps because I was awed by the possessions and opportunities that came with war. I watched as Phnom Penh, surrounded by the Khmer Rouge, turned from a city of several hundred thousand to an island of more than two million people who were refugees or displaced persons in their own homeland.

In April, 1975 during the Cambodian New Year, my fate and that of seven million of my brothers and sisters were decided by the Khmer Rouge. On the morning of April 14, the radio stopped broadcasting its normal programs. The Khmer Rouge took over the radio station and told us that we were going to be bombed by the enemies. They told us to take only a few possessions and leave the city immediately.

We put my mother, who was in the city to help my sister with her new baby, into the car with my sister, her baby, and my son. My brother-in-law drove the car through masses of people as they walked out of the city. The lines went on for miles and miles, and along the side of the road there were signs of what would happen to people who did not cooperate with our new leaders. The car quickly ran out of gas, but we were able to push it as the crowds moved slowly.

Each day on the road I watched my family move closer to death. My brother grew angry as he starved, and my sister grew desperate for food, eating anything she could get her hands on. I had more food than they because I worked periodically in the fields. After she gave birth to her daughter, my sister was not able to work, so I tried to share food with her and my mother, but my mother would take the little bit that I gave her and give it to my brother.

One day the Khmer Rouge took my sister away for stealing some food and locked her up in prison and tortured her daily. Because she had been caring for my son, he was locked up in the cage with her. I heard this news from people working in the field, but when I was finally able to get to her, she had been taken to the hospital. The Khmer Rouge hospitals were places where people were taken to die. I knew when I saw her that she did not have long. She begged the Khmer Rouge to let me stay with her while she died, but they refused and forced me back to work. When I came back, her bed was empty. Now I was alone with my son.

Life no longer seemed real, and I no longer had any feelings. Everywhere around me people looked like walking skeletons. I knew that there was a place for killing close to us, and we could hear people crying in the night. In the day, Khmer Rouge would be wearing the clothes of the dead. Even in those terrible times, some people were able to remain compassionate. My dear friend would take some of her rice and save it for my son who was so thin that he could hardly hold his head up. She risked her life for me and for many others, and her compassion gave me the courage to stay alive. This spirit appeared in many places—even one of the Khmer Rouge leaders would sneak small bits of food for me.

Finally, we heard that the Vietnamese had come into the country and that the Khmer Rouge planned to kill all of us. They were having people dig big holes, which we knew would be our graves. I didn't know what to do. I didn't know where to run to. Then, the Khmer Rouge leader came to us at night and told us to get ready to leave. I didn't know whom to trust, so I prayed and followed him. He led us out of the concentration camp to a safe place.

In May of 1979, my son, my niece, and I escaped with hundreds of people and walked through the forest for eleven days. Even though I was very skinny, I was strong enough to carry my son on my back. When we arrived at my father's house, I saw one of my sisters standing in the doorway; she looked at us as though we were strangers. I said, "Sister, don't you know me?" Then she recognized my voice and started to cry.

After two months, food became so scarce I knew I had to go to the Thai border. My sisters gave me the few pieces of gold and jewelry they still had to buy food. One sister also told me she had had a dream: I would meet an obstacle on my trip to the border, but it would be all right because she saw a monk standing right next to me.

I promised my son that I would bring him some candy and left early in the morning without saying good-bye to my father. The trip to the border was more dangerous than I could have ever imagined. An old soldier led me and my friend through minefields where dead bodies marked the way. All of a sudden, shooting began between the Cambodian and Vietnamese troops. I ran for hours until I reached the border. The camps at the border offered little safety, but my feet had swollen so much from running that all of my toenails had fallen off and I could hardly walk.

It was at that time that the Red Cross came into the camp and began taking the sick to a new camp inside Thailand. My friend was very ill with a fever, and I went with her on the truck into a camp with thousands of people called Khao-I-Dang. Soon after we arrived, we were greeted by doctors and nurses from all over the world. They treated us with great kindness and respect, and asked that anyone who could understand English or French come help them at the hospital.

I had studied English before the time of the Khmer Rouge and was fluent in French and thought I might help because I had learned some nursing skills when I was living in my town. I began to work in the German hospital run by the German Catholic Relief Service. Soon I was assisting with surgery, and people were being brought in from the border where the fighting was becoming heavy. We worked day and night alongside doctors and nurses who had no thought for their own comfort. Their kindness and compassion gave me hope for my own life and reminded me of the way life was before our suffering.

There is no question that life in the refugee camps was hard, but now we had hope. The price I paid for my hope was the knowledge that I could not return to my home. I would have to go to a new country and make a new life so that I could support my son and my family. Every time I moved to a new camp, I found people who shared my feelings and understood how hard it was for us to lose our families and our country. The compassion I experienced in the camps was an experience that influenced what I did once I reached the United States.

I arrived in the United States all alone and was sent to Chicago to live with people I had never met before. I decided not to stay there and in August of 1981 moved to Connecticut to live close to a nurse I had met in the camps. It was my hope that she would help me get work helping others. In Connecticut, I met other people who had worked in the camps; they too had been changed by their experiences and wanted to continue to work with refugees. Together, we made a plan to start an organization that could bring some of the compassion from the camps to the refugees who were coming into the United States. Thus, Khmer Health Advocates (KHA) was born.

We started Khmer Health Advocates in 1982 to provide health care for Cambodians who were just coming to the United States, and to advocate for people in the camps. KHA is a treatment program for victims of torture and is committed to the health of the Cambodian family, especially here in the United States. As stated in its brochure, its focus is

> the thousands of Cambodians who had fled a decade of war, starvation and torture in their homeland, and had arrived as refugees in the United States. Traumatized and suffering from multiple health problems, the refugees needed special help to cope with life in their new country and new language, and to begin the process of healing.

Its mission is to provide

> essential health services to survivors of the Cambodian holocaust living in Connecticut and Southern New England. On a local level, KHA provides community based advocacy services, and also offers health education on a national level.

Our thoughts were never far from the people who were left behind. I knew that by working hard in an organization like this, I could survive the yearning that I felt for my son and my family.

We all worked for Khmer Health Advocates as volunteers, so I had to find other jobs to support myself and to send money home. I began working for a resettlement agency, where I helped new families coming into the country. I watched as people who had stayed so strong in the camps, began to fall apart in the safety of their new homes. It didn't take me long to feel like I didn't know what I was doing and needed to learn new ways to help my people. I was very lucky to find two mentors to help me understand my own story and to look at ways to help Cambodian families.

The Venerable Maha Ghosananda is a Cambodian monk who was studying in India when Cambodia fell to the Khmer Rouge. He is currently one of the prelates of the Cambodian Buddhist church in Cambodia and is well known for his *dhammayātrās,* or peace walks.

He, like most Cambodians, lost family members at the hands of the Khmer Rouge, but unlike most Cambodians, he was willing to listen to the terrible stories of refugees who had come out of the country in 1979. This he did day after day. He never turned away from a refugee and he treated the rich and the poor alike, understanding the suffering that each person held in his or her heart.

Every story he heard convinced him of the need for compassion and hope. His unconditional acceptance of everyone taught me important lessons about therapy and how to approach a family in need. He showed me how to defuse anger with acceptance and how to help people put their deepest concerns into words.

Everywhere Maha Ghosananda goes there is laughter—even when people are describing their greatest tragedies. People who are around him feel at peace. While I know that I cannot provide the same conditions in my therapy, I also know that I want to do therapy in a way that makes people relaxed and feel good about themselves. I learned how to do this from watching my other mentor, Ivan Borzormeny Nagy.

Dr. Nagy is one of the original founders of a school of family therapy. He came to the United States from Hungary after World War II and has a deep understanding of what war does to families. He also believes that the family is the most important resource in a person's life. This philosophy is important to me because, as a Cambodian, I find it difficult to think of myself outside of my family.

Dr. Nagy's form of family therapy is called contextual family therapy; as its name implies, it calls for the therapist to look at where a family comes from. "What is the story of the individual and of the family?" "What have they lived through?" "What events have made them the family that they are?" "What resources do they have, and who owes what to whom?" He uses the concept of family legacies to explain how we pass on behavior and values to the next generation. I came to understand how loyalty to family members is sometimes hidden, but that it is always a factor in how we behave.

Like the Venerable Maha Ghosananda, Dr. Nagy taught me never to judge a family. He showed me that I had the power to help a family if I focused on learning the truth rather than accepting what only appeared to be the truth. I see this over and over again when the court sends us patients who are accused of child abuse or domestic violence. Very often, people have already judged the situation and decided who is to blame in a family.

Dr. Nagy taught me a technique for helping family members talk about their lives. He said that he always starts dealing with new clients by asking them how they help each other; this very simple question was the first question he asked me about my family. No one had ever asked me this before, and the question filled me with tears because I had tried, very hard, to help my family. I remembered how I tried to get food for my mother and sister, and how I worked hard to stay alive so that my son would not be alone. Remembering in this way is very different from recalling all of the horror of my family dying. I was able to remember my mother's face, and I knew that I did exactly what she wanted me to do when I used the little strength I had to keep myself alive and take care of my son.

Over the years, I have become more and more convinced of the importance of encouraging people to talk about what happened to them by focusing on their desire to help. The idea of helping is based on compassion, which is the root of Buddhism. For me it means being connected to other people and feeling what they feel and allowing them to feel what I feel. Compassion works well to heal people who have been tortured, and often it is the only way to help.

Cambodians call what happened in Cambodia the *Mahantdorai.* It means the time of great destruction. It refers not only to the time of the Khmer Rouge, but also to the period of the late 1960s during the civil war and the bombing of our country. It also refers to the time after the Khmer Rouge when violence continued in the minefields of Cambodia and in the refugee camps.

I don't know why this evil happened, but my mother believed that the Khmer Rouge had lost its way. She thought that years of war had confused people and she felt that confused people are capable of behaving in very destructive, violent ways. The more cruel and violent the Khmer Rouge became, the more convinced my mother was that we had to concentrate on our survival. She warned us not to allow ourselves to be lost in anger and hatred. I think she feared the loss of compassion more than she feared the Khmer Rouge.

The Khmer Rouge took the path of evil. They lost their way. They lost their connection with the power of Buddhism and their connection to other people. They were only able to inflict cruelty and pain because they no longer felt anything. Every survivor that I have ever interviewed has described how she was forbidden to show emotions during the Khmer Rouge era. Any sign of tears or sorrow was punishable by death. The Khmer Rouge used to say that if you cried when someone was killed or died, it was because you too were the enemy, but we all knew that the Khmer Rouge was afraid of the power of tears. Frightened people are very dangerous.

This loss of connection is the Khmer Rouge legacy. It is what people fear the most and yet it is an inevitable part of life for us today. Our bodies and minds have grown accustomed to feeling numb whenever we are frightened or reminded of our experiences. Parents describe how their children are disconnected from them, and children describe how impossible it is to get their parents' attention.

For those working with Cambodian survivors, there is no doubt that the signs of trauma and injury are everywhere. Cambodians are mentally and physically sicker than other refugees. As a community we are disorganized, and our families are poorer than others. Families are breaking apart because people cannot share anymore—we especially cannot share our sorrow. Children are disrespectful of parents who no longer teach them right from wrong and who do not have the energy to correct them. It is as though the Cambodian way of life is lost forever.

But, I have hope that this view is wrong. I see signs that people are becoming more connected to each other. Over the years, I have known so many people who work day and night trying to help our people. Every community has people who will get up in the middle of the night to take care of someone who is sick or in trouble. When the Welfare Reform Bill took away peoples' homes and their food, other people who were also poor shared whatever they had with neighbors and friends. These stories make me believe that what I cherish about Cambodian life is still alive.

Just as I believe that it is a miracle that so many Cambodians have survived, I am touched and proud to see that so many of the values that have come from our beliefs as Buddhists are still alive in our communities and especially in our young people. The goal of the Khmer Rouge was to control our bodies, our minds, and our spirits and to make us like them—without feelings and without compassion. Even though they used great power, they were never able to make this happen. For every act of violence, there were a hundred acts of kindness, even in the darkest days.

I never dreamed that my life would be like this. My vision of myself was to be a good wife and mother and to take care of my family. After all of the suffering, my strength still comes from Buddhism. It remains in my soul and spirit and it gives me strength to work hard in caring for my patients and my community. Everything that I give comes back to me a hundred times, and I find peace.

WOMEN'S HEALTH IN TIBETAN MEDICINE AND TIBET'S "FIRST" FEMALE DOCTOR

Vincanne Adams and Dashima Dovchin

Tibetan medicine is one of the oldest continuously used medical systems in the world. Its potential contributions to modern views of health and healing are enormous. Derived from centuries of experimentation, observation, and adaptation of a wide variety of medical techniques from India, China, and Persia, and combined with indigenous practices of the Tibetan plateau dating from the seventh century, Tibetan medicine continues today to update and improve itself without abandoning its commitment to Buddhist precepts or many of its foundational theories. Tibetan medicine is called *sowa rigpa* in Tibetan, which literally means "science of healing." Its principle texts, the *rGyud bzhi*, or *The Four Tantras,* date from the eleventh century, a period of renaissance in Tibetan medical sciences and in Tibetan Buddhism in general. Several of the main medical texts used in Tibetan medicine were translated from Sanskrit and eventually included in the Buddhist Tangyur (the canonical collection of Buddhist commentaries and treatises). Along with the classical Indian medical tradition, Tibetans adopted tantric Buddhist conceptions of the body, notably those of the famous *Kālacakra Tantra,* as well as certain pharmacological techniques derived from the alchemical arts. These borrowings were gradually adapted, enriched, and melded into a specifically Tibetan medical tradition closely allied with Buddhism.

In this essay, we will map out the link between Buddhism and Tibetan medicine in terms of medical theory, specifically, the conception of the body, physiology, and pathology. We will then focus on questions of women's health, and on the contribution of Tibet's first female doctor, the prominent Amchi Kandro Yangkar. We will also explore the relationship between religion and science as reflected in her life and work. Kandro Yangkar lived through a period of great social transformation in Tibet and helped build the department of women's medicine that is now part of Tibet's Mentsikhang (Tibetan Medical Hospital, College of Medicine and Astrology). Yangkar is of interest to us not only because of her contributions to women's health, but also because she is recognized today as Tibet's "first" and, among the medical community, one of its most revered female doctors. In her work, she exemplifies a Buddhist form of healing that Tibetan doctors today refer to as "compassionate" practice. This fact is made more remarkable by the enormous political and social difficulties she faced and the tumultuous times in which she lived.

Tibetan Medicine and Buddhism

Tibetan medicine has a strong relationship with Buddhist Dharma. Tibetan Buddhist tradition holds that the Buddha recognized the basic nature of existence as one of suffering, and set about addressing the elimination of this suffering by proposing certain courses of action that would remove its causes. All of the precepts relating to the identification of suffering and the removal of its causes are reflected in the medical disciplines. Thus, as a result of his enlightenment, the Buddha acquired the title "Supreme Physician." Tibetan medicine and Buddhist philosophy share a number of fundamental concepts concerning the status of the person and the material nature of the phenomenal world—concepts that differ substantially from Western thought. Included in the Buddha's efforts were specific proposals for eliminating suffering through medical practices that recognized, for example, the relative and conditioned nature of material phenomena and, thus, the utility of all phenomena (for example, animals, minerals, plants) in producing a state of health.

According to popular tradition, the canonical treatise on medicine, the *rGyud bzhi,* was expounded by the Buddha Śākyamuni who in his medical personification is known as Bhaiṣajyaguru. The arrival of these medical teachings in Tibet is traced to the Indian translator Candrānanda and the great Vairocana, who were in Tibet during the reign of King Trison Deutsen, and later to Yuthok Yontan Gompo, the elder, who is credited with codifying the teachings. The texts that are understood as the *rGyud bzhi* today were probably codified anew during the life of Yuthok Yontan Gompo, the younger, during the eleventh and twelfth centuries,[1] and supplemented in the centuries thereafter by many commentaries.

The central symbol in Tantra is the Medicine Buddha (Bhaiṣajyaguru), who emanates multicolored rays of light that cleanse living beings of negativity and heal physical suffering caused by humoral imbalance. In Tibetan medicine humoral balance is responsible for the prevention of diseases and the maintenance of good health. The translation of religious ideas and images associated with the Medicine Buddha into clinical practice occurs in at least two ways, each of which can illuminate the unique understanding of women in, and the unique contributions of women to, Buddhist healing. First, Tibetan Buddhism has specific theories about the nature of the material world that link morality, environment, and physiological function together in various approaches to gynecological disorders, suggesting approaches to women's health that may be uniquely Buddhist. Second, healers recognize the importance of their own actions as compassionate beings and the primacy of an individual's service to others. Such healing practices are exemplified in Tibet's "first" female physician.

Translating Buddhist Ideology into Medical Theory: An Overview

The theoretical and practical foundations of Tibetan medicine are set forth in a fundamental treatise entitled the *rGyud bzhi*, or *The Four Tantras.* In addition to *The Four Tantras*, there are several widely used medical compendiums, and one of them, *The Blue Beryl Treatise*, is a unique collection of commentaries and illustrations from medical treatises produced in the seventeenth century as aide-mémoire for Tibetan physicians in training. Materials such as these present an approach to healing in which Buddhist doctrine forms the basis for theories of physiology and pathology, as well as of approaches to diagnosis and healing. For example, Buddhism assumes that the universe is impermanent and constantly changing. This idea is translated into medical theories about the physical world and the way in which coarse phenomena are related to one another as follows: Tibetan medicine states that the human body adjusts to infinite changes of state automatically, but that it is possible for imbalances to arise when external influences and the body's inner balances are not in harmony.

In Tibetan medicine, this lack of harmony is seen to be caused by the action of twenty-five factors, including the five elements, the six tastes, and the secondary characteristics. Taking as an example the five-element theory, all matter in the macro and microcosmic worlds is formed of the five cosmo-physical elements of earth *(sa)*, water *(chu)*, fire *(me)*, wind *(rlung)*, and space *(nammkha)*. The body likewise is composed of these same five basic cosmo-physical elements. Disorders involve a disharmony or a loss of equilibrium that is set in place by the increase or decrease of these elements in the body or in the environment.[2]

Because each individual represents a unique combination of these elements, and because individual health is determined by the maintenance of homeostasis, an excess of one or more elements can cause illness, that is, a disturbance of natural balance. Homeostasis is determined by the harmonious interaction of the body's three humors (literally, "faults"): wind *(rlung)*, bile *(mkhris pa)*, and phlegm *(bad kan)*. The three humors ensure the body's healthy physiological functioning by regulating the elemental composition of the body through organs and channels. The three humors are not separate entities, nor are they best viewed as organs or organ systems, but rather as systemic principles or energies related to natural phenomena like heat, cold, and movement, which are also in constant flux. They stand in clear and definite relation to each other and, when functioning normally, have appropriate physiological characteristics. When their functions are disturbed, their characteristics turn pathological.

Buddhist ideas are translated into medical theory in two ways, the first of which is via the system of the humors. The specific quality and strength of the humors is determined not only by the quality of elements present in the fetal tissues (themselves affected by the quality of the mother's and father's regenerative fluids, by congenital conditions, and by the mother's diet), but also by the presence of the three poisons of greed, anger, and ignorance, which are manifested in the fetal formation in the form of the humors, that is, wind, bile, and phlegm, respectively. In other words, the development of the humors in the fetus is dependent in part upon the quality of the karma (that is, the quality of one's moral existence) transferred from one's past life.

In this way, Tibetan medicine proposes a relationship between religious morality and physiology in that the presence of the poisons is an outcome of past deeds. The human body is thus, by its mere existence, an expression of spiritual and moral potential. It represents a combination of the five elements, which result from a mingling of the mother's and father's reproductive essences, brought to life or "ignited" by a life force, the *srog*, which contains the individual's karmic potential. It is this force that quickens physical tissue and gives rise to the humors and thereafter to the bodily complex as the humors act on the elemental constituents of the body. In sum, past morality is expressed in the quality, strength, or vitality of one's physiology.

The second way in which religious ideas are expressed in Tibetan medicine is in the relationship between the humors and the elements, such that morally relevant phenomena are seen as having physiological effects. This is the corollary to the theory of the fetal formation of the humors. Tibetan medicine relates theological precepts to physiological properties by positing a correspondence between the five elements and the humors or poisons: wind (in the sense of desire) corresponds to the wind humor and to the element wind; bile (in the sense of aversion) corresponds to the bile humor and the element fire; and phlegm (in the sense of ignorance) to the phlegm humor and the elements of earth and water.

The three humors support each other and keep the body in equilibrium. For example, the enormous heat produced by bile must be balanced by phlegm. At the same time, body tissues must be protected from the stress, wear, and tear created by wind, and appropriate fluids moved by winds ensure that the products of the biochemical processes, as enlivened by heat, are properly distributed throughout the body. In this sense, phlegm is the main category or principal of homeostasis.

In some accounts, the wind humor is the vital force; bile is the vital energy, and phlegm is the corrective force.

Additionally, each of the humors is seen as having its own characteristics. Wind *(rlung)* is seen as having a neutral character and assists bile and phlegm in their functions involving motion or movement of any type. Wind is of five types depending on both the place where it occurs in the body (for example, life-sustaining, ascending, pervading, fire-like equalizing, or downward expelling) and the function it is related to: breathing, spitting, muscular activity, speech, menstruation, urination, and relaying sensory input. The wind humor is directly related to mind and is always involved in mental or emotional illness. Since wind controls breathing, muscular activity, and movement, it can be realized as an air or as a pressure, energy, or force. Because of its qualities, wind is considered the main force in the body's function, the "leader" of the three humors, and is the most sensitive and responsive of the three. In Tibetan medicine, stress disorders such as blood pressure and emotional disturbances are considered wind disorders. Being associated with the poison of desire, it is symbolically represented by a copulating couple, suggesting that sexual desire is paradigmatic for all desire, whether in the form of lust and greed or simple longing and attachment.

The bile *(mkhris pa)* humor has the nature of the element fire, and also consists of five types. Bile does not simply refer to the secretion of the liver, but includes all liver disorders and the metabolism. It regulates the digestion of food and plays a large role in nutrition processes that eventually constitute the seven physical constituents: nutritional essence, blood, flesh, fat, bone, marrow, and regenerative fluid. Bile also influences the health of the skin, metabolism, and eye sight, and reflects the health of digestive metabolism, vital energy, and heat. Being associated with the poison of anger or aversion, it is depicted symbolically by two figures in combat with one another.

Finally, phlegm *(bad kan)* also has five types and consists of the elements water and earth. Its primary function is to regulate the body's tissue metabolism and the structural integrity of the body. The phlegm humor supports stability and weight, is responsible for sexual potency and fertility, and for resistance to illness. It is also related to emotional capacities such as patience, inner strength, and lack of desire, but is also considered a product of ignorance. It is represented by a sleeping figure (who is unaware of the ultimate causes of his or her suffering).

Here, what can be noted is that the humors themselves correspond to emotional or mental states in ways that implicate bodily function. In this system of medicine, emotional states are not subordinate to physical function—they are constitutive of it. Moreover, disruptive emotional states are seen to have physical symptoms and, more important, are also understood in terms of their moral implications and the context of human relations. All three humors can be explained in terms of theories about the causes of disease and the development of disorders.

One cause of disorders is innate predisposition. Time, location, diagnosis, and treatment of diseases are considered in Tibetan medicine in relation to the balance of the three humors. In a given individual, one of the humors can predominate over the others. Because of this, we can classify the human body into seven groups on the basis of natural predominance: those having a natural predominance of one of wind, bile, or phlegm; those with a predominance of a particular combination, such as wind-bile, wind-phlegm, or phlegm-bile; and those with a predominance of all three. In Tibetan medicine this system of the natural dominance and interaction of the humors is essential to the diagnosis and treatment of diseases.

Added to the humoral system is one of constitutional pulses: the male pulse is similar to wind; the female pulse is similar to bile; and the neuter pulse is similar to phlegm. These pulses represent the temperament and constitution of the person, and thus may be thought of as similar to blood type in biomedicine, in the sense that blood type differs in each person, is critical to diagnosis, and is the basis on which grave mistakes in treatment can be made.

The predominance of a particular humor makes the body differentially susceptible to various illnesses depending on a person's constitution. The constitution of each one of the humors is different and, accordingly, personal temperaments associated with them are different as well. For example, someone who has a predominance of wind is prone to insomnia and irritability. A person with a dominance of fire is usually of medium build, hot tempered, and likely to suffer from heat. This person might be more susceptible to disturbing or conflictual relations with others. A person with a dominance of water and earth elements (phlegm humor) is strong, plump, good-natured, and not bothered by heat, but is unclear about the ultimate sources of his or her unhappiness or happiness. In contrast, a person with wind dominance is slender and shy, and feels very comfortable in the heat, but may tend toward anxiousness and is easily disappointed. Changing one's climate or environmental condition can produce different reactions in different people, depending on their humoral character. Engaging in religious practices can aid in calming the mind, or in mitigating the effects of predominant constitutions; also helpful are eating specified foods and using appropriate medicines.

Imbalances in the humors are triggered by a number of factors beyond innate predominance, including diet, behavior, perception, karma, and demons, and seasonal, climactic, or environmental factors. When an imbalance occurs, the body becomes prone to diseases, harm, and increasing suffering. For example, when a disorder of bile occurs, the seven physical constituents are heated. Bile is located in the central part of the body, and when disturbed, it rises to the upper body. When a phlegm disorder occurs, body heat is reduced and smothered. Phlegm has an earth and water nature and is located in the upper part of the body. When disorder occurs, the phlegm descends to the lower body—and are responsible for colds. Wind is common to both cold and heat and pervades the entire body to promote both heat and cold disorders. It assists whichever of the two, bile or phlegm, is more dominant. If a phlegm disturbance is dominant, wind acts to produce a cold disorder in order to balance the properties of heat and cold.

Tibetan medicine thus combines psychological (or personality) factors with physical factors. Psychological factors exist in relation to—even as a result of—physical factors. But Tibetan medicine is also concerned with the emotional and, ultimately, the moral dimensions of humoral function, recalling this medical system's religious foundations. A person with wind problems may perceive that the circumstances he or she is living in are difficult, even if they are not ostensibly so to others, and this perception, because it translates into physiological imbalances, can eventually produce disease, or it can augment and exacerbate disorders caused by other factors. Similarly, living in ostensibly stressful or traumatic conditions can produce imbalances because they are stressful and can produce corresponding physical disorders.

Imbalance can be caused by climactic, dietary, or social conditions in a two-way relationship between external and internal functioning. For example, a person who reacts with anger to certain situations might be doing so because of a humoral imbalance. Likewise a person who fails to react with equanimity to ostensibly difficult situations can effect a change in his or her humoral composition, creating minor imbalances, which can become chronic if the causal situation persists or if the body is assaulted by other imbalancing forces (in diet or climate, for example). Thus, someone who has little ability to tame his or her emotions may suffer from imbalances as a result of his or her personal perceptions of a situation. The subtle links between perceptions and physiology in Tibetan medicine make for a medical system that proposes empirical relationships between social and physical environment, mind, body—and morality.

The moral dimensions of this equation are the least often discussed, operating as they do at the level of implicit cultural assumption as much as overt medical theory. Again, morality pertains to one's actions and intentions toward others. It is when one is disturbed by the actions of others, or when one causes others suffering by being angry or desirous, for example, that these humoral effects are aroused—that is, the humoral effects are brought on by the activity of the three poisons represented by the humors. In this system, emotional states are relevant not just to the individual and his or her physiology, but also to others. It is because the poisons result in benefit or harm to others that the individual who expresses them also, inevitably, suffers from them. Anger and desire manifest in the individual psyche can also be manifest in relationships with others, just as these relationships can in turn influence perception. In other words, such emotions are ultimately of moral importance at the same time that they are implicated in bodily function.

Thus, for example, a good Tibetan physician is attentive to his or her demeanor with a patient since if fear or worry is aroused by the doctor, these emotions can exacerbate or even cause imbalances (by the action of the winds and other humors) in the patient. Here, the idea is not simply that a physician must be sensitive to the perceptions of the patient lest those perceptions interfere with the health of the patient—the doctor must also recognize that whatever effect he or she ultimately produces in the patient will, by the action of karma and by the action of arousing emotional responses in him- or herself, have an outcome on the doctor's own health (if not in this life then in future lives). This religious orientation is implicit in Tibetan medicine where it works as a cultural ideal and as a basis upon which to establish the links between karma, the humors, the poisons, and health.

In practice, this means that although Tibetan doctors recognize that their patients' suffering is ultimately tied to the suffering of worldly existence—to possessing a body and living according to the push and pull of desire and aversion caused by ignorance—they also recognize the limitations of their own intervention in relation to religious practices. Thus, Tibetan physicians may sometimes recommend a visit to a lama or a religious teacher for certain intractable health problems to those who would obviously be aided by religious training. At the same time, Tibetan physicians recognize that, because the poisons manifest themselves physically—through processes affected by emotional, social, and environmental circumstances, all of which are based on the five elements—they can be effectively addressed by medical intervention, and especially by medicines made up of the same five elements as the body. Tibetan medicine does not substitute for but rather supplements formal religious training.

This does not mean that Tibetan physicians do not, depending on their own level of training and expertise, prescribe meditation or other religious ritual activities to calm the mind and help maintain or restore homeostasis. Sometimes, they recognize the need to use medicines as a first order intervention in order to restore balance and calm to the patient's humors so that he or she can proceed to meditate or undertake religious training. The corollary to this is that the potency of Tibetan medicines is believed to derive not simply from the ingredients but also from the blessings they receive from qualified lama physicians.

On Women's Health

A final example of the moral and religious foundations of Tibetan medicine can be seen in the diagnosis and treatment of women's disorders. The *rGyud bzhi* enumerates thirty-two gynecological disorders, and various physicians have added new disorders to this list in their commentaries over the years. Gynecological disorders include five womb disorders caused by wind, bile, phlegm, blood, and various combinations of these; nine types of womb tumors; two types of womb parasites; and sixteen types of menstruation disorders. During menopause, moreover, there are conditions related to the lungs, heart, liver, spleen, gall bladder, kidneys, small intestine, large intestine, stomach, bones, breasts, and head, making a total of thirty-two named gynecological diseases. In women's health, disorders most often start from menstrual blood and become chronic disorders accompanied by wind. Wind affects many internal organs, but especially the liver. If the liver is functioning properly and its wind element is flowing smoothly, the emotional state will be happy and easy going, and the person will be in good spirits and freely able to express her emotions. If the wind element is obstructed and deviates from a normal state, it will affect the emotional state of the woman, causing anger and irritability. In pathology, if wind rebels upward causing the rise of liver-fire, the person will be very irritable and suffer from headaches. When wind deviates, it can impair the movement of blood in the vessels, thus affecting the uterus and resulting in irregular and painful menstruation along with premenstrual tension with distention of the breasts.

Wind, moreover, can easily interfere with the liver function of ensuring the smooth flow of blood. The supply of blood in the liver can become depleted, leading ultimately to an imbalance of blood stasis or equilibrium. When the liver-blood process stagnates, the flow of blood in the vessels will also stagnate and affect menstrual function. The chief manifestation of the stasis of blood in the uterus is dark and clotted menstrual blood. Blood stasis always leads to pain and, in this pattern, pain relates primarily to distention. This pattern can also give rise to fibroid blood masses in the uterus. Lack of blood results in scanty periods or no periods at all, such as in early menopause.

Since wind is also closely tied to emotions, we can also understand women's problems in terms of mental disturbances. The emotions of anger and distress are related to liver function and to the element of fire, the bile humor. Wind and fire tend to affect the mind by causing anxiety, irritability, mental agitation, insomnia, or mental illness. When fire moves upward it agitates the blood, causing bleeding. Fire's nature is to rise upward to the head, where it can dry up fluids, damage blood, and affect the mind. Thus, a woman who is living in conditions that persistently arouse anger or fear can suffer from menstrual irregularities, or ultimately growths in her uterus. In Tibet today, it is not hard to find women who suffered great trauma during the Cultural Revolution and who, because of the resulting anxiety, developed chronic wind imbalances and eventually menstrual dysfunction and growths in the uterus.

Other social factors such as government-sponsored relocation to damp or moist regions of Tibet from dry arid zones or new labor requirements whereby people are working in water for long periods of time can also result in chronic wind-phlegm imbalances in some women that persist for long periods of time. An increase in phlegm activity affects water flow, and kidney temperature associated with cold, and also blood flow, resulting in abdominal, back, and arthritic pain. Here, the psychological effects of social conditions cause wind to exacerbate the activity of phlegm.

Finally, a common problem among young Tibetan women today is inflammation of the pelvic region due to wind-bile imbalances. These problems typically stem from dietary changes, whereby young people are exposed to more varied foods, but especially hot chili peppers consumed in enormous quantities, and also to changing behavior, especially sexual and reproductive behaviors. Increased practice of birth control, especially use of I.U.D.s, more frequent intercourse with multiple partners, and abortions are all implicated in the production of wind-bile disorders and fevers with inflammation of the uterus, fallopian tubes, and/or ovaries. Here, wind imbalance can augment the bile's activity, thus producing heat, resulting in heat-based fevers. Agitation of the blood in the reproductive tract is associated with inflammation.

In all cases, the Tibetan physician focuses on physical imbalances that can be remedied by dietary, behavioral, medicinal, or external therapies (the latter includes moxibustion, massage, incense, and cupping), but it is also possible to understand these health problems as related to the three poisons under the influence of external factors. Wind disorders are particularly exemplary. In the case of suffering caused by the Cultural Revolution, or government policies of relocation, new labor or work requirements, or even policies on reproduction and population, women's health is affected directly. First, the action of the elements (such as cold or water in the environment or hot foods in the diet) can be detrimental to homeostasis. The disturbance of winds, caused both by imbalance of the other humors and by emotional responses to perceptions of one's situation—that is, an inability to respond effectively to these circumstances in ways that are not harmful to one's health—are also secondarily implicated in causing disorders. Women who suffered great losses such as the death of family members or long separations from them because of imprisonment during the Cultural Revolution, often developed humoral imbalances that resulted in chronic diseases.

Young women in urban Tibet today might also be understood as suffering from wind disorders in relation to the poison of desire, specifically unfulfilled desires, brought on by rapid social change. Since imbalances of wind are related to unfulfilled desires, it is possible to read increased sexuality as a form of grasping for satisfaction that ultimately, under modern conditions requiring birth control, abortions, or multiple sexual partners, can harm a woman's health.

Generally, Tibetan doctors treat disease with gentle methods. The techniques of healing address not only the particular disease the patient is suffering from but also its side effects. Thus, treatments consisting of herbal remedies are effective not only in rectifying humoral imbalance but also in changing one's perceptions of a given social situation, enabling one to better cope with it. Tibetan doctors are well known for the tremendous number of different medicines they have for wind disorders. The herb most used to treat wind disorders is black aloe wood or eagle-wood (Aquilaria agallocha), which is also the most favored minor tranquilizer among the Tibetan community.

To summarize, Tibetan humoral medical theory weaves together Buddhist ideas in a complicated understanding of the elemental composition of worldly phenomena, associating physiology with mental, physical, social, environmental, and moral states or conditions. A good doctor in the tradition of Tibetan medicine must not only be armed with an extensive body of knowledge, but must also possess a variety of personal qualities. We believe these qualities are amply demonstrated in one of Tibet's most famous female doctors, Kandro Yangkar.

Kandro Yangkar, Tibet's "First" Female Doctor

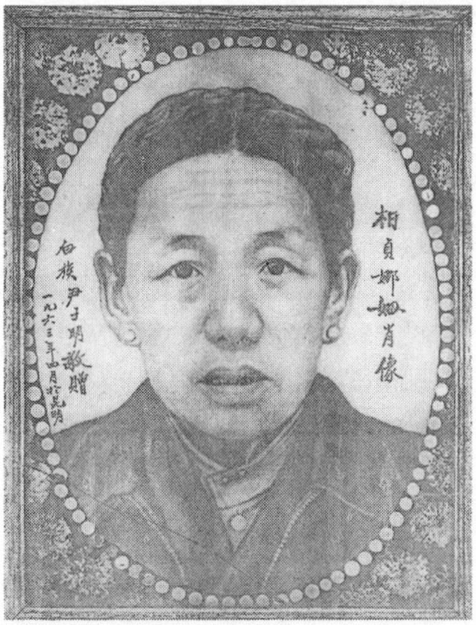

Kandro Yangkar (with permission of Dr. Jamphel Kunkyab, Yangkar's son)

In Rechung Rinpoche's translation of the *rGyud bzhi,* we find an account of the personal qualities required of a good doctor as they were probably taught during the time of Kandro Yankar (1904–1972/3). The requirements include the following:[3]

1. Intelligence: One wishing to become a good doctor must be intelligent and have a deep comprehension, quick understanding, and good memory. He must be able to read and write in order to learn all about medicine and master the medical texts. His teacher must be one who knows all about medicine and is able to explain everything, not hiding any knowledge from the student. He must be an understanding and kind-hearted person and generally knowledgeable in every field. The student should obey and be patient with his teacher, and coordinate with his fellow-students to help one another in their studies and not be lazy.
2. Compassion: One wishing to become a good doctor must always think of being helpful to all beings. He must have a sympathetic mind and must not be partial,

but treat all alike. He should wish happiness for all and have the desire to obtain enlightenment. One with such a good mind will have no trouble in his medical practice.
3. Bedside manner: Doctors must have a pleasant nature and be understanding and able to give encouragement and confidence to patients. They must be well versed in medicine and able to diagnose diseases without difficulty. A doctor should be familiar with the customs and usages of the common man, know how to talk and behave, and have some knowledge of religion. He should not be selfish and should have pity for the poor. He should look after a patient well until the patient has fully recovered. A doctor who has all the above qualities will attain fame and prosperity. A good doctor is like a protector and deliverer of those who are helpless; he is a representative of the Medicine Buddha and of the lineage of the teachers of medicine.

Kandro Yangkar was surely not the first female doctor to live and work in Tibet, there were numerous well-known female doctors trained in the family lineage tradition common throughout the Tibetan cultural region. But Kandro Yangkar was the first woman to come under the tutelage of Tibet's most famous twentieth-century monastic physician-scholar, Khenrab Norbu. And she was the first to practice in Tibet's first non-monastic medical college, the Mentsikhang, which was established in 1916. For these reasons, she is called Tibet's first female physician. In the story of her life one finds evidence that she embodied many of the ideals of a Buddhist healer as noted in the *rGyud bzhi.* Her recognition in Tibet today is testimony to her contribution to the preservation of this medical system, even while supporting its modernization during a period of great social upheaval. The story of her life that follows was told in rather glowing terms by one of her children. Although his account has not been corroborated by comparison with other sources, we believe that it is an honest account and can be read as his memory of her life and of her contributions as a healer.

Kandro Yangkar was from the Kham region in eastern Tibet. Here there was an incarnate lama called the Rinpoche Jedung, an important teacher of the Taklung Kagyupa order. He possessed a set of the writings of Jedung Champa Chungne, who was famed for his medical skills. Champa Chungne had two daughters. The elder daughter had two daughters of her own. The younger of these two granddaughters of Champa Chungne was Yangkar.

Yangkar was born in 1904 in the area of Powo, in a place that used to be called Pema Gyu. Powo Kanam Deba was the *chogyal,* or religious leader of this area. When Yangkar was twelve years old, her family moved to Kham Riwoche. Her grandfather, Champa Chungne, a *rinpoche,* was sent to Kham to build a monastery at Riwoche. In Kham, Yangkar became a nun. She donned nun's clothes and started studying the five sciences: Sanskrit, debate, Buddhism, medicine, and painting. She had already started learning some medicine from her father (who was a doctor), as was common in families of medical practitioners.

By the time she was thirteen, she could already write Tibetan very well. At that time, however, in 1917, political turmoil broke out: Kham Riwoche came under occupation by the Chinese military as the result of a border dispute.[4] The family and all of her grandfather's followers from the monastery had to leave the area. They went to Chamdo to live, but had a hard time surviving there, and were forced to beg for a living. Soon, the people of her grandfather's lineage remaining at his original home in Taklung requested that they return, since many of his followers were still there. This area is now called Phenpo Lhundrup Dzong. By 1920, Champa Chungne had passed away in Taklung, and the family came to Lhasa, where they finally got permission to return to Kham Riwoche. Once in Riwoche, Yangkar was taken under wing of Chame Rinpoche, the Kagyu lama, who was the sixth reincarnation of the Chame lama. He "adopted" her and gave her the name of Kandro.

Having learned a great deal from her doctor father, Kandro Yangkar was already qualified to practice healing at a very young age. Like her father, who had had many teachers from Derge, Lhasa, including various *rinpoches*, Kandro Yangkar also had many teachers during her lifetime. She learned medicine from her maternal grandfather, her father, and her lama, the Chame Rinpoche, as well as from her mother who knew a little medicine.

The director of the Mentsikhang (College of Medicine and Astrology) in Lhasa at that time was Khenrab Norbu. It so happens that he sent two students to Kandro Yangkar's grandfather, Champa Chungne, while he was still alive, in order to study with him. Champa Chungne taught these students, and when they were finished studying and had become doctors, he sent a message through them back to the Mentsikhang saying that he now had one request of his own. His request was that Khenrab Norbu teach his "daughter" (actually granddaughter) Kandro Yangkar to study eye medicine.

Years passed, and Kandro Yangkar was traveling as the adopted daughter of the Chame Rinpoche. She went to Bhutan, India, Nepal, and many other places on behalf of the *rinpoche*. While traveling, one of her tasks was to collect ingredients for use in medicines. One day, her travels brought her to Lhasa, to the Mentsikhang, in order to purchase medicines that were made available to family-based doctors there. When the doctors in Lhasa met her, they asked her identity, and Khenrab Norbu asked, "Who is this? Is this a Khamba woman? Because previously I got a request from a Khamba lama that I should teach her how to do eye medicine." The answer was "Yes, she is that one." With this, he invited her to stay in Lhasa to study eye medicine, and she became Khenrab Norbu's personal student, and he, her main teacher. She did not do anything that was not his wish and soon she became his model apprentice. Not only was she a brilliant student who was devoted to her teachers, but she had an extremely sharp memory as well, and could memorize a long prayer book in just thirteen or fourteen hours, during the course of a single day. As an eye doctor, she traveled widely—to Nepal, Sikkim, Kalimpong, and Calcutta—and patients from all over gradually began to come to Tibet seeking treatment from her.

Eventually, she married the Chame Rinpoche, and together they had three daughters. Her eldest daughter is still in Kham Riwoche, but her other two daughters have died. After the *rinpoche*, she had a second husband, with whom she had a daughter, and then a third husband, who was from Lhasa and descended from the Shakapba family.

Kandro Yangkar's main virtue was that she was extremely generous. She always thought of helping others and used to have patients come right into her own home for treatment. She would feed them, take care of them, diagnose their illnesses, give them medicines, and then, after treating them, she would even give them money for their journey back home. Moreover, Kandro Yangkar used to rent rooms from well-known, wealthy families in Lhasa in order to house and treat patients needing ongoing care. Sometimes her patients could pay quite a lot of money and did so out of gratitude for her services, but, when patients had no money, nothing would be asked of them.

Yangkar would often travel great distances to treat patients. She always went, and because she was a very tall and heavy woman, only the family horses could carry her. She used to take several servants with her to help look after patients, even those living at a great distance. No matter how important a matter was at home, if there was a patient who needed her, she would leave everything to attend the sick.

Kandro Yangkar was open to all sorts of new ideas and practices, even medical theories from outside the Tibetan tradition. She explored many new ideas on her visits to other places. When she was in India, for example, she asked famous doctors there to teach her about injections and stitching wounds and would always practice with them to see what she could learn. She always wanted to learn surgery but was told by the doctors that they couldn't teach her because in Tibet she would not be able to practice without modern equipment and sterile conditions. She also used to purchase the medicinal ingredients from where they were the best, that is, the most potent, and would then compound her own medicines. If the medical ingredients were better from India, for example, she would buy them from India. If they were better from Bhutan, she would buy them from there. She also used penicillin and new medicines, but in using both traditional and modern medicines, she would research thoroughly their ingredients and the proper manner of their preparation and use.

She was also very well organized and kept clear records of the problems and successful outcomes of her work. She used to follow up on all of her patients to find out the current status of their illnesses. Today, one can meet people who still remember being treated successfully by her—some who, for example, had eye surgery thirty years ago and can still thread a needle today.

The following story is an example of her generosity. Sometime in the 1940s, there was an epidemic in the Chamdo area in which many people died. At that time, no other doctor would go there because he was afraid of being infected. Kandro Yangkar, however, went. A certain lady was so stricken with the disease that she had no control over her bowel movements or urination. No one would take care of her because she was considered the dirtiest and worst case. When Kandro Yangkar went to her, however, she scrubbed her and nursed her lovingly back to health, surprising all around her. To this day, many people in Chamdo remember her for this.

In 1948, the family moved back to Kham Riwoche, but Kandro Yangkar still traveled extensively for her work. In 1952 or 1953, she was called to Bhutan by the then king, the current king's grandfather, as the royal family of Bhutan had been connected to Kandro Yangkar's family since the time of her grandfather. (Her grandfather had been the then king's lama and was the one who gave him his *dbang* initiations.) At this time, the king was suffering from eye problems and called Kandro Yangkar to come and treat him. He told her that he had invited many Western doctors to look at his eyes but that none of them could help. He then requested her to stay at court until he could shoot an arrow right at the target, for only then would he be satisfied that his eyesight was perfect. Yangkar placed her son in the care of a Bhutanese family living in Lhasa and went to help the king, and did, in fact, take care of his eyes until he could shoot an arrow accurately at the target.

On another occasion, there was an epidemic of smallpox in Tsurphu, the seat of the Karmapa, and a lot of people were sick and dying. The Karmapa wrote to Kandro Yangkar, telling her she must come and treat these patients. She left immediately, but her own people said that she was crazy for doing it, not only because she herself would get infected, but because her children would be harmed as well. At that time, however, she didn't think of herself or her children, but only of the problems present in the community; moreover, she was convinced that she herself would not get sick. In 1958, in the midst of all the chaos in Tibet, Khenrab Norbu himself developed eye problems. Kandro Yangkar received a letter from his office requesting that she return to take care of his eyes. She left her young son in the monastery enrolled as a monk and went immediately to Lhasa to take care of Khenrab Norbu.

From that time on, she became one of the main practitioners of medicine in the Mentsikhang and was known, despite the political turmoil around her, as a doctor who had a wonderful outlook on life. She was a jovial, light-hearted, and fun-loving person, who never appeared awkward, sad, or in despair about the things around her. She loved to sing the songs she had learned on her travels and had a very lovely voice. Although she was connected to a number of aristocratic families of her time and did many things with them, she was never arrogant about her good fortune. She always worked for others, and because she was very skilled with her hands and could cut and sew clothes, she would call the tailors to her home and help them with the cutting and sewing.

During the years that she was at the Mentsikhang, many problems developed. One problem was that Kandro Yangkar was renowned for her skill in eye surgery, and patients requested her treatment first. Patients who were treated unsuccessfully by other doctors would become disgruntled and suggest that, had they gone to her first, they would have been cured. Eventually, in 1962, jealous people voiced so many criticisms about the way things were run that Mentsikhang shut down the eye surgery department. This happened at a time when medicine in general was perceived to be elitist and extraneous to the communist project.

Nevertheless, Kandro Yangkar continued treating patients. On one occasion, she saw a poor farmer's family in the street. Because the father couldn't see due to eye problems, the mother was carrying all three of her young children in her arms. When Kandro Yangkar saw this, she felt so bad that she rented a room in Tengyeling, near the monastery, and asked the family to stay there. She personally treated the father's eyes and nursed him until he was strong again. When news of this reached the administration, however, Kandro Yangkar and her whole family were reprimanded and told not to do such things again. After this scolding, she never practiced privately again.

During 1962, after the Mentsikhang eye department shut down, Kandro Yangkar was assigned to work in the children's ward and then from 1963 onward she was assigned to work in the newly established women's health section. One reason given for her transfer to the women's section was a very specific incident. Some time in 1961, when Khenrab Norbu was still alive, a Chinese leader came with his wife to visit Lhasa. The wife visited the Mentsikhang, telling Khenrab Norbu that although she had been married for eighteen years, she still could not get pregnant, and she wondered if the Tibetan doctors could help her. Khenrab Norbu called on Kandro Yangkar and made her responsible for treating the Chinese woman. After receiving medicine from Yangkar, the wife was able to conceive, and from that time onward, there was much talk of Kandro Yangkar's expertise in women's medicine. The fact that the women's ward itself was established at about this same time and that she was the first woman to work in the Mentsikhang contributed to her reputation.

Kandro Yangkar was also well known for her compounding skills. She used to make her own medicines for problems that were difficult to cure. The medicines she invented were known for being effective, and they were often given her name. After her reprimand for her treatment of the farmer's family, however, the practice of naming medicines after the doctor who devised them was prohibited.

In general, during the next years Yangkar was very committed to serving the community and helping people. But life became much more difficult in Tibet in the years that followed. It was a time of terrible turmoil during which Yangkar was not allowed to work as a physician. Because she was from a family connected to the aristocracy, she was considered to be from a "bad family." Being classified that way placed her among the people who were prohibited from working at all between about 1968 and 1970.

In the early 1970s, Kandro Yangkar became sick. She was said to have had an accident involving a fall from a ladder while she was cleaning windows, which damaged her leg. Her leg never completely healed, and for the rest of her life she was unable to walk properly. What made the injury worse was that she wasn't allowed to receive good medical treatment. Medicines at that time were regulated, and access was given only by permission and only to some. Kandro Yangkar's leg became increasingly worse, and she eventually became paralyzed. During her illness, and fearful about the future of her medical tradition, she requested that the administration choose somebody she could teach and to whom she could transmit her knowledge before she died. She knew that there wasn't any point in teaching her own children because they would not be allowed to practice medicine as they were from the wrong class. But she did want them to choose somebody, and eventually the authorities sent her two students who are still practicing medicine today.

Kandro Yangar wrote many treatises on women's health, including a codification of disorders and new treatments, and a commentary on the *rGyud bzhi* specifically concerned with women's health. Unfortunately, many of her writings were destroyed during the Cultural Revolution and these works are unrecoverable today. Nevertheless, Kandro Yangkar's work and achievements are recognized by many contemporary scholars of Tibetan medicine, but more importantly, by many common people throughout Tibet. Although most of her writings were destroyed and although she apparently suffered a great deal during her time, she has today begun to be rehabilitated by the current administration and is highly regarded by those who have followed her.

The story of Kandro Yangkar's life conveys her commitment to many of the ideals of the Buddhist approach to healing: she combined a form of selfless, compassionate practice with a use of sharp memory and great devotion to teachers. She devoted her skills not only to the faculty of vision but to the health of women, and because of these she enjoys a great reputation today. The sort of healing and motivation Kandro Yangkar exemplified is slowly making a comeback in contemporary Tibet and, in some small way, they are still alive among practitioners in the Mentsikhang today. That the benefits of such a medical approach are far-reaching and enduring is perhaps best testified by the experience of Yangkar's son, who in his travels, is most happy to discover people who once knew and were cured by his mother and who, in meeting him, are always good to him in return.

Notes

1. Gerken (1999).
2. See Clark (1995) and Clifford (1984), for extensive and accessible translations of portions of the medical Tantras.
3. Rechung Rinpoche (1973), 91–92.
4. Goldstein (1989), 83.

BIBLIOGRAPHY

Ackerly, J., and K., Blake. "The Suppression of a People: Accounts of Torture and Imprisonment in Tibet." *Physicians for Human Rights* (November 1989).

Addiss, Stephen. *The Art of Zen.* New York: Abrams, 1989.

Addy, Premen. "British and Indian Strategic Perceptions of Tibet." In *Resistance and Reform,* edited by Barnett and Akiner. Bloomington: Indiana University Press, 1994.

Agarwal, Bina. *A Field of One's Own: Gender and Land Rights in South Asia.* Cambridge: Cambridge University Press, 1994.

Altekar, A.S. *The Position of Women in Hindu Civilization: From Prehistoric Times to the Present Day.* 1956. Reprint, New Delhi: Motilal Banarsidass, 1978.

Ambedkar, B.R. *The Buddha and His Dhamma.* Bombay: Siddharth College Publication, 1957.

———. "On the Awakening of Women." In *Thus Spoke Ambedkar.* Edited and compiled by Bhagawan Das. Vol 2. Bangalore: Ambedkar Sahitya Prakashana, 1969.

———. *The Untouchables: Who Were They? And Why They Became Untouchables.* Delhi: Amrit Book Co., 1948.

Anan Kōshiki. Reprint, Kyoto: Kaibashoin, 1986.

Arai, Paula. *Women Living Zen: Japanese Sōtō Buddhist Nuns.* New York: Oxford University Press, 1999.

———. "Zen Nuns: Living Treasures of Japanese Buddhism." Ph.D. dissertation, Harvard University, 1993.

Argüelles, José, and Miriam Argüelles. *Mandala.* Boston: Shambhala, 1995.

Asad, Talal. *Genealogies of Religion: Discipline and Reasons of Power in Christianity and Islam.* Baltimore: Johns Hopkins University Press, 1993.

Aston, W. G., trans. *Nihongi.* Rutland, VT: Tuttle, 1972.

Atkinson, J. M., and S. Errington, eds. *Power and Difference: Gender in Island Southeast Asia.* Stanford: Stanford University Press, 1990.

Avedon, John. F., and Fernand Meyer. *The Buddha's Art of Healing.* New York: Rizzoli International Publications, 1998.

Aziz, Barbara. "Moving Towards a Sociology of Tibet." In *Essays on Women and Tibet,* edited by Janice D. Willis. Ithaca: Snow Lion, 1987.

Banerjee, Anukul Chandra, trans. *Sarvāstivāda Literature.* Calcutta: K.L. Mukhopadhyay, 1957.

Barnes, Nancy J. "Buddhist Women and the Nuns' Order in Asia." In *Engaged Buddhism: Buddhist Liberation Movements in Asia,* edited by Christopher S. Queen and Sallie B. King. Albany, NY: State University of New York Press, 1996.

———. "Women in Buddhism." In *Today's Woman in World Religions,* edited by A. Sharma. Albany: State University of New York Press, 1994.

———. "Buddhism." In *Women in World Religions,* edited by A. Sharma. Albany: State University of New York Press, 1987.

Barnett, Robbert. "The Role of Nuns in Tibetan Protest." *Preliminary Notes.* Tibet Information Network (October 17, 1989).

Barnett, Robert, and Shirin Akiner, eds. *Resistance and Reform in Tibet.* 1994. Reprint, Delhi: Motilal Banarsidass, 1996.

Barraud, C., et al. *Of Relations and the Dead: Four Societies Viewed from the Angle of Their Exchanges.* Translated by S. J. Suffern. Providence, Rhode Island: Berg, 1994.

Bartholomeusz, Tessa. "First Among Equals: Buddhism and the Sri Lankan State." In *Buddhism and Politics in Twentieth-Century Asia,* edited by I. Harris. London: Pinter, 1999.

———. "The Female Mendicant in Sri Lanka." In *Buddhism, Sexuality, and Gender,* edited by José Ignacio Cabezón. Albany: State University of New York Press, 1992.

———. "Views From the Monastery Kitchen." *Kailash* 4, no. 2 (1976): 155–67.

———. *Women under the Bo Tree: Buddhist Nuns in Sri Lanka.* 1994. Reprint, Cambridge: Cambridge University Press, 1995.

———. "Mothers of Buddhas, Mothers of Nations: Kumaratunga and her Meteoric Rise to Power in Sri Lanka." *Journal of Feminist Studies* 25, no. 1 (spring 1999): 211–25.

Bartholomeusz, Tessa, and Chandra R. de Silva, ed. *Buddhist Fundamentalism and Minority Identities in Sri Lanka.* Albany: State University of New York Press, 1998.

Batchelor, Martine. *Principles of Zen.* San Francisco: Thorsons, 1999.

———. *Walking on Lotus Flowers.* San Francisco: Thorsons/HarperCollins, 1996.

Bechert, Heinz. *Buddhismus, Staat und Gesellshcaft in den Ländern des Theravāda Buddhismus.* Frankfurt: A. Metzner, Wiesbaden: O. Harrasowitz, 1993–96.

———. "Theravāda Buddhist Sangha: Some General Observations on Historical and Political Factors in Its Development." *Journal of Asian Studies* 29 (1970): 761–78.

Bell, Catherine. *Ritual: Perspectives and Dimensions.* New York: Oxford University Press, 1997.

———. *Ritual Theory, Ritual Practice.* New York: Oxford University Press, 1992.

Benisti, Mireille. "Observations concernant le stūpa no. 2 de Sanci." *Bulletin d'êtudes Indienne* 4 (1986): 165–70.

Beyer, Stephan. *The Cult of Tārā: Magic and Ritual in Tibet.* Berkeley: University of California Press, 1978.

Blakiston, Hilary. [Padmasuri]. *But Little Dust: Life amongst the "Ex-Untouchables."* 2nd ed. Birmingham: Windhorse, 1997.

Bloch, Maurice. "Language, Anthropology, and Cognitive Science." *Man* 26 (1991): 183–98.

Bond, George D. *The Buddhist Revival in Sri Lanka: Religious Tradition, Reinterpretation and Response.* Columbia: University of South Carolina Press, 1988.

Bourdieu, Pierre. *Language and Symbolic Power.* Cambridge, MA: Harvard University Press, 1991.

Bowie, Catherine. "The Alchemy of Charity: Of Class and Buddhism in Northern Thailand." *American Anthropologist* 100, no. 2 (1998): 469–81.

Brauen, Martin. *The Mandala: Sacred Circle in Tibetan Buddhism.* Boston: Shambhala, 1997.

Brink, J., and J. Mencher. *Mixed Blessings: Gender and Religious Fundamentalism Cross Culturally.* New York: Routledge, 1997.

Broch-Due, V., I. Rudie, and T. Bleie, eds. *Carved Flesh/Cast Selves: Gendered Symbols and Social Practice.* Oxford: Berg Publishers, 1993.

Bunnag, J. *Buddhist Monk, Buddhist Layman: A Study of Urban Monastic Organisation in Central Thailand.* Cambridge: Cambridge University Press, 1973.

Cabezón, José Ignacio. "Buddhist Principles in the Tibetan Liberation Movement." In *Engaged Buddhism: Buddhist Liberation Movements in Asia,* edited by Christopher S. Queen and Sallie B. King. Albany: State University of New York Press, 1996.

Carpenter, J. Estlin, ed. *The Dīgha Nikāya,* Vol. 3. 1911. Rpt. London: The Pali Text Society, 1976.

Carrithers, Michael. *The Forest Monks of Sri Lanka: An Anthropological and Historical Study.* Delhi: Oxford University Press, 1983.

———. "The Modern Ascetics of Lanka and the Pattern of Change in Buddhism." *Man* 14 (1979): 294–310.

Census Office of India. 1981 District Census Handbook: Kargil (Village and Town Directory), n.p., 1981.

Chalmers, Robert, ed. *The Majjhima Nikāya.* Vols. 2 and 3. 1896, 1899. Reprint, London: The Pali Text Society, 1977.

Chandra, Lokesh. *Tibetan Mandalas (Vajravali and Tantra-samuccaya).* International Academy of Indian Culture. New Delhi: Crescent Printing Works, 1995.

Chatham, Doris Clark. "Rasa and Sculpture." In *Kaladarsana: American Studies in the Art of India,* edited by J.G. Williams. New Delhi: Oxford and IBH Publishing Co., 1981.

Chattopadhyaya, Alaka. *Atiśa and Tibet: Life and Works of Dipamkara Srijñana in Relation to the History and Religion of Tibet.* New Delhi: Motilal Banarsidass, 1981.

Chayat, Roko Sherry, ed. *Subtle Sound: The Zen Teachings of Maurine Stuart.* Boston: Shambhala Publications, 1996.

Chodron, Thubten, ed. *Blossoms of the Dharma: Living as a Buddhist Nun.* Berkeley, CA: North Atlantic Books, 2000.

———. "Preparing for Ordination: Reflections for Westerners Considering Monastic Ordination in the Tibetan Buddhist Tradition." In *Life as a Western Buddhist Nun.* Seattle, 1997.

Cixous, Helen. "Castration or Decapitation?" *Signs* 7, no. 1 (1981): 41–55.

Clark, Barry. *The Quintessence Tantras of Tibetan Medicine.* Translated by Barry Clark. Ithaca, NY: Snow Lion Publications, 1995.

Clifford, Terry. *Tibetan Buddhist Medicine and Psychiatry: The Diamond Healing.* York Beach, ME: S. Weiser, 1984.

Collins, Stephen. *Selfless Persons: Imagery and Thought in Theravada Buddhism.* 1982. Reprint, Cambridge: Cambridge University Press, 1990.

Cook, N.M. "The Position of Nuns in Thai Buddhism: The Parameters of Religious Recognition." M.A. thesis, Australian National University, 1981.

Cort, John. "Art, Religion, and Material Culture: Some Reflections on Method." *Journal of the American Academy of Religion* 44, no.3 (1996): 613–32

Criddle, Joan D., and Teeda Butt Mam. *To Destroy You Is No Loss.* New York: Atlantic Monthly Press, 1987.

Crook, John, and Henry Osmaston. *Himalayan Buddhist Villages.* New Delhi: Motilal Banarsidass, 1994.

Cunningham, Alexander. *The Bhilsa Topes; or, Buddhist Monuments of Central India.* London: 1854. Reprint, New Delhi: Munshiram Manoharlal, 1997.

Daniels, Christine. "Defilement and Purification: Tibetan Buddhist Pilgrims at Bodhnath, Nepal." Ph.D. dissertation, Oxford University, 1994.

Dani, A.H. *Indian Palaeography.* Oxford: Clarendon Press, 1963.

Daorueng, P. "Sole Sisters." *Far Eastern Economic Review* (September, 1998).

Das, Chandra. *A Tibetan-English Dictionary.* Reprint, Delhi: Book Faith India, 1995.

De Silva, R., and H. Kawanami. "Women in Buddhism: Unity and Diversity." In *Sakyadhītā Newsletter,* International Association of Buddhist Women. Vol. 9, 1, no. 1, S.1–3 (summer 1998).

Dehejia, Vidya. *Early Buddhist Rock Temples: A Chronology.* London: Thames and Hudson, and Ithaca, N.Y.: Cornell University Press, 1972.

———. "The Collective and Popular Basis of Early Buddhist Patronage: Sacred Monuments, 100 B.C.–250 A.D." In *The Powers of Art: Patronage in Indian Culture*, edited by B.S. Miller. Delhi: 1992.

———, ed. *Unseen Presence: The Buddha and Sanchi.* Mumbai: Marg Publications, 1996.

Deutsch, Elliot, trans. and ed. *The Bhagavad Gita.* New York: Holt, Rhinehart and Winston, n.d.

Devendra, Kusuma. "The Dasa Sil Nun: A Study of Women's Buddhist Religious Movement in Sri Lanka with an Outline of Its Historical Antecedents." Typescript, 1987.

dGe 'dun Chos 'phel. *The Dhammapada.* Translated by Elizabeth Cook. Berkeley: Dharma Publishing, 1995.

Dōgen. *Dōgen Zenji Zenshū.* 2 vols. Edited by Ōkubo Dōshū. Tokyo: Chikuma Shobō, 1969–1970.

Donden, Yeshi. *Health through Balance: An Introduction to Tibetan Medicine.* Edited and translated by J. Hopkins. Translated by L. Rabgay and A. Wallace. Ithaca, NY: Snow Lion Publications, 1986.

———. *Materia Medica.* Translated by G. Tshering. Tibetan Medicine, a Publication for the Study of Tibetan Medicine. Series no. 1. Dharamsala: n.p., 1980.

———. *Methods of Treatment in Tibetan Medicine.* Translated by G. Tshering. Tibetan Medicine, a Publication for the Study of Tibetan Medicine. Series no. 1. Dharamsala: n.p., 1980.

Donden, Yeshi, and Sonam Topgay. *Pulse Diagnosis in Tibetan Medicine.* Tibetan Medicine, a Publication for the Study of Tibetan Medicine. Series no. 1. Dharamsala: n.p., 1980.

Douglas, M. *Purity and Danger: An Analysis of the Concept of Pollution and Taboo.* 1994. Reprint, London: Routledge, 1996.

Doyle, Tara N. *"Bodh Gaya: Journeys to the Diamond Throne and the Feet of Gayasur."* Ph.D. dissertation, Harvard University, 1997.

Dresser, Marianne, ed. *Buddhist Women on the Edge: Contemporary Perspectives from the Western Frontier.* Berkeley: North Atlantic Books, 1996.

Eberhardt, N., ed. *Gender, Power, and the Construction of the Moral Order: Studies from the Thai Periphery*. Madison: University of Wisconsin, Center for Southeast Asian Studies, 1988.

Ebie Gimyō. "Anan Kōshiki." In *Sōtō-shū Jissen Sōsho.* Vol. 8. Edited by Sōtō-shū Jissen Sōsho Hensan Iinkai. Kiyomizu-shi, Shizouka Prefecture: Daizōsha, 1985.

Eck, Diana. *Darshan: Seeing the Divine Image in India.* New York: Columbia University Press, 1985.

———. *Encountering God: A Spiritual Journey from Bozeman to Banares.* Boston: Beacon Press, 1993.

Eilberg-Schwartz, Howard, and Wendy Doniger, eds. *Off With Her Head: The Denial of Women's Identity in Myth, Religion, and Culture.* Berkeley: University of California Press, 1995.

Eliade, Mircea. *The Sacred and the Profane: The Nature of Religion.* Reprint, New York: Harcourt Brace, 1987.

Enloe, Cynthia. *Bananas, Beaches and Bases: Making Feminist Sense of International Politics.* Berkeley: University of California Press, 1989.

———. "Some of the Best Soldiers Wear Lipstick." In *Living with Contradictions: Controversies in Feminist Social Ethics,* edited by A. M. Jaggar. Boulder: Westview, 1994.

Epstein, Larry, and Peng Wenbin. "Ritual, Ethnicity, and Generational Identity." In *Buddhism in Contemporary Tibet Religious Revival and Cultural Identity,* edited by M.C. Goldstein and M.T. Kapstein. Berkeley: University of California Press, 1998.

Evers, Hans-Deiter. "'Monastic Landlordism' in Ceylon: A Traditional System in a Modern Setting." *Journal of Asian Studies* 28, no. 4 (1969): 685–92.

Fa-hien. *A Record of Buddhistic Kingdoms.* Translated by J. Legge. Oxford: 1886. Reprint, New York: Dover Publications, 1965.

Falk, Nancy. "The Case of the Vanishing Nuns: The Fruits of Ambivalence in Ancient Indian Buddhism." In *Unspoken Worlds: Women's Religious Lives in Non-Western Cultures,* edited by N. Falk and R. Gross. San Francisco: Harper & Row, 1980.

Falk, Nancy A., and Rita M. Gross, eds. *Unspoken Worlds: Women's Religious Lives.* Belmont: Wadsworth Publishing, 1989.

Föhrer-Haimendorf, C. "A Nunnery in Nepal." *Kailash* 4, no. 2 (1976): 121–54.

Faure, Bernard. *Chan Insights and Oversights: An Epistemological Critique of the Chan Tradition.* Princeton: Princeton University Press, 1993.

———. *The Rhetoric of Immediacy: A Cultural Critique of Ch'an/Zen Buddhism.* Princeton: Princeton University Press, 1991.

Feer, M. Leon, ed. *The Saṃyutta Nikāya.* Pts. 1, 2, 4, 5. 1884, 1888, 1894, 1898. Reprint, London: The Pali Text Society, 1973, 1976, 1989, 1990.

Findly, Ellison Banks, comp. *The Nuns' Circle: Global Re-visioning of Women in Sacred Practice,* with essays by Judy Dworin, Ellison Banks Findly, Melissa Kerin, and Ann Norton. Hartford, CT: Trinity College, 1998.

Fox, Mathew. *Illuminations of Hildegard of Bingen.* Santa Fe: Bear and Company, 1985.

Findly, Ellison Banks. "Ānanda's Case for Women." *International Journal of Indian Studies* 3, no. 2 (July–December 1993): 1–31.

———. "Ānanda's Hindrance: Faith (saddhā) in Early Buddhism." *Journal of Indian Philosophy* 20 (1992): 13–33.

———. "Gārgī at the King's Court: Women and Philosophic Innovation in Ancient India." In *Women, Religion and Social Change,* edited by Ellison Banks Findly and Yvonne Yazbeck Haddad. Albany: State University of New York Press, 1985.

———. "Women and the Practice of Giving: The Housemistress at the Door as a Vedic and Buddhist Paradigm." In *Debating Gender,* edited by Laurie Patton. New York: Oxford University Press, 2000.

———. "Women and the *arahant* Issue in Early Pāli Literature." *Journal of Feminist Studies in Religion* 15, no. 1 (spring 1999): 57–76.

Friedman, Leonore. *Meetings with Remarkable Women: Buddhist Teachers in America.* Boston: Shambala, 1987.

Furuki, Yoshiko. *The White Plum: A Biography of Ume Tsuda, Pioneer in the Higher Education of Japanese Women.* New York: Weatherhill, 1991.

Gangōji Garan Engi. *Jisha Engi.* Compiled by S. Tokutarō. Tokyo: Iwanami Shoten, 1975.

Geertz, Clifford. *Negara: The Theater State in Bali.* Princeton: Princeton University Press, 1980.

Geiger, Wilhelm, trans. *The Mahāvaṃsa.* Colombo: Government Press, 1986.

Gerke, Barbara. "On the History of the Two Tibetan Medical Schools Janglug and Zurlug." *Ayurvijnana* 6 (1999): 17–24.

Getty, Alice. *The Gods of Northern Buddhism: Their History and Iconography.* Oxford: Clarendon, 1928. Reprint, New York: Dover Publications, 1988.

Gittinger, Mattiebelle, and H. Leedom Lefferts, Jr. "Textiles and the Tai Experience in Southeast Asia." Washington, D.C.: The Textile Museum, 1992.

Gold, Peter. *Navajo and Tibetan Sacred Wisdom: Circle of the Spirit.* Rochester, VT: Inner Traditions International, 1994.

Golde, Peggy, ed. *Women in the Field: Anthropological Experiences.* Reprint, Berkeley: University of California Press, 1986.

Goldstein, Melvyn C. *A History of Modern Tibet, 1913–1951.* University of California Press, 1989.

Goldstein, Melvyn C., and Matthew T. Kapstein, eds. *Buddhism in Contemporary Tibet: Religious Revival and Cultural Identity.* Berkeley: University of California Press, 1998.

Gombrich, Richard. *Theravada Buddhism: A Social History from Ancient Benares to Modern Colombo.* New York: Routledge, 1988.

Gombrich, Richard, and Gananath Obeysekere. *Buddhism Transformed: Religious Change in Sri Lanka.* Princeton: Princeton University Press, 1988. Reprint, Delhi: Princeton University Press, 1990.

Gómez, Luis, and Hiram W. Woodmard, Jr. *Barabudur: History and Significance of a Buddhist Monument.* Berkeley: Asian Humanities Press, 1981.

Goonatilake, H. "Buddhist Nuns' Protests, Struggle, and the Reinterpretation of Orthodoxy in Sri Lanka." In *Mixed Blessings: Gender and Religious Fundamentalism Cross Culturally,* edited by J. Brink and J. Mencher. New York: Routledge, 1997.

Goonesekera, S. "Status of Women in the Family Law of Sri Lanka." In *Women at the Crossroads: A Sri Lankan Perspective,* edited by Sirima Kiribamune and Vidyamali Samarasinghe. New Delhi: Vikas, 1990.

Greenbaum, Suzanne W. "Dykil-Khor: Center and Periphery-Mapping the Spheres of the Buddha: A Three Dimensional Maṇḍala." M.A. thesis, Wesleyan University, 1997.

Gross, Rita M. *Buddhism After Patriarchy: A Feminist History, Analysis, and Reconstruction of Buddhism.* Albany: State University of New York Press, 1993.

Gunawardene, R.A.L.H. *Robe and Plough: Monasticism and Economic Interest in Early and Medieval Sri Lanka.* Tucson: University of Arizona Press, 1979.

———. "Subtile Silks of Ferreous Firmness: Buddhist Nuns in Ancient and Medieval Sri Lanka and their Role in the Propagation of Buddhism." *Sri Lanka Journal of the Humanities* 14, nos. 1–2 (1988): 1–59.

Guru, Gopal. "Dalit Women Talk Differently." *Economic and Political Weekly* 35 (1995): 2548–50.

Gutschow, Kim. "An Economy of Merit: Women and Buddhist Monasticism in Zangskar, Northwest India." Ph.D. dissertation, Harvard University, 1998.

———. "Unfocussed Merit-Making in Zangskar: A Socio-Economic Account of Karsha Nunnery." *The Tibet Journal* 22, no 2 (1997): 30–58.

Haddad, Yvonne Yazbeck, and Ellison Banks Findly. *Women, Religion and Social Change.* Albany: State University of New York Press, 1985.

Hamilton, Roy. *Hues of the Rainbow.* Los Angeles: Fowler Museum of Cultural History, University of California at Los Angeles, 1998.

Hanh, Thich Nhat. *For a Future to Be Possible.* Berkeley: Parallax Press, 1993.

Hantrakul, S. "Prostitution in Thailand." In *Development and Displacement: Women in Southeast Asia,* edited by G Chandler, N. Sullivan, and J. Branson. Clayton, Victoria: Centre of Southeast Asian Studies, Monash University, 1988.

Hardy, E., ed. *The Aṅguttara Nikāya.* Pts. 3, 4, 5. 1897, 1899, 1900. Reprint, London: The Pali Text Society, 1976, 1979.

Hare, E.M., trans. *The Book of the Gradual Sayings.* Vols. 3 and 4. 1934, 1935. Reprint, Oxford: The Pali Text Society, 1988, 1989.

Havnevik, Hanna. "The Role of Nuns in Contemporary Tibet." In *Resistance and Reform in Tibet,* edited by R. Barnett and S. Akiner. Bloomington: Indiana University Press, 1994.

———. *Tibetan Buddhist Nuns: History, Cultural Norms and Social Reality.* Oslo: Norwegian University Press for the Institute for Comparative Research in Human Culture and Oxford, 1989.

Henry, Patrick, and Donald Swearer. *For the Sake of the World: The Spirit of Buddhist and Christian Monasticism.* Minneapolis: Fortress Press, 1989.

Hewison, K., ed. *Political Change in Thailand: Democracy and Participation.* London: Routledge, 1997.

Hirakawa, Akira, trans. *Monastic Discipline for the Buddhist Nuns.* An English translation of the Chinese Text of the *Mahāsaṅghika-Bhikṣuṇī-Vinaya.* Patna: K. P. Jayaswal Research Institute, 1982.

Hopkirk, Peter. *The Great Game: On Secret Service in High Asia.* London: Murray, 1990.

Horner, Isaline B., trans. *The Book of the Discipline (Vinaya-Pitaka).* Vols. 1–6. London: Oxford University Press, 1938–66. Reprint, London: The Pali Text Society, 1982–88.

———. *The Middle Length Sayings.* Vols. 1–3. 1954–59. Reprint, London: The Pali Text Society, 1977, 1987, 1989.

———. *Women Under Primitive Buddhism: Laywomen and Almswomen.* London: 1930. Reprint, Delhi: Motilal Banarsidass, 1975, 1990.

Hotchkiss, Brian, ed. *Buddhism in America: Proceedings of the First Buddhism in America Conference.* Rutland, VT: Tuttle, 1998.

Huber, Toni. "Why Can't Women Climb Pure Crystal Mountain? Remarks on Gender, Ritual, and Space at Tsa Ri." In *Tibetan Studies: Proceedings of the Sixth Seminar of the I.A.T.S.*, edited by P. Kvaerne. Oslo: Institute for Comparative Research in Human Culture, 1994.

"Human Rights Update." *Dharamsala: Tibetan Centre for Human Rights and Democracy* 2, no. 24 (December, 1997); 3, no. 5 (March, 1998); 3, no. 7 (April, 1998).

Hundanov, L. L., and T. B Batomunkieva. "Tibetan Medicine." *Prometei* (1993): 115–16.

Irigaray, Luce. *Sexes and Genealogies.* New York: Columbia University Press, 1987.

Irvine, Walter. "Decline of Village Spirit Cults and Growth of Urban Spirit Mediumship: The Persistence of Spirit Beliefs, the Position of Women and Modernization." *Mankind* 14, no. 4 (1984): 315–24.

Ishikawa, Rikizan. "Chūsei Bukkyō ni okeru Ni no Isō nitsuite: Tokuni Shoki Sōtō Shūkyōdan no Jirei o Chūshin toshite." Part 1. *Komazawa Daigaku Kenkyūjo Nenpō* 3 (March, 1992): 141–53.

Ishikawa, Rikizan. "Chūsei Bukkyō ni okeru Ni no Isō nitsuite: Tokuni Shoki Sōtō Shūkyōdan no Jirei o Chūshin toshite." Part 2. *Komazawa Daigaku Kenkyūjo Nenpō* 4 (March, 1993): 63–80.

———. "Dōgen no 'Nyoshin Fujōbutsu Ron' nitsuite Jūni Makibon Shōbōgenzō no Seikaku o Meguru Oboegaki." *Komazawa Daigaku Kenkyūjo Nenpō* 1 (March 1990): 88–123.

Jackson, David, and Janice Jackson. *Tibetan Thangka Painting: Methods and Materials.* London: Serindia, 1984.

Jackson, P.A. *Buddhadasa: A Buddhist Thinker for the Modern World.* Bangkok: The Siam Society, 1988.

———. *Buddhism, Legitimation, and Conflict: The Political Functions of Urban Thai Buddhism.* Singapore: Institute of Southeast Asian Studies, 1989.

———. *Dear Uncle Go: Male Homosexuality in Thailand.* Bangkok: Bua Luang Books, 1995.

———. "Withering Centre, Flourishing Margins: Buddhism's Changing Political Roles." In *Political Change in Thailand: Democracy and Participation*, edited by K. Hewison. London: Routledge, 1997.

Jaggar, Allison M., ed. *Living with Contradictions: Controversies in Feminist Social Ethics.* Boulder: Westview Press, 1994.

Jaini, Padmanabh S. *Gender and Salvation: Jaina Debates on the Spiritual Liberation of Women.* Berkeley: University of California Press, 1991.

Jamison, Stephanie W. *Sacrificed Wife; Sacrificer's Wife.* New York: Oxford University Press, 1996.

Jampa Tsedroen, B. *A Brief Survey of the Vinaya: Its Origin, Transmission and Arrangement from the Tibetan Point of View with Comparisons to the Theravāda and Dharmagupta Traditions.* Hamburg: Foundation for Tibetan Buddhist Studies, Dharma Edition, 1992.

Jaschka, H. *A Tibetan-English Dictionary.* Reprint, Delhi: Motilal Banarsidass, 1995.

Jayawardena, Kumari. "Some Aspects of Religious and Cultural Identity and the Construction of Sinhala Buddhist Womanhood." In *Religion and Political Conflict in South Asia: India, Pakistan, and Sri Lanka*, edited by Douglas Allen. Delhi: Oxford University Press, 1993.

Jordt, Ingrid. "Bhikkhuni, Thilashin, and Mae-chi: Women Who Renounce the World in Burma, Thailand, and the Classical Buddhist Texts." *Crossroads* 4, no. 1 (1988): 31–9.

Kabilsingh, Chatsumarn. "Buddhism and the Status of Women." *Southeast Asian Review* 7 (1982): 63–74.

———, trans. *The Bhikkhunī Pāṭimokkha of the Six Schools*. Bangkok: n.p., 1991.

———. "The Role of Women in Buddhism." In *Sakyadhītā: Daughters of the Buddha*, edited by K.L. Tsomo. Ithaca, NY: Snow Lion Publications, 1988.

———. *Thai Women in Buddhism*. Berkeley: Parallax Press, 1991.

Kakar, Sudhir. *Shamans, Mystics and Doctors: A Psychological Inquiry into India and Its Healing Traditions*. 1982. Reprint, Delhi: Oxford University Press, 1990.

Kane, Pandurang Vaman. *History of Dharmaśāstra*. Reprint, Poona: Bhandarkar Oriental Research Institute, 1974.

Kapstein, Matthew. "Weaving the World: The Ritual Art of the Pata in Pala Buddhism and Its Legacy in Tibet." *History of Religions* 34, no. 3 (February, 1995): 241–63.

Karim, W. J. *'Male' and 'Female' in Developing Southeast Asia*. Washington, D.C.: Berg Publishers, 1995.

Katsuura, R. *Onna no shinjin (The Faith of Women)*. Tokyo: Heibonsha, 1995.

Kawanami, Hiroko. "The Religious Standing of Burmese Buddhist Nuns (thilashin): The Ten Precepts and Religious Respect Words." *The Journal of the International Association of Buddhist Studies* 13, 1 (1990): 17–40.

———. "Buddhist Nuns in Transition: The Case of Burmese thila-shin." In *Indian Insights: Buddhism, Brahmanism and Bhakti*, edited by P. Connolly and S. Hamilton. London: Luzac Oriental, 1997.

Keer, Dhananjay. *Dr. Ambedkar: Life and Mission*. 1954. Reprint, Bombay: Popular Prakashan, 1962.

Kemper, Steven. "The Buddhist Monkhood, the Law and the State in Colonial Sri Lanka." *Comparative Studies in Society and History* 26 (1984): 401–27.

———. *The Presence of the Past*. Ithaca: Cornell University Press, 1990.

Keyes, Charles F. "Ambiguous Gender: Male Initiation in a Northern Thai Buddhist Society." In *Gender and Religion: On the Complexity of Symbols*, edited by C. W. Bynum, S. Harrell, and P. Richman. Boston: Beacon Press, 1986.

———. *Isan: Regionalism in Northeast Thailand*. Interim Report Series no. 10,

Program in Southeast Asian Studies. Ithaca, New York: Cornell University Press, 1967.

———. *The Golden Peninsula.* 1996. Reprint, Chiang Mai: Silkworm Books, 1997.

———. "Mother or Mistress but Never a Monk: Buddhist Notions of Female Gender in Rural Thailand." *American Ethnologist* 11, no. 2 (1984): 223–41.

———. *Thailand: Buddhist Kingdom as Modern Nation-State.* Boulder and London: Westview Press, 1987.

Khaydav, Ts., Zh. Tsognemekh, and B. Baldan. *The Medicinal Plants of the Mongolian Peoples Republic.* Ulan Bator, Mongolia: Academy of Sciences, 1962.

Khin, T. "Providence and Prostitution: Image and Reality for Women in Buddhist Thailand." *Change* (1980): International Reports.

King, Sallie. "Conclusion." In *Engaged Buddhism: Buddhist Liberation Movements in Asia,* edited by Christopher S. Queen and Sallie B. King. Albany: State University of New York Press, 1996.

———, trans and ed. *Passionate Journey: The Spiritual Autobiography of Satomi Myōdō.* 1987. Reprint, Albany: State University of New York Press, 1993.

King, Ursula, ed. *Religion and Gender.* Oxford: Blackwell, 1995.

———, ed. *Women in the World's Religions: Past and Present.* New York: Paragon House, 1987.

Kirsch, A. T. "Buddhism, Sex-Roles, and the Thai Economy." In *Women of Southeast Asia.* Occasional Paper No. 9, edited by P. Van Esterik. DeKalb: Northern Illinois University, Center for Southeast Asian Studies, 1982.

———. "Complexity and the Thai Religious System: An Interpretation." *Journal of Asian Studies* 36, no. 2 (1977): 241–66.

———. "Text and Context: Buddhist Sex Roles/Culture of Gender Revisited." *American Ethnologist* 12, no. 2 (1985): 302–20.

Klausner, W. J. *Thai Culture in Transition.* Bangkok: The Siam Society, 1997.

———. *Reflections on Thai Culture: Collected Writings of William Klausner.* Bangkok: Siam Society, 1993.

Klein, Anne C. *Meeting the Great Bliss Queen: Buddhists, Feminists and the Art of the Self.* Boston: Beacon Press, 1995.

———. "Persons and Possibilities." In *Buddhist Women on the Edge: Contemporary Perspectives from the Western Frontier*, edited by M. Dresser. Berkeley: North Atlantic Books, 1996.

Kojima, Kendō. *Bikuni no Jisei: Fune ni Kazamu.* Tokyo: Meibun Insatsu, 1985.

Komazawa Daigakunai Zengaku Daijiten Hensanjo, ed. *Zengaku Daijiten.* 3 vols. 1978. Reprint, Tokyo: Taishukan Shoten, 1985.

Komin, S. *Psychology of the Thai People: Values and Behavioural Patterns.* Bangkok, 1991.

Kondo, Dorinne. *Crafting Selves: Power, Gender, and Discourses of Identity in a Japanese Workplace.* Chicago: University of Chicago, 1990.

Kramrisch, Stella. "The Art of Nepal and Tibet." In *Philadelphia Museum of Art Bulletin* 5, no. 265 (spring 1960): 23–38.

Kuan-chung, Lo. *Three Kingdoms: China's Epic Drama.* Translated and edited by M. Roberts. New York: Pantheon Books, 1976.

Kuoch, T., M. Scully, and R. Miller. "Healing the Wounds of the Mahantdorai." In *Refugee Women and Their Mental Health: Shattered Societies, Shattered Lives*, edited by E. Cole. New York: Harrington Park Press, 1992.

Kusan Sunim. *The Way of Korean Zen.* Translated by Martine Fages and edited by Stephen Batchelor. New York: Weatherhill, 1985.

Lama, Gega. *Principles of Tibetan Art.* Darjeeling, West Bengal: Jamyang Singe, 1983.

Lang, Karen. "Lord Death's Snare: Gender-Related Imagery in the Theragāthā and the Therīgāthā." *Journal of Feminist Studies in Religion* 2, no. 2 (fall 1986): 63–79.

———. "Shaven Heads and Loose Hair: Buddhist Attitudes Toward Hair and Sexuality." In *Off With Her Head: The Denial of Women's Identity in Myth, Religion, and Culture*, edited by H. Eilberg-Schwartz and W. Doniger. Berkeley: University of California Press, 1995.

Law, B. C. "Bhikshunis in Indian Inscriptions." *Epigraphia Indica* 25 (1939): 31–34.

Leach, Edmund. "Magical Hair." *Journal of the Royal Anthropological Institute* 83 (1958): 147–64.

Leacock, Eleanor Banks. *Myths of Male Dominance: Collected Articles of Women Cross-Culturally.* New York: Monthly Review Press, 1981.

Lebra, Joyce, Joy Paulson, and Elizabeth Powers, eds. *Women in Changing Japan.* Stanford: Stanford University Press, 1976.

Lebra, Takie. *Japanese Women: Constraint and Fulfillment.* Honolulu: University of Hawai'i Press, 1984.

Lefferts, Leedom. "Baan Dong Phong: Land Tenure and Social Organization in a Northeast Thai Village." Ph.D. dissertation, University of Colorado, Boulder, 1974.

———. "Clothing the Serpent: Transformations of the Naak in Thai-Lao Theravāda Buddhism." In *The Transformative Power of Cloth in Southeast Asia,* edited by L. Milgram and P. Van Esterik. Toronto: The Museum for Textiles, 1994.

———. "The Power of Women's Decisions: Textiles in Tai Dam and Thai-Lao Theravada Buddhist Funerals." *Southeast Asian Journal of Social Science* 21, no. 2 (1993): 111–29.

———. "The Ritual Importance of the Mundane: White Cloth Among the Tai of Southeast Asia." *Expedition* 38, no.1 (1996): 37–50.

———. "Textiles in the Service of Thai Buddhism." In *Textiles and the Tai Experience in Southeast Asia,* edited by M. Gittinger and H.L. Lefferts, Jr. Washington, DC: Textile Museum, 1992.

Leidy, Denise Patry, and Robert Thurman. *Mandala: The Architecture of Enlightenment.* Boston: Shambhala Press, 1998.

Lemonnier, Pierre. "The Study of Material Culture Today: Toward an Anthropology of Technical Systems." *Journal of Anthropological Archaeology* 5 (1986): 147–86.

Levering, Miriam. "The Dragon Girl and the Abbess of Mo-Shan: Gender and Status in the Ch'an Buddhist Tradition." *Journal of the International Association of Buddhist Studies* 5, no. 1 (1982): 19–35.

———. "Lin-chi (Rinzai) Ch'an and Gender: The Rhetoric of Equality and the Rhetoric of Heroism." In *Buddhism, Sexuality, and Gender,* edited by José Ignacio Cabezón. Albany: State University of New York Press, 1992.

———. "Women, the State, and Religion Today in the People's Republic of China." In *Today's Woman in World Religions,* edited by A. Sharma. Albany: State University of New York Press, 1994.

Levine, Sarah. "Growth of the Monastic Community 1980–2000." In "Rebuilding Buddhism," edited by David Gellner and Sarah Levine. Typescript.

Ligaa, U. *The Methods of Uses of Medicinal Plants in Mongolian Traditional Medicine and Prescriptions.* Ulan Bator, Mongolia: 1996.

Lilley, Mary E., ed. *The Apadāna of the Khuddaka Nikāya, Part II, Therī-Apadāna.* London: Oxford University Press for the Pali Text Society, 1927.

Ling, T. *A Dictionary of Buddhism: Indian and South-East Asian.* Calcutta, New Delhi: K. P. Bagchi, 1981.

Lopez, David. *Prisoners of Shangri-La: Tibetan Buddhism and the West.* Chicago: The University of Chicago Press, 1998.

Lüders, Heinrich, ed. *Bharhut Inscriptions.* Revised by E. Waldschmidt and M. A. Mehendale. Ootacamund: Government Epigraphist for India, 1963.

Ludú Daw Ama. "Típítaká-dará Thathana Míhki-gyì." *Níkaya Thathana-pyú Ahapwé* (1982): 352–65.

Lutzker, Mary-Ann. "Mayumi Oda: Goddess Banners." *Orientations* (February, 1990): 46–52.

Lux, E. Thomas. "The Thai-Lao Family System and Domestic Cycle of Northeastern Thailand." *Journal of the National Research Council of Thailand* 5, nos. 1–4 (1969): 1–17.

Lynch, Owen M. "Dalit Buddhism: The Liberate Bodh Gaya Movement." *Dalit International Newsletter* 3, no 1 (1998): 1, 4, 10–11.

———. "Dr. B.R. Ambedkar: Myth and Charisma." In *The Untouchables in Contemporary India,* edited by J.M. Mahar. Tucson: University of Arizona Press, 1972.

———. *The Politics of Untouchability: Social Mobility and Social Change in a City of India.* New York: Columbia University Press, 1969.

Maitrani (Marathi magazine). Mumbai: n.p., n.d.

Maitreya, Balangoda Ananda, and Rose Kramer. "The Dhammapada." *Omni* 16, no. 4 (1988).

Makley, Charlene E. "Gendered Practices and the Inner Sanctum: The Reconstruction of Tibetan Sacred Space in 'China's Tibet.'" *The Tibet Journal* 19, no. 2 (summer 1994): 61–94.

Malalgoda, Kitsiri. *Buddhism in Sinhalese Society, 1750–1900*. Berkeley: University of California Press, 1976.

Marchand, Marianne, and Jane Parpart, eds. *Feminism/Postmodernism/Development*. New York: Routledge, 1995.

Marcus, George, and Michael Fischer. *Anthropology as Cultural Critique: An Experimental Moment in the Human Sciences*. Chicago: University of Chicago Press, 1986.

"Mark of a Man." *Samakali* (newsletter of Women for Peace). (Jan.–Feb., 1997): 11.

Marshall, John, Alfred Foucher, and N. G. Majumdar. *The Monuments of Sanchi*. London: Probsthain, 1940. Reprint, Delhi: Swati Publications, 1982.

Martin, Daniel Preston. *Mandala Cosmogony: Human Body, Good Thought and the Revelation of Secret Mother Tantra of Bon*. Wiesbaden: Harrassowitz, 1994.

Mauss, Marcell. *The Gift: The Form and Reason for Exchange in Archaic Societies*. Translated by W. D. Halls. New York: Routledge, 1989

McDonald, M. "Dipa Ma: A Memorial." *The Inquiring Mind* 6, no. 4 (winter/spring 1990): 19.

Men-Tsee-Khang. *Fundamentals of Tibetan Medicine*. New Delhi: Nehru House, 1997.

Miller, Beatrice D. "Views of Women's Roles in Buddhist Tibet." In *Studies in History of Buddhism*, edited by A.K. Navain. New Delhi: B.R. Publishing Co., 1980.

Mills, Mary Beth. "Gendered Encounters with Modernity: Labor Migrants and Marriage Choices in Contemporary Thailand." *Identities* 5, no. 3 (1999): 1–34.

———. "Attack of the Widow Ghosts: Gender, Death, and Modernity in Northeast Thailand." In *Bewitching Women, Pious Men: Gender and Body Politics in Southeast Asia,* edited by A. Ong and M. Peletz. Berkeley: University of Chicago Press, 1995.

Mitra, Debala. "Discovery and Restoration of the Monuments." In *Unseen Presence, The Buddha and Sanchi,* edited by V. Dehejia. Mumbai: Marg Publications, 1996.

———. *Sanchi*. 1957. Reprint, New Delhi: Archaeological Survey of India, 1992.

Moore, F. J., C. T. Alton, H. L. Lefferts, S. Soonthornpasuch, and R. E. Suttor.

"Rural Roads in Thailand." *Project Impact Evaluation 13*. Washington, D.C.: Agency for International Development, 1980.

Moore, Henrietta L. *A Passion for Difference*. Cambridge: Polity Press, 1994.

———. *Feminism and Anthropology*. Cambridge: Polity Press, 1988.

Morris, Richard, ed. *The Aṅguttara Nikāya*. Pts. 1 and 2. 1885, 1888. Pt. 1, 2nd ed., revised by A.K. Warder.

Mulder, Neils. *Everyday Life in Thailand: An Interpretation*. Bangkok: Duang Kamol, 1979.

Müller, E., ed. *Paramatthadīpanī. Dhammapāla's Commentary on the Therīgāthā*. London: Henry Frowde, for the Pali Text Society, 1893.

Murcott, Susan, trans. *The First Buddhist Women: Translations and Commentary on the Therigatha*. Berkeley: Parallax Press, 1991.

Nakamura, Hajime, ed. *Bukkyō-go Daijiten*. 3 vols. Tokyo: Tokyo Shoseki, 1981.

Nakamura, Kyōko. "Revelatory Experience in the Female Life Cycle: A Biographical Study of Women Religionists in Modern Japan." *Japanese Journal of Religious Studies* 8, nos. 3–4 (September–December 1981): 187–205.

———, ed. "Women and Religion in Japan." *Japanese Journal of Religious Studies* 10, nos. 2–3 (June–Sept. 1983).

Nandámala Bíwunthá. *Thameikdàw-dayá Hsaya-gyì Daw Malayi*. Rangoon: Nyún Sapei-daik, 1980.

Nattier, Jan. "Visible and Invisible: The Politics of Representation in Buddhist America." *Tricycle: The Buddhist Review* 5, no. 1 (fall 1995): 42–49.

Neelsen, John P. "Gender, Caste and Power in a Transitional Society." In *Gender, Caste and Power in South Asia: Social Status and Mobility in a Transitional Society*, edited by John P. Neelsen. New Delhi: Manohar, 1991.

Ngaosyvathn, M. "Buddhism, Merit Making, and Gender: The Competition for Salvation in Laos." In *'Male' and 'Female' in Developing Southeast Asia*, edited by W.J. Karim. Washington, D.C.: Berg Publishers, 1995.

Ngor, H. *A Cambodian Odyssey*. New York: MacMillan, 1987.

Nishiguchi, J. *Onna no chikara (The Strength of Women)*. Tokyo: Heibonsha, 1987.

Nishiguchi, J., and K. Ōsumi, eds. *Ama to Amadera*. Tokyo: Heibonsha, 1989.

Nihon Bukkyō Gakkai, ed. *Bukkyō to Josei.* Kyoto: Hyōraku-ji Shoten, 1991.

Njammasch, Marlene. "Der navakammika und seine Stellung in der Hierarchie der buddhistischen Kloster." *Schriften zur Geschichte und Kultur des alten Orients* 1 (1974): 279–93.

Norman, K. R. "The Value of the Pali Tradition." *'Jagajjyoti' Buddha Jayanti Annual.* Calcutta: (1984): 1–9.

———, trans. *The Elders' Verses II: Therīgāthā.* London: Luzac and Company, for the Pali Text Society, 1971.

Obeyesekere, Gananath. *Medusa's Hair: An Essay on Personal Symbols and Religious Experience.* Chicago: University of Chicago Press, 1981.

Oda, Mayumi. *Goddesses.* Berkeley, CA: Lancaster-Miller Publishers, 1981.

Ōgishi, Sakichi. *Gyōten no Hibiki: Kifun Yakushi-dō to Aichi Senmon Nisōdō no Rekishi.* Nagoya: Kaikoku Kōsoku, 1981

Oldenberg, Herman, ed. *The Vinaya Piṭakam.* Vols. 1–5. London: 1879, 1880, 1881, 1882, 1883. Reprint, London: The Pali Text Society, 1969, 1977, 1984, 1982.

Oldenberg, Herman, and Richard Pischel, eds. *The Thera- and Therīgāthā.* London: 1883. Reprint, Oxford: The Pali Text Society, 1990.

Olschak, Blanche Christine, and Geshe Thupten Wangyal. *Mystic Art of Ancient Tibet.* 1973. Reprint, Boston: Shambhala, 1987.

Omvedt, Gail. *Dalit Visions: The Anti-caste Movement and the Construction of an Indian Identity.* Delhi: Orient Longman, 1995

Ong, A., and M. Peletz, eds. *Bewitching Women, Pious Men: Gender and Body Politics in Southeast Asia.* Berkeley: University of Chicago Press, 1995.

Ortner, Sherry. "Sherpa Purity." *American Anthropologist* 75 (1973): 49–63.

———. *Making Culture: The Politics and Erotics of Culture.* Boston: Beacon, 1996.

Paul, Diana. *Women in Buddhism: Images of the Feminine in Mahayana Tradition.* Berkeley: Asian Humanities Press, 1979. Reprint, Berkeley: University of California Press, 1985.

Peiris, Noeyal. "The Romantic and Heroic Story of Vihara Maha Devi." *The Buddhist* 4, no. 3 (September–October, 1984): 25.

"People's Republic of China: Persistent Human Rights Violations in Tibet." *Amnesty International* (May 1995).

Phongpaichit, P. *Rural Women in Thailand: From Peasant Girls to Bangkok Masseuses.* Geneva: International Labour Office, 1982.

Pierce, Lori. "Outside In: Buddhism in America." In *Buddhist Women on the Edge: Contemporary Perspectives from the Western Frontier*, edited by Marianne Dresser. Berkeley: North Atlantic Books, 1996.

Pollitt, K. *Reasonable Creatures: Essays on Women and Feminism.* New York: Alfred A. Knopf, 1995.

Pran, Dith, ed. *Children of Cambodia's Killing Fields.* New Haven: Yale University Press, 1997.

The Profound Path of Peace. International Kagyu Sangha Association, no. 12 (February, 1993).

Queen, Christopher S. "Introduction." In *Engaged Buddhism: Buddhist Liberation Movements in Asia,* edited by Chistopher S. Queen and Sallie B. King. Albany: State University of New York Press, 1996.

Raghu, V., and L. Chandra. *Tibetan Mandalas: Vajravali and Tantra-samuccaya.* International Academy of Indian Culture. New Delhi: Aditya Prakashan, 1995.

Rahula, Walpola. *What the Buddha Taught.* New York: Grove Press, 1974.

Ram, Nandu. *Beyond Ambedkar: Essays on Dalits in India.* Delhi: Har Anand, 1995.

Rawson, Philip. *Sacred Tibet.* London: Thames and Hudson, 1991.

Ray, Reginald A. *Buddhist Saints in India: A Study in Buddhist Values and Orientations.* New York: Oxford University Press, 1994.

Rhie, Marilyn, and Robert A. F. Thurman. *Wisdom and Compassion: The Sacred Art of Tibet.* New York: Harry N. Abrams, 1991.

Rhys Davids, C.A.F., trans. *Psalms of the Early Buddhists, Part II Psalms of the Sisters.* Translation Series No. 1, the Pali Text Society. London, Henley, and Boston: Routledge & Kegan Paul, 1980.

Rhys Davids, C.A.F., and K. R. Norman, trans. *Poems of Early Buddhist Nuns.* Reprint, Oxford: The Pali Text Society, 1976. London: The Pali Text Society, 1989.

Rhys Davids, C.A.F., and Suriyagoda Sumangala Thera, trans. *The Book of Kindred Sayings, Pt. 1.* 1917. Reprint, Oxford: The Pali Text Society, 1989.

Rhys Davids, C.A.F., and F.H. Woodward, trans. *The Book of Kindred Sayings, Pt. 2.* 1922. Reprint, London: The Pali Text Society, 1982.

Rhys Davids, C.A.F., and T.W. Rhys Davids, trans. *Dialogues of the Buddha,* Pts. 2, 3. 1910, 1921. Reprint, Oxford, London: The Pali Text Society, 1989, 1977.

Rhys Davids, T.W., and J. Estlin Carpentier, eds. *The Dīgha Nikāya,* Vol. 2. 1903. Reprint, London: The Pali Text Society, 1982.

Rhys Davids, T.W., and William Stede, eds. *The Pali Text Society's Pali-English Dictionary.* 1921–1925. Reprint, London: The Pali Text Society, 1986.

Riaboff, Isabelle. "Le Roi et le Moine: figures et principe's de et de sa legitimation au Zanskar (Himalaya Occidental)." Ph.D. dissertation, Universite de Paris, 1997.

Rinpoche, Rechung. *Tibetan Medicine.* Translated by J. Kunzang. Berkeley: University of California Press, 1973.

Roland, Alan. *In Search of Self in India and Japan: Toward a Cross-Cultural Psychology.* Princeton: Princeton University Press, 1988.

Sahlins, M. "The Sadness of Sweetness: The Native Anthropology of Western Cosmology." *Current Anthropology* 37, no. 3 (1996): 395–428.

Salgado, N. "Ways of Knowing and Transmitting Religious Knowledge: Case Studies of Theravada Buddhist Nuns." *Journal of the International Association of Buddhist Studies* 19, no. 1 (1996): 61–80.

Sangharakshita, B. *Ambedkar and Buddhism.* Glasgow: Windhorse, 1986.

Schieffelin, Edward L. *The Sorrow of the Lonely and the Burning of the Dancers.* New York: St. Martin's Press, 1976.

Schopen, Gregory. "Archaeology and Protestant Presuppositions in the Study of Indian Buddhism." *History of Religions* 31 (August, 1991–May, 1992): 1–23.

———. *Bones, Stones, and Buddhist Monks, Collected Papers on the Archaeology, Epigraphy, and Texts of Monastic Buddhism in India.* Honolulu: University of Hawai'i Press, 1997.

———. "Ritual Rights and Bones of Contention: More on Monastic Funerals and Relics in the *Mūlasarvāstivāda-Vinaya.*" *Journal of Indian Philosophy* 22 (1994): 60–61.

———. "The Suppression of Nuns and the Ritual Murder of their Special Dead in Two Buddhist Monastic Texts." *Journal of Indian Philosophy* 24 (1996): 563–92.

———. "What's in a Name: The Religious Function of Donative Inscriptions." In *Unseen Presence, The Buddha and Sanchi,* edited by V. Dehejia. Mumbai: Marg Publications, 1996.

Sen, K., and M. Stivens. *Gender and Power in Affluent Asia.* London: Routledge, 1998.

Shakapa, Tsepon W.D. *Tibet: A Political History.* 1967. Reprint, New Haven: Yale University Press, 1980.

Shakya, Tsering. "The Development of Modern Tibetan Studies." *In Resistance and Reform in Tibet,* edited by R. Barnett and S. Akiner. Bloomington: Indiana University Press, 1994.

Sivaraksa, S. *A Buddhist Vision For Renewing Society.* Bangkok: Thai Inter-Religious Commission For Development, 1994.

Smith, Warren W. "The Nationalities Policy of the Chinese Communist Party and the Socialist Transformation of Tibet." In *Resistance and Reform in Tibet,* edited by R. Barnett and S. Akiner. Bloomington: Indiana University Press, 1994.

Snellgrove, David. *Indo-Tibetan Buddhism.* Vol. 1. Boston: Shambhala, 1987.

Snodgrass, Adrian. *The Symbolism of the Stūpa.* Studies in Southeast Asia. Ithaca: Cornell University, 1985.

Sohni, Malati. "Dhamma Jyotī pad yātrā (Dhamma Jyoti Foot Pilgrimage)." In *Dhamma jyotī smārikā (Dhamma Jyoti Souvenir).* Agra: Indian Buddhist Conference, Agra Region, 1992

Soonthorndhada, A. "Individual Role Behavior, Expectations and Adaptations: Past to Present." In *Changing Roles and Statuses of Women in Thailand: A Documentary Assessment,* edited by B. Yoddumnern-Attig. Bangkok: Institute for Population and Social Research, Mahidol University, 1992.

Sōtōshū Zensho Kankōkai, ed. *Sōtōshū Zensho.* 1929–1935. 18 vols. Tokyo: Sōtōshū Shūmuchō, 1970–73.

Sponberg, Alan. "Attitudes toward Women and the Feminine in Early Buddhism." In *Buddhism, Sexuality, and Gender,* edited by José Ignacio Cabezón. New York: State University of New York Press, 1992.

———. "TBMSG: A Dhamma Revolution in Contemporary India." In *Engaged Buddhism: Buddhist Liberation Movements in Asia,* edited by Christopher S. Queen and Sallie B. King. Albany: State University of New York Press, 1996.

Strenski, Ivan. "On Generalized Exchange and the Domestication of the Sangha." *Man* 18 (1983): 463–77.

"Striking Hard: Torture in Tibet." *Physicians for Human Rights* (October 1997).

Suksamran, S. *Buddhism and Political Legitimacy.* Bangkok: Research Division, Chulalongkorn University, 1993.

Swearer, Donald K. "Folk Buddhism." In *The Encyclopedia of Religion*, edited by Mircea Eliade. Vol. 5. New York: Macmillan.

Szymusiak, M. *The Stones Cry Out.* New York: Hill and Wang, 1986.

Taddei, Maurizio. "The First Beginnings: Sculptures on Stūpa 2." In *Unseen Presence, The Buddha and Sanchi*, edited by Vidya Dehejia. Mumbai: Marg Publications, 1996.

Tajima, Hakudō. *Dōgen Keizan Ryō Zenji no Nisōkan.* Nagoya: Sōtō-shū Kōtō Nigakurin Shuppanbu, 1953.

———, ed. *Rokujūnen no Ayumi (A Path of Sixty Years).* Nagoya, Japan: Kingusha, 1963.

———. *Sōtō-shū Nisō-shi.* Tokyo: Sanyosha, 1955.

Tambiah, Stanley J. *Buddhism and the Spirit Cults in Northeast Thailand.* Cambridge: Cambridge University Press, 1970

———. *The Buddhist Saints of the Forest and the Cult of Amulets: A Study in Charisma, Hagiography, Sectarianism, and Millennial Buddhism.* Cambridge: Cambridge University Press, 1984.

———. *World Conqueror and World Renouncer.* Cambridge: Cambridge University Press, 1976.

Tanabe, S. "Spirits, Power, and the Discourse of Female Gender: The Phi Meng Cult of Northern Thailand." In *Thai Constructions of Knowledge*, edited by Manas Chitkasem and Andrew Turton. London, 1994.

Tansubhapol, Kulcharee. "The Silent Nunhood Finds a Voice." *Newsletter on International Buddhist Women's Activities* 11.2, no. 42 (January–March, 1995): 7–9.

Tantiwiramanond, D., and S. R. Pandey. *By Women, for Women: A Study of Women's Organizations in Thailand.* Singapore: Institute of Southeast Asian Studies, 1991.

———. "New Opportunities or New Inequalities: Development Issues and Women's Lives in Thailand." Paper presented at the Sixth International Conference on Thai Studies, Chiang Mai, 1996.

———. "The Status and Role of Thai Women in the Pre-Modern Period: A Historical and Cultural Perspective." *Sojourn* 2, no. 1 (1987): 125–49.

Tapontsang, Adhe, as told to Joy Blakeslee. *Ama Adhe, The Voice That Remembers: The Heroic Story of a Woman's Fight to Free Tibet.* Boston: Wisdom Publications, 1997.

Taylor, J. "Buddhist Revitalization, Modernization, and Social Change in Contemporary Thailand." *Sojourn* 8, no. 1 (1993): 62–91.

———. *Forest Monks and Nation-State: An Anthropological and Historical Study of Northeastern Thailand.* Singapore: Institute of South East Asian Studies, 1993.

Tegchok, Geshe. *Monastic Rites.* London: Wisdom Publications, 1985.

Tenzin Gyatso, H.H. Dalai Lama XIV. *Freedom in Exile: The Autobiography of the Dalai Lama.* New York: Harper Collins, 1990.

———. *Advice from Buddha Shakyamuni Concerning a Monk's Discipline.* Dharamsala, India: Library of Tibetan Works and Archives, 1982.

Terwiel, B. J. *Monks and Magic: An Analysis of Religious Ceremonies in Central Thailand.* Bangkok: White Lotus, 1994.

Thamel, K.M. Lily Beatrice. "A Study of the Dasa-Sil Maniyo (Consecrated Women) in the Buddhist Society of Sri Lanka." M.A. thesis, University of the Philippines, 1983.

Tharchin, Sermey Geshe Lobsang. *Kindudrayana and the Wheel of Life.* New Jersey: Mahayana Sutra and Tantra Press, 1989.

Thorbek, S. *Voices from the City: Women of Bangkok.* New Jersey: Zed Books, 1987.

Tibetan Medicine: History, Methodology of Studies and Prospects of Use. Collected Articles. Ulan-Ude: 1989.

Tiyavanich, K. *Forest Recollections: Wandering Monks in Twentieth-Century Thailand.* University of Hawai'i Press, 1997.

Trenckner, V., ed. *The Majjhima Nikāya.* Vol. 1. London: The Pali Text Society, 1988.

———. *Milindapañho: Being Dialogues Between King Milinda and the Buddhist Sage Nāgasena.* London: Williams and Norgate, 1880.

Trungpa, Chögyam. *Orderly Chaos: The Mandala Principle.* Edited by Sherab Chödzin. Boston: Shambhala, 1991.

Tsering, Tashi, and Philippa Russell. "An Account of the Buddhist Ordination of Women." *Cho Yang* 1, no. 1 (1986): 21–30.

Tsomo, Karma Lekshe, ed. *Buddhism through American Women's Eyes.* Ithaca, New York: Snow Lion Publications, 1995.

———, ed. *Sakyadhītā, Daughters of the Buddha.* Ithaca, NY: Snow Lion Publications, 1988.

———. *From Untouchable to Dalit: Essays on the Ambedkar Movement.* 1992. Reprint, New Delhi: Manohar, 1998.

———. "Tibetan Anis: The Nun's Life In Tibet." In *Feminine Ground: Essays on Women and Tibet,* edited by Janice D. Willis. Ithaca: Snow Lion Publications, 1989.

———. "Tibetan Nuns and Nunneries." In *Feminine Ground: Essays on Women and Tibet.* Ithaca, NY: Snow Lion Publications, 1989.

———. *Sisters in Solitude: Two Traditions of Buddhist Monastic Ethics for Women.* Albany: State University of New York Press, 1996.

———. "Stri Dalit Sahitya: The New Voice of Women Poets." In *Images of Women in Maharashtrian Literature and Religion,* edited by Anne Feldhaus. Albany: State University of New York Press, 1996.

Tucci, Giuseppe. *Tibetan Painted Scrolls.* Vol 2. Bangkok: SDI Publications, 1999.

Turner, Victor. *Image and Pilgrimage in Christian Culture.* New York: Columbia University Press, 1978.

———. *The Ritual Process: Structure and Anti-Structure.* New York: Aldine, 1982.

Tworkov, Helen. *Zen in America.* San Francisco: North Point Press, 1989.

Ueda Yoshie. *Chōmon Nisō Monogatari.* Tokyo: Kokusho Kankōkai, 1979.

United States State Department. "Human Rights Report on China," 1997.

Vajiranavarorasa, S. *Ordination Procedure.* Bangkok: Mahamakutarajavidyalaya, 1989.

Van Esterik, J. "Rewriting Gender and Development Anthroplogy in Southeast Asia." In *"Male" and "Female" in Developing Southeast Asia,* edited by W. J. Karim. Washington D.C.: Berg, 1995.

Van Esterik, Penny, ed. *Women of Southeast Asia.* Occasional Paper No. 9. DeKalb: Northern Illinois University, Center for Southeast Asian Studies, 1982a.

———. *Women of Southeast Asia.* Occasional Paper No. 9. DeKalb: Northern Illinois University, Center for Southeast Asian Studies, 1982b.

———. *Women of Southeast Asia.* Occasional Paper No. 17. DeKalb: Northern Illinois University, Center for Southeast Asian Studies, 1996.

Varela, Francisco J., ed. *Sleeping, Dreaming, and Dying: An Exploration of Consciousness with The Dalai Lama.* Boston: Wisdom Publications, 1997.

Vitali, Roberto. *The Kingdoms of Gu-ge Pu-hrang: According to mNga'-ris rgyal rabs by Gu-ge Mkhan-chen Ngag-dbang-grags-pa.* New Delhi: Indraprashta Press, 1996.

Watkins, Joanne C. *Spirited Women.* New York: Columbia University Press, 1996.

Weber, Max. *The Religion of India.* Translated by H. Gerth and D. Martindale. New York: Free Press, 1958.

Wijayaratna, M. *Buddhist Monastic Life According to the Texts of the Theravada Tradition.* Translated by C. Grangier and S. Collins. Cambridge: Cambridge University Press, 1990.

Willis, Janice D. "Buddhism and Race: An African American Baptist-Buddhist Perspective." In *Buddhist Women on the Edge: Contemporary Perspectives from the Western Frontier,* edited by Marianne Dresser. Berkeley: North Atlantic Books, 1996.

———. "Nuns and Benefactresses: The Role of Women in the Development of Buddhism." In *Women, Religion and Social Change,* edited by Yvonne Yazbeck Haddad and Ellison Banks Findly. Albany: State University of New York Press, 1985.

———, ed. *Feminine Ground: Essays on Women and Tibet.* Ithaca: Snow Lion, 1987.

Willson, Martin. *In Praise of Tārā: Songs to the Saviouress.* London: Wisdom Publications, 1986.

"Women and Buddhism—A Special Issue of Spring Wind: Buddhist Cultural Forum." *Spring Wind-Buddhist Cultural Forum* 6, no.1 (1986): 2–3.

"Women in Black." *Samakali* (newsletter for Women for Peace) (January–February, 1997): 10.

"Women in Peace Work." *Sama Yamaya (Time of Peace).* Internet edition of the newsletter of the National Peace Council of Sri Lanka. No. 6 (April/July 1998).

Woodward, F.L. trans. *The Book of the Gradual Sayings*. Vols. 1, 2 and 5. 1932, 1933, 1936. Vol. 1. Reprint, Oxford: The Pali Text Society, 1989; vols. 2 and 5. Reprint, London: The Pali Text Society, 1982, 1986.

———, trans. *The Book of Kindred Sayings*. Pts. 4, 5. 1927, 1930. Rpt., London, Oxford: The Pali Text Society, 1980, 1990.

Wurst, Rotraut. "Die Töchter des Buddha." In *Mandala: Buddhismus Heute*. 3 (Dec. 1995): 36–8.

———. "Die Töchter des Buddha." Konferenz des Frauennetzwerkes Sakyadhītā. In *Spirita: Zeitschrift für Religionswissenschaft* 9 (February 1995): 34–6.

———. "Erstes Treffen von Sakyadhītā Deutschland." In *Graswurzen. Buddhistische Vierteljahresschrift* 3, no. 4 (winter 1996): 6.

———. "Aufgaben und Zielsetzungen von Sakyadhītā im Westen." Paper at the international symposium *Frauen im Buddhismus*, at the Johann Wolfgang Goethe-Universität, Frankfurt a. M. Feb. 7–9, 1997.

Wurst, Rotraut, and Gabrielle Müller, ed. *Sakyadhītā: Frauen im Buddhismus*. No. 1, 1997.

———. "Auf den Spuren von Buddha: Frauen im Buddhismus." Paper in a meeting of the *Altenholzer Kulturkreis*, March 1998.

Wyatt, David. *Thailand: A Short History*. New Haven: Yale University Press, 1984

Yalman, N. "The Ascetic Buddhist Monks of Ceylon." *Ethnology* 1 (1962): 315–28.

Yamazaki, G. "The Spread of Buddhism in the Mauryan Age, with Special Reference to the Mahinda Legend." *Acta Asiatica* 43 (1982): 1–16.

Yoddumnern-Attig, B. *Changing Roles and Statuses of Women in Thailand: A Documentary Assessment*. Bangkok: Institute for Population and Social Research, Mahidol University, 1992.

Yongyuth, M. "Spiritual Solace." *The Nation* 16, no. 2 (1997).

Zelliot, Eleanor. "Buddhist Women of the Contemporary Maharashtrian Conversion Movement." In *Buddhism, Sexuality and Gender*, edited by José Ignacio Cabezón. Albany: State University of New York, 1985.

———. *From Untouchable to Dalit: Essays on Ambedkar Movement*. Delhi: Manohar, 1992.

———. "Bibliography on Untouchability." In *The Untouchables in Contemporary India*, edited by J. Michael Mahar. Tucson: University of Arizona Press, 1972.

Zoku Sōtōshū Zensho Kankōkai, ed. *Zoku Sōtōshū Zensho*. 10 vols. Tokyo: Sōtōshū Shūmuchō, 1974–77.

Zopa, Lama Thubtin, and George Chumoff. *Nyung Na: The Means of Achievement of the Eleven-Faced Great Compassionate One, Avalokiteshvara*. Boston: Wisdom Publications, 1995.

LIST OF CONTRIBUTORS

VINCANNE ADAMS is an associate professor of anthropology at Princeton University. She received a Ph.D. from the University of California at Berkeley in 1989 and has been working and writing on the peoples and medical practices of Tibet and the Nepal Himalayas since 1982. She is the author of *Tigers of the Snow and Other Virtual Sherpas: An Ethnography of Himalayan Encounters* and *Doctors for Democracy: Health Professionals in the Nepal Revolution.*

PAULA KANE ROBINSON ARAI is a professor of religious studies at Vanderbilt University. She received a Ph.D. from Harvard University in 1993, with a dissertation on female monastic traditions in Japanese Zen Buddhism. She has received numerous academic grants and honors, and her publications focus on nuns of the Sōtō school in contemporary Japan as well as on related ritual and healing practices. She is the author of *Women Living Zen: Japanese Sōtō Buddhist Nuns.*

NANCY J. BARNES is a professor of art history at the University of Hartford. She received a Ph.D. from the University of Toronto in 1976, with a dissertation on early Mahāyāna Buddhism in China. Her numerous publications focus on Buddhist art and archaeology, early Buddhist thought and practice, and women in Buddhist literature and inscriptions, with a special interest in nuns of China and India.

TESSA J. BARTHOLOMEUSZ is a professor of religion at Florida State University. She received a Ph.D. from the University of Virginia in 1991, with a dissertation on women renunciants in contemporary Sri Lanka. In addition to a number of articles and reviews, she has written several books, including *Women under the Bo Tree: Buddhist Nuns in Sri Lanka,* and co-edited *Buddhist Fundamentalism and Minority Identities in Sri Lanka.*

MARTINE BATCHELOR is a former nun in the Korean Zen tradition, now a lay Buddhist living in England. She is coordinator of a year-long program in Buddhist studies at Sharpham College in Totnes, Devon, and is the author of several books, including *Walking on Lotus Flowers: Buddhist Women Living, Loving, and Meditating* and *Principles of Zen.*

SARAH D. BUIE is a professor of graphic design at Clark University. She received her M.F.A. in graphic design from Yale University in 1978, and has designed and curated numerous exhibitions for museums and university galleries, including several on Buddhist cultures. Her publications on Asian subjects include works on textiles, Tibetan space, and the *maṇḍala* archetype. She is currently working on an anthology about spatial archetypes, with an emphasis on the environment.

BHIKṢUṆĪ THUBTEN CHODRON is a Western Buddhist nun in the Tibetan tradition. She received a B.A. from the University of California at Los Angeles and, after traveling through Europe, North Africa, and Asia, received *śramaṇerikā* (novice) ordination in 1977 and *bhikṣuṇī* (full) ordination in Taiwan in 1986. She has studied, practiced, and taught Buddhism world-wide for many years, and currently lives and teaches in Seattle with the Dharma Friendship Foundation. Her books include *Open Heart, Clear Heart; What Color is Your Mind; Taming the Monkey Mind;* and *Blossoms of the Dharma: Living as a Buddhist Nun.*

DASHIMA DOVCHIN is a physician trained in Tibetan medicine, who received her M.D. from the Medical University of Mongolia in 1982. She has conducted research at the Institute of Traditional Medicine, Academy of Sciences of Mongolia, where she studied Tibetan medicinal plants. Currently, she specializes in liver, neurological, and gynecological disorders, and has a private practice at Manual Therapy Associates in Dallas, Texas.

JUDY DWORIN is professor of theater and dance at Trinity College. She founded the dance program at Trinity in 1971, and received her M.A. in dance and education from Goddard College in 1975. Her many performance works with the Judy Dworin Performance Ensemble have been presented throughout the country, as well as in Taiwan and Bulgaria, and have been reviewed in major national publications. Her works focus on a variety of issues, including gender and the environment, and she has collaborated with such Asian artists as Manhong Kang and Hi-ah Park.

MONICA LINDBERG FALK is a Ph.D. candidate at Göteborg University, Sweden, in social anthropology, and she teaches at the Centre for East and Southeast Asian Studies at the same university. Her research deals with questions on gender relations and Buddhism, and her thesis focuses on Buddhist nuns in Thailand.

ELLISON BANKS FINDLY is a professor of religion and Asian studies at Trinity College. She received a Ph.D. in South Asian religions at Yale University in 1978, and has published widely in Vedic, Mughal, and early Buddhist studies. She is co-editor, with Yvonne Yazbeck Haddad, of *The Islamic Impact* and *Women, Religion and Social Change,* and is the author of *Nur Jahan: Empress of Mughal India.* She is currently finishing a book on *dāna* entitled *Giving and Getting: Relations Between Donors and Renunciants in Pali Buddhism.*

TRUDY GOODMAN has studied in the Zen and *vipassanā* traditions since 1974. She is a child psychologist, and is on the board of directors of the Barre Center for Buddhist Studies. She currently lives and practices in Taos, New Mexico.

KIM GUTSCHOW belongs to the Harvard University Society of Fellows. She received her Ph.D. from Harvard in 1998 in anthropology, with a dissertation on women and liminality in Zangskar (northwest India) based on more than thirty-seven months of fieldwork. Her publications focus on kinship, land, and water use in Zangskar, as well as on a variety of issues concerning women in Tibetan Buddhism.

HIROKO KAWANAMI is a lecturer in Buddhist studies at Lancaster University. She received a Ph.D. from the London School of Economics and Political Science in social anthropology in 1991, and publishes on Buddhist women in Myanmar, in both English and Japanese publications.

MELISSA R. KERIN is a research associate for the Center for the Study of World Religions at Harvard University. She received an M.T.S. in religious studies from Harvard in 1999, where she focused on women sacred artists and Buddhism. She has traveled extensively in Nepal and India. While a Trinity undergraduate in 1993 and a Watson Fellow from 1994 to 1995, she worked and lived with the nuns from the Keydong Thuk-Che-Cho Ling Nunnery as they learned *thangka* and sand *maṇḍala* techniques.

THEANVY KUOCH is a founder and the executive director of Khmer Health Advocates, a national Cambodian health organization located in West Hartford, Connecticut. She arrived in the United States in 1981 as a refugee and received her Masters degree in family therapy and refugee mental health from Goddard College in 1984. Currently, she is a clinician with the KHA mental health team and is an advocate for the health issues of survivors of torture. She has received national and international awards for her work. Her publications focus on mental health issues of survivors of massive trauma especially among women and children.

H. LEEDOM LEFFERTS, JR., is a professor of anthropology at Drew University. He received a Ph.D. in anthropology from the University of Colorado in 1974, and has done extensive ethnographic and archeological work in Thailand, Laos, Cambodia, Vietnam, and southern China. He has published numerous articles and monographs on textile culture and on Buddhist women in Southeast Asia, and has collaborated on several major textile exhibitions.

OWEN M. LYNCH is a professor of anthropology at New York University. He received his Ph.D. in anthropology from Columbia University in 1966, and has done extensive fieldwork among Dalits in India. Recipient of numerous awards and holder of many professional offices on the national level, he has published voluminously on untouchability, caste, democracy, development, social change, and urban and village sociology in India. Among his books are *The Politics of Untouchability* and *Divine Passions: The Social Construction of Emotion in India.*

HELENA NORBERG-HODGE is the founder and director of the Ladakh Project and the International Society for Ecology and Culture. For over two decades she has worked in Ladakh promoting community regeneration, environmental sustainability, and decentralized economic development. She helped to compile the first English-Ladakhi dictionary, and set up the first non-governmental organizations in the region. She is the author of *Ancient Futures: Learning from Ladakh.*

ANN WOOD NORTON is a professor of art history at Providence College. She received a diploma from the C. G. Jung Institute for Analytical Psychology in Zurich in 1974, and a Ph.D. in Asian art history from the Institute of Fine Arts, New York University, in 1981, with a dissertation on the Jaina *Samavasaraṇa.* She has curated a number of Asian art exhibits in New England, and publishes on South Asian art and religion.

HI-AH PARK is a professor of theater and dance at Trinity College. She has studied Korean classical music and dance at the National Classical Music and Dance Institute and the Seoul National University, College of Music, in Korea. She received an M.A. in dance ethnology from the University of California at Los Angeles in 1978. She has taught and performed all over the world and, in 1981, was initiated as a Korean shaman, a practice she combines with Buddhism.

NIRMALA S. SALGADO is a professor of religion at Augustana College, Rock Island. She received her Ph.D. in religion from Northwestern University in 1992. She began her research on Buddhist nuns in Sri Lanka in 1984 while working as a research officer at the International Center for Ethnic Studies in Colombo. She has published several articles on Buddhist nuns in Sri Lanka.

AMY SCHMIDT is one of the resident teachers at the Insight Meditation Center in Barre, Massachusetts, and was formerly a resident Dhamma coordinator at the Insight Meditation Society in San Lorenzo, New Mexico. She received an M.S. in social work from the University of Washington in 1984, and is a licensed clinician in social work with a specialty in Alzheimer's disease. She has been practicing *vipassanā* for sixteen years and teaching it for six, and has lived in a variety of spiritual communities. She is currently writing a full-length biography of Dipa Ma Barua.

KATE LILA WHEELER is a former Burmese nun who now, as a lay Buddhist, is a novelist and short story writer. She is listed among *Granta's* twenty best young American novelists, is a PEN/Faulkner nominee, and has received the O. Henry and Whiting Awards for her short fiction. Author of *Not Where I Started From,* she has just finished a new novel entitled *When Mountains Walked,* published by Houghton Mifflin.

JAMES WHITEHILL is a professor of religious studies at Stephens College. He received his Ph.D. from Drew University, and served as a Fulbright senior lecturer in Japan from

1991–92 in the area of environmental philosophy, theology, and ethics. He is a founding member of the Columbia Zen Center, and his recent publications focus on Buddhist ethics especially in response to the American context and Western ethical traditions.

JANICE D. WILLIS is a professor of religion at Wesleyan University. She received her Ph.D. from Columbia University in 1976, with a dissertation on the *Tattvārthapatalam* of Asaṇga's *Bodhisattvabhūmi.* She was named the Walter A. Crowell University Professor of the Social Sciences at Wesleyan in 1992, and has published numerous articles on Tibetan Buddhism, Buddhist philosophy, and women in Buddhism. Among her books are *The Diamond Light of the Eastern Dawn: An Introduction to Tibetan Buddhism; On Knowing Reality: The Tattvārtha Chapter of Asaṇga's Bodhisattvabhūmi; Feminine Ground: Essays on Women and Tibet;* and *Enlightened Beings: Life Stories from the Ganden Oral Tradition.*

ROTRAUT WURST has been a member of Sakyadhītā, the International Network of Buddhist Women, since 1988, and was director of Sakyadhītā Europe from 1995 to 1997. She has just received her Ph.D. from the Johann Wolfgang Goethe-Universität in Berlin, where she studied women in Tibetan Buddhism. She began her fieldwork on Tibetan nuns in exile in 1990, and from 1991 to 1995 visited nunneries and monasteries in India, Nepal, and Ladakh.

SERINITY YOUNG is a professor of religious studies at Southern Methodist University. She received a Ph.D. from Columbia University in 1990 in Tibetan Buddhism, and is the recipient of numerous grants and awards. She has traveled widely in Asia and is the author of many articles on women, Buddhism, dreams, and symbols. She is the editor of *The Encyclopedia of Women and World Religion* and *An Anthology of Sacred Texts by and About Women,* and is the author of *Dreaming in the Lotus: Buddhist Dream Narrative, Imagery, and Practice.*

ELEANOR ZELLIOT is Laird Bell Professor of History emerita at Carleton College. She received her Ph.D. from the University of Pennsylvania in 1969 and has traveled widely in India. She has published voluminously in the field of Dalit culture, movements, and literature and is the author of several books including *The Experience of Hinduism: Essays on Religion in Maharashtra; From Untouchable to Dalit: Essays on the Ambedkar Movement;* and *An Anthology of Dalit Literature.*

INDEX

Compassion, 430–31, 449–50
customary, 113–14
dispassionate, 10
quality required of a good physician, 443–44
Conferences on Buddhist Women, 99
Conrad D'aoud, Emilie, 401
Consumerism, avoiding, 91
Continuity, for Buddhist women, 13
Continuum dance studio, 401
Cooking meditation, 219
Cooray, Reginald, 291
Cūḷapanthaka, 145, 150–51
Cullavagga, 142
Cultural Revolution (Tibet), 441–42, 449
Cundī, 147
Customary compassion, nuns practicing, 113–14

Dadon, 343
Dagyon, Tenzin, 334
Ḍākinī, the Sky Goer, 369
Dalai Lama, the Fourteenth, 6, 12, 94, 99, 105, 229–31, 239–40n, 328–29, 339, 357
pictures of destroyed, 235, 241n
Dalit Buddhist women, 10–11, 247–57, 259–74
writing by, 268
Damásari, Daw, 161–62
D'aoud, Emilie Conrad, 401
Deba, Powo Kanam, 444
Desire, transcending, 206–7
Deskit, 244
Dhamma
as an antidote, 94
and conversion of women, 147
and Dalit women's movement, 271
definition, 30
first taught at Sarnath, 19
impropriety of teaching to women, 145
men and women having equal privilege of hearing, 144
and position of nuns in Thailand, 157
preaching, 18
taking refuge in, 51
and Tibetan medicine, 434
and Western Buddhists, 81, 89, 90, 92, 93
Dhammacāriṇīs, 261–63, 273n
Dhammacārīs, 273n
Dhammadinnā, 148
Dhammasarīyā, title of, 166
Dhānañjānī, 147
Dhani, Shantabai, 265
Dharma. *See* Dhamma
Dharmagupta Vinaya, 96n
Diaspora, Tibetan nuns in, 363–69
Difficulties, transforming into the Path, 83–85
Disciplinary rules, 117n
limitations imposed on Buddhist women in, 3–4
Discrimination. *See* Limitations imposed on Buddhist women
Dispassionate compassion, 10
Divination, experiences with, 395–96, 422–23
Dōgen, 120–21, 128, 129n
"Dolkar," 236–37, 239
Dolkar, Yangchen, 319, 326, 328
Dolma, Tsultrim, 238
Dolma Ling Nunnery, 2, 388
Donative inscriptions, 32–34n
Dorje, Lama Thupten Gyalsten, 305–6, 312–13
Douangsavanh, Ammala, 12, 366, 367, 372
Dovchin, Dashima, 13, 482
Dreaming Me: An African American Baptist-Buddhist Journey, 309
Dworin, Judy, 1, 3, 12, 482

ABOUT WISDOM

Wisdom Publications, a not-for-profit publisher, is dedicated to making available authentic Buddhist works by the world's leading Buddhist scholars. We publish our titles with the appreciation of Buddhism as a living philosophy and with the special commitment to preserve and transmit important works from all the major Buddhist traditions.

If you would like more information or a copy of our mail-order catalog, please contact us at:

Wisdom Publications
199 Elm Street
Somerville, Massachusetts 02144 USA
Telephone: (617) 776-7416 • Fax: (617) 776-7841
Email: info@wisdompubs.org • www.wisdompubs.org

THE WISDOM TRUST

As a not-for-profit publisher, Wisdom Publications is dedicated to the publication of fine Dharma books for the benefit of all sentient beings and dependent upon the kindness and generosity of sponsors in order to do so. If you would like to make a donation to Wisdom, please do so through our Somerville office. If you would like to sponsor the publication of a book, please write or e-mail us for more information.

Thank you.

Wisdom Publications is a non-profit, charitable 501(c)(3) organization and a part of the Foundation for the Preservation of the Mahayana Tradition (FPMT).